MEDITERRANEAN DIET COOKBOOK FOR BEGINNERS 2021

1000+ Everyday recipes ready in less than 45 minutes | 14 Days meal-plan to build new habits and an healthier lifestyle for the entire family |

Table of Contents

Introduction 1

Chapter 1. Breakfast Recipes 2

Chapter 2. Salads, Sides, and Vegetables 19

Chapter 3. Soups 37

Chapter 4. Sandwiches, Pizzas, and Wraps 57

Chapter 5. Pasta, Rice & Grains Recipes 78

Chapter 6. Meat Recipes 99

Chapter 7. Poultry Recipes 119

Chapter 8. Egg Recipes 138

Chapter 9. Fish and Seafood Recipes 157

Chapter 10. Sauce, Dip, And Dressing Recipes 176

Chapter 11. Snack Recipes 187

Chapter 12. Dessert Recipes 202

Chapter 13. Drinks and Smoothies 220

Chapter 14. 14-Day Meal Plan 233

Conclusion 234

Introduction

The Mediterranean diet is considered to be one of the healthiest ways to eat, and for a good reason: it includes fruits, vegetables, whole grains, olive oil, beans, nuts, and seeds. Without dairy products or red meat! Not only this, but the diet is also generally low in fat and high in protein. It's amazing that no one thought of this before because it makes so much sense! The only drawback is that there are numerous misconceptions about what the Mediterranean diet entails.

In this book, I'd like to address some of the most frequently asked questions and misconceptions about the Mediterranean diet. To begin, let's start with what the Mediterranean diet does NOT include:

- It doesn't include all carbs. This is a common misconception. While it certainly includes a good number of whole grains, fruits, and vegetables, it doesn't include all carbs – only those that are high in calories, such as bread, cereals, rice, pasta, and potatoes.
- It doesn't include all fats. The diet is really quite low in fat, although it does include some olive oil. I would use extra virgin olive oil whenever possible (you can see here how to choose the best).
- It doesn't include all dairy products. Milk, yogurt, and cheese are definitely part of this meal plan, but as long as you eat the proper amounts (low) of these foods, your body won't face any problems whatsoever. This is especially true if you eat yogurt.
- It doesn't include red meat. While the Mediterranean diet does not include red meat, it does include fish. In fact, fish is a really big part of this diet. It includes cold-water fish such as salmon, tuna, and mackerel. The best way to prepare these fish is to grill them or bake them in the oven with salt, pepper, and olive oil.
- It doesn't include sweets. This is true but in moderation, of course. Sweets are a treat, not a daily food. In fact, the Mediterranean diet recommends that you enjoy sweets on only one day of the week!
- It doesn't include sodas or other beverages with high sugar content. The Mediterranean diet does not include drinks such as sodas, sweetened fruit juice, or fruit juice flavored drinks. Alcohol is also strongly discouraged for obvious reasons, and water should be your main beverage choice instead.
- It doesn't include superfoods. Superfoods such as mushrooms, avocados, olives, and other fatty foods that are high in calories but low in nutrients are not included in the Mediterranean diet. It doesn't mean that these foods don't provide many health benefits. They do, and they are an important part of this diet, just not at all times of the day.
- It doesn't include all grains (some versions do include quinoa or amaranth). Grains such as quinoa, amaranth, and millet are considered "super grains" because they have a high protein content and phytochemicals that help fight disease. While I do highly recommend eating these grains in moderation, they are not at all included in the Mediterranean diet plan.
- It doesn't include all vegetables (some versions do include root vegetables). Carrots, beets, onions, and sweet potatoes are all considered important components of this diet. The reason they aren't included is that the only way to digest these foods properly is from the skin. Cook them as you would any other vegetable and enjoy! Some people do, however, have problems digesting beets and/or onions. In this case, it's recommended to avoid these vegetables altogether or to blanche them first.
- It doesn't include all fruits (some versions do include apples). Fruits such as blueberries, oranges, and apples are considered to be very important parts of the Mediterranean diet as they contain a lot of vitamins and antioxidants. Fruit juices, on the other hand, are discouraged because they have a high sugar content and can lead to weight gain. It should also be noted that dried fruits should be avoided at all times because they are much higher in calories than raw or fresh fruit.
- It does not include all varieties of fish (some versions do include oily fish). The Mediterranean diet structure includes oily fish such as salmon, mackerel, and sardines. However, some people have problems digesting these types of seafood. In this case, it's recommended to avoid them altogether or to only eat smaller portions on a daily basis.

Chapter 1. Breakfast Recipes

1. Mediterranean Bowl

Preparation Time: 10 Minutes
Cooking Time: 5 Minutes
Servings: 1
Ingredients:
- 1 tablespoon olive oil
- 1-pound asparagus, trimmed and roughly chopped
- 1 cups kale, shredded
- 1 cups Brussels sprouts, shredded
- 1/4 cup hummus
- 1 avocado, peeled, pitted and sliced
- 3 scallops
- 1 egg, soft boiled, peeled and sliced

For the dressing:
- 1 tablespoons lemon juice
- 1 garlic clove, minced
- 1 teaspoons Dijon mustard
- 1 tablespoons olive oil
- Salt and black pepper to the taste

Directions:
1. Heat up a pan with 2 tablespoons oil over medium-high heat, add the asparagus and the scallops. Sauté for 5 minutes, stirring often.
2. In a bowl, combine the other 2 tablespoons oil with the lemon juice, garlic, mustard, salt and pepper and whisk well.
3. In a salad bowl, combine the asparagus with the kale, sprouts, hummus, scallops, avocado and eggs and toss gently.
4. Add the dressing, toss and serve for breakfast.

Nutrition:
Calories: 323
Fats: 21 g
Fibers: 10.9 g
Carbs: 24.8 g

2. Berry Oats

Preparation Time: 5 Minutes
Cooking Time: 0 Minutes
Servings: 1
Ingredients:
- ½ cup rolled oats
- 1 cup almond milk
- ¼ cup chia seeds
- A pinch of cinnamon powder
- 2 teaspoons honey
- 1 cup berries, pureed
- 1 tablespoon yogurt

Directions:
1. In a bowl, combine the oats with the milk and the rest of the ingredients except the yogurt, toss, divide into bowls, top with the yogurt and serve cold for breakfast.

Nutrition:
Calories: 420
Fats: 30.3 g
Fibers: 7.2 g
Carbs: 35.3 g
Proteins: 6.4 g

3. Stuffed Tomatoes

Preparation Time: 10 Minutes
Cooking Time: 15 Minutes
Servings: 1
Ingredients:
- 1 tablespoons olive oil
- 2 tomatoes, insides scooped
- 1/8 cup almond milk
- 2 eggs
- 1/4 cup parmesan, grated
- Salt and black pepper to the taste
- 1 tablespoons rosemary, chopped

Directions:
1. Grease a pan with the oil and arrange the tomatoes inside.
2. Crack an egg in each tomato, divide the milk and the rest of the ingredients, introduce the pan in the oven and bake at 375 degrees F for 15 minutes.
3. Serve for breakfast right away.

Nutrition:
Calories: 276
Fats: 20.3 g
Fibers: 4.7 g
Carbs: 13.2 g
Proteins: 13.7 g

4. Watermelon "Pizza"

Preparation Time: 10 Minutes
Cooking Time: 0 Minutes
Servings: 1
Ingredients:
- 1 watermelon slice cut 1-inch thick and then from the center cut into 4 wedges resembling pizza slices
- 2 kalamata olives, pitted and sliced
- 1-ounce feta cheese, crumbled
- 1/4 tablespoon balsamic vinegar
- 1/2 teaspoon mint, chopped

Directions:
1. Arrange the watermelon "pizza" on a plate, sprinkle the olives and the rest of the ingredients on each slice and serve right away for breakfast.

Nutrition:
Calories: 90
Fats: 3 g
Fibers: 1 g
Carbs: 14 g
Proteins: 2 g

5. Avocado Chickpea Pizza

Preparation Time: 20 Minutes
Cooking Time: 20 Minutes
Servings: 1
- Ingredients:
- 1/2 cups chickpea flour
- A pinch of salt and black pepper
- 1/2 cups water
- 1 tablespoons olive oil
- 1/2 teaspoon onion powder
- 1/2 teaspoon garlic, minced
- 1 tomato, sliced
- 1 avocado, peeled, pitted and sliced

- 2 ounces gouda, sliced
- ¼ cup tomato sauce
- 1 tablespoon green onion, chopped

Directions:

1. In a bowl, mix the chickpea flour with salt, pepper, water, oil, onion powder and garlic, stir well until you obtain a dough, knead a bit, put in a bowl, cover and leave aside for 20 minutes.
2. Transfer the dough to a working surface, shape a bit circle, transfer it to a baking sheet lined with parchment paper and bake at 425 degrees F for 10 minutes.
3. Spread the tomato sauce over the pizza, also spread the rest of the ingredients and bake at 400 degrees F for 10 minutes more.
4. Cut and serve for breakfast.

Nutrition:
Calories: 416
Fats: 24.5 g
Fibers: 9.6 g
Carbs: 36.6 g
Proteins: 15.4 g

6.   Stuffed Sweet Potato

Preparation Time: 10 Minutes
Cooking Time: 40 Minutes
Servings: 1
Ingredients:

- 2 sweet potatoes, pierced with a fork
- 3 ounces canned chickpeas, drained and rinsed
- 1 small red bell pepper, chopped
- 1 tablespoon lemon zest, grated
- 1 tablespoons lemon juice
- 1 tablespoons olive oil
- 1 teaspoon garlic, minced
- 1 tablespoon oregano, chopped
- 1 tablespoons parsley, chopped
- A pinch of salt and black pepper
- 1 avocado, peeled, pitted and mashed
- ¼ cup water
- ¼ cup tahini paste

Directions:

1. Arrange the potatoes on a baking sheet lined with parchment paper, bake them at 400 degrees F for 40 minutes, cool them down and cut a slit down the middle in each.
2. In a bowl, combine the chickpeas with the bell pepper, lemon zest, half of the lemon juice, half of the oil, half of the garlic, oregano, half of the parsley, salt and pepper, toss and stuff the potatoes with this mix.
3. In another bowl, mix the avocado with the water, tahini, the rest of the lemon juice, oil, garlic and parsley, whisk well and spread over the potatoes.
4. Serve cold for breakfast.

Nutrition:
Calories: 308
Fats: 2 g
Fibers: 8 g
Carbs: 38 g
Proteins: 7 g

7.   Tuna Salad

Preparation Time: 10 Minutes
Cooking Time: 0 Minutes
Servings: 1
Ingredients:

- 6 ounces canned tuna in water, drained and flaked
- 1/8 cup roasted red peppers, chopped
- 1 tablespoons caper, drained
- 4 kalamata olives, pitted and sliced
- 1 tablespoons olive oil
- 1/2 tablespoon parsley, chopped
- 1/2 tablespoon lemon juice
- A pinch of salt and black pepper

Directions:

1. In a bowl, combine the tuna with roasted peppers and the rest of the ingredients, toss, divide between plates and serve for breakfast.

Nutrition:
Calories: 250
Fats: 17.3 g
Fibers: 0.8 g
Carbs: 2.7 g
Proteins: 10.1 g

8.   Veggie Quiche

Preparation Time: 6 Minutes
Cooking Time: 55 Minutes
Servings: 1
Ingredients:

- 1/4 cup sun-dried tomatoes, chopped
- 1 prepared small pie crust
- 1 tablespoon avocado oil
- 1 yellow onion, chopped
- 2 garlic cloves, minced
- 1/4 cups spinach, chopped
- 1/2 red bell pepper, chopped
- 1/8 cup kalamata olives, pitted and sliced
- 1/2 teaspoon parsley flakes
- 1/2 teaspoon oregano, dried
- 1/4 cup feta cheese, crumbled
- 1 egg, whisked
- 1/2 cups almond milk
- 1/2 cup cheddar cheese, shredded
- Salt and black pepper to the taste

Directions:

1. Heat up a pan with the oil over medium-high heat, add the garlic and onion and sauté for 3 minutes.
2. Add the bell pepper and sauté for 3 minutes more.
3. Add the olives, parsley, spinach, oregano, salt and pepper and cook everything for 5 minutes.
4. Add tomatoes and the cheese, toss and take off the heat.
5. Arrange the pie crust on a pie plate, pour the spinach and tomatoes mix inside and spread.
6. In a bowl, mix the eggs with salt, pepper, milk and half of the cheese, whisk and pour over the mixture in the pie crust.
7. Sprinkle the remaining cheese on top and bake at 375 degrees F for 40 minutes.
8. Cool the quiche down, slice and serve for breakfast.

Nutrition:
Calories: 211
Fats: 14.4 g

Fibers: 1.4 g
Carbs: 12.5 g
Proteins: 8.6 g

9. Veggie Stuffed Hash Browns

Preparation Time: 10 minutes
Cooking Time: 20 minutes
Servings: 4
Ingredients:
- Olive oil cooking spray
- 1 tablespoon plus 2 teaspoons olive oil, divided
- 4 ounces (113 g) baby bella mushrooms, diced
- 1 scallion, white parts and green parts, diced
- 1 garlic clove, minced
- 2 cups shredded potatoes
- 1/2 teaspoon salt
- 1/4 teaspoon black pepper
- 1 Roma tomato, diced
- 1/2 cup shredded Mozzarella

Directions:
1. Preheat the air fryer to 380°F (193°C). Lightly coat the inside of a 6-inch cake pan with olive oil cooking spray.
2. In a small skillet, heat 2 teaspoons olive oil over medium heat. Add the mushrooms, scallion, and garlic, and cook for 4 to 5 minutes, or until they have softened and are beginning to show some color. Remove from heat.
3. Meanwhile, in a large bowl, combine the potatoes, salt, pepper, and the remaining tablespoon olive oil. Toss until all potatoes are well coated.
4. Pour half of the potatoes into the bottom of the cake pan. Top with the mushroom mixture, tomato, and Mozzarella. Spread the remaining potatoes over the top.
5. Bake in the air fryer for 12 to 15 minutes, or until the top is golden brown.
6. Remove from the air fryer and allow to cool for 5 minutes before slicing and serving.

Nutrition:
Calories: 173
Fats: 0.95 g
Fibers: 5.5 g
Carbs: 36.22 g
Proteins: 9.1 g

10. Feta and Pepper Frittata

Preparation Time: 10 minutes
Cooking Time: 20 minutes
Servings: 4
Ingredients:
- Olive oil cooking spray
- 8 large eggs
- 1 medium red bell pepper, diced
- 1/2 teaspoon salt
- 1/2 teaspoon black pepper
- 1 garlic clove, minced
- 1/2 cup feta, divided

Directions:
1. Preheat the air fryer to 360°F (182°C). Lightly coat the inside of a 6-inch round cake pan with olive oil cooking spray.
2. In a large bowl, beat the eggs for 1 to 2 minutes, or until well combined.

3. Add the bell pepper, salt, black pepper, and garlic to the eggs, and mix together until the bell pepper is distributed throughout.
4. Fold in 1/4 cup of the feta cheese.
5. Pour the egg mixture into the prepared cake pan, and sprinkle the remaining 1/4 cup of feta over the top.
6. Place into the air fryer and bake for 18 to 20 minutes, or until the eggs are set in the center.
7. Remove from the air fryer and allow to cool for 5 minutes before serving.

Nutrition:
Calories: 166
Fats: 13.11 g
Fibers: 0.3 g
Carbs: 3.56 g
Proteins: 8.37 g

11. Tomato, Herb, and Goat Cheese Frittata

Preparation Time: 15 minutes
Cooking Time: 25 minutes
Servings: 2
Ingredients:
- 1 tablespoon olive oil
- 1/2-pint cherry or grape tomatoes
- 2 garlic cloves, minced
- 5 large eggs, beaten
- 3 tablespoons unsweetened almond milk
- 1/2 teaspoon salt
- Pinch freshly ground black pepper
- 2 tablespoons minced fresh oregano
- 2 tablespoons minced fresh basil
- 2 ounces (57 g) crumbled goat cheese (about 1/2 cup)

Directions:
1. Heat the oil in a nonstick skillet over medium heat. Add the tomatoes. As they start to cook, pierce some of them so they give off some of their juice. Reduce the heat to medium-low, cover the pan, and let the tomatoes soften.
2. When the tomatoes are mostly softened and broken down, remove the lid, add the garlic and continue to sauté.
3. In a medium bowl, combine the eggs, milk, salt, pepper, and herbs and whisk well to combine.
4. Turn the heat up to medium-high. Add the egg mixture to the tomatoes and garlic, then sprinkle the goat cheese over the eggs.
5. Cover the pan and let cook for about 7 minutes.
6. Uncover the pan and continue cooking for another 7 to 10 minutes, or until the eggs are set. Run a spatula around the edge of the pan to make sure they won't stick.
7. Let the frittata cool for about 5 minutes before serving. Cut it into wedges and serve.

Nutrition:
Calories: 299
Fats: 25.1 g
Fibers: 0.2 g
Carbs: 5.87 g
Proteins: 12.31 g

12. Prosciutto Breakfast Bruschetta

Preparation Time: 10 minutes
Cooking Time: 20 minutes
Servings: 4
Ingredients:
- 1/4 teaspoon kosher or sea salt
- 6 cups broccoli rabe, stemmed and chopped (about 1 bunch)
- 1 tablespoon extra-virgin olive oil
- 2 garlic cloves, minced (about 1 teaspoon)
- 1-ounce (28 g) prosciutto, cut or torn into ½-inch pieces
- 1/4 teaspoon crushed red pepper
- Nonstick cooking spray
- 3 large eggs
- 1 tablespoon unsweetened almond milk
- 1/4 teaspoon freshly ground black pepper
- 4 teaspoons grated Parmesan or Pecorino Romano cheese
- 1 garlic clove, halved
- 8 slices baguette-style whole-grain bread or 4 slices larger Italian-style whole-grain bread

Directions:
1. Bring a large stockpot of water to a boil. Add the salt and broccoli rabe, and boil for 2 minutes. Drain in a colander.
2. In a large skillet over medium heat, heat the oil. Add the garlic, prosciutto, and crushed red pepper, and cook for 2 minutes, stirring often. Add the broccoli rabe and cook for an additional 3 minutes, stirring a few times. Transfer to a bowl and set aside.
3. Place the skillet back on the stove over low heat and coat with nonstick cooking spray.
4. In a small bowl, whisk together the eggs, milk, and pepper. Pour into the skillet. Stir and cook until the eggs are soft scrambled, 3 to 5 minutes. Add the broccoli rabe mixture back to the skillet along with the cheese. Stir and cook for about 1 minute, until heated through. Remove from the heat.
5. Toast the bread, then rub the cut sides of the garlic clove halves onto one side of each slice of the toast. (Save the garlic for another recipe.) Spoon the egg mixture onto each piece of toast and serve.

Nutrition:
Calories: 312
Fats: 10.12 g
Fibers: 7.8 g
Carbs: 39.17 g
Proteins: 17.02 g

13. Prosciutto, Avocado, and Veggie Sandwiches

Preparation Time: 10 minutes
Cooking Time: 0 minutes
Servings: 4
Ingredients:
- 8 slices whole-grain or whole-wheat bread
- 1 ripe avocado, halved and pitted
- 1/4 teaspoon freshly ground black pepper
- 1/4 teaspoon kosher or sea salt
- 4 romaine lettuce leaves, torn into 8 pieces total
- 1 large, ripe tomato, sliced into 8 rounds
- 2 ounces (57 g) prosciutto, cut into 8 thin slices

Directions:
1. Toast the bread and place on a large platter.
2. Scoop the avocado flesh out of the skin into a small bowl. Add the pepper and salt. Using a fork or a whisk, gently mash the avocado until it resembles a creamy spread. Spread the avocado mash over all 8 pieces of toast.
3. To make one sandwich, take one slice of avocado toast, and top it with a lettuce leaf, tomato slice, and prosciutto slice. Top with another slice each of lettuce, tomato, and prosciutto, then cover with a second piece of avocado toast (avocado-side down on the prosciutto). Repeat with the remaining ingredients to make three more sandwiches and serve.

Nutrition:
Calories: 133
Fats: 11.28 g
Fibers: 4.1 g
Carbs: 6.13g
Proteins: 3.89 g

14. Apple Muffins

Preparation Time: 10 minutes
Cooking Time: 15 minutes
Servings: 5
Ingredients
- 2 eggs
- 1 cup oat flour
- ½ teaspoon salt
- 2 tablespoon stevia
- 3 apples, washed and peeled
- ½ cup skim milk
- 1 tablespoon olive oil
- ½ teaspoon baking soda
- 1 teaspoon apple cider vinegar

Directions:
1. Beat the eggs in the mixing bowl and whisk them well.
2. Add the skim milk, salt, baking soda, stevia, and apple cider vinegar.
3. Stir the mixture carefully.
4. Grate the apples and add the grated mixture in the egg mixture.
5. Stir it carefully and add the oat flour.
6. Add the olive oil and blend into a smooth batter
7. Preheat the oven to 350 F.
8. Fill each muffin form halfway with the batter and place the muffins in the oven.
9. Cook the dish for 15 minutes. Remove the cooked muffins from the oven.
10. Cool the cooked muffins well and serve them.

Nutrition: Calories: 200, Fat: 6.0g, Carbs: 32.4g, Protein: 11.7g

15. Egg Butter

Preparation time: 5 Minutes
Cooking time: 20 Minutes
Servings: 4
Ingredients:
- 4 eggs
- 4 tablespoons butter
- 1 teaspoon salt

Directions:
1. Cover the air fryer basket with foil and place the eggs there. Transfer the air fryer basket into the air

fryer and cook the eggs for 17 minutes at 320°Fahrenheit.
2. When the time is over, remove the eggs from the air fryer basket and put them in cold water to chill them. After this, peel the eggs and chop them up finely.
3. Combine the chopped eggs with butter and add salt. Mix it until you get the spread texture. Serve the egg butter with the keto almond bread.

Nutrition: Calories: 164, Fat: 8.5g, Carbs: 2.67g, Protein: 3g

16. Honey Almond Ricotta Spread with Peaches

Preparation Time: 5 minutes
Cooking Time: 8 minutes
Servings: 4
Ingredients:
- 1/2 cup Fisher Sliced Almonds
- 1 cup whole milk ricotta
- 1/4 teaspoon almond extract
- zest from an orange, optional
- 1 teaspoon honey
- hearty whole-grain toast
- English muffin or bagel
- extra Fisher sliced almonds
- sliced peaches
- extra honey for drizzling

Directions:
1. Cut peaches into a proper shape and then brush them with olive oil. After that, set it aside.
2. Take a bowl; combine the ingredients for the filling. Set aside.
3. Then just pre-heat grill to medium.
4. Place peaches cut side down onto the greased grill.
5. Close lid cover and then just grill until the peaches have softened, approximately 6-10 minutes, depending on the size of the peaches.
6. Then you will have to place peach halves onto a serving plate.
7. Put a spoon of about 1 tablespoon of ricotta mixture into the cavity (you are also allowed to use a small scooper).
8. Sprinkle it with slivered almonds, crushed amaretti cookies, and honey.
9. Decorate with the mint leaves.

Nutrition: calories 140, fat 7, fiber 6, carbs 22, protein 7

17. Quinoa & Dried Fruit

Preparation Time: 10 minutes
Cooking Time: 15 minutes
Servings: 4
Ingredients:
- 3 c. water
- 1 c. quinoa
- ¼ c. walnuts
- 8 dried apricots
- 4 dried figs
- 1 tsp. cinnamon

Directions:
1. In a pot, mix water and quinoa and let simmer for 15 minutes, until the water evaporates.
2. Chop dried fruit.
3. When quinoa is cooked, stir in all other ingredients.

4. Serve cold. Add milk, if desired.
Nutrition: calories 254, fat 8, fiber 6, carbs44, protein 14

18. Chia Carrot Oatmeal

Preparation Time: 10 minutes
Cooking Time: 10 minutes
Servings: 6
Ingredients:
- 1 cup steel-cut oats
- 1/4 cup chia seeds
- 1 cup carrot, grated
- 1 1/2 tsp ground cinnamon
- 4 cups almond milk

Directions:
1. Spray instant pot from inside with cooking spray.
2. Add all ingredients except chia seeds into the instant pot and stir well.
3. Seal pot with lid and cook on high for 10 minutes.
4. Once done, allow to release pressure naturally for 10 minutes then release remaining using quick release. Remove lid.
5. Stir in chia seeds and serve.

Nutrition: Calories 434 Fat 39.4 g Carbs 20.9 g Protein 5.8 g

19. Parmesan Sandwiches

Preparation time: 25 minutes
Cooking time: 10 minutes
Servings: 2
Ingredients
- 1/2 cup all-purpose flour
- 1 large egg lightly beaten
- 3/4 cup of breadcrumbs
- 3 tablespoons grated parmesan cheese
- 2 boneless and skinless chicken breast halves (5 ounces each)
- 1/8 teaspoon salt
- 1/8 teaspoon pepper
- 2 tablespoons of olive oil
- 2 Italian bread rolls, divided
- 2 slices of provolone cheese
- 1/3 cup of marinara sauce or other meatless pasta sauce, heated

Direction:
1. Place the flour and egg in separate, shallow containers. Mix the breadcrumbs in another bowl with parmesan cheese.
2. Pound the chicken with ½-in. wooden hammer. Thickness Sprinkle with salt and pepper. Dip the chicken in the flour to cover both sides; shake off the excess. Dip the egg into the crumb mixture.
3. Heat the oil in a large frying pan over medium heat. Add the chicken; Bake until chicken is golden and chicken is no longer pink, 4 to 5 minutes per side. Serve in sandwiches with provolone cheese and sauce.

Nutrition:
Calories: 669, Fat: 32g, Saturated fat: 10g, Cholesterol: 198mg, Sodium: 1124mg, Carbohydrates: 45g, Sugars: 3g, Fiber: 3g, Protein: 48g.

20. Cobb Salad

Preparation time: 20 minutes
Cooking time: 12 minutes
Servings: 6 servings
Ingredients

- 6 slices of bacon
- 3 eggs
- 1 cup Iceberg lettuce, grated
- 3 cups cooked minced chicken meat
- 2 tomatoes, seeded and minced
- 3/4 cup of blue cheese, crumbled
- 1 avocado - peeled, pitted and diced
- 3 green onions, minced
- 1 bottle (8 oz.) Ranch Vinaigrette

Direction:
1. Place the eggs in a pan and cover them completely with cold water. Boil the water. Cover and remove from heat and let the eggs rest in hot water for 10 to 12 minutes. Remove from hot water, let cool, peel, and chop.
2. Put the bacon in a big, deep frying pan. Bake over medium heat until smooth. Drain, crumble, and reserve.
3. Divide the grated lettuce into separate plates.
4. Spread chicken, eggs, tomatoes, blue cheese, bacon, avocado, and green onions in rows on lettuce.
5. Sprinkle with your favorite vinaigrette and enjoy.
Nutrition:
Per serving: 525 calories; 39.9 g fat; 10.2 g carbohydrates; 31.7 g of protein; 179 mg cholesterol; 915 mg of sodium.

21. Mini Frittatas

Preparation time: 5 minutes
Cooking time: 15 minutes
Servings: 12
Ingredients:
- 1 yellow onion, chopped
- 1 cup parmesan, grated
- 1 yellow bell pepper, chopped
- 1 red bell pepper, chopped
- 1 zucchini, chopped
- Salt and black pepper to the taste
- 8 eggs, whisked
- A drizzle of olive oil
- 2 tablespoons chives, chopped

Directions:
1. Heat up a pan with the oil over medium-high heat, add the onion, the zucchini and the rest of the ingredients except the eggs and chives and sauté for 5 minutes stirring often.
2. Divide this mix on the bottom of a muffin pan, pour the eggs mixture on top, sprinkle salt, pepper and the chives and bake at 350 degrees F for 10 minutes.
3. Serve the mini frittatas for breakfast right away.
Nutrition: calories 55, fat 3, fiber 0.7, carbs 3.2, protein 4.2

22. Sun-Dried Tomatoes Oatmeal

Preparation time: 10 minutes
Cooking time: 25 minutes
Servings: 4
Ingredients:
- 3 cups water
- 1 cup almond milk
- 1 tablespoon olive oil
- 1 cup steel-cut oats
- ¼ cup sun-dried tomatoes, chopped
- A pinch of red pepper flakes

Directions:
1. In a pan, mix the water with the milk, bring to a boil over medium heat.
2. Meanwhile, heat up a pan with the oil over medium-high heat, add the oats, cook them for about 2 minutes and transfer m to the pan with the milk.
3. Stir the oats, add the tomatoes and simmer over medium heat for 23 minutes.
4. Divide the mix into bowls, sprinkle the red pepper flakes on top and serve for breakfast.
Nutrition: calories 170, fat 17.8, fiber 1.5, carbs 3.8, protein 1.5

23. Quinoa Muffins

Preparation time: 10 minutes
Cooking time: 30 minutes
Servings: 12
Ingredients:
- 1 cup quinoa, cooked
- 6 eggs, whisked
- Salt and black pepper to the taste
- 1 cup Swiss cheese, grated
- 1 small yellow onion, chopped
- 1 cup white mushrooms, sliced
- ½ cup sun-dried tomatoes, chopped

Directions:
1. In a bowl, combine the eggs with salt, pepper and the rest of the ingredients and whisk well.
2. Divide this into a silicone muffin pan, bake at 350 degrees F for 30 minutes and serve for breakfast.
Nutrition: calories 123, fat 5.6, fiber 1.3, carbs 10.8, protein 7.5

24. Quinoa and Eggs Pan

Preparation time: 10 minutes
Cooking time: 23 minutes
Servings: 4
Ingredients:
- 4 bacon slices, cooked and crumbled
- A drizzle of olive oil
- 1 small red onion, chopped
- 1 red bell pepper, chopped
- 1 sweet potato, grated
- 1 green bell pepper, chopped
- 2 garlic cloves, minced
- 1 cup white mushrooms, sliced
- ½ cup quinoa
- 1 cup chicken stock
- 4 eggs, fried
- Salt and black pepper to the taste

Directions:
1. Heat up a pan with the oil over medium-low heat, add the onion, garlic, bell peppers, sweet potato and the mushrooms, toss and sauté for 5 minutes.
2. Add the quinoa, toss and cook for 1 more minute.
3. Add the stock, salt and pepper, stir and cook for 15 minutes.
4. Divide the mix between plates, top each serving with a fried egg, sprinkle some salt, pepper and crumbled bacon and serve for breakfast.
Nutrition: calories 304, fat 14, fiber 3.8, carbs 27.5, protein 17.8

25. Scrambled Eggs

Preparation time: 10 minutes
Cooking time: 10 minutes
Servings: 2
Ingredients:
- 1 yellow bell pepper, chopped
- 8 cherry tomatoes, cubed
- 2 spring onions, chopped
- 1 tablespoon olive oil
- 1 tablespoon capers, drained
- 2 tablespoons black olives, pitted and sliced
- 4 eggs
- A pinch of salt and black pepper
- ¼ teaspoon oregano, dried
- 1 tablespoon parsley, chopped

Directions:
1. Heat up a pan with the oil over medium-high heat, add the bell pepper and spring onions and sauté for 3 minutes.
2. Add the tomatoes, capers and the olives and sauté for 2 minutes more.
3. Crack the eggs into the pan, add salt, pepper and the oregano and scramble for 5 minutes more.
4. Divide the scramble between plates, sprinkle the parsley on top and serve.

Nutrition: calories 249, fat 17, fiber 3.2, carbs 13.3, protein 13.5

26. Banana and Quinoa Casserole

Preparation time: 10 minutes
Cooking time: 1 hour and 20 minutes
Servings: 8
Ingredients:
- 3 cups bananas, peeled and mashed
- ¼ cup pure maple syrup
- ¼ cup molasses
- 1 tablespoon cinnamon powder
- 2 teaspoons vanilla extract
- 1 teaspoon cloves, ground
- 1 teaspoon ginger, ground
- ½ teaspoon allspice, ground
- 1 cup quinoa
- ¼ cup almonds, chopped
- 2 and ½ cups almond milk

Directions:
1. In a baking dish, combine the bananas with the maple syrup, molasses and the rest of the ingredients, toss and bake at 350 degrees F for 1 hour and 20 minutes.
2. Divide the mix between plates and serve for breakfast.

Nutrition: calories 213, fat 4.1, fiber 4, carbs 41, protein 4.5

27. Spiced Chickpeas Bowls

Preparation time: 10 minutes
Cooking time: 30 minutes
Servings: 4
Ingredients:
- 15 ounces canned chickpeas, drained and rinsed
- ¼ teaspoon cardamom, ground
- ½ teaspoon cinnamon powder
- 1 and ½ teaspoons turmeric powder
- 1 teaspoon coriander, ground
- 1 tablespoon olive oil
- A pinch of salt and black pepper
- ¾ cup Greek yogurt
- ½ cup green olives, pitted and halved
- ½ cup cherry tomatoes, halved
- 1 cucumber, sliced

Directions:
1. Spread the chickpeas on a lined baking sheet, add the cardamom, cinnamon, turmeric, coriander, the oil, salt and pepper, toss and bake at 375 degrees F for 30 minutes.
2. In a bowl, combine the roasted chickpeas with the rest of the ingredients, toss and serve for breakfast.

Nutrition: calories 519, fat 34.5, fiber 13.3, carbs 49.8, protein 12

28. Cheesy Yogurt

Preparation time: 4 hours and 5 minutes
Cooking time: 0 minutes
Servings: 4
Ingredients:
- 1 cup Greek yogurt
- 1 tablespoon honey
- ½ cup feta cheese, crumbled

Directions:
1. In a blender, combine the yogurt with the honey and the cheese and pulse well.
2. Divide into bowls and freeze for 4 hours before serving for breakfast.

Nutrition: calories 161, fat 10, fiber 0, carbs 11.8, protein 6.6

29. Scrambled Pancake Hash

Preparation time: 5 Minutes
Cooking time: 10 Minutes
Servings: 4
Ingredients:
- 1 egg
- ¼ cup heavy cream
- 5 tablespoons butter
- 1 cup coconut flour
- 1 teaspoon ground ginger
- 1 teaspoon salt
- 1 tablespoon apple cider vinegar
- 1 teaspoon baking soda

Directions:
1. Combine the salt, baking soda, ground ginger and flour in a mixing bowl. In a separate bowl crack, the egg into it. Add butter and heavy cream.
2. Mix well using a hand mixer. Combine the liquid and dry mixtures and stir until smooth.
3. Preheat your air fryer to 400°Fahrenheit. Pour the pancake mixture into the air fryer basket tray. Cook the pancake hash for 4-minutes.
4. After this, scramble the pancake hash well and continue to cook for another 5-minutes more. When dish is cooked, transfer it to serving plates, and serve hot!

Nutrition: Calories: 178, Fat: 13.3g, Carbs: 10.7g, Protein: 4.4g

30. Warm Pumpkin Oats

Preparation Time: 10 minutes
Cooking Time: 10 minutes
Servings: 4
Ingredients:
- 1 cup steel-cut oats
- 1/4 tsp ground cinnamon
- 2 1/2 tbsp maple syrup
- 1 tsp vanilla
- 2 cups unsweetened almond milk
- 1/4 cup pumpkin puree
- 1 cup pumpkin coffee creamer
- Pinch of salt

Directions:
1. Spray instant pot from inside with cooking spray.
2. Add oats, almond milk, coffee creamer, vanilla, and salt into the instant pot and stir well.
3. Seal pot with a lid and select manual and set timer for 10 minutes.
4. Once done, allow to release pressure naturally for 10 minutes then release remaining using quick release. Remove lid.
5. Add remaining ingredients and stir well.
6. Serve and enjoy.

Nutrition: calories 140, fat 4, fiber 3, carbs27, protein 6

31. Pear Oatmeal

Preparation Time: 10 minutes
Cooking Time: 13 minutes
Servings: 4
Ingredients:
- 1 cup steel-cut oatmeal
- 2 cups of water
- 1/4 tsp vanilla
- 2 tbsp maple syrup
- 1 1/4 tsp pumpkin pie spice
- 2 pears, peeled and diced
- Pinch of salt

Directions:
1. Spray instant pot from inside with cooking spray.
2. Add pears, pumpkin pie spice, and maple syrup into the instant pot and stir well and cook on sauté mode for 2 minutes.
3. Add remaining ingredients and stir well.
4. Seal pot with a lid and select manual and set timer for 10 minutes.
5. Once done, allow to release pressure naturally for 10 minutes then release remaining using quick release. Remove lid.
6. Stir well and serve.

Nutrition: calories 70, fat 4, fiber 4, carbs 30, protein 2

32. Almond Peach Oatmeal

Preparation Time: 10 minutes
Cooking Time: 10 minutes
Servings: 2
Ingredients:
- 1 cup unsweetened almond milk
- 2 cups of water
- 1 cup oats
- 2 peaches, diced
- Pinch of salt

Directions:
1. Spray instant pot from inside with cooking spray.
2. Add all ingredients into the instant pot and stir well.
3. Seal pot with a lid and select manual and set timer for 10 minutes.
4. Once done, allow to release pressure naturally for 10 minutes then release remaining using quick release. Remove lid.
5. Stir and serve.

Nutrition: calories 234, fat 5, fiber 4, carbs43, protein8

33. Breakfast Cobbler

Preparation Time: 10 minutes
Cooking Time: 12 minutes
Servings: 4
Ingredients:
- 2 lbs. apples, cut into chunks
- 1 1/2 cups water

- 1/4 tsp nutmeg
- 1 1/2 tsp cinnamon
- 1/2 cup dry buckwheat
- 1/2 cup dates, chopped
- Pinch of ground ginger

Directions:
1. Spray instant pot from inside with cooking spray.
2. Add all ingredients into the instant pot and stir well.
3. Seal pot with a lid and select manual and set timer for 12 minutes.
4. Once done, release pressure using quick release. Remove lid.
5. Stir and serve.

Nutrition: calories 195, fat 3, fiber 1, carbs 50 , protein 4

34. Eggs & Hash & Cheese

Preparation Time: 5 minutes
Cooking Time: 2 minutes
Servings: 1
Ingredients:
- 1 egg
- ½ c. shredded hash browns
- 2 tbsps. cheddar cheese
- Salt

Pepper
Directions:
1. Grease a microwaveable bowl with olive oil spray and fill with hash browns. Microwave for 1 minute, and add salt and pepper to taste.
2. Stir in an egg and beat well. Microwave for 45 seconds.
3. Sprinkle cheese over the top.

Nutrition: calories 210 , fat 15 , fiber 3 , carbs 7 , protein16

35. Edamame & Sweet Pea Hummus

Preparation Time: 5 minutes
Cooking Time: 2 minutes
Servings: 2
Ingredients:
- ½ c. edamame
- ½ c. peas
- 2 tbsps. Tahini
- 1 minced garlic clove
- 2 tbsps. chopped mint
- 3 tbsps. olive oil
- 2 wheat tortillas
- 2 eggs

Directions:
1. Blend the first 5 ingredients and 1 Tbsp. of olive oil in a food processor. Spread evenly over the wheat tortillas.
2. Coat pan with remaining olive oil and cook the eggs. When ready, put one egg on each tortilla.

Nutrition: calories 400, fat 30 , fiber3 , carbs 40, protein 20

36. Muffin Pan Frittatas

Preparation Time: 10 minutes
Cooking Time: 15 minutes
Servings: 6
Ingredients:
- 6 eggs
- ½ c. milk
- 1 c. cheddar cheese

- ¾ c. chopped zucchini
- ¼ c. chopped red bell pepper
- 2 tbsps. sliced red onion
- Pepper

Directions:
1. Preheat oven to 350°F.
2. Mix the milk, eggs, and pepper. Then mix in other ingredients.
3. Spray cooking spray on a muffin tin and distribute the prepared mixture evenly between the cups. Bake for 15 min.

Nutrition: calories 149 , fat 10 , fiber 1 , carbs3 , protein 12

37. Carrot Rice Pudding

Preparation Time: 10 minutes
Cooking Time: 15 minutes
Servings: 4
Ingredients:
- 1 cup of rice
- 1 cup carrot, grated
- 1/4 tsp ground nutmeg
- 1 tsp vanilla
- 3 cups unsweetened almond milk
- Pinch of salt

Directions:
1. Spray instant pot from inside with cooking spray.
2. Add all ingredients into the instant pot and stir well.
3. Seal pot with lid and cook on high for 15 minutes.
4. Once done, allow to release pressure naturally for 10 minutes then release remaining using quick release. Remove lid.
5. Stir and serve.

Nutrition: Calories 214 Fat 3 g Carbs 41.4 g Protein 4.3 g

38. Healthy Carrot Soup

Preparation Time: 10 minutes
Cooking Time: 10 minutes
Servings: 4
Ingredients:
- 1 3/4 lbs. carrots, chopped
- 1 tsp coriander powder
- 1 onion, chopped
- 1 tbsp olive oil
- 4 cups vegetable stock
- 1/4 cup fresh coriander, chopped
- Pepper
- Salt

Directions:
1. Add oil into the inner pot of instant pot and set the pot on sauté mode.
2. Add onion and sauté until onion is softened.
3. Add remaining ingredients and stir well.
4. Seal pot with lid and cook on high for 5 minutes.
5. Once done, allow to release pressure naturally for 10 minutes then release remaining using quick release. Remove lid.
6. Blend soup using an immersion blender until smooth.
7. Serve and enjoy.

Nutrition: Calories 129 Fat 3.6 g Carbohydrates 23 g Protein 2.3 g

39. Creamy Squash Cauliflower Soup

Preparation Time: 10 minutes
Cooking Time: 8 minutes
Servings: 6
Ingredients:
- 1 cauliflower head, cut into florets
- 1 bell pepper, diced
- 1 small butternut squash, peeled and chopped
- 1/2 tsp dried parsley
- 1/2 tsp dried mix herbs
- 1 cup vegetable stock
- 1/4 cup yogurt
- 1 onion, chopped
- Pepper
- Salt

Directions:
1. Add all ingredients except yogurt into the instant pot.
2. Seal pot with lid and cook on high for 8 minutes.
3. Once done, release pressure using quick release. Remove lid.
4. Stir in yogurt and blend soup using an immersion blender until smooth.
5. Serve and enjoy.

Nutrition: Calories 54 Fat 0.3 g Carbohydrates 11.3 g Protein 2.5 g

40. Zucchini and Quinoa Pan

Preparation time: 10 minutes
Cooking time: 20 minutes
Servings: 4
Ingredients:
- 1 tablespoon olive oil
- 2 garlic cloves, minced
- 1 cup quinoa
- 1 zucchini, roughly cubed
- 2 tablespoons basil, chopped
- ¼ cup green olives, pitted and chopped
- 1 tomato, cubed
- ½ cup feta cheese, crumbled
- 2 cups water
- 1 cup canned garbanzo beans, drained and rinsed
- A pinch of salt and black pepper

Directions:
1. Heat up a pan with the oil over medium-high heat, add the garlic and quinoa and brown for 3 minutes.
2. Add the water, zucchinis, salt and pepper, toss, bring to a simmer and cook for 15 minutes.
3. Add the rest of the ingredients, toss, divide everything between plates and serve for breakfast.

Nutrition: calories 310, fat 11, fiber 6, carbs 42, protein 11

41. Ham Muffins

Preparation Time: 10 minutes
Cooking Time: 15 minutes
Servings: 6
Ingredients:
- 9 ham slices
- 5 eggs, whisked
- 1/3 cup spinach, chopped
- ¼ cup feta cheese, crumbled
- ½ cup roasted red peppers, chopped
- A pinch of salt and black pepper
- 1 and ½ tbsp. basil pesto
- Cooking spray

Directions:
1. Grease a muffin tin with cooking spray and line each muffin mould with 1 and ½ ham slices.
2. Divide the peppers and the rest of the ingredients except the eggs, pesto, salt and pepper into the ham cups.
3. In a bowl, mix the eggs with the pesto, salt and pepper, whisk and pour over the peppers mix.
4. Bake the muffins in the oven at 400°F for 15 minutes and serve for breakfast.
Nutrition: Calories 109 g, Fat 6.7 g, Carbs 1.8 g, Protein 9.3 g

42. Avocado Spread

Preparation Time: 5 minutes
Cooking Time: 0 minutes
Servings: 8
Ingredients:
• 2 avocados, peeled, pitted and roughly chopped
• 1 tbsp. sun-dried tomatoes, chopped
• 2 tbsp. lemon juice
• 3 tbsp. cherry tomatoes, chopped
• ¼ cup red onion, chopped
• 1 tsp. oregano, dried
• 2 tbsp. parsley, chopped
• 4 kalamata olives, pitted and chopped
• A pinch of salt and black pepper
Directions:
1. Put the avocados in a bowl and mash with a fork.
2. Add the rest of the ingredients, stir to combine and serve as a morning spread.
Nutrition:
Calories 110,
Fat 10.5 g,
Fiber 3.6 g,
Carbs 5.6 g,
Protein 1.4 g

43. Artichokes and Cheese Omelet

Preparation Time: 10 minutes
Cooking Time: 8 minutes
Servings: 1
Ingredients:
• 1 tsp. avocado oil
• 1 tbsp. almond milk
• 2 eggs, whisked
• A pinch of salt and black pepper
• 2 tbsp. tomato, cubed
• 2 tbsp. kalamata olives, pitted and sliced
• 1 artichoke heart, chopped
• 1 tbsp. tomato sauce
• 1 tbsp. feta cheese, crumbled

Directions:
1. In a bowl, combine the eggs with the milk, salt, pepper and the rest of the ingredients except the avocado oil and whisk well.
2. Heat up a pan with the avocado oil over medium-high heat, add the omelet mix, spread into the pan, cook for 4 minutes, flip, cook for 4 minutes more, transfer to a plate and serve.
Nutrition:
Calories 303,
Fat 17.5 g,
Fiber 9.6 g,
Carbs 6.6 g,
Protein 15.4 g

44. Walnut Poached Eggs

Preparation Time: 10 minutes
Cooking Time: 10 minutes
Servings: 2
Ingredients:
• 2 slices whole grain bread toasted
• 1 oz sun-dried tomato, sliced
• 1 tbsp. cream cheese
• 1/3 tsp. minced garlic
• 2 slices prosciutto
• 2 eggs
• 1 tbsp. walnuts
• ½ cup fresh basil
• 1 oz Parmesan, grated
• 3 tbsp. olive oil
• ¼ tsp. ground black pepper
• 1 cup water, for cooking
Directions:
1.   Pour water in the saucepan and bring it to boil.
2.   Then crack eggs in the boiling water and cook them for 3-4 minutes or until the egg whites are white.
3.   Meanwhile, churn together minced garlic and cream cheese.
4.   Spread the bread slices with the cream cheese mixture.
5.   Top them with the sun-dried tomatoes.
6.   Make the pesto sauce: Blend together ground black pepper, Parmesan, olive oil, and basil. When the mixture is homogenous, pesto is cooked.
7.   Carefully transfer the poached eggs over the sun-dried tomatoes and sprinkle with pesto sauce.
8.   The poached eggs should be hot while serving.
Nutrition:
Calories 317,
Fat 36.5 g,
Fiber 3.6 g,
Carbs 17.6 g,
Protein 17.4 g

45. Almond Cream Cheese Bake

Preparation Time: 10 minutes
Cooking Time: 2 hours
Servings: 4
Ingredients:
• 1 cup cream cheese
• 4 tbsp. honey
• 1 oz almonds, chopped
• ½ tsp. vanilla extract
• 3 eggs, beaten
• 1 tbsp. semolina
Directions:
1.   Put beaten eggs in the mixing bowl.
2.   Add cream cheese, semolina, and vanilla extract.
3.   Blend the mixture with the help of the hand mixer until it is fluffy.
4.   After this, add chopped almonds and mix up the mass well.
5.   Transfer the cream cheese mash in the non-sticky baking mold.
6.   Flatten the surface of the cream cheese mash well.
7.   Preheat the oven to 325°F.
8.   Cook the breakfast for 2 hours.
9.   The meal is cooked when the surface of the mash is light brown.
10.   Chill the cream cheese mash little and sprinkle with honey.

Nutrition:
Calories 352,
Fat 22.5 g,
Fiber 1.6 g,
Carbs 7.6 g,
Protein 10.4 g

46. Chili Egg Cups

Preparation Time: 15 minutes
Cooking Time: 15 minutes
Servings: 4
Ingredients:
- 1 tsp. chives, chopped
- 4 eggs
- 1 tsp. tomato paste
- 1 tbsp. Plain yogurt
- ½ tsp. butter, softened
- ¼ tsp. chili flakes
- ½ oz Cheddar cheese, shredded

Directions:
1. Preheat the oven to 365°F.
2. Brush the muffin molds with the softened butter from inside.
3. Then mix up together Plain yogurt with chili flakes and tomato paste.
4. Crack the eggs in the muffin molds.
5. After this, carefully place the tomato paste mixture over the eggs and top with Cheddar cheese.
6. Sprinkle the eggs with chili flakes and place in the preheated oven.
7. Cook the egg cups for 15 minutes.
8. Then check if the eggs are solid and remove them from the oven.
9. Chill the egg cups till the room temperature and gently remove from the muffin molds.
Nutrition:
Calories 85,
Fat 6.5 g,
Fiber 0.6 g,
Carbs 0.6 g,
Protein 6.4 g

47. Dill Eggs Mix

Preparation Time: 10 minutes
Cooking Time: 15 minutes
Servings: 2
Ingredients:
- 2 eggs
- 2 oz Feta cheese
- 1 tsp. fresh dill, chopped
- 1 tsp. butter
- ½ tsp. olive oil
- ¼ tsp. onion powder
- ¼ tsp. chili flakes

Directions:
1. Toss butter in the skillet.
2. Add olive oil and bring to boil.
3. After this, crack the eggs in the skillet.
4. Sprinkle them with chili flakes and onion powder.
5. Then preheat the oven to 360°F.
6. Transfer the skillet with eggs in the oven and cook for 10 minutes.
7. Then crumble Feta cheese and sprinkle it over the eggs.
8. Bake the eggs for 5 minutes more.
Nutrition:
Calories 185,

Fat 13.5 g,
Fiber 0.6 g,
Carbs 2.6 g,
Protein 15.4 g

48. Hummus and Tomato Sandwich

Preparation Time: 10 minutes
Cooking Time: 2 minutes
Servings: 3
Ingredients:
- 6 whole grain bread slices
- 1 tomato
- 3 Cheddar cheese slices
- ½ tsp. dried oregano
- 1 tsp. green chili paste
- ½ red onion, sliced
- 1 tsp. lemon juice
- 1 tbsp. hummus
- 3 lettuce leaves

Directions:
1. Slice tomato into 6 slices.
2. In the shallow bowl mix up together dried oregano, green chili paste, lemon juice, and hummus.
3. Spread 3 bread slices with the chili paste mixture.
4. After this, place the sliced tomatoes on them.
5. Add sliced onion, Cheddar cheese, and lettuce leaves.
6. Cover the lettuce leaves with the remaining bread slices to get the sandwiches.
7. Preheat the grill to 365°F.
8. Grill the sandwiches for 2 minutes.
Nutrition:
Calories 269,
Fat 12.5 g,
Fiber 9.6 g,
Carbs 25.6 g,
Protein 13.4 g

49. Buttery Pancakes

Preparation Time: 10 minutes
Cooking Time: 10 minutes
Servings: 5
Ingredients:
- 1 cup wheat flour, whole-grain
- 1 tsp. baking powder
- 1 tsp. lemon juice
- 3 eggs, beaten
- ¼ cup Splenda
- 1 tsp. vanilla extract
- 1/3 cup blueberries
- 1 tbsp. olive oil
- 1 tsp. butter
- 1/3 cup milk

Directions:
1. In the mixer bowl, combine together baking powder, wheat flour, lemon juice, eggs, Splenda, vanilla extract, milk, and olive oil.
2. Blend the liquid until it is smooth and homogenous.
3. After this, toss the butter in the skillet and melt it.
4. With the help of the ladle pour the pancake batter in the hot skillet and flatten it in the shape of the pancake.
5. Sprinkle the pancake with the blueberries gently and cook for 1.5 minutes over the medium heat.
6. Then flip the pancake onto another side and cook it for 30 seconds more.

7. Repeat the same steps with all remaining batter and blueberries.
8. Transfer the cooked pancakes in the serving plate.
Nutrition:
Calories 152,
Fat 7.5 g,
Fiber 3.6 g,
Carbs 30.6 g,
Protein 7.4 g

50. Cream Olive Muffins

Preparation Time: 15 minutes
Cooking Time: 20 minutes
Servings: 6
Ingredients:
• ½ cup quinoa, cooked
• 2 oz Feta cheese, crumbled
• 2 eggs, beaten
• 3 kalamata olives, chopped
• ¾ cup heavy cream
• 1 tomato, chopped
• 1 tsp. butter, softened
• 1 tbsp. wheat flour, whole grain
• ½ tsp. salt
Directions:
1. In the mixing bowl whisk eggs and add Feta cheese.
2. Then add chopped tomato and heavy cream.
3. After this, add wheat flour, salt, and quinoa.
4. Then add kalamata olives and mix up the ingredients with the help of the spoon.
5. Brush the muffin molds with the butter from inside.
6. Transfer quinoa mixture in the muffin molds and flatten it with the help of the spatula or spoon if needed.
7. Cook the muffins in the preheated to 355°F oven for 20 minutes.
Nutrition:
Calories 165,
Fat 10.5 g,
Fiber 1.6 g,
Carbs 11.6 g,
Protein 5.4 g

51. Herbed Fried Eggs

Preparation Time: 6 minutes
Cooking Time: 7 minutes
Servings: 2
Ingredients:
• 4 eggs
• 1 tbsp. butter
• ½ tsp. chives, chopped
• ½ tsp. fresh parsley, chopped
• 1/3 tsp. fresh dill, chopped
• ¾ tsp. sea salt
Directions:
1. Toss butter in the skillet and bring it to boil.
2. Then crack the eggs in the coiled butter and sprinkle with sea salt.
3. Cook the eggs with the closed lid for 2 minutes over the medium heat.
4. Then open the lid and sprinkle them with parsley, dill, and chives.
5. Cook the eggs for 3 minutes more over the medium heat.
6. Carefully transfer the cooked meal in the plate. Use the wooden spatula for this step.

Nutrition:
Calories 177,
Fat 14.5 g,
Fiber 0.6 g,
Carbs 0.6 g,
Protein 11.4 g

52. Chili Scramble

Preparation Time: 15 minutes
Cooking Time: 15 minutes
Servings: 4
Ingredients:
• 3 tomatoes
• 4 eggs
• ¼ tsp. of sea salt
• ½ chili pepper, chopped
• 1 tbsp. butter
• 1 cup water, for cooking
Directions:
1. Pour water in the saucepan and bring it to boil.
2. Then remove water from the heat and add tomatoes.
3. Let the tomatoes stay in the hot water for 2-3 minutes.
4. After this, remove the tomatoes from water and peel them.
5. Place butter in the pan and melt it.
6. Add chopped chili pepper and fry it for 3 minutes over the medium heat.
7. Then chop the peeled tomatoes and add into the chili peppers.
8. Cook the vegetables for 5 minutes over the medium heat. Stir them from time to time.
9. After this, add sea salt and crack the eggs
10. Stir (scramble) the eggs well with the help of the fork and cook them for 3 minutes over the medium heat.
Nutrition:
Calories 177,
Fat 7.5 g,
Fiber 1.6 g,
Carbs 4.6 g,
Protein 6.4 g

53. Couscous and Chickpeas Bowls

Preparation Time: 10 minutes
Cooking Time: 6 minutes
Servings: 4
Ingredients:
• ¾ cup whole wheat couscous
• 1 yellow onion, chopped
• 1 tbsp. olive oil
• 1 cup water
• 2 garlic cloves, minced
• 15 oz. canned chickpeas, drained and rinsed
• A pinch of salt and black pepper
• 15 oz. canned tomatoes, chopped
• 14 oz. canned artichokes, drained and chopped
• ½ cup Greek olives, pitted and chopped
• ½ tsp. oregano, dried
• 1 tbsp. lemon juice
Directions:
1. Put the water in a pot, bring to a boil over medium heat, add the couscous, stir, take off the heat, cover the pan, leave aside for 10 minutes and fluff with a fork.
2. Heat up a pan with the oil over medium-high heat, add the onion and sauté for 2 minutes.

3.   Add the rest of the ingredients, toss and cook for 4 minutes more.
4.   Add the couscous, toss, divide into bowls and serve for breakfast.
Nutrition:
Calories 540,
Fat 10.5 g,
Fiber 9.6 g,
Carbs 51.6 g,
Protein 11.4 g

54.   Banana Oats

Preparation Time: 10 minutes
Cooking Time: 0 minutes
Servings: 2
Ingredients:
- 1 banana, peeled and sliced
- 1¾ cup almond milk
- ½ cup cold brewed coffee
- 2 dates, pitted
- 2 tbsp. cocoa powder
- 1 cup rolled oats
- 1 and ½ tbsp. chia seeds

Directions:
1.   In a blender, combine the banana with the milk and the rest of the ingredients, pulse, divide into bowls and serve for breakfast.
Nutrition:
Calories 451
Fat 25.1 g,
Fiber 9.9 g,
Carbs 55.4 g,
Protein 9.3 g

55.   Slow-cooked Peppers Frittata

Preparation Time: 10 minutes
Cooking Time: 3 hours
Servings: 6
Ingredients:
- ½ cup almond milk
- 8 eggs, whisked
- Salt and black pepper to the taste
- 1 tsp. oregano, dried
- 1 and ½ cups roasted peppers, chopped
- ½ cup red onion, chopped
- 4 cups baby arugula
- 1 cup goat cheese, crumbled
- Cooking spray

Directions:
1. In a bowl, combine the eggs with salt, pepper and the oregano and whisk.
2. Grease your slow cooker with the cooking spray, arrange the peppers and the remaining ingredients inside and pour the eggs mixture over them.
3. Put the lid on and cook on Low for 3 hours.
4. Divide the frittata between plates and serve.
Nutrition:
Calories 259,
Fat 20.2,
Fiber 1,
Carbs 4.4,
Protein 16.3

56.   Avocado Toast

Preparation Time: 10 minutes
Cooking Time: 0 minutes
Servings: 2

Ingredients:
- 1 tbsp. goat cheese, crumbled
- 1 avocado, peeled, pitted and mashed
- A pinch of salt and black pepper
- 2 whole wheat bread slices, toasted
- ½ tsp. lime juice
- 1 persimmon, thinly sliced
- 1 fennel bulb, thinly sliced
- 2 tsp. honey
- 2 tbsp. pomegranate seeds

Directions:
1.   In a bowl, combine the avocado flesh with salt, pepper, lime juice and the cheese and whisk.
2.   Spread this onto toasted bread slices, top each slice with the remaining ingredients and serve for breakfast.
Nutrition:
Calories 348,
Fat 20.8 g
Fiber 12.3 g,
Carbs 38.7 g,
Protein 7.1 g

57.   Veggie Breakfast Bowl

Preparation Time: 5 minutes
Cooking Time: 2 minutes
Servings: 1
Ingredients:
- 1 egg
- 1 tbsp. water
- 2 tbsps. shredded mozzarella cheese
- 2 tbsps. diced mushrooms
- ¼ c. baby spinach
- 2 tbsps. cherry tomatoes

Directions:
1.   Mix all ingredients excluding the cheese in a greased microwaveable bowl.
2.   Microwave for 1 minute or until the egg is cooked.
3.   Sprinkle shredded cheese over the top.
Nutrition: calories 100, fat 6 , fiber 1 , carbs 2 , protein 10

58.   Apple Peanut Butter Oatmeal

Preparation Time: 15 minutes
Cooking Time: 8 hours
Servings: 4
Ingredients:
- 1 c. steel-cut oats
- ¼ c. brown sugar
- ½ tsp. cinnamon
- ¼ c. peanut butter
- 1 tsp. vanilla extract
- 2 diced apples
- Salt

Directions:
1.   Grease a slow cooker with cooking spray.
2.   Add all ingredients to the crockpot except apples, mix well.
3.   Add apples to the top of the mixture and cook on low for 8 hours.
Nutrition: calories 320 , fat 11 , fiber 2 , carbs 50 , protein 13

59.   Buckwheat Breakfast Bowls

Preparation Time: 10 minutes
Cooking Time: 15 minutes
Servings: 4
Ingredients:

- 1 cup buckwheat
- 1 tsp ground cinnamon
- 1 tbsp almonds, chopped
- 1 tbsp walnuts, chopped
- 1 cup heavy cream
- 2 cups almond milk

Directions:
1. Spray instant pot from inside with cooking spray.
2. Add all ingredients into the instant pot and stir well.
3. Seal pot with lid and cook on high for 15 minutes.
4. Once done, allow to release pressure naturally for 10 minutes then release remaining using quick release. Remove lid.
5. Stir and serve.

Nutrition: calories 575, fat 43 , fiber 4 , carbs49 , protein 10

60. Baked Omelet Mix

Preparation time: 10 minutes
Cooking time: 45 minutes
Servings: 12
Ingredients:
- 12 eggs, whisked
- 8 ounces spinach, chopped
- 2 cups almond milk
- 12 ounces canned artichokes, chopped
- 2 garlic cloves, minced
- 5 ounces feta cheese, crumbled
- 1 tablespoon dill, chopped
- 1 teaspoon oregano, dried
- 1 teaspoon lemon pepper
- A pinch of salt
- 4 teaspoons olive oil

Directions:
1. Heat up a pan with the oil over medium-high heat, add the garlic and the spinach and sauté for 3 minutes.
2. In a baking dish, combine the eggs with the artichokes and the rest of the ingredients.
3. Add the spinach mix as well, toss a bit, bake the mix at 375 degrees F for 40 minutes, divide between plates and serve for breakfast.

Nutrition: calories 186, fat 13, fiber 1, carbs 5, protein 10

61. Greek Beans Tortillas

Preparation time: 5 minutes
Cooking time: 20 minutes
Servings: 4
Ingredients:
- 1 red onion, chopped
- 2 garlic cloves, minced
- 1 tablespoon olive oil
- 1 green bell pepper, sliced
- 3 cups canned pinto beans, drained and rinsed
- 2 red chili peppers, chopped
- 4 tablespoon parsley, chopped
- 1 teaspoon cumin, ground
- A pinch of salt and black pepper
- 4 whole wheat Greek tortillas
- 1 cup cheddar cheese, shredded

Directions:
1. Heat up a pan with the oil over medium heat, add the onion and sauté for 5 minutes.
2. Add the rest of the ingredients except the tortillas and the cheese, stir and cook for 15 minutes.
3. Divide the beans mix on each Greek tortilla, also divide the cheese, roll the tortillas and serve for breakfast.

Nutrition: calories 673, fat 14.9, fiber 23.7, carbs 75.4, protein 39

62. Baked Cauliflower Hash

Preparation time: 10 minutes
Cooking time: 25 minutes
Servings: 4
Ingredients:
- 4 cups cauliflower florets
- 1 tablespoon olive oil
- 2 cups white mushrooms, sliced
- 1 cup cherry tomatoes, halved
- 1 yellow onion, chopped
- 2 garlic cloves, minced
- ¼ teaspoon garlic powder
- 3 tablespoons basil, chopped
- 3 tablespoons mint, chopped
- 1 tablespoon dill, chopped

Directions:
1. Spread the cauliflower florets on a baking sheet lined with parchment paper, add the rest of the ingredients, introduce in the oven at 350 degrees F and bake for 25 minutes.
2. Divide the hash between plates and serve for breakfast.

Nutrition: calories 367, fat 14.3, fiber 3.5, carbs 16.8, protein 12.2

63. Bacon, Spinach and Tomato Sandwich

Preparation time: 5 minutes
Cooking time: 0 minutes
Servings: 1
Ingredients:
- 2 whole-wheat bread slices, toasted
- 1 tablespoon Dijon mustard
- 3 bacon slices
- Salt and black pepper to the taste
- 2 tomato slices
- ¼ cup baby spinach

Directions:
1. Spread the mustard on each bread slice, divide the bacon and the rest of the ingredients on one slice, top with the other one, cut in half and serve for breakfast.

Nutrition: calories 246, fat 11.2, fiber 4.5, carbs 17.5, protein 8.3

64. Veggie Salad

Preparation time: 5 minutes
Cooking time: 0 minutes
Servings: 4
Ingredients:
- 2 tomatoes, cut into wedges
- 2 red bell peppers, chopped
- 1 cucumber, chopped
- 1 red onion, sliced
- ½ cup kalamata olives, pitted and sliced
- 2 ounces feta cheese, crumbled
- ¼ cup lime juice
- ½ cup olive oil
- 2 garlic cloves, minced
- 1 tablespoon oregano, chopped
- Salt and black pepper to the taste

Directions:
1. In a large salad bowl, combine the tomatoes with the peppers and the rest of the ingredients except the cheese and toss.

2. Divide the salad into smaller bowls, sprinkle the cheese on top and serve for breakfast.
Nutrition: calories 327, fat 11.2, fiber 4.4, carbs 16.7, protein 6.4

65. Salmon and Bulgur Salad

Preparation time: 25 minutes
Cooking time: 10 minutes
Servings: 4
Ingredients:
- 1-pound salmon fillet, skinless and boneless
- 1 tablespoon olive oil
- 1 cup bulgur
- 1 cup parsley, chopped
- ¼ cup mint, chopped
- 3 tablespoons lemon juice
- 1 red onion, sliced
- Salt and black pepper to the taste
- 2 cup hot water

Directions:
1. Heat up a pan with half of the oil over medium heat, add the salmon, some salt and pepper, cook for 5 minutes on each side, cool down, flake and put in a salad bowl.
2. In another bowl, mix the bulgur with hot water, cover, leave aside for 25 minutes, drain and transfer to the bowl with the salmon.
3. Add the rest of the ingredients, toss and serve for breakfast.
Nutrition: calories 321, fat 11.3, fiber 7.9, carbs 30.8, protein 27.6

66. Herbed Quinoa and Asparagus

Preparation time: 10 minutes
Cooking time: 0 minutes
Servings: 4
Ingredients:
- 3 cups asparagus, steamed and roughly chopped
- 1 tablespoon olive oil
- 3 tablespoons balsamic vinegar
- 1 and ¾ cups quinoa, cooked
- 2 teaspoons mustard
- Salt and black pepper to the taste
- 5 ounces baby spinach
- ½ cup parsley, chopped
- 1 tablespoon thyme, chopped
- 1 tablespoon tarragon, chopped

Directions:
1. In a salad bowl, combine the asparagus with the quinoa, spinach and the rest of the ingredients, toss and keep in the fridge for 10 minutes before serving for breakfast.
Nutrition: calories 323, fat 11.3, fiber 3.4, carbs 16.4, protein 10

67. Cinnamon Apple and Lentils Porridge

Preparation time: 5 minutes
Cooking time: 10 minutes
Servings: 4
Ingredients:
- ½ cup walnuts, chopped
- 2 green apples, cored, peeled and cubed
- 3 tablespoons maple syrup
- 3 cups almond milk
- ½ cup red lentils
- ½ teaspoon cinnamon powder
- ½ cup cranberries, dried
- 1 teaspoon vanilla extract

Directions:
1. Put the milk in a pot, heat it up over medium heat, add the walnuts, apples, maple syrup and the rest of the ingredients, toss, simmer for 10 minutes, divide into bowls and serve.
Nutrition: calories 150, fat 2, fiber 1, carbs 3, protein 5

68. Lentils and Cheddar Frittata

Preparation time: 10 minutes
Cooking time: 15 minutes
Servings: 4
Ingredients:
- 1 red onion, chopped
- 2 tablespoons olive oil
- 1 cup sweet potatoes, boiled and chopped
- ¾ cup ham, chopped
- 4 eggs, whisked
- ¾ cup lentils, cooked
- 2 tablespoons Greek yogurt
- Salt and black pepper to the taste
- ½ cup cherry tomatoes, halved
- ¾ cup cheddar cheese, grated

Directions:
1. Heat up a pan with the oil over medium heat, add the onion, stir and sauté for 2 minutes.
2. Add the rest of the ingredients except the eggs and the cheese, toss and cook for 3 minutes more.
3. Add the eggs, sprinkle the cheese on top, cover the pan and cook for 10 minutes more.
4. Slice the frittata, divide between plates and serve.
Nutrition: calories 274, fat 17.3, fiber 3.5, carbs 8.9, protein 11.4

69. Seeds and Lentils Oats

Preparation time: 10 minutes
Cooking time: 50 minutes
Servings: 4
Ingredients:
- ½ cup red lentils
- ¼ cup pumpkin seeds, toasted
- 2 teaspoons olive oil
- ¼ cup rolled oats
- ¼ cup coconut flesh, shredded
- 1 tablespoon honey
- 1 tablespoon orange zest, grated
- 1 cup Greek yogurt
- 1 cup blackberries

Directions:
1. Spread the lentils on a baking sheet lined with parchment paper, introduce in the oven and roast at 370 degrees F for 30 minutes.
2. Add the rest of the ingredients except the yogurt and the berries, toss and bake at 370 degrees F for 20 minutes more.
3. Transfer this to a bowl, add the rest of the ingredients, toss, divide into smaller bowls and serve for breakfast.
Nutrition: calories 204, fat 7.1, fiber 10.4, carbs 27.6, protein 9.5

70. Orzo and Veggie Bowls

Preparation time: 10 minutes
Cooking time: 0 minutes
Servings: 4
Ingredients:
- 2 and ½ cups whole-wheat orzo, cooked
- 14 ounces canned cannellini beans, drained and rinsed
- 1 yellow bell pepper, cubed

- 1 green bell pepper, cubed
- A pinch of salt and black pepper
- 3 tomatoes, cubed
- 1 red onion, chopped
- 1 cup mint, chopped
- 2 cups feta cheese, crumbled
- 2 tablespoons olive oil
- ¼ cup lemon juice
- 1 tablespoon lemon zest, grated
- 1 cucumber, cubed
- 1 and ¼ cup kalamata olives, pitted and sliced
- 3 garlic cloves, minced

Directions:

1. In a salad bowl, combine the orzo with the beans, bell peppers and the rest of the ingredients, toss, divide the mix between plates and serve for breakfast.

Nutrition: calories 411, fat 17, fiber 13, carbs 51, protein 14

71. Lemon Peas Quinoa Mix

Preparation time: 10 minutes
Cooking time: 20 minutes
Servings: 4
Ingredients:
- 1 and ½ cups quinoa, rinsed
- 1-pound asparagus, steamed and chopped
- 3 cups water
- 2 tablespoons parsley, chopped
- 2 tablespoons lemon juice
- 1 teaspoon lemon zest, grated
- ½ pound sugar snap peas, steamed
- ½ pound green beans, trimmed and halved
- A pinch of salt and black pepper
- 3 tablespoons pumpkin seeds
- 1 cup cherry tomatoes, halved
- 2 tablespoons olive oil

Directions:

1. Put the water in a pot, bring to a boil over medium heat, add the quinoa, stir and simmer for 20 minutes.
2. Stir the quinoa, add the parsley, lemon juice and the rest of the ingredients, toss, divide between plates and serve for breakfast.

Nutrition: calories 417, fat 15, fiber 9, carbs 58, protein 16

72. Walnuts Yogurt Mix

Preparation time: 10 minutes
Cooking time: 0 minutes
Servings: 6
Ingredients:
- 2 and ½ cups Greek yogurt
- 1 and ½ cups walnuts, chopped
- 1 teaspoon vanilla extract
- ¾ cup honey
- 2 teaspoons cinnamon powder

Directions:

1. In a bowl, combine the yogurt with the walnuts and the rest of the ingredients, toss, divide into smaller bowls and keep in the fridge for 10 minutes before serving for breakfast.

Nutrition: calories 388, fat 24.6, fiber 2.9, carbs 39.1, protein 10.2

73. Stuffed Pita Bread

Preparation time: 5 minutes
Cooking time: 15 minutes
Servings: 4
Ingredients:
- 1 and ½ tablespoons olive oil

- 1 tomato, cubed
- 1 garlic clove, minced
- 1 red onion, chopped
- ¼ cup parsley, chopped
- 15 ounces canned fava beans, drained and rinsed
- ¼ cup lemon juice
- Salt and black pepper to the taste
- 4 whole wheat pita bread pockets

Directions:

1. Heat up a pan with the oil over medium heat, add the onion, stir and sauté for 5 minutes.
2. Add the rest of the ingredients, stir and cook for 10 minutes more
3. Stuff the pita pockets with this mix and serve for breakfast.

Nutrition: calories 382, fat 1.8, fiber 27.6, carbs 66, protein 28.5

74. Farro Salad

Preparation time: 5 minutes
Cooking time: 4 minutes
Servings: 2
Ingredients:
- 1 tablespoon olive oil
- A pinch of salt and black pepper
- 1 bunch baby spinach, chopped
- 1 avocado, pitted, peeled and chopped
- 1 garlic clove, minced
- 2 cups farro, already cooked
- ½ cup cherry tomatoes, cubed

Directions:

1. Heat up a pan with the oil over medium heat, add the spinach, and the rest of the ingredients, toss, cook for 4 minutes, divide into bowls and serve.

Nutrition: calories 157, fat 13.7, fiber 5.5, carbs 8.6, protein 3.6

75. Cranberry and Dates Squares

Preparation time: 30 minutes
Cooking time: 0 minutes
Servings: 10
Ingredients:
- 12 dates, pitted and chopped
- 1 teaspoon vanilla extract
- ¼ cup honey
- ½ cup rolled oats
- ¾ cup cranberries, dried
- ¼ cup almond avocado oil, melted
- 1 cup walnuts, roasted and chopped
- ¼ cup pumpkin seeds

Directions:

1. In a bowl, mix the dates with the vanilla, honey and the rest of the ingredients, stir well and press everything on a baking sheet lined with parchment paper.
2. Keep in the freezer for 30 minutes, cut into 10 squares and serve for breakfast.

Nutrition: calories 263, fat 13.4, fiber 4.7, carbs 14.3.protein 3.5

76. Cheesy Eggs Ramekins

Preparation time: 10 minutes
Cooking time: 10 minutes
Servings: 2
Ingredients:
- 1 tablespoon chives, chopped
- 1 tablespoon dill, chopped
- A pinch of salt and black pepper

- 2 tablespoons cheddar cheese, grated
- 1 tomato, chopped
- 2 eggs, whisked
- Cooking spray

Directions:

1. In a bowl, mix the eggs with the tomato and the rest of the ingredients except the cooking spray and whisk well.

2. Grease 2 ramekins with the cooking spray, divide the mix into each ramekin, bake at 400 degrees F for 10 minutes and serve.

Nutrition: calories 104, fat 7.1, fiber 0.6, carbs 2.6, protein 7.9

77. Quinoa and Eggs Salad

Preparation time: 5 minutes
Cooking time: 0 minutes
Servings: 4
Ingredients:
- 4 eggs, soft boiled, peeled and cut into wedges
- 2 cups baby arugula
- 2 cups cherry tomatoes, halved
- 1 cucumber, sliced
- 1 cup quinoa, cooked
- 1 cup almonds, chopped
- 1 avocado, peeled, pitted and sliced
- 1 tablespoon olive oil
- ½ cup mixed dill and mint, chopped
- A pinch of salt and black pepper
- Juice of 1 lemon

Directions:

1. In a large salad bowl, combine the eggs with the arugula and the rest of the ingredients, toss, divide between plates and serve for breakfast.

Nutrition: calories 519, fat 32.4, fiber 11, carbs 43.3, protein 19.1

78. Breakfast Potato Salad

Preparation Time: 10 minutes
Cooking Time: 15 minutes
Servings: 4
Ingredients:
- 1 lb. baby potatoes, peeled and cut in half
- 1 cup vegetable stock
- 2 tbsp balsamic vinegar
- 2 tbsp olive oil
- 1 tbsp rosemary, chopped
- 4 eggs, hard-boiled, peeled and cut into wedges
- 2 tbsp green onion, chopped
- Pepper
- Salt

Directions:

1. Pour the stock into the instant pot then place steamer basket in the pot.
2. Add potato into the basket.
3. Seal pot with lid and cook on high for 15 minutes.
4. Once done, allow to release pressure naturally for 10 minutes then release remaining using quick release. Remove lid.
5. Transfer potato into the large mixing bowl. Add remaining ingredients to the bowl and mix well.
6. Serve and enjoy.

Nutrition: calories 198, fat12, , carbs 16 , protein 8

79. Cauliflower Fritters

Preparation time: 10 minutes
Cooking time: 50 minutes
Servings: 4
Ingredients:
- 30 ounces canned chickpeas, drained and rinsed
- 2 and ½ tablespoons olive oil
- 1 small yellow onion, chopped
- 2 cups cauliflower florets chopped
- 2 tablespoons garlic, minced
- A pinch of salt and black pepper

Directions:

1. Spread half of the chickpeas on a baking sheet lined with parchment pepper, add 1 tablespoon oil, season with salt and pepper, toss and bake at 400 degrees F for 30 minutes.

2. Transfer the chickpeas to a food processor, pulse well and put the mix into a bowl.

3. Heat up a pan with the ½ tablespoon oil over medium-high heat, add the garlic and the onion and sauté for 3 minutes.

4. Add the cauliflower, cook for 6 minutes more, transfer this to a blender, add the rest of the chickpeas, pulse, pour over the crispy chickpeas mix from the bowl, stir and shape medium fritters out of this mix.

5. Heat up a pan with the rest of the oil over medium-high heat, add the fritters, cook them for 3 minutes on each side and serve for breakfast.

Nutrition: calories 333, fat 12.6, fiber 12.8, carbs 44.7, protein 13.6

80. Rum-raisin Arborio Pudding

Preparation time: 15 minutes
Cooking Time: 4 Hours
Servings: 2
Ingredients:
- ¾ cup Arborio rice
- 1 can evaporated milk
- ½ cup raisins
- ¼ teaspoon nutmeg, grated
- 1½ cups water
- 1/3 cup sugar
- ¼ cup dark rum
- sea salt or plain salt

Directions:

1. Start by mixing rum and raisins in a bowl and set aside.
2. Then, heat the evaporated milk and water in a saucepan and then simmer.
3. Now, add sugar and stir until dissolved.
4. Finally, convert this milk mixture into a slow cooker and stir in rice and salt. Cook on low heat for hours.
5. Now, stir in the raisin mixture and nutmeg and let sit for 10 minutes.
6. Serve warm.

Nutrition: Calories: 3, Total Fat: 10.1g, Saturated Fat: 5.9, Cholesterol: 36 mg, Sodium: 161 mg, Total Carbohydrate: 131.5 g, Dietary Fiber: 3.3 g, Total Sugars: 54.8 g, Protein: 14.4 g, Vitamin D: 0 mcg, Calcium: 372 mg, Iron: 2 mg, Potassium: 7

Chapter 2. Salads, Sides, and Vegetables

81. Arugula Salad

Preparation Time: 5 minutes
Cooking Time: 0 minute
Servings: 4
Ingredients:
- 4 cups arugula leaves
- 1 cup cherry tomatoes
- .25 cup pine nuts
- 1 tbsp. rice vinegar
- 2 tbsp. olive/grapeseed oil
- .25 cup grated parmesan cheese
- Black pepper & salt (as desired)
- 1 large sliced avocado

Directions:
1. Peel and slice the avocado.
2. Rinse and dry the arugula leaves, grate the cheese, and slice the cherry tomatoes into halves.
3. Combine the arugula, pine nuts, tomatoes, oil, vinegar, salt, pepper, and cheese.
4. Toss the salad to mix and portion it onto plates with the avocado slices to serve.
5. Serve.
Nutrition:
Calories: 257
Fat: 23 g
Protein: 6.1 g

82. Chickpea Salad

Preparation Time: 15 minutes
Cooking Time: 0 minute
Servings: 4
Ingredients:
- 15 oz. cooked chickpeas
- 1 diced Roma tomato
- ½ of 1 diced green medium bell pepper
- 1 tbsp. fresh parsley
- 1 small white onion
- .5 tsp. minced garlic
- 1 lemon juiced

Directions:
1. Chop the tomato, green pepper, and onion.
2. Mince the garlic.
3. Combine each of the fixings into a salad bowl and toss well.
4. Cover the salad to chill for at least 15 minutes in the fridge.
5. Serve when ready.
Nutrition:
Calories: 163
Fat: 7 g
Protein: 4 g

83. Chopped Israeli Mediterranean Pasta Salad

Preparation Time: 15 minutes
Cooking Time: 2 minutes
Servings: 8
Ingredients:
- .5 lb. small bow tie or other small pasta
- 1/3 cup Cucumber
- 1/3 cup Radish
- 1/3 cup Tomato
- 1/3 cup yellow bell pepper
- 1/3 cup orange bell pepper
- 1/3 cup Black olives
- 1/3 cup Green olives
- 1/3 cup Red onions
- 1/3 cup Pepperoncini
- 1/3 cup Feta cheese
- 1/3 cup fresh thyme leaves
- (1 tsp.) dried oregano

Dressing:
- 0.25 cup + more, olive oil
- 1 lemon juice

Directions:
1. Slice the green olives into halves.
2. Dice the feta and pepperoncini and finely dice the remainder of the veggies.
3. Prepare a pot of water with the salt and simmer the pasta until it's "Al dente" (checking at two minutes under the listed time).
4. Rinse and drain in cold water.
5. Combine a small amount of oil with the pasta.
6. Add the salt, pepper, oregano, thyme, and veggies.
7. Pour in the rest of the oil, lemon juice, and mix and fold in the grated feta.
8. Pop it into the fridge within two hours, best if overnight.
9. Taste test and adjust the seasonings to your liking.
10. Add fresh thyme.
11. Serve.
Nutrition:
Calories: 65
Fat: 5.6 g
Protein: 0.8 g

84. Feta Tomato Salad

Preparation Time: 5 minutes
Cooking Time: 0 minute
Servings: 4
Ingredients:
- 2 tbsp. balsamic vinegar
- .5 tsp. freshly minced basil (1.5 tsp.) or dried
- .5 tsp. salt
- .5 cup coarsely chopped sweet onion
- 2 tbsp. Olive oil
- 1 lb. cherry or grape tomatoes
- .25 cup crumbled feta cheese

Directions:
1. Whisk the salt, basil, and vinegar.
2. Toss the onion into the vinegar mixture for 5 minutes
3. Slice the tomatoes into halves and stir in the tomatoes, feta cheese, and oil to serve.
4. Serve.
Nutrition:
Calories: 121
Fat: 9 g
Protein: 3 g

85. Greek Pasta Salad

Preparation Time: 5 minutes
Cooking Time: 11 minutes
Servings: 4
Ingredients:
- 1 cup penne pasta

- 1.5 tsp. lemon juice
- 2 tbsp. red wine vinegar
- 1 garlic clove
- 1 tsp. dried oregano
- Black pepper and sea salt (as desired)
- .33 cup olive oil
- 5 halved cherry tomatoes
- 1/2 of 1 small red onion
- 1/2 of 1 green & red bell pepper each
- ¼ of 1 cucumber
- .25 cup black olives
- .25 cup crumbled feta cheese

Directions:
1. Slice the cucumber and olives.
2. Chop/dice the onion, peppers, and garlic and slice the tomatoes into halves.
3. Arrange a large pot with water and salt using the high-temperature setting.
4. Once it's boiling, add the pasta and cook for 11 minutes.
5. Rinse it using cold water and drain it in a colander.
6. Whisk the oil, juice, salt, pepper, vinegar, oregano, and garlic.
7. Combine the cucumber, cheese, olives, peppers, pasta, onions, and tomatoes in a large salad dish.
8. Add the vinaigrette over the pasta and toss.
9. Chill in the fridge (covered) for about 3 hours and serve as desired.
10. Serve.
Nutrition:
Calories: 307
Fat: 23.6 g
Protein: 5.4 g

86.   Apples and Pomegranate Salad

Preparation Time: 10 minutes
Cooking Time: 0 minute
Servings: 4
Ingredients:
- 3 big apples, cored and cubed
- 1 cup pomegranate seeds
- 3 cups baby arugula
- 1 cup walnuts, chopped
- 1 tbsp. olive oil
- 1 tsp. white sesame seeds
- 2 tbsp. apple cider vinegar

Directions:
1. Mix the apples with the arugula and the rest of the ingredients in a bowl,
2. Toss and serve cold.
3. Serve.
Nutrition:
Calories: 160
Fat: 4.3 g
Protein: 10 g

87.   Mediterranean Chicken Bites

Preparation Time: 10 minutes
Cooking Time: 10 minutes
Servings: 4
Ingredients:
- 20 ounces canned pineapple slices
- A drizzle of olive oil
- 3 cups chicken thighs
- A tbsp. of smoked paprika

Directions:
1. Situate pan over medium-high heat, add pineapple slices, cook them for a few minutes on each side, transfer to a cutting board, cool them down, and cut into medium cubes.
2. Heat another pan with a drizzle of oil over medium-high heat, rub chicken pieces with paprika, add them to the pan and cook for 5 minutes on each side.
3. Arrange chicken cubes on a platter, add a pineapple piece on top of each and stick a toothpick in each.
4. Serve.
Nutrition:
Calories: 120
Fat: 3 g
Protein: 2 g

88.   Pork and Greens Salad

Preparation Time: 10 minutes
Cooking Time: 15 minutes
Servings: 4
Ingredients:
- 1-pound pork chops
- 8 ounces white mushrooms, sliced
- ½ cup Italian dressing
- 6 cups mixed salad greens
- 6 ounces jarred artichoke hearts, drained
- Salt and black pepper to the taste
- ½ cup basil, chopped
- 1 tbsp. olive oil

Directions:
1. Heat a pan with the oil over medium-high heat, add the pork, and brown for 5 minutes.
2. Add the mushrooms, stir and sauté for 5 minutes more.
3. Add the dressing, artichokes, salad greens, salt, pepper, and basil, cook for 4-5 minutes, divide everything into bowls.
4. Serve.
Nutrition:
Calories: 235
Fat: 5 g
Protein: 11 g

89.   Creamy Chicken Salad

Preparation Time: 10 minutes
Cooking Time: 0 minute
Servings: 6
Ingredients:
- 20 ounces chicken meat
- ½ cup pecans, chopped
- 1 cup green grapes
- ½ cup celery, chopped
- 2 ounces canned mandarin oranges, drained

For the Creamy Cucumber Salad Dressing:
- 1 cup Greek yogurt cucumber, chopped garlic clove
- 1 tsp. lemon juice

Directions:
1. In a bowl, mix cucumber with salt, pepper to taste, lemon juice, garlic, and yogurt, and stir very well.
2. In a salad bowl, mix chicken meat with grapes, pecans, oranges, and celery.
3. Add cucumber salad dressing, toss to coat, and keep in the fridge until you serve it.
4. Serve.
Nutrition:
Calories: 200
Fat: 3 g
Protein: 8 g

90. Cheese Beet Salad

Preparation Time: 15 minutes
Cooking Time: 0 minute
Servings: 4
Ingredients:
- 6 red beets
- 3 ounces feta cheese
- 2 tbsp. olive oil
- 2 tbsp. balsamic vinegar

Directions:
1. Combine everything together.
2. Serve.
Nutrition:
Calories: 230
Protein: 7.3 g
Fat: 12 g

91. Beef Tartar

Preparation Time: 10 minutes
Cooking Time: 0 minute
Servings: 1
Ingredients:
- 1 shallot, chopped
- 4 ounces beef fillet
- 5 small cucumbers
- 1 egg yolk
- 2 tsp. mustard
- 1 tbsp. parsley
- 1 parsley spring

Directions:
1. Incorporate meat with shallot, egg yolk, salt, pepper, mustard, cucumbers, and parsley.
2. Stir well and arrange on a platter.
3. Garnish with the chopped parsley spring
4. Serve.
Nutrition:
Calories: 210
Fat: 3 g
Protein: 8 g

92. Orange Celery Salad

Preparation Time: 16 minutes
Cooking Time: 0 minute
Servings: 6
Ingredients:
- 1 tbsp. lemon juice, fresh
- ¼ tsp. sea salt, fine
- ¼ tsp. black pepper
- 1 tbsp. olive brine
- 1 tbsp. olive oil
- ¼ cup red onion, sliced
- ½ cup green olives
- 2 oranges, peeled & sliced
- 3 celery stalks, sliced diagonally in ½ inch slices

Directions:
1. Put your oranges, olives, onion, and celery in a shallow bowl.
2. Stir oil, olive brine, and lemon juice, pour this over your salad.
3. Season with salt and pepper before serving.
4. Serve.
Nutrition:
Calories: 65
Protein: 2 g
Fat: 0.2 g

93. Pilaf with Cream Cheese

Preparation Time: 11 minutes
Cooking Time: 34 minutes
Servings: 6
Ingredients:
- 2 cups yellow long grain rice, parboiled
- 1 cup onion
- 4 green onions
- 3 tbsp. butter
- 3 tbsp. vegetable broth
- 2 tsp. cayenne pepper
- 1 tsp. paprika
- ½ tsp. cloves, minced
- 2 tbsp. mint leaves
- 1 bunch of fresh mint leaves to garnish
- 1 tbsp. olive oil

Cheese Cream:
- 3 tbsp. olive oil
- Sea salt & black pepper to taste
- 9 ounces cream cheese

Directions:
1. Start by heating your oven to 360°F (180°C) and then get out a pan.
2. Heat your butter and olive oil together and cook your onions and spring onions for two minutes.
3. Add in your salt, pepper, paprika, cloves, vegetable broth, rice, and remaining seasoning.
4. Sauté for three minutes.
5. Wrap with foil and bake for another half hour.
6. Allow it to cool.
7. Mix in the cream cheese, cheese, olive oil, salt, and pepper.
8. Serve your pilaf garnished with fresh mint leaves.
9. Serve.
Nutrition:
Calories: 364
Protein: 5 g
Fat: 30 g

94. Easy Spaghetti Squash

Preparation Time: 13 minutes
Cooking Time: 45 minutes
Servings: 6
Ingredients:
- 2 spring onions, chopped fine
- 3 cloves garlic, minced
- 1 zucchini, diced
- 1 red bell pepper, diced
- 1 tbsp. Italian seasoning
- 1 tomato, small & chopped fine
- 1 tbsp. parsley, fresh & chopped
- Pinch lemon pepper
- Dash sea salt, fine
- 4 ounces feta cheese, crumbled
- 3 Italian sausage links, casing removed
- 2 tbsp. olive oil
- 1 spaghetti sauce, halved lengthwise

Directions:
1. Prep oven to 350°F (180°C), and get out a large baking sheet.
2. Coat it with cooking spray and then put your squash on it with the cut side down.
3. Bake at 350°F (180°C) for 45 minutes. It should be tender.

4. Turn the squash over and bake for 5 more minutes.
5. Scrape the strands into a larger bowl.
6. Cook tbsp. of olive oil in a skillet and then add in your Italian sausage.
7. Cook at 8 minutes before removing it and placing it in a bowl.
8. Add another tbsp. of olive oil to the skillet and cook your garlic and onions until softened. This will take 5 minutes.
9. Throw in your Italian seasoning, red peppers, and zucchini, and cook for another 5 minutes. Your vegetables should be softened.
10.   Mix in your feta cheese and squash, cooking until the cheese has melted.
11.   Stir in your sausage and then season with lemon pepper and salt.
12.   Serve with parsley and tomato.
13.   Serve.
Nutrition:
Calories: 423
Protein: 18 g
Fat: 30g

95. Passion Fruit and Spicy Couscous

Preparation Time: 15 minutes
Cooking Time: 15 minutes
Servings: 4
Ingredients:
- 1 pinch of salt
- 1 pinch of allspice
- 1 tsp. of mixed spice
- 1 cup of boiling water
- 2 tsp. of extra-virgin olive oil
- ½ cup of full-fat Greek yogurt
- ½ cup of honey
- 1 cup of couscous
- 1 tsp. of orange zest
- 2 oranges, peeled and sliced
- 2 tbsp. of passion fruit pulp
- ½ cup of blueberries
- ½ cup of walnuts, roasted and unsalted
- 2 tbsp. of fresh mint

Directions:
1. In a mixing bowl, combine the salt, allspice, mixed spice, honey, couscous, and boiling water.
2. Cover the bowl and allow to rest for 5 to 10 minutes, or until the water has been absorbed.
3. Using a fork, give the mixture a good stir, then add the diced walnuts.
4. In a separate bowl, combine the passion fruit, yogurt, and orange zest.
5. To serve, dish the couscous up into four bowls, add the yogurt mixture, and top with the sliced orange, blueberries, and mint leaves.
Nutrition:
Calories: 100
Fat: 10.5 g
Protein: 2.1 g

96. Springtime Quinoa Salad

Preparation Time: 10 minutes
Cooking Time: 25 minutes
Servings: 4
Ingredients:
For Vinaigrette:
- 1 pinch of salt
- 1 pinch of black pepper
- ½ tsp. of dried thyme
- ½ tsp. of dried oregano
- ¼ cup of extra-virgin olive oil
- 1 tbsp. of honey
- 1 lemon juice
- 1 clove of garlic, minced
- 2 tbsp. of fresh basil, diced

For Salad:
- 1 ½ cups of cooked quinoa
- 4 cups of mixed leafy greens
- ½ cup of Kalamata olives halved and pitted
- ¼ cup of sun-dried tomatoes, diced
- ½ cup of almonds, raw, unsalted, and diced

Directions:
1. Combine all the vinaigrette ingredients together, either by hand or using a blender or food processor.
2. Set the vinaigrette aside in the refrigerator.
3. In a large salad bowl, combine the salad ingredients.
4. Drizzle the vinaigrette over the salad.
5. Serve.
Nutrition:
Calories: 201
Fat: 13 g
Protein: 4 g

97. Spaghetti Niçoise

Preparation Time: 15 minutes
Cooking Time: 20 minutes
Servings: 4
Ingredients:
For Pasta:
- 1 pinch of salt
- 1 pinch of black pepper
- ½ tsp. of chili flakes
- 8 oz. of spaghetti
- 14 oz. of canned tuna chunks in oil
- 1/3 cup of Kalamata olives
- 8 oz. of cherry tomatoes
- 3 oz. of arugula
- ½ cup of pine nuts

For Dressing:
- 1 pinch of salt
- 1 pinch of black pepper
- 2 tbsp. of extra-virgin olive oil
- 1 tbsp. of Dijon mustard
- ¼ cup of lemon juice
- 1 tbsp. of lemon zest
- 1 clove of garlic, minced
- 1 tbsp. of capers

Directions:
1. Stir all the ingredients for the dressing.
2. Cook the pasta according to the package instructions.
3. Boil the eggs, deshell, and cut them in half. Set this aside.
4. Rinse and drain the cooked pasta.
5. Add the remaining ingredients, give it a toss, top with the eggs, and then drizzle with the mustard dressing.
6. Serve
Nutrition:
Calories: 287
Fat: 14 g
Protein: 4 g

98. Tomato Poached Fish with Herbs and Chickpeas

Preparation Time: 20 minutes
Cooking Time: 20 minutes
Servings: 2
Ingredients:

- 1 pinch of salt
- 1 pinch of black pepper
- 4 sprigs of fresh oregano
- 4 sprigs of fresh dill
- 1 ½ cups of water
- 1 cup of white wine
- 2 tbsp. of extra-virgin olive oil
- 1 tbsp. of tomato paste
- 2 cloves of garlic
- 2 shallots
- 1 lemon
- 1 lemon zest
- 14 oz. can of chickpeas
- 8 oz. of cherry tomatoes
- 1 Fresno pepper
- 1 lb. of cod

Directions:
1. Situate saucepan over high heat, cook olive oil, garlic, and shallots for two minutes.
2. Add the salt, pepper, tomato paste, cherry tomatoes, chickpeas, and Fresno pepper.
3. Stir in the water and wine. Place the fish into the center of the pan, ensuring it is submerged in the liquid.
4. Sprinkle the lemon zest over the broth, then add the lemon slices and fresh herbs.
5. Place a lid onto the saucepan and allow the broth to simmer for 5 to 10 minutes, depending on the thickness of the cut of fish.
6. When cooked, remove from the heat and serve over basmati rice.
7. Top with a few toasted pistachios for added texture.
8. Serve.
Nutrition:
Calories: 351
Fat: 21 g
Protein: 9 g

99. Rosemary Beets

Preparation Time: 10 minutes
Cooking Time: 20 minutes
Servings: 4
Ingredients:

- 4 medium beets
- 1/3 cup balsamic vinegar
- 1 tsp. rosemary, chopped
- 1 garlic clove, minced
- ½ tsp. Italian seasoning
- 1 tbsp. olive oil

Directions:
1. Place pan with the oil over medium heat, add the beets and the rest of the ingredients, toss, and cook for 20 minutes.
2. Divide the mix between plates.
3. Serve.
Nutrition:
Calories: 165
Fat: 3.4 g
Protein: 2.3 g

100. White Bean and Tuna Salad

Preparation Time: 10 minutes
Cooking Time: 8 minutes
Servings: 4
Ingredients:

- 1 (12 ounce) can solid white albacore tuna, drained
- 1 (16 ounce) can Great Northern beans, drained and rinsed
- 1 (2.25 ounce) can sliced black olives, drained
- 1 teaspoon dried oregano
- 1/2 teaspoon finely grated lemon zest
- 1/4 medium red onion, thinly sliced
- 3 tablespoons lemon juice
- 3/4-pound green beans, trimmed and snapped in half
- 4 large hard-cooked eggs, peeled and quartered
- 6 tablespoons extra-virgin olive oil
- Salt and ground black pepper, to taste

Directions:
1. Place a saucepan on medium high fire. Add a cup of water and the green beans. Cover and cook for 8 minutes. Drain immediately once tender.
2. In a salad bowl, whisk well oregano, olive oil, lemon juice, and lemon zest. Season generously with pepper and salt and mix until salt is dissolved.
3. Stir in drained green beans, tuna, beans, olives, and red onion. Mix thoroughly to coat.
4. Adjust seasoning to taste.
5. Spread eggs on top.
6. Serve and enjoy.
Nutrition: Calories: 551; Protein: 36.3g; Carbs: 33.4g; Fat: 30.3g

101. Mediterranean Spaghetti

Preparation time: 10 minutes
Cooking time: 10 minutes
Servings: 2
Ingredients:
- 1/3 cup broccoli
- 7 oz. whole grain spaghetti
- 2 oz. Parmesan, shaved
- ½ tsp. ground black pepper
- 1 cup water, for cooking
Directions:
1. Chop the broccoli into the small florets.
2. Pour water in the pan. Bring it to boil.
3. Add broccoli florets and spaghetti.
4. Close the lid and then cook the ingredients for 10 minutes.
5. Then drain water. Add ground black pepper and shaved Parmesan. Shake the spaghetti well.
Nutrition
Calories 430 Fat 8.8g Fiber 9.3g Carbs 72.4g Protein 23.6 g

102. Hummus Pasta

Preparation time: 10 minutes
Cooking time: 15 minutes
Servings: 4
Ingredients:
- 10 oz. soba noodles
- ½ tsp. Italian seasoning
- ¼ tsp. sage
- ¾ tsp. ground coriander
- 4 tsp. hummus

- 1 tsp. butter, softened
- 2 cups water, for cooking

Directions:

1. Pour water in the pan. Bring the liquid to boil.
2. Add soba noodles, sage, and ground coriander.
3. Boil the noodles for 15 minutes over the medium-high heat. The cooked soba noodles should be tender.
4. Then drain water.
5. Mix up together soba noodles, butter, and Italian seasoning.
6. Place the cooked pasta in the bowls and top with hummus.

Nutrition
Calories 256
Fat 2.1g
Fiber 0.3g
Carbs 53.6g
Protein 10.6g

103. Mushroom and Garlic Spaghetti

Preparation time: 10 minutes
Cooking time: 20 minutes
Servings: 4
Ingredients:

- ½ cup white mushrooms, chopped
- 3 garlic cloves, diced
- 2 tbsp. sesame oil
- ½ tsp. chili flakes
- 1 tsp. salt
- 1 tsp. dried marjoram
- 10 oz. whole grain buckwheat spaghetti
- 1 cup water, for cooking

Directions:

1. Pour sesame oil in the skillet and heat it up.
2. Add mushrooms and garlic. Mix up well.
3. Sprinkle the vegetables with chili flakes, salt, and dried marjoram.
4. Pour water in the pan and bring to boil.
5. Add buckwheat spaghetti and cook them according to the direction of the manufacturer.
6. Drain water from spaghetti and transfer them in the mushroom mixture.
7. Mix up spaghetti well and cook for 5 minutes over the medium-low heat.

Nutrition
Calories 303
Fat 8.7g
Fiber 5.2g
Carbs 52.4g
Protein 10.4 g

104. Pasta with Creamy Sauce

Preparation time: 10 minutes
Cooking time: 7 minutes
Servings: 2
Ingredients:

- 7 oz. quinoa pasta
- 1 tbsp. fresh dill, chopped
- 1 tbsp. fresh cilantro, chopped
- ½ tsp. ground black pepper
- 1 oz. Parmesan, grated
- ½ cup milk
- 1 cup water, for cooking

Directions:

1. Pour water in the pan and bring it to boil.
2. Add quinoa pasta and boil it for 2 minutes. Drain the water.

3. Sprinkle pasta with dill, cilantro, and ground black pepper.
4. Then bring to boil milk and mix it up with Parmesan. Stir well until cheese is melted.
5. Pour the milk sauce over the pasta.

Nutrition
Calories 252
Fat 6.3g
Fiber 2.8g
Carbs 39g
Protein 10.9 g

105. Feta Macaroni

Preparation time: 15 minutes
Cooking time: 25 minutes
Servings: 4
Ingredients:

- 5 oz. whole grain macaroni
- 4 oz. Feta cheese, crumbled
- 2 eggs, beaten
- ½ tsp. chili pepper
- 1 tsp. almond butter
- 1 cup water, for cooking

Directions:

1. Mix up together water and macaroni and boil according to the directions of the manufacturer.
2. Then drain water.
3. Add almond butter, chili pepper, and Feta cheese. Mix up well.
4. Transfer the mixture in the casserole mold and flatten well.
5. Pour beaten eggs over the macaroni and bake for 10 minutes at 355F.

Nutrition
Calories 262 Fat 11.4g
Fiber 4.2g
Carbs 27.2g
Protein 13.9g

106. Broccoli Puree

Preparation time: 10 minutes
Cooking time: 15 minutes
Servings: 6
Ingredients:

- 1-pound broccoli, trimmed
- 1 cup chicken stock
- 1 tsp. butter
- 1 tsp. salt

Directions:

1. Line the baking tray with baking paper.
2. Cut the broccoli into the florets and place them on the baking paper.
3. Sprinkle them with salt and bake for 10 minutes at 360F.
4. Meanwhile, pour chicken stock in the pan and bring it to boil.
5. Add baked cauliflower florets and boil them until soft.
6. Then drain ½ part of chicken stock. You can leave less liquid if the broccoli is juicy.
7. Mash the broccoli until you get a soft and fluffy texture.
8. Add butter and mix up with the help of the spoon.

Nutrition: Calories 33 Fat 1g Fiber 2g Carbs 5.1g Protein 2.2g

107. Margherita Slices

Preparation Time: 5 minutes
Cooking Time: 15 Minutes
Servings: 4
Ingredients:
- 1 Tomato, Cut into 8 Slices
- 1 Clove Garlic, Halved
- 1 tbsp. Olive Oil
- ¼ tsp. Oregano
- 1 Cup Mozzarella, Fresh & Sliced
- ¼ Cup Basil Leaves, Fresh, Tron & Lightly Packed
- Sea Salt & Black Pepper to Taste
- 2 Hoagie Rolls, 6 Inches Each

Directions:
1. Start by heating your oven broiler to high. Your rack should be four inches under the heating element.
2. Place the sliced bread on a rimmed baking sheet. Broil for a minute. Your bread should be toasted lightly. Brush each one down with oil and rub your garlic over each half.
3. Place the bread back on your baking sheet. Distribute the tomato slices on each one, and then sprinkle with oregano and cheese.
4. Bake for one to two minutes, but check it after a minute. Your cheese should be melted.
5. Top with basil and pepper before serving.

Nutrition:
Calories: 297
Protein: 12 g
Fat: 11 g
Carbs: 38 g

108. Vegetable Panini

Preparation Time: 15 minutes
Cooking Time: 25 Minutes
Servings: 4
Ingredients:
- 2 tbsp. Olive Oil, Divided
- ¼ Cup Onion, Diced
- 1 Cup Zucchini, Diced
- 1 ½ Cups Broccoli, Diced
- ¼ tsp. Oregano
- Sea Salt & Black Pepper to Taste
- 12 Oz. Jar Roasted Red Peppers, Drained & Chopped Fine
- 2 tbsp. Parmesan Cheese, Grated
- 1 Cup Mozzarella, Fresh & Sliced
- 2-Foot-Long Whole Grain Italian Loaf, Cut into 4 Pieces

Directions:
1. Heat your oven to 450°F, and then get out a baking sheet. Heat the oven with your baking sheet inside.
2. Get out a bowl and mix your broccoli, zucchini, oregano, pepper, onion and salt with a tbsp. of olive oil.
3. Remove your baking sheet from the oven and coat it in a nonstick cooking spray. Spread the vegetable mixture over it to roast for five minutes. Stir halfway through.
4. Take it from the oven, and add your red pepper, and sprinkle with parmesan cheese. Mix everything together.
5. Get out a panini maker or grill pan, placing it over medium-high heat. Heat up a tbsp. of oil.
6. Spread the bread horizontally on it, but don't cut it all the way through. Fill with the vegetable mix, and then a slice of mozzarella cheese on top.
7. Close the sandwich and cook like you would a normal panini. With a press it should grill for five minutes. For a grill pan cook for two and a half minutes per side. Repeat for the remaining sandwiches.

Nutrition:

Calories: 352
Protein: 16 g
Fat: 15 g
Carbs: 45 g

109. Baked Tomato

Preparation Time: 7 minutes
Cooking Time: 25 Minutes
Servings: 4
Ingredients:
- Whole grain bread
- Salt and pepper to taste
- 1 tbsp. of finely chopped basil
- 2 cloves of garlic. Finely chopped
- Extra virgin oil
- 2 large tomatoes

Directions:
1. Preheat your oven to 400°F.
2. Use the olive oil to brush the bottom of a baking dish. Set aside.
3. Slice the tomatoes into a thickness of a ½ inch. Lay the tomato pieces into the baking dish that you had prepared earlier. Sprinkle some basil and garlic on top of the tomatoes, season with pepper and salt to taste.
4. Then drizzle the slices of tomatoes with olive oil and then place the baking dish into the oven. Bake for about 20-25 minutes.
5. Remove from the oven, give it a few seconds to cool down and then serve and enjoy.
6. Tip: The tomato juice and olive oil at the bottom of the pan can be used as a dipping sauce. So, if you want, you can put it into a small bowl and enjoy it with warm whole grain bread.

Nutrition:
Calories: 342
Protein: 16 g
Fat: 10 g
Carbs: 45 g

110. Mediterranean Humus Filled Roasted Veggies

Preparation Time: 7 minutes
Cooking Time: 25 Minutes
Servings: 12
Ingredients:
- 6 pitted kalamata olives quartered
- ½ cup (2oz.) of feta cheese
- 1 cup of hummus
- 2 tbsp. of olive oil
- 1 medium red bell pepper
- 1 small zucchini (6 inch)

Directions:
1. Heat a closed medium sized contact grill at 375°F for about 5 minutes.
2. Cut the summer squash and zucchini into half lengthwise. Use a spoon to scoop out the seeds from the two vegetables and discard the seeds.
3. Cut the red bell pepper around the stem and remove the stem and the seeds; cut them into quarters and set aside.
4. Use olive oil to brush the bell pepper, squash and zucchini pieces. Once done, place them on the grill. Do not close the grill.
5. Cook them for 4-6 minutes and turn only once. The vegetables should be tender by the end of the sixth minute. Remove from the grill and let them cool for 2 minutes. Cut the vegetables into 1-inch pieces.

6. Use a spoon to scoop 2 tbsp. of humus onto each piece of vegetable. Light drizzle the vegetables with cheese and top it with one piece of olive. Serve cold or warm.
Nutrition:
Calories: 342
Protein: 10 g
Fat: 15 g
Carbs: 35 g

111. Melon Salad

Preparation Time: 10 minutes
Cooking Time: 20 Minutes
Servings: 6
Ingredients:
- ¼ tsp. Sea Salt
- ¼ tsp. Black Pepper
- 1 tbsp. Balsamic Vinegar
- 1 Cantaloupe, Quartered & Seeded
- 12 Watermelon, Small & Seedless
- 2 Cups Mozzarella Balls, Fresh
- 1/3 Cup Basil, Fresh & Torn
- 2 tbsp. Olive Oil
Directions:
1. Get out a melon baller and scoop out balls of cantaloupe, and the put them in a colander over a serving bowl.
2. Use your melon baller to cut the watermelon as well, and then put them in with your cantaloupe.
3. Allow your fruit to drain for ten minutes, and then refrigerate the juice for another recipe. It can even be added to smoothies.
4. Wipe the bowl dry, and then place your fruit in it.
5. Add in your basil, oil, vinegar, mozzarella and tomatoes before seasoning with salt and pepper.
6. Gently mix and serve immediately or chilled.
Nutrition:
Calories: 218
Protein: 10 g
Fat: 13 g
Carbs: 17 g

112. Roasted Broccoli Salad

Preparation Time: 30 Minutes
Cooking Time: 30 minutes
Servings: 4
Ingredients:
- 1 lb. Broccoli, Cut into Florets & Stem Sliced
- 3 tbsp. Olive Oil, Divided
- 1 Pint Cherry Tomatoes
- 1 ½ Tsp. Honey, Raw & Divided
- 3 Cups Cubed Bread, Whole Grain
- 1 tbsp. Balsamic Vinegar
- ½ tsp. Black Pepper
- ¼ tsp. Sea Salt, Fine
- Grated Parmesan for Serving
Directions:
1. Preheating your oven set at 450, and then get out a rimmed baking sheet. Place it in the oven to heat up.
2. Drizzle your broccoli with a tbsp. of oil, and toss to coat.
3. Remove the baking sheet form the oven, and spoon the broccoli on it. Leave oil it eh bottom of the bowl and add in your tomatoes, toss to coat, and then toss your tomatoes with a tbsp. of honey. Pour them on the same baking sheet as your broccoli.
4. Roast for fifteen minutes, and stir halfway through your cooking time.
5. Add in your bread, and then roast for three more minutes.

6. Whisk two tbsp. of oil, vinegar, and remaining honey. Season with salt and pepper. Pour this over your broccoli mix to serve.
Nutrition:
Calories: 226
Protein: 7 g
Fat: 12 g
Carbs: 26 g

113. Tomato Salad

Preparation Time: 5 minutes
Cooking Time: 20 Minutes
Servings: 4
Ingredients:
- 1 Cucumber, Sliced
- ¼ Cup Sun Dried Tomatoes, Chopped
- 1 lb. Tomatoes, Cubed
- ½ Cup Black Olives
- 1 Red Onion, Sliced
- 1 tbsp. Balsamic Vinegar
- ¼ Cup Parsley, Fresh & Chopped
- 2 tbsp. Olive Oil
- Sea Salt & Black Pepper to Taste
Directions:
1. Get out a bowl and combine all of your vegetables together. To make your dressing mix all your seasoning, olive oil and vinegar.
2. Toss with your salad and serve fresh.
Nutrition:
Calories: 126
Protein: 2.1 g
Fat: 9.2 g
Carbs: 11.5 g

114. Feta Beet Salad

Preparation Time: 5 minutes
Cooking Time: 5 Minutes
Servings: 4
Ingredients:
- 6 Red Beets, Cooked & Peeled
- 3 Oz. Feta Cheese, Cubed
- 2 tbsp. Olive Oil
- 2 tbsp. Balsamic Vinegar
Directions:
1. Combine everything, and then serve.
Nutrition:
Calories: 230
Protein: 7.3 g
Fat: 12 g
Carbs: 26.3 g

115. Cauliflower & Tomato Salad

Preparation Time: 5 minutes
Cooking Time: 15 Minutes
Servings: 4
Ingredients:
- 1 Head Cauliflower, Chopped
- 2 tbsp. Parsley, Fresh & chopped
- 2 Cups Cherry Tomatoes, Halved
- 2 tbsp. Lemon Juice, Fresh
- 2 tbsp. Pine Nuts
- Sea Salt & Black Pepper to Taste
Directions:
1. Mix your lemon juice, cherry tomatoes, cauliflower, and parsley, and then season. Top with pine nuts, and mix well before serving.
Nutrition:

Calories: 64
Protein: 2.8 g
Fat: 3.3 g
Carbs: 7.9 g

116. Wrapped Chopped Salad

Preparation time: 15 minutes
Servings: 4
Ingredients:

- 1 cup Monterey Jack cheese, shredded
- 1 avocado, chopped
- ½ cup radish, chopped
- 2 cups lettuce, teared
- 1 tomato, chopped
- 4 whole wheat tortillas
- 1 teaspoon olive oil
- ¼ teaspoon dried oregano
- ¼ teaspoon garlic powder
- ½ oz Plain yogurt
- ¼ teaspoon salt

Directions:

1. In the mixing bowl mix up together avocado, radish, lettuce, and tomato. Add cheese.
2. For the dressing: in the shallow bowl, whisk together salt, Plain yogurt, garlic powder, dried oregano, and olive oil.
3. Pour the dressing over the salad and give a good shake.
4. Then spoon the salad mixture down the center of every tortilla and wrap/roll them.
5. The cooked lunch should be served immediately; otherwise, it will not be crunchy.

Nutrition: Calories 340, Fat 20.7, Fiber 7, Carbs 28.9, Protein 12.5

117. Beet and Caper Salad

Preparation time: 5 minutes
Cooking time: 25 minutes
Servings: 4
Ingredients

- 4 medium beets
- 2 tablespoons of rice wine vinegar

For Dressing

- Small bunch parsley, stems removed
- 1 large garlic clove
- ½ teaspoon salt
- Pinch of black pepper
- 1 tablespoon extra-virgin olive oil
- 2 tablespoons capers

Directions:

1. Pour 1 cup of water into your steamer basket and place it on the side
2. Snip the tops of your beets and wash them well
3. Put the beets in your steamer basket
4. Place the steamer basket in your Instant Pot and lock the lid
5. Let it cook for about 25 minutes at high pressure
6. Once done, release the pressure naturally
7. While it is being cooked, take a small jar and add chopped up parsley and garlic alongside olive oil, salt, pepper and capers
8. Shake it vigorously to prepare your dressing
9. Open the lid once the pressure is released and check the beets for doneness using a fork
10. Take the steamer basket to your sink and run it under cold water
11. Use your finger to brush off the skin of the beets
12. Use a plastic cutting board and slice up the beets
13. Arrange them on a platter and sprinkle some vinegar on top

Nutrition: calories 230, fat 12, fiber 1, carbs 11, protein 2

118. Linguine and Brussels sprouts

Preparation time: 10 minutes
Cooking time: 25 minute
Servings: 4
Ingredients:

- 8 ounces whole-wheat linguine
- 1/3 cup, plus 2 tablespoons extra-virgin olive oil, divided
- 1 medium sweet onion, diced
- 2 to 3 garlic cloves, smashed
- 8 ounces Brussels sprouts, chopped
- ½ cup chicken stock, as needed
- 1/3 cup dry white wine
- ½ cup shredded Parmesan cheese
- 1 lemon, cut in quarters

Direction:

1. Bring a large pot of water to a boil and cook the pasta according to package directions. Drain, reserving 1 cup of the pasta water. Mix the cooked pasta with 2 tablespoons of olive oil, then set aside.
2. In a large sauté pan or skillet, heat the remaining 1/3 cup of olive oil on medium heat. Add the onion to the pan and cook for about 5 minutes, until softened. Add the smashed garlic cloves and cook for 1 minute, until fragrant.
3. Add the Brussels sprouts and cook covered for 15 minutes. Add chicken stock as needed to prevent burning. Once Brussels sprouts have wilted and are fork-tender, add white wine and cook down for about 7 minutes, until reduced.
4. Add the pasta to the skillet and add the pasta water as needed.
5. Serve with the Parmesan cheese and lemon for squeezing over the dish right before eating.

Nutrition: Calories: 530; Carbs: 95.4g; Protein: 5.0g; Fat: 16.5g

119. Minty Melon & Fruity Feta with Cool Cucumber

Preparation time: 15 minutes
Cooking time: 0 minutes
Servings: 4
Ingredients:

- 3-cups watermelon cubes
- 2-pcs tomatoes, diced
- 1-pc lemon, zested and juiced
- 1-pc cucumber, peeled, seeded & diced
- ½-cup fresh mint, roughly chopped
- ½-bulb red onion, sliced
- ¼-cup olive oil
- Salt and pepper
- 1/3-cup crumbled feta cheese

Directions:

1. Combine and mix the watermelon, tomatoes, lemon juice, lemon zest, cucumber, mint, red onion, and olive oil in a large mixing bowl.

Sprinkle over the salt and pepper. Toss to combine evenly.

2. Serve chilled with a sprinkling of crumbled feta cheese.

Nutrition: Calories: 205 Fats: 15.5g Fiber: 3.3g Carbohydrates: 18.5g Protein: 3.7g

120. Creamy Chickpea Sauce with Whole-Wheat Fusilli

Preparation time: 15 minutes
Cooking time: 20 minute
Servings: 4
Ingredients:

- ¼ cup extra-virgin olive oil
- ½ large shallot, chopped
- 5 garlic cloves, thinly sliced
- 1 (15-ounce) can chickpeas, drained and rinsed, reserving ½ cup canning liquid
- Pinch red pepper flakes
- 1 cup whole-grain fusilli pasta
- ¼ teaspoon salt
- 1/8 teaspoon freshly ground black pepper
- ¼ cup shaved fresh Parmesan cheese
- ¼ cup chopped fresh basil
- 2 teaspoons dried parsley
- 1 teaspoon dried oregano
- Red pepper flakes

Direction:

1. In a medium pan, heat the oil over medium heat, and sauté the shallot and garlic for 3 to 5 minutes, until the garlic is golden. Add ¾ of the chickpeas plus 2 tablespoons of liquid from the can, and bring to a simmer.
2. Remove from the heat, transfer into a standard blender, and blend until smooth. At this point, add the remaining chickpeas. Add more reserved chickpea liquid if it becomes thick.
3. Bring a large pot of salted water to a boil and cook pasta until al dente, about 8 minutes. Reserve ½ cup of the pasta water, drain the pasta, and return it to the pot.
4. Add the chickpea sauce to the hot pasta and add up to ¼ cup of the pasta water. You may need to add more pasta water to reach your desired consistency.
5. Place the pasta pot over medium heat and mix occasionally until the sauce thickens. Season with salt and pepper.
6. Serve, garnished with Parmesan, basil, parsley, oregano, and red pepper flakes.

Nutrition: Calories: 230; Carbs: 20.4g; Protein: 8.0g; Fat: 18.5g

121. Courgette, Fennel, and Orange Salad

Preparation Time: 15 minutes
Cooking time: 0 minutes
Servings: 4
Ingredients

- 1 orange
- 2 small courgettes (green or yellow)
- 2 small fennel bulbs
- 2 teaspoon sherry vinegar
- 4 tablespoon olive oil
- 1 Baby Gem lettuce, washed and leaves separated
- juice ½ lemon

Direction:

1. Cut the peel off the orange. Remove any pith. Slice the orange and halve each slice. Ideally, you should be cutting the orange on a plate or the chopping board since we are going to collect the juice left over from the cutting.
2. Take the fennel and remove any outer leaves that are tough. Cut the cores into halves and then slice them as thinly as you can.
3. Remove the ends of the courgettes and shave thin and long slices using a vegetable peeler. You can toss away the watery and seedy centers.
4. Take a small bowl and mix together olive oil, vinegar, and the orange juice left over on the plate or chopping board.
5. Take out another bowl and mix the courgette, fennel, orange slices, and lettuce leaves.
6. Serve the fennel mixture and top it with the orange juice dressing.

Nutrition:
Calories: 170 calories
Protein: 3 g
Total Fat: 12 g
Carbohydrate: 10 g

122. Potato Salad

Preparation Time: 10 minutes
Cooking time: 15 minutes
Servings: 4
Ingredients

- 1 small onion, thinly sliced
- 1 tablespoon olive oil
- 1 garlic clove, crushed
- 100 g roasted red pepper sliced
- 25 g black olive, sliced
- 1 teaspoon fresh oregano
- 200 g canned cherry tomatoes
- 300 g new potato, halved if large
- handful basil leaves, torn

Direction:

1. Take out a saucepan and place it over medium heat. Pour the olive oil into it and allow it to heat. Add the onions and cook for about 10 minutes, or until the onions have become soft.
2. Add oregano and garlic. Cook for another 1 minute.
3. Add the peppers and tomato. Let the mixture simmer for about 10 minutes.
4. Use a pan and place it over medium-high heat. Bring it to a boil and then add the potatoes into the water. Cook the potatoes for about 15 minutes, or until they turn tender. Drain the potatoes.
5. Take out a small bowl and add the pepper and tomato sauce into it. Toss in the potatoes and mix well.
6. Serve your salad with a sprinkle of basil and olives.

Nutrition:
Calories: 111 calories
Protein: 3 g
Total Fat: 4 g
Carbohydrate: 16 g

123. Tomato, Cucumber, and Feta Salad

Preparation Time: 10 minutes
Cooking time: 0 minutes
Servings: 4
Ingredients

- 3 tablespoons extra-virgin olive oil
- ½ teaspoon Dijon mustard

- 4 medium Persian cucumbers, thinly sliced crosswise
- 1 teaspoon chopped fresh oregano, plus extra for garnish
- 1 ½ tablespoons red-wine vinegar
- 1 cup (8 ounces) tomatoes, cut into wedges
- 1/4 teaspoon salt
- 1 1/2 ounces feta cheese, crumbled

Direction:
1. Take out a medium bowl and combine oregano, vinegar, mustard, and salt.
2. Drizzle the oil on top. Add tomatoes, cucumbers, and feta.
3. Mix them well and serve with oregano leaves toppings, if you prefer.
4. Refrigerate if you are planning to serve later.

Nutrition:
Calories: 153 calories
Protein: 3 g
Total Fat: 13.1 g
Carbohydrate: 6.1 g

124. Goat Cheese Stuffed Tomatoes

Preparation Time: 10 minutes
Cooking time: 0 minutes
Servings: 4
Ingredients
- 6-8 arugula leaves
- 3 ounces crumbled feta cheese
- 2 medium ripe tomatoes
- extra-virgin olive oil to drizzle
- balsamic vinegar to drizzle
- 1 red onion, very thinly sliced for garnish
- fresh chopped parsley for garnish
- salt and freshly ground pepper to taste

Direction:
1. Arrange the arugula leaves in the center of a plate.
2. Remove the tops and the core of the tomatoes. Ideally, you should remove the top first and scoop out the core.
3. Fill the tomatoes with feta cheese. Add salt and pepper, to taste
4. Drizzle with olive oil and balsamic vinegar.
5. Garnish with chopped parsley and red onion.
6. Serve at room temperature.

Nutrition:
Calories: 142 calories
Protein: 7 g
Total Fat: 13.1 g
Carbohydrate: 7 g

125. Classic Tabbouleh

Preparation Time: 10 minutes
Cooking time: 10 minutes (Additional 5-10 minutes if you decide to roast the pine nuts)
Servings: 4
Ingredients
- ¾ cup bulgur
- 2 cups freshly chopped parsley
- 1½ cups water
- ½ cup fresh lemon juice
- ½ cup extra-virgin olive oil
- ½ red bell pepper, diced
- 3 ripe plum tomatoes, peeled, seeded, and diced
- 1 large cucumber, peeled, seeded, and diced

- ¾ cup chopped scallions, white and green parts
- ½ green bell pepper, diced
- ½ cup finely chopped fresh mint
- handful of greens for serving
- seasoned pita wedges
- sea salt and freshly ground pepper to taste

Direction:
1. Preheat the oven to around 375° F.
2. Take a medium-sized bowl and add the asparagus with 2 tablespoons of salt and olive oil.
3. Take out a baking dish and add the asparagus. Place the tray in the oven and roast for about 10 minutes, or until the asparagus becomes tender.
4. Take out the asparagus and set aside.
5. Use another medium-sized bowl and add garlic, lime juice, orange juice, and remaining 2 tablespoons of olive oil. Whisk all the ingredients together. Add salt and pepper to taste.
6. Take the lettuce and split it into 6 plates. Take out the asparagus and place it on top of the lettuce.
7. Pour the dressing over the asparagus and lettuce salad. Top the salad with basil and pine nuts. Add a small amount of Romano cheese for garnish, if you prefer.
8. You can also toast the pine nuts in the oven. Use the method below:
9. Take out a baking tray and line it with a non-stick baking sheet. Add the pine nuts on top.
10. Bake at 375 degrees for about 5-10 minutes, or until the nuts are lightly browned.
11. Remove from the oven and set aside to cool.
12. Add the nuts to the salad as a topping.

Nutrition:
Calories: 177 calories
Protein: 12 g
Total Fat: 11 g
Carbohydrate: 28 g

126. Mediterranean Greens

Preparation Time: 10 minutes
Cooking time: None
Servings: 4
Ingredients
- 6 cups assorted fresh mixed greens (such as radicchio, arugula, watercress, baby spinach, and romaine)
- 1 small red onion, thinly sliced
- 20 cherry tomatoes, halved
- ¼ cup dried cranberries
- ¼ cup chopped walnuts
- crumbled feta cheese
- freshly ground pepper to taste
- 2 tablespoons balsamic vinegar
- 2 cloves fresh garlic, finely minced
- 4 tablespoons extra-virgin olive oil
- 1 tablespoon water
- ½ teaspoon crushed dried oregano

Direction:
1. Take out a large salad bowl, combine walnuts, greens, tomatoes, onion, and cranberries. Gently toss.
2. For the dressing, combine water, vinegar, oregano, olive oil, and garlic. Mix the ingredients well. Pour over the salad and lightly toss.
3. Add feta cheese as garnish, if preferred.

4. Add pepper to taste.

Nutrition:
Calories: 140 calories
Protein: 2 g
Total Fat: 12 g
Carbohydrate: 6 g

127. North African Zucchini Salad

Preparation Time: 10 minutes
Cooking time: 0 minutes
Servings: 4
Ingredients
- 1-pound firm green zucchini, thinly sliced
- ½ teaspoon ground cumin
- 2 cloves fresh garlic, finely minced
- juice from 1 large lemon
- 1 tablespoon extra-virgin olive oil
- 1½ tablespoons plain low-fat yogurt
- crumbled feta cheese
- finely chopped parsley for garnish
- salt and freshly ground pepper to taste

Direction:
1. Add the zucchini into a large saucepan and steam it for about 2-5 minutes, or until it becomes tender and crispy. Place the zucchini under cold water and drain well.
2. Take out a large bowl and mix cumin, olive oil, lemon juice, garlic, and yogurt. Add salt and pepper to taste.
3. Add the zucchini into the mixture in the bowl and toss gently.
4. Serve with feta cheese and parsley as garnish.

Nutrition:
Calories: 140 calories
Protein: 2 g
Total Fat: 12 g
Carbohydrate: 6 g

128. Avocado Salad

Preparation Time: 10 minutes
Cooking time: 0 minutes
Servings: 3
Ingredients
- 1 small onion, finely chopped
- 1 large ripe avocado, pitted and peeled
- 2 tablespoons chopped fresh parsley
- 2 teaspoons fresh lime juice
- ½ small hot pepper, finely chopped (optional)
- 1 cup halved cherry tomatoes
- salt and freshly ground pepper to taste

Direction:
1. Start with the avocado and cut it into bite-sized pieces.
2. Add parsley, lime juice, tomatoes, onion, and hot pepper. Mix all the ingredients well. Add salt and pepper to taste.
3. Finally, add the avocado into the mixture and mix them well.

Nutrition:
Calories: 130 calories
Protein: 2 g
Total Fat: 10 g
Carbohydrate: 10 g

129. Tunisian Style Carrot Salad

Preparation Time: 15 minutes
Cooking time: 0 minutes
Servings: 6
Ingredients
- 10 medium carrots, peeled and sliced
- 1 cup crumbled feta cheese, divided
- 2 teaspoons caraway seed
- ¼ cup extra-virgin olive oil
- 6 tablespoons apple cider vinegar
- 5 teaspoons freshly minced garlic
- 1 tablespoon Harissa paste (choose the level of heat based on your preference)
- 20 pitted Kalamata olives, reserving some for garnish
- salt to taste

Direction:
1. Take out a medium saucepan and place it on medium heat. Fill it with water and add the carrots. Cook carrots until tender. Drain and cool the carrots under cold water. Drain again to remove any excess water.
2. Take out a large bowl and place the carrots in them.
3. Take out a mortar and combine salt, garlic, and caraway seeds. Grind them until they form a paste. Otherwise, you can also use a small bowl, preferably one not made out of glass for grind. The final option would be to toss the ingredients into a blender and pulse them.
4. Add vinegar and Harissa into the bowl with the carrots and mix them well.
5. Use a large spoon and mash the carrots. Add the garlic mixture into the carrot and mix again until they have all blended well. Add the olive oil and mix again.
6. Finally, add about ½ the feta cheese and all the olives and mix well again.
7. Take out a large bowl and add the salad to it. Top it with the remaining feta cheese.

Nutrition:
Calories: 138 calories
Protein: 7 g
Total Fat: 5 g
Carbohydrate: 13 g

130. Classic Greek Salad

Preparation Time: 15 minutes
Cooking time: None
Servings: 6
Ingredients
- 6 large firm tomatoes, quartered
- 20 Greek black olives
- ½ pound Greek feta cheese, cut into small cubes
- ½ head of escarole, shredded
- 3 tablespoons red wine vinegar
- ¼ cup extra-virgin olive oil
- 1 tablespoon dried oregano
- ½ English cucumber, peeled, seeded, and thinly sliced
- 2 cloves fresh garlic, finely minced
- ½ red onion, sliced
- 1 medium red bell pepper, seeded and sliced
- ¼ cup freshly chopped Italian parsley

- salt and freshly ground pepper to taste

Direction:

1. Take out a large bowl and add vinegar, oregano, olive oil, and garlic. Add salt and pepper to taste. Set aside the bowl.
2. In another large bowl, add onion, tomatoes, escarole, cucumber, bell pepper, and cheese and mix them well.
3. Take the vinegar mixture and pour it over the salad in the second bowl.
4. Top the salad with olives and parsley.

Nutrition:

Calories: 268 calories

Protein: 23 g

Total Fat: 17 g

Carbohydrate: 44 g

131. Caesar Salad

Preparation Time: 5 minutes

Cooking time: 0 minutes

Servings: 6

Ingredients

- 10 small pitted black olives, chopped
- 1-2 bunches romaine lettuce, cleaned and torn in pieces
- 2 teaspoons lemon juice
- 2½ teaspoons balsamic vinegar
- ½ cup grated parmesan cheese
- ½ cup nonfat plain yogurt
- 1 teaspoon worcestershire sauce
- ½ teaspoon anchovy paste
- 2 cloves freshly minced garlic

Direction:

1. Take out a large bowl and place romaine lettuce in it.
2. Take out your blended and add mix lemon juice, yogurt, garlic, anchovy paste, vinegar, worcestershire sauce, and ¼ cup parmesan cheese. Mix all the ingredients well until they are smooth.
3. Pour the yogurt mixture over the lettuce and toss lightly.
4. Top the salad with the remaining parmesan cheese.

Nutrition:

Calories: 49 calories

Protein: 4 g

Total Fat: 1 g

Carbohydrate: 4 g

132. Spanish Salad

Preparation Time: 10 minutes

Cooking time: 0 minutes

Servings: 6

Ingredients

- 2 bunches romaine lettuce, cleaned and trimmed
- 1 large sweet onion, thinly sliced
- 3 medium ripe tomatoes, chopped
- 3 tablespoons balsamic vinegar
- ¼ cup extra-virgin olive oil
- 1 red bell pepper, seeded and thinly sliced
- 1 green bell pepper, seeded and thinly sliced
- ¼ cup chopped and pitted black olives
- ¼ cup chopped and pitted marinated green olives
- salt and freshly ground pepper to taste

Direction:

1. Take out 6 plates and place romaine lettuce on them to form a base.
2. Add peppers, tomatoes, onion, and olives on top of each of the lettuce bases.
3. In a small bowl, combine olive oil and vinegar together. Add the dressing over the salad.
4. Add salt and pepper to taste, if preferred.

Nutrition:

Calories: 107 calories

Protein: 2 g

Total Fat: 9 g

Carbohydrate: 6 g

133. Parsley Couscous Salad

Preparation Time: 2 hours (refrigerate overnight if you are having in the morning)

Cooking time: 0 minutes

Servings: 4

Ingredients

- ¼ cup couscous
- 2 teaspoons extra-virgin olive oil
- ¼ cup water
- 2 teaspoons lemon zest
- 1 medium ripe tomato, peeled, seeded, and diced
- 2 tablespoons pine nuts
- 2 tablespoons fresh lemon juice
- ¼ cup finely chopped fresh flat parsley leaves
- 2 tablespoons finely chopped fresh mint leaves
- 2 heads Belgian endive, leaves for scooping
- whole wheat pita rounds, cut into wedges and toasted until crispy
- salt and freshly ground pepper to taste

Direction:

1. Take out a medium bowl and then combine lemon juice and water. All the mixture to stand for about 1 hour.
2. After the hour, add mint, parsley, lemon zest, olive oil, and pine nuts. Mix the ingredients well.
3. Add in the couscous to the mixture. Allow it to stand for about 1 hour. After 1 hour, add salt and pepper to taste.
4. Place couscous mixture in the center of a plate and top it with tomato. You can surround the couscous salad with toasted pita wedges and endive leaves, which makes for a wonderful presentation.
5. Refrigerator overnight so that you can have it the next day.

Nutrition:

Calories: 120 calories

Protein: 5 g

Total Fat: 2 g

Carbohydrate: 18 g

134. Cress and Tangerine Salad

Preparation Time: 15 minutes

Cooking time: None

Servings: 4

Ingredients

- 4 large sweet tangerines
- ¼ cup extra-virgin olive oil
- 2 large bunches watercress, washed and stems removed
- juice from 1 fresh lemon
- 10 cherry tomatoes, halved

- 16 pitted Kalamata olives
- Sea salt and freshly ground pepper to taste

Direction:
1. Take the tangerines and peel them into a medium-sized bowl. Make sure that you remove any pits and squeeze the pieces. You should have around ¼ cup of tangerine juice. Set pieces aside.
2. Take a large bowl and add lemon juice, tangerine juice, and olive oil. Mix them together and add salt and pepper for flavor, if you prefer.
3. Use paper towels to pat the cress dry. Add watercress, tomatoes, and olives to the bowl containing the tangerine slices (not to be confused with the bowl containing tangerine juice). Toss them lightly.
4. Pour the tangerine juice mixture on top. Mix well and serve.

Nutrition:
Calories: 195 calories
Protein: 3 g
Total Fat: 16 g
Carbohydrate: 14 g

135. Prosciutto and Figs Salad

Preparation Time: 10 minutes
Cooking time: 0 minutes
Servings: 4
Ingredients
- One 10-12-ounce package fresh baby spinach
- 1 small hot red chili pepper, finely diced
- 1 carton figs, stems removed and quartered
- ½ cup walnuts, coarsely chopped
- 1 tablespoon fresh orange juice
- 1 tablespoon honey
- 4 slices prosciutto, cut into strips
- shaved parmesan cheese for garnish

Direction:
1. Take your spinach and divide them into 4 equal portions. Each portion should be on a separate plate and will act as a base. Add quartered prosciutto, figs, and walnuts on each spinach as toppings.
2. For the dressing, take a small bowl and add honey, orange juice, and diced pepper. Add the mixture over the salad.
3. Finally, toss the salad lightly and use parmesan cheese for the garnish.

Nutrition:
Calories: 190 calories
Protein: 26 g
Total Fat: 9 g
Carbohydrate: 17 g

136. Garden Vegetables and Chickpeas Salad

Preparation Time: 10 minutes (or you can refrigerate it overnight)
Cooking time: 0 minutes
Servings: 4
Ingredients
- 2 tablespoons freshly squeezed lemon juice
- 1/8 teaspoon freshly ground pepper
- 1 cup cubed part-skim mozzarella cheese
- 1 tablespoon fresh basil leaf, snipped

- 1 (15-ounce) can chickpeas, rinsed and well drained
- 2 cups coarsely chopped fresh broccoli
- 2 cloves fresh garlic, finely minced
- ½ cup sliced fresh carrots
- 1 7½-ounce can dice tomatoes, undrained

Direction:
1. Use a large bowl and add garlic, basil, lemon juice, and ground pepper. Mix them well.
2. Add the chickpeas, carrots, tomatoes with juice, broccoli, and mozzarella cheese. Toss all the ingredients well.
3. You can serve immediately, or you can keep it refrigerated overnight.

Nutrition:
Calories: 195 calories
Protein: 16 g
Total Fat: 7 g
Carbohydrate: 24 g

137. Peppered Watercress Salad

Preparation Time: 5 minutes (or less)
Cooking time: None
Servings: 4
Ingredients
- 2 teaspoons champagne vinegar
- 2 bunches (about 8 cups) watercress, rinsed and rough stems removed
- 2 tablespoons extra-virgin olive oil
- salt and freshly ground pepper to taste

Direction:
1. Drain the watercress properly.
2. Take out a small bowl and then add salt, pepper, vinegar, and olive oil. Mix them well together.
3. Transfer the watercress to a bowl. Add the vinegar mixture into it and toss well.
4. Serve immediately.

Nutrition:
Calories: 67 calories
Protein: 4 g
Total Fat: 7 g
Carbohydrate: 1 g

138. Watermelon Salad

Preparation Time: 5 minutes
Cooking time: None
Servings: 4
Ingredients
- 2 cups cubed seedless watermelon
- 2 cups arugula
- 1 cup sliced cucumber, with skin on
- 3 tablespoons extra virgin olive oil
- 2 teaspoons white balsamic vinegar
- 4 ounces fresh feta cheese, cut into bite-sized pieces
- salt and freshly ground pepper to taste

Direction:
1. Take a small bowl and add watermelon, arugula, salt and pepper, cucumber, vinegar, feta, and olive oil.
2. Mix them well and serve immediately.

Nutrition:
Calories: 94 calories
Protein: 5 g
Total Fat: 7 g
Carbohydrate: 7 g

139. Watercress and Pear Salad

Preparation Time: 5 minutes
Cooking time: None
Servings: 4
Ingredients

- 4 ripe-but-firm smooth-skin pears
- 2 tablespoons toasted pecan halves
- 2 ounces crumbled blue cheese
- 2 cups watercress
- juice from 1 lemon
- honey to drizzle
- ¼ cup vinaigrette dressing

Direction:
1. Take each pear and core it. Leave the stem intact.
2. Take a medium sized bowl and add watercress, pecans, blue cheese, and vinaigrette. Mix all the ingredients well. Set aside.
3. Slice each pear in 4 horizontal slices. Use lemon juice to brush the cut sides.
4. For the next part, reassemble the pears into their original shape but with the salad mixture between each slice.
5. Add honey as a topping.

Nutrition:
Calories: 94 calories
Protein: 5 g
Total Fat: 7 g
Carbohydrate: 7 g

140. Cheesy Beet Salad

Preparation time: 10 minutes
Cooking time: 1 hour
Servings: 4
Ingredients:
- 4 beets, peeled and cut into wedges
- 3 tablespoons olive oil
- Salt and black pepper to the taste
- ¼ cup lime juice
- 8 slices goat cheese, crumbled
- 1/3 cup walnuts, chopped
- 1 tablespoons chive, chopped

Directions:
1. In a roasting pan, combine the beets with the oil, salt and pepper, toss and bake at 400 degrees F for 1 hour.
2. Cool the beets down, transfer them to a bowl, add the rest of the ingredients, toss and serve as a side salad.
Nutrition: calories 156, fat 4.2, fiber 3.4, carbs 6.5, protein 4

141. Vinegar Cucumber Mix

Preparation time: 10 minutes
Cooking Time: 0 Minutes
Servings: 6
Ingredients:
- 1 tablespoon olive oil
- 4 cucumbers, sliced
- Salt and black pepper to the taste
- 1 red onion, chopped
- 3 tablespoons red wine vinegar
- 1 bunch basil, chopped
- 1 teaspoon honey

Directions:
1. In a bowl, mix the vinegar with the basil, salt, pepper, the oil and the honey and whisk well.

2. In a bowl, mix the cucumber with the onion and the vinaigrette, toss and serve as a side salad.
Nutrition: calories 182, fat 7.8, fiber 2.1, carbs 4.3, protein 4.1

142. Crispy Fennel Salad

Preparation time: 10 minutes
Cooking Time: 15 Minutes
Servings: 2
Ingredients:
- 1 fennel bulb, finely sliced
- 1 grapefruit, cut into segments
- 1 orange, cut into segments
- 2 tablespoons almond slices, toasted
- 1 teaspoon chopped mint
- 1 tablespoon chopped dill
- Salt and pepper to taste
- 1 tablespoon grape seed oil

Directions:
1. Mix the fennel bulb with the grapefruit and orange segments on a platter.
2. Top with almond slices, mint and dill then drizzle with the oil and season with salt and pepper.
3. Serve the salad as fresh as possible.
Nutrition: Per Serving:Calories:104 Fat:0.5g Protein:3.1g Carbohydrates:25.5g

143. Red Beet Feta Salad

Preparation time: 10 minutes
Cooking Time: 15 Minutes
Servings: 4
Ingredients:
- 6 red beets, cooked and peeled
- 3 oz. feta cheese, cubed
- 2 tablespoons extra virgin olive oil
- 2 tablespoons balsamic vinegar

Directions:
1. Combine the beets and feta cheese on a platter.
2. Drizzle with oil and vinegar and serve right away.
Nutrition: Per Serving: Calories: 230 Fat: 12.0g Protein: 7.3g Carbohydrates: 26.3g

144. Cheesy Potato Mash

Preparation time: 10 minutes
Cooking Time: 20 Minutes
Servings: 8
Ingredients:
- 2 pounds gold potatoes, peeled and cubed
- 1 and ½ cup cream cheese, soft
- Sea salt and black pepper to the taste
- ½ cup almond milk
- 2 tablespoons chives, chopped

Directions:
1. Put potatoes in a pot, add water to cover, add a pinch of salt, bring to a simmer over medium heat, cook for 20 minutes, drain and mash them.
2. Add the rest of the ingredients except the chives and whisk well.
3. Add the chives, stir, divide between plates and serve as a side dish.
Nutrition: calories 243, fat 14.2, fiber 1.4, carbs 3.5, protein 1.4

145. Provencal Summer Salad

Preparation time: 10 minutes
Cooking Time: 25 Minutes
Servings: 4

Ingredients:
- 1 zucchini, sliced
- 1 eggplant, sliced
- 2 red onions, sliced
- 2 tomatoes, sliced
- 1 teaspoon dried mint
- 2 garlic cloves, minced
- 2 tablespoons balsamic vinegar
- Salt and pepper to taste

Directions:

1. Season the zucchini, eggplant, onions and tomatoes with salt and pepper. Cook the vegetable slices on the grill until browned.
2. Transfer the vegetables in a salad bowl then add the mint, garlic and vinegar.
3. Serve the salad right away.

Nutrition Info: Per Serving: Calories: 74 Fat: 0.5g Protein: 3.0g Carbohydrates: 16.5g

146. Sunflower Seeds And Arugula Garden Salad

Preparation time: 5 minutes
Cooking Time: 0 Minutes
Servings: 6
Ingredients:
- ¼ tsp black pepper
- ¼ tsp salt
- 1 tsp fresh thyme, chopped
- 2 tbsp sunflower seeds, toasted
- 2 cups red grapes, halved
- 7 cups baby arugula, loosely packed
- 1 tbsp coconut oil
- 2 tsp honey
- 3 tbsp red wine vinegar
- ½ tsp stone-ground mustard

Directions:

1. In a small bowl, whisk together mustard, honey and vinegar. Slowly pour oil as you whisk.
2. In a large salad bowl, mix thyme, seeds, grapes and arugula.
3. Drizzle with dressing and serve.

Nutrition Info: Calories per serving: 86.7; Protein: 1.6g; Carbs: 13.1g; Fat: 3.1g

147. Ginger Pumpkin Mash

Preparation time: 1 hour
Cooking Time: 30 Minutes
Servings: 4
Ingredients:
- 10 oz pumpkin, peeled
- ½ teaspoon butter
- ¾ teaspoon ground ginger
- 1/3 teaspoon salt

Directions:

1. Chop the pumpkin into the cubes and bake in the preheated to the 360F oven for 30 minutes or until the pumpkin is soft.
2. After this, transfer the pumpkin cubes in the food processor.
3. Add butter, salt, and ground ginger.
4. Blend the vegetable until you get puree or use the potato masher for this step.

Nutrition: Per Serving: calories 30, fat 0.7, fiber 2.1, carbs 6, protein 0.8

148. Yogurt Peppers Mix

Preparation time: 20 minutes
Cooking Time: 15 Minutes
Servings: 4
Ingredients:
- 2 red bell peppers, cut into thick strips
- 2 tablespoons olive oil
- 3 shallots, chopped
- 3 garlic cloves, minced
- Salt and black pepper to the taste
- ½ cup Greek yogurt
- 1 tablespoon cilantro, chopped

Directions:

1. Heat up a pan with the oil over medium heat, add the shallots and garlic, stir and cook for 5 minutes.
2. Add the rest of the ingredients, toss, cook for 10 minutes more, divide the mix between plates and serve as a side dish.

Nutrition: calories 274, fat 11, fiber 3.5, protein 13.3, carbs 6.5

149. Lemony Carrots

Preparation time: 1 hour
Cooking Time: 40 Minutes
Servings: 4
Ingredients:
- 3 tablespoons olive oil
- 2 pounds baby carrots, trimmed
- Salt and black pepper to the taste
- ½ teaspoon lemon zest, grated
- 1 tablespoon lemon juice
- 1/3 cup Greek yogurt
- 1 garlic clove, minced
- 1 teaspoon cumin, ground
- 1 tablespoon dill, chopped

Directions:

1. In a roasting pan, combine the carrots with the oil, salt, pepper and the rest of the ingredients except the dill, toss and bake at 400 degrees F for 20 minutes.
2. Reduce the temperature to 375 degrees F and cook for 20 minutes more.
3. Divide the mix between plates, sprinkle the dill on top and serve.

Nutrition: calories 192, fat 5.4, fiber 3.4, carbs 7.3, protein 5.6

150. Roasted Vegetable Salad

Preparation time: 20 minutes
Cooking Time: 30 Minutes
Servings: 6
Ingredients:
- ½ pound baby carrots
- 2 red onions, sliced
- 1 zucchini, sliced
- 2 eggplants, cubed
- 1 cauliflower, cut into florets
- 1 sweet potato, peeled and cubed
- 1 endive, sliced
- 3 tablespoons extra virgin olive oil
- 1 teaspoon dried basil
- Salt and pepper to taste
- 1 lemon, juiced
- 1 tablespoon balsamic vinegar

Directions:

1. Combine the vegetables with the oil, basil, salt and pepper in a deep-dish baking pan and cook in the preheated oven at 350F for 25-30 minutes.

2. When done, transfer in a salad bowl and add the lemon juice and vinegar.

3. Serve the salad fresh.

Nutrition: Per Serving:Calories:164 Fat:7.6g Protein:3.7g Carbohydrates:24.2g

151. Chicken Kale Soup

Preparation time: 20 minutes
Cooking Time: 6 Hours 10 Minutes
Servings: 6
Ingredients:
- 2poundschicken breast, skinless
- 1/3cuponion
- 1tablespoonolive oil
- 14ounceschicken bone broth
- ½ cup olive oil
- 4 cups chicken stock
- ¼ cup lemon juice
- 5ouncesbaby kale leaves
- Salt, to taste

Directions:
1. Season chicken with salt and black pepper.
2. Heat olive oil over medium heat in a large skillet and add seasoned chicken.
3. Reduce the temperature and cook for about 15 minutes.
4. Shred the chicken and place in the crock pot.
5. Process the chicken broth and onions in a blender and blend until smooth.
6. Pour into crock pot and stir in the remaining ingredients.
7. Cook on low for about 6 hours, stirring once while cooking.

Nutrition: Calories: 261 Carbs: 2g Fats: 21g Proteins: 14.1g Sodium: 264mg Sugar: 0.3g

152. Mozzarella Pasta Mix

Preparation time: 5 minutes
Cooking Time: 15 Minutes
Servings: 2
Ingredients:
- 2 oz whole grain elbow macaroni
- 1 tablespoon fresh basil
- ¼ cup cherry size Mozzarella
- ½ cup cherry tomatoes, halved
- 1 tablespoon olive oil
- 1 teaspoon dried marjoram
- 1 cup water, for cooking

Directions:
1. Boil elbow macaroni in water for 15 minutes. Drain water and chill macaroni little.
2. Chop fresh basil roughly and place it in the salad bowl.
3. Add Mozzarella, cherry tomatoes, dried marjoram, olive oil, and macaroni.
4. Mix up salad well.

Nutrition Info: Per Serving: calories 170, fat 9.7, fiber 1.1, carbs 15, protein 6

153. Quinoa Salad

Preparation time: 10 minutes
Cooking Time: 20 Minutes
Servings: 2 Cups
Ingredients:
- 2 cups red quinoa
- 4 cups water
- 1 (15-oz.) can chickpeas, drained
- 1 medium red onion, chopped (1/2 cup)
- 3 TB. fresh mint leaves, finely chopped

- 1/4 cup extra-virgin olive oil
- 3 TB. fresh lemon juice
- 1/2 tsp. salt
- 1/2 tsp. fresh ground black pepper

Directions:
1. In a medium saucepan over medium-high heat, bring red quinoa and water to a boil. Cover, reduce heat to low, and cook for 20 minutes or until water is absorbed and quinoa is tender. Let cool.
2. In a large bowl, add quinoa, chickpeas, red onion, and mint.
3. In a small bowl, whisk together extra-virgin olive oil, lemon juice, salt, and black pepper.
4. Pour dressing over quinoa mixture, and stir well to combine.
5. Serve immediately, or refrigerate and enjoy for up to 2 or 3 days.

154. Couscous And Toasted Almonds

Preparation time: 5 minutes
Cooking Time: 10 Minutes
Servings: 4
Ingredients:
- 1 cup (about 200 g) whole-grain couscous
- 400 ml boiling water
- 1 tablespoon extra-virgin olive oil
- 1/2 red onion, chopped
- 1/2 teaspoon ground ginger,
- 1/2 teaspoon ground cinnamon and
- 1/2 teaspoon ground coriander
- 2 tablespoons blanched almonds, toasted, and chopped

Directions:
1. Preheat the oven to 110C.
2. In a casserole, toss the couscous with the olive oil, onion, spices, salt and pepper. Stir in the boiling water, cover, and bake for 10 minutes. Fluff using a fork. Scatter the nuts over the top and then serve. Pair with harira.

Nutrition Info: Per Serving:261.23 cal,8 g total fat (1 g sat. fat), 37 g carb, 7 g protein, 1 g sugar, and 6.85 mg sodium.

155. Spanish Tomato Salad

Preparation time: 10 minutes
Cooking Time: 15 Minutes
Servings: 4
Ingredients:
- 1-pound tomatoes, cubed
- 2 cucumbers, cubed
- 2 garlic cloves, chopped
- 1 red onion, sliced
- 2 anchovy fillets
- 1 tablespoon balsamic vinegar
- 1 pinch chili powder
- Salt and pepper to taste

Directions:
1. Combine the tomatoes, cucumbers, garlic and red onion in a bowl.
2. In a mortar, mix the anchovy fillets, vinegar, chili powder, salt and pepper.
3. Drizzle the mixture over the salad and mix well.
4. Serve the salad fresh.

Nutrition: Per Serving: Calories: 61 Fat: 0.6g Protein: 3.0g Carbohydrates: 13.0g

156. Chickpeas And Beets Mix

Preparation time: 10 minutes
Cooking Time: 25 Minutes
Servings: 4
Ingredients:
- 3 tablespoons capers, drained and chopped
- Juice of 1 lemon
- Zest of 1 lemon, grated
- 1 red onion, chopped
- 3 tablespoons olive oil
- 14 ounces canned chickpeas, drained
- 8 ounces beets, peeled and cubed
- 1 tablespoon parsley, chopped
- Salt and pepper to the taste

Directions:
1. Heat up a pan with the oil over medium heat, add the onion, lemon zest, lemon juice and the capers and sauté for 5 minutes.
2. Add the rest of the ingredients, stir and cook over medium-low heat for 20 minutes more.
3. Divide the mix between plates and serve as a side dish.
Nutrition: calories 199, fat 4.5, fiber 2.3, carbs 6.5, protein 3.3

157. Roasted Bell Pepper Salad With Anchovy Dressing

Preparation time: 15 minutes
Cooking Time: 20 Minutes
Servings: 4
Ingredients:
- 8 roasted red bell peppers, sliced
- 2 tablespoons pine nuts
- 1 cup cherry tomatoes, halved
- 2 tablespoons chopped parsley
- 4 anchovy fillets
- 1 lemon, juiced
- 1 garlic clove
- 1 tablespoon extra-virgin olive oil
- Salt and pepper to taste

Directions:
1. Combine the anchovy fillets, lemon juice, garlic and olive oil in a mortar and mix them well.
2. Mix the rest of the ingredients in a salad bowl then drizzle in the dressing.
3. Serve the salad as fresh as possible.
Nutrition: Per Serving: Calories: 81 Fat: 7.0g Protein: 2.4g Carbohydrates: 4.0g

158. Warm Shrimp And Arugula Salad

Preparation time: 10 minutes
Cooking Time: 20 Minutes
Servings: 4
Ingredients:
- 2 tablespoons extra virgin olive oil
- 2 garlic cloves, minced
- 1 red pepper, sliced
- 1-pound fresh shrimps, peeled and deveined
- 1 orange, juiced
- Salt and pepper to taste
- 3 cups arugula

Directions:
1. Heat the oil in a frying pan and stir in the garlic and red pepper. Cook for 1 minute then add the shrimps.
2. Cook for 5 minutes then add the orange juice and cook for another 5 more minutes.

3. When done, spoon the shrimps and the sauce over the arugula.
4. Serve the salad fresh.
Nutrition: Per Serving:Calories:232 Fat:9.2g Protein:27.0g Carbohydrates:10.0g

159. Cheesy Tomato Salad

Preparation time: 5 minutes
Cooking Time: 0 Minutes
Servings: 4
Ingredients:
- 2 pounds tomatoes, sliced
- 1 red onion, chopped
- Sea salt and black pepper to the taste
- 4 ounces feta cheese, crumbled
- 2 tablespoons mint, chopped
- A drizzle of olive oil

Directions:
1. In a salad bowl, mix the tomatoes with the onion and the rest of the ingredients, toss and serve as a side salad.
Nutrition: calories 190, fat 4.5, fiber 3.4, carbs 8.7, protein 3.3

160. Garlic Cucumber Mix

Preparation time: 10 minutes
Cooking Time: 0 Minutes
Servings: 4
Ingredients:
- 2 cucumbers, sliced
- 2 spring onions, chopped
- 2 tablespoons olive oil
- 3 garlic cloves, grated
- 1 tablespoon thyme, chopped
- Salt and black pepper to the taste
- 3 and ½ ounces goat cheese, crumbled

Directions:
1. In a salad bowl, mix the cucumbers with the onions and the rest of the ingredients, toss and serve after keeping it in the fridge for 15 minutes.
Nutrition Info: calories 140, fat 5.4, fiber 4.3, carbs 6.5, protein 4.8

Chapter 3. Soups

161. Italian Broccoli and Potato Soup

Preparation Time: 10 minutes
Cooking Time: 45 minutes
Servings: 4
Ingredients:
- 1-pound broccoli, cut into florets
- 2 potatoes, peeled, chopped
- 4 cups vegetable broth
- 1/2 teaspoon dried rosemary
- 1/2 teaspoon salt
- 1/2 cup sour cream

Directions:
1. Place broccoli and potatoes in the pot. Pour the broth and seal the lid. Cook on Soup/Broth for 20 minutes on high. Do a quick release and remove to a blender.
2. Pulse to combine and stir in sour cream and add salt.

Nutrition:
Calories: 123
Fat: 13 g
Fiber: 58 g
Carbs: 11 g
Protein: 12 g

162. Broccoli Soup with Gorgonzola

Preparation Time: 10 minutes
Cooking Time: 35 Minutes
Servings: 4
Ingredients:
- 8 ounces Gorgonzola cheese, crumbled
- 1 cup broccoli, finely chopped
- 4 cups water
- 1 tablespoon olive oil
- 1/2 cup full-fat milk
- 1 tablespoon parsley, finely chopped
- 1/2 teaspoon salt
- 1/4 teaspoon black pepper, ground

Directions:
1. Add all ingredients to the pot, seal the lid, and cook on Soup/Broth mode for 30 minutes on High Pressure. Do a quick release. Remove the lid and sprinkle with fresh parsley. Serve warm.

Nutrition:
Calories: 132
Fat: 11 g
Fiber: 50 g
Carbs: 18 g
Protein: 12 g

163. Comfort Food Soup

Preparation Time: 10 minutes
Cooking Time: 30 Minutes
Servings: 8
Ingredients:
- 1 cup yellow split peas
- 1 cup red lentils
- 1 large onion, chopped roughly
- 2 carrots, peeled and chopped roughly
- 5 garlic cloves, chopped
- 1 1/2 teaspoon ground cumin
- Salt and black pepper,
- 8 cup chicken broth
- 2 tablespoons fresh lemon juice

Directions:
1. In the pot of Instant Pot, place all the ingredients except for the lemon juice and stir to merge.
2. Close the lid and place the pressure.
3. Cook for 30 minutes.
4. Select "Cancel" and do a "Natural" release.
5. Remove the lid and stir in lemon juice.
6. Serve hot.

Nutrition:
Calories: 226
Carbohydrates: 34.3 g
Protein: 17.7 g
Fat: 2.1 g
Sodium: 801 mg
Fiber: 14.5 g

164. Comfy Meal Stew

Preparation Time: 20 minutes
Cooking Time: 1 hour 6 minutes
Servings: 8
Ingredients:
- 1/4 cups flour
- Salt and black pepper
- 2 pounds lamb shoulder, cut into 1-inch cubes
- 2 tablespoons olive oil
- 1/2 cups celery, chopped
- 1/2 cups carrots, peeled and chopped
- 1/2 cups fennel, chopped
- 1/2 cups leeks, sliced
- 1 teaspoon dried rosemary, crushed
- 2 tablespoons brandy
- 1 can diced tomatoes
- 1 can chickpeas, drained and rinsed
- 2 cups beef broth
- 1 bay leaf
- 2 tablespoons fresh parsley, chopped

Directions:
1. Merge together the flour, salt, and black pepper.
2. Add the lamb cubes and toss to coat well.
3. Place the oil in the instant Pot and select "Sauté." Then add the lamb cubes in 2 batches and cook for about 4-5 minutes.
4. With a slotted spoon, transfer the lamb cubes into a bowl.
5. In the pot, add the celery, carrots, fennel, and cook for about 5 minutes.
6. Stir in the rosemary and brandy and cook for about 1 minute, scraping up any browned bits from the bottom.
7. Select "Cancel" and stir in the cooked lamb cubes, tomatoes, chickpeas, broth, and bay leaf.
8. Cook for about 45 minutes.
9. Select "Cancel" and do a "Natural" release.
10.   Remove the lid and serve hot with the garnishing of parsley.

Nutrition:
Calories: 478
Carbohydrates: 28.5 g
Protein: 49.7 g
Fat: 17.4 g
Sodium: 634 mg
Fiber: 5.7 g

165. Exciting Chickpeas Soup

Preparation Time: 10 minutes
Cooking Time: 8 Minutes
Servings: 6
Ingredients:
- 2 tablespoons olive oil
- 1 cup onion, chopped
- 4-5 garlic cloves, crushed
- 1 cup carrot, peeled and chopped
- 1 cup celery stalk, chopped
- 2 cans chickpeas, drained and rinsed
- 1 can fire-roasted tomatoes
- 2 tablespoons tomato paste
- 1 tablespoon sun-dried tomatoes
- 1/2 teaspoon ground cinnamon
- 2 teaspoons ground cumin
- 2 teaspoons paprika
- 2 teaspoons ground coriander
- Salt and black pepper
- 4 cups vegetable broth
- 2 cups fresh baby spinach, chopped
- 1 tablespoon fresh lemon juice

Directions:
1. In the pot of Instant Pot, place all the ingredients except for spinach and lemon juice and stir to merge.
2. Cook for about 8 minutes.
3. Select "Cancel" and do a "Natural" release for about 10 minutes.
4. Detach the lid and mash some beans with a potato masher.
5. Whip in the spinach and lemon juice and set aside for about 5 minutes before serving.

Nutrition:
Calories: 352
Carbohydrates: 50.5 g
Protein: 18.2 g
Fat: 9.9 g
Sodium: 938 mg
Fiber: 14 g

166. Classic Napoli Sauce

Preparation Time: 10 minutes
Cooking Time: 45 minutes
Servings: 4
Ingredients:
- 1-pound mushrooms
- 2 cups canned tomatoes, diced
- 1 carrot, chopped
- 1 onion, chopped
- 1 celery stick, chopped
- 1 tablespoon olive oil
- 1 teaspoon salt
- 1/2 teaspoon paprika
- 1 teaspoon fish sauce
- 1 cup water

Directions:
1. Heat olive oil on Sauté. Stir-fry carrot, onion, celery, and paprika, for 5 minutes. Merge all remaining ingredients, except for the tomatoes, and cook for 5-6 more minutes, until the meat is slightly browned. Seal the lid.
2. Cook on High Pressure for 20 minutes. When done, release the steam naturally, for about 10 minutes. Hit Sauté, and cook for 7-8 minutes to thicken the sauce.

Nutrition:
Calories: 269
Carbohydrates: 41.5 g

Protein: 11.4 g
Fat: 9.5 g
Sodium: 549 mg
Fiber: 9 g

167. Winter Dinner Stew

Preparation Time: 5 minutes
Cooking Time: 14 Minutes
Servings: 6
Ingredients:
- 3 tablespoons extra-virgin olive oil
- 1 small onion
- 1 small green bell pepper
- 1 1/2 cups tomatoes, chopped
- 2 garlic cloves, minced
- 1/4 cups fresh cilantro, chopped and divided
- 2 bay leaves
- 2 teaspoons paprika
- Salt and black pepper
- 1 cup fish broth
- 1-pound shrimp, peeled and deveined
- 12 littleneck clams
- 1 1/2 pounds cod fillets, cut into 2-inch chunks

Directions:
1. Place the oil in the Instant Pot and select "Sauté." Then add the onion, bell pepper, tomatoes, garlic, 2 tablespoons of cilantro, bay leaves, paprika, salt, and black pepper, and cook for about 3-4 minutes.
2. Select "Cancel" and stir in the broth.
3. Submerge the clams and shrimps into the vegetable mixture and top with the cod fillets.
4. Cook for about 10 minutes.
5. Select "Cancel" and do a "Natural" release for about 10 minutes, then do a "Quick" release.
6. Remove the lid and serve hot with the garnishing of the remaining cilantro.

Nutrition:
Calories: 450
Carbohydrates: 6.2 g
Protein: 79.3 g
Fat: 11.9 g
Sodium: 487 mg
Fiber: 1.4 g

168. Meatless-Monday Chickpeas Stew

Preparation Time: 10 minutes
Cooking Time: 16 minutes
Servings: 8
Ingredients:
- 1/4 cups olive oil
- 1 onion, chopped
- 7 garlic cloves, chopped finely
- 1 teaspoon ground cinnamon
- 1 1/2 teaspoon ground cumin
- 2 teaspoons sweet paprika
- 1/8 teaspoon cayenne pepper
- 3 cans chickpeas, rinsed and drained
- 1 can diced tomatoes
- 1 cup carrots, peeled and chopped
- 4 cups low-sodium vegetable broth
- Salt and ground black pepper
- 7 ounces fresh baby spinach

Directions:
1. Place the oil in the Instant Pot and select "Sauté." Then add the onion and cook for about 3-4 minutes.
2. Attach the garlic and cook for about 1 minute.
3. Attach the spices and cook for about 1 minute.

4. Select "Cancel" and stir in the chickpeas, diced tomatoes with juice, carrots, and broth.

5. Detach the lid and with a potato masher, mash the most of the stew.

6. Add the spinach and stir until wilted.

7. Serve immediately.

Nutrition:

Calories: 279

Carbohydrates: 42.5 g

Protein: 10.4 g

Fat: 8.5 g

Sodium: 549 mg

Fiber: 9 g

169. Fragrant Fish Stew

Preparation Time: 10 minutes

Cooking Time: 15 minutes

Servings: 4

Ingredients:

- 4 tablespoons extra-virgin olive oil, divided
- 1 medium red onion, sliced thinly
- 4 garlic cloves, chopped
- 1/2 cups dry white wine
- 1/2 pounds red potatoes, cubed
- 1 can diced tomatoes with juices
- 1/8 teaspoon red pepper
- Salt and black pepper
- 1 bottled clam juice
- 2 1/2 cups water
- 2 pounds sea bass, cut into 2-inch pieces
- 2 tablespoons fresh dill, chopped
- 2 tablespoons fresh lemon juice

Directions:

1. Place 2 tablespoons Of the oil in the Instant Pot and select "Sauté." Then add the onion.

2. Attach the garlic and cook for about 1 minute.

3. Attach the wine and cook for about 1 minute, scraping up any browned bits from the bottom.

4. Select "Cancel" and stir in the potatoes, tomatoes with juices, red pepper flakes, salt, black pepper, clam juice, and water.

5. Detach the lid and select "Sauté."

6. Stir in the fish pieces and cook for about 5 minutes.

7. Select "Cancel" and stir in the dill and lemon juice.

8. Serve hot.

Nutrition:

Calories: 533

Carbohydrates: 24.8 g

Protein: 56.8 g

Fat: 20.4 g

Sodium: 458 mg

Fiber: 3.4 g

170. Bright Green Soup

Preparation Time: 3 minutes

Cooking Time: 7 minutes

Servings: 4

Ingredients:

- 2 tablespoons olive oil
- 1 large celery stalk, chopped
- 1 medium onion, chopped finely
- 1-pound broccoli, chopped
- 2 medium white potatoes, peeled and cubed
- 2 large garlic cloves, chopped
- 4 cups vegetable broth
- Salt and black pepper
- 1/2 cups coconut cream

- 1 tablespoon fresh lemon juice

Directions:

1. Place the oil in the instant Pot and select "Sauté." Then add the celery and onion and cook for about 3-4 minutes.

2. Select "Cancel" and stir in the remaining ingredients except for lemon juice.

3. Choose "Cancel" and do a "Natural" release for about 5 minutes, then do a "Quick" release.

4. Detach the lid and with an immersion blender, blend the soup until smooth.

5. Whip in the coconut cream and lemon juice and serve.

Nutrition:

Calories: 294

Carbohydrates: 30.1 g

Protein: 11 g

Fat: 16.1 g

Sodium: 856 mg

Fiber: 6.9 g

171. Parsley Garden Vegetable Soup

Preparation Time: 10 minutes

Cooking Time: 42 minutes

Servings: 8

Ingredients:

- 2 tablespoons olive oil
- 1 cup leeks, chopped
- 2 garlic cloves, minced
- 8 cups vegetable stock
- 1 carrot, diced
- 1 potato, diced
- 1 celery stalk, diced
- 1 cup mushrooms
- 1 cup broccoli florets
- 1 cup cauliflower florets
- 1/2 red bell pepper, diced
- 1/4 head green cabbage, chopped
- 1/2 cup green beans
- 1/2 salt, or more to taste
- 1/2 teaspoon ground black pepper
- 1/2 cup fresh parsley, chopped

Directions:

1. Heat oil on Sauté. Add in garlic and onion and cook for 6 minutes until slightly browned. Add in the stock, carrot, celery, broccoli, bell pepper, green beans, salt, cabbage, cauliflower, mushrooms, potato, and pepper.

2. Seal the lid; cook on high for 6 minutes. Release pressure naturally for about 5 minutes. Stir in parsley and serve.

Nutrition:

Calories: 310

Carbohydrates: 21.1 g

Protein: 12 g

Fat: 13.1 g

Sodium: 321 mg

Fiber: 6.9 g

172. Lamb and Spinach Soup

Preparation Time: 10 minutes

Cooking Time: 50 minutes

Servings: 5

Ingredients:

- 1 pound of lamb shoulder, cut into bite-sized pieces
- 10 ounces fresh spinach leaves, chopped
- 3 eggs, beaten
- 5 cups vegetable broth
- 3 tablespoons olive oil
- 1 teaspoon salt

Directions:

1. Place in your instant pot the lamb along with the remaining ingredients. Seal the lid, press Soup/Broth, and cook for 30 minutes on High Pressure.
Nutrition:
Calories: 310
Carbohydrates: 21.1 g
Protein: 12 g
Fat: 13.1 g
Sodium: 321 mg
Fiber: 6.9 g

173. Effortless Chicken Rice Soup

Preparation Time: 10 minutes
Cooking Time: 20 minutes
Servings: 4
Ingredients:
• 1-pound chicken breast, boneless, skinless, cut into pieces
• 1 large carrot, chopped
• 1 onion, chopped
• 1/4 cup rice
• 1 potato, finely chopped
• 1/2 teaspoon salt
• 1 teaspoon cayenne pepper
• A handful of parsley, finely chopped
• 3 tablespoons olive oil
• 4 cups chicken broth
Directions:
1. Add all ingredients, except parsley, to the pot, and seal the lid. Cook on Soup/Broth for 15 minutes on high. Do a quick pressure and release. Stir in fresh parsley and serve.
Nutrition:
Calories: 213
Carbohydrates: 24 g
Protein: 16 g
Fat: 15 g
Sodium: 213 mg
Fiber: 10.9 g

174. Spanish Fall Soup

Preparation Time: 10 minutes
Cooking Time: 34 minutes
Servings: 4
Ingredients:
• 3 sweet potatoes, chopped
• 1 teaspoon sea salt
• 2 fennel bulb, chopped
• 16 ounces pureed pumpkin
• 1 large onion, chopped
• 1 tablespoon coconut oil
• 4 cups water
• 1 tablespoon sour cream
Directions:
1. Heat the oil on Sauté, add onion and fennel bupounds Cook until tender and translucent. Merge the remaining ingredients and cover the lid.
2. Cook on high pressure for 25 minutes. Do a quick release, transfer the soup to a blender, and blend for 20 seconds until creamy. Top with sour cream and serve.
Nutrition:
Calories: 213
Carbohydrates: 24 g
Protein: 16 g
Fat: 15 g
Sodium: 213 mg
Fiber: 10.9 g

175. Toe-warming Lamb Stew

Preparation Time: 10 minutes
Cooking Time: 34 minutes
Servings: 5
Ingredients:
• 2 pounds lamb shoulder, cubed
• Salt and black pepper
• 1 tablespoon olive oil
• 1 tablespoon butter
• 1 cup onion, chopped
• 2-3 garlic cloves, minced
• 1 tablespoon ginger paste
• 1 teaspoon ground coriander
• 1 teaspoon ground cinnamon
• 1/4-1/2 cups water
• 8 dried apricots
• 8 dates, pitted
• 2 tablespoons slivered almonds
• 1 tablespoon orange zest
• 1/2 tablespoon honey
• 1 teaspoon ras el hanout
Directions:
1. Use the lamb cubes with salt and pepper lightly.
2. Place the oil and butter in the instant Pot and select "Sauté". Then add the lamb cubes in 2 batches and cook for about 4-5 minutes or until browned.
3. With a slotted spoon, transfer the lamb cubes into a bowl.
4. In the pot, add the onion, garlic, ginger paste, coriander, and cinnamon, and cook for about 4-5 minutes.
5. Add the water and cook for about 1 minute, scraping up any browned bits from the bottom.
6. Select "Cancel" and stir in the lamb cubes.
7. Choose "Manual" and cook under "High Pressure" for about 25 minutes.
8. Select "Cancel" and carefully do a "Natural" release.
9. Remove the lid and stir in the remaining ingredients.
10.   Select "Sauté" and cook for about 5-10 minutes or until the desired thickness of sauce.
11.   Select "Cancel" and serve hot.
Nutrition:
Calories: 483
Carbohydrates: 22.3 g
Protein: 53 g
Fat: 20.1 g
Sugar: 16.3 g
Sodium: 188 mg
Fiber: 3 g

176. Sweet and Savory Stew

Preparation Time: 10 minutes
Cooking Time: 1 hour
Servings: 8
Ingredients:
• 3 tablespoons olive oil
• 1 1/2 onions, minced
• 3 pounds beef stew meat, cubed
• 1 1/2 teaspoon ground cinnamon
• 3/4 teaspoon paprika
• 3/4 teaspoon ground turmeric
• 1/4 teaspoon ground allspice
• 1/4 teaspoon ground ginger
• 1 1/2 cups beef broth
• 1 1/2 tablespoon honey
• 1 1/2 cups dried apricots, halved and soaked in hot water until softened and drained
• 1/3 cups almond slivers, toasted

Directions:
1. Place the oil in Instant Pot and select "Sauté." Then add the onion and cook for about 3-4 minutes.
2. Stir in the beef and cook for about 3-4 minutes or until browned completely.
3. Whisk in the spices and cook for about 2 minutes.
4. Select "Cancel" and stir in the broth and honey.
5. Choose "Meat/Stew" and just use the default time of 50 minutes.
6. Choose "Cancel" and do a "Natural" release for about 15 minutes, then do a "Quick" release.
7. Remove the lid and stir in the apricot halves.
8. Serve with the topping of almond slivers.
Nutrition:
Calories: 428
Carbohydrates: 10.1 g
Protein: 54 g
Fat: 18.4 g
Sodium: 257 mg
Fiber: 1.9 g

177. Feta-topped Potato Gazpacho

Preparation Time: 10 minutes
Cooking Time: 25 minutes
Servings: 4
Ingredients:
- 3 large leeks
- 3 tablespoons butter
- 1 onion, thinly chopped
- 1-pound potatoes, chopped
- 5 cups vegetable stock
- 2 teaspoons lemon juice
- 1/4 teaspoon nutmeg
- 1/4 teaspoon ground coriander
- 1 bay leaf
- 5 ounces feta, crumbled
- 1 1/2 Salt and white pepper
- 1/3 Freshly snipped chives, to garnish
Directions:
1. Remove most of the green parts of the leeks. Slice the white parts very finely. Melt butter on Sauté, and stir-fry leeks and onion for 5 minutes without browning. Add potatoes, stock, juice, nutmeg, coriander, and bay leaf.
2. Choose Manual/Pressure Cook and set the timer to 10 minutes. Cook on high pressure. Do a quick release and discard the bay leaf. Season to taste, add feta. Serve the soup sprinkled with freshly snipped chives.
Nutrition:
Calories: 428
Carbohydrates: 10.1 g
Protein: 54 g
Fat: 18.4 g
Sodium: 257 mg
Fiber: 1.9 g

178. White Bean Pomodoro Soup

Preparation Time: 10 minutes
Cooking Time: 40 minutes
Servings: 4
Ingredients:
- 2 pounds tomatoes, diced
- 1 cup white beans, pre-cooked
- 1 small onion, diced
- 2 garlic cloves, crushed
- 1 cup heavy cream
- 1 cup vegetable broth
- 2 tablespoons fresh parsley, finely chopped

- 1/4 teaspoon black pepper, ground
- 2 tablespoons extra virgin olive oil
- 1/2 teaspoon salt
Directions:
1. Warm oil on Sauté mode. Stir-fry onion and garlic on Sauté for 2 minutes. Add tomatoes, beans, broth, 3 cups of water, parsley, salt, pepper, and a little bit of sugar to balance the bitterness.
2. Seal the lid and cook on Soup/Broth for 30 minutes on High Pressure. Release the pressure naturally for 10 minutes. Present with a dollop of sour cream and chopped parsley to serve.
Nutrition:
Calories: 400
Carbohydrates: 15 g
Protein: 58 g
Fat: 18.4 g
Sodium: 300 mg
Fiber: 1.9 g

179. Power Green Soup

Preparation Time: 10 minutes
Cooking Time: 35 minutes
Servings: 3
Ingredients:
- 1-pound fresh Brussels sprouts, rinsed, halved, chopped
- 6 ounces fresh baby spinach, rinsed, torn, chopped
- 1 teaspoon sea salt
- 1 tablespoon whole milk
- 3 tablespoons sour cream
- 1 tablespoon fresh celery, chopped
- 3 cups water
- 1 tablespoon butter
Directions:
1. Add all ingredients to the Instant Pot. Protect the lid and set the steam release. Press Soup/Broth and cook for 30 minutes on high. Do a quick release. Transfer to a food processor and blend well to combine.
Nutrition:
Calories: 325
Carbohydrates: 21 g
Protein: 34 g
Fat: 21 g
Sodium: 213 mg
Fiber: 4 g

180. Creamy Asparagus Soup

Preparation Time: 10 minutes
Cooking Time: 40 minutes
Servings: 4
Ingredients:
- 2 pounds fresh asparagus, trimmed, 1-inch thick
- 2 onions, peeled and finely chopped
- 1 cup heavy cream
- 4 cups vegetable broth
- 2 tablespoons butter
- 1 tablespoon vegetable oil
- 1/2 teaspoon salt
- 1/2 teaspoon dried oregano
- 1/2 teaspoon paprika
Directions:
1. Warm butter and oil on Sauté. Stir-fry the onions for 2 minutes, until translucent. Add asparagus, oregano, salt, and paprika. Stir well and cook for a few minutes until the asparagus softens. Pour in the broth. Seal the lid and cook on Soup/Broth for 20 minutes on high. Do a quick release and whisk in the heavy cream. Serve chilled or warm.

Nutrition:
Calories: 312
Carbohydrates: 25 g
Protein: 34 g
Fat: 21 g
Sodium: 213 mg
Fiber: 8 g

181. Greek Lemon Chicken Soup

Preparation time: 10 minutes
Cooking time: 45 minutes
Servings: 4
Ingredients
For The Soup
- 2 Chicken legs
- 4 shallots, chopped
- Salt: 2 ½ tsp.
- Olive oil, as needed
- 2 carrots, diagonal slices
- Black pepper, to taste
- Dried acini di pepe: 1/3 cup
- 3 celery ribs, cut into large pieces
- 1 lemon's juice
- Fresh dill & thyme (15 sprigs each)
- 3-4 minced garlic cloves
- 3 egg yolks
For The Dill + Chive Oil
- Olive oil: ¾ cup
- Chives: ¼ cup, chopped
- Dill: half cup, chopped
- Salt: half tsp.
- Minced garlic clove
- Half lemon's juice
Direction:
1. In a Dutch oven, add oil on medium flame. Season the chicken with salt and pepper.
2. Sear the chicken for 3 to 5 minutes on each side. Take out on a plate.
3. In the same pot, sauté onion and garlic with salt. Add celery and carrots, cook for 2 to 3 minutes in between.
4. Add thyme, dill cook, until fragrant.
5. Add water (4 cups), let it come to a boil. Turn the heat low and simmer for 60 minutes until the chicken is tender.
6. In a food processor, add chives, garlic, dill pulse until chopped.
7. As it is chopping, slowly drizzle olive oil. Add lemon juice and salt. Take out in a bowl.
8. Shred the chicken into bite-size pieces. Take out the dill, chives and celery ribs.
9. Turn the heat high, add pepe and season with salt, let it come to a boil, turn the heat low and simmer.
10. Make sure pepe is tender. Add more liquid (water) if needed, but it needs to be thick.
11. When pepe is ready, add the chicken back in the pot, heat it through.
12. Turn the heat off. Add whisked egg yolks (at room temperature) slowly in the soup, and stir.
13. Add seasoning and serve with oil.
Nutrition: 216 Cal | 8 g Fat | 19.3 g Carbs | 18.4 g Protein

182. Chicken & Spinach Soup

Preparation time: 30 minutes
Cooking time: 35 minutes
Servings: 5
Ingredients
- Olive oil: 3 tbsp.
- 2 Chicken breast boneless & skinless, sliced into cubes

- 1 minced garlic clove
- Carrot: half cup, diced
- Grated parmesan cheese: ¼ cup
- Chicken broth: 5 cups
- Dried marjoram: 1 ½ tsp.
- 1 can of (~15-oz.) Cannellini beans, rinsed
- Fresh basil leaves: 1/3 cup
- Baby spinach: 1 cup, chopped
- Black pepper, to taste
Direction:
1. In a Dutch oven, add oil (2 tbsp.). Sauté onion, add chicken, cook for 3-4 minutes.
2. Add garlic and cook for 60 seconds. Add marjoram, broth and let it boil.
3. Turn the heat and let it simmer for five minutes until the chicken is cooked.
4. Take chicken out on a board. Add beans, spinach and let it come to a boil. Cook for five minutes.
5. In a food processor, add the rest of the ingredients and pulse into a coarse paste. Add water (a little) if necessary.
6. Cut chicken into smaller pieces, add pesto and chicken in the pot.
7. Adjust seasoning, and serve right away.
Nutrition: 227 Cal | 1.7 g Fat | 18 g Carbs | 19.4 g Protein

183. Chicken & Chickpea Soup

Preparation time: 20 minutes
Cooking time: 4-8 hours
Servings: 6
Ingredients
- Dried chickpeas: 1 1/2 cups, soaked for 12 hours
- 1 Can of (15 oz.) Roasted diced tomatoes
- Tomato paste: 2 tbsp.
- 1 bay leaf
- Ground cumin: 4 tsp.
- Paprika: 4 tsp.
- 4 minced garlic cloves
- Chicken thighs: 2 pounds, with bone, skin removed
- 1 can of (14 oz.) Artichoke hearts, quartered
- 1 yellow onion, chopped
- Cayenne pepper: ¼ tsp.
- Water: 4 cups
- Ground pepper: ¼ tsp.
- Fresh parsley: 1/4 cup, chopped
- Oil cured olives: ¼ cup, halved
- Salt: half tsp.
Direction:
1. In a slow cooker (1 qt.), add chickpeas and the rest of the ingredients except for olives and artichokes, mix well.
2. Cook on high for 4 hours or on low for 8 hours.
3. Take chicken out and cool. Take out the bay leaf.
4. Add olives and artichoke to the cooker and mix, shred chicken and take bones out.
5. Put chicken back in, stir and serve.
Nutrition: 447 Cal | 8.5 g Fat | 43 g Carbs | 33 g Protein

184. Pasta e Fagioli Soup

Preparation time: 5 minutes
Cooking time: 7 hour & 30 minutes
Servings: 6
Ingredients
- 1 Can of (28-oz.) Crushed tomatoes
- 2 Carrots, sliced
- White beans: 1½ cups, soaked overnight & drained
- Fresh parsley: 1/3 cup, chopped

- 1 onion, diced
- 4 Minced garlic cloves
- Fresh thyme: 3 sprigs
- 1 parmesan rind
- 2 stalks celery, sliced
- Chicken broth: 4 cups
- Red pepper flakes, a pinch
- 1 bunch of kale, torn
- 1 bay leaf
- Dry white wine: half cup
- Fresh rosemary: 2 sprigs
- Salt & black pepper, to taste
- Short pasta: 1¼ cup

Direction:

1. In a slow cooker, add onion, garlic, tomatoes, beans, white wine, broth, carrots, rind and celery.
2. Add herbs, pepper flakes, and bay leaf. Cook on low for 7 hours.
3. Add salt and pepper. Add kale, pasta. Cook on high for half an hour.
4. Add parsley, and serve right away.

Nutrition: 379 Cal | 3 g Fat | 69 g Carbs | 21 g Protein

185. Turkey & White Bean Spinach Soup

Preparation time: 5 minutes
Cooking time: 25 minutes
Servings: 6
Ingredients
- Olive oil: 1 tbsp.
- Lemon juice: 1 tbsp.
- Parmesan: ¼ cup, shaved
- Diced yellow onion: half cup
- Fresh spinach: 3 cups
- Chicken broth: 5 cups
- Cannellini beans: 15.5 oz., rinsed
- Minced garlic: 1 tbsp.
- Salt & pepper, to taste
- Ground turkey: 1 pound
- Thyme: half tsp.

Direction:

1. In a dutch oven, add oil on medium flame. Sauté onion and garlic for five minutes.
2. Add broth and let it come to a boil.
3. Season the turkey with salt and pepper. Drop it in the broth in small pieces.
4. Add thyme and lemon juice, simmer for 15 minutes.
5. Turn the heat to low; before serving, add beans, spinach. Cook for 2 minutes.
6. Serve with bread.

Nutrition: 194 Cal | 5 g Fat | 14 g Carbs | 24 g Protein

186. Greek White Bean Soup with Orange & Olive Oil

Preparation time: 15 minutes
Cooking time: 30 minutes
Servings: 8
Ingredients
- 4 carrots, thinly sliced
- Dried oregano: half tsp.
- 5 celery sticks, thinly sliced
- Water: 2 cups
- Olive oil: 1 cup
- 1 bay leaf
- 3 orange, sliced with skin
- 1 onion, thinly sliced

- Tomato paste: 2 tbsp.
- 1 can of (15-oz.) white beans

Direction:

1. In a pan, sauté celery, onion and carrots. Add bay leaf and oregano.
2. Add tomato paste, orange slices, cook for two minutes.
3. Add beans (2 with liquids, 2 without liquid). Add water (2 cups).
4. Let it simmer for 30 to 40 minutes till the soup thickens.
5. Serve right away.

Nutrition: 162 Cal | 8 g Fat | 21 g Carbs | 6 g Protein

187. Mediterranean Cabbage Soup

Preparation time: 10 minutes
Cooking time: 20 minutes
Servings: 6
Ingredients
- Olive oil: 2 tbsp.
- Salt: half tsp.
- Chopped carrots: 1 cup
- Sugar: 2 tsp.
- Sliced fennel: 1 cup
- Chopped onion: half cup
- 1 Can of (15 oz.) Tomatoes with basil, oregano & garlic
- Minced garlic: 2 tsp.
- 1 can of (15 oz.) Cannellini beans, rinsed
- Ground coriander: half tsp.
- Fresh oregano: 1 tsp.
- Vegetable broth: 6 cups
- 1 green cabbage (small head), chopped

Direction:

1. In a pan, add oil on medium flame.
2. Sauté onion, carrots and fennel for five minutes.
3. Add salt, garlic and coriander, stir and cook for 60 seconds.
4. Add tomatoes, broth and let it come to a boil.
5. Add cabbage and turn the heat low. Cook for 20-25 minutes.
6. Add oregano, sugar and beans. Cook for three minutes.
7. Add zest and serve.

Nutrition: 205 Cal | 5.5 g Fat | 31 g Carbs | 6.2 g Protein

188. Minestrone

Preparation time: 35 minutes
Cooking time: 50 minutes
Servings: 8
Ingredients
- Olive oil: 3 tbsp.
- Kidney beans: 1 cup, drained
- 3 minced garlic cloves
- 5 carrots, thinly sliced
- Chicken broth: 2 cups
- Water: 2 cups
- 2 onions, diced
- Chopped celery: 2 cups
- 1 Can of (15 oz.) Green beans
- Tomato sauce: 4 cups
- Red wine: half cup
- Chopped fresh oregano: 1 tbsp.
- Baby spinach: 2 cups
- Salt & pepper to taste
- 3 Zucchinis, half-moons
- Chopped fresh basil: 2 tbsp.
- Seashell pasta: half cup

Direction:
1. In a pot, sauté garlic for 2 to 3 minutes. Add onion and cook for 4 to 5 minutes.
2. Add carrots, celery and cook for 1-2 minutes.
3. Add broth, tomato sauce, and water. Let it come to a boil; add red wine.
4. Turn the heat low and add the rest of the ingredients. Let it simmer for 30-40 minutes.
5. Cook pasta as per pack instructions.
6. Before serving, add pasta to the bottom of the bowl, pour soup on top. Serve with grated cheese on top.

Nutrition: 228 Cal |8.3 g Fat | 30 g Carbs |6.9 g Protein

189. Zucchini Basil Soup with Lemon

Preparation time: 10 minutes
Cooking time: 20 minutes
Servings: 4-6
Ingredients
- Butter: 2 tbsp.
- 1 lemon's zest
- 3 to 4 minced garlic cloves
- Basil: half cup
- 4 peeled zucchini, sliced into cubes
- 1 onion, diced
- Chicken broth: 3 cups
- Sea salt & pepper, to taste

Direction:
1. In a pot, add butter and sauté onion for five minutes.
2. Add garlic keep stirring for 1-2 minutes.
3. Add zucchini and cook for 4 to 5 minutes.
4. Add zest, broth and let it come to a boil. Turn the heat to low and simmer for ten minutes.
5. Add basil and mix. With a stick blender, puree the soup. Season with salt and pepper.
6. Serve right away.

Nutrition: 278 Cal |7 g Fat | 10 g Carbs |9 g Protein

190. Ravioli & Vegetable Soup

Preparation time: 10 minutes
Cooking time: 15 minutes
Servings: 4
Ingredients
- Olive oil: 1 tbsp.
- 1 Pack of (6-9 oz.) Ravioli
- 3 Minced garlic cloves
- 1 can of (15-oz.) Chicken broth
- Diced bell pepper & onion mix: 2 cups
- Crushed red pepper to taste
- 1 can of (28-oz.) Crushed tomatoes
- Diced zucchini: 2 cups
- Hot water: 1 1/2 cups
- Dried basil: 1 tsp.
- Pepper, to taste

Direction:
1. In a Dutch oven, add oil and sauté onion, pepper mix, garlic with pepper flakes. Cook for 1 minute.
2. Add water, basil, tomatoes and broth. Let it come to a boil.
3. Add ravioli and cook for three minutes (half time of the pack instructions).
4. Add zucchini and cook for 3 minutes, adjust seasoning and serve.

Nutrition: 261 Cal |8.3 g Fat | 32 g Carbs |10 g Protein

191. Chicken Vegetable Soup

Preparation time: 10 minutes
Cooking time: 60 minutes
Servings: 4-5
Ingredients
- Water: 4 cups
- 2 carrots, diced
- Half onion, chopped
- Cauliflower: ¼ head, chopped
- Olive oil: 2 tbsp.
- 4 minced garlic cloves
- Salt: 1 1/2 tsp.
- 6 chicken thighs (bone-in)
- 1 Zucchini, chopped
- 1 broccoli head, chopped
- 1 carton of (32 oz.) Chicken broth

Direction:
1. In a pot, add chicken and water. Let it come to a boil, turn the heat low. Simmer for half an hour.
2. Take off the foam if it appears on top.
3. In a pot, add oil. Sauté onions, carrots for 3 to 4 minutes. Add salt, garlic cook for 60 seconds.
4. Add chicken and broth to this pot. Let it come to a boil.
5. Turn the heat low and simmer for 1-4 hours. Turn off the heat.
6. Take chicken out, remove bones, skin and shred the meat.
7. Put chicken back in the pot. Add the rest of the vegetables on medium flame.
8. Let it simmer for 20-30 minutes.

192. Lentil Soup with Olive Oil & Orange

Preparation time: 30 minutes
Cooking time: 2 hours & 5 minutes
Servings: 6
Ingredients
- 2 minced garlic cloves
- Washed lentils: 1 pound
- Olive oil: 1 cup
- Water: 6 cups
- Tomato paste: 2 tbsp.
- 2 orange slices with peels
- 3 grated carrots
- 1bay leaf
- 1 grated onion
- Salt & pepper, to taste

Direction:
- In a pot, lentils with water. Boil for 15 minutes.
- Add the rest of the ingredients and cook for half an hour.
- Cook until lentils are tender; add more water if required.

Nutrition: 206 Cal |12.3 g Fat | 8 g Carbs |15.9 g Protein

193. White Bean Soup with Tomato & Shrimp

Preparation time: 10 minutes
Cooking time: 25 minutes
Servings: 6
Ingredients
- Olive oil: 3 tbsp.
- Ancho chile powder: 1 tsp.
- 1 can of (28 oz.) Peeled whole tomatoes
- Ground pepper: half tsp.
- Raw shrimp: 1 pound, peeled & deveined
- 1 onion, chopped

- Kalamata olives: ¼ cup, chopped
- Salt: half tsp.
- 1 can of (14 oz.) White beans
- 3 minced garlic cloves
- Crushed red pepper: ¼ tsp.
- Capers: 2 tbsp., chopped
- Chicken broth: 2 cups
- Small pasta: 2 oz.

Direction:
1. In a pan, add oil and cook shrimps with chile powder, salt and pepper (1/4 tsp. of each). Cook for three minutes. Take out on a plate
2. Add onion to the same pan, with the rest of the salt and pepper. Cook for 3-4 minutes.
3. Add garlic, red pepper and cook for 30 seconds.
4. Add broth, tomatoes, let it come to a boil. Turn the heat low and simmer for ten minutes.
5. Crush the tomatoes roughly. Add beans, also mash them roughly.
6. Let it boil again. Add pasta and cook for 1 oten minutes.
7. Add capers, olives and shrimps. Serve right away.

Nutrition: 266 Cal |3.2 g Fat | 22.7 g Carbs |18.5 g Protein

194. Chicken Leek Soup with White Wine

Preparation time: 15 minutes
Cooking time: 50 minutes
Servings: 4
Ingredients
- Chicken breast: 2 pounds, bite sizes pieces
- Olive oil: half cup
- 4 green onions, chopped
- White wine: 1 cup
- 1 Leek, sliced into thin rounds
- Nutmeg: 1/8 tsp.
- 4 celery sticks, diced
- Salt & pepper, to taste
- 1 small-head cabbage, thickly sliced
- Paprika: half tsp.
- Water: 3 cups

Direction:
1. In a pot, add olive oil. Add chicken and cook for few minutes until lightly browned.
2. Add vegetables and cook for 1 minute.
3. Add cabbage, cook until fork tender. Add spices and water, mix.
4. Cook for 45 minutes, at low.
5. Serve right away.

Nutrition: 287 Cal | 9 g Fat | 4 g Carbs |12.3 g Protein

195. Chickpea & Spinach Stew

Preparation time: 10 minutes
Cooking time: 20 minutes
Servings: 4
Ingredients
- 2 cans of (15 oz.) chickpeas, rinsed
- Ground turkey: 12 oz.
- Olive oil: 1 tbsp.
- Crushed red pepper: half tsp.
- 1onion, diced
- Fennel seeds: half tsp., crushed
- Spinach: 3 cups
- 2 carrots, chopped
- Dried oregano: half tsp.
- 4minced garlic cloves
- Salt: 1/8 tsp.
- Tomato paste: 3 tbsp.

- 1 carton of (32 oz.) Chicken broth
- Ground pepper: ¼ tsp.

Direction:
1. In a bowl, mash one can of chickpeas with a potato masher.
2. In a pan, add oil and cook turkey, fennel seeds, red pepper and oregano for 2-3 minutes.
3. Add garlic, onion, and carrots, cook for 3-4 minutes. Add tomato paste and cook for 30 seconds.
4. Add whole, mashed chickpeas, broth, salt and pepper. Mix and let it simmer.
5. Cook until vegetables are soft for ten minutes.
6. Turn the heat to medium, add spinach, cook for 1-2 minutes.
7. Pour soup into bowls and serve with grated cheese on top.

Nutrition: 401 Cal | 13 g Fat | 41.3 g Carbs |32.4 g Protein

196. Harissa Bean Stew

Preparation time: 20 minutes
Cooking time: 55 minutes
Servings: 6
Ingredients
Harissa
- Vegetable oil: half cup
- Ground caraway: 1 tsp.
- Smoked paprika: 2 tbsp.
- Ground coriander: 1 tbsp.
- Cayenne pepper: half-1 tsp.
- 6 minced garlic cloves
- Ground cumin: 2 tbsp.
- Kosher salt: 1 tsp.
Bean Stew
- Diced tomatoes: 1 cup, canned
- Chopped carrots: 1 cup
- Dried 15 bean mix: 1½ cups, soaked & drained
- Chopped onion: 1 cup
- Kosher salt: 1 tsp.
- Ground turmeric: 1 tsp.
- Black pepper: half tsp.
- Harissa: 1-2 tbsp. (made above)
- Apple cider vinegar: 2 tbsp.
- Chopped celery: 1 cup
- Water: 2½ cups
- Chopped fresh parsley: half cup

Direction:
1. To make harissa. In a bowl, add all the ingredients, whisk well.
2. Microwave for 60 seconds; after 30 seconds, stir and microwave till it is bubbly and hot.
3. Let it cool completely.
4. In an instant pot, add all the ingredients except for the vinegar. Mix and close the lid.
5. Cook manually for half an hour on high pressure. Do the quick release after it is done cooking.
6. Puree the soup with a hand mixer. Add parsley and vinegar.
7. Serve right away.

Nutrition: 202 Cal | 1 g Fat | 38 g Carbs |13 g Protein

197. Freekeh Vegetable Soup

Preparation time: 10 minutes
Cooking time: 45 minutes
Servings: 8
Ingredients
- Freekeh: 1 cup

- 1 Kohlrabi, diced
- 2 Carrots, chopped
- Kosher salt: 1 tsp.
- 2 Zucchinis, diced
- Black pepper: half tsp.
- 1 onion, chopped
- 3 Minced garlic cloves
- Olive oil: 3 tbsp.
- Cayenne pepper: ¼ tsp.
- Chicken broth: 8 cups
- Chopped fresh oregano: 2 tsp.

Direction:
1. In a bowl, cover the freekeh with cold water.
2. In a pot (4-5 qt.), add oil, sauté onion for 6-8 minutes. Add carrots, kohlrabi, cook for five minutes, season with salt and pepper.
3. Add garlic, and cook for 60 seconds.
4. Drain and wash freekeh and add in the pot.
5. Add the rest of the ingredients. Let it come to a boil.
6. Turn the heat low and simmer for 25-30 minutes.
7. Adjust seasoning and serve right away.

Nutrition: 227 Cal | 9 g Fat | 28 g Carbs | 11 g Protein

198. Greek Easter Lamb Soup

Preparation time: 20 minutes
Cooking time: 100 minutes
Servings: 6
Ingredients
- 2 bunches of dill, chopped
- Olive oil: half cup
- Head of romaine lettuce, thinly sliced
- 10 green onions, diced
- Lamb: 2 lbs., bone in
- Water: 5 cups
- 3 eggs
- Salt & pepper, to taste
- 3 lemons' juice

Direction:
1. Cut lamb into smaller pieces, or cut just the meat and save the bone.
2. In a pan, add oil and add lamb, bone cook for ten minutes.
3. Add green onion, cook for three minutes.
4. Add water, let it come to a boil, turn the heat low and simmer for half an hour.
5. Add herbs, salt and pepper. Simmer for 1 hour.
6. Whisk lemon juice and eggs in a bowl.
7. Add some broth to the whisked egg and mix. Turn the heat off.
8. Mix the broth and add egg mixture.
9. Do not cover the pot; let it rest for few minutes. Serve.

Nutrition: 301 Cal | 18.1 g Fat | 12 g Carbs | 27 g Protein

199. Chicken & White Bean Soup

Preparation time: 10 minutes
Cooking time: 15 minutes
Servings: 6
Ingredients
- Olive oil: 2 tsp.
- 1 Can of (15 oz.) Cannellini beans, rinsed
- 1 roasted chicken (2-pound), without skin & bone, shredded
- 3 leeks, white & light green parts only, sliced into ¼" rounds
- 3 Cans of (14 oz.) Chicken broth

- Chopped fresh sage: 1 tbsp.
- Water: 2 cups

Direction:
1. In a Dutch oven, add oil on medium flame.
2. Add leeks and sauté for three minutes. Add sage, and cook for 30 seconds.
3. Add water, broth and let it come to a boil.
4. Add the rest of the ingredients, cook for three minutes and serve.

Nutrition: 248 Cal | 5.8 g Fat | 14.8 g Carbs | 35.1 g Protein

200. Celery & Parmesan Minestrone

Preparation time: 10 minutes
Cooking time: 35 minutes
Servings: 6
Ingredients
- Olive oil: 2 tbsp.
- Diced onion: half cup
- Black pepper: half tsp.
- Diced carrot: half cup
- 1 can of (15 oz.) Diced tomatoes
- Grated parmigiano cheese: ¼ cup, packed
- 3 minced garlic clove
- Celery seed: 1 tsp.
- Cooked chickpeas: 1 3/4 cups
- Vegetable/chicken broth: 4 cups
- Diced celery: 2 cups + half cup celery leaves
- Whole-wheat orzo: 1/3 cup

Direction:
1. Sauté onion, celery seed, celery, pepper, garlic and carrots. Cook for ten minutes, keep stirring.
2. Add broth, let it boil. Add pasta and cook for 8-10 minutes.
3. Add chickpeas, tomatoes, cheese (1/4 cup), celery leaves (half).
4. Cook for 3-5 minutes, on medium flame. Serve with celery leaves and cheese.

Nutrition: 198 Cal | 6.8 g Fat | 24.2 g Carbs | 9.6 g Protein

201. Lamb and Chickpeas Stew

Preparation time: 10 minutes
Cooking time: 1 hour and 20 minutes
Servings: 6
Ingredients:
- 1 and ½ pounds lamb shoulder, cubed
- 3 tablespoons olive oil
- 1 cup yellow onion, chopped
- 1 cup carrots, cubed
- 1 cup celery, chopped
- 3 garlic cloves, minced
- 4 rosemary springs, chopped
- 2 cups chicken stock
- 1 cup tomato puree
- 15 ounces canned chickpeas, drained and rinsed
- 10 ounces baby spinach
- 2 tablespoons black olives, pitted and sliced
- A pinch of salt and black pepper

Directions:
1. Heat up a pot with the oil over medium-high heat, add the meat, salt and pepper and brown for 5 minutes.
2. Add carrots, celery, onion and garlic, stir and sauté for 5 minutes more.
3. Add the rosemary, stock, chickpeas and the other ingredients except the spinach and olives, stir and cook for 1 hour.

4. Add the rest of the ingredients, cook the stew over medium heat for 10 minutes more, divide into bowls and serve.

Nutrition: calories 340, fat 16, fiber 3, carbs 21, protein 19

202. Chorizo and Lentils Stew

Preparation time: 10 minutes
Cooking time: 35 minutes
Servings: 4
Ingredients:
- 4 cups water
- 1 cup carrots, sliced
- 1 yellow onion, chopped
- 1 tablespoon extra-virgin olive oil
- ¾ cup celery, chopped
- 1 and ½ teaspoon garlic, minced
- 1 and ½ pounds gold potatoes, roughly chopped
- 7 ounces chorizo, cut in half lengthwise and thinly sliced
- 1 and ½ cup lentils
- ½ teaspoon smoked paprika
- ½ teaspoon oregano
- Salt and black pepper to taste
- 14 ounces canned tomatoes, chopped
- ½ cup cilantro, chopped

Directions:
1. Heat a saucepan with oil over medium high heat, add onion, garlic, celery and carrots, stir and cook for 4 minutes.
2. Add the chorizo, stir and cook for 1 minute more.
3. Add the rest of the ingredients except the cilantro, stir, bring to a boil, reduce heat to medium-low and simmer for 25 minutes.
4. Divide the stew into bowls and serve with the cilantro sprinkled on top. Enjoy!

Nutrition: calories 400, fat 16, fiber 13, carbs 58, protein 24

203. Lamb and Potato Stew

Preparation time: 10 minutes
Cooking time: 2 hours
Servings: 4
Ingredients:
- 2 and ½ pounds lamb shoulder, boneless and cut in small pieces
- Salt and black pepper to taste
- 1 yellow onion, chopped
- 3 tablespoons extra virgin olive oil
- 3 tomatoes, grated
- 1 and ½ cups chicken stock
- ½ cup dry white wine
- 1 bay leaf
- 2 and ½ pounds gold potatoes, cut into medium cubes
- ¾ cup green olives

Directions:
1. Heat a saucepan with the oil over medium high heat, add the lamb, brown for 10 minutes, transfer to a platter and keep warm for now.
2. Heat the pan again, add onion, stir and cook for 4 minutes.
3. Add tomatoes, stir, reduce heat to low and cook for 15 minutes.
4. Return lamb meat to pan, add wine and the rest of the ingredients except the potatoes and olives, stir, increase heat to medium high, bring to a boil, reduce heat again, cover pan and simmer for 30 minutes.
5. Add potatoes and olives, stir, cook for 1 more hour., divide into bowls and serve.

Nutrition: calories 450, fat 12, fiber 4, carbs 33, protein 39

204. Meatball and Pasta Soup

Preparation time: 10 minutes
Cooking time: 40 minutes
Servings: 4
Ingredients:
- 12 ounces pork meat, ground
- 12 ounces veal, ground
- Salt and black pepper to taste
- 1 garlic clove, minced
- 2 garlic cloves, sliced
- 2 teaspoons thyme, chopped
- 1 egg, whisked
- 3 ounces Manchego, grated
- 2 tablespoons extra virgin olive oil
- 1/3 cup panko
- 4 cups chicken stock
- A pinch of saffron
- 15 ounces canned tomatoes, crushed
- 1 tablespoons parsley, chopped
- 8 ounces pasta

Directions:
1. In a bowl, mix veal with pork, 1 garlic clove, 1 teaspoon thyme, ¼ teaspoon paprika, salt, pepper to taste, egg, manchego, panko, stir very well and shape medium meatballs out of this mix.
2. Heat a pan with 1 ½ tablespoons oil over medium high heat, add half of the meatballs, cook for 2 minutes on each side, transfer to paper towels, drain grease and put on a plate. Repeat this with the rest of the meatballs.
3. Repeat this with the rest of the meatballs.
4. Heat a saucepan with the rest of the oil, add sliced garlic, stir and cook for 1 minute.
5. Add the remaining ingredients and the meatballs, stir, reduce heat to medium low, cook for 25 minutes and season with salt and pepper.
6. Cook pasta according to instructions, drain, put in a bowl and mix with ½ cup soup.
7. Divide pasta into soup bowls, add soup and meatballs on top, sprinkle parsley all over and serve.

Nutrition: calories 380, fat 17, fiber 2, carbs 28, protein 26

205. Peas Soup

Preparation time: 10 minutes
Cooking time: 10 minutes
Servings: 4
Ingredients:
- 1 teaspoon shallot, chopped
- 1 tablespoon butter
- 1-quart chicken stock
- 2 eggs
- 3 tablespoons lemon juice
- 2 cups peas
- 2 tablespoons parmesan, grated
- Salt and black pepper to taste

Directions:
1. Heat a saucepan with the butter over medium high heat, add shallot, stir and cook for 2 minutes.
2. Add stock, lemon juice, some salt and pepper and the whisked eggs .
3. Add more salt and pepper to taste, peas and parmesan cheese, stir, cook for 3 minutes, divide into bowls and serve.

Nutrition: calories 180, fat 39, fiber 4, carbs 10, protein 14

206. Minty Lamb Stew

Preparation time: 10 minutes
Cooking time: 1 hour and 45 minutes
Servings: 4
Ingredients:
- 3 cups orange juice
- ½ cup mint tea
- Salt and black pepper to taste
- 2 pounds lamb shoulder chops
- 1 tablespoon mustard, dry
- 3 tablespoons canola oil
- 1 tablespoon ras el hanout
- 1 carrot, chopped
- 1 yellow onion, chopped
- 1 celery rib, chopped
- 1 tablespoon ginger, grated
- 28 ounces canned tomatoes, crushed
- 1 tablespoon garlic, minced
- 2-star anise
- 1 cup apricots, dried and cut in halves
- 1 cinnamon stick
- ½ cup mint, chopped
- 15 ounces canned chickpeas, drained
- 6 tablespoons yogurt

Directions:
1. Put orange juice in a saucepan, bring to a boil over medium heat, take off heat, add tea leaves, cover and leave aside for 3 minutes, strain this and leave aside.
2. Heat a saucepan with 2 tablespoons oil over medium high heat, add lamb chops seasoned with salt, pepper, mustard and rasel hanout, toss, brown for 3 minutes on each side and transfer to a plate.
3. Add remaining oil to the saucepan, heat over medium heat, add ginger, onion, carrot, garlic and celery, stir and cook for 5 minutes.
4. Add orange juice, star anise, tomatoes, cinnamon stick, lamb, apricots, stir and cook for 1 hour and 30 minutes.
5. Transfer lamb chops to a cutting board, discard bones and chop.
6. Bring sauce from the pan to a boil, add chickpeas and mint, stir and cook for 10 minutes.
7. Discard cinnamon and star anise, divide into bowls and serve with yogurt on top.
Nutrition: calories 560, fat 24, fiber 11, carbs 35, protein 33

207. Spinach and Orzo Soup

Preparation time: 10 minutes
Cooking time: 10 minutes
Servings: 4
Ingredients:
- ½ cup orzo
- 6 cups chicken soup
- 1 and ½ cups parmesan, grated
- Salt and black pepper to taste
- 1 and ½ teaspoon oregano, dried
- ¼ cup yellow onion, finely chopped
- 3 cups baby spinach
- 2 tablespoons lemon juice
- ½ cup peas, frozen

Directions:
1. Heat a saucepan with the stock over high heat, add oregano, orzo, onion, salt and pepper, stir, bring to a boil, cover and cook for 10 minutes.
2. Take soup off the heat, add salt and pepper to taste and the rest of the ingredients , stir well and divide into soup bowls. Serve right away.
Nutrition: calories 201, fat 5, fiber 3, carbs 28, protein 17

208. Minty Lentil and Spinach Soup

Preparation time: 10 minutes
Cooking time: 30 minutes
Servings: 6
Ingredients:
- 2 tablespoons olive oil
- 1 yellow onion, chopped
- A pinch of salt and black pepper
- 2 garlic cloves, minced
- 1 teaspoon coriander, ground
- 1 teaspoon cumin, ground
- 1 teaspoon sumac
- 1 teaspoon red pepper, crushed
- 2 teaspoons mint, dried
- 1 tablespoon flour
- 6 cups veggie stock
- 3 cups water
- 12 ounces spinach, torn
- 1 and ½ cups brown lentils, rinsed
- 2 cups parsley, chopped
- Juice of 1 lime

Directions:
1. Heat up a pot with the oil over medium heat, add the onions, stir and sauté for 5 minutes.
2. Add garlic, salt, pepper, coriander, cumin, sumac, red pepper, mint and flour, stir and cook for another minute.
3. Add the stock, water and the other ingredients except the parsley and lime juice, stir, bring to a simmer and cook for 20 minutes.
4. Add the parsley and lime juice, cook the soup for 5 minutes more, ladle into bowls and serve.
Nutrition: calories 170, fat 7, fiber 6, carbs 22, protein 8

209. Chicken and Apricots Stew

Preparation time: 10 minutes
Cooking time: 2 hours and 10 minutes
Servings: 4
Ingredients:
- 3 garlic cloves, minced
- 1 tablespoon parsley, chopped
- 20 saffron threads
- 3 tablespoons cilantro, chopped
- Salt and black pepper to taste
- 1 teaspoon ginger, ground
- 2 tablespoons olive oil
- 3 red onions, thinly sliced
- 4 chicken drumsticks
- 5 ounces apricots, dried
- 2 tablespoons butter
- ¼ cup honey
- 2/3 cup walnuts, chopped
- ½ cinnamon stick

Directions:
1. Heat a pan over medium high heat, add saffron threads, toast them for 2 minutes, transfer to a bowl, cool down and crush.
2. Add the chicken pieces, 1 tablespoon cilantro, parsley, garlic, ginger, salt, pepper, oil and 2 tablespoons water, toss really well and keep in the fridge for 30 minutes.
3. Arrange onion on the bottom of a saucepan.
4. Add chicken and marinade, add 1 tablespoon butter, place on stove over medium high heat and cook for 15 minutes.
5. Add ¼ cup water, stir, cover pan, reduce heat to medium-low and simmer for 45 minutes.

6. Heat a pan over medium heat, add 2 tablespoons honey, cinnamon stick, apricots and ¾ cup water, stir, bring to a boil, reduce to low and simmer for 15 minutes.

7. Take off heat, discard cinnamon and leave to cool down.

8. Heat a pan with remaining butter over medium heat, add remaining honey and walnuts, stir, cook for 5 minutes and transfer to a plate.

9. Add chicken to apricot sauce, also season with salt, pepper and the rest of the cilantro stir, cook for 10 minutes and serve on top of walnuts.

Nutrition: calories 560, fat 10, fiber 4, carbs 34, protein 44

210. Fish and Veggie Stew

Preparation time: 10 minutes
Cooking time: 1 hour and 30 minutes
Servings: 4
Ingredients:
• 6 lemon wedges, pulp separated and chopped and some of the peel reserved
• 2 tablespoons parsley, chopped
• 2 tomatoes, cut in halves, peeled and grated
• 2 tablespoons cilantro, chopped
• 2 garlic cloves, minced
• ½ teaspoon paprika
• 2 tablespoons water
• ½ cup water
• ½ teaspoon cumin, ground
• Salt and black pepper to taste
• 4 bass fillets
• ¼ cup olive oil
• 3 carrots, sliced
• 1 red bell pepper, sliced lengthwise and thinly cut in strips
• 1 and ¼ pounds potatoes, peeled and sliced
• ½ cup olives
• 1 red onion, thinly sliced
Directions:
1. In a bowl, mix tomatoes with lemon pulp, cilantro, parsley, cumin, garlic, paprika, salt, pepper, 2 tablespoons water, 2 teaspoons oil and the fish, toss to coat and keep in the fridge for 30 minutes.
2. Heat a saucepan with the water and some salt over medium high heat, add potatoes and carrots, stir, cook for 10 minutes and drain.
3. Heat a pan over medium heat, add bell pepper and ¼ cup water, cover, cook for 5 minutes and take off heat.
4. Coat a saucepan with remaining oil, add potatoes and carrots, ¼ cup water, onion slices, fish and its marinade, bell pepper strips, olives, salt and pepper, toss gently, cook for 45 minutes, divide into bowls and serve.
Nutrition: calories 440, fat 18, fiber 8, carbs 43, protein 30

211. Tomato Soup

Preparation time: 60 minutes
Cooking time: 2 minutes
Servings: 4
Ingredients:
• ½ green bell pepper, chopped
• ½ red bell pepper, chopped
• 1 and ¾ pounds tomatoes, chopped
• ¼ cup bread, torn
• 9 tablespoons extra virgin olive oil
• 1 garlic clove, minced
• 2 teaspoons sherry vinegar
• Salt and black pepper to taste
• 1 tablespoon cilantro, chopped
• A pinch of cumin, ground

Directions:
1. In a blender, mix green and red bell peppers with tomatoes, salt, pepper, 6 tablespoons oil, and the other ingredients except the bread and cilantro, and pulse well. Keep in the fridge for 1 hour.
2. Heat up a pan with remaining oil over medium high heat, add bread pieces, and toast them for 1 minute.
3. Divide cold soup into bowls, top with bread cubes and cilantro then serve.
Nutrition: calories 260, fat 23, fiber 2, carbs 11, protein 2

212. Chickpeas Soup

Preparation time: 10 minutes
Cooking time: 35 minutes
Servings: 4
Ingredients:
• 1 bunch kale, leaves torn
• Salt and black pepper to taste
• 3 tablespoons olive oil
• 1 celery stalk, chopped
• 1 yellow onion, chopped
• 1 carrot, chopped
• 30 ounces canned chickpeas, drained
• 14 ounces canned tomatoes, chopped
• 1 bay leaf
• 3 rosemary sprigs
• 4 cups veggie stock
Directions:
1. In a bowl, mix kale with half of the oil, salt and pepper, toss to coat., spread on a lined baking sheet, cook at 425 degrees F for 12 minutes and leave aside to cool down.
2. Heat a saucepan with remaining oil over medium high heat, add carrot, celery, onion, some salt and pepper, stir and cook for 5 minutes.
3. Add the rest of the ingredients, toss and simmer for 20 minutes.
4. Discard rosemary and bay leaf, puree using a blender and divide into soup bowls. Top with roasted kale and serve.
Nutrition: calories 360, fat 14, fiber 11, carbs 53, protein 14

213. Fish Soup

Preparation time: 10 minutes
Cooking time: 35 minutes
Servings: 6
Ingredients:
• 2 garlic cloves, minced
• 2 tablespoons olive oil
• 1 fennel bulb, sliced
• 1 yellow onion, chopped
• 1 pinch saffron, soaked in some orange juice for 10 minutes and drained
• 14 ounces canned tomatoes, peeled
• 1 strip orange zest
• 6 cups seafood stock
• 10 halibut fillet, cut into big pieces
• 20 shrimp, peeled and deveined
• 1 bunch parsley, chopped
• Salt and white pepper to taste
Directions:
1. Heat a saucepan with oil over medium high heat, add onion, garlic and fennel, stir and cook for 10 minutes.
2. Add saffron, tomatoes, orange zest and stock, stir, bring to a boil and simmer for 20 minutes.
3. Add fish and shrimp, stir and cook for 6 minutes..
4. Sprinkle parsley, salt and pepper, divide into bowls and serve.
Nutrition: calories 340, fat 20, fiber 3, carbs 23, protein 45

214. Chili Watermelon Soup

Preparation time: 4 hours
Cooking time: 5 minutes
Servings: 4
Ingredients:
- 3 pounds watermelon, sliced
- ½ teaspoon chipotle chili powder
- 2 tablespoons olive oil
- Salt to taste
- 1 tomato, chopped
- 1 tablespoon shallot, chopped
- ¼ cup cilantro, chopped
- 1 small cucumber, chopped
- 1 small Serrano chili pepper, chopped
- 3 and ½ tablespoons lime juice
- ¼ cup crème Fraiche
- ½ tablespoon red wine vinegar

Directions:
1. In a bowl, mix 1 tablespoon oil with chipotle powder, stir and brush the watermelon with this mix.
2. Put the watermelon slices preheated grill pan over medium high heat, grill for 1 minute on each side, cool down, chop and put in a blender.
3. Add cucumber and the rest of the ingredients except the vinegar and the lime juice and pulse well.
4. Transfer to bowls, top with lime juice and vinegar, keep in the fridge for 4 hours and then serve.

Nutrition: calories 115, fat 0, fiber 2, carbs 18, protein 2

215. Shrimp Soup

Preparation time: 30 minutes
Cooking time: 5 minutes
Servings: 6
Ingredients:
- 1 English cucumber, chopped
- 3 cups tomato juice
- 3 jarred roasted red peppers, chopped
- ½ cup olive oil
- 2 tablespoons sherry vinegar
- 1 teaspoon sherry vinegar
- 1 garlic clove, mashed
- 2 baguette slices, cut into cubes and toasted
- Salt and black pepper to taste
- ½ teaspoon cumin, ground
- ¾ pounds shrimp, peeled and deveined
- 1 teaspoon thyme, chopped

Directions:
1. In a blender, mix cucumber with tomato juice, red peppers and pulse well, bread, 6 tablespoons oil, 2 tablespoons vinegar, cumin, salt, pepper and garlic, pulse again, transfer to a bowl and keep in the fridge for 30 minutes.
2. Heat a saucepan with 1 tablespoon oil over high heat, add shrimp, stir and cook for 2 minutes.
3. Add thyme, and the rest of the ingredients, cook for 1 minute and transfer to a plate. .
4. Divide cold soup into bowls, top with shrimp and serve. Enjoy!

Nutrition: calories 230, fat 7, fiber 10, carbs 24, protein 13

216. Halibut and Veggies Stew

Preparation time: 10 minutes
Cooking time: 50 minutes
Servings: 4
Ingredients:
- 1 yellow onion, chopped
- 2 tablespoons oil
- 1 fennel bulb, stalks removed, sliced and roughly chopped
- 1 carrot, thinly sliced crosswise
- 1 red bell pepper, chopped
- 2 garlic cloves, minced
- 3 tablespoons tomato paste
- 16 ounces canned chickpeas, drained
- ½ cup dry white wine
- 1 teaspoon thyme, chopped
- A pinch of smoked paprika
- Salt and black pepper to taste
- 1 bay leaf
- 2 pinches saffron
- 4 baguette slices, toasted
- 3 and ½ cups water
- 13 mussels, debearded
- 11 ounces halibut fillets, skinless and cut into chunks

Directions:
1. Heat a saucepan with the oil over medium high heat, add fennel, onion, bell pepper, garlic, tomato paste and carrot, stir and cook for 5 minutes. .
2. Add wine, stir and cook for 2 minutes. Add the rest of the ingredients except the halibut and mussels, stir, bring to a boil, cover and boil for 25 minutes.
3. Add, halibut and mussels, cover and simmer for 6 minutes more.
4. Discard unopened mussels, ladle into bowls and serve with toasted bread on the side.

Nutrition: calories 450, fat 12, fiber 13, carbs 47, protein 34

217. Cucumber Soup

Preparation time: 10 minutes
Cooking time: 6 minutes
Servings: 4
Ingredients:
- 3 bread slices
- ¼ cup almonds
- 4 teaspoons almonds
- 3 cucumbers, peeled and chopped
- 3 garlic cloves, minced
- ½ cup warm water
- 6 scallions, thinly sliced
- ¼ cup white wine vinegar
- 3 tablespoons olive oil
- Salt to taste
- 1 teaspoon lemon juice
- ½ cup green grapes, cut in halves

Directions:
1. Heat a pan over medium high heat, add almonds, stir, toast for 5 minutes, transfer to a plate and leave aside.
2. Soak bread in warm water for 2 minutes, transfer to a blender, add almost all the cucumber, salt, the oil, garlic, 5 scallions, lemon juice, vinegar and half of the almonds and pulse well.
3. Ladle soup into bowls, top with reserved ingredients and 2 tablespoons grapes and serve.

Nutrition: calories 200, fat 12, fiber 3, carbs 20, protein 6

218. Chickpeas, Tomato and Kale Stew

Preparation time: 10 minutes
Cooking time: 30 minutes
Servings: 4
Ingredients:
- 1 yellow onion, chopped
- 1 tablespoon extra-virgin olive oil
- 2 cups sweet potatoes, peeled and chopped
- 1 ½ teaspoon cumin, ground

- 4-inch cinnamon stick
- 14 ounces canned tomatoes, chopped
- 14 ounces canned chickpeas, drained
- 1 ½ teaspoon honey
- 6 tablespoons orange juice
- 1 cup water
- Salt and black pepper to taste
- ½ cup green olives, pitted
- 2 cups kale leaves, chopped

Directions:
1. Heat a saucepan with the oil over medium high heat, add onion, cumin and cinnamon stir and cook for 5 minutes.
2. Add potatoes and the rest of the ingredients except the kale, stir, cover, reduce heat to medium-low and cook for 15 minutes.
3. Add kale , stir, cover again and cook for 10 minutes more. Divide into bowls and serve.
Nutrition: calories 280, fat 6, fiber 9, carbs 53, protein 10

219. Chicken and Rice Soup

Preparation time: 10 minutes
Cooking time: 30 minutes
Servings: 4
Ingredients:
- ½ cup water
- Salt and black pepper to taste
- 6 cups chicken stock
- ¼ cup lemon juice
- 1 chicken breast, boneless, skinless and cut into thin strips
- ½ cup white rice
- 6 tablespoons mint, chopped

Directions:
1. Put the water in a saucepan, add salt, ½ cup stock, stir, bring to a boil over medium heat, add rice, stir, reduce temperature to low, cover, simmer for 20 minutes, take off heat and cool down.
2. Put remaining stock in another saucepan, bring to a boil over medium heat, add chicken, rice and the rest of the ingredients, stir, simmer for 10 minutes more, divide into bowls and serve.
Nutrition: calories 180, fat 2, fiber 1, carbs 21, protein 20

220. Veggie Stew

Preparation time: 10 minutes
Cooking time: 50 minutes
Servings: 4
Ingredients:
- 3 eggplants, chopped
- Salt and black pepper to taste
- 6 zucchinis, chopped
- 2 yellow onions, chopped
- 3 red bell peppers, chopped
- 56 ounces canned tomatoes, chopped
- A handful black olives, pitted and chopped
- A pinch of allspice, ground
- A pinch of cinnamon, ground
- 1 teaspoon oregano, dried
- A drizzle of honey
- 1 tablespoon garbanzo bean flour mixed with 1 tablespoon water
- A drizzle of olive oil
- A pinch of red chili flakes
- 3 tablespoons Greek yogurt

Directions:
1. Heat a saucepan with the oil over medium high heat, add bell peppers, onions, some salt and pepper, stir and sauté for 4 minutes.

2. Add eggplant and the rest of the ingredients except the flour, olives, chili flakes and the yogurt, stir, bring to a boil, cover, reduce heat to medium-low and cook for 45 minutes.
3. Add the remaining ingredients except the yogurt, stir, cook for 1 minute, divide into bowls and serve with some Greek yogurt on top.
Nutrition: calories 80, fat 2, fiber 4, carbs 12, protein 3

221. Chunky Mediterranean Soup

Preparation time: 25 minutes
Cooking Time: 35 minutes
Servings: 8
Ingredients:
- 2 tablespoons extra virgin olive oil
- 1 shallot, chopped
- 2 garlic cloves, minced
- 1 eggplants, peeled and cubed
- 1 zucchini, cubed
- 2 red bell peppers, cored and diced
- 1 can diced tomatoes
- 1 can white beans, drained
- 8 cups water
- 1 thyme sprig
- 1 oregano sprig
- Salt and pepper to taste
- 1 lemon, juiced
- 2 tablespoons chopped parsley

Directions:
1. Heat the oil in a soup pot and stir in the shallot and garlic.
2. Add the eggplants, zucchini and bell peppers and cook for 5 minutes then stir in the rest of the ingredients, except the lemon juice and parsley.
3. Season with salt and pepper and cook on low heat for 25 minutes.
4. Add the lemon juice and cook for 5 more minutes.
5. Serve the soup warm and fresh.
Nutrition per serving
Calories:151
Fat:4.0g
Protein:7.5g
Carbohydrates:23.5g

222. Minty Green Pea Soup

Preparation time: 16 minutes
Cooking Time: 19 minutes
Servings: 6
Ingredients:
- 2 tablespoons olive oil
- 2 shallots, chopped
- 2 garlic cloves, chopped
- 1-pound green peas
- 4 mint leaves, chopped
- ½ teaspoon dried oregano
- 2 cups vegetable stock
- 1 cup water
- Salt and pepper to taste
- 1 tablespoon lemon juice
- ¼ cup heavy cream

Directions:
1. Heat the oil in a soup pot and stir in the shallots and garlic. Cook for 2 minutes until softened then add the green peas, mint, oregano, stock and water.
2. Add salt and pepper to taste and cook on low heat for 15 minutes.
3. Stir in the lemon juice and cook for 2 additional minutes.

4. When done, remove from heat and stir in the cream.
5. Puree the soup with an immersion blender until creamy and smooth.
6. Serve the soup warm or chilled.
Nutrition per serving
Calories:129
Fat:6.9g
Protein:4.7g
Carbohydrates:13.0g

223. Spinach Orzo Soup

Preparation time: 18 minutes
Cooking time : 27 minutes
Servings: 8
Ingredients:
- 2 tablespoons extra virgin olive oil
- 2 shallots, chopped
- 2 garlic cloves, chopped
- 1 green bell pepper, cored and diced
- 1 yellow bell pepper, cored and diced
- 4 cups baby spinach
- 1 cup green peas
- 2 cups vegetable stock
- 4 cups water
- 2 tablespoons lemon juice
- Salt and pepper to taste
- ¼ cup orzo

Directions:
1. Heat the oil in a soup pot and stir in the shallots and garlic.
2. Cook for 2 minutes then add the rest of the ingredients and season with salt and pepper.
3. Cook on low heat for 25 minutes.
4. Serve the soup warm or chilled.
Nutrition per serving
Calories:83
Fat:3.9g
Protein:2.6g
Carbohydrates:9.9g

224. Spiced Lentil Stew

Preparation time: 13 minutes
Cooking Time: 32 minutes
Servings: 8
Ingredients:
- 2 tablespoons extra virgin olive oil
- 2 shallots, chopped
- 2 garlic cloves, chopped
- 2 red bell peppers, cored and diced
- 2 carrots, diced
- 1 celery stalk, diced
- ½ teaspoon mustard seeds
- ½ teaspoon cumin seeds
- 1 can crushed tomatoes
- 3 cups vegetable stock
- 3 cups water
- 1 cup green lentils
- Salt and pepper to taste
- Yogurt for serving

Directions:
1. Heat the oil in a soup pot and stir in the shallots and garlic. Cook for 2 minutes then add the rest of the ingredients.
2. Adjust the taste with salt and pepper and cook on low heat for 30 minutes.

3. Serve the soup warm and fresh, topped with plain yogurt or freshly chopped parsley.
Nutrition per serving
Calories:143
Fat:4.0g
Protein:7.3g
Carbohydrates:20.2g

225. Spanish Meatball Soup

Preparation time: 20 minutes
Cooking Time: 1 hour
Servings: 8
Ingredients:
- 2 tablespoons olive oil
- 1 onion, chopped
- 2 garlic cloves, chopped
- 2 red bell peppers, cored and diced
- 2 carrots, diced
- 1 celery stalk, diced
- 2 cups vegetable stock
- 6 cups water
- 1-pound ground veal
- 1 egg
- 2 tablespoons chopped parsley
- 1 can crushed tomatoes
- Salt and pepper to taste

Directions:
1. Heat the oil in a soup pot and stir in the onion, garlic, bell peppers, carrots, celery, stock and water. Season with salt and pepper and bring to a boil.
2. In the meantime, mix the veal, egg and parsley in a bowl. Form small meatballs and place them in the boiling liquid.
3. Add the tomatoes and adjust the taste with salt and pepper.
4. Cook on low heat for 20 minutes.
5. Serve the soup war and fresh.
Nutrition per serving
Calories:166
Fat:8.5g
Protein:15.6g
Carbohydrates:6.5g

226. Sweet and Sour Rhubarb Lentil Soup

Preparation time: 20 minutes
Cooking Time: 25 minutes
Servings: 6
Ingredients:
- 2 tablespoons olive oil
- 1 shallot, chopped
- 1 garlic clove, chopped
- 1 green bell pepper, cored and diced
- 1 yellow bell pepper, cored and diced
- 1 carrot, diced
- 1 celery stalk, diced
- 1 cup green lentils
- 4 rhubarb stalks, sliced
- 2 cups vegetable stock
- 6 cups water
- ½ cup diced tomatoes
- Salt and pepper to taste
- 1 thyme sprig
- 1 oregano sprig

Directions:
1. Heat the oil in a soup pot and stir in the shallot, garlic, bell peppers, carrot and celery.

2. Cook for 5 minutes until softened then add the lentils, rhubarb, stock and water, as well as tomatoes.
3. Season with salt and pepper and add the thyme and oregano sprig.
4. Cook on low heat for 20 minutes.
5. Serve the soup warm or chilled.
Nutrition per serving
Calories:184
Fat:5.3g
Protein:9.4g
Carbohydrates:25.6g

227. Lamb Veggie Soup

Preparation time: 25 minutes
Cooking Time: 1 hour 5 minutes
Servings: 8
Ingredients:
- 1 ½ pound lamb shoulder, cubed
- 2 tablespoons olive oil
- 2 shallots, chopped
- 2 carrots, diced
- 2 celery stalks, diced
- ¼ teaspoon grated ginger
- 2 cups cauliflower florets
- ½ cup green peas
- 4 cups vegetable stock
- 6 cups water
- 1 thyme sprig
- 1 oregano sprig
- 1 basil sprig
- Salt and pepper to taste
- 1 can crushed tomatoes
- 2 tablespoons lemon juice

Directions:
1. Heat the oil in a soup pot and stir in the lamb shoulder.
2. Cook for 5 minutes on all sides then add the water and stock.
3. Cook for 40 minutes then add the rest of the ingredients and season with salt and pepper.
4. Continue cooking for another 20 minutes then serve the soup fresh.
Nutrition per serving
Calories:221
Fat:9.9g
Protein:25.7g
Carbohydrates:6.5g

228. Creamy Chickpea Soup

Preparation time: 28 minutes
Cooking Time: 17 minutes
Servings: 4
Ingredients:
- 2 tablespoons olive oil
- 1 shallot, chopped
- 1 celery stalk, diced
- 1 can chickpeas, drained
- 1 can crushed tomatoes
- 2 cups vegetable stock
- 2 cups water
- Salt and pepper to taste
- ½ cup Greek yogurt

Directions:
1. Heat the oil in a soup pot and stir in the shallot and celery. Cook for 2 minutes until softened then add the chickpeas, tomatoes, stock and water, as well as salt and pepper.

2. Cook on low heat for 15 minutes.
3. Remove from heat and stir in the yogurt. Puree the soup with an immersion blender until creamy and smooth.
4. Serve the soup fresh.
Nutrition per serving
Calories:260
Fat:10.1g
Protein:10.7g
Carbohydrates:33.9g

229. Fresh Gazpacho

Preparation time: 10 minutes
Cooking Time: 10 minutes
Servings: 6
Ingredients:
- 2 pounds tomatoes, peeled and cubed
- 1 red bell pepper, cored and diced
- 1 celery stalk, sliced
- 2 garlic cloves, chopped
- 2 whole wheat bread slices
- 3 tablespoons extra virgin olive oil
- 1 teaspoon sherry vinegar
- 1 pinch cumin powder
- Salt and pepper to taste
- Chopped cilantro for serving

Directions:
1. Combine the tomatoes, bell pepper, celery, garlic, bread, oil, vinegar and cumin in a blender.
2. Add salt and pepper to taste and puree the soup with an immersion blender or until smooth.
3. Pour the soup into serving bowls right away.
Nutrition per serving
Calories:119
Fat:7.7g
Protein:2.8g
Carbohydrates:11.4g

230. Cream of Bell Pepper Soup

Preparation Time: 20 minutes
Cooking time: 22 minutes
Servings: 6
Ingredients:
- 2 tablespoons olive oil
- 1 sweet onion, chopped
- 1 celery stalk, chopped
- 1 garlic clove, chopped
- 2 jars roasted red bell peppers, sliced
- 1 can diced tomatoes
- 2 cups vegetable stock
- Salt and pepper to taste
- 1 thyme sprig

Directions:
1. Heat the oil in a soup pot and stir in the onion, celery and garlic. Cook for 2 minutes then add the rest of the ingredients.
2. Season with salt and pepper and cook on low heat for 20 minutes.
3. When done, remove the thyme sprig and puree the soup with an immersion blender.
4. Serve the soup warm or chilled.
Nutrition per serving
Calories:53
Fat:4.8g
Protein:0.5g
Carbohydrates:2.9g

231. Watermelon Gazpacho

Preparation Time: 25 minutes
Cooking time 0 minutes
Servings: 4
Ingredients:
- 6 oz. seedless watermelon
- 4 tomatoes, peeled and cubed
- 1 red pepper, seeded
- 1 shallot
- 1 garlic clove
- 1 lime, juiced
- 1 cup ice cubes
- Salt and pepper to taste
- 1 teaspoon sherry vinegar

Directions:
1. Combine all the ingredients in a blender.
2. Add salt and pepper and pulse until smooth and creamy.
3. Pour the soup into bowls and serve chilled.

Nutrition per serving
Calories:52
Fat:0.4g
Protein:1.9g
Carbohydrates:12.2g

232. Mediterranean Sausage Soup

Preparation time: 30 minutes
Cooking Time: 30 minutes
Servings: 8
Ingredients:
- 2 tablespoons olive oil
- 4 chicken sausages, halved
- 2 shallots, chopped
- 1 garlic clove, chopped
- 2 red bell peppers, cored and diced
- 1 zucchini, cubed
- 2 cups cauliflower florets
- 1 can diced tomatoes
- 2 cups vegetable stock
- 6 cups water
- Salt and pepper to taste
- ½ teaspoon dried oregano
- ½ teaspoon dried basil
- ½ teaspoon dried thyme

Directions:
1. Heat the oil in a soup pot and stir in the sausages. Cook for 5 minutes then stir in the rest of the ingredients.
2. Add salt and pepper to taste and cook on low heat for 25 minutes.
3. Serve the soup warm and fresh.

Nutrition per serving
Calories:56
Fat:3.7g
Protein:1.4g
Carbohydrates:5.3g

233. Spicy Chorizo Soup

Preparation time: 30 minutes
Cooking Time: 30 minutes
Servings: 6
Ingredients:
- 2 tablespoons olive oil
- 2 chorizo links, sliced
- 1 shallot, chopped
- 1 garlic clove, chopped
- 1 red bell peppers, cored and diced
- 2 carrots, diced
- 1 yellow bell pepper, cored and diced
- 1 can white beans, drained
- 1 can diced tomatoes
- 2 cups vegetable stock
- 6 cups water
- 1 thyme sprig
- 1 red pepper, chopped
- Salt and pepper to taste

Directions:
1. Heat the oil in a soup pot.
2. Stir in the chorizo links and cook for 5 minutes then add the rest of the ingredients and season with salt and pepper.
3. Cook on low heat for 25 minutes.
4. When done, serve the soup warm.

Nutrition per serving
Calories:277
Fat:12.8g
Protein:13.8g
Carbohydrates:27.6g

234. White Bean Kale Soup

Preparation time: 28 minutes
Cooking Time: 32 minutes
Servings: 8
Ingredients:
- 2 tablespoons olive oil
- 1 shallot, chopped
- 2 garlic cloves, chopped
- 1 red pepper, chopped
- 1 celery stalk, diced
- 2 carrots, diced
- 1 can white beans, drained
- 2 tablespoons lemon juice
- 1 can diced tomatoes
- 2 cups vegetable stock
- 6 cups water
- Salt and pepper to taste
- 1 bunch kale, shredded

Directions:
1. Heat the oil in a soup pot and stir in the shallot, garlic, red pepper, celery and carrots. Cook for 2 minutes until softened.
2. Add the rest of the ingredients and season with salt and pepper.
3. Cook on low heat for 30 minutes.
4. Serve the soup warm or chilled.

Nutrition per serving
Calories:136
Fat:3.8g
Protein:6.8g
Carbohydrates:19.8g

235. Chorizo Cod Soup

Preparation time: 20 minutes
Cooking Time: 25 minutes
Servings: 6
Ingredients:
- 2 tablespoons olive oil
- 2 chorizo links, sliced
- 1 shallot, chopped
- 2 yellow bell pepper, cored and diced
- 1 carrot, diced

- 1 leek, sliced
- 1 can diced tomatoes
- 2 cups vegetable stock
- 4 cups water
- 4 cod fillets
- 1 thyme sprig
- Salt and pepper to taste
- Chopped parsley for serving

Directions:

1. Heat the oil in a soup pot. Stir in the chorizo links and cook for 5 minutes.
2. Add the rest of the ingredients, except the cod fillets.
3. Season with salt and pepper and cook for 15 minutes.
4. Add the cod and cook for another 5 minutes.
5. Serve the soup warm, topped with chopped parsley.

Nutrition per serving

Calories:162

Fat:12.5g

Protein:5.8g

Carbohydrates:7.0g

236. Tomato Haddock Soup

Preparation time: 3 minutes

Cooking Time: 27 minutes

Servings: 6

Ingredients:

- 2 tablespoons olive oil
- 1 shallot, chopped
- 2 garlic cloves, minced
- 1 celery stalk, diced
- 4 tomatoes, peeled and diced
- 2 cups vegetable stock
- 2 cups water
- 1 teaspoon sherry vinegar
- 4 haddock fillets, cubed
- 1 thyme sprig
- 1 bay leaf
- ½ teaspoon dried oregano
- Salt and pepper to taste

Directions:

1. Heat the oil in a soup pot and stir in the shallot and garlic. Cook for 2 minutes until fragrant.
2. Add the celery, tomatoes, stock, water, vinegar, thyme and bay leaf, as well as oregano, salt and pepper.
3. Cook for 15 minutes then add the haddock and cover the pot with a lid.
4. Cook for another 10 minutes on low heat.
5. Serve the soup warm and fresh.

Nutrition per serving

Calories:172

Fat:5.8g

Protein:25.2g

Carbohydrates:4.3g

237. Cucumber Yogurt Gazpacho

Preparation Time: 20 minutes

Cooking time: 0 minutes

Servings: 6

Ingredients:

- 4 cucumbers, partially peeled
- 1 cup seedless white grapes
- 2 tablespoon sliced almonds
- 1 cup ice cubes
- 2 garlic cloves
- 1 tablespoon chopped dill

- 2 tablespoons cream cheese
- ½ cup plain yogurt
- 2 tablespoons extra virgin olive oil
- Salt and pepper to taste
- 1 tablespoon lemon juice

Directions:

1. Combine the cucumbers with the rest of the ingredients in a blender.
2. Add salt and pepper and pulse until smooth and creamy.
3. Serve the gazpacho as fresh as possible.

Nutrition per serving

Calories:111

Fat:7.3g

Protein:3.3g

Carbohydrates:9.9g

238. Cold Avocado Soup

Preparation time: 20 minutes

Cooking Time: 0 minutes

Servings: 6

Ingredients:

- 2 avocados, peeled and pitted
- 4 cucumbers, peeled
- ½ cup plain yogurt
- 1 cup water
- 2 tablespoons lemon juice
- 2 garlic cloves
- 2 fresh basil leaves
- 2 tablespoons extra virgin olive oil
- 2 mint leaves
- 1 shallot, chopped
- Salt and pepper to taste

Directions:

1. Combine all the ingredients in a blender.
2. Add salt and pepper to taste and pulse until smooth and creamy.
3. Pour the soup into bowls and serve right away.

Nutrition per serving

Calories:226

Fat:18.3g

Protein:4.0g

Carbohydrates:15.2g

239. Creamy Roasted Vegetable Soup

Preparation time: 20 minutes

Cooking Time: 45 minutes

Servings: 8

Ingredients:

- 2 red onions, sliced
- 1 zucchini, sliced
- 2 tomatoes, sliced
- 2 potatoes, sliced
- 2 garlic cloves
- 2 tablespoons olive oil
- 1 teaspoon dried basil
- 1 teaspoon dried oregano
- 4 cups vegetable stock
- 8 cups water
- Salt and pepper to taste
- 1 bay leaf
- 1 thyme sprig

Directions:

1. Combine the onions, zucchini, tomatoes, potatoes, garlic, oil, basil and oregano in a deep-dish baking pan.

2. Season with salt and pepper and cook in the preheated oven at 400F for 30 minutes or until golden brown.
3. Transfer the vegetables in a soup pot and add the stock and water.
4. Stir in the bay leaf and thyme sprig and cook for 15 minutes.
5. When done, remove the thyme and bay leaf and puree the soup with an immersion blender.
6. Serve the soup warm and fresh.
Nutrition per serving
Calories:92
Fat:3.8g
Protein:2.0g
Carbohydrates:13.9g

240. Mixed Chicken Soup

Preparation time: 40 minutes
Cooking Time: 1 hour 5 minutes
Servings: 8
Ingredients:

- 1 whole chicken, cut into smaller pieces
- 1 sweet onion, chopped
- 2 celery stalks, sliced
- 2 carrots, sliced
- 2 red bell peppers, cored and diced
- 1 zucchini, cubed
- 2 potatoes, peeled and cubed
- 2 tomatoes, peeled and diced
- 2 cups vegetable stock
- 8 cups water
- Salt and pepper to taste
- 1 tablespoon lemon juice
- 2 tablespoons chopped parsley for serving

Directions:
1. Combine the chicken with stock and water in a pot. Add salt and pepper and cook on low heat for 40 minutes.
2. Add the rest of the ingredients and continue cooking for another 20-25 minutes.
3. When done, remove from heat and stir in the parsley.
4. Serve the soup warm and fresh.
Nutrition per serving
Calories:103
Fat:1.6g
Protein:7.3g
Carbohydrates:15.4g

Chapter 4. Sandwiches, Pizzas, and Wraps

241. Falafel Balls with Tahini Sauce

Preparation time: 2 hours 20 minutes
Cooking time: 20 minutes
Serving: 4
Ingredients:
Tahini Sauce:
- ½ cup tahini
- 2 tablespoons lemon juice
- ¼ cup finely chopped flat-leaf parsley
- 2 cloves garlic, minced
- ½ cup cold water, as needed

Falafel:
- 1 cup dried chickpeas, soaked overnight, drained
- ¼ cup chopped flat-leaf parsley
- ¼ cup chopped cilantro
- 1 large onion, chopped
- 1 teaspoon cumin
- ½ teaspoon chili flakes
- 4 cloves garlic
- 1 teaspoon sea salt
- 5 tablespoons almond flour
- 1½ teaspoons baking soda, dissolved in 1 teaspoon water
- 2 cups peanut oil
- 1 medium bell pepper, chopped
- 1 medium tomato, chopped
- 4 whole-wheat pita bread

Direction:
1. Combine the ingredients for the tahini sauce in a small bowl. Stir to mix well until smooth.
2. Wrap the bowl in plastic and refrigerate until ready to serve.

Make the Falafel
3. Put the chickpeas, parsley, cilantro, onion, cumin, chili flakes, garlic, and salt in a food processor. Pulse to mix well but not puréed.
4. Add the flour and baking soda to the food processor, then pulse to form a smooth and tight dough.
5. Put the dough in a large bowl and wrap in plastic. Refrigerate for at least 2 hours to let it rise.
6. Divide and shape the dough into walnut-sized small balls.
7. Pour the peanut oil in a large pot and heat over high heat until the temperature of the oil reaches 375°F (190°C).
8. Drop 6 balls into the oil each time, and fry for 5 minutes or until golden brown and crispy. Turn the balls with a strainer to make them fried evenly.
9. Transfer the balls on paper towels with the strainer, then drain the oil from the balls.
10.   Roast the pita bread in the oven for 5 minutes or until golden brown, if needed, then stuff the pitas with falafel balls and top with bell peppers and tomatoes. Drizzle with tahini sauce and serve immediately.
Nutrition Per Serving
calories: 574 | fat: 27.1g | protein: 19.8g | carbs: 69.7g | fiber: 13.4g | sodium: 1246mg

242. Glazed Mushroom and Vegetable Fajitas

Preparation time: 20 minutes
Cooking time: 20 minutes
Serving: 6
Ingredients:
Spicy Glazed Mushrooms:
- 1 teaspoon olive oil
- 1 (10- to 12-ounce / 284- to 340-g) package cremini mushrooms, rinsed and drained, cut into thin slices
- ½ to 1 teaspoon chili powder
- Sea salt and freshly ground black pepper, to taste
- 1 teaspoon maple syrup

Fajitas:
- 2 teaspoons olive oil
- 1 onion, chopped
- Sea salt, to taste
- 1 bell pepper, any color, deseeded and sliced into long strips
- 1 zucchini, cut into large matchsticks
- 6 whole-grain tortilla
- 2 carrots, grated
- 3 to 4 scallions, sliced
- ½ cup fresh cilantro, finely chopped

Direction:
Make the Spicy Glazed Mushrooms
1. Heat the olive oil in a nonstick skillet over medium heat until shimmering.
2. Add the mushrooms and sauté for 10 minutes or until tender.
3. Sprinkle the mushrooms with chili powder, salt, and ground black pepper. Drizzle with maple syrup. Stir to mix well and cook for 5 to 7 minutes or until the mushrooms are glazed. Set aside until ready to use.
Make the Fajitas
4. Heat the olive oil in the same skillet over medium heat until shimmering.
5. Add the onion and sauté for 5 minutes or until translucent. Sprinkle with salt.
6. Add the bell pepper and zucchini and sauté for 7 minutes or until tender.
7. Meanwhile, toast the tortilla in the oven for 5 minutes or until golden brown.
8. Allow the tortilla to cool for a few minutes until they can be handled, then assemble the tortilla with glazed mushrooms, sautéed vegetables and remaining vegetables to make the fajitas. Serve immediately.
Nutrition Per Serving
calories: 403 | fat: 14.8g | protein: 11.2g | carbs: 7.9g | fiber: 7.0g | sodium: 230mg

243. Cheesy Fig Pizzas with Garlic Oil

Preparation time: 1 day 40 minutes
Cooking time: 10 minutes
Serving: 2 pizzas
Ingredients:
Dough:
- 1 cup almond flour
- 1½ cups whole-wheat flour
- ¾ teaspoon instant or rapid-rise yeast

- 2 teaspoons raw honey
- 1¼ cups ice water
- 2 tablespoons extra-virgin olive oil
- 1¾ teaspoons sea salt

Garlic Oil:
- 4 tablespoons extra-virgin olive oil, divided
- ½ teaspoon dried thyme
- 2 garlic cloves, minced
- 1/8 teaspoon sea salt
- ½ teaspoon freshly ground pepper

Topping:
- 1 cup fresh basil leaves
- 1 cup crumbled feta cheese
- 8 ounces (227 g) fresh figs, stemmed and quartered lengthwise
- 2 tablespoons raw honey

Direction:

Make the Dough

1. Combine the flours, yeast, and honey in a food processor, pulse to combine well. Gently add water while pulsing. Let the dough sit for 10 minutes.
2. Mix the olive oil and salt in the dough and knead the dough until smooth. Wrap in plastic and refrigerate for at least 1 day.

Make the Garlic Oil

3. Heat 2 tablespoons of olive oil in a nonstick skillet over medium-low heat until shimmering.
4. Add the thyme, garlic, salt, and pepper and sauté for 30 seconds or until fragrant. Set them aside until ready to use.

Make the Pizzas

5. Preheat the oven to 500°F (260°C). Grease two baking sheets with 2 tablespoons of olive oil.
6. Divide the dough in half and shape into two balls. Press the balls into 13- inch rounds. Sprinkle the rounds with a tough of flour if they are sticky.
7. Top the rounds with the garlic oil and basil leaves, then arrange the rounds on the baking sheets. Scatter with feta cheese and figs.
8. Put the sheets in the preheated oven and bake for 9 minutes or until lightly browned. Rotate the pizza halfway through.
9. Remove the pizzas from the oven, then discard the bay leaves. Drizzle with honey. Let sit for 5 minutes and serve immediately.

Nutrition Per Serving (1 pizza)

calories: 1350 | fat: 46.5g | protein: 27.5g | carbs: 221.9g | fiber: 23.7g | sodium: 2898mg

244. Mashed Grape Tomato Pizzas

Preparation time: 10 minutes
Cooking time: 20 minutes
Serving: 6
Ingredients:
- 3 cups grape tomatoes, halved
- 1 teaspoon chopped fresh thyme leaves
- 2 garlic cloves, minced
- ¼ teaspoon kosher salt
- ¼ teaspoon freshly ground black pepper
- 1 tablespoon extra-virgin olive oil
- ¾ cup shredded Parmesan cheese
- 6 whole-wheat pita bread

Direction:

1. Preheat the oven to 425°F (220°C).
2. Combine the tomatoes, thyme, garlic, salt, ground black pepper, and olive oil in a baking pan.

3. Roast in the preheated oven for 20 minutes. Remove the pan from the oven, mash the tomatoes with a spatula and stir to mix well halfway through the cooking time.
4. Meanwhile, divide and spread the cheese over each pita bread, then place the bread in a separate baking pan and roast in the oven for 5 minutes or until golden brown and the cheese melts.
5. Transfer the pita bread onto a large plate, then top with the roasted mashed tomatoes. Serve immediately.

Nutrition Per Serving

calories: 140 | fat: 5.1g | protein: 6.2g | carbs: 16.9g | fiber: 2.0g | sodium: 466mg

245. Vegetable and Cheese Lavash Pizza

Preparation time: 15 minutes
Cooking time: 11 minutes
Serving: 4
Ingredients:
- 2 (12 by 9-inch) lavash bread
- 2 tablespoons extra-virgin olive oil
- 10 ounces (284 g) frozen spinach, thawed and squeezed dry
- 1 cup shredded fontina cheese
- 1 tomato, cored and cut into ½-inch pieces
- ½ cup pitted large green olives, chopped
- ¼ teaspoon red pepper flakes
- 3 garlic cloves, minced
- ¼ teaspoon sea salt
- ¼ teaspoon ground black pepper
- ½ cup grated Parmesan cheese

Direction:

1. Preheat oven to 475°F (246°C).
2. Brush the lavash bread with olive oil, then place them on two baking sheet. Heat in the preheated oven for 4 minutes or until lightly browned. Flip the bread halfway through the cooking time.
3. Meanwhile, combine the spinach, fontina cheese, tomato pieces, olives, red pepper flakes, garlic, salt, and black pepper in a large bowl. Stir to mix well.
4. Remove the lavash bread from the oven and sit them on two large plates, spread them with the spinach mixture, then scatter with the Parmesan cheese on top.
5. Bake in the oven for 7 minutes or until the cheese melts and well browned.
6. Slice and serve warm.

Nutrition Per Serving

calories: 431 | fat: 21.5g | protein: 20.0g | carbs: 38.4g | fiber: 2.5g | sodium: 854mg

246. Dulse, Avocado, and Tomato Pitas

Preparation time: 10 minutes
Cooking time: 30 minutes
Serving: 4 pitas
Ingredients:
- 2 teaspoons coconut oil
- ½ cup dulse, picked through and separated
- Ground black pepper, to taste
- 2 avocados, sliced
- 2 tablespoons lime juice
- ¼ cup chopped cilantro
- 2 scallions, white and light green parts, sliced
- Sea salt, to taste
- 4 (8-inch) whole wheat pitas, sliced in half
- 4 cups chopped romaine
- 4 plum tomatoes, sliced

Direction:

1. Heat the coconut oil in a nonstick skillet over medium heat until melted.

2. Add the dulse and sauté for 5 minutes or until crispy. Sprinkle with ground black pepper and turn off the heat. Set aside.

3. Put the avocado, lime juice, cilantro, and scallions in a food processor and sprinkle with salt and ground black pepper. Pulse to combine well until smooth.

4. Toast the pitas in a baking pan in the oven for 1 minute until soft.

5. Transfer the pitas to a clean work surface and open. Spread the avocado mixture over the pitas, then top with dulse, romaine, and tomato slices.

6. Serve immediately.

Nutrition Per Serving (1 pita)

calories: 412 | fat: 18.7g | protein: 9.1g | carbs: 56.1g | fiber: 12.5g | sodium: 695mg

247. Greek Vegetable Salad Pita

Preparation time: 10 minutes
Cooking time: 0 minutes
Serving: 4
Ingredients:

- ½ cup baby spinach leaves
- ½ small red onion, thinly sliced
- ½ small cucumber, deseeded and chopped
- 1 tomato, chopped
- 1 cup chopped romaine lettuce
- 1 tablespoon extra-virgin olive oil
- ½ tablespoon red wine vinegar
- 1 teaspoon Dijon mustard
- 1 tablespoon crumbled feta cheese
- Sea salt and freshly ground pepper, to taste
- 1 whole-wheat pita

Direction:

1. Combine all the ingredients, except for the pita, in a large bowl. Toss to mix well.

2. Stuff the pita with the salad, then serve immediately.

Nutrition Per Serving

calories: 137 | fat: 8.1g | protein: 3.1g | carbs: 14.3g | fiber: 2.4g | sodium: 166mg

248. Artichoke and Cucumber Hoagies

Preparation time: 10 minutes
Cooking time: 15 minutes
Serving: 1
Ingredients:

- 1 (12-ounce / 340-g) whole grain baguette, sliced in half horizontally
- 1 cup frozen and thawed artichoke hearts, roughly chopped
- 1 cucumber, sliced
- 2 tomatoes, sliced
- 1 red bell pepper, sliced
- 1/3 cup Kalamata olives, pitted and chopped
- ¼ small red onion, thinly sliced
- Sea salt and ground black pepper, to taste
- 2 tablespoons pesto
- Balsamic vinegar, to taste

Direction:

1. Arrange the baguette halves on a clean work surface, then cut off the top third from each half. Scoop some insides of the bottom half out and reserve as breadcrumbs.

2. Toast the baguette in a baking pan in the oven for 1 minute to brown lightly.

3. Put the artichokes, cucumber, tomatoes, bell pepper, olives, and onion in a large bowl. Sprinkle with salt and ground black pepper. Toss to combine well.

4. Spread the bottom half of the baguette with the vegetable mixture and drizzle with balsamic vinegar, then smear the cut side of the baguette top with pesto. Assemble the two baguette halves.

5. Wrap the hoagies in parchment paper and let sit for at least an hour before serving.

Nutrition Per Serving (1 hoagies)

calories: 1263 | fat: 37.7g | protein: 56.3g | carbs: 180.1g | fiber: 37.8g | sodium: 2137mg

249. Brown Rice and Black Bean Burgers

Preparation time: 20 minutes
Cooking time: 40 minutes
Serving: 8 burgers
Ingredients:

- 1 cup cooked brown rice
- 1 (15-ounce / 425-g) can black beans, drained and rinsed
- 1 tablespoon olive oil
- 2 tablespoons taco or Harissa seasoning
- ½ yellow onion, finely diced
- 1 beet, peeled and grated
- 1 carrot, peeled and grated
- 2 tablespoons no-salt-added tomato paste
- 2 tablespoons apple cider vinegar
- 3 garlic cloves, minced
- ¼ teaspoon sea salt
- Ground black pepper, to taste
- 8 whole-wheat hamburger buns

Toppings:

- 16 lettuce leaves, rinsed well
- 8 tomato slices, rinsed well
- Whole-grain mustard, to taste

Direction:

1. Line a baking sheet with parchment paper.

2. Put the brown rice and black beans in a food processor and pulse until mix well. Pour the mixture in a large bowl and set aside.

3. Heat the olive oil in a nonstick skillet over medium heat until shimmering.

4. Add the taco seasoning and stir for 1 minute or until fragrant.

5. Add the onion, beet, and carrot and sauté for 5 minutes or until the onion is translucent and beet and carrot are tender.

6. Pour in the tomato paste and vinegar, then add the garlic and cook for 3 minutes or until the sauce is thickened. Sprinkle with salt and ground black pepper.

7. Transfer the vegetable mixture to the bowl of rice mixture, then stir to mix well until smooth.

8. Divide and shape the mixture into 8 patties, then arrange the patties on the baking sheet and refrigerate for at least 1 hour.

9. Preheat the oven to 400°F (205°C).

10.   Remove the baking sheet from the refrigerator and allow to sit under room temperature for 10 minutes.

11.   Bake in the preheated oven for 40 minutes or until golden brown on both sides. Flip the patties halfway through the cooking time.

12.	Remove the patties from the oven and allow to cool for 10 minutes.

13.	Assemble the buns with patties, lettuce, and tomato slices. Top the filling with mustard and serve immediately.

Nutrition Per Serving (1 burger)
calories: 544 | fat: 20.0g | protein: 15.8g | carbs: 76.0g | fiber: 10.6g | sodium: 446mg

250. Classic Socca

Preparation time: 10 minutes
Cooking time: 10 minutes
Serving: 4
Ingredients:
- 1½ cups chickpea flour
- ½ teaspoon ground turmeric
- ½ teaspoon sea salt
- ½ teaspoon ground black pepper
- 2 tablespoons plus
- 2 teaspoons extra-virgin olive oil
- 1½ cups water

Direction:
1. Combine the chickpea flour, turmeric, salt, and black pepper in a bowl. Stir to mix well, then gently mix in 2 tablespoons of olive oil and water. Stir to mix until smooth.
2. Heat 2 teaspoons of olive oil in an 8-inch nonstick skillet over medium- high heat until shimmering.
3. Add half cup of the mixture into the skillet and swirl the skillet so the mixture coat the bottom evenly.
4. Cook for 5 minutes or until lightly browned and crispy. Flip the socca halfway through the cooking time. Repeat with the remaining mixture.
5. Slice and serve warm.

Nutrition Per Serving
calories: 207 | fat: 10.2g | protein: 7.9g | carbs: 20.7g | fiber: 3.9g | sodium: 315mg

251. Alfalfa Sprout and Nut Rolls

Preparation time: 40 minutes
Cooking time: 0 minutes
Serving: 16 bite-size pieces
Ingredients:
- 1 cup alfalfa sprouts
- 2 tablespoons Brazil nuts
- ½ cup chopped fresh cilantro
- 2 tablespoons flaked coconut
- 1 garlic clove, minced
- 2 tablespoons ground flaxseeds
- Zest and juice of 1 lemon
- Pinch cayenne pepper
- Sea salt and freshly ground black pepper, to taste
- 1 tablespoon melted coconut oil
- 2 tablespoons water
- 2 whole-grain wraps

Direction;
1. Combine all ingredients, except for the wraps, in a food processor, then pulse to combine well until smooth.
2. Unfold the wraps on a clean work surface, then spread the mixture over the wraps. Roll the wraps up and refrigerate for 30 minutes until set.
3. Remove the rolls from the refrigerator and slice into 16 bite-sized pieces, if desired, and serve.

Nutrition Per Serving (1 piece)
calories: 67 | fat: 7.1g | protein: 2.2g | carbs: 2.9g | fiber: 1.0g | sodium: 61mg

252. Mini Pork and Cucumber Lettuce Wraps

Preparation time: 20 minutes
Cooking time: 0 minutes
Serving: 12 wraps
Ingredients:
- 8 ounces (227 g) cooked ground pork
- 1 cucumber, diced
- 1 tomato, diced
- 1 red onion, sliced
- 1 ounce (28 g) low-fat feta cheese, crumbled
- Juice of 1 lemon
- 1 tablespoon extra-virgin olive oil
- Sea salt and freshly ground pepper, to taste
- 12 small, intact iceberg lettuce leaves

Direction:
1. Combine the ground pork, cucumber, tomato, and onion in a large bowl, then scatter with feta cheese. Drizzle with lemon juice and olive oil, and sprinkle with salt and pepper. Toss to mix well.
2. Unfold the small lettuce leaves on a large plate or several small plates, then divide and top with the pork mixture.
3. Wrap and serve immediately.

Nutrition Per Serving (1 warp)
calories: 78 | fat: 5.6g | protein: 5.5g | carbs: 1.4g | fiber: 0.3g | sodium: 50mg

253. Mushroom and Caramelized Onion Musakhan

Preparation time: 20 minutes
Cooking time: 1 hour 5 minutes
Serving: 4
Ingredients:
- 2 tablespoons sumac, plus more for sprinkling
- 1 teaspoon ground allspice
- ½ teaspoon ground cardamom
- ½ teaspoon ground cumin
- 3 tablespoons extra-virgin olive oil, divided
- 2 pounds (907 g) portobello mushroom caps, gills removed, caps halved and sliced ½ inch thick
- 3 medium white onions, coarsely chopped
- ¼ cup water
- Kosher salt, to taste
- 1 whole-wheat Turkish flatbread
- ¼ cup pine nuts
- 1 lemon, wedged

Direction:
1. Preheat the oven to 350°F (180°C).
2. Combine 2 tablespoons of sumac, allspice, cardamom, and cumin in a small bowl. Stir to mix well.
3. Heat 2 tablespoons of olive oil in an oven-proof skillet over medium-high heat until shimmering.
4. Add the mushroom to the skillet and sprinkle with half of sumac mixture. Sauté for 8 minutes or until the mushrooms are tender. You may need to work in batches to avoid overcrowding. Transfer the mushrooms to a plate and set side.
5. Heat 1 tablespoon of olive oil in the skillet over medium-high heat until shimmering.
6. Add the onion and sauté for 20 minutes or until caramelized. Sprinkle with remaining sumac mixture, then cook for 1 more minute.

7. Pour in the water and sprinkle with salt. Bring to a simmer.

8. Turn off the heat and put the mushroom back to the skillet.

9. Place the skillet in the preheated oven and bake for 30 minutes.

10. Remove the skillet from the oven and let the mushroom sit for 10 minutes until cooled down.

11. Heat the Turkish flatbread in a baking dish in the oven for 5 minutes or until warmed through.

12. Arrange the bread on a large plate and top with mushrooms, onions, and roasted pine nuts. Squeeze the lemon wedges over and sprinkle with more sumac. Serve immediately.

Nutrition Per Serving
calories: 336 | fat: 18.7g | protein: 11.5g | carbs: 34.3g | fiber: 6.9g | sodium: 369mg

254. Red Pepper Coques with Pine Nuts

Preparation time: 1 day 40 minutes
Cooking time: 45 minutes
Serving: 4 coques
Ingredients:
Dough:
- 3 cups almond flour
- ½ teaspoon instant or rapid-rise yeast
- 2 teaspoons raw honey
- 1 1/3 cups ice water
- 3 tablespoons extra-virgin olive oil
- 1½ teaspoons sea salt

Red Pepper Topping:
- 4 tablespoons extra-virgin olive oil, divided
- 2 cups jarred roasted red peppers, patted dry and sliced thinly
- 2 large onions, halved and sliced thin
- 3 garlic cloves, minced
- ¼ teaspoon red pepper flakes
- 2 bay leaves
- 3 tablespoons maple syrup
- 1½ teaspoons sea salt
- 3 tablespoons red whine vinegar

For Garnish:
- ¼ cup pine nuts (optional)
- 1 tablespoon minced fresh parsley

Direction:
Make the Dough

1. Combine the flour, yeast, and honey in a food processor, pulse to combine well. Gently add water while pulsing. Let the dough sit for 10 minutes.

2. Mix the olive oil and salt in the dough and knead the dough until smooth. Wrap in plastic and refrigerate for at least 1 day.

Make the Topping

3. Heat 1 tablespoon of olive oil in a nonstick skillet over medium heat until shimmering.

4. Add the red peppers, onions, garlic, red pepper flakes, bay leaves, maple syrup, and salt. Sauté for 20 minutes or until the onion is caramelized.

5. Turn off the heat and discard the bay leaves. Remove the onion from the skillet and baste with wine vinegar. Let them sit until ready to use.

Make the Coques

6. Preheat the oven to 500°F (260°C). Grease two baking sheets with 1 tablespoon of olive oil.

7. Divide the dough ball into four balls, then press and shape them into equal-sized oval. Arrange the ovals on the baking sheets and pierce each dough about 12 times.

8. Rub the ovals with 2 tablespoons of olive oil and bake for 7 minutes or until puffed. Flip the ovals halfway through the cooking time.

9. Spread the ovals with the topping and pine nuts, then bake for an additional 15 minutes or until well browned.

10. Remove the coques from the oven and spread with parsley. Allow to cool for 10 minutes before serving.

Nutrition Per Serving (1 coque)
calories: 658 | fat: 23.1g | protein: 3.4g | carbs: 112.0g | fiber: 6.2g | sodium: 1757mg

255. Ritzy Garden Burgers

Preparation time: 1 hour 30 minutes
Cooking time: 30 minutes
Serving: 6
Ingredients:
- 1 tablespoon avocado oil
- 1 yellow onion, diced
- ½ cup shredded carrots
- 4 garlic cloves, halved
- 1 (15 ounces / 425 g) can black beans, rinsed and drained
- 1 cup gluten-free rolled oats
- ¼ cup oil-packed sun-dried tomatoes, drained and chopped
- ½ cup sunflower seeds, toasted
- 1 teaspoon chili powder
- 1 teaspoon paprika
- 1 teaspoon ground cumin
- 1/2 cup fresh parsley, stems removed
- ¼ teaspoon ground red pepper flakes
- ¾ teaspoon sea salt
- ¼ teaspoon ground black pepper
- ¼ cup olive oil

For Serving:
- 6 whole-wheat buns, split in half and toasted
- 2 ripe avocados, sliced
- 1 cup kaiware sprouts or mung bean sprouts
- 1 ripe tomato, sliced

Direction:

1. Line a baking sheet with parchment paper.

2. Heat 1 tablespoon of avocado oil in a nonstick skillet over medium heat.

3. Add the onion and carrots and sauté for 10 minutes or until the onion is caramelized.

4. Add the garlic and sauté for 30 seconds or until fragrant.

5. Transfer them into a food processor, then add the remaining ingredients, except for the olive oil. Pulse until chopped fine and the mixture holds together. Make sure not to purée the mixture.

6. Divide and form the mixture into six 4-inch diameter and ½-inch thick patties.

7. Arrange the patties on the baking sheet and wrap the sheet in plastic. Put the baking sheet in the refrigerator and freeze for at least an hour until firm.

8. Remove the baking sheet from the refrigerator, let them sit under room temperature for 10 minutes.

9. Heat the olive oil in a nonstick skillet over medium-high heat until shimmering.

10. Fry the patties in the skillet for 15 minutes or until lightly browned and crispy. Flip the patties halfway through the

cooking time. You may need to work in batches to avoid overcrowding.

11. Assemble the buns with patties, avocados, sprouts, and tomato slices to make the burgers.

Nutrition Per Serving

calories: 613 | fat: 23.1g | protein: 26.2g | carbs: 88.3g | fiber: 22.9g | sodium: 456mg

256. Roasted Tomato Panini

Preparation time: 15 minutes
Cooking time: 3 hours 6 minutes
Serving: 2
Ingredients:

- 2 teaspoons olive oil
- 4 Roma tomatoes, halved
- 4 cloves garlic
- 1 tablespoon Italian seasoning   Sea salt and freshly ground pepper, to taste
- 4 slices whole-grain bread
- 4 basil leaves
- 2 slices fresh Mozzarella cheese

Direction:

1. Preheat the oven to 250°F (121°C). Grease a baking pan with olive oil.
2. Place the tomatoes and garlic in the baking pan, then sprinkle with Italian seasoning, salt, and ground pepper. Toss to coat well.
3. Roast in the preheated oven for 3 hours or until the tomatoes are lightly wilted.
4. Preheat the panini press.
5. Make the panini: Place two slices of bread on a clean work surface, then top them with wilted tomatoes. Sprinkle with basil and spread with Mozzarella cheese. Top them with remaining two slices of bread.
6. Cook the panini for 6 minutes or until lightly browned and the cheese melts. Flip the panini halfway through the cooking.
7. Serve immediately.

Nutrition Per Serving

calories: 323 | fat: 12.0g | protein: 17.4g | carbs: 37.5g | fiber: 7.5g | sodium: 603mg

257. Samosas in Potatoes

Preparation time: 20 minutes
Cooking time: 30 minutes
Serving: 8
Ingredients:

- 4 small potatoes
- 1 teaspoon coconut oil
- 1 small onion, finely chopped
- 1 small piece ginger, minced
- 2 garlic cloves, minced
- 2 to 3 teaspoons curry powder
- Sea salt and freshly ground black pepper, to taste
- ¼ cup frozen peas, thawed
- 2 carrots, grated
- ¼ cup chopped fresh cilantro

Direction:

1. Preheat the oven to 350°F (180°C).
2. Poke small holes into potatoes with a fork, then wrap with aluminum foil.
3. Bake in the preheated oven for 30 minutes until tender.
4. Meanwhile, heat the coconut oil in a nonstick skillet over medium-high heat until melted.

5. Add the onion and sauté for 5 minutes or until translucent.
6. Add the ginger and garlic to the skillet and sauté for 3 minutes or until fragrant.
7. Add the curry powder, salt, and ground black pepper, then stir to coat the onion. Remove them from the heat.
8. When the cooking of potatoes is complete, remove the potatoes from the foil and slice in half.
9. Hollow to potato halves with a spoon, then combine the potato fresh with sautéed onion, peas, carrots, and cilantro in a large bowl. Stir to mix well.
10.   Spoon the mixture back to the tomato skins and serve immediately.

Nutrition Per Serving (1 samosa)

calories: 131 | fat: 13.9g | protein: 3.2g | carbs: 8.8g | fiber: 3.0g | sodium: 111mg

258. Spicy Black Bean and Poblano Dippers

Preparation time: 20 minutes
Cooking time: 21 minutes
Serving: 8
Ingredients:

- 2 tablespoons avocado oil, plus more for brushing the dippers
- 1 (15 ounces / 425 g) can black beans, drained and rinsed
- 1 poblano, deseeded and quartered
- 1 jalapeño, halved and deseeded
- ½ cup fresh cilantro, leaves and tender stems

- 1 yellow onion, quartered
- 2 garlic cloves
- 1 teaspoon chili powder
- 1 teaspoon ground cumin
- 1 teaspoon sea salt
- 24 organic corn tortillas

Direction:

1. Preheat the oven to 400°F (205°C). Line a baking sheet with parchment paper and grease with avocado oil.
2. Combine the remaining ingredients, except for the tortillas, in a food processor, then pulse until chopped finely and the mixture holds together. Make sure not to purée the mixture.
3. Warm the tortillas on the baking sheet in the preheated oven for 1 minute or until softened.
4. Add a tablespoon of the mixture in the middle of each tortilla. Fold one side of the tortillas over the mixture and tuck to roll them up tightly to make the dippers.
5. Arrange the dippers on the baking sheet and brush them with avocado oil.
1. Bake in the oven for 20 minutes or until well browned. Flip the dippers halfway through the cooking time.
6. Serve immediately.

Nutrition Per Serving

calories: 388 | fat: 6.5g | protein: 16.2g | carbs: 69.6g | fiber: 13.5g | sodium: 340mg

259. Spicy Tofu Tacos with Cherry Tomato Salsa

Preparation time: 20 minutes
Cooking time: 11 minutes
Serving: 4 tacos
Ingredients:
Cherry Tomato Salsa:

- ¼ cup sliced cherry tomatoes
- ½ jalapeño, deseeded and sliced
- Juice of 1 lime
- 1 garlic clove, minced
- Sea salt and freshly ground black pepper, to taste
- 2 teaspoons extra-virgin olive oil

Spicy Tofu Taco Filling:
- 4 tablespoons water, divided
- ½ cup canned black beans, rinsed and drained
- 2 teaspoons fresh chopped chives, divided
- ¾ teaspoon ground cumin, divided
- ¾ teaspoon smoked paprika, divided
- Dash cayenne pepper (optional)
- ¼ teaspoon sea salt
- ¼ teaspoon freshly ground black pepper
- 1 teaspoon extra-virgin olive oil
- 6 ounces (170 g) firm tofu, drained, rinsed, and pressed
- 4 corn tortillas
- ¼ avocado, sliced
- ¼ cup fresh cilantro

Direction:
Make the Cherry Tomato Salsa
1. Combine the ingredients for the salsa in a small bowl. Stir to mix well. Set aside until ready to use.
Make the Spicy Tofu Taco Filling
2. Add 2 tablespoons of water into a saucepan, then add the black beans and sprinkle with 1 teaspoon of chives, ½ teaspoon of cumin, ¼ teaspoon of smoked paprika, and cayenne. Stir to mix well.
3. Cook for 5 minutes over medium heat until heated through, then mash the black beans with the back of a spoon. Turn off the heat and set aside.
4. Add remaining water into a bowl, then add the remaining chives, cumin, and paprika. Sprinkle with cayenne, salt, and black pepper. Stir to mix well. Set aside.
5. Heat the olive oil in a nonstick skillet over medium heat until shimmering.
6. Add the tofu and drizzle with taco sauce, then sauté for 5 minutes or until the seasoning is absorbed. Remove the tofu from the skillet and set aside.
7. Warm the tortillas in the skillet for 1 minutes or until heated through.
8. Transfer the tortillas onto a large plate and top with tofu, mashed black beans, avocado, cilantro, then drizzle the tomato salsa over. Serve immediately.
Nutrition Per Serving (1 taco)
calories: 240 | fat: 9.0g | protein: 11.6g | carbs: 31.6g | fiber: 6.7g | sodium: 195mg

260. Super Cheeses and Mushroom Tart

Preparation time: 30 minutes
Cooking time: 1 hour 30 minutes
Serving: 4 to 6
Ingredients:
Crust:
- 1¾ cups almond flour
- 1 tablespoon raw honey
- ¾ teaspoon sea salt
- ¼ cup extra-virgin olive oil
- 1/3 cup water

Filling:
- 2 tablespoons extra-virgin olive oil, divided
- 1 pound (454 g) white mushrooms, trimmed and sliced thinly

- Sea salt, to taste
- 1 garlic clove, minced
- 2 teaspoons minced fresh thyme
- ¼ cup shredded Mozzarella cheese
- ½ cup grated Parmesan cheese
- 4 ounces (113 g) part-skim ricotta cheese
- Ground black pepper, to taste
- 2 tablespoons ground basil

Direction:
Make the Crust
1. Preheat the oven to 350°F (180°C).
2. Combine the flour, honey, salt and olive oil in a large bowl. Stir to mix well. Gently mix in the water until a smooth dough forms.
3. Drop walnut-size clumps from the dough in the single layer on a tart pan. Press the clumps to coat the bottom of the pan.
4. Bake the crust in the preheated oven for 50 minutes or until firm and browned. Rotate the pan halfway through.
Make the Filling
5. While baking the crust, heat 1 tablespoon of olive oil in a nonstick skillet over medium-high heat until shimmering.
6. Add the mushrooms and sprinkle with ½ teaspoon of salt. Sauté for 15 minutes or until tender.
7. Add the garlic and thyme and sauté for 30 seconds or until fragrant.
Make the Tart
8. Meanwhile, combine the cheeses, salt, ground black pepper, and 1 tablespoon of olive oil in a bowl. Stir to mix well.
9. Spread the cheese mixture over the crust, then top with the mushroom mixture.
10. Bake in the oven for 20 minutes or until the cheeses are frothy and the tart is heated through. Rotate the pan halfway through the baking time.
11. Remove the tart from the oven. Allow to cool for at least 10 minutes, then sprinkle with basil. Slice to serve.
Nutrition Per Serving
calories: 530 | fat: 26.6g | protein: 11.7g | carbs: 63.5g | fiber: 4.6g | sodium: 785mg

261. Mediterranean Veggie Sandwich

Preparation Time: 5 minutes
Cooking time 0 minutes
Serving: 1 sandwich
Ingredients
- ¼ cup of hummus
- ¼ medium red onion (or pickled onions)
- 2 slices of whole-grain bread
- 1 carrot
- ½ cup of microgreens, or spinach, lettuce (greens of any type)
- 2 tablespoons feta

Direction:
1. Thinly slice the onion and shred the carrot.
2. Spread the hummus on one slice of bread, then layer the onions, shredded carrot, crumbled feta, and microgreens. Top with the second slice.
3. Serve with more hummus or tea for a hearty breakfast.
Tips
Replace the feta with some olives if you want to make it vegetarian.
Use good bread such as artisan multigrain bread or sourdough.

While the recipe calls for hummus, any creamy spread such as pesto or avocado dip will do.

Of course, you can include any toppings you want to this sandwich and truly make it your own.

Nutrition Per Serving

calories: 365| fat: 8.95g | protein: 15.06g | carbs: 56.84g | fiber: 10.9g | sodium: 509mg

262. Falafel Pita Sandwich

Preparation Time: 15 minutes

Cooking time 25 minutes

Serving: 2 people

Ingredients

- 2 loaves pita bread
- 1 tablespoon extra-virgin olive oil
- 6 cooked falafel balls
- ¾ medium tomato, diced
- 1/3 medium cucumber, diced
- ½ medium onion, sliced
- 2 tablespoons fresh chopped parsley
- Tahini or tzatziki sauce to taste

Direction:

1. Heat a pan over medium-high heat. Coat it with olive oil and warm the pita bread for two minutes on each side. Once it starts browning a little, it's ready.

2. Slice the warm pita to reveal the pocket and stuff each loaf with three falafel balls, a spoonful of diced tomatoes, onions, and cucumber.

3. Top it off with a generous drizzling of tahini or tzatziki sauce and parsley.

4. Enjoy.

Tips

Falafel is typically fried. However, you can bake it if you are looking for a healthier option.

Add done feta for tangy creaminess and tabbouleh salad for extra crunch, flavor, and texture.

Alternatively, you can make a simple dressing for your sandwiches: take ½ cup of yogurt, ¼ cup olive oil, lime or lemon juice, ½ cup of chopped cilantro, salt, and pepper to taste. Blend everything together and use this herb dressing on the sandwiches.

Nutrition Per Serving

calories: 119| fat: 8.95g | protein: 3.32g | carbs: 18.56g | fiber: 1.6g | sodium: 215mg

263. Greek Chicken Wrap

Preparation Time: 20 minutes

Cooking time 0 minutes

Servings: 4

Ingredients

- 1 medium tomato, thinly sliced
- 2 tablespoon olives, coarsely chopped
- 1 1/3 crumbled feta
- ½ tablespoon of fresh oregano
- ½ tablespoon of olive oil
- 1/8 teaspoon of red pepper
- 2/3 cups of shredded chicken
- 1 small cucumber chopped
- 1 tablespoon of lemon/lime juice
- 4 tablespoons of hummus
- 4 whole-wheat tortillas

Direction:

1. In a salad bowl, add the tomatoes, oregano, pepper, chicken, lemon juice, feta, olives, and cucumber. Toss them to combine well.

2. Spread one tablespoon of hummus or any spread you want over one side of the tortilla and top it with the chicken mixture.

3. Roll the wrap up, slice it in half and enjoy.

Tips

Look for rotisserie chicken and premake the shredded chicken, which you can use for other sandwiches, pasta, salads, and soups.

Nutrition Per Serving

calories: 489| fat: 22.44g | protein: 44.62g | carbs: 25.46g | fiber: 5.1g | sodium: 855mg

264. Caprese on Toast

Preparation Time: 15 minutes

Cooking time 5 minutes

Serving: 4 people

Ingredients

- 4 slices of whole-grain bread or sourdough
- 5 oz soft mozzarella sliced into ¼-inch thick slices
- 1 garlic clove
- 1½ tablespoon fresh basil
- 1 medium-large tomato sliced into ¼ inch slices
- 1½ teaspoon of virgin olive oil
- Salt and black pepper to taste

Direction:

1. In a pan, add olive oil and garlic and toast the bread slices on one side.

2. Place the mozzarella slices, bay leaves, and tomato slices on the toasted side.

3. Drizzle more virgin olive oil and season with salt and black pepper to taste.

4. Enjoy.

Nutrition Per Serving

calories: 166| fat: 4.28g | protein: 12.42g | carbs: 19.86g | fiber: 3.3g | sodium: 601mg

265. Smoked Salmon and Mozzarella Cheese pizza

Preparation time: 15 min

Cooking time: 30 min

Servings: 8

Ingredients

• 1 flat wrap 1 tablespoon fresh Basil Pesto Sauce or a market-fresh basil pesto

• 4 slices of smoked nova (about 2 ounces)

• 2 tablespoons coarsely chopped red onion

• ¼ cup shredded part-skim mozzarella cheese Dried oregano flakes to sprinkle

Direction:

1. Preheat the oven to 350°F. Spread the wrap on a baking sheet and gently spread the pesto sauce on the wrap's top.

2. Cover the salmon over the pesto and the onion and mozzarella cheese. Sprinkle with oregano and bake until the cheese melts and starts to bubble at 350 degrees F. Remove and serve from the oven.

Nutrition Per Serving

calories: 106| fat: 3.63g | protein: 3.24g | carbs: 16.86g | fiber: 1.1g | sodium: 9mg

266. Broccoli and Pecorino Flat Bread Pizzas

Preparation time: 10

Cooking time: 30 min

Servings: 8

Ingredients

• 4 oval, trans fat–free whole grain flatbread 30 fresh broccoli florets, thinly sliced

- 2 tablespoons olive oil
- 3 cloves fresh garlic, thinly sliced ½ teaspoon crushed red hot pepper flakes nor to taste Salt and freshly ground pepper to taste 1 cup shaved fresh Pecorino Romano (about 4 ounces)

Direction:

1. Preheat the oven to 400°F. On 2 rimmed baking sheets, put the flatbread. Toss broccoli, olive oil, garlic, hot pepper flakes, salt, and pepper together in a bowl to taste. Scatter equally on flatbread with broccoli mixture and scatter with Pecorino shavings.

2. Bake until the flatbread are crispy and broccoli brown, about 15 minutes, at 400 degrees F.

Nutrition Per Serving

calories: 12| fat: 0.62g | protein: 0.94g | carbs: 0.78g | fiber: 0.1g | sodium: 24mg

267. Assorted Mushroom and Swiss

Preparation time: 15 min
Cooking time: 30 min
Servings: 8
Ingredients

- 1 flat wrap
- 1 tablespoon extra-virgin olive oil
- ½ cup sliced assorted mushrooms
- 2 tablespoons chopped scallions, white and green parts
- 2 teaspoons fresh garlic paste
- Freshly ground pepper to taste
- 1-ounce shredded light Swiss cheese
- 1 tablespoon dried thyme, finely crushed

Direction:

1. Preheat the oven to 350°F. Place the wrap and set it aside on a baking sheet. In a heavy-bottomed pan, melt a small quantity of olive oil.

2. Add some onions, garlic sauce, scallions, and pepper. Sauté for 2-3 minutes before mushrooms and scallions soften, stirring sometimes.

3. Remove from the heat and uniformly distribute the mixture over the wrap. Distribute the Swiss cheese and scatter with thyme over the mushroom mixture. Place it in the oven and bake until the cheese melts at 350 degrees F. Remove and serve from the oven.

Nutrition Per Serving

calories: 18| fat: 1.51g | protein: 0.66g | carbs: 0.63g | fiber: 0.1g | sodium: 73mg

268. Fresh Basil and Mozzarella Cheese Pizza

Preparation time: 15 min
Cooking time: 30 min
Servings: 8
Ingredients

- 1 flat wrap
- 1 teaspoon finely minced fresh garlic ¼ cup fresh Traditional Pizza Sauce
- or a market sauce like Dei Fratelli ¼ cup shredded part-skim mozzarella cheese 4 slices fresh tomato
- 4–6 fresh whole basil leaves

Direction:

1. Preheat the oven to 350°F. Place the wrap on a baking sheet. Combine the garlic with the pizza sauce and scatter uniformly over the wrap.

2. Cover the sauce with the mozzarella cheese first, then the tomato and basil slices. Bake until the cheese melts at 350 degrees F. Remove and serve from the oven.

Nutrition Per Serving

calories: 65| fat: 1g | protein: 11.24g | carbs: 2.59g | fiber: 0.6g | sodium: 303mg

269. Baby Shrimp and Mozzarella Cheese Pizza

Preparation time: 15 min
Cooking time: 30 min
Servings: 8
Ingredients

- 1 flat wrap
- 1 tablespoon fresh Basil Pesto Sauce or a market-fresh basil pesto
- ½ cup cooked baby salad shrimp, defrosted (if frozen) and well-drained
- 4small pitted black olives, drained and sliced
- ¼ cup shredded part-skim
- mozzarella cheese Dried chives to sprinkle

Direction:

1. Preheat the oven to 350°F. On a baking sheet, place the cover and distribute the pesto uniformly over the surface of the wrap.

2. Scatter the shrimp over the pesto, add the olives and add the mozzarella cheese to the top.

3. Sprinkle the chives over the cheese and bake until the cheese melts and starts bubbling at 350 degrees F. Remove and serve from the oven.

Nutrition Per Serving

calories: 152| fat: 11.4g | protein: 10.91g | carbs: 0.73g | fiber: 0.1g | sodium: 190mg

270. Pizza Margherita

Preparation time: 15 min
Cooking time: 30 min
Servings: 8
Ingredients

- Thin Crust Pizza Dough 4 Roma tomatoes, thinly sliced
- Salt and freshly ground pepper to taste ½ cup yellow sweet pepper, thinly
- sliced ¾ cup shredded part-skim mozzarella cheese, about 3 ounces 4–5
- snipped fresh basil leaves
- 1/4 cup freshly grated Parmesan cheese 1 tablespoon extra-virgin olive oil

Direction:

1. Preheat the oven to 450°F. For pizza dough, follow Instructions and roll out to a 12-15-inch round. Place dough on a pizza pan that is scarcely oiled. Range the tomatoes nearly to the edge of the crust on the rolled-out dough. Sprinkle with pepper and salt to taste.

2. Cover with yellow pepper tomatoes, mozzarella cheese, basil cheese, parmesan cheese, and drizzle over the top with olive oil. Bake for 8 to 10 minutes at 450 degrees F or until the crust is crisp and the cheeses are melted.

Nutrition Per Serving

calories: 16| fat: 0.55g | protein: 1.65g | carbs: 1.08g | fiber: 0g | sodium: 45mg

271. Tomato, Eggplant, and Basil pizza

Preparation time: 15 min
Cooking time: 30 min
Servings: 8
Ingredients

- Crispy Thin Whole Wheat Pizza Dough
- 1 large eggplant
- 6 cloves fresh garlic, minced
- 2 tablespoons extra-virgin olive oil 5 medium tomatoes, seeded and chopped

- 3 tablespoons chopped fresh basil
- Pinch of crushed red-hot pepper flakes 3 cups crumbled non-fat feta cheese
- Salt and freshly ground pepper to taste 1/3 cup freshly grated Parmesan cheese for garnish Fresh rosemary, finely chopped (optional)

Direction:

1. Preheat the oven to 425°F. For pizza dough, follow Instructions and roll out to a 12-15-inch round. Place a round of pizza on a scarcely oiled pizza pan. Break the eggplant halfway down the middle, but not through the flesh. Place it in a separate pan and bake for 20 to 30 minutes. The flesh is withered, and the eggplant is tender.

2. Remove to a plate and set aside; slice crosswise into thin slices when cooled. In a pan, sauté garlic over low heat in 1 tablespoon of olive oil until softened.

3. Add the onions, basil and flakes of hot pepper. Gently spray the pizza dough with 1/2 teaspoon of olive oil, cover with the tomato mixture, then the feta cheese, and arrange the eggplant slices' pinwheel pattern, slightly overlapping the slices. Season the pizza with salt and pepper and drizzle over the eggplant with the remaining olive oil. Bake for 10 to 15 minutes at 425 degrees F until the pizza crust is crisp. If wanted, garnish the top of the pizza with Parmesan cheese and rosemary.

Nutrition Per Serving

calories: 150| fat: 7.7g | protein: 6.19g | carbs: 15.23g | fiber: 5.4g | sodium: 155mg

272. Spicy Sweet Pepper Pizza

Preparation time: 15 min
Cooking time: 30 min
Servings: 8
Ingredients

- Whole Wheat Pizza Dough
- 1 tablespoon extra-virgin olive oil
- 3 large red bell peppers, seeded and thinly sliced 3 large yellow bell peppers,
- seeded and thinly sliced 2 cloves fresh garlic, minced
- 1 tablespoon chopped fresh thyme
- Salt and freshly ground pepper to taste Crushed red-hot pepper flakes to taste
- 1 cup shredded part-skim mozzarella cheese

Direction

1. Preheat the oven to 500°F.

2. Ignore the pizza dough Instructions and roll out to a 12-15-inch round. Place the dough on a pizza pan that is completely oiled. In a heavy-bottomed skillet, heat the olive oil and sauté the red and yellow bell peppers and garlic until tender, about 10 minutes. Mix thyme, salt and pepper to taste, and flakes of sweet pepper.

3. Spread the pepper mixture over the pizza dough, scatter the mozzarella cheese over the pepper mixture, and bake for 20-25 minutes at 500 degrees F until the crust is crisp and the cheese melts.

Nutrition Per Serving

calories: 56| fat: 3.23g | protein: 3.8g | carbs: 3.06g | fiber: 0.4g | sodium: 367mg

273. Wild Mushroom Pizza

Preparation time: 15 min
Cooking time: 30 min
Servings: 8
Ingredients

- Thin Crust Pizza Dough 3 ounces dried porcini mushrooms
- 1-quart warm water

- 2 tablespoons extra-virgin olive oil 4 cloves fresh garlic, finely minced 1 cup
- fresh button mushrooms, cleaned and thinly sliced 1 cup fresh shiitake or
- other wild mushrooms 4 tablespoons white wine
- 1 tablespoon low-sodium soy sauce
- ½ teaspoon dried thyme
- ½ teaspoon dried rosemary
- Salt and freshly ground pepper to taste 3 tablespoons chopped fresh parsley
- 8 ounces shredded smoked provolone cheese

Direction:

1. Preheat oven to 425 degrees F. Follow Instructions for pizza dough; when ready, roll it out to a 15-inch round. Place on scantly oiled pizza pan. Soak the dried mushrooms in warm water for 30 minutes.

2. After soaking, squeeze excess liquid from mushrooms and chop coarsely. Strain soaking water through a cheesecloth and set aside. Heat 1 tablespoon of olive oil over medium heat in a heavy-bottomed skillet and add half of the garlic. Sauté garlic, often stirring until it becomes golden. Add dried and fresh mushrooms, sauté for about 5 minutes until they begin to release their liquid, and then add wine and soy sauce. Continue to sauté until the wine evaporates. Add soaking liquid to mushrooms, thyme, rosemary, remaining garlic, and salt and pepper to taste. Increase heat; continue cooking and stirring until most of the liquid has evaporated and mushrooms have become glazed.

3. Add parsley and remove from heat. Brush pizza dough with remaining olive oil. Evenly spread provolone cheese over crust. Spread mushroom mixture over cheese and bake at 425 degrees F for roughly 8–10 minutes, until crust is crisp and cheese is melted.

Nutrition Per Serving

calories: 419| fat: 35.74g | protein: 20.37g | carbs: 4.06g | fiber: 0.5g | sodium: 948mg

274. Sundried Tomato and Anchovy Pizza

Preparation time: 15 min
Cooking time: 30 min
Servings: 8
Ingredients

- Crispy Thin Whole Wheat Pizza Dough 1 red onion, thinly sliced
- 8 sundried tomatoes in oil, chopped
- 1 tablespoon fresh basil leaves, broken in pieces 1 can (2 ounces) anchovy
- fillets, chopped, oil reserved 1 clove fresh garlic, minced
- 1 cup fresh part-skim mozzarella cheese, shredded Salt and freshly ground
- pepper to taste Finely chopped fresh parsley for garnish (optional)

Direction:

1. Preheat oven to 425 degrees F. Follow Instructions for pizza dough; when ready, roll out to a 15-inch round. Place on scantly oiled pizza pan.

2. Top pizza crust dough with onion, sundried tomatoes, basil, anchovies, garlic, and mozzarella cheese. Salt and pepper to taste and bake at 425 degrees F until crust is crisp and cheese is melted. Garnish with parsley, if desired.

Nutrition Per Serving

calories: 43| fat: 2.45g | protein: 3.56g | carbs: 1.72g | fiber: 0g | sodium: 31mg

275. Crispy Thin Whole Wheat Pizza Dough

Preparation time: 15 min
Cooking time: 20 min
Serving: 8 slices 15-inch crust servings
Ingredients
- 2/3 cup + 1–2 tablespoons all-purpose unbleached flour, divided 1 package
- active dry yeast
- 1/8 teaspoon salt
- ½ cup warm water
- 1 teaspoon extra-virgin olive oil
- ½ cup whole wheat flour
- Non-stick olive oil cooking spray

Direction:
1. Combine half a cup of all-purpose flour, yeast, and salt in a mixing dish. Add water and olive oil and mix for around 2-3 minutes at high rpm. Stir in the whole wheat flour using a wooden spoon. Move the mixture to a finely floured surface and knead as you build the mixture with 1-2 extra tablespoons of all-purpose flour.
2. Into a slightly rigid, but still smooth and elastic ball. Put the dough in a clean bowl, cover it and place it for about 10 minutes in a warm location. Lightly coat the pizza pan with cooking oil.
3. Roll the dough into a 15-inch circle on a thinly floured board, put on the pizza pan, and top with the sauce and ingredients of your choice. Bake for about 10 minutes at 425 degrees F or until the crust is crispy.

Nutrition Per Serving
calories: 66| fat: 0.56g | protein: 2.08g | carbs: 13.4g | fiber: 1.1g | sodium: 44mg

276. Whole Wheat Pizza Dough

Preparation time: 15 min
Cooking time: 20 min
Serving: 8 slices 15-inch crust servings
Ingredients
- 2½ teaspoons active dry yeast
- 1½ teaspoons low-calorie baking sweetener
- 1 teaspoon salt
- 2 tablespoons extra-virgin olive oil
- ½ cup lukewarm water
- 2 cups whole wheat flour
- 3–4 tablespoons extra flour for kneading

Direction:
1. Mix the yeast, sweetener, salt, olive oil, and water together in a cup. For 10 minutes, set aside; the mixture will turn cloudy and thick. Create a well in the middle of the whole wheat flour as this occurs.
2. Add the yeast mixture and fold it gradually into the flour and, if necessary, add more lukewarm water. Knead the dough until it is smooth and put the dough in a lightly oiled bowl.
3. A clean towel. Place the dough for around 45 minutes in a heated environment or until its size doubles. Roll the dough into a 15-inch circle on a thinly floured board, put on the pizza pan, and top with the sauce and ingredients of your choice. Bake until the crust is crispy at 500 degrees F.

Nutrition Per Serving
calories: 132| fat: 2.54g | protein: 4.79g | carbs: 24.48g | fiber: 3.6g | sodium: 323mg

277. Thin Crust Pizza Dough

Preparation time: 15 min
Cooking time: 20 min
Serving: 8 slices 15-inch crust servings
Ingredients
- 1 2/3 cups unbleached all-purpose flour ½ teaspoon salt
- 1 package dry active yeast
- 2 tablespoons extra-virgin olive oil ½ cup warm water
- Olive oil to lightly coat pan

Direction:
1. In a wide bowl, put the flour, salt, and yeast and combine with a wooden spoon. In the middle, make a well and add olive oil and water. Function gradually from the sides of the bowl of flour as the mixture becomes smooth, pliable, moist dough. Sprinkle a little extra flour with the paste if it's too wet; just don't dry the dough.
2. Move the dough to a lightly floured surface and knead for around 10 minutes; if necessary, apply very small quantities of flour until the dough is smooth and elastic. Rub a small amount of olive oil over the surface of the dough, then put it back in a clean bowl, cover it with a rag, and put it for around 1 hour in a warm environment or until the dough has increased in size.
3. Remove the dough from the surface to a gently floured surface, knead for another 2 minutes, and roll it out into a 15-inch circle. Put on a pizza pan and top with the option of sauce and ingredients. Bake until the crust is crispy, at 425 degrees F.

Nutrition Per Serving
calories: 304| fat: 23.46g | protein: 2.91g | carbs: 19.92g | fiber: 0.7g | sodium: 465mg

278. Traditional Pizza Sauce

Preparation time: 15 min
Cooking time: 20 min
Serving: 1
Ingredients
- 2 tablespoons extra-virgin olive oil 3 cloves fresh garlic, peeled and sliced 5 medium tomatoes, seeded and chopped 2 sprigs fresh rosemary
- Salt and freshly ground pepper to taste Pinch of sugar

Direction:
1. Add the olive oil and garlic and cook until tender in a heavy skillet over medium-high heat.
2. Add tomatoes, rosemary, salt, pepper and sugar; gently increase the heat and cook fast, stirring regularly (about 15-20 minutes) before the juices thicken. Via a food mill, placed sauce, letting pulp flow through. Return to low heat if the sauce is too thin, and simmer until the consistency is needed.

Nutrition Per Serving
calories: 100| fat: 8.67g | protein: 3.39g | carbs: 3.87g | fiber: 1.8g | sodium: 124mg

279. Fiery Tomato and Basil Pizza Sauce

Preparation time: 15 min
Cooking time: 20 min
Serving: 1
Ingredients
- 1 tablespoon extra-virgin olive oil
- 4 cloves fresh garlic, chopped
- 5 medium tomatoes, seeded and chopped 3 tablespoons fresh chopped basil
- Salt and freshly ground pepper to taste Pinch of sugar
- ¼ teaspoon crushed red hot pepper flakes

Direction:
1. Heat the olive oil in a skillet over medium-high heat, and sauté the garlic.
2. Add the tomatoes, boil them and stir for 5 minutes or so. Mix the basil, salt and pepper, sugar, and hot pepper flakes in a separate bowl and add them to the tomato mixture.
Nutrition Per Serving
calories: 187| fat: 7.34g | protein: 6.44g | carbs: 28.89g | fiber: 7.8g | sodium: 154mg

280. Spicy Garlic, Olive Oil, and Sundried Tomato Pizza Sauce

Preparation time: 15 min
Cooking time: 20 min
Serving: 1
Ingredients
• ¼ cup extra-virgin olive oil
• 4 cloves fresh garlic, minced
• ¼ teaspoon crushed red hot pepper flakes 6 jumbo pitted black olives, diced
• 8 sundried tomatoes in oil, drained and diced Salt and freshly ground pepper to taste
Direction:
1. Heat olive oil in a medium-sized skillet over medium-high heat,
2. Garlic is added and sautéed until translucent. Add hot pepper flakes, olives, sundried tomatoes, salt and pepper to taste; boil for 3-5 minutes over very low heat.
Nutrition Per Serving
calories: 232| fat: 23.28g | protein: 1.2g | carbs: 5.04g | fiber: 0.4g | sodium: 467mg

281. Halibut Sandwiches Mediterranean Style

Preparation time: 15 minutes
Cooking Time: 23 minutes
Servings: 4
INGREDIENTS
• 2 packed cups arugula or 2 oz. Grated zest of 1 large lemon
• 1 tbsp capers, drained and mashed
• 2 tbsp fresh flat leaf parsley, chopped
• ¼ cup fresh basil, chopped
• ¼ cup sun dried tomatoes, chopped
• ¼ cup reduced fat mayonnaise
• 1 garlic clove, halved
• 1 pc of 14 oz of ciabatta loaf bread with ends trimmed and split in half, horizontally
• 2 tbsp plus 1 tsp olive oil, divided Kosher salt and freshly ground pepper
• 2 pcs or 6 oz halibut fillets, skinned
• Cooking spray
DIRECTIONS
1. Heat oven to 4500F. With cooking spray, coat a baking dish.
2. Season halibut with a pinch of pepper and salt plus rub with a tsp of oil and place on baking dish. Then put in oven and bake until cooked or for ten to fifteen minutes.
3. Remove from oven and let cool. Get a slice of bread and coat with olive oil the sliced portions. Put in oven and cook until golden, around six to eight minutes.
4. Remove from heat and rub garlic on the bread. Combine the following in a medium bowl: lemon

zest, capers, parsley, basil, sun dried tomatoes and mayonnaise.
5. Then add the halibut, mashing with fork until flaked.
6. Spread the mixture on one side of bread, add arugula and cover with the other bread half and serve.
NUTRITION: Calories: 125; Carbs: 8.0g; Protein: 3.9g; Fat: 9.2g

282. Open Face Egg and Bacon Sandwich

Preparation time: 5 minutes
Cooking Time: 20 minutes
Servings: 1
INGREDIENTS
• ¼ oz reduced fat cheddar, shredded
• ½ small jalapeno, thinly sliced
• ½ whole grain English muffin, split
• 1 large organic egg
• 1 thick slice of tomato
• 1-piece turkey bacon
• 2 thin slices red onion
• 4-5 sprigs fresh cilantro
• Cooking spray
• Pepper to taste
DIRECTIONS
1. On medium fire, place a skillet, cook bacon until crisp tender and set aside.
2. In same skillet, drain oils, and place ½ of English muffin and heat for at least a minute per side.
3. Transfer muffin to a serving plate. Coat the same skillet with cooking spray and fry egg to desired doneness. Once cooked, place egg on top of muffin.
4. Add cilantro, tomato, onion, jalapeno and bacon on top of egg. Serve and enjoy.
NUTRITION: Calories: 245; Carbs: 24.7g; Protein: 11.8g; Fat: 11g

283. Sandwich with Spinach and Tuna Salad

Preparation time: 5 minutes
Cooking Time: 0 minutes
Servings: 4
INGREDIENTS
• 1 cup fresh baby spinach
• 8 slices 100% whole wheat sandwich bread
• ¼ tsp freshly ground black pepper
• ½ tsp salt
• free seasoning blend
• Juice of one lemon
• 2 tbsp olive oil
• ½ tsp dill weed
• 2 ribs celery, diced
DIRECTIONS
1. In a medium bowl, mix well dill weed, celery, onion, cucumber and tuna. Add lemon juice and olive oil and mix thoroughly.
2. Season with pepper and salt-free seasoning blend.
3. To assemble sandwich, you can toast bread slices, on top of one bread slice layer ½ cup tuna salad, top with ¼ cup spinach and cover with another slice of bread.
4. Repeat procedure to remaining ingredients, serve and enjoy.

NUTRITION: Calories: 272.5; Carbs: 35.9g; Protein: 10.4g; Fat: 9.7g

284. Grilled Sandwich with Goat Cheese

Preparation time: 20 minutes
Cooking Time: 8 minutes
Servings: 4
INGREDIENTS
- ½ cup soft goat cheese
- 4 Kaiser rolls 2-oz
- ¼ tsp freshly ground black pepper
- ¼ tsp salt
- 1/3 cup chopped basil
- Cooking spray
- 4 big Portobello mushroom caps
- 1 yellow bell pepper, cut in half and seeded
- 1 red bell pepper, cut in half and seeded
- 1 garlic clove, minced
- 1 tbsp olive oil
- ¼ cup balsamic vinegar

DIRECTIONS
1. In a large bowl, mix garlic, olive oil and balsamic vinegar.
2. Add mushroom and bell peppers. Gently mix to coat.
3. Remove veggies from vinegar and discard vinegar mixture.
4. Coat with cooking spray a grill rack and the grill preheated to medium high fire.
5. Place mushrooms and bell peppers on the grill and grill for 4 minutes per side.
6. Remove from grill and let cool a bit. Into thin strips, cut the bell peppers.
7. In a small bowl, combine black pepper, salt, basil and sliced bell peppers.
8. Horizontally, cut the Kaiser rolls and evenly spread cheese on the cut side. Arrange 1 Portobello per roll, top with 1/3 bell pepper mixture and cover with the other half of the roll.
9. Grill the rolls as you press down on them to create a Panini like line on the bread. Grill until bread is toasted.

NUTRITION: Calories: 317; Carbs: 41.7g; Protein: 14.0g; Fat: 10.5g

285. Sandwich with Hummus

Preparation time: 5 minutes
Cooking Time: 0 minutes
Servings: 4
INGREDIENTS
- 4 cups alfalfa sprouts
- 1 cup cucumber sliced 1/8 inch thick
- 4 red onion sliced ¼-inch thick
- 8 tomatoes sliced ¼-inch thick
- 2 cups shredded Bibb lettuce
- 12 slices 1-oz whole wheat bread
- 1 can 15.5-oz chickpeas, drained
- 2 garlic cloves, peeled
- ¼ tsp salt
- ½ tsp ground cumin
- 1 tbsp tahini
- 1 tbsp lemon juice
- 2 tbsp water
- 3 tbsp plain fat free yogurt

DIRECTIONS
1. In a food processor, blend chickpeas, garlic, salt, cumin, tahini, lemon juice, water and yogurt until smooth to create hummus.
2. On 1 slice of bread, spread 2 tbsp hummus, top with 1 onion slice, 2 tomato slices, ½ cup lettuce, another bread slice, 1 cup sprouts, ¼ cup cucumber and cover with another bread slice.
3. Repeat procedure for the rest of the ingredients.

NUTRITION: Calories: 407; Carbs: 67.7g; Protein: 18.8 g; Fat: 6.8g

286. Cheese & Cucumber Mini Sandwiches

Preparation Time: 5 minutes
Cooking time: 0 minutes
Serving: 4
INGREDIENTS
- 4 bread slices
- 1 cucumber, sliced
- 2 tbsp cream cheese, soft
- 1 tbsp chives, chopped
- ¼ cup hummus
- Salt and black pepper to taste

DIRECTIONS
1. In a bowl, mix hummus, cream cheese, chives, salt, and pepper until well combined.
2. Spread the mixture onto bread slices.
3. Top with cucumber and cut each sandwich into three pieces. Serve immediately.

NUTRITION Per Serving: Calories 190, Fat 13g, Carbs 5g, Protein 9g

287. Watermelon Pizza

Preparation time: 10 minutes
Cooking time: 0 minutes
Servings: 2
INGREDIENTS
- 9 oz watermelon slice
- 1 tablespoon Pomegranate sauce
- 2 oz Feta cheese, crumbled
- 1 tablespoon fresh cilantro, chopped

DIRECTIONS
1. Place the watermelon slice in the plate and sprinkle with crumbled Feta cheese. Add fresh cilantro. After this, sprinkle the pizza with Pomegranate juice generously.
2. Cut the pizza into the servings.

NUTRITION: Calories 143, fat 6.2, fiber 0.6, carbs 18.4, protein 5.1

288. Morning Pizza with Sprouts

Preparation time: 15 minutes
Cooking time: 20 minutes
Servings: 6
INGREDIENTS
- ½ cup wheat flour, whole grain
- 2 tablespoons butter, softened
- ¼ teaspoon baking powder
- ¾ teaspoon salt
- 5 oz chicken fillet, boiled
- 2 oz Cheddar cheese, shredded
- 1 teaspoon tomato sauce
- 1 oz bean sprouts

DIRECTIONS

1. Make the pizza crust: mix up together wheat flour, butter, baking powder, and salt.
2. Knead the soft and non-sticky dough.
3. Add more wheat flour if needed.
4. Leave the dough for 10 minutes to chill.
5. Then place the dough on the baking paper.
6. Cover it with the second baking paper sheet.
7. Roll up the dough with the help of the rolling pin to get the round pizza crust. After this, remove the upper baking paper sheet.
8. Transfer the pizza crust in the tray. Spread the crust with tomato sauce.
9. Then shred the chicken fillet and arrange it over the pizza crust.
10. Add shredded Cheddar cheese. Bake pizza for 20 minutes at 355F.
11. Then top the cooked pizza with bean sprouts and slice into the servings.

NUTRITION: Calories 157, fat 8.8, fiber 0.3, carbs 8.4, protein 10.5

289. Keto BBQ Chicken Pizza Soup

Preparation time: 30 minutes
Cooking time: 90 minutes
Servings: 6
INGREDIENTS

- 6 chicken legs
- 1 medium red onion, diced
- 4 garlic cloves
- 1 large tomato, unsweetened
- 4 cups green beans
- ¾ cup BBQ Sauce
- 1½ cups mozzarella cheese, shredded
- ¼ cup ghee
- 2 quarts water
- 2 quarts chicken stock
- Salt and black pepper, to taste
- Fresh cilantro, for garnishing

DIRECTIONS

1. Put chicken, water and salt in a large pot and bring to a boil.
2. Reduce the heat to medium-low and cook for about 75 minutes.
3. Shred the meat off the bones using a fork and keep aside.
4. Put ghee, red onions and garlic in a large soup and cook over a medium heat.
5. Add chicken stock and bring to a boil over a high heat.
6. Add green beans and tomato to the pot and cook for about 15 minutes.
7. Add BBQ Sauce, shredded chicken, salt and black pepper to the pot.
8. Ladle the soup into serving bowls and top with shredded mozzarella cheese and cilantro to serve.

NUTRITION: Calories: 449 Carbs: 7.1g Fats: 32.5g Proteins: 30.8g Sodium: 252mg Sugar: 4.7g

290. Coconut Flour Pizza

Preparation time: 15 minutes
Cooking Time: 20 minutes
Servings: 4
INGREDIENTS

- 2 tablespoons psyllium husk powder
- ¾ cup coconut flour
- 1 teaspoon garlic powder
- ½ teaspoon salt
- ½ teaspoon baking soda
- 1 cup boiling water
- 1 teaspoon apple cider vinegar
- 3 eggs
- Toppings
- 3 tablespoons tomato sauce
- 1½ oz. Mozzarella cheese
- 1 tablespoon basil, freshly chopped

DIRECTIONS

1. Preheat the oven to 350 degrees F and grease a baking sheet. Mix coconut flour, salt, psyllium husk powder, and garlic powder until fully combined.
2. Add eggs, apple cider vinegar, and baking soda and knead with boiling water.
3. Place the dough out on a baking sheet and top with the toppings.
4. Transfer in the oven and bake for about 20 minutes. Dish out and serve warm.

NUTRITION: Calories: 173 Carbs: 16.8g Fats: 7.4g Proteins: 10.4g Sodium: 622mg Sugar: 0.9g

291. Keto Pepperoni Pizza

Preparation time: 40 minutes
Cooking time: 25 minutes
Servings: 4
INGREDIENTS

- Crust
- 6 oz. mozzarella cheese, shredded
- 4 eggs Topping
- 1 teaspoon dried oregano
- 1½ oz. pepperoni
- 3 tablespoons tomato paste
- 5 oz. mozzarella cheese, shredded
- Olives

DIRECTIONS :

1. Preheat the oven to 400 degrees F and grease a baking sheet.
2. Whisk together eggs and cheese in a bowl and spread on a baking sheet. Transfer in the oven and bake for about 15 minutes until golden.
3. Remove from the oven and allow it to cool.
4. Increase the oven temperature to 450 degrees F.
5. Spread the tomato paste on the crust and top with oregano, pepperoni, cheese, and olives on top.
6. Bake for another 10 minutes and serve hot.

NUTRITION: Calories: 356 Carbs: 6.1g Fats: 23.8g Proteins: 30.6g Sodium: 790mg Sugar: 1.8g

292. BBQ Chicken Pizza

Preparation time: 30 minutes
Cooking time: 13 minutes
Servings: 4
INGREDIENTS
Dairy Free Pizza Crust

- 6 tablespoons
- Parmesan cheese
- 6 large eggs
- 3 tablespoons psyllium husk powder
- Salt and black pepper, to taste
- 1½ teaspoons Italian seasoning

Toppings

- 6 oz. rotisserie chicken, shredded

- 4 oz. cheddar cheese
- 1 tablespoon mayonnaise
- 4 tablespoons tomato sauce
- 4 tablespoons BBQ sauce

DIRECTIONS
1. Preheat the oven to 400 degrees F and grease a baking dish.
2. Place all Pizza Crust ingredients in an immersion blender and blend until smooth.
3. Spread dough mixture onto the baking dish and transfer in the oven.
4. Bake for about 10 minutes and top with favorite toppings.
5. Bake for about 3 minutes and dish out.

NUTRITION: Calories: 356 Carbs: 2.9g Fats: 24.5g Proteins: 24.5g Sodium: 396mg Sugar: 0.6g

293. Fresh Bell Pepper Basil Pizza

Preparation time: 25 minutes
Cooking time: 20 minutes
Servings: 3
INGREDIENTS
Pizza Base
- ½ cup almond flour
- 2 tablespoons cream cheese
- 1 teaspoon Italian seasoning
- ½ teaspoon black pepper
- 6 ounces mozzarella cheese
- 2 tablespoons psyllium husk
- 2 tablespoons fresh Parmesan cheese
- 1 large egg
- ½ teaspoon salt

Toppings
- 4 ounces cheddar cheese, shredded
- ¼ cup Marinara sauce
- 2/3 medium bell pepper
- 1 medium vine tomato
- 3 tablespoons basil, fresh chopped

DIRECTIONS:
1. Preheat the oven to 400 degrees F and grease a baking dish.
2. Microwave mozzarella cheese for about 30 seconds and top with the remaining pizza crust. Add the remaining pizza ingredients to the cheese and mix together.
3. Flatten the dough and transfer in the oven.
4. Bake for about 10 minutes and remove pizza from the oven.
5. Top the pizza with the toppings and bake for another 10 minutes.
6. Remove pizza from the oven and allow to cool.

NUTRITION: Calories: 411 Carbs: 6.4g Fats: 31.3g Proteins: 22.2g Sodium: 152mg Sugar: 2.8g

294. Apple and Ham Flatbread Pizza

Preparation time: 15 mins
Cooking time: 15 minutes
Servings: 8
INGREDIENTS
For the crust:
- ¾ cup almond flour
- ½ teaspoon sea salt
- 2 cups mozzarella cheese, shredded
- 2 tablespoons cream cheese
- 1/8 teaspoon dried thyme

For the topping:
- ½ small red onion, cut into thin slices
- 4 ounces low carbohydrate ham, cut into chunks
- Salt and black pepper, to taste
- 1 cup Mexican blend cheese, grated
- ¼ medium apple, sliced
- 1/8 teaspoon dried thyme

DIRECTIONS
1. Preheat the oven to 425 degrees F and grease a 12-inch pizza pan.
2. Boil water and steam cream cheese, mozzarella cheese, almond flour, thyme, and salt. When the cheese melts enough, knead for a few minutes to thoroughly mix dough.
3. Make a ball out of the dough and arrange in the pizza pan. Poke holes all over the dough with a fork and transfer in the oven.
4. Bake for about 8 minutes until golden brown and reset the oven setting to 350 degrees F.
5. Sprinkle ¼ cup of the Mexican blend cheese over the flatbread and top with onions, apples, and ham.
6. Cover with the remaining ¾ cup of the Mexican blend cheese and sprinkle with the thyme, salt, and black pepper.
7. Bake for about 7 minutes until cheese is melted and crust is golden brown. Remove the flatbread from the oven and allow to cool before cutting. Slice into desired pieces and serve.

NUTRITION: Calories: 179 Carbs: 5.3g Fats: 13.6g Proteins: 10.4g Sodium: 539mg Sugar: 2.1g

295. Basil & Artichoke Pizza

Preparation Time: 1 hour
Cooking time: 20 minutes
Serving: 4
INGREDIENTS
- 1 cup canned passata
- 2 cups flour
- 1 cup lukewarm water
- 1 pinch of sugar
- 1 tsp active dry yeast
- ¾ tsp salt 2 tbsp olive oil
- 1 ½ cups frozen artichoke hearts
- ¼ cup grated Asiago cheese
- ½ onion, minced
- 3 garlic cloves, minced
- 1 tbsp dried oregano
- 1 cup sun-dried tomatoes, chopped
- ½ tsp red pepper flakes
- 5-6 basil leaves, torn

DIRECTIONS
1. Sift the flour and salt in a bowl and stir in yeast. Mix lukewarm water, olive oil, and sugar in another bowl.
2. Add the wet mixture to the dry mixture and whisk until you obtain a soft dough. Place the dough on a lightly floured work surface and knead it thoroughly for 4-5 minutes until elastic. Transfer the dough to a greased bowl.
3. Cover with cling film and leave to rise for 50-60 minutes in a warm place until doubled in size. Roll out the dough to a thickness of around 12 inches.
4. Preheat oven to 400 F. Warm oil in a saucepan over medium heat and sauté onion and garlic for

3-4 minutes. Mix in tomatoes and oregano and bring to a boil.
5. Decrease the heat and simmer for another 5 minutes.
6. Transfer the pizza crust to a baking sheet. Spread the sauce all over and top with artichoke hearts and sun-dried tomatoes. Scatter the cheese and bake for 15 minutes until golden.
7. Top with red pepper flakes and basil leaves and serve sliced.

NUTRITION Per Serving: Calories 254, Fat 9.5g, Carbs 34.3g, Protein 8g

296. Pepperoni Fat Head Pizza

Preparation Time: 20 minutes
Cooking time: 15 minutes
Serving: 4
INGREDIENTS
- 2 cups flour
- 1 cup lukewarm water
- 1 pinch of sugar
- 1 tsp active dry yeast
- ¾ tsp salt
- 2 tbsp olive oil
- 1 tsp dried oregano
- 2 cups mozzarella cheese
- 1 cup sliced pepperoni

DIRECTIONS
1. Sift the flour and salt in a bowl and stir in yeast. Mix lukewarm water, olive oil, and sugar in another bowl.
2. Add the wet mixture to the dry mixture and whisk until you obtain a soft dough. Place the dough on a lightly floured work surface and knead it thoroughly for 4-5 minutes until elastic.
3. Transfer the dough to a greased bowl. Cover with cling film and leave to rise for 50-60 minutes in a warm place until doubled in size.
4. Roll out the dough to a thickness of around 12 inches. Preheat oven to 400 F. Line a round pizza pan with parchment paper.
5. Spread the dough on the pizza pan and top with the mozzarella cheese, oregano, and pepperoni slices.
6. Bake in the oven for 15 minutes or until the cheese melts. Remove the pizza, slice and serve.

NUTRITION Per Serving: Calories 229; Fats 7.1g; Carbs 0.4g; Protein 36.4g

297. Spanish-Style Pizza de Jamon

Preparation time: 30 minutes
Cooking Time: 15 minutes
Serving: 4
INGREDIENTS
For the crust
- 2 cups flour
- 1 cup lukewarm water
- 1 pinch of sugar
- 1 tsp active dry yeast
- ¾ tsp salt
- 2 tbsp olive oil
For the topping
- ½ cup tomato sauce
- ½ cup sliced mozzarella cheese
- 4 oz jamon serrano, sliced

- 7 fresh basil leaves

DIRECTIONS
1. Sift the flour and salt in a bowl and stir in yeast. Mix lukewarm water, olive oil, and sugar in another bowl.
2. Add the wet mixture to the dry mixture and whisk until you obtain a soft dough.
3. Place the dough on a lightly floured work surface and knead it thoroughly for 4-5 minutes until elastic.
4. Transfer the dough to a greased bowl.
5. Cover with cling film and leave to rise for 50-60 minutes in a warm place until doubled in size. Roll out the dough to a thickness of around 12 inches.
6. Preheat the oven to 400 F. Line a pizza pan with parchment paper. Spread the tomato sauce on the crust.
7. Arrange the mozzarella slices on the sauce and then the jamon serrano.
8. Bake for 15 minutes or until the cheese melts.
9. Remove from the oven and top with the basil. Slice and serve warm.

NUTRITION Per Serving: Calories 160; Fats 6.2g; Carbs 0.5g; Protein 21.9g

298. Dill Salmon Salad Wraps

Preparation Time: 20 minutes
Cooking Time: 60 minutes
Servings: 2
Ingredients:
• 1-pound salmon filet, cooked and flaked, or 3 (5-ounce) cans salmon
• ½ cup diced carrots (about 1 carrot)
• ½ cup diced celery (about 1 celery stalk)
• 3 tablespoons chopped fresh dill
• 3 tablespoons diced red onion (a little less than 1/8 onion)
• 2 tablespoons capers
• 1½ tablespoons extra-virgin olive oil
• 1 tablespoon aged balsamic vinegar
• ½ teaspoon freshly ground black pepper
• ¼ teaspoon kosher or sea salt
• 4 whole-wheat flatbread wraps or soft whole-wheat tortillas
Directions:
1. In a large bowl, mix together the salmon, carrots, celery, dill, red onion, capers, oil, vinegar, pepper, and salt.
2. Divide the salmon salad among the flatbread. Fold up the bottom of the flatbread, then roll up the wrap and serve.
Nutrition: Calories: 336; Total Fat: 16g; Saturated Fat: 2g; Cholesterol: 67mg; Sodium: 628mg; Total Carbohydrates: 23g; Fiber: 5g; Protein: 32g

299. Chicken Parmesan Wraps

Preparation Time: 10 minutes
Cooking Time: 20 minutes
Servings: 2
Ingredients:
• Nonstick cooking spray
• 1-pound boneless, skinless chicken breasts
• 1 large egg
• ¼ cup buttermilk
• 2/3 cup whole-wheat panko or whole-wheat bread crumbs
• ½ cup grated Parmesan cheese (about 1½ ounces)
• ¾ teaspoon garlic powder, divided

- 1 cup canned low-sodium or no-salt-added crushed tomatoes
- 1 teaspoon dried oregano
- 6 (8-inch) whole-wheat tortillas, or whole-grain spinach wraps
- 1 cup fresh mozzarella cheese (about 4 ounces), sliced
- 1½ cups loosely packed fresh flat-leaf (Italian) parsley, chopped

Directions:

1. Preheat the oven to 425°F. Line a large, rimmed baking sheet with aluminum foil. Place a wire rack on the aluminum foil, and spray the rack with nonstick cooking spray. Set aside.
2. Put the chicken breasts in a large, zip top plastic bag. With a rolling pin or meat mallet, pound the chicken so it is evenly flattened, about ¼ inch thick.
3. Slice the chicken into six portions. (It's fine if you have to place 2 smaller pieces together to form six equal portions.)
4. In a wide, shallow bowl, whisk together the egg and buttermilk. In another wide, shallow bowl, mix together the panko crumbs, Parmesan cheese, and ½ teaspoon of garlic powder.
5. Dip each chicken breast portion into the egg mixture and then into the Parmesan crumb mixture, pressing the crumbs into the chicken so they stick. Place the chicken on the prepared wire rack.
6. Bake the chicken for 15 to 18 minutes, or until the internal temperature of the chicken reads 165°F on a meat thermometer and any juices run clear.
7. Transfer the chicken to a cutting board, and slice each portion diagonally into ½-inch pieces.
8. In a small, microwave-safe bowl, mix together the tomatoes, oregano, and the remaining ¼ teaspoon of garlic powder.
9. Cover the bowl with a paper towel and microwave for about 1 minute on high, until very hot. Set aside.
10. Wrap the tortillas in a damp paper towel or dishcloth and microwave for 30 to 45 seconds on high, until warmed.
11. To assemble the wraps, divide the chicken slices evenly among the six tortillas and top with the cheese.
12. Spread 1 tablespoon of the warm tomato sauce over the cheese on each tortilla, and top each with about ¼ cup of parsley.
13. To wrap each tortilla, fold up the bottom of the tortilla, then fold one side over and fold the other side over the top. Serve the wraps immediately, with the remaining sauce for dipping.

Nutrition: Calories: 373; Total Fat: 10g; Saturated Fat: 4g; Cholesterol: 95mg; Sodium: 591 mg; Total Carbohydrates: 33g; Fiber: 8g; Protein: 30g

300. Plum Wraps

Preparation time: 15 minutes
Cooking Time: 10 Minutes
Servings: 4
Ingredients:
- 4 plums
- 4 prosciutto slices
- ¼ teaspoon olive oil

Directions:

1. Preheat the oven to 375F. Wrap every plum in prosciutto slice and secure with a toothpick (if needed). Place the wrapped plums in the oven and bake for 10 minutes.

Nutrition: Calories 62 Fat 2.2g Carbs 8g Protein 4.3g

301. Fried Egg, Bacon And Cheese Sandwich

Preparation time: 10 minutes
Cooking Time: 5 Minutes
Serving: 1
Ingredients
- Bacon 10 g
- White bread ½ pieces
- Edam cheese 20 g
- Tomatoes 1 piece
- Mayonnaise 1 tablespoon
- Butter 10 g
- Chicken egg 1 piece
- Lettuce leaves 3 pieces

Direction:

1. Fry thin slices of bacon until golden brown.
2. Heat the bread and spread one half of the sandwich with mayonnaise (you can make it yourself), put cheese, tomato slices, bacon and lettuce on the second.
3. Meanwhile, in butter, fry a little fried eggs - such that the yolk is half-cooked.

Nutrition: Calories 77 Fat 5.07g Carbs 6.65g Protein 2.71g

302. Sandwiches With Tuna And Cheese

Preparation time: 30 minutes
Cooking Time: 10 Minutes
Serving: 8
Ingredients
- Canned tuna in own juice 1 can
- Bread for toasts 8 slices
- Emmental cheese 200 g
- Pink pepper to taste
- Capers ½ teaspoon
- Butter 20 g
- Cucumbers ½ pieces

Direction:

1. Put the tuna together with the juice in a bowl and knead it with your hands. Sprinkle with pink Mauritius pepper (it is as fragrant as black, but less hot), add capers and mix. Put grated emmental (or other cheese to taste - edam, for example, or gouda) and mix again.
2. Heat the pan over medium heat and lightly dry the bread on both sides. Then lightly grease all the pieces on one side with butter, put the tuna-cheese mixture, combine the halves of the sandwiches - and again send to the skillet. There they should spend a couple of minutes under the lid - the idea is to melt the cheese and grab the fish mass.

Nutrition: Calories 87 Fat 1.8g Carbs 13.66g Protein 3.98g

303. Tuna sandwich

Preparation time: 5 minutes
Cooking Time: 20 Minutes
Serving: 4
Ingredients
- Canned tuna in its own juice 2 cans
- Light mayonnaise ¼ g
- Granular mustard 2 tablespoons
- Chives 1 bunch
- Sweet red onion 1 head
- Celery 1 stalk
- Green apples 1 piece
- Cucumbers 1 piece
- Chicken egg (large) 2 pieces
- Green salad to taste

Direction:
1. Any bread you like: ciabatta, baguette, black, Borodino. It's best to fry it a little without oil or make toasts (we use toasts).
2. Drain the tuna, chop finely and mix all the ingredients.
3. Put on a toast decorated with a leaf of salad, cover with a second piece of bread.
Nutrition: Calories 59 Fat 0.75g Carbs 13.04g Protein 1.78g

304. Bacon Club Sandwich

Preparation time: 15 minutes
Cooking Time: 10 Minutes
Serving: 6
INGREDIENTS
• Bacon 400 g
• Meat 8 pieces
• 4-piece cheese
• Red onion 1 piece
• Mayonnaise 100 g
• White bread 8 slices
• Tomatoes 8 pieces
• Green salad 4 pieces
Direction:
1. In a pan, fry slices of bread on one side. On the non-roasted side, we smear the mayonnaise.
2. Put cheese and bacon on top, then meat.
3. Then two slices of tomato, chopped onion, lettuce.
Nutrition: Calories 103 Fat 0.9g Carbs 19.59g Protein 4.56g

305. Sandwiches With Salmon And Rondele Cheese

Preparation time: 1 hour
Cooking Time: 5 Minutes
Serving: 10
INGREDIENTS
• Rondele cheese 95 g
• Olive oil 2 teaspoons
• White bread 8 slices
• Balsamic vinegar 2 teaspoons
• Dill 8 stems
• Lightly salted salmon 4 pieces
• Lettuce leaves 4 pieces
• Ground black pepper to taste
Direction:
1. Put the cheese in a bowl, add olive oil and balsamic vinegar, mix. Pepper to taste, add finely chopped tops of four branches of dill, mix again.
2. Put four slices of bread on a sheet of lettuce, spread on top with cheese. Spread the remaining bread with cheese.
3. Put a slice of salmon on bread with lettuce and cover with the remaining pieces of bread. Top with a sprig of dill.
Nutrition: Calories 65 Fat 1.41g Carbs 10.69g Protein 2.6g

306. Herring Sandwich

Preparation time: 5 minutes
Cooking Time: 5 Minutes
Serving: 1
INGREDIENTS
• Bun 3 pieces
• Herring fillet 6 pieces
• ½ sweet onion
• Pickled cucumbers 3 pieces
Direction:
1. Finely chop the onion. Cut the cucumbers into thin slices.
2. Cut herring fillets into small pieces.

3. Put herring fillet on both sides of the bun - top and bottom. Sprinkle with onion and cover with cucumber.
Nutrition: Calories 3136 Fat 206.47g Carbs 117.03g Protein 192.97g

307. Chicken And Tomato Sandwich

Preparation time: 10 minutes
Cooking Time: 10 Minutes
Serving: 1
INGREDIENTS
• 2 toast bread
• Chicken fillet 1 piece
• Gouda cheese 1 piece
• Buko cheese 30 g
• Tomatoes 1 piece
• Green salad 1 bunch
Direction:
1. Boil chicken fillet. Cut lengthwise 1-2 cm.
2. Spread bread with cheese buko.
3. On the lower bread, put gouda cheese and a slice of chicken.
4. On the top - salad leaf and a slice of tomato.
5. Connect the sandwich.
Nutrition: Calories 87 Fat 6.12g Carbs 1.12g Protein 6.68g

308. Smoked Salmon Avocado Sandwiches

Preparation time: 20 minutes
Cooking Time: 30 Minutes
Serving: 1
INGREDIENTS
• Avocado 1 piece
• Light mayonnaise 1 tablespoon
• ½ teaspoon lemon juice
• Freshly ground black pepper to taste
• 8whole grain bread
• Smoked Salmon 60 g
• Cucumbers 1 piece
Direction:
1. Peel and cut avocados into thin slices. Cut the cucumber into thin circles.
2. In a small bowl, combine mayonnaise, lemon juice, and a little black pepper.
3. Spread the bread with the sauce. Half the avocado slices, thinly sliced fish and cucumber. Top with the remaining bread and gently squeeze. Cut each in half diagonally.
Nutrition: Calories 395 Fat 34.56g Carbs 22.12g Protein 6.11g

309. Turkey, Cheese And Arugula Sandwich

Preparation time: 20 minutes
Cooking Time: 30 Minutes
Serving: 4-6
INGREDIENTS
• Rye bread 2 slices
• Turkey fillet 50 g
• Tomatoes 2 pieces
• Arugula to taste
• Emmental cheese 20 g
Direction:
1. Boil the turkey fillet.
2. Put the fillet on the bottom bread, on top - a slice of tomato and cover everything with a slice of cheese.
3. Turn the top bread, put a second slice of cheese and tomato.

4. Send the butter to the microwave for 30 seconds.

5. Between the butters put arugula or some other greenery and connect the two halves.

Nutrition: Calories 15769 Fat 1452.33g Carbs 4.4g Protein 622.45g

310. Thin Pizza Dough

Preparation time: 30 minutes
Cooking Time: 1 hour
Serving: 10
INGREDIENTS
• Wheat flour 175 g
• Salt to taste
• 1 tablespoon olive oil
• Dry yeast 1 teaspoon
• Water 125 ml
Direction:

1. Combine flour, salt and yeast in a food processor. Combine oil and water in a jug. Without turning off the combine, pour in liquid and knead a homogeneous dough. Transfer to a table sprinkled with flour and knead the dough for 2-3 minutes.

2. Transfer the dough into a bowl and grease the outside with olive oil. Cover the bowl with cling film and place in a warm place for 40 minutes until the dough is doubled.

3. Knead the dough again for 1-2 minutes. Roll out the dough into a circle of 30 cm and put on a baking sheet. Squeeze 2 cm from the edge to make a crust and fill with the filling of your choice.

Nutrition:
calorie content 200 kcal
squirrels 4.6 gram
fats 5,6 gram
carbohydrates 33.3gram

311. Olive Oil Pizza Dough

Preparation time: 20 minutes
Cooking Time: 30 minutes
Serving: 1
INGREDIENTS
• Water 2/3 cup
• Wheat flour 2 cups
• Dry yeast 1 teaspoon
• Salt 1 teaspoon
• 1 tablespoon olive oil
Direction:

1. Pour the yeast with warm water. Stir the mixture properly so that there are no lumps.

2. Pour 2 cups flour and salt into a large bowl. Add yeast and knead the dough.

3. Put the dough out of the bowl on a dry, floured surface, and continue to knead, adding flour if necessary, until the dough is soft and elastic (about 10 minutes).

4. Lightly grease a large bowl with olive oil. Put the dough in a bowl, turning it so that the entire surface is smeared with oil.

5. Cover with a film and place in a warm, without drafts, place for 1.5 hours (until the dough increases about 2 times).

6. Flatten the dough with your fists. Divide into 2 parts and roll into balls.

Nutrition:
calorie content392kcal
squirrels9.8gram
fats6.3gram
carbohydrates75,4gram

312. Crispy Pizza Dough

Preparation time: 15 minutes
Cooking Time: 30 minutes
Serving: 12
INGREDIENTS
• Wheat flour 2 cups
• 2 tablespoons olive oil
• ½ cup milk
• Chicken egg 2 pieces
• Salt pinch
Direction:

1. Heat milk, add eggs and butter, stir.

2. Constantly mixing, pour the milk mixture into the flour, add salt

3. Knead the dough for about 10 minutes to make it elastic.

Nutrition:
calorie content495 kcal
squirrels 13.8 gram
fats 15.4 gram
carbohydrates 76.3 gram

313. Thin Crispy Pizza Dough

Preparation time: 1 hour
Cooking Time: 1 hour 30 minutes
Serving: 4
INGREDIENTS
• Wheat flour 250 g
• Cane sugar 0.3 teaspoon
• Dry yeast 4 g
• 0.4 teaspoon salt
• Water 125 ml
Direction:

1. Prepare the dough. To do this, mix yeast, sugar and 2 tablespoons of warm water in a bowl. Then add 2 tablespoons of flour, mix well again, cover with a towel and put in a warm place for 30 minutes. Watch the dough, it happens that it is ready in 10 minutes!

2. Pour flour into a bowl, make a depression in the middle. Put the dough in the recess, salt, add about 125 ml of warm water. Knead for about 10-15 minutes until the dough is soft, smooth and elastic. It should not stick to your hands, so you may need to add a little flour or water.

3. Cover the dough with a towel and put in a warm place for 1 hour. It should increase in volume by about half.

4. Making a crunch! Heat the oven to 200 degrees, grease the pizza dish with olive oil, roll it out with a diameter of about 28 cm, put it in the mold, form the sides (or not), grease with tomato sauce and put in the oven for about 5 minutes.

5. Then remove, distribute the rest of the filling and bake for another 20 minutes. Due to the fact that the dough is slightly baked at the beginning, it will become crispy, but at the same time it will not burn!

Nutrition:
calorie content 221kcal
squirrels 6.2gram
fats 0.8gram
carbohydrates 48gram

314. Yeast Pizza Dough

Preparation time: 35 minutes
Cooking Time: 20 minutes
Serving: 1
INGREDIENTS
• Wheat flour 2 cups
• Vegetable oil 1 tablespoon

- Fresh yeast 20 g
- Sugar 1 teaspoon
- Salt 1 teaspoon

Direction:

1. In one glass of warm water, dilute 20 grams of yeast (or 1/3 sachet of dry yeast). Leave to stand for 10 minutes.

2. Add 1 tablespoon of vegetable oil, pour all this into 2 cups flour, add salt and sugar.

3. Knead the dough well.

Nutrition:

calorie content 394 kcal

Squirrels 9.8 Gram

Fats 5.8 Gram

Carbohydrates 76.9 Gram

315. Green Veggie Sandwiches

Preparation time: 20 minutes

Cooking time: 0 minutes

Serving: 2

Ingredients:

Spread:

- 1 (15-ounce / 425-g) can cannellini beans, drained and rinsed
- 1/3 cup packed fresh basil leaves
- 1/3 cup packed fresh parsley
- 1/3 cup chopped fresh chives
- 2 garlic cloves, chopped
- Zest and juice of ½ lemon
- 1 tablespoon apple cider vinegar

Sandwiches:

- 4 whole-grain bread slices, toasted
- 8 English cucumber slices
- 1 large beefsteak tomato, cut into slices
- 1 large avocado, halved, pitted, and cut into slices
- 1 small yellow bell pepper, cut into slices
- 2 handfuls broccoli sprouts
- 2 handfuls fresh spinach

Direction:

1. In a food processor, combine the cannellini beans, basil, parsley, chives, garlic, lemon zest and juice, and vinegar. Pulse a few times, scrape down the sides, and purée until smooth. You may need to scrape down the sides again to incorporate all the basil and parsley. Refrigerate for at least 1 hour to allow the flavors to blend.

Assemble the Sandwiches

2. Build your sandwiches by spreading several tablespoons of spread on each slice of bread. Layer two slices of bread with the cucumber, tomato, avocado, bell pepper, broccoli sprouts, and spinach. Top with the remaining bread slices and press down lightly.

3. Serve immediately.

Nutrition Per Serving

calories: 617 | fat: 21.1g | protein: 28.1g | carbs: 86.1g | fiber: 25.6g | sodium: 593mg

316. Easy Pizza Pockets

Preparation time: 10 minutes

Cooking time: 0 minutes

Serving: 2

Ingredients:

- ½ cup tomato sauce
- ½ teaspoon oregano
- ½ teaspoon garlic powder
- ½ cup chopped black olives
- 2 canned artichoke hearts, drained and chopped

- 2 ounces (57 g) pepperoni, chopped
- ½ cup shredded Mozzarella cheese
- 1 whole-wheat pita, halved

Direction:

1. In a medium bowl, stir together the tomato sauce, oregano, and garlic powder.

2. Add the olives, artichoke hearts, pepperoni, and cheese. Stir to mix.

3. Spoon the mixture into the pita halves and serve.

Nutrition Per Serving

calories: 375 | fat: 23.5g | protein: 17.1g | carbs: 27.1g | fiber: 6.1g | sodium: 1080mg

317. Mushroom-Pesto Baked Pizza

Preparation time: 5 minutes

Cooking time: 15 minutes

Serving: 2

Ingredients:

- 1 teaspoon extra-virgin olive oil
- ½ cup sliced mushrooms
- ½ red onion, sliced
- Salt and freshly ground black pepper
- ¼ cup store-bought pesto sauce
- 2 whole-wheat flatbread
- ¼ cup shredded Mozzarella cheese

Direction:

1. Preheat the oven to 350ºF (180ºC).

2. In a small skillet, heat the oil over medium heat. Add the mushrooms and onion, and season with salt and pepper. Sauté for 3 to 5 minutes until the onion and mushrooms begin to soften.

3. Spread 2 tablespoons of pesto on each flatbread.

4. Divide the mushroom-onion mixture between the two flatbread. Top each with 2 tablespoons of cheese.

5. Place the flatbread on a baking sheet and bake for 10 to 12 minutes until the cheese is melted and bubbly. Serve warm.

Nutrition Per Serving

calories: 348 | fat: 23.5g | protein: 14.2g | carbs: 28.1g | fiber: 7.1g | sodium: 792mg

318. Tuna and Hummus Wraps

Preparation time: 10 minutes

Cooking time: 0 minutes

Serving: 2

Ingredients:

Hummus:

- 1 cup from 1 (15-ounce / 425-g) can low-sodium chickpeas, drained and rinsed
- 2 tablespoons tahini
- 1 tablespoon extra-virgin olive oil
- 1 garlic clove
- Juice of ½ lemon
- ¼ teaspoon salt
- 2 tablespoons water

Wraps:

- 4 large lettuce leaves
- 1 (5-ounce / 142-g) can chunk light tuna packed in water, drained
- 1 red bell pepper, seeded and cut into strips
- 1 cucumber, sliced

Direction:

Make the Hummus

1. In a blender jar, combine the chickpeas, tahini, olive oil, garlic, lemon juice, salt, and water. Process until smooth. Taste and adjust with additional lemon juice or salt, as needed.

Make the Wraps

2. On each lettuce leaf, spread 1 tablespoon of hummus, and divide the tuna among the leaves. Top each with several strips of red pepper and cucumber slices.

3. Roll up the lettuce leaves, folding in the two shorter sides and rolling away from you, like a burrito. Serve immediately.

Nutrition Per Serving

calories: 192 | fat: 5.1g | protein: 26.1g | carbs: 15.1g | fiber: 4.1g | sodium: 352mg

319. Chickpea Lettuce Wraps

Preparation time: 15 minutes
Cooking time: 0 minutes
Serving 2
Ingredients:

- 1 (15-ounce / 425-g) can chickpeas, drained and rinsed well
- 1 celery stalk, diced
- ½ shallot, minced
- 1 green apple, cored and diced
- 3 tablespoons tahini (sesame paste)
- 2 teaspoons freshly squeezed lemon juice
- 1 teaspoon raw honey
- 1 teaspoon Dijon mustard
- Dash salt
- Filtered water, to thin
- 4 romaine lettuce leaves

Direction:

1. In a medium bowl, stir together the chickpeas, celery, shallot, apple, tahini, lemon juice, honey, mustard, and salt. If needed, add some water to thin the mixture.

2. Place the romaine lettuce leaves on a plate. Fill each with the chickpea filling, using it all. Wrap the leaves around the filling. Serve immediately.

Nutrition Per Serving

calories: 397 | fat: 15.1g | protein: 15.1g | carbs: 53.1g | fiber: 15.3g | sodium: 409mg

320. Zucchini Hummus Wraps

Preparation time: 15 minutes
Cooking time: 6 minutes
Serving: 2
Ingredients:

- 1 zucchini, ends removed, thinly sliced lengthwise
- ½ teaspoon dried oregano
- ¼ teaspoon freshly ground black pepper
- ¼ teaspoon garlic powder
- ¼ cup hummus
- 2 whole wheat tortillas
- 2 Roma tomatoes, cut lengthwise into slices
- 1 cup chopped kale
- 2 tablespoons chopped red onion
- ½ teaspoon ground cumin

Direction:

1. In a skillet over medium heat, place the zucchini slices and cook for 3 minutes per side. Sprinkle with the oregano, pepper, and garlic powder and remove from the heat.

2. Spread 2 tablespoons of hummus on each tortilla. Lay half the zucchini in the center of each tortilla. Top with tomato slices, kale, red onion, and ¼ teaspoon of cumin. Wrap tightly and serve.

Nutrition Per Serving

calories: 248 | fat: 8.1g | protein: 9.1g | carbs: 37.1g | fiber: 8.1g | sodium: mg

Chapter 5. Pasta, Rice & Grains Recipes

321. Greek Rice Salad

Preparation time:20 mins
Cooking time :45 mins
Servings:8
Ingredients
- one cup of uncooked long grain brown rice
- 2 1/2 cup of water
- 1 avocado - peeled, pitted, and diced
- ¼ cup of lemon juice
- 2 vine-ripened tomatoes, diced
- 1 1//2 cup of diced English cucumbers
- 1/3 cup of diced red onion
- ½ cup of crumbled feta cheese
- ¼ cup of sliced Kalamata olives
- ¼ cup of chopped fresh mint
- 3 tbsp olive oil
- 1 tsp lemon zest
- ½ tsp minced garlic
- ½ tsp kosher salt
- ½ tsp ground black pepper
Directions
1. Heat the earthy colored rice and water to the point of boiling in a pan over high warmth. Diminish the warmth to medium-low, cover, and stew until the rice is delicate and the fluid has been ingested, 45 to 50 minutes; eliminate from warmth and permit to cool, cushioning every so often with a fork.
2. Throw the avocado and lemon squeeze together in a huge bowl. Add the tomatoes, cucumber, onion, feta, olives, mint, olive oil, lemon zing, garlic, salt, and pepper to the bowl; daintily throw the blend until equitably consolidated. Crease the cooled rice delicately into the combination. Serve promptly or chill as long as 60 minutes; the plate of mixed greens doesn't last well for over a day as the tomato and cucumber start to deliver their juices and the plate of mixed greens gets watery.
Nutrition:
Calories: 222 kcal
Fat: 12.52 g
Carbohydrates: 23.19 g
Protein: 5.52 g

322. Creamy Roasted Red Pepper Pasta

Preparation Time: 5 Min
Cooking Time: 15 Min
Serving: 6
Ingredients
- 1 rigatoni pasta (or pasta of your choice)
- 1/2 cup of Stock (chicken or vegetable)
- 1 cup of Heavy cream
- 8Fresh basil leaves
- 12 ozJar roasted red peppers, liquid drained
- 1/2 tsp Salt
- 1/2 tsp Red pepper flakes
- 1/2 cup of Grated parmesan cheese
Direction:
1. In a high velocity blender add hefty cream, stock, simmered red peppers, basil, salt and red pepper chips. Mix until smooth.
2. Cook pasta until still somewhat firm (around 6 minutes). Eliminate from warmth and channel.
3. In a similar pot the pasta was cooked in, add your smooth broiled red pepper sauce and bring to a delicate stew over medium-low warmth. Add the parmesan cheddar and depleted pasta and cook for another 1-2 minutes, mixing continually. Eliminate from warmth and serve hot finished off with additional parmesan cheddar and new basil. Appreciate!
Nutrition:
Calories: 124 kcal
Fat: 10 g
Carbohydrates: 5.55 g
Protein: 3.83 g

323. Tomato Basil Rice

Preparation Time: 10 Minutes
Cooking Time: 30 Minutes
Servings: 4
Ingredients
- 1 tbsp olive oil
- ½ cup of onion diced
- 1 cup of white rice
- 2 cup of chicken broth
- one ripe tomato diced with juices, plus extra for garnish
- 2 cloves garlic minced
- salt and pepper to taste
- 3 tbsp parmesan cheese grated, divided
Direction:
1. In a medium pan, cook onion in olive oil until it starts to mollify, around four minutes. Add rice and cook tow- three minutes or until the rice begins to brown a touch.
2. Mix in chicken stock, tomatoes (with any juices), and garlic. Add salt and pepper to taste.
3. Heat to the point of boiling, cover and lessen warmth to a stew. Cook 20 minutes without lifting the top.
4. Eliminate from warmth and rest 5 minutes prior to eliminating the cover. Add 2 tbsp parmesan cheddar and basil. Blend well.
5. Spot in a bowl, embellish with outstanding parmesan cheddar, extra basil and new tomatoes whenever wanted.
Nutrition:
Calories: 419 kcal
Fat: 13.02 g
Carbohydrates: 42.12 g
Protein: 30.63 g

324. Easy Canned Tuna Pasta

Preparation Time: 5 Mins
Cooking Time: 10 Mins
Serving: 2
Ingredients
- 2 tbsp olive oil
- 2 large cloves garlic minced
- 1 can tuna, drained I prefer tuna packed in oil
- 1 tsp lemon juice
- 1 tbsp fresh parsley chopped
- Salt & pepper to taste
- 4 ounces uncooked pasta (I used spaghetti)
Direction:
1.Warmth up a salted pot of water for your pasta and cook it still genuinely firm as per bundle headings. Prep your different decorations while it cooks.
2.Exactly when the pasta is close being ready, add the oil to a little dish over medium warmth. Exactly when the oil is hot, add the garlic and cook it for 30 seconds.
3. Blend in the fish, lemon juice, and parsleys. Permit it to warm through.

4.At the point when the pasta is done, add a bit of the pasta water to the sauce and a while later channel the pasta and toss with the sauce. Season with salt and pepper depending on the situation. Discretionary: serve pasta with newly ground parmesan cheddar and lemon zing.
Nutrition:
Calories: 276 kcal
Fat: 14.79 g
Carbohydrates: 19.24 g
Protein: 18.24 g

325. Vegan Spaghetti Alla Puttanesca

Preparation Time: 10 mins
Cooking Time: 20 mins
Serving: 2
Ingredients
Puttanesca sauce
• 1 large can of chunky tomato sauce (I recommend Muir Glen brand) or diced tomatoes
• 1/3 cup of chopped Kalamata olives
• 1/3 cup of capers
• 1 tbsp Kalamata olive brine (from your jar of olives)
• 1 tbsp caper brine (from your jar of capers)
• 3 cloves garlic, pressed or minced
• ¼ tsp red pepper flakes
• 1 tbsp olive oil
• ½ cup of chopped fresh parsley leaves and divided
• Freshly ground black pepper
• Salt, if necessary
Everything else
• eight ounces whole grain spaghetti, or an equivalent combination of spaghetti and zucchini noodles
Direction:
1. In a medium pot, join the pureed tomatoes, olives, tricks, olive bring, escapade brackish water, garlic and red pepper drops. Carry the blend to a stew over medium-high warmth, at that point decrease warmth to medium and stew, mixing frequently, for 20 minutes.
2. Eliminate the sauce from warmth, and mix in the olive oil and practically the entirety of the cleaved parsley, saving some to sprinkle on the completed dishes. Season to taste with newly ground dark pepper and salt, if fundamental (the sauce was at that point bounty pungent for me, so I didn't add any salt).
3. While the sauce cooks, bring an enormous pot of salted water to bubble and cook your spaghetti as indicated by bundle headings. Channel and return it to the pot.
4. In case you're adding zucchini noodles, spiralize the zucchini with a spiralizer (here's the manner by which), or transform the zucchini into noodles with a julienne peeler, or mesh the zucchini the long path on an enormous box grater.
5. When the entirety of your parts are prepared, pour the sauce over the pasta and mix to join. Mix in the zucchini noodles, if utilizing (in the event that you plan on having extras, store additional zucchini noodles independently, as they siphon water once they come into contact with pungent fixings). Gap into singular dishes and top each bowl with a light sprinkle of parsley. Serve right away.
Nutrition:
Calories: 211 kcal
Fat: 13.33g
Carbohydrates: 18.59 g
Protein: 7.04 g

326. Italian Style Mac And Cheese

Preparation time: 10 mins
Cooking time: 18 mins
Serving: 2
Ingredients
• 1 lb. penne
• ¼ cup of butter unsalted
• ¼ cup of all-purpose flour
• 1 tbsp Italian seasoning
• 2 cup of milk
• 3 cup of cheese shredded, such as mozzarella, provolone
• 1 cup of Parmesan cheese freshly grated
• ½ tsp red pepper flakes
Direction:
1. Cook Pasta: Cook the pasta in an enormous salted pot of bubbling water as indicated by bundle guidelines, until still somewhat firm. Channel, flush with cold water and put away.
2. Make Sauce: In an enormous pot or Dutch stove, dissolve the margarine over medium warmth. Add the flour and Italian flavoring and whisk. Cook for 2 minutes while whisking consistently.
3. Finish Sauce: Add the milk and rush until it thickens. Mix in the cheeses and rush until very much consolidated and smooth.
4. Add Pasta: Add the penne to the pot and throw well ensuring the pasta is completely canvassed in sauce.
5. Trimming and Serve: Garnish with red pepper chips and serve.
Nutrition:
Calories: 1571 kcal
Fat: 107.14g
Carbohydrates: 68.43 g
Protein: 83.08 g

327. Ita Chicken, Pasta In Creamy White Wine sauce

Preparation Time: 10 mins
Cooking Time: 20 mins
Serving: 2
Ingredients
For cooking chicken:
• four boneless skinless chicken breasts (halved horizontally and paper towel dried)
• 1/2 cup of flour
• 1 tsp salt
• ¼ tsp black pepper
• 1 tsp garlic powder
• 2 tsp Italian seasoning
• 2 tbsp olive oil
Pasta:
• 12 oz of spaghetti
• White Wine Parmesan Sauce:
• 4 tbsp butter
• one small yellow onion (or use 1/2 onion) chopped
• 4 garlic cloves minced
• 2 scallions chopped
• 2 small tomatoes diced
• 1 tbsp flour
• 1 cup of heavy cream
• 1 cup of white wine
• ½ cup of Parmesan cheese shredded
• 1 tsp Italian Seasoning
• 1/2 tsp salt more to taste
• ¼ tsp crushed red pepper flakes

Direction:
1. Planning CHICKEN BREASTS: Make sure to slice chicken bosoms evenly to make them slight. Paper towel dry the chicken.
2. In a huge bowl, consolidate flour, salt, dark pepper, garlic powder and Italian flavoring. Mix well to mix. Utilizing a fork or utensils, coat the chicken bosoms in the flour combination by squeezing into the blend with utensils and afterward flipping the chicken over to cover the opposite side. Put away.
3. COOKING CHICKEN BREASTS: Heat 2 tbsp of olive oil in a huge skillet over medium-high warmth. At the point when the skillet is hot, place flour canvassed chicken chests in the skillet And cook for four to five mins on each side, until splendid gritty shaded on the different sides and cooked through, turning once between cooking, around 8-10 minutes. Kill chicken from dish and set aside.
4. SAUCE: Add margarine, diced yellow onion and minced garlic cloves to skillet. Cook medium high until onions and garlic are clear, around 2 mins. Next add cleaved scallions and tomatoes. Add 1 tbsp flour to dish and rush to join.
5. Presently add substantial cream, wine, Italian Seasoning, salt and red pepper pieces. Carry combination to a stewing point and afterward add ½ cup of destroyed Parmesan cheddar. Utilize a whisk or a wooden spoon and blend it in until you have a smooth combination.
6. COOKING PASTA as indicated by your bundle directions in pungent water. I like pasta that is neither hard nor unnecessarily fragile, so I by and large cook it Al Dente. Channel, however don't flush.
7. Last ASSEMBLY: Add cooked pasta to the skillet with the sauce and mix to join on low warmth for 2-4 minutes. Taste and add salt, if necessary. Return chicken skillet on top of the pasta and grant it to prepare for an additional 5 minutes.
8. SERVE chicken either on top or close to pasta and sprinkle with Parmesan cheddar, whenever wanted.
Nutrition:
Calories: 1668 kcal
Fat: 112.05g
Carbohydrates: 91/73 g
Protein: 75.66 g

328. Herbed Polenta

Preparation time: 10 min
Cooking: 25 min
Serving: 2
Ingredients
- Deselect All
- 6 cup of water
- 2 tsp salt
- 1 3/4 cup of yellow cornmeal
- 3/4 cup of grated Parmesan
- 3/4 cup of whole milk
- 6 tbsp (3/4 stick) unsalted butter
- 3 tbsp chopped fresh Italian parsley leaves
- 2 tsp finely chopped fresh rosemary leaves
- 2 tsp chopped fresh thyme leaves
- 1/2 tsp freshly ground black pepper
Directions
Warmth the water to the purpose of bubbling in a profound huge pot. Add 2 tsps. of salt. One small step at a time surge in the cornmeal. Lessen the warmth to low and cook until the blend thickens and the cornmeal is delicate, mixing frequently, around 15 minutes. Eliminate from the warmth. Add the cheddar, milk, margarine, parsley, rosemary,

thyme, and pepper, and mix until the spread and cheddar soften. Move the polenta to a bowl and serve.
Nutrition:
Calories: 956 kcal
Fat: 32.99g
Carbohydrates: 133.68 g
Protein: 29.31 g

329. Shrimp Pesto Pasta

Preparation Time10 minutes
Cooking Time: 10 minutes
Servings:4
Ingredients
- 10 ounces dry spaghetti can also use linguine or fettuccine
- 3/4 cup of basil pesto
- one-pound medium to large shrimp peeled and deveined
- 1 tbsp olive oil
- 1 tsp Italian seasoning (or equal parts garlic powder dried basil and dried oregano)
- salt and pepper to taste
- 1/4 cup of parmesan cheese
- 1 cup of cherry tomatoes halved
- Optional garnish: chopped parsley
Direction:
1. Heat an enormous pot of salted water to the point of boiling and cook the pasta as indicated by bundle headings.
2. While t pasta is cooking, set up the shrimp.
3. Warmth the olive oil in a huge dish over high warmth. Add the shrimp and sprinkle with Italian flavoring, salt and pepper.
4. Cook for tow-four minutes or until shrimp are essentially pink and dim. Mood killer the warmth.
5. Channel the pasta and add it to the container with the shrimp. Mix in the pesto.
6. Add the cherry tomatoes and parmesan cheddar to the container. Enhancement with slashed parsley whenever wanted.
Nutrition:
Calories: 347 kcal
Fat: 6.55g
Carbohydrates: 59.27 g
Protein: 12.65 g

330. Mexican Quinoa Stuffed Sweet Potatoes

Preparation Time: 5 minutes
Cooking Time: 40 minutes
Servings:4
Ingredients
- 2 large sweet potatoes
- 1 tbsp olive oil
- 1/4 cup of chopped red onion
- 1/4 cup of chopped bell pepper
- 1/2 cup of frozen corn
- 1/2 cup of cooked quinoa
- one cup of canned black beans drained & rinsed
- 1 tbsp chili powder
- 1 tsp cumin
- 1/2 tsp smoked paprika
- Sea salt to taste
to garnish:
- 1 avocado mashed
- Tahini
- Hot sauce
- Chopped cilantro

Direction:
1. Preheat the broiler to 400°F. Spot yams on a preparing sheet and prick with a fork. Spot in the stove and heat for 40 minutes.
2. In the interim, heat the oil in an enormous skillet. Add the onion and pepper and sauté until delicate, around 5 minutes.
3. Add corn, quinoa, dark beans and flavors and cook 2 - 3 additional minutes.
4. At the point when yams are fork delicate, eliminate from broiler and let rest for 5 minutes. Cut into equal parts and spot every half on a plate. Top with quinoa combination, avocado and a sprinkle of the two tahini and hot sauce. Get done with a sprinkle of cilantro and appreciate!
Nutrition:
Calories: 332 kcal
Fat: 13.77g
Carbohydrates: 44.93 g
Protein: 10.42 g

331. Mediterranean Three Bean Quinoa Salad

Preparation Time: 15 Mins
Cooking Time: 20 Mins
Servings:8
Ingredients
For the Salad:
- 1 cup of quinoa
- 2 cup of water
- ½ lb. green beans trimmed and snapped into 2-inch pieces
- one can garbanzo beans drained and rinsed
- 1 white beans, drained and rinsed
- one red bell pepper seeds removed and chopped
- one yellow bell pepper seeds removed and chopped
- cup of chopped seedless cucumber
- one cup of grape tomatoes cut in half
- 1/4 cup of diced red onion
- 1/4 cup of crumbled feta cheese
- 1/3 cup of kalamata olives pitted and sliced in half
- 1/4 cup of chopped fresh basil
For the Dressing:
- 1/4 cup of olive oil
- 1 tbsp balsamic vinegar
- 2 garlic cloves pressed
- 1/4 tsp dried basil
- 1/4 tsp dried oregano
- Kosher salt and freshly ground black pepper
Direction:
1 In a medium pot, heat quinoa and water to the point of boiling. Cover, diminish warmth to low, and stew until for 15 minutes, or until quinoa is delicate. Eliminate from warmth and let represent 5 minutes, covered. Eliminate top and cushion with a fork. Move quinoa to an enormous bowl.
2 Meanwhile, whiten the green beans. Heat an enormous pot of salted water point of boiling. Add the green beans and cook until delicate fresh, around 2 minutes. Channel the green beans and spot in a bowl of ice water. Channel well and wipe off.
3 Add the green beans, garbanzo beans, white beans, peppers, cucumbers, tomatoes, red onion, feta cheddar, olives, and basil the bowl with the quinoa.
4 In a little bowl, whisk together the olive oil, balsamic vinegar, garlic, basil, oregano, salt, and pepper. Pour dressing over the serving of mixed greens and delicately mix

until salad is covered with dressing. Season with extra salt and pepper serve.
5 Note-on the off chance that you have an Instant Pot , you can cook the quinoa in your Instant Pot. It just requires one moment.
Nutrition:
Calories: 228 kcal
Fat: 10.55g
Carbohydrates: 27.52 g
Protein: 6.83 g

332. Buffalo Quinoa Bites

Preparation Time: 15 minutes
Cooking Time: 15 minutes
Serving: 16 bites
Ingredients
- 2 cup of cooked quinoa
- 1 cup of cannellini beans mashed
- 3/4 cup of panko bread crumbs
- 1 large egg lightly beaten
- 1/2 cup of bison wing sauce isolated
- 1/2 tsp salt
- 1 tsp pepper
- 2 oz. crumbled blue cheese
Direction:
1 In a huge bowl consolidate the quinoa, pounded cannellini beans, bread scraps, egg, salt, pepper and 1/4 cup of wild ox sauce.
2 Mix well to soak the fixings and afterward structure into 16 equivalent size balls. (I utilized a 2 tbsp treat scoop)
3 Flatten each ball into a flapjack shape in the palm of your hand. Spot a touch of blue cheddar disintegrates into the middle, at that point overlap the sides up to encase the cheddar in the focal point of the ball. Crush firmly to seal.
4 Air fry balls in a solitary even layer at 375 degrees for 8 minutes. Pivot the balls and proceed with air singing for 8 additional minutes until firm.
5 Toss quinoa chomps into residual wild ox wing sauce. Serve.
Nutrition:
Calories: 54 kcal
Fat: 1.86g
Carbohydrates: 7.08 g
Protein: 2.38 g

333. Loaded Lebanese Rice: Hashweh

Preparation Time: 20 mins
Cooking Time: 30 mins
Serving: 2
Ingredients
- 1 ½ cup of medium grain rice
- Olive oil
- one small red onion, finely chopped
- one lb. lean ground beef or lean ground lamb
- 1 ¾ tsp ground allspice, divided
- ½ tsp minced garlic
- ¾ tsp ground cloves, divided
- ¾ tsp ground cinnamon, divided
- salt and pepper
- ½ cup of fresh parsley leaves, roughly chopped
- 1/3 to 1/2 cup of pine nuts, toasted
- 1/3 to ½ cup of slivered almonds, toasted
- ½ cup of dark raisins
Direction:
1 .Absorb the rice cool water for 15 minutes or until you are adequately prepared to break one grain rice between your

thumb and index fingers. At the point when prepared, channel well.

2. Meanwhile, heat one tbsp of olive oil in a substantial cooking pot. Add slashed red onions, cook on medium-high warmth momentarily, at that point add the ground meat. Season the meat blend with 1 ¼ tsp allspice, minced garlic, ½ tsp ground cloves, ½ tsp ground cinnamon, salt and pepper. Throw together to join. Cook until the meat is completely carmelized (8-10 minutes). Channel.

3 .Top the meat with rice. Season the rice with little salt and the rest of the allspice, ground cloves and cinnamon. Add 2 ½ cup of of water and 1 tbsp of olive oil to cover the rice.

4 .Turn warmth to high and carry the fluid to a moving bubble. Let bubble until the fluid has altogether decreased (see picture underneath).

5 .Now go warmth to low and cover; let cook for 20 minutes or until dampness has totally been ingested and the rice is not, at this point hard nor tacky. Eliminate from warmth and put away for 10 minutes.

6 .Uncover the rice pot and spot an enormous round serving platter on the launch of the rice pot. Cautiously flip the pot substance onto the platter with the goal that the meat layer presently beat the rice.

7 .Garnish with parsley, toasted pine nuts, almonds and raisins. Appreciate.

Nutrition:
Calories: 1185kcal
Fat: 51.32g
Carbohydrates: 119.33 g
Protein: 64.6 g

334. Linguine With Brie & Raw Tomato Sauce

Preparation Time 10 Min
Cooking Time 5 Min
Servings 4 To 6
Ingredients
• 3 large vine-ripened tomatoes, cut into wedges
• three oz low-fat Brie cheese, cubed, rind removed and discarded
• 2 loosely packed cup of baby arugula or spinach leaves
• 1/2 loosely packed cup of torn fresh basil leaves
• 1/4 cup of grated low-fat Parmesan cheese
• tow green onions, green parts only, thinly sliced
• tow tbsp extra-virgin olive oil
• 2 tbsp balsamic vinegar
• Sea salt a fresh ground black pepper, to taste
• 12 oz whole-wheat linguine
• three tbsp toasted pine nuts or slivered unsalted almonds
Direction:
1. In an enormous bowl, throw tomatoes, Brie, arugula, basil, Parmesan, onions, oil, vinegar, salt and pepper; put away.

2. Heat an enormous pot of water to the point of boiling. Add linguine and cook as indicated by bundle headings. Hold 3/4 cup of pasta cooking water; channel. Promptly add pasta and 1/2 cup of saved pasta cooking water to tomato-Brie combination; let stand immaculate for 1 moment, at that point throw to consolidate. Add nuts and step by step amount to 1/4 cup of held pasta cooking water if important and as wanted to make a rich sauce; throw to cover.

Nutrition:
Calories: 167kcal
Fat: 6.25g
Carbohydrates: 21.02 g
Protein: 8.69 g

335. Greek Chicken Pasta

Preparation time:15 mins
Cooking time:15 mins
Servings:6
Ingredients
• 1 (16 ounce) package linguine pasta
• ½ cup of chopped red onion
• 1 tbsp olive oil
• 2 cloves garlic, crushed
• one-pound skinless, boneless chicken breast meat - cut into bite-size pieces
• 1 (14 ounce) can marinated artichoke hearts, drained and chopped
• 1 large tomato, chopped
• ½ cup of crumbled feta cheese
• 3 tbsp chopped fresh parsley
• 2 tbsp lemon juice
• 2 tsps. dried oregano
• salt and pepper to taste
• 2 lemons, wedged, for garnish
Directions
Stage 1
   1. Heat a huge pot of softly salted water to the point of boiling. Cook pasta in bubbling water until delicate yet firm to the piece, 8 to 10 minutes; channel.
Stage 2
   2. Warmth olive oil in a colossal skillet over medium-high warmth . Add onion and garlic; sauté until fragrant, around 2 minutes. Mix in the chicken and cook, mixing every so often, until chicken is not, at this point pink the middle and the juices run clear, around 5 to 6 minutes.
Stage 3
   3. Lessen warmth to medium-low; add artichoke hearts, tomato, feta cheddar, parsley, lemon juice, oregano, and cooked pasta. Cook and mix until warmed through, around 2 to 3 minutes. Eliminate from heat, season with salt and pepper, and embellishment with lemon wedges.

Nutrition:
Calories: 187kcal
Fat: 8.12g
Carbohydrates: 7.59 g
Protein: 21.15 g

336. Herbed Rice

Preparation time:5 minutes
Cooking time :20 minutes
Serving: 2
Ingredients
• 2 Tbsp butter
• 1 tsp dried onion or ¼ C finely chopped onion
• 1 tsp salt
• black pepper a few shakes
• 1 tsp garlic minced
• ¼ cup of fresh lemon juice
• 3 cup of chicken broth
• 1½ cup of basmati rice
• 1/2 tsp rosemary, basil, thyme, dill (use less dill), oregano, or parsley use your favorite combo, If using fresh herbs use 2 times as much. Only use 3-4 different herbs at a time.
• fresh parsley for garnish

Direction:
1. In a dish over medium warmth liquefy margarine and include onion just as salt and pepper.
2. Mix until onion is delicate.
3. Include garlic and cook briefly more.
4. Include chicken stock and lemon juice and spice blend alongside the rice. I utilized 1 tsp basil, 1/2 tsp thyme and 1 tsp parsley.
5. Mix until combined as one.
6. Heat to the point of boiling and cover and diminish heat.
7. Cook covered for around 20 minutes or until rice is delicate.
8. Embellishment for certain new spices whenever wanted.
Nutrition:
Calories: 1032kcal
Fat: 58.1g
Carbohydrates: 56.86 g
Protein: 94.22 g

337. Creamy Baked Mac And Cheese

Preparation Time: 20 minutes
Cooking Time: 15 minutes
Serving: 2
Ingredients
• 1 lb. dried elbow pasta
• 1/2 cup of unsalted butter
• 1/2 cup of all-purpose flour
• 1 1/2 cup of whole milk
• 2 1/2 cup of half and half
• 4 cup of grated medium sharp cheddar cheese divided (measured after grating)
• 2 cup of grated Gruyere cheese divided (measured after grating)
• 1/2 Tbsp. salt
• 1/2 tsp. black pepper
• 1/4 tsp. paprika
Direction:
1. Preheat stove to 325 degrees F and oil a 3 qt heating dish (9x13"). Put away.
2. Heat a huge pot of salted water to the point of boiling. When bubbling, add dried pasta and cook 1 moment not exactly the bundle coordinates for still somewhat firm. Channel and sprinkle with a tad of olive oil to hold back from staying.
3. While water is coming up to an air pocket, crush cheeses and put together to mix, by then parcel into three stores. Roughly 3 cup of for the sauce, 1/2 cup of for the internal layer, and 1/2 cup of for the garnish.
4. Liquefy margarine in a huge pan over MED heat. Sprinkle in flour and race to join. Blend will look like wet sand. Cook for roughly 1 moment, whisking regularly. Gradually pour in around 2 cup of or so of the milk/creamer, while whisking continually, until smooth. Gradually pour in the leftover milk/creamer, while whisking continually, until joined and smooth.
5. Keep on warming over MED heat, whisking regularly, until thickened to an exceptionally thick consistency. It ought to nearly be the consistency of a semi dispersed dense soup.
6. Eliminate from the warmth and mix in flavors and 1/2 cup of the cheeses, blending to soften and join. Mix in another 1/2 cup of cheddar, and mix until totally softened and smooth.
7. In an enormous blending bowl, join depleted pasta with cheddar sauce, mixing to consolidate completely. Pour half of the pasta combination into the pre-arranged preparing dish. Top with 1/2 cup of ground cheeses, at that point top

that with the leftover pasta blend. Sprinkle the top with the last 1/2 cup of cheddar and heat for 15 minutes, until messy is effervescent and gently brilliant earthy colored.
Nutrition:
Calories: 1563kcal
Fat: 85.25g
Carbohydrates: 137.99 g
Protein: 63.49 g

338. Pasta Puttanesca

Preparation Time:20 minutes
Cooking time: 10 minutes
Serving: 3 to 6
Ingredients
• Salt to taste
• 3 tbsp olive oil
• three or more cloves garlic, lightly smashed and peeled
• 3 or more anchovy fillets
• 1 28-ounce can whole plum tomatoes
• Freshly ground black pepper to taste
• ½ cup of pitted black olives, preferably oil-cured
• 2 tbsp capers
• Crushed red pepper flakes to taste
• 1-pound linguine or other long pasta
Direction:
1. Carry pot of water to bubble and salt it. Warm 2 tbsp oil with garlic and anchovies in skillet over medium-low warmth. Cook, blending infrequently, until garlic is delicately brilliant.
2. Channel tomatoes and smash with fork or hands. Add skillet, with some salt and pepper. Raise warmth to medium-high and cook, mixing infrequently, until tomatoes separate and blend gets sassy, around 10 minutes. Mix in olives, tricks and red pepper drops, and keep on stewing.
3. Cook pasta, mixing once in a while, until it is delicate however not soft. Channel rapidly and throw with sauce and remaining tbsp of oil. Taste and change flavors as essential, embellish with spices on the off chance that you like, and serve.
Nutrition:
Calories: 293kcal
Fat: 8.74g
Carbohydrates: 53.54 g
Protein: 3.39 g

339. Italian Chicken Pasta

Preparation Time: 10 minutes
Cooking Time: 9 minutes
Servings: 8
Ingredients:
• 1 lb. chicken breast, skinless, boneless, and cut into chunks
• 1/2 cup cream cheese
• 1 cup mozzarella cheese, shredded
• 1 1/2 tsp Italian seasoning
• 1 tsp garlic, minced
• 1 cup mushrooms, diced
• 1/2 onion, diced
• 2 tomatoes, diced
• 2 cups of water
• 16 oz whole wheat penne pasta
• Pepper
• Salt

Directions:
1. Add all ingredients except cheeses into the inner pot of instant pot and stir well.
2. Seal pot with lid and cook on high for 9 minutes.
3. Once done, allow to release pressure naturally for 5 minutes then release remaining using quick release. Remove lid.
4. Add cheeses and stir well and serve.

Nutrition: calories 328, fat 9, fiber 4, carbs 40, protein 24

340. Delicious Greek Chicken Pasta

Preparation Time: 10 minutes
Cooking Time: 10 minutes
Servings: 6
Ingredients:
- 2 chicken breasts, skinless, boneless, and cut into chunks
- 1/2 cup olives, sliced
- 2 cups vegetable stock
- 12 oz Greek vinaigrette dressing
- 1 lb. whole grain pasta
- Pepper
- Salt

Directions:
1. Add all ingredients into the inner pot of instant pot and stir well.
2. Seal pot with lid and cook on high for 10 minutes.
3. Once done, release pressure using quick release. Remove lid.
4. Stir well and serve.

Nutrition: calories 320, fat 24, fiber 4, carbs 11, protein 19

341. Long-Grain Rice Congee & Vietnamese Chicken

Preparation time: 10 minutes
Cooking time: 1 hour 15 minutes
Servings: 4
Ingredients
- 1/8 cup uncooked jasmine rice
- 1 whole chicken (2.5 lb.)
- 3 pieces of fresh ginger root
- 1 stalk of lemongrass
- 1 tablespoon of salt
- 1/4 cup chopped coriander
- 1/8 cup chopped fresh chives
- ground black pepper to taste
- 1 lime, cut into 8 quarters

Direction:
1. Place the chicken in a pan. Pour enough water to cover the chicken. Add ginger, lemongrass, and salt; bring to a boil. Lower the heat, cover and let it simmer for 1 hour to an hour and a half.
2. Filter the broth and put the broth back in a pan. Allow the chicken to cool, then remove the bones and skin and tear into small pieces; put aside.
3. Add the rice to the broth and bring to a boil. Turn the heat to medium and cook for 30 minutes, stirring occasionally. Adjust if necessary with extra water or salt. The congee is done, but you can still cook for 45 minutes for better consistency.
4. Pour the congee into bowls and garnish with chicken, coriander, chives, and pepper. Squeeze the lime juice to taste.

Nutrition: Per serving: 642 calories; 42.3 g fat; 9.8 g of carbohydrates; 53 g of protein; 210 mg cholesterol; 1943 mg of sodium

342. Wild Rice Soup & Creamy Chicken

Preparation time: 5 minutes
Cooking time: 20 minutes
Servings: 8
Ingredients
- 4 cups of chicken broth
- 2 cups of water
- 2 half-cooked and boneless chicken breast, grated
- 1 pack (4.5 ounces) of long-grain fast-cooking rice with a spice pack
- 1/2 teaspoon of salt
- 1/2 teaspoon of ground black pepper
- 3/4 cup flour
- 1/2 cup butter
- 2 cups thick cream

Direction:
1. Combine broth, water, and chicken in a large saucepan over medium heat. Bring to a boil, stir in the rice, and save the seasoning package. Cover and remove from heat.
2. In a small bowl, mix the flour with salt and pepper. Using a medium-sized pan, melt some butter over medium heat. Stir the contents of the herb bag until the mixture bubbles. Reduce the heat and add the flour mixture to the tablespoon to form a roux. Stir the cream little by little until it is completely absorbed and smooth. Bake until thick, 5 minutes.
3. Add the cream mixture to the stock and rice — Cook over medium heat for 10 to 15 minutes.

Nutrition Per serving: 462 calories; 36.5 grams of fat; 22.6 g carbohydrates; 12 g of protein; 135 mg cholesterol; 997 mg of sodium.

343. Best Spanish Rice

Preparation time: 10 minutes
Cooking time: 25 minutes
Servings: 5
Ingredients
- 2 tablespoons oil
- 2 tablespoons chopped onion
- 1 1/2 cups uncooked white rice
- 2 cups chicken broth
- 1 cup chunky salsa

Direction:
1. Heat the oil in a large frying pan over medium heat. Stir the onion and cook until tender, about 5 minutes.
2. Mix the rice in a pan, stirring often. When the rice starts to brown, stir in the chicken stock and salsa. Lower the heat, cover, and simmer for 20 minutes until liquid is absorbed.

Nutrition: Per serving: 286 calories; 6.2 g fat; 50.9 g carbohydrates; 5.7 g of protein; 2 mg of cholesterol; 697 mg of sodium.

344. Classic Rice Pilaf

Preparation time: 10 minutes
Cooking time: 13 minutes
Servings: 6
Ingredients
- 2 tablespoons butter
- 2 tablespoons olive oil
- 1/2 onion, minced
- 2 cups long-grain white rice

- 3 cups chicken broth
- 1 1/2 teaspoons of salt
- 1 pinch of saffron (optional)
- 1/4 teaspoon of cayenne pepper

Direction:

1. Preheat the oven to 175 ° C (350 ° F).
2. Heat the butter until it reaches liquid form.
3. Add melted butter and olive oil in a large saucepan over medium heat.
4. Add and cook minced onion, continuously stirring until the onion is light brown in color, 7 to 8 minutes. Remove from the heat.
5. Combine rice and onion in a 9 x 13-inch baking dish on a baking sheet. Mix well to cover the rice.
6. Mix chicken broth, salt, saffron, and cayenne pepper in a pan. Bring to a boil, reduce the heat and simmer for 5 minutes.
7. Pour the chicken stock mixture over the rice in the casserole and mix. Spread the mixture evenly over the bottom of the pan. Cover firmly with sturdy aluminum foil.
8. Bake in the preheated oven for 35 minutes. Remove from the oven and leave under cover for 10 minutes. Remove the aluminum foil and stir with a fork to separate the rice grains.

Nutrition Per serving: 312 calories; 9.1 g of fat; 51.7 g of carbohydrates; 5 g of protein; 11 mg cholesterol; 956 mg of sodium

345. Sarah's Rice Pilaf

Preparation time: 10 minutes
Cooking time: 25 minutes
Servings: 4 servings
Ingredients
- 2 tablespoons butter
- 1/2 cup orzo
- 1/2 cup diced onion
- 2 cloves finely chopped garlic
- 1/2 cup uncooked white rice
- 2 cups of chicken broth

Direction:

1. Melt the butter in a frying pan with a lid on medium heat. Boil and mix the orzo pasta golden brown.
2. Stir in the onion and cook until it is transparent, then add the garlic and cook for 1 minute.
3. Stir in the rice and chicken broth. Turn up the heat and bring to a boil. Lower the heat to medium, cover, and simmer until the rice is soft and the liquid is absorbed for 20 to 25 minutes. Remove from heat and let stand for 5 minutes, then stir with a fork.

Nutrition: Per serving: 244 calories; 6.5 g of fat; 40 g carbohydrates; 5.9 g of protein; 18 mg cholesterol; 524 mg of sodium.

346. Homemade Fried Rice

Preparation time: 10 minutes
Cooking time: 10 minutes
Servings: 8
Ingredients
- 1 1/2 cup uncooked white rice
- 3 tablespoons sesame oil
- 1 small onion, minced
- 1 clove of garlic, minced
- 1 cup peeled shrimp
- 1/2 cup diced ham
- 1 cup chopped cooked chicken fillet
- 2 celery stalks, minced

- 2 carrots, peeled and diced
- 1 green pepper, minced
- 1/2 cup of green peas
- 1 beaten egg
- 1/4 cup soy sauce

Direction:

1. Cook the rice according to the instructions on the package.
2. While cooking rice, heat a wok or large frying pan over medium heat. Pour in the sesame oil and sauté in the onion until golden brown. Add the garlic, shrimp, ham, and chicken. Cook until the shrimp are pink.
3. Reduce the heat and stir in celery, carrot, green pepper, and peas. Bake until the vegetables are soft. Stir in the beaten egg and cook until the egg is scrambled and firm.
4. When the rice is cooked, mix it with the vegetables and soy sauce.

Nutrition Per serving: 236 calories; 8.4 g fat; 26.4 g carbohydrates; 13 g of protein; 59 mg cholesterol; 603 mg of sodium

347. Cranberry Rice

Preparation time: 5 minutes
Cooking time: 55 minutes
Servings: 6
Ingredients
- 2/3 cup uncooked brown rice
- 1 1/2 cups water
- 2 tablespoons canned cranberry sauce
- 1/2 cup of dried cranberries
- salt and black pepper to taste
- 1/4 cup chopped pecans

Direction:

1. Bring the brown rice and 1 1/2 cups of water to a boil in a pan over high heat. Reduce heat to low, cover, and simmer until the rice is soft and almost all of the liquid has been absorbed for 45 to 50 minutes.
2. Squash the cranberry sauce in a small bowl with a fork and mix with the brown rice. Cover and let steam for about 5 minutes.
3. Put the dried cranberries in a bowl microwave and cook them on high heat in the microwave for about 30 seconds. Stir the cranberries into the rice. Season with salt and black pepper; sprinkle with pecans.

Nutrition:

Per serving: 129 calories; 3.7 g of fat; 23.4 grams of carbohydrates; 1.6 g of protein; 0 mg of cholesterol; 4 mg of sodium.

348. Kickin' Rice

Preparation time: 10 minutes
Cooking time: 23 minutes
Servings: 6
Ingredients
- 1 tablespoon of vegetable oil
- 1 cup of long-grain white rice
- 1 can of chopped green peppers
- 1 teaspoon of ground black pepper
- 2 cups of chicken broth

Direction:

1. Heat the vegetable oil in a pan over medium heat. Stir the rice in hot oil.
2. Add the green peppers and keep cooking until the rice starts to turn a little brown, 2 to 3 minutes.
3. Season the rice with pepper. Pour the stock into the pan; bring to a boil.

4. Reduce the heat to low, cover the pan and cook until the broth has been absorbed and the rice is soft, about 20 minutes.
Nutrition:
Per serving: 83 calories; 2.6 g fat; 13 grams of carbohydrates 1.9 g of protein; 2 mg of cholesterol; 757 mg of sodium.

349. Garlic Rice

Preparation time: 5 minutes
Cooking time: 3 minutes
Servings: 4
Ingredients
- 2 tablespoons vegetable oil
- 1 1/2 tablespoons chopped garlic
- 2 tablespoons ground pork
- 4 cups cooked white rice
- 1 1/2 teaspoons of garlic salt
- ground black pepper to taste

Direction:
1. Heat the oil in a large frying pan over medium heat. When the oil is hot, add the garlic and ground pork. Boil and stir until garlic is golden brown.
2. Stir in cooked white rice and season with garlic salt and pepper. Bake and stir until the mixture is hot and well mixed for about 3 minutes.
Nutrition:
Per serving: 293 calories; 9 g fat; 45.9 g carbohydrates; 5.9 g of protein; 6 mg cholesterol; 686 mg of sodium

350. Sweet Rice

Preparation time: 10 minutes
Cooking time: 40 minutes
Servings: 6
Ingredients
- 1 cup uncooked long-grain white rice
- 2 tablespoons unsalted butter
- 2 cups of water
- 2 cups of whole milk
- 1 tablespoon of all-purpose flour
- 1/3 cup white sugar
- 1 egg
- 1 1/2 teaspoon vanilla extract
- 1 cup whole milk
- 2/3 cup thick cream
- 1/2 cup raisins (optional)
- 1/2 teaspoon ground cinnamon

Direction:
1. Add rice and butter to water in a large saucepan and bring to boil over high heat. Once it begins to bubble, lower the heat to medium, cover, and simmer until the rice is soft and the liquid is absorbed for 20 to 25 minutes.
2. Mix 2 cups of milk, flour, sugar, egg, and vanilla extract in a bowl and pour the milk mixture over the cooked rice. Mix and simmer for 15 minutes over low heat.
3. Stir in 1 cup of whole milk, cream, raisins, and cinnamon until it is well mixed and let it cool for a few minutes.
Nutrition:
Per serving: 418 calories; 18.7 grams of fat; 54.3 g carbohydrates; 8.6 g of protein; 90 mg of cholesterol; 76 mg of sodium.

351. Gourmet Mushroom Risotto

Preparation time: 20 minutes
Cooking time: 25 minutes
Servings: 6
Ingredients
- 1 kg Portobello mushrooms, minced,
- 1 pound of white mushrooms, minced
- 2 shallots, diced
- 3 tablespoons olive oil, divided
- 1 1/2 cup Arborio rice
- Salt and black pepper to taste
- 1/2 cup dry white wine
- 4 tablespoons butter
- 3 tablespoons finely chopped chives
- 6 cups chicken broth, divided
- 1/3 cup of freshly grated Parmesan cheese

Direction:
1. Heat the broth in a saucepan over low heat.
2. Heat 2 tablespoons of olive oil in a huge saucepan over medium heat. Stir in the mushrooms and cook until soft, about 3 minutes. Now remove the mushrooms and their liquid and set aside.
3. Put 1 tablespoon of olive oil in the pan and stir in the shallots. Cook for 1 minute and add the rice, stirring, to cover with oil for about 2 minutes. When the rice has turned a pale golden color, pour the wine constantly, stirring until the wine is completely absorbed.
4. Add 1/2 cup of rice broth and mix until the broth has been absorbed. Continue to add 1/2 cup of broth at a time, constantly stirring, until the liquid is absorbed and the rice is al dente, about 15 to 20 minutes.
5. Then remove from the heat and stir in the mushrooms with their liquid, butter, chives, and Parmesan cheese. Season with salt and pepper.
Nutrition:
Per serving: 431 calories; 16.6 g fat; 56.6 g carbohydrates; 11.3 g of protein; 29 mg of cholesterol; 1131 mg of sodium.

352. John's Beans and Rice

Preparation time: 20 minutes
Cooking time: 17 minutes
Servings: 8
Ingredients
- 1 lb. dry red beans
- 1 tablespoon of vegetable oil
- 12 grams of andouille sausage, diced
- 1 cup finely chopped onion
- 3/4 cup chopped celery
- 3/4 cup poblano peppers
- 4 cloves of garlic, minced
- 2 pints of chicken broth or more if necessary
- 1 smoked ham shank
- 2 bay leaves
- 1 teaspoon dried thyme
- 1/2 teaspoon cayenne pepper
- 1 teaspoon freshly ground black pepper
- 2 tablespoons chopped green onion,
- 4 cups cooked white rice

Direction:
1. Place the beans in a large container and cover them with a few centimeters of cold water; soak overnight. Drain and rinse.
2. Heat the vegetable oil in a large saucepan over medium heat. Cook and stir sausage in hot oil for 5 to 7 minutes. Stir in onion, celery, and poblano pepper in sausage; cook and stir until the vegetables soften and start to become transparent, 5 to 10 minutes. Add the garlic to the sausage mixture; cook and stir until fragrant, about 1 minute.
3. Stir in brown beans, chicken broth, ham shank, bay leaf, black pepper, thyme, cayenne pepper, and sausage mixture;

bring to a boil, reduce the heat and stir occasionally, for an hour and a half.

4. Season with salt and simmer until the beans are soft, the meat is soft, and the desired consistency is achieved, 1 1/2 to 2 hours more. Season with salt.

5. Put the rice in bowls, place the red bean mixture on the rice and garnish with green onions.

Nutrition:

Per serving: 542 calories; 20.5 grams of fat; 62.9 g carbohydrates; 25.9 g of protein; 46 mg cholesterol; 1384 mg of sodium.

353. Creamy Chicken & Wild Rice Soup

Preparation time: 10 minutes
Cooking time: 20 minutes
Servings: 8
Ingredients

- 2 cups of water
- 4 cups chicken broth
- 2 boneless chicken fillet and cooked, grated
- 1 pack (4.5 oz) long-grain fast-cooking rice with a spice pack
- ½ teaspoon of salt
- ½ teaspoon of ground black pepper
- ¾ cup of all-purpose flour
- ½ cup of butter
- 2 cups thick cream

Direction:

1. Combine broth, water, and chicken in a large saucepan over medium heat. Bring to a boil, stir in the rice, and save the seasoning package. Cover and remove from heat.

2. Combine salt, pepper, and flour in a small bowl. Melt the butter in a medium-sized pan over medium heat. Stir the contents of the herb bag until the mixture bubbles. Reduce the heat and add the flour mixture to the tablespoon to form a roux. Stir the cream little by little until it is completely absorbed and smooth. Bake until thick, 5 minutes.

3. Add the cream mixture to the stock and rice. Cook over medium heat for 10 to 15 minutes.

Nutrition:

Per serving: 462 calories; 36.5 g total fat; 135 mg cholesterol; 997 mg of sodium. 22.6 g carbohydrates; 12 g of protein;

354. Carrot Rice

Preparation time: 5 minutes
Cooking time: 20 minutes
Servings: 6
Ingredients

- 2 cups of water
- 1 cube chicken broth
- 1 grated carrot
- 1 cup uncooked long-grain rice

Direction:

1. Bring the water to a boil in a medium-sized saucepan over medium heat. Place in the bouillon cube and let it dissolve.

2. Stir in the carrots and rice and bring to a boil again.

3. Lower the heat, cover, and simmer for 20 minutes.

4. Remove from heat and leave under cover for 5 minutes.

Nutrition:

Per serving: 125 calories; 0.3 g of fat; 27.1 g carbohydrates; 2.7 g of protein; <1 mg cholesterol; 199 mg of sodium.

355. Rice Sauce

Preparation time: 15 minutes
Cooking time: 30 minutes
Servings: 6
Ingredients

- 3 cups of cooked rice
- 1 1/4 cup grated Monterey Jack cheese, divided
- 1 cup canned or frozen corn
- 1/2 cup of milk
- 1/3 cup of sour cream
- 1/2 cup chopped green onions

Direction:

1. Preheat the oven to 175 ° C (350 ° F).

2. Combine rice, a cup of cheese, corn, milk, sour cream, and green onions in a medium-sized bowl. Put in a 1-liter baking dish and sprinkle the rest of the cheese over it.

3. Bake in the preheated oven for 25 to 30 minutes or until cheese is melted and the dish is hot.

Nutrition:

Per serving: 253 calories; 10.7 g of fat; 29.7 g of carbohydrates; 9.8 g of protein; 28 mg cholesterol; 225 mg of sodium.

356. Brown Rice

Preparation time: 5 minutes
Cooking time: 30 minutes
Servings: 4
Ingredients

- 1 1/2 cup uncooked long-grain white rice
- 1 (14 grams) beef broth
- 1 condensed soup of French onions
- 1/4 cup melted butter
- 1 tablespoon Worcestershire sauce
- 1 tablespoon dried basil leaves

Direction:

1. Preheat the oven to 175 ° C (350 ° F).

2. In a 2-quarter oven dish, combine rice, broth, soup, butter, Worcestershire sauce, and basil.

3. Cook for 1 hour, stirring after 30 minutes.

Nutrition:

Per serving: 425 calories; 13.5 grams of fat; 66.2 g carbohydrates; 8.8 g of protein; 33 mg cholesterol; 1091 mg of sodium

357. Rice Lasagna

Preparation time: 20 minutes
Cooking time: 30 minutes
Servings: 8
Ingredients

- 1-pound ground beef
- spaghetti sauce in 1 (26 oz) jars
- 3 cups cooked rice, cooled, 1/2 teaspoon garlic powder
- 2 eggs, lightly beaten, 3/4 cup grated Parmesan cheese, divided
- 2 1/4 cup grated mozzarella cheese
- 2 cups of cottage cheese

Direction:

1. Preheat the oven to 190 ° C.

2. Heat a large frying pan over medium heat. Fry and stir the meat in a hot pan until golden brown and crumbly, 5 to 7 minutes; drain the fat and discard it. Add the spaghetti sauce and garlic powder.

3. Mix the rice, eggs, and 1/4 cup Parmesan cheese in a bowl. Mix 2 cups mozzarella, cottage cheese, and 1/4 cup Parmesan cheese in another bowl.

4. Spread half of the rice mixture in a 3-liter baking dish, followed by half of the cheese mixture and half of the meat sauce. Repeat the layers. Sprinkle 1/4 cup Parmesan cheese and 1/4 cup mozzarella on the last layer of meat sauce.

5. Bake in the preheated oven until cheese has melted and the sauce is bubbling, 20 to 25 minutes.

Nutrition:
Per serving: 461 calories; 20.3 g of fat; 35.3 g carbohydrates; 32 g of protein; 118 mg of cholesterol; 975 mg of sodium

358. Rice Milk

Preparation time: 5 minutes
Cooking time: 3 minutes
Servings: 4
Ingredients
- 4 cups cold water
- 1 cup cooked rice
- 1 teaspoon vanilla extract (optional)

Direction:
1. Combine water, cooked rice, and vanilla extract in a blender; blend until smooth, about 3 minutes.
2. Chill before serving.

Nutrition:
Per serving: 54 calories; 0.1 g fat; 11.3 g carbohydrates; 1.1 g protein; 0 mg cholesterol; 8 mg sodium.

359. Pasta Fazool (Pasta e Fagioli)

Preparation time: 10 minutes
Cooking time: 30 minutes
Servings: 2
Ingredients
- 1 tablespoon of olive oil,
- 12 ounces of Italian sweet bulk sausage
- 1 celery stem, diced
- 1/2 yellow onion, chopped
- 3/4 cup dry macaroni
- 1/4 cup tomato puree
- 3 cups chicken broth or more if necessary, divided
- salt and freshly ground black pepper
- 1/4 teaspoon of ground red pepper flakes
- 1/4 teaspoon dried oregano
- 3 cups finely chopped chard
- 1 can cannellini (15 oz), drained
- 1/4 cup grated Parmesan-Reggiano cheese

Direction:
1. Heat the oil in a frying pan over medium heat. Brown the sausage by cutting it into small pieces, about 5 minutes. Return the heat to medium. Add diced celery and chopped onion. Bake until the onions are transparent, 4 to 5 minutes. Add the dry pasta. Boil and stir for 2 minutes.
2. Stir the tomato puree until smooth, 2 to 3 minutes. Add 3 cups of broth. Turn up the heat and let it simmer.
3. Season with salt, black pepper, pepper flakes, and oregano.
4. Lower heat once soup comes to a boil, then let it simmer for about 5 minutes, often stirring. Check the consistency of the soup and add stock if necessary.
5. Place the chopped chard in a bowl. And soak with cold water to rinse the leaves; some grain will fall to the bottom of the bowl. Transfer the chard to a colander to drain briefly; add to the soup. Boil and stir until the leaves fade, 2 to 3 minutes.

6. Stir in the white beans; keep cooking, stir until the pasta is cooked, 4 or 5 minutes. Remove from heat and stir in the grated cheese. Serve garnished with grated cheese, if desired.

Nutrition:
Per serving: 888 calories; 43.8 g of fat; 77.3 g carbohydrates; 43.8 g of protein; 84 mg of cholesterol; 4200 mg of sodium.

360. Pasta Orecchiette Pasta

Preparation time: 15 minutes
Cooking time: 25 minutes
Servings: 2
Ingredients
- 2 tablespoons olive oil
- 1/2 onion, salt, diced to taste
- 8 grams of spicy Italian sausage
- 3 1/2 cups low-sodium chicken broth, divided
- 1 1/4 cup orecchiette pasta
- 1/2 cup of arugula
- 1/4 cup finely grated Parmigiano-Reggiano cheese

Direction:
1. Heat the olive oil in a deep-frying pan over medium heat. Cook and stir the onion with a pinch of salt in hot oil until the onion is soft and golden brown, 5 to 7 minutes. Stir the sausages with onions; cook and stir until the sausages are golden brown, 5 to 7 minutes.
2. Pour 1 1/2 cup chicken stock into the sausage mixture and bring to a boil. Add the pasta to the orecchiette; boil and mix the pasta in a warm broth, add the remaining broth when the liquid is absorbed until the pasta is well cooked, and most of the broth is absorbed, about 15 minutes.
3. Spread the pasta in bowls and sprinkle with Parmigiano-Reggiano cheese.

Nutrition:
Per serving: 662 calories; 39.1 grams of fat; 46.2 g carbohydrates; 31.2 g of protein; 60 mg cholesterol; 1360 mg of sodium.

361. Bell Peppers 'n Tomato-Chickpea Rice

Preparation time: 18 minutes
Cooking Time: 35 minutes
Serving: 4
Ingredients:
- 2 tablespoons olive oil
- 1/2 chopped red bell pepper
- 1/2 chopped green bell pepper
- 1/2 chopped yellow pepper
- 1/2 chopped red pepper
- 1 medium onion, chopped
- 1 clove garlic, minced
- 2 cups cooked jasmine rice
- 1 teaspoon tomato paste
- 1 cup chickpeas
- salt to taste
- 1/2 teaspoon paprika
- 1 small tomato, chopped
- Parsley for garnish

Directions for Cooking:
1) In a large mixing bowl, whisk well olive oil, garlic, tomato paste, and paprika. Season with salt generously.
2) Mix in rice and toss well to coat in the dressing.
3) Add remaining ingredients and toss well to mix.
4) Let salad rest to allow flavors to mix for 15 minutes.
5) Toss one more time and adjust salt to taste if needed.

6) Garnish with parsley and serve.
Nutrition:
Calories per serving: 490; Carbs: 93.0g; Protein: 10.0g; Fat: 8.0g

362. Seafood and Veggie Pasta

Preparation time: 20 minutes
Cooking Time: 20 minutes
Serving: 4,
Ingredients:
- ¼ tsp pepper
- ¼ tsp salt
- 1 lb. raw shelled shrimp
- 1 lemon, cut into wedges
- 1 tbsp butter
- 1 tbsp olive oil
- 2 5-oz cans chopped clams, drained (reserve 2 tbsp clam juice)
- 2 tbsp dry white wine
- 4 cloves garlic, minced
- 4 cups zucchini, spiraled (use a veggie spiralizer)
- 4 tbsp Parmesan Cheese
- Chopped fresh parsley to garnish

Directions for Cooking:
1) Ready the zucchini and spiralize with a veggie spiralizer. Arrange 1 cup of zucchini noodle per bowl. Total of 4 bowls.
2) On medium fire, place a large nonstick saucepan and heat oil and butter.
3) For a minute, sauté garlic. Add shrimp and cook for 3 minutes until opaque or cooked.
4) Add white wine, reserved clam juice and clams. Bring to a simmer and continue simmering for 2 minutes or until half of liquid has evaporated. Stir constantly.
5) Season with pepper and salt. And if needed add more to taste.
6) Remove from fire and evenly distribute seafood sauce to 4 bowls.
7) Top with a tablespoonful of Parmesan cheese per bowl, serve and enjoy.
Nutrition:
Calories per Serving: 324.9; Carbs: 12g; Protein: 43.8g; Fat: 11.3g

363. Breakfast Salad From Grains and Fruits

Preparation time: 15 minutes
Cooking Time: 20 minutes
Serving: 6
Ingredients:
- ¼ tsp salt
- ¾ cup bulgur
- ¾ cup quick cooking brown rice
- 1 8-oz low fat vanilla yogurt
- 1 cup raisins
- 1 Granny Smith apple
- 1 orange
- 1 Red delicious apple
- 3 cups water

Directions for Cooking:
1) On high fire, place a large pot and bring water to a boil.
2) Add bulgur and rice. Lower fire to a simmer and cook for ten minutes while covered.
3) Turn off fire, set aside for 2 minutes while covered.
4) In baking sheet, transfer and evenly spread grains to cool.

5) Meanwhile, peel oranges and cut into slices. Chop and core apples.
6) Once grains are cool, transfer to a large serving bowl along with fruits.
7) Add yogurt and mix well to coat.
8) Serve and enjoy.
Nutrition:
Calories per Serving: 48.6; Carbs: 23.9g; Protein: 3.7g; Fat: 1.1g

364. Puttanesca Style Bucatini

Preparation time: 10 minutes
Cooking Time: 40 minutes
Serving: 4
Ingredients:
- 1 tbsp capers, rinsed
- 1 tsp coarsely chopped fresh oregano
- 1 tsp finely chopped garlic
- 1/8 tsp salt
- 12-oz bucatini pasta
- 2 cups coarsely chopped canned no-salt-added whole peeled tomatoes with their juice
- 3 tbsp extra virgin olive oil, divided
- 4 anchovy fillets, chopped
- 8 black Kalamata olives, pitted and sliced into slivers

Directions for Cooking:
1) Cook bucatini pasta according to package directions. Drain, keep warm, and set aside.
2) On medium fire, place a large nonstick saucepan and heat 2 tbsp oil.
3) Sauté anchovies until it starts to disintegrate.
4) Add garlic and sauté for 15 seconds.
5) Add tomatoes, sauté for 15 to 20 minutes or until no longer watery. Season with 1/8 tsp salt.
6) Add oregano, capers, and olives.
7) Add pasta, sautéing until heated through.
8) To serve, drizzle pasta with remaining olive oil and enjoy.
Nutrition:
Calories per Serving: 207.4; Carbs: 31g; Protein: 5.1g; Fat: 7g

365. Cinnamon Quinoa Bars

Preparation time: 15 minutes
Cooking Time: 30 minutes
Serving: 4
Ingredients:
- 2 ½ cups cooked quinoa
- 4 large eggs
- 1/3 cup unsweetened almond milk
- 1/3 cup pure maple syrup
- Seeds from ½ whole vanilla bean pod or 1 tbsp vanilla extract
- 1 ½ tbsp cinnamon
- 1/4 tsp salt

Directions for Cooking:
1) Preheat oven to 3750F.
2) Combine all ingredients into large bowl and mix well.
3) In an 8 x 8 Baking pan, cover with parchment paper.
4) Pour batter evenly into baking dish.
5) Bake for 25-30 minutes or until it has set. It should not wiggle when you lightly shake the pan because the eggs are fully cooked.
6) Remove as quickly as possible from pan and parchment paper onto cooling rack.
7) Cut into 4 pieces.

8) Enjoy on its own, with a small spread of almond or nut butter or wait until it cools to enjoy the next morning.
Nutrition:
Calories per serving: 285; Carbs: 46.2g; Protein: 8.5g; Fat: 7.4g

366. Creamy Alfredo Fettuccine

Preparation time: 20 minutes
Cooking Time: 25 minutes
Serving: 4
Ingredients:
- Grated parmesan cheese
- ½ cup freshly grated parmesan cheese
- 1/8 tsp freshly ground black pepper
- ½ tsp salt
- 1 cup whipping cream
- 2 tbsp butter
- 8 oz dried fettuccine, cooked and drained
Directions for Cooking:
1) On medium high fire, place a big fry pan and heat butter.
2) Add pepper, salt and cream and gently boil for three to five minutes.
3) Once thickened, turn off fire and quickly stir in ½ cup of parmesan cheese. Toss in pasta, mix well.
4) Top with another batch of parmesan cheese and serve.
Nutrition:
Calories per Serving: 202; Carbs: 21.1g; Protein: 7.9g; Fat: 10.2g

367. Greek Couscous Salad and Herbed Lamb Chops

Preparation time: 20 minutes
Cooking Time: 30 minutes
Serving: 4
Ingredients:
- ¼ tsp salt
- ½ cup crumbled feta
- ½ cup whole wheat couscous
- 1 cup water
- 1 medium cucumber, peeled and chopped
- 1 tbsp finely chopped fresh parsley
- 1 tbsp minced garlic
- 2 ½ lbs. lamb loin chops, trimmed of fat
- 2 medium tomatoes, chopped
- 2 tbsp finely chopped fresh dill
- 2 tsp extra virgin olive oil
- 3 tbsp lemon juice
Directions for Cooking:
1) On medium saucepan, add water and bring to a boil.
2) In a small bowl, mix salt, parsley, and garlic. Rub onto lamb chops.
3) On medium high fire, place a large nonstick saucepan and heat oil.
4) Pan fry lamb chops for 5 minutes per side or to desired doneness. Once done, turn off fire and keep warm.
5) On saucepan of boiling water, add couscous. Once boiling, lower fire to a simmer, cover and cook for two minutes.
6) After two minutes, turn off fire, cover and let it stand for 5 minutes.
7) Fluff couscous with a fork and place into a medium bowl.
8) Add dill, lemon juice, feta, cucumber, and tomatoes in bowl of couscous and toss well to combine.
9) Serve lamb chops with a side of couscous and enjoy.
Nutrition:

Calories per Serving: 524.1; Carbs: 12.3g; Protein: 61.8g; Fat: 25.3g

368. Spanish Rice Casserole with Cheesy Beef

Preparation time: 15 minutes
Cooking Time: 32 minutes
Serving: 2
Ingredients:
- 2 tablespoons chopped green bell pepper
- 1/4 teaspoon Worcestershire sauce
- 1/4 teaspoon ground cumin
- 1/4 cup shredded Cheddar cheese
- 1/4 cup finely chopped onion
- 1/4 cup chile sauce
- 1/3 cup uncooked long grain rice
- 1/2-pound lean ground beef
- 1/2 teaspoon salt
- 1/2 teaspoon brown sugar
- 1/2 pinch ground black pepper
- 1/2 cup water
- 1/2 (14.5 ounce) can canned tomatoes
- 1 tablespoon chopped fresh cilantro
Directions for Cooking:
1) Place a nonstick saucepan on medium fire and brown beef for 10 minutes while crumbling beef. Discard fat.
2) Stir in pepper, Worcestershire sauce, cumin, brown sugar, salt, chile sauce, rice, water, tomatoes, green bell pepper, and onion. Mix well and cook for 10 minutes until blended and a bit tender.
3) Transfer to an ovenproof casserole and press down firmly. Sprinkle cheese on top and cook for 7 minutes at 4000F preheated oven. Broil for 3 minutes until top is lightly browned.
4) Serve and enjoy with chopped cilantro.
Nutrition:
Calories per serving: 460; Carbohydrates: 35.8g; Protein: 37.8g; Fat: 17.9g

369. Tasty Lasagna Rolls

Preparation time: 15 minutes
Cooking Time: 20 minutes
Serving: 6
Ingredients:
- ¼ tsp crushed red pepper
- ¼ tsp salt
- ½ cup shredded mozzarella cheese
- ½ cups parmesan cheese, shredded
- 1 14-oz package tofu, cubed
- 1 25-oz can of low-sodium marinara sauce
- 1 tbsp extra virgin olive oil
- 12 whole wheat lasagna noodles
- 2 tbsp Kalamata olives, chopped
- 3 cloves minced garlic
- 3 cups spinach, chopped
Directions for Cooking:
1) Put enough water on a large pot and cook the lasagna noodles according to package instructions. Drain, rinse and set aside until ready to use.
2) In a large skillet, sauté garlic over medium heat for 20 seconds. Add the tofu and spinach and cook until the spinach wilts. Transfer this mixture in a bowl and add parmesan olives, salt, red pepper and 2/3 cup of the marinara sauce.
3) In a pan, spread a cup of marinara sauce on the bottom. To make the rolls, place noodle on a surface and spread ¼

cup of the tofu filling. Roll up and place it on the pan with the marinara sauce. Do this procedure until all lasagna noodles are rolled.

4) Place the pan over high heat and bring to a simmer. Reduce the heat to medium and let it cook for three more minutes. Sprinkle mozzarella cheese and let the cheese melt for two minutes. Serve hot.

Nutrition:
Calories per Serving: 304; Carbs: 39.2g; Protein: 23g; Fat: 19.2g

370. Tortellini Salad with Broccoli

Preparation time: 20 minutes
Cooking Time: 20 minutes
Serving: 12
Ingredients:
- 1 red onion, chopped finely
- 1 cup sunflower seeds
- 1 cup raisins
- 3 heads fresh broccoli, cut into florets
- 2 tsp cider vinegar
- ½ cup white sugar
- ½ cup mayonnaise
- 20-oz fresh cheese filled tortellini

Directions for Cooking:
1) In a large pot of boiling water, cook tortellini according to manufacturer's instructions. Drain and rinse with cold water and set aside.
2) Whisk vinegar, sugar and mayonnaise to create your salad dressing.
3) Mix together in a large bowl red onion, sunflower seeds, raisins, tortellini and broccoli. Pour dressing and toss to coat.
4) Serve and enjoy.

Nutrition:
Calories per Serving: 272; Carbs: 38.7g; Protein: 5.0g; Fat: 8.1g

371. Simple Penne Anti-Pasto

Preparation time: 10 minutes
Cooking Time: 15 minutes
Serving: 4
Ingredients:
- ¼ cup pine nuts, toasted
- ½ cup grated Parmigiano-Reggiano cheese, divided
- 8oz penne pasta, cooked and drained
- 1 6oz jar drained, sliced, marinated and quartered artichoke hearts
- 1 7 oz jar drained and chopped sun-dried tomato halves packed in oil
- 3 oz chopped prosciutto
- 1/3 cup pesto
- ½ cup pitted and chopped Kalamata olives
- 1 medium red bell pepper

Directions for Cooking:
1) Slice bell pepper, discard membranes, seeds and stem. On a foiled lined baking sheet, place bell pepper halves, press down by hand and broil in oven for eight minutes. Remove from oven, put in a sealed bag for 5 minutes before peeling and chopping.
2) Place chopped bell pepper in a bowl and mix in artichokes, tomatoes, prosciutto, pesto and olives.
3) Toss in ¼ cup cheese and pasta. Transfer to a serving dish and garnish with ¼ cup cheese and pine nuts. Serve and enjoy!

Nutrition:

Calories per Serving: 606; Carbs: 70.3g; Protein: 27.2g; Fat: 27.6g

372. Red Quinoa Peach Porridge

Preparation time: 30 minutes
Cooking Time: 30 minutes
Serving: 1
Ingredients:
- ¼ cup old fashioned rolled oats
- ¼ cup red quinoa
- ½ cup milk
- 1 ½ cups water
- 2 peaches, peeled and sliced

Directions for Cooking:
1) On a small saucepan, place the peaches and quinoa. Add water and cook for 30 minutes.
2) Add the oatmeal and milk last and cook until the oats become tender.
3) Stir occasionally to avoid the porridge from sticking on the bottom of the pan.

Nutrition:
Calories per Serving: 456.6; Carbs: 77.3g; Protein: 16.6g; Fat: 9g

373. Spaghetti With Garlic, Olive Oil, And Red Pepper

Preparation time: 5 minutes
Cooking time: 10 minutes
Serving: 2
Ingredients:
- Salt
- 8 ounces spaghetti
- ¼ cup extra-virgin olive oil
- 4 garlic cloves, 3 lightly smashed and 1 minced
- ½ teaspoon red pepper flakes
- ¼ cup grated Parmesan cheese
- 1 tablespoon chopped fresh flat-leaf parsley

Direction:
1.Bring a large pot of water to a boil over high heat. Once boiling, salt the water to your liking, stir, and return to a boil. Add the spaghetti and cook according to package directions until al dente. Drain, reserving about ½ cup of the cooking water.
2.In a large skillet, heat the olive oil over low heat. Add the smashed garlic cloves and cook until golden brown. Remove the garlic from the pan and discard.
3.Add the red pepper flakes to the garlic-infused oil and warm for 1 minute before turning off the heat.
4.Once the spaghetti is cooked, add it to the pan.
5.Add the minced garlic and toss the spaghetti in the oil to coat. Add the reserved pasta water, a little at a time, as needed to help everything combine.
6.Sprinkle with the Parmesan and parsley.
COOKING TIP: When making pasta, it is important to salt the water for a flavorful dish generously. I generally use about 2 tablespoons of salt per pound of pasta. Add the salt after the water boils, stir to dissolve, and wait for the water to return to a boil, then add the pasta.

Nutrition Per Serving:
CALORIES: 722; Total Fat: 32g; Saturated Fat: 6g; Protein: 19g; Total Carbohydrates: 89g; Fiber: 4g; Sugar: 3g; Cholesterol: 11mg

374. Roasted Tomato Sauce With Pasta

Preparation time: 5 minutes
Cooking time: 35 minutes
Serving: 2
Ingredients:

- 4 large tomatoes, quartered
- 4 garlic cloves, unpeeled
- 3 basil sprigs, plus more for garnish
- 3 tablespoons extra-virgin olive oil
- 1 teaspoon salt, plus more for the pasta water
- ½ teaspoon freshly ground black pepper
- 8 ounces whole wheat pasta
- ¼ cup grated Parmesan or Romano cheese

Direction:
1. Preheat the oven to 450°F.
2. Put the tomatoes, garlic cloves, and basil sprigs in a small baking dish. Add the olive oil, salt, and pepper and toss to coat. Push the basil to the bottom so that it doesn't dry out.
3. Roast for 30 minutes.
4. Meanwhile, bring a large pot of water to boil over high heat. Once boiling, salt the water to your liking, stir, and return to a boil. Add the pasta and cook for 1 to 2 minutes less than the package directions for al dente, as it will continue to cook later with the sauce. Drain, reserving about ½ cup of the cooking water.
5. Remove the tomatoes from the oven. Discard the basil. Squeeze the roasted garlic from their skins and discard the skins.
6. Using a potato masher or large spoon, mash the tomato mixture. Be careful, as it will be hot and the juices can squirt out at you. Pull out any tomato skins; they should slip right off after being roasted.
7. Transfer the tomato mixture to a large skillet, set over medium-low heat, and add the cooked pasta. Toss, adding the reserved cooking water as needed to achieve the desired consistency.
8. Add the Parmesan. Continue to cook for 2 to 3 minutes, until everything is blended.
9. Garnish with fresh basil.
Nutrition PER SERVING:
CALORIES: 727; Total Fat: 26g; Saturated Fat: 5g; Protein: 22g; Total Carbohydrates: 102g; Fiber: 8g; Sugar: 13g; Cholesterol: 11mg

375. Pasta Primavera

Preparation time: 15 minutes
Cooking time: 15 minutes
Serving 4
Ingredients:

- 1 teaspoon salt, plus more for the pasta water
- 1-pound rotini
- 1 bell pepper (any color), seeded and cut into thin strips
- ½ cup broccoli florets
- 1-pint cherry or grape tomatoes, halved
- 2 carrots, shredded
- ½ cup fresh or frozen peas
- 1 scallion, thinly sliced
- 4 garlic cloves, thinly sliced
- ¼ cup extra-virgin olive oil
- ¼ teaspoon freshly ground black pepper
- ½ cup grated Parmesan or Romano cheese
- ½ cup chopped fresh flat-leaf parsley
- ½ teaspoon red pepper flakes

Direction:
1. Bring a large pot of water to a boil over high heat. Once boiling, salt the water to your liking, stir, and return to a boil. Add the rotini and cook according to package directions until al dente. Drain, reserving about ½ cup of the cooking water.
2. Meanwhile, in a large skillet, combine the bell pepper and broccoli. Add a few tablespoons of water, cover, and cook for about 5 minutes, until they start to soften. Drain any remaining water from the pan.
3. Add the tomatoes, carrots, peas, scallion, garlic, olive oil, salt, and black pepper. Stir to coat all the vegetables and cook for 3 minutes.
4 Add the cooked pasta, Parmesan, parsley, and red pepper flakes. Toss to combine, adding the reserved cooking water a little at a time as needed to thin out the sauce.
Nutrition PER SERVING:
CALORIES: 651; Total Fat: 19g; Saturated Fat: 4g; Protein: 21g; Total Carbohydrates: 99g; Fiber: 7g; Sugar: 7g; Cholesterol: 11mg

376. Lemon Linguine

Preparation time: 5 minutes
Cooking time: 10 minutes
Serving 2
Ingredients:

- Salt
- 8 ounces linguine
- 1/3 cup grated Parmesan or Romano cheese
- 1/3 cup extra-virgin olive oil
- ¼ cup freshly squeezed lemon juice
- Chopped fresh basil, for garnish

Direction:
1. Bring a large pot of water to a boil over high heat. Once boiling, salt the water to your liking, stir, and return to a boil. Add the linguine and cook according to package directions until al dente. Drain, reserving about ½ cup of the cooking water.
2. In a large bowl, whisk together the Parmesan, olive oil, and lemon juice.
3. Add the cooked pasta to the bowl and toss to combine. Add a little of the reserved cooking water as needed to help meld the flavors.
4. Garnish with fresh basil.
COOKING TIP: This pasta makes a perfect side dish for Greek Sheet Pan Chicken (here).
Nutrition PER SERVING:
CALORIES: 812; Total Fat: 42g; Saturated Fat: 8g; Protein: 20g; Total Carbohydrates: 89g; Fiber: 4g; Sugar: 4g; Cholesterol: 14mg

377. Fusilli Arrabbiata

Preparation time: 5 minutes
Cooking time: 20 minutes
Serving: 4
Ingredients:

- 3 tablespoons extra-virgin olive oil
- 1 small onion, finely chopped
- Splash dry red wine (optional)
- ½ serrano pepper, seeded and minced
- 2 garlic cloves, minced
- 1 (28-ounce) can crushed tomatoes
- 1 (6-ounce) can tomato paste
- ¾ cup water
- ½ to 1 teaspoon red pepper flakes

- 1 tablespoon dried oregano
- 1 teaspoon dried basil
- 1 teaspoon salt, plus more for the pasta water
- ½ teaspoon freshly ground black pepper
- 1-pound fusilli or rotini
- ¼ cup grated Parmesan or Romano cheese

Direction:

1. In a large, deep skillet, heat the olive oil over medium heat. Add the onion and cook for about 3 minutes, until just starting to soften.
2. Add a little red wine (if using) and cook for about 3 minutes, until the alcohol is burned off.
3. Add the serrano pepper and garlic and cook for about 1 minute, until fragrant.
4. Pour in the crushed tomatoes and stir everything together. Add the tomato paste and water and stir until the paste is blended in.
5. Add the red pepper flakes. You may want to do this a little at a time until you get your desired level of heat. You can always add more, but you can't take it out.
6. Season with the oregano, basil, salt, and black pepper.
7. Bring the sauce to a boil, then reduce the heat to a simmer.
8. Bring a large pot of water to a boil over high heat. Once boiling, salt the water to your liking, stir, and return to a boil. Add the fusilli and cook according to package directions until al dente. Drain.
9. Ladle the sauce over the pasta and top with the Parmesan cheese.

Nutrition PER SERVING:

CALORIES: 619; Total Fat: 14g; Saturated Fat: 3g; Protein: 21g; Total Carbohydrates: 104g; Fiber: 10g; Sugar: 15g; Cholesterol: 5mg

378. Spaghetti With Anchovy Sauce

Preparation time: 5 minutes
Cooking time: 10 minutes
Serving: 4
Ingredients:
- Salt
- 1-pound spaghetti
- ¼ cup extra-virgin olive oil
- 1 (2-ounce) can oil-packed anchovy fillets, undrained
- 3 garlic cloves, minced
- ¼ cup chopped fresh flat-leaf parsley
- 1 teaspoon red pepper flakes
- ¼ teaspoon freshly ground black pepper
- 1 tablespoon bread crumbs

Direction:

1. Bring a large pot of water to a boil over high heat. Once boiling, salt the water to your liking, stir, and return to a boil. Add the spaghetti and cook according to package directions until al dente. Drain, reserving about ½ cup of the cooking water.
2. Meanwhile, in a large skillet, heat the olive oil over low heat. Add the anchovy fillets with their oil and the garlic. Cook for 7 to 10 minutes, until the pasta is ready, stirring until the anchovies melt away and form a sauce.
3. Add the spaghetti, parsley, red pepper flakes, black pepper, and a little of the reserved cooking water, as needed, and toss to combine all the ingredients.
4. Sprinkle with the bread crumbs.

Nutrition PER SERVING:

CALORIES: 581; Total Fat: 17g; Saturated Fat: 3g; Protein: 19g; Total Carbohydrates: 87g; Fiber: 4g; Sugar: 3g; Cholesterol: 12mg

379. Vegetable Rice Bake

Preparation time: 15 minutes
Cooking time: 50 minutes
Serving: 4
Ingredients:
- 1½ teaspoons paprika
- 1½ teaspoons dried thyme
- 1 teaspoon Italian Herb Blend
- 1 teaspoon salt
- 1 teaspoon freshly ground black pepper
- 2 carrots, chopped
- 1 turnip, peeled and chopped
- 2 garlic cloves, minced
- 1½ cups long-grain white rice
- 1½ cups chicken broth
- 1½ cups water
- 1 head broccoli, cut into florets
- 2 ears corn, husks and silks removed, cut into thirds
- 1 red onion, cut into large chunks
- 1 red bell pepper, seeded and cut into chunks
- ¼ cup extra-virgin olive oil

Direction:

1. Preheat the oven to 400°F.
2. In a small bowl, combine the paprika, thyme, Italian herb blend, salt, and pepper.
3. In a 9-by-13-inch baking pan, combine the carrots, turnip, garlic, rice, broth, and water. Stir in 1 teaspoon of the spice mix. Cover with aluminum foil and bake for 20 minutes.
4. In a large bowl, combine the broccoli, corn pieces, red onion, and bell pepper. Add the olive oil and the remaining 5 teaspoons of spice mix and toss to coat.
5. Remove the baking pan from the oven and remove the foil. Increase the oven temperature to 425°F.
6. Scatter the broccoli and corn mixture over the surface of the rice mixture. Be sure to cover the top fully so that the rice stays hidden underneath.
7. Return the dish to the oven, uncovered, and bake for 30 minutes.

Nutrition PER SERVING:

CALORIES: 653; Total Fat: 23g; Saturated Fat: 4g; Protein: 30g; Total Carbohydrates: 86g; Fiber: 8g; Sugar: 6g; Cholesterol: 38mg

380. Baked Chicken Paella

Preparation time: 15 minutes
Cooking time: 1 hour 15 minutes
Serving: 4
Ingredients:
- 2 tablespoons extra-virgin olive oil
- 2 boneless, skinless chicken breasts, cut into bite-size pieces
- 1 teaspoon salt
- 1 teaspoon freshly ground black pepper
- 1 hot Italian pork sausage, sliced
- 1 medium onion, sliced
- 1 red or green bell pepper, seeded and sliced
- 3 garlic cloves, chopped
- ¼ cup dry white wine
- 1 cup Arborio rice

- 3 cups chicken broth, divided
- 1 cup canned or cooked chickpeas
- 1 cup baby spinach
- 2 large eggs, beaten

Direction:

1. Preheat the oven to 350°F.

2. In a large ovenproof skillet or braising pan, heat the olive oil over medium heat. Add the chicken and season with the salt and pepper. Brown the chicken on both sides, about 5 minutes total, then transfer to a plate.

3. Add the sausage, onion, bell pepper, and garlic to the skillet and cook for about 10 minutes, until the sausage is browned and the vegetables are softened. Transfer to the plate with the chicken.

4. Pour in the wine and deglaze the skillet, stirring to scrape up any browned bits on the bottom. Add the rice and mix with the wine until coated.

5. Add 1 cup of chicken broth, stir, and cook for 5 minutes.

6. Add the chickpeas and another 1 cup of broth and stir again. Return the browned chicken to the skillet on top of the rice and chickpeas.

7. Add the sausage, onion, and bell pepper mixture on top of the chicken. Push the chicken, sausage, and vegetables down into the rice and chickpea mixture, but do not stir. Add the remaining 1 cup of chicken broth and bring to a boil.

8. Cover the skillet, transfer to the oven, and bake for 40 minutes.

9. Uncover the skillet and take a peek at the dish. If it looks dry, add 1/3 cup water to the skillet. Add the spinach and push it down into the mixture slightly. Pour the beaten eggs on top.

10. Return to the oven and bake for another 10 minutes, uncovered, until the egg is completely cooked.

11. Let rest for 5 minutes before serving.

Nutrition PER SERVING:

CALORIES: 539; Total Fat: 21g; Saturated Fat: 5g; Protein: 30g; Total Carbohydrates: 52g; Fiber: 5g; Sugar: 3g; Cholesterol: 166mg

381. Pesto Zucchini Noodles

Preparation Time: 10 minutes
Cooking Time: 30 minutes
Servings: 4
Ingredients:
- 4 zucchinis, spiralized
- 1 tbsp avocado oil
- 2 garlic cloves, chopped
- 2/3 cup olive oil
- 1/3 cup parmesan cheese, grated
- 2 cups fresh basil
- 1/3 cup almonds
- 1/8 tsp. black pepper
- 3/4 tsp. sea salt

Directions:

1. Add zucchini noodles into a colander and sprinkle with ¼ teaspoon of salt.

2. Cover and let sit for 30 minutes.

3. Drain zucchini noodles well and pat dry.

4. Preheat the oven to 400°F.

5. Place almonds on a parchment-lined baking sheet and bake for 6-8 minutes.

6. Transfer toasted almonds into the food processor and process until coarse.

7. Add olive oil, cheese, basil, garlic, pepper, and remaining salt in a food processor with almonds and process until pesto texture.

8. Cook avocado oil in a large pan over medium-high heat.

9. Add zucchini noodles and cook for 4-5 minutes.

10. Pour pesto over zucchini noodles, mix well and cook for 1 minute.

11. Serve immediately with baked salmon.

Nutrition:

525 Calories

47g Fat

17g Protein

382. Herbed Wild Rice

Preparation Time: 10 minutes
Cooking Time: 4 to 6 hours
Servings: 8
Ingredients:
- 3 cups wild rice, rinsed and drained
- 6 cups roasted vegetable broth
- 1 onion, chopped
- ½ teaspoon salt
- ½ teaspoon dried thyme leaves
- ½ teaspoon dried basil leaves
- 1 bay leaf
- 1/3 cup chopped fresh flat-leaf parsley

Directions:

1. In a 6-quart slow cooker, mix the wild rice, vegetable broth, onion, salt, thyme, basil, and bay leaf.

2. Cover and cook on low for 4 to 6 hours, or until the wild rice is tender but still firm.

3. You can cook this dish longer until the wild rice pops, taking about 7 to 8 hours.

4. Remove and discard the bay leaf.

5. Stir in the parsley and serve.

Nutrition:

258 Calories

2g Fat

6g Protein

383. Barley Risotto

Preparation Time: 15 minutes
Cooking Time: 7 to 8 hours
Servings: 8
Ingredients:
- 2 ¼ cups hulled barley, rinsed
- 1 onion, finely chopped
- 4 garlic cloves, minced
- 1 (8-ounce) package button mushrooms, chopped
- 6 cups low-sodium vegetable broth
- ½ teaspoon dried marjoram leaves
- 1/8 teaspoon freshly ground black pepper
- 2/3 cup grated Parmesan cheese

Directions:

1. In a 6-quart slow cooker, mix the barley, onion, garlic, mushrooms, broth, marjoram, and pepper.

2. Cover and cook on low for 7 to 8 hours, or until the barley has absorbed most of the liquid and is tender, and the vegetables are tender.

3. Stir in the Parmesan cheese and serve.

Nutrition:

288 Calories

6g Fat

13g Protein

384. Risotto with Green Beans, Sweet Potatoes, and Peas

Preparation Time: 20 minutes
Cooking Time: 4 to 5 hours
Servings: 8
Ingredients:
- 1 large sweet potato, peeled and chopped
- 1 onion, chopped
- 5 garlic cloves, minced
- 2 cups short-grain brown rice
- 1 teaspoon dried thyme leaves
- 7 cups low-sodium vegetable broth
- 2 cups green beans, cut in half crosswise
- 2 cups frozen baby peas
- 3 tablespoons unsalted butter
- ½ cup grated Parmesan cheese

Directions:
1. In a 6-quart slow cooker, mix the sweet potato, onion, garlic, rice, thyme, and broth.
2. Cover and cook at low for 3 to 4 hours.
3. Mix in the green beans and frozen peas.
4. Cover and cook on low for 30 to 40 minutes or until the vegetables are tender.
5. Stir in the butter and cheese. Cover and cook on low for 20 minutes, then stir and serve.

Nutrition:
385 Calories 10g Fat 10g Protein

385. Maple Lemon Tempeh Cubes

Preparation Time: 10 minutes
Cooking Time: 30 to 40 minutes
Servings: 4
Ingredients:
- Tempeh; 1 packet
- Coconut oil; 2 to 3 teaspoons
- Lemon juice; 3 tablespoons
- Maple syrup; 2 teaspoons
- Bragg's Liquid Aminos or low-sodium tamari or (optional); 1 to 2 teaspoons
- Water; 2 teaspoons
- Dried basil; ¼ teaspoon
- Powdered garlic; ¼ teaspoon
- Black pepper (freshly grounded); to taste

Directions:
1. Heat your oven to 400 ° C.
2. Cut your tempeh block into squares in bite form.
3. Cook coconut oil at medium to high heat in a non-stick skillet.
4. When melted and heated, add the tempeh and cook on one side for 2-4 minutes, or until the tempeh turns down into a golden-brown color.
5. Flip the tempeh bits, and cook for 2-4 minutes.
6. Mix the lemon juice, tamari, maple syrup, basil, water, garlic, and black pepper while tempeh is browning.
7. Drop the mixture over tempeh, then swirl to cover the tempeh.
8. Sauté for 2-3 minutes, then turn the tempeh and sauté 1-2 minutes more.
9. The tempeh, on both sides, should be soft and orange.

Nutrition:
22 Carbohydrates 17g Fats 21g Protein

386. Quinoa with Vegetables

Preparation Time: 10 minutes
Cooking Time: 5 to 6 hours
Servings: 8
Ingredients:
- 2 cups quinoa, rinsed and drained
- 2 onions, chopped
- 2 carrots, peeled and sliced
- 1 cup sliced cremini mushrooms
- 3 garlic cloves, minced
- 4 cups low-sodium vegetable broth
- ½ teaspoon salt
- 1 teaspoon dried marjoram leaves
- 1/8 teaspoon freshly ground black pepper

Directions:
1. In a 6-quart slow cooker, mix all of the ingredients.
2. Cover and cook on low for 5 to 6 hours, or until the quinoa and vegetables are tender.
3. Stir the mixture and serve.

Nutrition:
204 Calories
3g Fat
7g Protein

387. Beef with Broccoli or Cauliflower Rice

Preparation Time: 10 minutes
Cooking Time: 30 minutes
Servings: 2
Ingredients:
- 1 lb. raw beef round steak, cut into strips.
- 1 tbsp + 2 tsp. low sodium soy sauce
- 1 Splenda packet
- ½ c. water
- 1 ½ c. broccoli florets
- 1 tsp. sesame or olive oil
- 2 cups cooked, grated cauliflower or frozen riced cauliflower

Directions:
1. Stir steak with soy sauce and let sit for about 15 minutes.
2. Heat oil over medium-high heat and stir-fry beef for 3-5 minutes or until browned.
3. Remove from pan.
4. Place broccoli, Splenda, and water.
5. Cover and cook for 5 minutes or until broccoli starts to turn tender, stirring sometimes.
6. Add beef back in and heat up thoroughly.
7. Serve the dish with cauliflower rice.

Nutrition:
16g Fats
9g Protein
211 Calories

388. Chicken Zucchini Noodles

Preparation Time: 10 minutes
Cooking Time: 25 minutes
Servings: 2
Ingredients:
- 1 large zucchini, spiralized
- 1 chicken breast, skinless & boneless
- ½ tbsp jalapeno, minced
- 2 garlic cloves, minced
- ½ tsp. ginger, minced
- ½ tbsp fish sauce
- 2 tbsp coconut cream

- ½ tbsp honey
- ½ lime juice
- 1 tbsp peanut butter
- 1 carrot, chopped
- 2 tbsp cashews, chopped
- ¼ cup fresh cilantro, chopped
- 1 tbsp olive oil
- Pepper
- Salt

Directions:
1. Cook olive oil in a pan over medium-high heat.
2. Season chicken breast with pepper and salt.
3. Once the oil is hot, add chicken breast into the pan and cook for 3-4 minutes per side or until cooked.
4. Remove chicken breast from pan.
5. Shred chicken breast with a fork and set aside.
6. In a small bowl, mix peanut butter, jalapeno, garlic, ginger, fish sauce, coconut cream, honey, and lime juice.
7. Set aside.
8. In a large mixing bowl, combine spiralized zucchini, carrots, cashews, cilantro, and shredded chicken.
9. Pour peanut butter mixture over zucchini noodles and toss to combine.
10.   Serve immediately and enjoy.

Nutrition:
353 Calories
21g Fat
25g Protein

389. Spinach and Feta Pasta

Preparation Time: 15 minutes
Cooking Time: 25 minutes
Servings: 4
Ingredients:
- 8 ounces uncooked penne pasta
- 1-ounce olive oil
- 2 ounces onion, chopped
- 1 minced garlic clove
- 24 ounces tomatoes, chopped
- 8 ounces fresh mushrooms, sliced
- 16 ounces packed spinach leaves
- A pinch of salt and pepper
- 1 pinch red pepper flakes
- 8 ounces crumbled feta cheese

Directions:
1. Boil salted water and cook pasta for 5-10 minutes or until the noodles are soft but firm to the taste. Drain the water from the pot.
2. Heat oil in a large frying pan on medium-high heat. Sauté onion and garlic until translucent.
3. Add tomatoes, mushrooms, spinach, salt, pepper, and red flakes in the pan and mix thoroughly, cooking for 2-3 minutes or until mixture is heated through.
4. Reduce heat and add pasta and cheese. Stir thoroughly until heated completely and serve.

Nutrition:
17g Protein
4.6g Fats
233 Calories

390. Slow Cooker Spaghetti

Preparation Time: 10 minutes
Cooking Time: 20 minutes
Servings: 8
Ingredients:
- 1-ounce olive oil
- 2 chopped small onions

- 4 ounces Italian sausage
- 16 ounces ground beef
- 1 teaspoon Italian seasoning, dried
- ½ teaspoon marjoram, dried
- 1 teaspoon of garlic powder
- 29-ounce canned tomato sauce
- 6 ounces canned tomato paste
- 1 4 ½ ounces canned Italian-style tomatoes, diced
- 1 4 ½ ounces canned Italian-style tomatoes, stewed
- ¼ teaspoon thyme leaves, dried
- ¼ teaspoon basil, dried
- ½ teaspoon of dried oregano
- 1/3-ounce garlic powder
- ½ -ounce white sugar

Directions:
1. Warm oil in a large frying pan on medium heat. Sautee onions and sausage in the oil until onions are translucent and sausage is browned evenly.
2. Move the sausage and onion into the pot of your slow cooker.
3. Cook marjoram, ground beef, seasoning, and 1 teaspoon of garlic in the same frying pan for 10 minutes or until meat is crumbly and browned evenly.
4. Transfer beef to the slow cooker. Stir in the rest of the ingredients to the mixture in the slow cooker and cook on low for 8 hours.

Nutrition:
343 Calories 29g Protein 9g Fat

391. Shrimp and Tomato Linguini

Preparation Time: 10 minutes
Cooking Time: 20 minutes
Servings: 6
Ingredients:
- 1-ounce extra-virgin olive oil
- 3 minced garlic cloves
- 32 ounces tomatoes, diced
- 8 ounces dry white wine
- 1-ounce butter
- A pinch of salt and black pepper
- 16 ounces uncooked linguine pasta
- 16 ounces medium shrimp, peeled and deveined
- 1 teaspoon Cajun seasoning
- 1-ounce extra-virgin olive oil

Directions:
1. Cook 1 oz of olive oil in a large stockpot on medium heat.
2. Sauté garlic in the oil for 2 minutes, then add tomatoes and wine to the garlic and oil.
3. Cook the mixture for 30 minutes, stirring frequently, then add butter, salt, and pepper.
4. Use a big pot of salted water and cook the linguine for 10-12 minutes or until al dente.
5. Drain water from the pool and set noodles aside.
6. Sprinkle shrimp with seasoning, salt, and pepper, and cook in a frying pan with 1 ounce of olive oil on medium heat.
7. Stir for 5 minutes or until pink in the center.
8. Add shrimp to the pasta sauce, then toss with the linguine in a large bowl and serve.

Nutrition:
10.7g Fats
3.8g Protein
204 Calories

392. Chicken and Pasta Casserole

Preparation Time: 15 minutes
Cooking Time: 20 minutes
Servings: 6
Ingredients:
- 8 ounces dry fusilli pasta
- 1 ½ ounces olive oil
- 6 chicken tenderloins, cut into bite-sized chunks
- 1 tablespoon dried minced onion
- A pinch of salt and pepper
- A bit of garlic powder
- ½ -ounce basil, dried
- ½ -ounce parsley, dried
- 10 3/4 ounces condensed cream of chicken soup
- 10 3/4 ounces condensed cream of mushroom soup
- 16 ounces frozen mixed vegetables
- 8 ounces bread crumbs
- 1-ounce Parmesan cheese, grated
- 1-ounce melted butter

Directions:
1. Preheat oven to 400 degrees Fahrenheit.
2. Lightly coat a baking dish with cooking spray.
3. Boil a large pot of the salted water and cook fusilli noodles for 10 minutes or until tender but firm to the bite.
4. Drain water out of the pot.
5. Heat oil in a large frying pan on medium heat. Cook chicken in the oil with onion, salt, pepper, garlic powder, basil, and parsley for 20 minutes or until juices run clear.
6. Stir in pasta, soups, and vegetables. Pour the mixture into the baking dish.
7. Mix bread crumbs, parmesan, and butter in a small bowl and spread over the pasta.
8. Bake for 20 minutes.
Nutrition:
416 Calories 33g Protein 18g Fat

393. Egg and Wild Rice Casserole

Preparation Time: 20 minutes
Cooking Time: 5 to 7 hours
Servings: 6
Ingredients:
- 3 cups plain cooked wild rice or Herbed Wild Rice
- 2 cups sliced mushrooms
- 1 red bell pepper
- 1 onion, minced
- 2 garlic cloves, minced
- 11 eggs
- 1 teaspoon dried thyme leaves
- ¼ teaspoon salt
- 1 ½ cups shredded Swiss cheese

Directions:
1. In a 6-quart slow cooker, layer the wild rice, mushrooms, bell pepper, onion, and garlic.
2. In a huge bowl, scourge eggs with thyme and salt. Pour into the slow cooker. Top with the cheese.
3. Cover and cook on low for 5 to 7 hours, or until a food thermometer registers 165°F and the casserole is set.
Nutrition:
360 Calories 17g Fat 24g Protein

394. Vegetarian Zucchini Lasagna

Preparation Time: 12 minutes
Cooking Time: 10 minutes
Servings:: 6
Ingredients:
- 1 ¼ lbs. zucchini, sliced into lasagna
- ¼ c. chopped fresh spinach
- 1 ½ c. low-sodium marinara sauce
- 2/3 c. mozzarella cheese, shredded
- 1 c. part-skim ricotta cheese
- Fresh basil for garnish

Directions:
1. Preheat the oven to 375° F for 5 mins.
2. Place the zucchini slices in a dish and layer with spinach, marinara sauce, mozzarella, and ricotta cheese. Repeat the process until several layers are formed.
3. Top with basil.
4. Place in the oven and bake for 10 mins.
Nutrition:
128 Calories
12.2g Protein
2.6g Fat

395. Cauliflower with Kale Pesto

Preparation Time: 17 minutes
Cooking Time: 2 minutes
Servings:: 6
Ingredients:
- 3 c. cauliflower, cut into florets
- 3 c. raw kale, stems removed
- 2 c. fresh basil
- 2 tbsp. extra virgin olive oil
- 3 tbsp. lemon juice
- 3 cloves of garlic
- ¼ tsp. salt

Directions:
1. Pour enough water into a pot and bring to a boil over medium flame. Blanch the cauliflower for 2 mins. Drain, then place in a bowl of ice-cold water for 5 mins. Drain again.
2. In a blender, add the rest of the ingredients. Pulse until smooth.
3. Pour the pesto over the cooked cauliflower.
Nutrition:
4 Calories
1.8g Protein
5.3g Fat

396. Mediterranean Broccoli Alfredo

Preparation Time: 9 minutes
Cooking Time: 2 minutes
Servings:: 4
Ingredients:
- 2 heads of broccoli, cut into florets
- 2 tbsp. lemon juice, freshly squeezed
- ½ c. cashew, soaked for 2 hrs. in water then drained
- 2 tbsp. white miso, low sodium
- 2 tsp. Dijon mustard
- Freshly cracked black pepper

Directions:
1. Boil water in a pot over a medium flame. Blanch the broccoli for 2 minutes, then place in a bowl of iced water. Drain.
2. In a food processor, place the remaining ingredients and pulse until smooth.
3. Pour the Alfredo sauce over the broccoli. Toss to coat with the sauce.
Nutrition:
359 Calories 10.6g Protein 8.4g Fat

397. Garlic Shrimp Zucchini Noodles

Preparation Time: 11 minutes
Cooking Time: 4 minutes
Servings:: 5
Ingredients:
- 16 oz. uncooked shrimps, shelled and deveined
- 1 tbsp. olive oil
- 1 c. cherry tomatoes, cut in half
- 8 c. zucchini strips
- 2 tbsp. minced garlic
- 1 tsp. dried oregano
- ½ tsp. chili powder
- ½ tsp. salt

Directions:
1. Brush the shrimps with olive oil. Place on a skillet and cook for 2 minutes on all sides or until pink. Set aside.
2. Put the rest of the ingredients in a bowl and add the shrimps. Season with salt, then toss to coat the ingredients.

Nutrition:
142 Calories
19.7g Protein
4.2g Fat

398. Spaghetti Squash with Buffalo Sauce

Preparation Time: 9 minutes
Cooking Time: 15 minutes
Servings: 6
Ingredients:
- 1 lb. skinless and boneless chicken breasts
- ½ c. chicken stock, low sodium
- ½ c. red hot sauce
- ½ tsp. garlic powder
- 2 ½ lbs. spaghetti squash, halved and seeded
- 8 oz. cream cheese, low sodium

Directions:
1. Situate chicken breasts in a deep saucepan. Stir in the stock, hot sauce, and garlic powder. Mix to combine all ingredients.
2. Place a rack or a steamer on top of the pot and place the spaghetti squash.
3. Cover with lid.
4. Boil and simmer for 10 to 15 mins.
5. Once cooked, take the spaghetti squash out of the steamer, and allow to rest. Using a fork, scrape the spaghetti squash and place it on a plate.
6. Mix in the cream cheese into the chicken sauce.
7. Pour the sauce over the spaghetti squash.

Nutrition:
273 Calories
21.6g Protein
3.2g Fat

399. Skinny Shrimp Scampi with Zucchini Noodles

Preparation Time: 11 minutes
Cooking Time: 8 minutes
Servings: 8
Ingredients:
- 1 tsp. olive oil
- 1 tbsp. minced garlic
- 1-lb. jumbo shrimps, shelled and deveined
- ¼ tsp. crushed red pepper flakes
- 5 tbsp. water
- 2 tbsp. lemon juice, freshly squeezed
- 2 medium zucchinis, spiralized into noodles then blanched
- Chopped parsley for garnish

Directions:
1. Cook oil in a saucepan over medium flame.
2. Sauté the garlic for 30 secs. before adding in the shrimps. Stir for another 30 secs. before putting in the red pepper flakes, water, and lemon juice.
3. Allow cooking for 3 mins. while stirring constantly. Season with salt and pepper if desired.
4. Place the blanched zucchini on a plate and pour the shrimps on top.
5. Garnish with parsley if desired.

Nutrition:
136 Calories
23.9g Protein
1.8g Fat

400. Classic Greek Lentils & Rice

Preparation Time: 10 minutes
Cooking Time: 16 minutes
Servings: 6
Ingredients:
- 1/3 cup lentils, soak for 1-2 hours
- 2 cups vegetable stock
- 1/2 tsp ground coriander
- 1/4 tsp ground cumin
- 1 cup of brown rice
- 2 tbsp olive oil
- 2 cups onion, sliced
- Salt

Directions:
1. Add oil into the inner pot of instant pot and set the pot on sauté mode.
2. Add onion and sauté for 5-10 minutes.
3. Add the rest of the ingredients and stir well.
4. Seal pot with lid and cook on high for 6 minutes.
5. Once done, allow to release pressure naturally for 10 minutes then release remaining using quick release. Remove lid.
6. Serve and enjoy.

Nutrition: calories 270, fat 12, fiber 1, carbs 10, protein 20

Chapter 6. Meat Recipes

401. Tasty Beef and Broccoli

Preparation Time: 10 minutes
Cooking Time: 15 minutes
Servings: 4
Ingredients:
- 1 and ½ lbs. of flanks steak, cut into strips
- 1 tablespoon of olive oil
- 1 tablespoon of tamari sauce
- 1 cup of beef stock
- 1-pound of broccoli, florets separated

Directions:
1. Combine the steak strips with oil and tamari, toss and set aside for 10 minutes. Select your instant pot on sauté mode, place beef strips and brown them for 4 minutes on each side. Stir in stock, cover the pot again and cook on high for 8 minutes. Stir in broccoli, cover and cook on high for 4 minutes more. Portion everything between plates and serve. Enjoy!

Nutrition:
Calories: 312 kcal
Fat: 5 g
Carbohydrates: 20 g
Protein: 4 g

402. Beef Corn Chili

Preparation Time: 8–10 minutes
Cooking Time: 30 minutes
Servings: 8
Ingredients:
- 2 small onions, chopped (finely)
- ¼ cup of canned corn
- 1 tablespoon of oil
- 10 ounces of lean ground beef
- 2 small chili peppers, diced

Directions:
1. Turn on the instant pot. Click "SAUTE." Pour the oil then stir in the onions, chili pepper, and beef; cook until turn translucent and softened. Pour the 3 cups water in the Cooking pot; mix well.
2. Seal the lid. Select "MEAT/STEW." Adjust the timer to 20 minutes. Allow to cook until the timer turns to zero.
3. Click "CANCEL" then "NPR" for natural pressure release for about 8–10 minutes. Open, then place the dish in serving plates. Serve.

Nutrition:
Calories: 94 kcal
Fat: 5 g
Carbohydrates: 2 g
Protein: 7 g

403. Balsamic Beef Dish

Preparation Time: 5 minutes
Cooking Time: 55 minutes
Servings: 8
Ingredients:
- 3 pounds of chuck roast
- 3 garlic cloves, thinly sliced
- 1 tablespoon of oil
- 1 teaspoon of flavored vinegar
- ½ teaspoon of pepper
- ½ teaspoon of rosemary
- 1 tablespoon of butter
- ½ teaspoon of thyme
- ¼ cup of balsamic vinegar
- 1 cup of beef broth

Directions:
1. Slice the slits in the roast and stuff in garlic slices all over. Combine flavored vinegar, rosemary, pepper, thyme and rub the mixture over the roast. Select the pot on sauté mode and mix in oil, allow the oil to heat up. Cook both side of the roast.
2. Take it out and set aside. Stir in butter, broth, balsamic vinegar and deglaze the pot. Return the roast and close the lid, then cook on HIGH pressure for 40 minutes.
3. Perform a quick release. Serve!

Nutrition:
Calories: 393 kcal
Fat: 15 g
Carbohydrates: 25 g
Protein: 37 g

404. Soy Sauce Beef Roast

Preparation Time: 8 minutes
Cooking Time: 35 minutes
Servings: 2–3
Ingredients:
- ½ teaspoon of beef bouillon
- 1 ½ teaspoon of rosemary
- ½ teaspoon of minced garlic
- 2 pounds of roast beef
- 1/3 cup of soy sauce

Directions:
1. Combine the soy sauce, bouillon, rosemary, and garlic together in a mixing bowl.
2. Turn on your instant pot. Place the roast, and pour enough water to cover the roast; gently stir to mix well. Seal it tight.
3. Click "MEAT/STEW" Cooking function; set pressure level to "HIGH" and set the Cooking time to 35 minutes. Let the pressure to build to cook the ingredients. Once done, click "CANCEL" setting then click "NPR" Cooking function to release naturally the pressure.
4. Gradually open the lid, and shred the meat. Mix in the shredded meat back in the potting mix and stir well. Transfer in serving containers. Serve warm.

Nutrition:
Calories: 423 kcal
Fat: 14 g
Carbohydrates: 12 g
Protein: 21 g

405. Rosemary Beef Chuck Roast

Preparation Time: 5 minutes
Cooking Time: 45 minutes
Servings: 5–6
Ingredients:
- 3 pounds of chuck beef roast
- 3 garlic cloves
- ¼ cup of balsamic vinegar
- 1 sprig fresh rosemary
- 1 sprig fresh thyme
- 1 cup of water
- 1 tablespoon of vegetable oil
- Salt and pepper to taste

Directions:
1. Chop slices in the beef roast and place the garlic cloves in them. Rub the roast with the herbs, black pepper, and salt.

Preheat your instant pot using the sauté setting and pour the oil. When warmed, mix in the beef roast and stir-cook until browned on all sides. Add the remaining ingredients; stir gently.

2. Seal tight and cook on high for 40 minutes using manual setting. Allow the pressure release naturally, about 10 minutes. Uncover and put the beef roast the serving plates, slice and serve.

Nutrition:
Calories: 542 kcal
Fat: 11.2 g
Carbohydrates: 8.7 g
Protein: 55.2 g

406. Pork Chops and Tomato Sauce

Preparation Time: 10 minutes
Cooking Time: 20 minutes
Servings: 4
Ingredients:
- 4 pork chops, boneless
- 1 tablespoon of soy sauce
- ¼ teaspoon of sesame oil
- 1 and ½ cups of tomato paste
- 1 yellow onion
- 8 mushrooms, sliced
Directions:
1. In a bowl, mix the pork chops with soy sauce and sesame oil, toss and leave aside for 10 minutes. Set your instant pot on sauté mode, add pork chops and brown them for 5 minutes on each side.
2. Stir in onion, and cook for 1–2 minutes more. Add tomato paste and mushrooms, toss, cover and cook on high for 8–9 minutes. Divide everything between plates and serve. Enjoy!

Nutrition:
Calories: 300 kcal
Fat: 7 g
Carbohydrates: 18 g
Protein: 4 g

407. Slow Cooker Mediterranean Beef Hoagies

Preparation Time: 10 minutes
Cooking Time: 13 hours
Servings: 6
Ingredients:
- 3 pounds of Beef top round roast fatless
- ½ teaspoon of Onion powder
- ½ teaspoon of Black pepper
- 3 cups of Low sodium beef broth
- 4 teaspoons of Salad dressing mix
- 1 Bay leaf
- 1 tablespoon of Garlic, minced
- 2 Red bell peppers, thin strips cut
- 16 ounces Pepperoncino
- 8 slices Sargento Provolone, thin
- 2 ounces of Gluten-free bread
- ½ teaspoon of salt
For seasoning:
- 1½ tablespoon of Onion powder
- 1½ tablespoon of Garlic powder
- 2 tablespoons of Dried parsley
- 1 tablespoon of stevia
- ½ teaspoon of Dried thyme
- 1 tablespoon of Dried oregano
- 2 tablespoons of Black pepper

- 1 tablespoon of Salt
- 6 Cheese slices
Directions:
1. Dry the roast with a paper towel. Combine black pepper, onion powder and salt in a small bowl and rub the mixture over the roast. Place the seasoned roast into a slow cooker.
2. Add broth, salad dressing mix, bay leaf, and garlic to the slow cooker. Combine it gently. Close and set to low cooking for 12 hours. After cooking, remove the bay leaf.
3. Take out the cooked beef and shred the beef meet. Put back the shredded beef and add bell peppers and. Add bell peppers and pepperoncino into the slow cooker. Cover the cooker and low cook for 1 hour. Before serving, top each of the bread with 3 ounces of the meat mixture. Top it with a cheese slice. The liquid gravy can be used as a dip.

Nutrition:
Calories: 442 kcal
Fat: 11.5 g
Carbohydrates: 37 g
Protein: 49 g

408. Roasted Sirloin Steak

Preparation Time: 10 minutes
Cooking Time: 30 minutes
Servings: 6
Ingredients:
- 2 lbs. sirloin steak, cut into 1" cubes
- 2 garlic cloves, minced
- 3 tablespoon fresh lemon juice
- 1 teaspoon dried oregano
- 1/4 cup water
- 1/4 cup olive oil
- 2 cups fresh parsley, chopped
- 1/2 teaspoon pepper
- 1 teaspoon salt
Directions:
1. Add all ingredients except beef into the large bowl and mix well.
2. Pour bowl mixture into the large zip-lock bag.
3. Add beef to the bag and shake well and refrigerate for 1 hour.
4. Preheat the oven 400 F.
5. Place marinated beef on a baking tray and bake in preheated oven for 30 minutes.
6. Serve and enjoy.

Nutrition: Calories 365 Fat 18.1 g Carbos 2 g Protein 46.6 g Cholesterol 135 mg

409. Lemon Pepper Pork Tenderloin

Preparation Time: 10 minutes
Cooking Time: 25 minutes
Servings: 4
Ingredients:
- 1 lb. pork tenderloin
- 3/4 teaspoon lemon pepper
- 2 teaspoon dried oregano
- 1 tablespoon olive oil
- 3 tablespoon feta cheese, crumbled
- 3 tablespoon olive tapenade
Directions:
1. Add pork, oil, lemon pepper, and oregano in a zip-lock bag and rub well and place in a refrigerator for 2 hours.
2. Remove pork from zip-lock bag. Using sharp knife make lengthwise cut through the center of the tenderloin.

3. Spread olive tapenade on half tenderloin and sprinkle with feta cheese.
4. Fold another half of meat over to the original shape of tenderloin.
5. Tie close pork tenderloin with twine at 2-inch intervals.
6. Grill pork tenderloin for 20 minutes.
7. Cut into slices and serve.

Nutrition: Calories 215 g Fat 9.1 g Carbs 1 g Protein 30.8

410. Jalapeno Lamb Patties

Preparation Time: 10 minutes
Cooking Time: 8 minutes
Servings: 4
Ingredients:
- 1 lb. ground lamb
- 1 jalapeno pepper, minced
- 5 basil leaves, minced
- 10 mint leaves, minced
- ¼ cup fresh parsley, chopped
- 1 cup feta cheese, crumbled
- 1 tablespoon garlic, minced
- 1 teaspoon dried oregano
- ¼ teaspoon pepper
- ½ teaspoon kosher salt

Directions:
1. Add all ingredients into the mixing bowl and mix until well combined.
2. Preheat the grill to 450 F.
3. Spray grill with cooking spray.
4. Make four equal shape patties from meat mixture and place on hot grill and cook for 3 minutes. Turn patties to another side and cook for 4 minutes.
5. Serve and enjoy.

Nutrition: Calories 317 Fat 16 g Carbs 3 g Protein 37.5

411. Lemon Chicken with Asparagus

Preparation time: 10 minutes
Cooking time: 10 minutes
Servings: 3-4
Ingredients
- 1 lb. boneless skinless chicken breasts
- 2 tablespoons honey + 2 tablespoons butter
- 1/4 cup flour
- 2 lemons, sliced
- 1/2 teaspoon salt, pepper to taste
- 1 teaspoon lemon pepper seasoning
- 1–2 cups asparagus, chopped
- 2 tablespoons butter

Directions:
1. Cut the chicken breast in half horizontally. In a shallow dish, mix 1/4 cup flour and salt and pepper to taste; toss the chicken breast until coated.
2. To a skillet, add 2 tablespoons of butter and melt over medium heat. Then add the coated chicken breast and cook each side for about 4-5 minutes, sprinkling both sides with lemon pepper.
3. Once chicken is completely cooked through and is golden brown, transfer it to a plate.
4. For Asparagus and Lemons:
5. To the pan, add 1–2 cups chopped asparagus; sauté until bright green for a few minutes.
6. Remove from the pan and keep it aside. Place the slices of lemon to the bottom of the pan and cook

each side until caramelized, for a few minutes without stirring.
7. Add a bit of butter along with the lemon slices. Take the lemons out of the pan and put them aside.
8. Serve the chicken with the asparagus and enjoy!

Nutrition: calories 230, fat 12, fiber 1, carbs 10, protein 28

412. Tender Chicken Quesadilla

Preparation time: 10 minutes
Cooking time: 20 minutes
Servings: 4
Ingredients:
- 2 bread tortillas
- 1 teaspoon butter
- 2 teaspoons olive oil
- 1 teaspoon Taco seasoning
- 6 oz chicken breast, skinless, boneless, sliced
- 1/3 cup Cheddar cheese, shredded
- 1 bell pepper, cut on the wedges

Directions:
1. Pour 1 teaspoon of olive oil in the skillet and add chicken.
2. Sprinkle the meat with Taco seasoning and mix up well.
3. Roast chicken for 10 minutes over the medium heat. Stir it from time to time.
4. Then transfer the cooked chicken in the plate.
5. Add remaining olive oil in the skillet.
6. Then add bell pepper and roast it for 5 minutes. Stir it all the time.
7. Mix up together bell pepper with chicken.
8. Toss butter in the skillet and melt it.
9. Put 1 tortilla in the skillet.
10. Put Cheddar cheese on the tortilla and flatten it.
11. Then add chicken-pepper mixture and cover it with the second tortilla.
12. Roast the quesadilla for 2 minutes from each side.
13. Cut the cooked meal on the halves and transfer in the serving plates.

Nutrition: Calories 167, Fat 8.2 g, Fiber 0.8 g, Carbs 16.4 g, Protein 24.2 g

413. Chicken and Chorizo Casserole

Preparation time: 5 minutes
Cooking time: 1 hour
Servings: 6
Ingredients:
- 6 chicken thighs
- 4 chorizo links, sliced
- 2 tablespoons olive oil
- 1 cup tomato juice
- 2 tablespoons tomato paste
- 1 bay leaf
- 1 teaspoon dried thyme
- Salt and pepper to taste

Directions:
1. Heat the oil in a skillet and add the chicken. Cook on all sides until golden then transfer the chicken in a deep-dish baking pan.
2. Add the rest of the ingredients and season with salt and pepper.
3. Cook in the preheated oven at 350F for 25 minutes.
4. Serve the casserole right away.

Nutrition: Calories: 424, Fat: 27.5g, Protein: 39.1g, Carbs: 3.6g

414. Chorizo White Bean Stew

Preparation time: 5 minutes
Cooking time: 1 hour
Servings: 8
Ingredients:
- 3 tablespoons olive oil
- 4 chorizo links, sliced
- 2 sweet onions, chopped
- 4 garlic cloves, minced
- 2 celery stalks, sliced
- 2 carrots, sliced
- 2 red bell peppers, cored and diced
- 2 tablespoons tomato paste
- 1 can diced tomatoes
- 2 cans white beans, drained
- 1 bay leaf
- 1 teaspoon sherry vinegar
- ½ teaspoon dried oregano
- 1 cup chicken stock
- Salt and pepper to taste

Directions:
1. Heat the oil in a deep saucepan and stir in the chorizo. Cook for 5 minutes then add the onions and garlic, as well as celery and carrots.
2. Cook for another 10 minutes to soften.
3. Add the rest of the ingredients then season with salt and pepper to taste.
4. Cook on low heat for 35-40 minutes.
5. Serve the stew right away or freeze it into individual portions for later serving.

Nutrition: Calories: 386, Fat: 17. Protein: 20, Carbs: 38.8

415. Olive Feta Beef

Preparation Time: 10 minutes
Cooking Time: 6 hours
Servings: 8
Ingredients:
- 2 lbs. beef stew meat, cut into half-inch pieces
- 1 cup olives, pitted and cut in half
- 30 oz can tomato, diced
- 1/2 cup feta cheese, crumbled
- 1/4 teaspoon pepper
- 1/2 teaspoon salt

Directions:
1. Add all ingredients into the crock pot and stir well.
2. Cover and cook on high for 6 hours.
3. Season with pepper and salt.
4. Stir well and serve.

Nutrition: calories 370, fat 12, fiber 1, carbs 10, protein 50

416. Italian Beef Casserole

Preparation Time: 10 minutes
Cooking Time: 1 hour 30 minutes
Servings: 6
Ingredients:
- 1 lb. lean stew beef, cut into chunks
- 3 teaspoon paprika
- 4 oz black olives, sliced
- 7 oz can tomato, chopped
- 1 tablespoon tomato puree
- 1/4 teaspoon garlic powder
- 2 teaspoon herb de Provence
- 2 cups beef stock
- 2 tablespoon olive oil

Directions:
1. Preheat the oven to 350 F.
2. Heat oil in a pan over medium heat.
3. Add meat to the pan and cook until brown.
4. Add stock, olives, tomatoes, tomato puree, garlic powder, herb de Provence, and paprika. Stir well and bring to boil.
5. Transfer meat mixture to the casserole dish.
6. Cover and cook in preheated oven for 1 1/2 hours.
7. Serve and enjoy.

Nutrition: Calories 228 Fat 11.6 g Carbs 6 g Protein 26 g Cholesterol 11 mg

417. Chicken Loaf

Preparation time: 10 minutes
Cooking time: 40 minutes
Servings: 4
Ingredients:
- 2 cups ground chicken
- 1 egg, beaten
- 1 tablespoon fresh dill, chopped
- 1 garlic clove, chopped
- ½ teaspoon salt
- 1 teaspoon chili flakes
- 1 onion, minced

Directions:
1. In the mixing bowl combine together all ingredient and mix up until you get smooth mass.
2. Then line the loaf dish with baking paper and put the ground chicken mixture inside.
3. Flatten the surface well.
4. Bake the chicken loaf for 40 minutes at 355F.
5. Then chill the chicken loaf to the room temperature and remove from the loaf dish.
6. Slice it.

Nutrition: Calories 167, Fat 6.2 g, Fiber 0.8 g, Carbs 3.4 g, Protein 32.2 g

418. Italian Beef Roast

Preparation Time: 10 minutes
Cooking Time: 50 minutes
Servings: 6
Ingredients:
- 2 1/2 lbs. beef roast, cut into chunks
- 1 cup chicken broth
- 1 cup red wine
- 2 tbsp Italian seasoning
- 2 tbsp olive oil
- 1 bell pepper, chopped
- 2 celery stalks, chopped
- 1 tsp garlic, minced
- 1 onion, sliced
- Pepper
- Salt

Directions:
1. Add oil into the instant pot and set the pot on sauté mode.
2. Add the meat into the pot and sauté until brown.
3. Add onion, bell pepper, and celery and sauté for 5 minutes.
4. Add remaining ingredients and stir well.
5. Seal pot with lid and cook on high for 40 minutes.
6. Once done, allow to release pressure naturally. Remove lid.

7. Stir well and serve.
Nutrition: calories 470, fat 24, fiber 4, carbs 6.0, protein 56

419. Delicious Chicken Casserole

Preparation Time: 10 minutes
Cooking Time: 20 minutes
Servings: 4
Ingredients:
- 1 lb. chicken breasts, skinless, boneless, & cubed
- 2 tsp paprika
- 3 tbsp tomato paste
- 1 cup chicken stock
- 4 tomatoes, chopped
- 1 small eggplant, chopped
- 1 tbsp Italian seasoning
- 2 bell pepper, sliced
- 1 onion, sliced
- 1 tbsp garlic, minced
- 1 tbsp olive oil
- Pepper
- Salt

Directions:
1. Add oil into the inner pot of instant pot and set the pot on sauté mode.
2. Season chicken with pepper and salt and add into the instant pot. Cook chicken until lightly golden brown.
3. Remove chicken from pot and place on a plate.
4. Add garlic and onion and sauté until onion is softened about 3-5 minutes.
5. Return chicken to the pot. Pour remaining ingredients over chicken and stir well.
6. Seal pot with lid and cook on high for 10 minutes.
7. Once done, release pressure using quick release. Remove lid.
8. Stir well and serve.
Nutrition: Calories 356 Fat 13.9 g Carbs 22.7 g Protein 36.

420. Mediterranean Pork Roast

Preparation Time: 10 minutes
Cooking Time: 8 hours and 10 minutes
Servings: 2
Ingredients:
- 2 tablespoons Olive oil
- 2 pounds Pork roast
- ½ teaspoon Paprika
- ¾ cup Chicken broth
- 2 teaspoons Dried sage
- ½ tablespoon Garlic minced
- ¼ teaspoon Dried marjoram
- ¼ teaspoon Dried Rosemary
- 1 teaspoon Oregano
- ¼ teaspoon Dried thyme
- 1 teaspoon Basil
- ¼ teaspoon Kosher salt

Directions:
1. In a small bowl mix broth, oil, salt, and spices. In a skillet pour olive oil and bring to medium-high heat. Put the pork into it and roast until all sides become brown.
2. Take out the pork after cooking and poke the roast all over with a knife. Place the poked pork roast into a 6-quart crock pot. Now, pour the small bowl mixture liquid all over the roast.
3. Seal crock pot and cook on low for 8 hours. After cooking, remove it from the crock pot on to a cutting board and shred into pieces. Afterward, add the shredded pork back into the crockpot. Simmer it another 10 minutes. Serve along with feta cheese, pita bread, and tomatoes.
Nutrition:
361 Calories
10.4g Fat
0.7g Carbohydrates
43.8g Protein

421. Beef Pizza

Preparation Time: 20 minutes
Cooking Time: 50 minutes
Servings: 2
Ingredients:
For Crust:
- 3 cups all-purpose flour
- 1 tablespoon sugar
- 2¼ teaspoons active dry yeast
- 1 teaspoon salt
- 2 tablespoons olive oil
- 1 cup warm water
For Topping:
- 1-pound ground beef
- 1 medium onion, chopped
- 2 tablespoons tomato paste
- 1 tablespoon ground cumin
- Salt and ground black pepper, as required
- ¼ cup water
- 1 cup fresh spinach, chopped
- 8 ounces artichoke hearts, quartered
- 4 ounces fresh mushrooms, sliced
- 2 tomatoes, chopped
- 4 ounces feta cheese, crumbled

Directions:
For crust:
1. Mix the flour, sugar, yeast and salt with a stand mixer, using the dough hook. Add 2 tablespoons of the oil and warm water and knead until a smooth and elastic dough is formed.
2. Make a ball of the dough and set aside for about 15 minutes.
3. Situate the dough onto a lightly floured surface and roll into a circle. Situate the dough into a lightly, greased round pizza pan and gently, press to fit. Set aside for about 10-15 minutes. Coat the crust with some oil. Preheat the oven to 400 degrees F.
For topping:
4. Fry beef in a nonstick skillet over medium-high heat for about 4-5 minutes. Mix in the onion and cook for about 5 minutes, stirring frequently. Add the tomato paste, cumin, salt, black pepper and water and stir to combine.
5. Put heat to medium and cook for about 5-10 minutes. Remove from the heat and set aside. Place the beef mixture over the pizza crust and top with the spinach, followed by the artichokes, mushrooms, tomatoes, and Feta cheese.
6. Bake until the cheese is melted. Pullout from the oven and keep aside for about 3-5 minutes before slicing. Cut into desired sized slices and serve.
Nutrition:
309 Calories
8.7g Fat
3.7g Carbohydrates
3.3g Protein

422. Beef & Bulgur Meatballs

Preparation Time: 20 minutes
Cooking Time: 28 minutes
Servings: 2
Ingredients:
- ¾ cup uncooked bulgur
- 1-pound ground beef
- ¼ cup shallots, minced
- ¼ cup fresh parsley, minced
- ½ teaspoon ground allspice
- ½ teaspoon ground cumin
- ½ teaspoon ground cinnamon
- ¼ teaspoon red pepper flakes, crushed
- Salt, as required
- 1 tablespoon olive oil

Directions:
1. In a large bowl of the cold water, soak the bulgur for about 30 minutes. Drain the bulgur well and then, squeeze with your hands to remove the excess water. In a food processor, add the bulgur, beef, shallot, parsley, spices and salt and pulse until a smooth mixture is formed.
2. Situate the mixture into a bowl and refrigerate, covered for about 30 minutes. Remove from the refrigerator and make equal sized balls from the beef mixture. Using big nonstick skillet, heat up the oil over medium-high heat and cook the meatballs in 2 batches for about 13-14 minutes, flipping frequently. Serve warm.

Nutrition:
228 Calories
7.4g Fat
0.1g Carbohydrates
3.5g Protein

423. Chicken with Caper Sauce

Preparation Time: 20 minutes
Cooking Time: 18 minutes
Servings: 2
Ingredients:
For Chicken:
- 2 eggs
- Salt and ground black pepper, as required
- 1 cup dry breadcrumbs
- 2 tablespoons olive oil
- 1½ pounds skinless, boneless chicken breast halves, pounded into ¾inch thickness and cut into pieces
For Capers Sauce:
- 3 tablespoons capers
- ½ cup dry white wine
- 3 tablespoons fresh lemon juice
- Salt and ground black pepper, as required
- 2 tablespoons fresh parsley, chopped

Directions:
1. For chicken: in a shallow dish, add the eggs, salt and black pepper and beat until well combined. In another shallow dish, place breadcrumbs. Soak the chicken pieces in egg mixture then coat with the breadcrumbs evenly. Shake off the excess breadcrumbs.
2. Cook the oil over medium heat and cook the chicken pieces for about 5-7 minutes per side or until desired doneness. With a slotted spoon, situate the chicken pieces onto a paper towel lined plate. With a piece of the foil, cover the chicken pieces to keep them warm.
3. In the same skillet, incorporate all the sauce ingredients except parsley and cook for about 2-3 minutes, stirring continuously. Drizzle parsley and remove from heat. Serve the chicken pieces with the topping of capers sauce.

Nutrition:
352 Calories
13.5g Fat
1.9g Carbohydrates
1.2g Protein

424. Slow Cooker Mediterranean Beef Roast

Preparation Time: 10 minutes
Cooking Time: 10 hours and 10 minutes
Servings: 2
Ingredients:
- 3 pounds Chuck roast, boneless
- 2 teaspoons Rosemary
- ½ cup Tomatoes, sun-dried and chopped
- 10 cloves Grated garlic
- ½ cup Beef stock
- 2 tablespoons Balsamic vinegar
- ¼ cup Chopped Italian parsley, fresh
- ¼ cup Chopped olives
- 1 teaspoon Lemon zest
- ¼ cup Cheese grits

Directions:
1. In the slow cooker, put garlic, sun dried tomatoes, and the beef roast. Add beef stock and Rosemary. Close the cooker and slow cook for 10 hours.
2. After cooking is over, remove the beef, and shred the meet. Discard the fat. Add back the shredded meat to the slow cooker and simmer for 10 minutes. In a small bowl combine lemon zest, parsley, and olives. Cool the mixture until you are ready to serve. Garnish using the refrigerated mix.
3. Serve it over pasta or egg noodles. Top it with cheese grits.

Nutrition:
314 Calories
19g Fat
1g Carbohydrate
32g Protein

425. Slow Cooker Mediterranean Beef with Artichokes

Preparation Time: 3 hours and 20 minutes
Cooking Time: 7 hours and 8 minutes
Servings: 2
Ingredients:
- 2 pounds Beef for stew
- 14 ounces Artichoke hearts
- 1 tablespoon Grape seed oil
- 1 Diced onion
- 32 ounces Beef broth
- 4 cloves Garlic, grated
- 14½ ounces Tinned tomatoes, diced
- 15 ounces Tomato sauce
- 1 teaspoon Dried oregano
- ½ cup Pitted, chopped olives
- 1 teaspoon Dried parsley
- 1 teaspoon Dried oregano
- ½ teaspoon Ground cumin
- 1 teaspoon Dried basil
- 1 Bay leaf
- ½ teaspoon Salt

Directions:
1. In a large non-stick skillet pour some oil and bring to medium-high heat. Roast the beef until it turns brown on both the sides. Transfer the beef into a slow cooker.

2. Add in beef broth, diced tomatoes, tomato sauce, salt and combine. Pour in beef broth, diced tomatoes, oregano, olives, basil, parsley, bay leaf, and cumin. Combine the mixture thoroughly.

3. Close and cook on low heat for 7 hours. Discard the bay leaf at the time serving. Serve hot.

Nutrition:

416 Calories

5g Fat

14.1g Carbohydrates

29.9g Protein

426. Skinny Slow Cooker Mediterranean Style Pot Roast

Preparation Time: 30 minutes

Cooking Time: 8 hours

Servings: 2

Ingredients:

- 4 pounds Eye of round roast
- 4 cloves Garlic
- 2 teaspoons Olive oil
- 1 teaspoon Freshly ground black pepper
- 1 cup Chopped onions
- 4 Carrots, chopped
- 2 teaspoons Dried Rosemary
- 2 Chopped celery stalks
- 28 ounces Crushed tomatoes in the can
- 1 cup Low sodium beef broth
- 1 cup Red wine
- 2 teaspoons Salt

Directions:

1. Season the beef roast with salt, garlic, and pepper and set aside. Pour oil in a non-stick skillet and bring to medium-high heat. Put the beef into it and roast until it becomes brown on all sides. Now, transfer the roasted beef into a 6-quart slow cooker. Add carrots, onion, rosemary, and celery into the skillet. Continue cooking until the onion and vegetable become soft.

2. Stir in the tomatoes and wine into this vegetable mixture. Add beef broth and tomato mixture into the slow cooker along with the vegetable mixture. Close and cook on low for 8 hours.

3. Once the meat gets cooked, remove it from the slow cooker and place it on a cutting board and wrap with an aluminum foil. To thicken the sauce, then transfer it into a saucepan and boil it under low heat until it reaches to the required consistency. Discard fats before serving.

Nutrition:

260 Calories

6g Fat

8.7g Carbohydrates

37.6g Protein

427. Chicken in Tomato-Balsamic Pan Sauce

Preparation Time: 10 minutes

Cooking Time: 20 minutes

Servings: 2

Ingredients

- 2 (8 oz. or 226.7 g each) boneless chicken breasts, skinless
- ½ tsp. salt
- ½ tsp. ground pepper
- 3 tbsps. extra-virgin olive oil
- ½ c. halved cherry tomatoes
- 2 tbsps. sliced shallot

- ¼ c. balsamic vinegar
- 1 tbsp. minced garlic
- 1 tbsp. toasted fennel seeds, crushed
- 1 tbsp. butter

Directions:

1. Slice the chicken breasts into 4 pieces and beat them with a mallet till it reaches a thickness of a ¼ inch. Use ¼ teaspoons of pepper and salt to coat the chicken. Heat two tablespoons of oil in a skillet and keep the heat to a medium. Cook the chicken breasts on each side for three minutes. Place it to a serving plate and cover it with foil to keep it warm.

2. Add one tablespoon oil, shallot, and tomatoes in a pan and cook till it softens. Add vinegar and boil the mix till the vinegar gets reduced by half. Put fennel seeds, garlic, salt, and pepper and cook for about four minutes. Pull it out from the heat and stir it with butter. Pour this sauce over chicken and serve.

Nutrition:

294 Calories

17g Fat

10g Carbohydrates

2g Protein

428. Brown Rice, Feta, Fresh Pea, and Mint Salad

Preparation Time: 10 minutes

Cooking Time: 25 minutes

Servings: 2

Ingredients

- 2 c. brown rice
- 3 c. water
- Salt
- 5 oz. or 141.7 g crumbled feta cheese
- 2 c. cooked peas
- ½ c. chopped mint, fresh
- 2 tbsps. olive oil
- Salt and pepper

Directions:

1. Place the brown rice, water, and salt into a saucepan over medium heat, cover, and bring to boiling point. Turn the lower heat and allow it to cook until the water has dissolved and the rice is soft but chewy. Leave to cool completely

2. Add the feta, peas, mint, olive oil, salt, and pepper to a salad bowl with the cooled rice and toss to combine   Serve and enjoy!

Nutrition:

613 Calories

18.2g Fat

45g Carbohydrates

12g Protein

429. Whole Grain Pita Bread Stuffed with Olives and Chickpeas

Preparation Time: 10 minutes

Cooking Time: 20 minutes

Servings: 2

Ingredients

- 2 wholegrain pita pockets
- 2 tbsps. olive oil
- 2 garlic cloves, chopped
- 1 onion, chopped
- ½ tsp. cumin
- 10 black olives, chopped
- 2 c. cooked chickpeas
- Salt and pepper

Directions:
1. Slice open the pita pockets and set aside Adjust your heat to medium and set a pan in place. Add in the olive oil and heat. Mix in the garlic, onion, and cumin to the hot pan and stir as the onions soften and the cumin is fragrant Add the olives, chickpeas, salt, and pepper and toss everything together until the chickpeas become golden
2. Set the pan from heat and use your wooden spoon to roughly mash the chickpeas so that some are intact and some are crushed Heat your pita pockets in the microwave, in the oven, or on a clean pan on the stove
3. Fill them with your chickpea mixture and enjoy!
Nutrition:
503 Calories
19g Fat
14g Carbohydrates
15.7g Protein

430. Roasted Carrots with Walnuts and Cannellini Beans

Preparation Time: 10 minutes
Cooking Time: 45 minutes
Servings: 2
Ingredients
• 4 peeled carrots, chopped
• 1 c. walnuts
• 1 tbsp. honey
• 2 tbsps. olive oil
• 2 c. canned cannellini beans, drained
• 1 fresh thyme sprig
• Salt and pepper
Directions:
1. Set oven to 400 F/204 C and line a baking tray or roasting pan with baking paper Lay the carrots and walnuts onto the lined tray or pan Sprinkle olive oil and honey over the carrots and walnuts and give everything a rub to make sure each piece is coated Scatter the beans onto the tray and nestle into the carrots and walnuts
2. Add the thyme and sprinkle everything with salt and pepper Set tray in your oven and roast for about 40 minutes.
3. Serve and enjoy
Nutrition:
385 Calories
27g Fat
6g Carbohydrates
18g Protein

431. Seasoned Buttered Chicken

Preparation Time: 10 minutes
Cooking Time: 20 minutes
Servings: 2
Ingredients
• ½ c. Heavy Whipping Cream
• 1 tbsp. Salt
• ½ c. Bone Broth
• 1 tbsp. Pepper
• 4 tbsps. Butter
• 4 Chicken Breast Halves
Directions:
1. Place cooking pan on your oven over medium heat and add in one tablespoon of butter. Once the butter is warm and melted, place the chicken in and cook for five minutes on either side. At the end of this time, the chicken should be cooked through and golden; if it is, go ahead and place it on a plate.

2. Next, you are going to add the bone broth into the warm pan. Add heavy whipping cream, salt, and pepper. Then, leave the pan alone until your sauce begins to simmer. Allow this process to happen for five minutes to let the sauce thicken up.
3. Finally, you are going to add the rest of your butter and the chicken back into the pan. Be sure to use a spoon to place the sauce over your chicken and smother it completely. Serve
Nutrition:
350 Calories
25g Fat
10g Carbohydrates
25g Protein

432. Double Cheesy Bacon Chicken

Preparation Time: 10 minutes
Cooking Time: 30 minutes
Servings: 2
Ingredients
• 4 oz. or 113 g. Cream Cheese
• 1 c. Cheddar Cheese
• 8 strips Bacon
• Sea salt
• Pepper
• 2 Garlic cloves, finely chopped
• Chicken Breast
• 1 tbsp. Bacon Grease or Butter
Directions:
1. Ready the oven to 400 F/204 C Slice the chicken breasts in half to make them thin
2. Season with salt, pepper, and garlic Grease a baking pan with butter and place chicken breasts into it. Add the cream cheese and cheddar cheese on top of the breasts
3. Add bacon slices as well Place the pan to the oven for 30 minutes Serve hot
Nutrition:
610 Calories
32g Fat
3g Carbohydrates
38g Protein

433. Shrimps with Lemon and Pepper

Preparation Time: 10 minutes
Cooking Time: 10 minutes
Servings: 2
Ingredients
• 40 deveined shrimps, peeled
• 6 minced garlic cloves
• Salt and black pepper
• 3 tbsps. olive oil
• ¼ tsp. sweet paprika
• A pinch crushed red pepper flake
• ¼ tsp. grated lemon zest
• 3 tbsps. Sherry or another wine
• 1½ tbsps. sliced chives
• Juice of 1 lemon
Directions:
1. Adjust your heat to medium-high and set a pan in place.
2. Add oil and shrimp, sprinkle with pepper and salt and cook for 1 minute Add paprika, garlic and pepper flakes, stir and cook for 1 minute. Gently stir in sherry and allow to cook for an extra minute
3. Take shrimp off the heat, add chives and lemon zest, stir and transfer shrimp to plates. Add lemon juice all over and serve

Nutrition:
140 Calories
1g Fat
5g Carbohydrates
18g Protein

434. Breaded and Spiced Halibut

Preparation Time: 5 minutes
Cooking Time: 25 minutes
Servings: 2
Ingredients
- ¼ c. chopped fresh chives
- ¼ c. chopped fresh dill
- ¼ tsp. ground black pepper
- ¾ c. panko breadcrumbs
- 1 tbsp. extra-virgin olive oil
- 1 tsp. finely grated lemon zest
- 1 tsp. sea salt
- 1/3 c. chopped fresh parsley
- 4 (6 oz. or 170 g. each) halibut fillets

Directions:
1. In a medium bowl, mix olive oil and the rest ingredients except halibut fillets and breadcrumbs
2. Place halibut fillets into the mixture and marinate for 30 minutes Preheat your oven to 400 F/204 C Set a foil to a baking sheet, grease with cooking spray Dip the fillets to the breadcrumbs and put to the baking sheet Cook in the oven for 20 minutes Serve hot

Nutrition:
667 Calories
24.5g Fat
2g Carbohydrates
54.8g Protein

435. Beef and Goat Cheese Stuffed Peppers

Preparation Time: 10 minutes
Cooking Time: 30 minutes
Serving: 4
Ingredients:
- 1-pound lean ground beef
- ½ cup cooked brown rice
- 2 Roma tomatoes, diced
- 3 garlic cloves, minced
- ½ yellow onion, diced
- 2 tablespoons fresh oregano, chopped
- 1 teaspoon salt
- ½ teaspoon black pepper
- ¼ teaspoon ground allspice
- 2 bell peppers, halved and seeded
- 4 ounces goat cheese
- ¼ cup fresh parsley, chopped

Direction:
1. Preheat the air fryer to 360°F.
2. In a large bowl, combine the ground beef, rice, tomatoes, garlic, onion, oregano, salt, pepper, and allspice. Mix well.
3. Divide the beef mixture equally into the halved bell peppers and top each with about 1 ounce (a quarter of the total) of the goat cheese.
4. Place the peppers into the air fryer basket in a single layer, making sure that they don't touch each other. Bake for 30 minutes.
5. Remove the peppers from the air fryer and top with fresh parsley before serving.

VARIATION TIP: You can substitute feta cheese for the goat cheese, if preferred.
Nutrition PER SERVING: Calories: 298; Total Fat: 12g; Saturated Fat: 7g; Protein: 32g; Total Carbohydrates: 17g; Fiber: 3g; Sugar: 2g; Cholesterol: 83mg

436. Herb-Roasted Beef Tips with Onions

Preparation Time: 5 minutes
Cooking Time: 10 minutes, plus 5 minutes to rest
Serving: 4
Ingredients:
- 1-pound rib eye steak, cubed
- 2 garlic cloves, minced
- 2 tablespoons olive oil
- 1 tablespoon fresh oregano
- 1 teaspoon salt
- ½ teaspoon black pepper
- 1 yellow onion, thinly sliced

Direction:
1. Preheat the air fryer to 380°F.
2. In a medium bowl, combine the steak, garlic, olive oil, oregano, salt, pepper, and onion. Mix until all of the beef and onion are well coated.
3. Put the seasoned steak mixture into the air fryer basket. Roast for 5 minutes. Stir and roast for 5 minutes more.
4. Let rest for 5 minutes before serving with some favorite sides.

INGREDIENT TIP: You can use any cut of beef you prefer, but note that many will require more tenderization prior to cooking so that they don't become tough.
Nutrition PER SERVING: Calories: 380; Total Fat: 28g; Saturated Fat: 11g; Protein: 28g; Total Carbohydrates: 3g; Fiber: 0g; Sugar: 1g; Cholesterol: 88mg

437. Easy Beef Kofta

Preparation Time: 10 minutes
Cooking Time: 10 minutes
Servings: 8
Ingredients:
- 2 lbs. ground beef
- 4 garlic cloves, minced
- 1 onion, minced
- 2 teaspoon cumin
- 1 cup fresh parsley, chopped
- ¼ teaspoon pepper
- 1 teaspoon salt

Directions:
1. Add all ingredients into the mixing bowl and mix until combined.
2. Roll meat mixture into the kabab shapes and cook in a hot pan for 4-6 minutes on each side or until cooked.
3. Serve and enjoy.

Nutrition: Calories 223 Fat 7.3 g Carbs 2.5 g Protein 35

438. Pork with Tomato & Olives

Preparation Time: 10 minutes
Cooking Time: 30 minutes
Servings: 6
Ingredients:
- 6 pork chops, boneless and cut into thick slices
- 1/8 teaspoon ground cinnamon
- 1/2 cup olives, pitted and sliced
- 8 oz can tomato, crushed
- 1/4 cup beef broth

- 2 garlic cloves, chopped
- 1 large onion, sliced
- 1 tablespoon olive oil

Directions:
1. Heat olive oil in a pan over medium-high heat.
2. Place pork chops in a pan and cook until lightly brown and set aside.
3. Cook garlic and onion in the same pan over medium heat, until onion is softened.
4. Add broth and bring to boil over high heat.
5. Return pork to pan and stir in crushed tomatoes and remaining ingredients.
6. Cover and simmer for 20 minutes.
7. Serve and enjoy.

Nutrition: Calories 321 Fat 23 g Carbs 7 g S Protein 19 g

439. Lamb Stuffed Tomatoes with Herbs

Preparation time:5 minutes
Cooking time:1 hour
Servings: 6
Ingredients:
- 6 large tomatoes
- 1-pound ground lamb
- ¼ cup white rice
- 2 shallots, chopped
- 2 garlic cloves, minced
- 1 tablespoon chopped dill
- 1 tablespoon chopped parsley
- 1 tablespoon chopped cilantro
- 1 teaspoon dried mint
- Salt and pepper to taste
- 1 tablespoon lemon juice
- 2 tablespoons olive oil
- 1 cup vegetable stock

Directions:
1. Mix the lamb, rice, shallots, garlic, dill, parsley, cilantro and mint in a bowl. Add salt and pepper to taste.
2. Remove the top of each tomato then carefully remove the flesh, leaving the skins intact.
3. Chop the flesh finely and place it in a deep heavy saucepan. Add the lemon juice, as well as salt and pepper to taste.
4. Stuff the tomatoes with the lamb mixture and place them all in the pan.
5. Drizzle with oil then pour in the stock.
6. Cover with a lid and cook on low heat for 35 minutes.
7. Serve the tomatoes right away.

Nutrition: Calories: 248, Fat: 10.7g, Protein: 23.7g, Carbs: 14.6g

440. Chicken Lentil Stew

Preparation Time: 10 minutes
Cooking Time: 25 minutes
Servings: 6
Ingredients:
- 2 lbs. chicken thighs, boneless & skinless
- 1 tbsp olive oil
- 1 cup onion, chopped
- 4 cups chicken stock
- 8 oz green lentils, soak for 1 hour
- 28 oz can tomato, diced
- Pepper
- Salt

Directions:
1. Add oil into the inner pot of instant pot and set the pot on sauté mode.
2. Add onion and sauté for 5 minutes.
3. Add the rest of the ingredients and stir well.
4. Seal pot with lid and cook on high for minutes.
5. Once done, release pressure using quick release. Remove lid.
6. Shred chicken using a fork.
7. Stir well and serve.

Nutrition: calories 479, fat 14, fiber 4, carbs 30, protein 55

441. Braised Veal Shanks

Preparation time: 10 minutes
Cooking time: 2 hours
Serving: 4
Ingredients:
- 4 veal shanks, bone in
- ½ cup flour
- 4 tablespoons extra-virgin olive oil
- 1 large onion, chopped
- 5 cloves garlic, sliced
- 2 teaspoons salt
- 1 tablespoon fresh thyme
- 3 tablespoons tomato paste
- 6 cups water
- Cooked noodles, for serving (optional)

Direction:
1. Preheat the oven to 350°F (180°C).
2. Dredge the veal shanks in the flour.
3. Pour the olive oil into a large oven-safe pot or pan over medium heat; add the veal shanks. Brown the veal on both sides, about 4 minutes each side. Remove the veal from pot and set aside.
4. Add the onion, garlic, salt, thyme, and tomato paste to the pan and cook for 3 to 4 minutes. Add the water, and stir to combine.
5. Add the veal back to the pan, and bring to a simmer. Cover the pan with a lid or foil and bake for 1 hour and 50 minutes. Remove from the oven and serve with cooked noodles, if desired.

Nutrition:
calories: 400 | fat: 19g | protein: 39g | carbs: 18g | fiber: 2g | sodium: 1368mg

442. Ground Pork Stuffed Peppers

Preparation time: 20 minutes
Cooking Time: 40 Minutes
Servings: 4
Ingredients:
- 6 bell peppers, deveined
- 1 tablespoon vegetable oil 1 shallot, chopped
- 1/2 garlic clove, minced
- 1/2-pound ground pork
- 1/3-pound ground veal 1 ripe tomato, chopped
- 1/2 teaspoon mustard seeds
- Sea salt and ground black pepper, to taste

Direction:
1. Parboil the peppers for 5 minutes.
2. Heat the vegetable oil in a frying pan that is preheated over a moderate heat. Cook the shallot and garlic for 3 to 4 minutes until they've softened.
3. Stir in the ground meat and cook, breaking apart with a fork, for about 6 minutes. Add the chopped tomatoes, mustard seeds, salt, and pepper.

4. Continue to cook for 5 minutes or until heated through. Divide the filling between the peppers and transfer them to a baking pan.
5. Bake in the preheated oven at 36degrees F approximately 25 minutes.
6. Storing
7. Place the peppers in airtight containers or Ziploc bags; keep in your refrigerator for up to 3 to 4 days.
8. For freezing, place the peppers in airtight containers or heavy-duty freezer bags. Freeze up to 2 to 3 months. Defrost in the refrigerator. Bon appétit!

Nutrition: 2 Calories; 20.5g Fat; 8.2g Carbs; 18.2g Protein; 1.5g Fiber

443. Honey Pork Chops

Preparation time: 10 minutes
Cooking time: 16 minutes
Serving: 4
Ingredients:
- 4 pork chops, boneless or bone-in
- ¼ teaspoon salt
- 1/8 teaspoon freshly ground black pepper
- 3 tablespoons extra-virgin olive oil
- 5 tablespoons low-sodium chicken broth, divided
- 6 garlic cloves, minced
- ¼ cup honey
- 2 tablespoons apple cider vinegar

Direction:
1. Season the pork chops with salt and pepper and set aside.
2. In a large sauté pan or skillet, heat the oil over medium-high heat. Add the pork chops and sear for 5 minutes on each side, or until golden brown.
3. Once the searing is complete, move the pork to a dish and reduce the skillet heat from medium-high to medium. Add 3 tablespoons of chicken broth to the pan; this will loosen the bits and flavors from the bottom of the skillet.
4. Once the broth has evaporated, add the garlic to the skillet and cook for 15 to 20 seconds, until fragrant. Add the honey, vinegar, and the remaining 2 tablespoons of broth. Bring the heat back up to medium-high and continue to cook for 3 to 4 minutes.
5. Stir periodically; the sauce is ready once it's thickened slightly. Add the pork chops back into the pan, cover them with the sauce, and cook for 2 minutes. Serve.

Nutrition: calories: 302 | fat: 16g | protein: 22g | carbs: 19g | fiber: 0g | sodium: 753mg

444. Mediterranean Grilled Skirt Steak

Preparation time: 10 minutes
Cooking time: 10 minutes
Serving: 4
Ingredients:
- 1-pound (454 g) skirt steak
- 1 teaspoon salt
- ½ teaspoon freshly ground black pepper
- 2 cups prepared hummus
- 1 tablespoon extra-virgin olive oil
- ½ cup pine nuts

Direction:
1. Preheat a grill, grill pan, or lightly oiled skillet to medium heat.

2. Season both sides of the steak with salt and pepper.
3. Cook the meat on each side for 3 to 5 minutes; 3 minutes for medium, and 5 minutes on each side for well done. Let the meat rest for 5 minutes.
4. Slice the meat into thin strips.
5. Spread the hummus on a serving dish, and evenly distribute the beef on top of the hummus.
6. In a small saucepan, over low heat, add the olive oil and pine nuts. Toast them for 3 minutes, constantly stirring them with a spoon so that they don't burn.
7. Spoon the pine nuts over the beef and serve.

Nutrition :calories: 602 | fat: 41g | protein: 42g | carbs: 20g | fiber: 8g | sodium: 1141mg

445. Beef Kefta

Preparation time: 10 minutes
Cooking time: 5 minutes
Serving: 4
Ingredients:
- 1 medium onion
- 1/3 cup fresh Italian parsley
- 1-pound (454 g) ground beef
- ¼ teaspoon ground cumin
- ¼ teaspoon cinnamon
- 1 teaspoon salt
- ½ teaspoon freshly ground black pepper

Direction:
1. Preheat a grill or grill pan to high.
2. Mince the onion and parsley in a food processor until finely chopped.
3. In a large bowl, using your hands, combine the beef with the onion mix, ground cumin, cinnamon, salt, and pepper.
4. Divide the meat into 6 portions. Form each portion into a flat oval.
5. Place the patties on the grill or grill pan and cook for 3 minutes on each side.

Nutrition:
calories: 203
fat: 10g
protein: 24g
carbs: 3g
fiber: 1g
sodium: 655mg

446. Beef and Potatoes with Tahini Sauce

Preparation time: 10 minutes
Cooking time: 30 minutes
Serving: 4 to 6
Ingredients:
- 1-pound (454 g) ground beef
- 2 teaspoons salt, divided
- ½ teaspoon freshly ground black pepper
- 1 large onion, finely chopped
- 10 medium golden potatoes
- 2 tablespoons extra-virgin olive oil
- 3 cups Greek yogurt
- 1 cup tahini
- 3 cloves garlic, minced
- 2 cups water

Direction:
1. Preheat the oven to 450°F (235°C).

2. In a large bowl, using your hands, combine the beef with 1 teaspoon salt, black pepper, and the onion.
3. Form meatballs of medium size (about 1-inch), using about 2 tablespoons of the beef mixture. Place them in a deep 8-by-8-inch casserole dish.
4. Cut the potatoes into ¼-inch-thick slices. Toss them with the olive oil.
5. Lay the potato slices flat on a lined baking sheet.
6. Put the baking sheet with the potatoes and the casserole dish with the meatballs in the oven and bake for 20 minutes.
7. In a large bowl, mix together the yogurt, tahini, garlic, remaining 1 teaspoon salt, and water; set aside.
8. Once you take the meatballs and potatoes out of the oven, use a spatula to transfer the potatoes from the baking sheet to the casserole dish with the meatballs, and leave the beef drippings in the casserole dish for added flavor.
9. Reduce the oven temperature to 375°F (190°C) and pour the yogurt tahini sauce over the beef and potatoes. Return it to the oven for 10 minutes. Once baking is complete, serve warm with a side of rice or pita bread.

Nutrition: calories: 1078 | fat: 59g | protein: 58g | carbs: 89g | fiber: 11g | sodium: 1368mg

447. Mediterranean Lamb Bowls

Preparation time: 15 minutes
Cooking time: 15 minutes
Serving: 2
Ingredients:
- 2 tablespoons extra-virgin olive oil
- ¼ cup diced yellow onion
- 1-pound (454 g) ground lamb
- 1 teaspoon dried mint
- 1 teaspoon dried parsley
- ½ teaspoon red pepper flakes
- ¼ teaspoon garlic powder
- 1 cup cooked rice
- ½ teaspoon za'atar seasoning
- ½ cup halved cherry tomatoes
- 1 cucumber, peeled and diced
- 1 cup store-bought hummus
- 1 cup crumbled feta cheese
- 2 pita bread, warmed (optional)

Direction:
1. In a large sauté pan or skillet, heat the olive oil over medium heat and cook the onion for about 2 minutes, until fragrant. Add the lamb and mix well, breaking up the meat as you cook. Once the lamb is halfway cooked, add mint, parsley, red pepper flakes, and garlic powder.
2. In a medium bowl, mix together the cooked rice and za'atar, then divide between individual serving bowls. Add the seasoned lamb, then top the bowls with the tomatoes, cucumber, hummus, feta, and pita (if using).

Nutrition:
calories: 1312 | fat: 96g | protein: 62g | carbs: 62g | fiber: 12g | sodium: 1454mg

448. Smoked Pork Sausage

Preparation time: 20 minutes
Cooking Time: 15 Minutes
Servings: 6
Ingredients:
- 3/4-pound smoked pork sausage, ground
- 1 teaspoon ginger-garlic paste
- 2 tablespoons scallions, minced
- 1 tablespoon butter, room temperature
- 1 tomato, pureed
- 4 ounces mozzarella cheese, crumbled
- 2 tablespoons flaxseed meal
- 8 ounces cream cheese, room temperature
- Sea salt and ground black pepper, to taste

Direction:
1. Melt the butter in a frying pan over medium-high heat. Cook the sausage for about 4 minutes, crumbling with a spatula.
2. Add in the ginger-garlic paste, scallions, and tomato; continue to cook over medium-low heat for a further 6 minutes. Stir in the remaining Shopping List:.
3. Place the mixture in your refrigerator for 1 to 2 hours until firm. Roll the mixture into bite-sized balls.
4. Storing
5. Transfer the balls to the airtight containers and place in your refrigerator for up to 3 days.
6. For freezing, place in a freezer safe containers and freeze up to 1 month. Enjoy!

Nutrition: 383 Calories; 32. Fat; 5.1g Carbs; 16.7g Protein; 1.7g Fiber

449. Grilled Beef Kebabs

Preparation time: 15 minutes
Cooking time: 10 minutes
Serving: 6
Ingredients:
- 2 pounds (907 g) beef fillet
- 1½ teaspoons salt
- 1 teaspoon freshly ground black pepper
- ½ teaspoon ground allspice
- ½ teaspoon ground nutmeg
- 1/3 cup extra-virgin olive oil
- 1 large onion, cut into 8 quarters
- 1 large red bell pepper, cut into 1-inch cubes

Direction:
1. Preheat a grill, grill pan, or lightly oiled skillet to high heat.
2. Cut the beef into 1-inch cubes and put them in a large bowl.
3. In a small bowl, mix together the salt, black pepper, allspice, and nutmeg.
4. Pour the olive oil over the beef and toss to coat the beef. Then evenly sprinkle the seasoning over the beef and toss to coat all pieces.
5. Skewer the beef, alternating every 1 or 2 pieces with a piece of onion or bell pepper.
6. To cook, place the skewers on the grill or skillet, and turn every 2 to 3 minutes until all sides have cooked to desired doneness, 6 minutes for medium-rare, 8 minutes for well done. Serve warm.

Nutrition:
calories: 485 | fat: 36g | protein: 35g | carbs: 4g | fiber: 1g | sodium: 1453mg

450. Turkey Wings With Gravy

Preparation time: 30 minutes
Cooking Time: 6 Hours
Servings: 6
Ingredients:

- 2 pounds turkey wings
- 1/2 teaspoon cayenne pepper
- 4 garlic cloves, sliced
- 1 large onion, chopped Salt and pepper, to taste
- 1 teaspoon dried marjoram
- 1 tablespoon butter, room temperature
- 1 tablespoon Dijon mustard

For the Gravy:

- 1 cup double cream
- Salt and black pepper, to taste
- 1/2 stick butter
- 3/4 teaspoon guar gum

Direction:
1. Rub the turkey wings with the Dijon mustard and tablespoon of butter. Preheat a grill pan over medium-high heat.
2. Sear the turkey wings for 10 minutes on all sides.
3. Transfer the turkey to your Crock pot; add in the garlic, onion, salt, pepper, marjoram, and cayenne pepper. Cover and cook on low setting for 6 hours.
4. Melt 1/2 stick of the butter in a frying pan. Add in the cream and whisk until cooked through.
5. Next, stir in the guar gum, salt, and black pepper along with cooking juices. Let it cook until the sauce has reduced by half.
6. Storing
7. Wrap the turkey wings in foil before packing them into airtight containers; keep in your refrigerator for up to 3 to 4 days.
8. For freezing, place the turkey wings in airtight containers or heavy-duty freezer bags. Freeze up to 2 to 3 months. Defrost in the refrigerator.
9. Keep your gravy in refrigerator for up to 2 days.

Nutrition: 280 Calories; 22.2g Fat; 4.3g Carbs; 15.8g Protein; 0.8g Fiber

451. Saucy Boston Butt

Preparation time: 30 minutes
Cooking Time: 1 Hour 20 Minutes
Servings: 8
Ingredients:

- 1 tablespoon lard, room temperature
- 2 pounds Boston butt, cubed
- Salt and freshly ground pepper
- 1/2 teaspoon mustard powder
- A bunch of spring onions, chopped
- 2 garlic cloves, minced
- 1/2 tablespoon ground cardamom
- 2 tomatoes, pureed
- 1 bell pepper, deveined and chopped
- jalapeno pepper, deveined and finely chopped
- 1/2 cup unsweetened coconut milk
- 2 cups chicken bone broth

Direction:
1. In a wok, melt the lard over moderate heat. Season the pork belly with salt, pepper and mustard powder.
2. Sear the pork for 8 to 10 minutes, stirring periodically to ensure even cooking; set aside, keeping it warm.
3. In the same wok, sauté the spring onions, garlic, and cardamom. Spoon the sautéed vegetables along with the reserved pork into the slow cooker.
4. Add in the remaining Shopping List:, cover with the lid and cook for 1 hour 10 minutes over low heat.
5. Storing
6. Divide the pork and vegetables between airtight containers or Ziploc bags; keep in your refrigerator for up to 3 to 5 days.
7. For freezing, place the pork and vegetables in airtight containers or heavy-duty freezer bags. Freeze up to 4 months. Defrost in the refrigerator. Bon appétit!

Nutrition: 369 Calories; 20.2g Fat; 2.9g Carbs; 41.3g Protein; 0.7g Fiber

452. Lamb Burgers

Preparation time: 15 minutes
Cooking time: 15 minutes
Serving: 4
Ingredients:

- 1-pound (454 g) ground lamb
- ½ small red onion, grated
- 1 tablespoon dried parsley
- 1 teaspoon dried oregano
- 1 teaspoon ground cumin
- 1 teaspoon garlic powder
- ½ teaspoon dried mint
- ¼ teaspoon paprika
- ¼ teaspoon kosher salt
- 1/8 teaspoon freshly ground black pepper
- Extra-virgin olive oil
- 4 pita bread, for serving (optional)
- Tzatziki sauce, for serving (optional)
- Pickled onions, for serving (optional)

Direction:
1. In a bowl, combine the lamb, onion, parsley, oregano, cumin, garlic powder, mint, paprika, salt, and pepper. Divide the meat into 4 small balls and work into smooth discs.
2. In a large sauté pan or skillet, heat a drizzle of olive oil over medium heat or brush a grill with oil and set it to medium. Cook the patties for 4 to 5 minutes on each side, until cooked through and juices run clear.
3. Enjoy lamb burgers in pitas, topped with tzatziki sauce and pickled onions (if using).

Nutrition:
calories: 328 | fat: 27g | protein: 19g | carbs: 2g | fiber: 1g | sodium: 215mg

453. Spare Ribs

Preparation time: 30 minutes
Cooking Time: 3 Hour 40 Minutes
Servings: 6,
Ingredients:

- 1 pounds spare ribs

- 1 garlic clove, minced
- 2 teaspoon dried marjoram
- 1 lime, halved
- Salt and ground black pepper, to taste

Direction:
1. Toss all Shopping List: in a ceramic dish.
2. Cover and let it refrigerate for 5 to 6 hours.
3. Roast the foil-wrapped ribs in the preheated oven at 275 degrees F degrees for about hours 30 minutes.
4. Storing
5. Divide the ribs into six portions. Place each portion of ribs in an airtight container; keep in your refrigerator for 3 to days.
6. For freezing, place the ribs in airtight containers or heavy-duty freezer bags. Freeze up to 4 to months. Defrost in the refrigerator and reheat in the preheated oven. Bon appétit!

Nutrition: 385 Calories; 29g Fat; 1.8g Carbs; 28.3g Protein; 0.1g Fiber

454. Cheesy Pork

Preparation time: 20 minutes
Cooking Time: 20 Minutes
Servings: 6
Ingredients:
- 1 tablespoon sesame oil
- 1 ½ pounds pork shoulder, cut into strips
- Himalayan salt and freshly ground black pepper, to taste
- 1/2 teaspoon cayenne pepper
- 1/2 cup shallots, roughly chopped
- 2 bell peppers, sliced
- 1/4 cup cream of onion soup
- 1/2 teaspoon Sriracha sauce
- 1 tablespoon tahini (sesame butter 1 tablespoon soy sauce
- 4 ounces gouda cheese, cut into small pieces

Direction:
1. Heat he sesame oil in a wok over a moderately high flame.
2. Stir-fry the pork strips for 3 to 4 minutes or until just browned on all sides. Add in the spices, shallots and bell peppers and continue to cook for a further 4 minutes.
3. Stir in the cream of onion soup, Sriracha, sesame butter, and soy sauce; continue to cook for to 4 minutes more.
4. Top with the cheese and continue to cook until the cheese has melted.
5. Storing
6. Place your stir-fry in six airtight containers or Ziploc bags; keep in your refrigerator for 3 to 4 days.
7. For freezing, wrap tightly with heavy-duty aluminum foil or freezer wrap. It will maintain the best quality for 2 to 3 months. Defrost in the refrigerator and reheat in your wok.

Nutrition: 424 Calories; 29.4g Fat; 3. Carbs; 34.2g Protein; 0.6g Fiber

455. Pulled Pork

Preparation time: 2 hours
Cooking Time: 6 Hours
Servings: 4
Ingredients:
- 1 ½ pounds pork shoulder
- 1 tablespoon liquid smoke sauce
- 1 teaspoon chipotle powder
- Au Jus gravy seasoning packet
- 2 onions, cut into wedges
- Kosher salt and freshly ground black pepper, taste

Direction:
1. Mix the liquid smoke sauce, chipotle powder, Au Jus gravy seasoning packet, salt and pepper. Rub the spice mixture into the pork on all sides.
2. Wrap in plastic wrap and let it marinate in your refrigerator for 3 hours.
3. Prepare your grill for indirect heat. Place the pork butt roast on the grate over a drip pan and top with onions; cover the grill and cook for about 6 hours.
4. Transfer the pork to a cutting board. Now, shred the meat into bite-sized pieces using two forks.
5. Storing
6. Divide the pork between four airtight containers or Ziploc bags; keep in your refrigerator for up to 3 to 5 days.
7. For freezing, place the pork in airtight containers or heavy-duty freezer bags. Freeze up to 4 months. Defrost in the refrigerator. Bon appétit!

Nutrition: 350 Calories; 11g Fat; 5g Carbs; 53.6g Protein; 2.2g Fiber

456. Brie-stuffed Meatballs

Preparation time: 20 minutes
Cooking Time: 25 Minutes
Servings: 5
Ingredients:
- 2 eggs, beaten
- 1-pound ground pork
- 1/3 cup double cream
- 1 tablespoon fresh parsley
- Kosher salt and ground black pepper
- 1 teaspoon dried rosemary
- 10 (1-inch cubes of brie cheese)
- 2 tablespoons scallions, minced
- 2 cloves garlic, minced

Direction:
1. Mix all Shopping List:, except for the brie cheese, until everything is well incorporated.
2. Roll the mixture into 10 patties; place a piece of cheese in the center of each patty and roll into a ball.
3. Roast in the preheated oven at 0 degrees F for about 20 minutes.
4. Storing
5. Place the meatballs in airtight containers or Ziploc bags; keep in your refrigerator for up to 3 to 4 days.
6. Freeze the meatballs in airtight containers or heavy-duty freezer bags. Freeze up to 3 to 4 months. To defrost, slowly reheat in a saucepan. Bon appétit!

Nutrition: 302 Calories; 13g Fat; 1.9g Carbs; 33.4g Protein; 0.3g Fiber

457. Pork in Cheese Sauce

Preparation time: 25 minutes
Cooking Time: 30 Minutes
Servings: 6
Ingredients:

- 2 pounds pork center cut loin roast, boneless and cut into 6 pieces
- 1 tablespoon coconut aminos
- 6 ounces blue cheese
- 1/3 cup heavy cream
- 1/3 cup port wine
- 1/3 cup roasted vegetable broth, preferably homemade 1 teaspoon dried hot chile flakes
- 1 teaspoon dried rosemary
- 1 tablespoon lard
- 1/2 shallot, chopped
- 2 garlic cloves, chopped
- Salt and freshly cracked black peppercorns, to taste

Direction:

1. Rub each piece of the pork with salt, black peppercorns, and rosemary.
2. Melt the lard in a saucepan over a moderately high flame. Sear the pork on all sides about 15 minutes; set aside.
3. Cook the shallot and garlic until they've softened. Add in port wine to scrape up any brown bits from the bottom.
4. Reduce the heat to medium-low and add in the remaining Shopping List:; continue to simmer until the sauce has thickened and reduced.
5. Storing
6. Divide the pork and sauce into six portions; place each portion in a separate airtight container or Ziploc bag; keep in your refrigerator for 3 to 4 days.
7. Freeze the pork and sauce in airtight containers or heavy-duty freezer bags. Freeze up to 4 months. Defrost in the refrigerator. Bon appétit!

Nutrition: 34Calories; 18.9g Fat; 1.9g Carbs; 40.3g Protein; 0.3g Fiber

458. Lamb Koftas

Preparation time: 30 minutes
Cooking time: 15 minutes
Serving 4
Ingredients:

- 1-pound (454 g) ground lamb
- 1/2 cup finely chopped fresh mint, plus 2 tablespoons
- 1/4 cup almond or coconut flour
- 1/4 cup finely chopped red onion
- 1/4 cup toasted pine nuts
- 2 teaspoons ground cumin
- 1 1/2 teaspoons salt, divided
- 1 teaspoon ground cinnamon
- 1 teaspoon ground ginger
- 1/2 teaspoon ground nutmeg
- 1/2 teaspoon freshly ground black pepper
- 1 cup plain whole-milk Greek yogurt
- 2 tablespoons extra-virgin olive oil
- Zest and juice of 1 lime

Direction:

1. Heat the oven broiler to the low setting. You can also bake these at high heat (450 to 475°F / 235 to 245°C) if you happen to have a very hot broiler. Submerge four wooden skewers in water and let soak at least 10 minutes to prevent them from burning.
2. In a large bowl, combine the lamb, 1/2 cup mint, almond flour, red onion, pine nuts, cumin, 1 teaspoon salt, cinnamon, ginger, nutmeg, and pepper and, using your hands, incorporate all the Shopping List: together well.
3. Form the mixture into 12 egg-shaped patties and let sit for 10 minutes.
4. Remove the skewers from the water, thread 3 patties onto each skewer, and place on a broiling pan or wire rack on top of a baking sheet lined with aluminum foil. Broil on the top rack until golden and cooked through, 8 to 12 minutes, flipping once halfway through cooking.
5. While the meat cooks, in a small bowl, combine the yogurt, olive oil, remaining 2 tablespoons chopped mint, remaining 1/2 teaspoon salt, and lime zest and juice and whisk to combine well. Keep cool until ready to use.
6. Serve the skewers with yogurt sauce.

Nutrition:
calories: 500 | fat: 42g | protein: 23g | carbs: 9g | fiber: 2g | sodium: 969mg

459. Lamb Burgers with Spicy Mayo

Preparation time: 15 minutes
Cooking time: 13 minutes
Serving 2
Ingredients:

- 1/2 small onion, minced
- 1 garlic clove, minced
- 2 teaspoons minced fresh parsley
- 2 teaspoons minced fresh mint
- 1/4 teaspoon salt
- Pinch freshly ground black pepper
- 1 teaspoon cumin
- 1 teaspoon smoked paprika
- 1/4 teaspoon coriander
- 8 ounces (227 g) lean ground lamb
- 2 tablespoons olive oil mayonnaise
- 1/2 teaspoon harissa paste, plus more or less to taste
- 2 hamburger buns or pitas, fresh greens, tomato slices (optional, for serving)

Direction:

1. Preheat the grill to medium-high, 350°F (180°C) to 400°F (205°C) and oil the grill grate. Alternatively, you can cook these in a heavy pan (cast iron is best) on the stovetop.
2. In a large bowl, combine the onion, garlic, parsley, mint, salt, pepper, cumin, paprika, and coriander. Add the lamb and, using your hands, combine the meat with the spices so they are evenly distributed. Form meat mixture into 2 patties.
3. Grill the burgers for 4 minutes per side, or until the internal temperature registers 160°F (71°C) for medium.
4. If cooking on the stovetop, heat the pan to medium-high and oil the pan. Cook the burgers for

5 to 6 minutes per side, or until the internal temperature registers 160°F (71°C).

5. While the burgers are cooking, combine the mayonnaise and harissa in a small bowl.

6. Serve the burgers with the harissa mayonnaise and slices of tomato and fresh greens on a bun or pita—or skip the bun altogether.

Nutrition:
calories: 381 | fat: 20g | protein: 22g | carbs: 27g | fiber: 2g | sodium: 653mg

460. Filet Mignon

Preparation time: 15 minutes
Cooking time: 16 minutes
Serving: 2
Ingredients:
- 2 (3-ounce / 85-g) pieces filet mignon
- 2 tablespoons olive oil, divided
- 8 ounces (227 g) baby bella (cremini) mushrooms, quartered
- 1/3 cup large shallot, minced
- 2 teaspoons flour
- 2 teaspoons tomato paste
- ½ cup red wine
- 1 cup low-sodium chicken stock
- ½ teaspoon dried thyme
- 1 sprig fresh rosemary
- 1 teaspoon herbes de Provence
- ¼ teaspoon salt
- ¼ teaspoon garlic powder
- ¼ teaspoon onion powder
- Pinch freshly ground black pepper

Direction:
1. Preheat the oven to 425°F (220°C) and set the oven rack to the middle position.

2. Remove the filets from the refrigerator about 30 minutes before you're ready to cook them. Pat them dry with a paper towel and let them rest while you prepare the mushroom sauce.

3. In a sauté pan, heat 1 tablespoon of olive oil over medium-high heat. Add the mushrooms and shallot and sauté for 10 minutes.

4. Add the flour and tomato paste and cook for another 30 seconds. Add the wine and scrape up any browned bits from the sauté pan. Add the chicken stock, thyme, and rosemary.

5. Stir the sauce so the flour doesn't form lumps and bring it to a boil. Once the sauce thickens, reduce the heat to the lowest setting and cover the pan to keep the sauce warm.

6. In a small bowl, combine the herbes de Provence, salt, garlic powder, onion powder, and pepper.

7. Rub the beef with the remaining 1 tablespoon of olive oil and season it on both sides with the herb mixture.

8. Heat an oven-safe sauté pan over medium-high heat. Add the beef and sear for 2½ minutes on each side. Then, transfer the pan to the oven for 5 more minutes to finish cooking. Use a meat thermometer to check the internal temperature and remove it at 130°F for medium-rare.

9. Tent the meat with foil and let it rest for 5 minutes before serving topped with the mushroom sauce.

Nutrition:
calories: 385

fat: 20g
protein: 25g
carbs: 15g
fiber: 0g
sodium: 330mg

461. Moist Shredded Beef

Preparation Time: 10 minutes
Cooking Time: 20 minutes
Servings: 8
INGREDIENTS
- 2 lbs. beef chuck roast, cut into chunks
- 1/2 tbsp dried red pepper
- 1 tbsp Italian seasoning
- 1 tbsp garlic, minced
- 2 tbsp vinegar
- 14 oz can fire-roasted tomatoes
- 1/2 cup bell pepper, chopped
- 1/2 cup carrots, chopped
- 1 cup onion, chopped
- 1 tsp salt

DIRECTIONS
1. Add all ingredients into the inner pot of instant pot and set the pot on sauté mode. Seal pot with lid and cook on high for 20 minutes.

2. Once done, release pressure using quick release. Remove lid.

3. Shred the meat using a fork. Stir well and serve.

NUTRITION:
Calories 456 Fat 32.7 g Carbohydrates 7.7 g Sugar 4.1 g Protein 31 g Cholesterol 118 mg

462. Hearty Beef Ragu

Preparation Time: 10 minutes
Cooking Time: 50 minutes
Servings: 4
INGREDIENTS
- 1 1/2 lbs. beef steak, diced
- 1 1/2 cup beef stock
- 1 tbsp coconut amino
- 14 oz can tomato, chopped
- 1/2 tsp ground cinnamon
- 1 tsp dried oregano
- 1 tsp dried thyme
- 1 tsp dried basil
- 1 tsp paprika
- 1 bay leaf
- 1 tbsp garlic, chopped
- 1/2 tsp cayenne pepper
- 1 celery stick, diced
- 1 carrot, diced
- 1 onion, diced
- 2 tbsp olive oil
- 1/4 tsp pepper
- 1 1/2 tsp sea salt

DIRECTIONS
1. Add oil into the instant pot and set the pot on sauté mode. Add celery, carrots, onion, and salt and sauté for 5 minutes.

2. Add meat and remaining ingredients and stir everything well. Seal pot with lid and cook on high for 30 minutes.

3. Once done, allow to release pressure naturally for 10 minutes then release remaining using quick release. Remove lid.

4. Shred meat using a fork. Set pot on sauté mode and cook for 10 minutes. Stir every 2-3 minutes. Serve and enjoy.

NUTRITION:
Calories 435 Fat 18.1 g Carbohydrates 12.3 g Sugar 5.5 g Protein 54.4 g Cholesterol 152 mg

463. Tasty Beef Stew

Preparation Time: 10 minutes
Cooking Time: 30 minutes
Servings: 4
INGREDIENTS
- 2 1/2 lbs. beef roast, cut into chunks
- 1 cup beef broth
- 1/2 cup balsamic vinegar
- 1 tbsp honey
- 1/2 tsp red pepper flakes
- 1 tbsp garlic, minced
- Pepper
- Salt

DIRECTIONS
1. Add all ingredients into the inner pot of instant pot and stir well. Seal pot with lid and cook on high for 30 minutes.
2. Once done, allow to release pressure naturally. Remove lid. Stir well and serve.

NUTRITION:
Calories 562 Fat 18.1 g Carbohydrates 5.7 g Sugar 4.6 g Protein 87.4 g Cholesterol 253 mg

464. Meatloaf

Preparation Time: 10 minutes
Cooking Time: 35 minutes
Servings: 6
INGREDIENTS
- 2 lbs. ground beef
- 2 eggs, lightly beaten
- 1/4 tsp dried basil
- 3 tbsp olive oil
- 1/2 tsp dried sage
- 1 1/2 tsp dried parsley
- 1 tsp oregano
- 2 tsp thyme
- 1 tsp rosemary
- Pepper
- Salt

DIRECTIONS
1. Pour 1 1/2 cups of water into the instant pot then place the trivet in the pot. Spray loaf pan with cooking spray.
2. Add all ingredients into the mixing bowl and mix until well combined. Transfer meat mixture into the prepared loaf pan and place loaf pan on top of the trivet in the pot.
3. Seal pot with lid and cook on high for 35 minutes.
4. Once done, allow to release pressure naturally for 10 minutes then release remaining using quick release. Remove lid. Serve and enjoy.

NUTRITION:
Calories 365 Fat 18 g Carbohydrates 0.7 g Sugar 0.1 g Protein 47.8 g Cholesterol 190 mg

465. Flavorful Beef Bourguignon

Preparation Time: 10 minutes
Cooking Time: 20 minutes
Servings: 4
INGREDIENTS
- 1 1/2 lbs. beef chuck roast, cut into chunks
- 2/3 cup beef stock
- 2 tbsp fresh thyme
- 1 bay leaf 1 tsp garlic, minced
- 8 oz mushrooms, sliced
- 2 tbsp tomato paste
- 2/3 cup dry red wine
- 1 onion, sliced
- 4 carrots, cut into chunks
- 1 tbsp olive oil
- Pepper
- Salt

DIRECTIONS
1. Add oil into the instant pot and set the pot on sauté mode. Add meat and sauté until brown. Add onion and sauté until softened.
2. Add remaining ingredients and stir well. Seal pot with lid and cook on high for 12 minutes.
3. Once done, allow to release pressure naturally. Remove lid. Stir well and serve.

NUTRITION:
Calories 744 Fat 51.3 g Carbohydrates 14.5 g Sugar 6.5 g Protein 48.1 g Cholesterol 175 mg

466. Delicious Beef Chili

Preparation Time: 10 minutes
Cooking Time: 35 minutes
Servings: 8
INGREDIENTS
- 2 lbs. ground beef
- 1 tsp olive oil
- 1 tsp garlic, minced
- 1 small onion, chopped
- 2 tbsp chili powder
- 1 tsp oregano
- 1/2 tsp thyme
- 28 oz can tomato, crushed
- 2 cups beef stock
- 2 carrots, chopped
- 3 sweet potatoes, peeled and cubed
- Pepper
- Salt

DIRECTIONS
1. Add oil into the instant pot and set the pot on sauté mode. Add meat and cook until brown. Add remaining ingredients and stir well.
2. Seal pot with lid and cook on high for 35 minutes.
3. Once done, allow to release pressure naturally. Remove lid. Stir well and serve.

NUTRITION:
Calories 302 Fat 8.2 g Carbohydrates 19.2 g Sugar 4.8 g Protein 37.1 g Cholesterol 101 mg

467. Rosemary Creamy Beef

Preparation Time: 10 minutes
Cooking Time: 40 minutes
Servings: 4
INGREDIENTS
- 2 lbs. beef stew meat, cubed

- 2 tbsp fresh parsley, chopped
- 1 tsp garlic, minced
- 1/2 tsp dried rosemary
- 1 tsp chili powder
- 1 cup beef stock
- 1 cup heavy cream
- 1 onion, chopped
- 1 tbsp olive oil
- Pepper
- Salt

DIRECTIONS
1. Add oil into the instant pot and set the pot on sauté mode. Add rosemary, garlic, onion, and chili powder and sauté for 5 minutes. Add meat and cook for 5 minutes.
2. Add remaining ingredients and stir well. Seal pot with lid and cook on high for 30 minutes.
3. Once done, allow to release pressure naturally for 10 minutes then release remaining using quick release. Remove lid. Serve and enjoy.

NUTRITION:
Calories 574 Fat 29 g Carbohydrates 4.3 g Sugar 1.3 g Protein 70.6 g Cholesterol 244 mg

468. Spicy Beef Chili Verde

Preparation Time: 10 minutes
Cooking Time: 23 minutes
Servings: 2
INGREDIENTS
- 1/2 lb. beef stew meat, cut into cubes
- 1/4 tsp chili powder
- 1 tbsp olive oil
- 1 cup chicken broth
- 1 Serrano pepper, chopped
- 1 tsp garlic, minced
- 1 small onion, chopped
- 1/4 cup grape tomatoes, chopped
- 1/4 cup tomatillos, chopped
- Pepper
- Salt

DIRECTIONS
1. Add oil into the instant pot and set the pot on sauté mode. Add garlic and onion and sauté for 3 minutes. Add remaining ingredients and stir well.
2. Seal pot with lid and cook on high for 20 minutes.
3. Once done, allow to release pressure naturally. Remove lid. Stir well and serve.

NUTRITION:
Calories 317 Fat 15.1 g Carbohydrates 6.4 g Sugar 2.6 g Protein 37.8 g Cholesterol 101 mg

469. Carrot Mushroom Beef Roast

Preparation Time: 10 minutes
Cooking Time: 40 minutes
Servings: 4
INGREDIENTS
- 1 1/2 lbs. beef roast
- 1 tsp paprika
- 1/4 tsp dried rosemary
- 1 tsp garlic, minced
- 1/2 lb. mushrooms, sliced
- 1/2 cup chicken stock
- 2 carrots, sliced
- Pepper

- Salt

DIRECTIONS
1. Add all ingredients into the inner pot of instant pot and stir well. Seal pot with lid and cook on high for 40 minutes.
2. Once done, allow to release pressure naturally for 10 minutes then release remaining using quick release. Remove lid. Slice and serve.

NUTRITION:
Calories 345 Fat 10.9 g Carbohydrates 5.6 g Sugar 2.6 g Protein 53.8 g Cholesterol 152 mg

470. Thyme Beef Round Roast

Preparation Time: 10 minutes
Cooking Time: 55 minutes
Servings: 8
INGREDIENTS
- 4 lbs. beef bottom round roast, cut into pieces
- 2 tbsp honey
- 5 fresh thyme sprigs
- 2 cups red wine
- 1 lb. carrots, cut into chunks
- 2 cups chicken broth
- 6 garlic cloves, smashed
- 1 onion, diced
- 1/4 cup olive oil
- 2 lbs. potatoes, peeled and cut into chunks
- Pepper
- Salt

DIRECTIONS
1. Add all ingredients except carrots and potatoes into the instant pot. Seal pot with lid and cook on high for 45 minutes.
2. Once done, release pressure using quick release. Remove lid. Add carrots and potatoes and stir well.
3. Seal pot again with lid and cook on high for 10 minutes.
4. Once done, allow to release pressure naturally. Remove lid. Stir well and serve.

NUTRITION:
Calories 648 Fat 21.7 g Carbohydrates 33.3 g Sugar 9.7 g Protein 67.1 g Cholesterol 200 mg

471. Jalapeno Beef Chili

Preparation Time: 10 minutes
Cooking Time: 40 minutes
Servings: 8
INGREDIENTS
- 1 lb. ground beef
- 1 tsp garlic powder
- 1 jalapeno pepper, chopped
- 1 tbsp ground cumin
- 1 tbsp chili powder
- 1 lb. ground pork
- 4 tomatillos, chopped
- 1/2 onion, chopped
- 5 oz tomato paste
- Pepper
- Salt

DIRECTIONS
1. Add oil into the instant pot and set the pot on sauté mode.
2. Add beef and pork and cook until brown. Add remaining ingredients and stir well.

3. Seal pot with lid and cook on high for 35 minutes.
4. Once done, allow to release pressure naturally. Remove lid. Stir well and serve.

NUTRITION:
Calories 217 Fat 6.1 g Carbohydrates 6.2 g Sugar 2.7 g Protein 33.4 g Cholesterol 92 mg

472. Beef with Tomatoes

Preparation Time: 10 minutes
Cooking Time: 40 minutes
Servings: 4
INGREDIENTS
- 2 lb. beef roast, sliced
- 1 tbsp chives, chopped
- 1 tsp garlic, minced
- 1/2 tsp chili powder
- 2 tbsp olive oil
- 1 onion, chopped
- 1 cup beef stock
- 1 tbsp oregano, chopped
- 1 cup tomatoes, chopped
- Pepper
- Salt

DIRECTIONS
1. Add oil into the instant pot and set the pot on sauté mode. Add garlic, onion, and chili powder and sauté for 5 minutes. Add meat and cook for 5 minutes.
2. Add remaining ingredients and stir well. Seal pot with lid and cook on high for 30 minutes.
3. Once done, allow to release pressure naturally for 10 minutes then release remaining using quick release. Remove lid. Stir well and serve.

NUTRITION:
Calories 511 Fat 21.6 g Carbohydrates 5.6 g Sugar 2.5 g Protein 70.4 g Cholesterol 203 mg

473. Tasty Beef Goulash

Preparation Time: 10 minutes
Cooking Time: 30 minutes
Servings: 2
INGREDIENTS
- 1/2 lb. beef stew meat, cubed
- 1 tbsp olive oil
- 1/2 onion, chopped
- 1/2 cup sun-dried tomatoes, chopped
- 1/4 zucchini, chopped
- 1/2 cabbage, sliced
- 1 1/2 tbsp olive oil
- 2 cups chicken broth
- Pepper
- Salt

DIRECTIONS
1. Add oil into the instant pot and set the pot on sauté mode.
2. Add onion and sauté for 3-5 minutes. Add tomatoes and cook for 5 minutes.
3. Add remaining ingredients and stir well. Seal pot with lid and cook on high for 20 minutes.
4. Once done, allow to release pressure naturally for 10 minutes then release remaining using quick release. Remove lid. Stir well and serve.

NUTRITION:
Calories 389 Fat 15.8 g Carbohydrates 19.3 g Sugar 10.7 g Protein 43.2 g Cholesterol 101 mg

474. Beef & Beans

Preparation Time: 10 minutes
Cooking Time: 30 minutes
Servings: 4
INGREDIENTS
- 1 1/2 lbs. beef, cubed
- 8 oz can tomato, chopped
- 8 oz red beans, soaked overnight and rinsed
- 1 tsp garlic, minced
- 1 1/2 cups beef stock
- 1/2 tsp chili powder
- 1 tbsp paprika
- 2 tbsp olive oil
- 1 onion, chopped
- Pepper
- Salt

DIRECTIONS
1. Add oil into the instant pot and set the pot on sauté mode. Add meat and cook for 5 minutes. Add garlic and onion and sauté for 5 minutes.
2. Add remaining ingredients and stir well. Seal pot with lid and cook on high for 25 minutes.
3. Once done, allow to release pressure naturally. Remove lid. Stir well and serve.

NUTRITION:
Calories 604 Fat 18.7 g Carbohydrates 41.6 g Sugar 4.5 g Protein 66.6 g Cholesterol 152 mg

475. Garlic Caper Beef Roast

Preparation Time: 10 minutes
Cooking Time: 40 minutes
Servings: 4
INGREDIENTS
- 2 lbs. beef roast, cubed
- 1 tbsp fresh parsley, chopped
- 1 tbsp capers, chopped
- 1 tbsp garlic, minced
- 1 cup chicken stock
- 1/2 tsp dried rosemary
- 1/2 tsp ground cumin
- 1 onion, chopped
- 1 tbsp olive oil
- Pepper
- Salt

DIRECTIONS
1. Add oil into the instant pot and set the pot on sauté mode. Add garlic and onion and sauté for 5 minutes.
2. Add meat and cook until brown. Add remaining ingredients and stir well.
3. Seal pot with lid and cook on high for 30 minutes.
4. Once done, allow to release pressure naturally. Remove lid. Stir well and serve.

NUTRITION:
Calories 470 Fat 17.9 g Carbohydrates 3.9 g Sugar 1.4 g Protein 69.5 g Cholesterol 203 mg

476. Cauliflower Tomato Beef

Preparation Time: 10 minutes
Cooking Time: 25 minutes
Servings: 2
INGREDIENTS
- 1/2 lb. beef stew meat, chopped
- 1 tsp paprika
- 1 tbsp balsamic vinegar
- 1 celery stalk, chopped
- 1/4 cup grape tomatoes, chopped
- 1 onion, chopped

- 1 tbsp olive oil
- 1/4 cup cauliflower, chopped
- Pepper
- Salt

DIRECTIONS
1. Add oil into the instant pot and set the pot on sauté mode. Add meat and sauté for 5 minutes. Add remaining ingredients and stir well.
2. Seal pot with lid and cook on high for 20 minutes.
3. Once done, allow to release pressure naturally. Remove lid. Stir and serve.

NUTRITION:
Calories 306 Fat 14.3 g Carbohydrates 7.6 g Sugar 3.5 g Protein 35.7 g Cholesterol 101 mg

477. Artichoke Beef Roast

Preparation Time: 10 minutes
Cooking Time: 45 minutes
Servings: 6
INGREDIENTS
- 2 lbs. beef roast, cubed
- 1 tbsp garlic, minced
- 1 onion, chopped
- 1/2 tsp paprika
- 1 tbsp parsley, chopped
- 2 tomatoes, chopped
- 1 tbsp capers, chopped
- 10 oz can artichokes, drained and chopped
- 2 cups chicken stock
- 1 tbsp olive oil
- Pepper
- Salt

DIRECTIONS
1. Add oil into the instant pot and set the pot on sauté mode. Add garlic and onion and sauté for 5 minutes. Add meat and cook until brown.
2. Add remaining ingredients and stir well. Seal pot with lid and cook on high for 35 minutes.
3. Once done, allow to release pressure naturally. Remove lid. Serve and enjoy.

NUTRITION:
Calories 344 Fat 12.2 g Carbohydrates 9.2 g Sugar 2.6 g Protein 48.4 g Cholesterol 135 mg

478. Greek Chuck Roast

Preparation Time: 10 minutes
Cooking Time: 35 minutes
Servings: 6
INGREDIENTS
- 3 lbs. beef chuck roast, boneless and cut into chunks
- 1/2 tsp dried basil
- 1 tsp oregano, chopped
- 1 small onion, chopped
- 1 cup tomatoes, diced
- 2 cups chicken broth
- 1 tbsp olive oil
- 1 tbsp garlic, minced
- Pepper
- Salt

DIRECTIONS
1. Add oil into the instant pot and set the pot on sauté mode. Add onion and garlic and sauté for 3-5 minutes. Add meat and sauté for 5 minutes.
2. Add remaining ingredients and stir well. Seal pot with lid and cook on high for 25 minutes.

3. Once done, allow to release pressure naturally. Remove lid. Serve and enjoy.

NUTRITION:
Calories 869 Fat 66 g Carbohydrates 3.2 g Sugar 1.5 g Protein 61.5 g Cholesterol 234 mg

479. Beanless Beef Chili

Preparation Time: 10 minutes
Cooking Time: 20 minutes
Servings: 4
INGREDIENTS
- 1 lb ground beef
- 1/2 tsp dried rosemary
- 1/2 tsp paprika
- 1 tsp garlic powder
- 1/2 tsp chili powder
- 1/2 cup chicken broth
- 1 cup heavy cream
- 1 tbsp olive oil
- 1 tsp garlic, minced
- 1 small onion, chopped
- 1 bell pepper, chopped
- 2 cups tomatoes, diced
- Pepper
- Salt

DIRECTIONS
1. Add oil into the instant pot and set the pot on sauté mode. Add meat, bell pepper, and onion and sauté for 5 minutes.
2. Add remaining ingredients except for heavy cream and stir well.
3. Seal pot with lid and cook on high for 5 minutes.
4. Once done, release pressure using quick release. Remove lid. Add heavy cream and stir well and cook on sauté mode for 10 minutes.
5. Serve and enjoy.

NUTRITION:
Calories 387 Fat 22.2 g Carbohydrates 9.5 g Sugar 5 g Protein 37.2 g Cholesterol 142 mg

480. Sage Tomato Beef

Preparation Time: 10 minutes
Cooking Time: 40 minutes
Servings: 4
INGREDIENTS
- 2 lbs beef stew meat, cubed
- 1/4 cup tomato paste
- 1 tsp garlic, minced
- 2 cups chicken stock
- 1 onion, chopped
- 2 tbsp olive oil 1
- tbsp sage, chopped
- Pepper
- Salt

DIRECTIONS
1. Add oil into the instant pot and set the pot on sauté mode. Add garlic and onion and sauté for 5 minutes. Add meat and sauté for 5 minutes.
2. Add remaining ingredients and stir well. Seal pot with lid and cook on high for 30 minutes.
3. Once done, allow to release pressure naturally. Remove lid. Serve and enjoy.

NUTRITION:
Calories 515 Fat 21.5 g Carbohydrates 7 g Sugar 3.6 g Protein 70 g Cholesterol 203 mg

Chapter 7. Poultry Recipes

481. Garlic Thyme Chicken Drumsticks

Preparation Time: 10 minutes
Cooking Time: 18 minutes
Serving: 4
Ingredients:
- 8 chicken drumsticks, skin-on
- 2 tbsp balsamic vinegar
- 2/3 cup can tomato, diced
- 6 garlic cloves
- 1 tsp lemon zest, grated
- 1 tsp dried thyme
- 1/4 tsp red pepper flakes
- 1 1/2 onions, cut into wedges
- 1 tbsp olive oil
- Pepper Salt

Directions:
1. Add oil into the inner pot of instant pot and set the pot on sauté mode. Add onion and 1/2 tsp salt and sauté for 2-3 minutes.
2. Add chicken, garlic, lemon zest, red pepper flakes, and thyme and mix well.
3. Add vinegar and tomatoes and stir well. Seal pot with lid and cook on high for 15 minutes.
4. Once done, release pressure using quick release. Remove lid. Stir well and serve.

Nutrition: Calories 220 Fat 8.9 g Carbohydrates 7.8 g Sugar 3.2 g Protein 26.4 g Cholesterol 81 mg

482. Chicken and Olives

Preparation time: 10 minutes
Cooking time: 15 minutes
Servings: 4
Ingredients:
- 4 chicken breasts, skinless and boneless
- 2 tablespoons garlic, minced
- 1 tablespoon oregano, dried
- Salt and black pepper to the taste
- 2 tablespoons olive oil
- ½ cup chicken stock
- Juice of 1 lemon
- 1 cup red onion, chopped
- 1 ½ cups tomatoes, cubed
- ¼ cup green olives, pitted and sliced
- A handful parsley, chopped

Directions:
1. Heat up a pan with the oil over medium-high heat, add the chicken, garlic, salt and pepper and brown for 2 minutes on each side.
2. Add the rest of the ingredients, toss, bring the mix to a simmer and cook over medium heat for 13 minutes.
3. Divide the mix between plates and serve.

Nutrition: calories 135, fat 5.8, fiber 3.4, carbs 12.1, protein 9.6

483. Tasty Turkey Chili

Preparation Time: 10 minutes
Cooking Time: 25 minutes
Serving: 4
Ingredients:
- 1 lb cooked turkey, shredded
- 2 cups chicken broth
- 1 tsp tomato paste
- 1 small onion, chopped
- 1 tbsp Italian seasoning
- 1 tsp garlic powder
- 1 tbsp cumin, roasted
- 1 tbsp chili powder cups tomatoes, crushed
- 1 tsp garlic, minced
- 14 oz can red beans, drained
- 14 oz can chickpeas, drained
- 1/2 cup corn
- 2 carrots, peeled and chopped
- 1/2 cup celery, chopped
- 1/4 cup edamame
- 2 tbsp olive oil
- Pepper
- Salt

Directions:
1. Add all ingredients into the instant pot and stir everything well. Seal pot with lid and cook on high for 15 minutes.
2. Once done, allow to release pressure naturally. Remove lid.
3. Set pot on sauté mode and cook for 5-10 minutes or until chili thicken. Stir well and serve.

Nutrition: Calories 593 Fat 18.1 g Carbohydrates 56 g Sugar 7.3 g Protein 50.9 g Cholesterol 88 mg

484. Chicken Bake

Preparation time: 10 minutes
Cooking time: 30 minutes
Servings: 4
Ingredients:
- 1 and ½ pounds chicken thighs, skinless, boneless and cubed
- 2 garlic cloves, minced
- 1 tablespoon oregano, chopped
- 2 tablespoons olive oil
- 1 tablespoon red wine vinegar
- ½ cup canned artichokes, drained and chopped
- 1 red onion, sliced
- 1-pound whole wheat fusili pasta, cooked
- ½ cup canned white beans, drained and rinsed
- ½ cup parsley, chopped
- 1 cup mozzarella, shredded
- Salt and black pepper to the taste

Directions:
1. Heat up a pan with half of the oil over medium-high heat, add the meat and brown for 5 minutes.
2. Grease a baking pan with the rest of the oil, add the browned chicken, and the rest of the ingredients except the pasta and the mozzarella.
3. Spread the pasta all over and toss gently. Sprinkle the mozzarella on top and bake at 425 degrees F for 25 minutes.
4. Divide the bake between plates and serve.

Nutrition: calories 195, fat 5.8, fiber 3.4, carbs 12.1, protein 11.6

485. Moist & Tender Turkey Breast

Preparation Time: 10 minutes
Cooking Time: 25 minutes
Serving: 8
Ingredients:
- 4 lbs turkey breast, bone-in
- 1 tsp Italian seasoning
- 2 tbsp olive oil
- 14 oz chicken broth
- 1 celery ribs, chopped
- 1 large onion, cut into wedges
- 3/4 lbs carrots, cut into pieces
- Pepper
- Salt

Directions:
1. Add carrots, celery, onion, and broth into the instant pot and stir well.
2. Coat turkey breast with oil and season with Italian seasoning, pepper, and salt and place on top of vegetables into the instant pot. Seal pot with lid and cook on high for 25 minutes.
3. Once done, allow to release pressure naturally for 10 minutes then release remaining using quick release. Remove lid. Slice and serve.

Nutrition: Calories 301 Fat 7.7 g Carbohydrates 15.9 g Sugar 11.1 g Protein 40.3 g Cholesterol 98 mg

486. Pesto Chicken Mix

Preparation time: 10 minutes
Cooking time: 40 minutes
Servings: 4
Ingredients:
- 4 chicken breast halves, skinless and boneless
- 3 tomatoes, cubed
- 1 cup mozzarella, shredded
- ½ cup basil pesto
- A pinch of salt and black pepper
- Cooking spray

Directions:
1. Grease a baking dish lined with parchment paper with the cooking spray. In a bowl, mix the chicken with salt, pepper and the pesto and rub well.
2. Place the chicken on the baking sheet, top with tomatoes and shredded mozzarella and bake at 400 degrees F for 40 minutes.
3. Divide the mix between plates and serve with a side salad.

Nutrition: calories 341, fat 20, fiber 1, carbs 4, protein 32

487. Sage Turkey Mix

Preparation time: 10 minutes
Cooking time: 40 minutes
Servings: 4
Ingredients
- 1 big turkey breast, skinless, boneless and roughly cubed
- Juice of 1 lemon
- 2 tablespoons avocado oil
- 1 red onion, chopped
- 2 tablespoons sage, chopped
- 1 garlic clove, minced
- 1 cup chicken stock

Directions
1. Heat up a pan with the avocado oil over medium-high heat, add the turkey and brown for 3 minutes on each side.
2. Add the rest of the ingredients, bring to a simmer and cook over medium heat for 35 minutes.
3. Divide the mix between plates and serve with a side dish.

Nutrition: Calories 382, fat 12.6, fiber 9.6, carbs 16.6, protein 33.2

488. Herb Garlic Chicken

Preparation Time: 10 minutes
Cooking Time: 12 minutes
Serving: 8
Ingredients:
- 4 lbs chicken breasts, skinless and boneless
- 1 tbsp garlic powder
- 2 tbsp dried Italian herb mix
- 2 tbsp olive oil
- 1/4 cup chicken stock
- Pepper
- Salt

Directions:
1. Coat chicken with oil and season with dried herb, garlic powder, pepper, and salt. Place chicken into the instant pot.
2. Pour stock over the chicken.
3. Seal pot with a lid and select manual and set timer for 12 minutes.
4. Once done, allow to release pressure naturally for 5 minutes then release remaining using quick release. Remove lid.
5. Shred chicken using a fork and serve.

Nutrition: Calories 502 Fat 20.8 g Carbohydrates 7.8 g Sugar 1 g Protein 66.8 g Cholesterol 202 mg

489. Chicken Wrap

Preparation time: 10 minutes
Cooking time: 0 minutes
Servings: 2
Ingredients:
- 2 whole wheat tortilla flatbread
- 6 chicken breast slices, skinless, boneless, cooked and shredded
- A handful baby spinach
- 2 provolone cheese slices
- 4 tomato slices
- 10 kalamata olives, pitted and sliced
- 1 red onion, sliced
- 2 tablespoons roasted peppers, chopped

Directions:
1. Arrange the tortillas on a working surface, and divide the chicken and the other ingredients on each.
2. Roll the tortillas and serve them right away.

Nutrition: calories 190, fat 6.8, fiber 3.5, carbs 15.1, protein 6.6

490. Turkey and Asparagus Mix

Preparation time: 10 minutes
Cooking time: 30 minutes
Servings: 4
Ingredients
- 1 bunch asparagus, trimmed and halved

- 1 big turkey breast, skinless, boneless and cut into strips
- 1 teaspoon basil, dried
- 2 tablespoons olive oil
- A pinch of salt and black pepper
- ½ cup tomato sauce
- 1 tablespoon chives, chopped

Directions
1. Heat up a pan with the oil over medium-high heat, add the turkey and brown for 4 minutes.
2. Add the asparagus and the rest of the ingredients except the chives, bring to a simmer and cook over medium heat for 25 minutes.
3. Add the chives, divide the mix between plates and serve.

Nutrition: Calories 337, fat 21.2, fiber 10.2, carbs 21.4, protein 17.6

491. Moroccan Spiced Chicken

Preparation Time: 10 minutes
Cooking Time: 20 minutes
Serving: 4
Ingredients:
- 1 lb chicken thighs, boneless and cut into chunks
- 1 cup can tomato, crushed
- 1/2 tsp red pepper flakes
- 1 tsp dried parsley
- 1/2 tsp coriander
- 1 tsp cumin
- 14 oz can chickpeas, drained and rinsed
- 2 tomatoes, chopped
- 1 tbsp garlic, minced
- 1 onion, sliced red peppers, diced
- 1 tbsp olive oil
- Pepper
- Salt

Directions:
1. Add oil into the inner pot of instant pot and set the pot on sauté mode. Add onion and garlic and sauté for 5 minutes.
2. Add chicken and cook for 5 minutes.
3. Add remaining ingredients and stir well. Seal pot with lid and cook on high for 10 minutes.
4. Once done, release pressure using quick release. Remove lid. Stir well and serve.

Nutrition : Calories 416 Fat 21.3 g Carbohydrates 32.3 g Sugar 4 g Protein 26.1 g Cholesterol 96 mg

492. Chicken and Artichokes

Preparation time: 10 minutes
Cooking time: 20 minutes
Servings: 4
Ingredients:
- 2 pounds chicken breast, skinless, boneless and sliced
- A pinch of salt and black pepper
- 4 tablespoons olive oil
- 8 ounces canned roasted artichoke hearts, drained
- 6 ounces sun-dried tomatoes, chopped
- 3 tablespoons capers, drained
- 2 tablespoons lemon juice

Directions:
1. Heat up a pan with half of the oil over medium-high heat, add the artichokes and the other

ingredients except the chicken, stir and sauté for 10 minutes.
2. Transfer the mix to a bowl, heat up the pan again with the rest of the oil over medium-high heat, add the meat and cook for 4 minutes on each side.
3. Return the veggie mix to the pan, toss, cook everything for 2-3 minutes more, divide between plates and serve.

Nutrition: calories 552, fat 28, fiber 6, carbs 33, protein 43

493. Easy Chicken Scampi

Preparation Time: 10 minutes
Cooking Time: 25 minutes
Serving: 4
Ingredients:
- 3 chicken breasts, skinless, boneless, and sliced
- 1 tsp garlic, minced
- 1 tbsp Italian seasoning
- 2 cups chicken broth
- 1 bell pepper, sliced
- 1/2 onion, sliced
- Pepper
- Salt

Directions:
1. Add chicken into the instant pot and top with remaining ingredients. Seal pot with lid and cook on high for 25 minutes.
2. Once done, release pressure using quick release. Remove lid.
3. Remove chicken from pot and shred using a fork.
4. Return shredded chicken to the pot and stir well. Serve over cooked whole grain pasta and top with cheese.

Nutrition :Calories 254 Fat 9.9 g Carbohydrates 4.6 g Sugar 2.8 g Protein 34.6 g Cholesterol 100 mg

494. Thyme Chicken and Potatoes

Preparation time: 10 minutes
Cooking time: 50 minutes
Servings: 4
Ingredients
- 1 tablespoon olive oil
- 4 garlic cloves, minced
- A pinch of salt and black pepper
- 2 teaspoons thyme, dried
- 12 small red potatoes, halved
- 2 pounds chicken breast, skinless, boneless and cubed
- 1 cup red onion, sliced
- ¾ cup chicken stock
- 2 tablespoons basil, chopped

Directions
1. In a baking dish greased with the oil, add the potatoes, chicken and the rest of the ingredients, toss a bit, introduce in the oven and bake at 400 degrees F for 50 minutes.
2. Divide between plates and serve.

Nutrition: Calories 281, fat 9.2, fiber 10.9, carbs 21.6, protein 13.6

495. Delicious Chicken Cacciatore

Preparation Time: 10 minutes
Cooking Time: 18 minutes
Serving: 6
Ingredients:
- 6 chicken thighs, skinless and boneless

- 1 tbsp fresh parsley, chopped
- 1 tbsp fresh basil, chopped
- 1/4 cup olives, pitted
- 1/2 tsp dried oregano
- 1/4 tsp dried thyme
- 1 1/2 tbsp garlic, minced
- 1 carrot, sliced
- 1 bell pepper, chopped
- 2 tbsp tomato paste
- 28 oz fire-roasted tomatoes, crushed
- 1/2 onion, chopped
- 1 tbsp olive oil
- Pepper
- Salt

Directions:
1. Add oil into the inner pot of instant pot and set the pot on sauté mode. Add onion and sauté for 3 minutes.
2. Add chicken and sauté for 3-5 minutes. Add remaining ingredients except for olives, parsley, and basil and stir well. Seal pot with lid and cook on high for 10 minutes.
3. Once done, allow to release pressure naturally. Remove lid. Add olives, parsley, and basil and stir well. Serve and enjoy.

Nutrition: Calories 375 Fat 13.9 g Carbohydrates 15.2 g Sugar 8.4 g Protein 43.1 g Cholesterol 130 mg

496. Lemon Olive Chicken

Preparation Time: 10 minutes
Cooking Time: 11 minutes
Serving: 8
Ingredients:
- 2 lbs chicken breasts, skinless and boneless
- 4 oz olives, pitted
- 2 lemons, quartered and remove seeds
- 1 cinnamon stick
- 1 tsp turmeric powder
- 1 tsp ground coriander
- 1 tsp ground ginger tsp ground cumin
- 1 1/2 tsp paprika
- 1/2 cup chicken broth
- 1 tbsp garlic, minced
- 1 tbsp olive oil onions, sliced
- Pepper
- Salt

Directions:
1. Add chicken, lemon, cinnamon, turmeric, coriander, ginger, cumin, paprika, pepper, and salt into the zip-lock bag.
2. Seal bag shake well and place in refrigerator overnight.
3. Add oil into the inner pot of instant pot and set the pot on sauté mode. Add garlic and onion and sauté for 5 minutes.
4. Add marinated chicken, broth, and olives and stir well.
5. Seal pot with lid and cook on high for 6 minutes. Once done, allow to release pressure naturally for 10 minutes then release remaining using quick release. Remove lid. Stir and serve.

Nutrition: Calories 271 Fat 12 g Carbohydrates 6.1 g Sugar 1.7 g Protein 33.9 g Cholesterol 101 mg

497. Perfect Chicken & Rice

Preparation Time: 10 minutes
Cooking Time: 25 minutes
Servings: 4
Ingredients:
- 1 lb chicken breasts, skinless and boneless
- 1 tsp olive oil
- 1 cup onion, diced
- 1 tsp garlic minced
- 4 carrots, peeled and sliced
- 1 tbsp Mediterranean spice mix
- 2 cups brown rice, rinsed
- 2 cups chicken stock
- Pepper
- Salt

Directions:
1. Add oil into the inner pot of instant pot and set the pot on sauté mode.
2. Add garlic and onion and sauté until onion is softened.
3. Add stock, carrot, rice, and Mediterranean spice mix and stir well.
4. Place chicken on top of rice mixture and season with pepper and salt. Do not mix.
5. Seal pot with a lid and select manual and set timer for 20 minutes.
6. Once done, allow to release pressure naturally for 10 minutes then release remaining using quick release. Remove lid.
7. Remove chicken from pot and shred using a fork.
8. Return shredded chicken to the pot and stir well.
9. Serve and enjoy.

Nutrition Calories 612 Fat 12.4 g Carbs 81.7 g Protein 41.1 g

498. Flavorful Cafe Rio Chicken

Preparation Time: 10 minutes
Cooking Time: 12 minutes
Servings: 6
Ingredients:
- 2 lbs chicken breasts, skinless and boneless
- 1/2 cup chicken stock
- 2 1/2 tbsp ranch seasoning
- 1/2 tbsp ground cumin
- 1/2 tbsp chili powder
- 1/2 tbsp garlic, minced
- 2/3 cup Italian dressing
- Pepper
- Salt

Directions:
1. Add chicken into the instant pot.
2. Mix together remaining ingredients and pour over chicken.
3. Seal pot with a lid and select manual and set timer for 12 minutes.
4. Once done, allow to release pressure naturally for 10 minutes then release remaining using quick release. Remove lid.
5. Shred the chicken using a fork and serve.

Nutrition: calories 327, fat 17, fiber 4, carbs 30, protein 44

499. Mango Salsa Chicken Burgers

Preparation Time: 15 minutes
Cooking Time: 10 minutes
Servings: 6
Ingredients:
- 1½ pounds ground turkey breast
- 1 teaspoon sea salt, divided
- ¼ teaspoon freshly ground black pepper
- 2 tablespoons extra-virgin olive oil
- 2 mangos, peeled, pitted, and cubed
- ½ red onion, finely chopped
- Juice of 1 lime
- 1 garlic clove, minced
- ½ jalapeño pepper, seeded and finely minced
- 2 tablespoons chopped fresh cilantro leaves

Directions:
1. Form the turkey breast into 4 patties and season with ½ teaspoon of sea salt and the pepper. Cook the olive oil in a nonstick skillet until it shimmers.
2. Add the turkey patties and cook for about 5 minutes per side until browned. While the patties cook, mix together the mango, red onion, lime juice, garlic, jalapeño, cilantro, and remaining ½ teaspoon of sea salt in a small bowl. Spoon the salsa over the turkey patties and serve.

Nutrition: 384 Calories3g Fat 27g Carbohydrates 34g Protein

500. Chicken and Orzo Soup

Preparation time: 10 minutes
Cooking time: 11 minutes
Servings: 4
Ingredients:
- ½ cup carrot, chopped
- 1 yellow onion, chopped
- 12 cups chicken stock
- 2 cups kale, chopped
- 3 cups chicken meat, cooked and shredded
- 1 cup orzo
- ¼ cup lemon juice
- 1 tablespoon olive oil

Directions:
1. Heat up a pot with the oil over medium heat, add the onion and sauté for 3 minutes.
2. Add the carrots and the rest of the ingredients, stir, bring to a simmer and cook for 8 minutes more.
3. Ladle into bowls and serve hot.

Nutrition: calories 300, fat 12.2, fiber 5.4, carbs 16.5, protein 12.2

501. Turkey and Cranberry Sauce

Preparation Time: 10 Minutes
Cooking Time: 50 Minutes
Servings: 4
Ingredients:
- 1 cup chicken stock
- 2 tablespoons avocado oil
- ½ cup cranberry sauce
- 1 big turkey breast, skinless, boneless and sliced
- 1 yellow onion, roughly chopped
- Salt and black pepper to the taste

Directions:
1. Heat up a pan with the avocado oil over medium-high heat, add the onion and sauté for 5 minutes.
2. Add the turkey and brown for 5 minutes more.
3. Add the rest of the ingredients, toss, introduce in the oven at 350 degrees F and cook for 40 minutes

Nutrition:
Calories:382,
Fat:12.6,
Fiber:9.6,
Carbs:26.6,
Protein:17.6

502. Herbed Almond Turkey

Preparation Time: 10 Minutes
Cooking Time: 40 Minutes
Servings: 4
Ingredients:
- 1 big turkey breast, skinless, boneless and cubed
- 1 tablespoon olive oil
- ½ cup chicken stock
- 1 tablespoon basil, chopped
- 1 tablespoon rosemary, chopped
- 1 tablespoon oregano, chopped
- 1 tablespoon parsley, chopped
- 3 garlic cloves, minced
- ½ cup almonds, toasted and chopped
- 3 cups tomatoes, chopped

Directions:
1. Warmth up a pan through the oil over medium-high heat, add the turkey and the garlic and brown for 5 minutes.
2. Add the stock in addition the rest of the fixings, bring to a simmer over medium heat and cook for 35 minutes.
3. Divide the mix between plates and serve.

Nutrition:
Calories:297,
Fat:11.2,
Fiber:9.2,
Carbs:19.4,
Protein:23.6

503. Thyme Chicken

Preparation Time: 10 Minutes
Cooking Time: 50 Minutes
Servings: 4
Ingredients:
- 1 tablespoon olive oil
- 4 garlic cloves, minced
- A pinch of salt and black pepper
- 2 teaspoons thyme, dried
- 12 small red potatoes, halved
- 2 pounds chicken breast, skinless, boneless and cubed
- 1 cup red onion, sliced
- ¾ cup chicken stock
- 2 tablespoons basil, chopped

Directions:
1. In a baking dish greased with the oil, add the potatoes, chicken and the rest of the ingredients, toss a bit, introduce in the oven and bake at 400 degrees F for 50 minutes.

Nutrition:
Calories:281,
Fat:9.2,
Fiber:10.9,
Carbs:21.6,
Protein:13.6

504. Turkey, Artichokes and Asparagus

Preparation Time: 10 Minutes
Cooking Time: 30 Minutes
Servings: 4
Ingredients:
- 2 turkey breasts, boneless, skinless and halved
- 3 tablespoons olive oil

- 1 and ½ pounds asparagus, trimmed and halved
- 1 cup chicken stock
- A pinch of salt and black pepper
- 1 cup canned artichoke hearts, drained
- ¼ cup kalamata olives, pitted and sliced
- 1 shallot, chopped
- 3 garlic cloves, minced
- 3 tablespoons dill, chopped

Directions:

1. Warmth up a pan through the oil over medium-high heat, add the turkey and the garlic and brown for 4 minutes on each side.
2. Add the asparagus, the stock and the rest of the ingredients except the dill, bring to a simmer and cook over medium heat for 20 minutes. Add the dill and serve.

Nutrition:

Calories:291,
Fat:16,
Fiber:10.3,
Carbs:22.8,
Protein:34.5

505. Lemony Turkey and Pine Nuts

Preparation Time: 10 Minutes
Cooking Time: 30 Minutes
Servings: 4
Ingredients:

- 2 turkey breasts, boneless, skinless and halved
- A pinch of salt and black pepper
- 2 tablespoons avocado oil
- Juice of 2 lemons
- 1 tablespoon rosemary, chopped
- 3 garlic cloves, minced
- ¼ cup pine nuts, chopped
- 1 cup chicken stock

Directions:

1. Warmth up a pan through the oil over medium-high heat, add the garlic and the turkey and brown for 4 minutes on each side.
2. Add the rest of the fixings, let it simmer and cook over medium heat for 20 minutes.
3. Divide the mix between plates and serve with a side salad.

Nutrition:

Calories:293,
Fat:12.4,
Fiber:9.3,
Carbs:17.8,
Protein:24.5

506. Yogurt Chicken and Red Onion Mix

Preparation Time: 10 Minutes
Cooking Time: 30 Minutes
Servings: 4
Ingredients:

- 2 pounds chicken breast, skinless, boneless and sliced
- 3 tablespoons olive oil
- ¼ cup Greek yogurt
- 2 garlic cloves, minced
- ½ teaspoon onion powder
- A pinch of salt and black pepper
- 4 red onions, sliced

Directions:

1. In a roasting pan, combine the chicken with the oil, the yogurt and the other ingredients, introduce in the oven at 375 degrees F and bake for 30 minutes.
2. Divide chicken mix between plates and serve hot.

Nutrition:

Calories:278,
Fat:15,
Fiber:9.2,
Carbs:15.1,
Protein:23.3

507. Chicken and Mint Sauce

Preparation Time: 10 Minutes
Cooking Time: 30 Minutes
Servings: 4
Ingredients:

- 2 and ½ tablespoons olive oil
- 2 pounds chicken breasts, skinless, boneless and halved
- 3 tablespoons garlic, minced
- 2 tablespoons lemon juice
- 1 tablespoon red wine vinegar
- 1/3 cup Greek yogurt
- 2 tablespoons mint, chopped
- A pinch of salt and black pepper

Directions:

1. Blend the garlic plus lemon juice and the other ingredients except the oil and the chicken and pulse well.
2. Warmth up a pan through the oil over medium-high heat, add the chicken and brown for 3 minutes on each side.
3. Add the mint sauce, introduce in the oven and bake everything at 370 degrees F for 25 minutes.

Nutrition:

Calories:278,
Fat;12,
Fiber:11.2,
Carbs:18.1,
Protein:13.3

508. Chicken and Sausage Mix

Preparation Time: 10 Minutes
Cooking Time: 50 Minutes
Servings: 4
Ingredients:

- 2 zucchinis, cubed
- 1-pound Italian sausage, cubed
- 2 tablespoons olive oil
- 1 red bell pepper, chopped
- 1 red onion, sliced
- 2 tablespoons garlic, minced
- 2 chicken breasts, boneless, skinless and halved
- Salt and black pepper to the taste
- ½ cup chicken stock
- 1 tablespoon balsamic vinegar

Directions:

1. Heat up a pan with half of the oil over medium-high heat, add the sausages, brown for 3 minutes on each side and transfer to a bowl.
2. Heat up the pan again with the rest of the oil over medium-high heat, add the chicken and brown for 4 minutes on each side.
3. Return the sausage, add the rest of the ingredients as well, bring to a simmer, introduce in the oven and bake at 400 degrees F for 30 minutes.
4. Divide everything between plates and serve.

Nutrition:

Calories:293,
Fat:13.1,
Fiber:8.1,
Carbs:16.6,
Protein:26.1

509. Oregano Turkey and Peppers

Preparation Time: 10 Minutes
Cooking Time: 1 Hour
Servings: 4
Ingredients:
- 2 red bell peppers, cut into strips
- 2 green bell peppers, cut into strips
- 1 red onion, chopped
- 4 garlic cloves, minced
- ½ cup black olives, pitted and sliced
- 2 cups chicken stock
- 1 big turkey breast, skinless, boneless and cut into strips
- 1 tablespoon oregano, chopped
- ½ cup cilantro, chopped

Directions:
1. In a baking pan, combine the peppers with the turkey and the rest of the ingredients, toss, introduce in the oven at 400 degrees F and roast for 1 hour.
2. Divide everything between plates and serve.
Nutrition:
Calories:229,
Fat:8.9,
Fiber:8.2,
Carbs:17.8,
Protein:33.6

510. Chicken and Mustard Sauce

Preparation Time: 10 Minutes
Cooking Time: 26 Minutes
Servings: 4
Ingredients:
- 1/3 cup mustard
- Salt and black pepper to the taste
- 1 red onion, chopped
- 1 tablespoon olive oil
- 1 and ½ cups chicken stock
- 4 chicken breasts, skinless, boneless, and halved
- ¼ teaspoon oregano, dried

Directions:
1. Heat up a pan with the stock over medium heat, add the mustard, onion, salt, pepper and the oregano, whisk, bring to a simmer and cook for 8 minutes.
2. Warmth up a pan through the oil over medium-high heat, add the chicken and brown for 3 minutes on each side.
3. Add chicken into the pan with the sauce, toss, simmer everything for 12 minutes more, divide between plates and serve.
Nutrition:
Calories:247,
Fat:15.1,
Fiber:9.1,
Carbs:16.6,
Protein:26.1

511. Coriander and Coconut Chicken

Preparation Time: 10 Minutes
Cooking Time: 30 Minutes
Servings: 4
Ingredients:
- 2 pounds chicken thighs, skinless, boneless and cubed
- 2 tablespoons olive oil
- Salt and black pepper to the taste
- 3 tablespoons coconut flesh, shredded
- 1 and ½ teaspoons orange extract
- 1 tablespoon ginger, grated
- ¼ cup orange juice

- 2 tablespoons coriander, chopped
- 1 cup chicken stock
- ¼ teaspoon red pepper flakes

Directions:
1. Warmth up a pan through the oil over medium-high heat, add the chicken and brown for 4 minutes on each side.
2. Add salt, pepper and the rest of the ingredients, bring to a simmer and cook over medium heat for 20 minutes.
3. Divide the mix between plates and serve hot.
Nutrition:
Calories:297,
Fat:14.4,
Fiber:9.6,
Carbs:22,
Protein:25

512. Saffron Chicken Thighs and Green Beans

Preparation Time: 10 Minutes
Cooking Time: 25 Minutes
Servings: 4
Ingredients:
- 2 pounds chicken thighs, boneless and skinless
- 2 teaspoons saffron powder
- 1-pound green beans, trimmed and halved
- ½ cup Greek yogurt
- Salt and black pepper to the taste
- 1 tablespoon lime juice
- 1 tablespoon dill, chopped

Directions:
1. In a roasting pan, combine the chicken with the saffron, green beans and the rest of the ingredients, toss a bit, introduce in the oven and bake at 400 degrees F for 25 minutes.
Nutrition:
Calories:274,
Fat:12.3,
Fiber:5.3,
Carbs:20.4,
Protein:14.3

513. Chicken and Olives Salsa

Preparation Time: 10 Minutes
Cooking Time: 25 Minutes
Servings: 4
Ingredients:
- 2 tablespoon avocado oil
- 4 chicken breast halves, skinless and boneless
- Salt and black pepper to the taste
- 1 tablespoon sweet paprika
- 1 red onion, chopped
- 1 tablespoon balsamic vinegar
- 2 tablespoons parsley, chopped
- 1 avocado, peeled, pitted and cubed
- 2 tablespoons black olives, pitted and chopped

Directions:
1. Heat up your grill over medium-high heat, add the chicken brushed with half of the oil and seasoned with paprika, salt and pepper, cook for 7 minutes on each side and divide between plates.
2. Meanwhile, in a bowl, mix the onion with the rest of the ingredients and the remaining oil, toss, add on top of the chicken and serve.
Nutrition:
Calories:289,
Fat:12.4,

Fiber:9.1,
Carbs:23.8,
Protein:14.3

514. Smoked and Hot Turkey Mix

Preparation Time: 10 Minutes
Cooking Time: 40 Minutes
Servings: 4
Ingredients:
- 1 red onion, sliced
- 1 big turkey breast, skinless, boneless and roughly cubed
- 1 tablespoon smoked paprika
- 2 chili peppers, chopped
- Salt and black pepper to the taste
- 2 tablespoons olive oil
- ½ cup chicken stock
- 1 tablespoon parsley, chopped
- 1 tablespoon cilantro, chopped

Directions:
1. Grease a roasting pan through the oil, add the turkey, onion, paprika and the rest of the ingredients, toss, introduce in the oven and bake at 425 degrees F for 40 minutes.
2. Divide the mix between plates and serve right away.
Nutrition:
Calories:310,
Fat:18.4,
Fiber:10.4,
Carbs:22.3,
Protein:33.4

515. Spicy Cumin Chicken

Preparation Time: 10 Minutes
Cooking Time: 25 Minutes
Servings: 4
Ingredients:
- 2 teaspoons chili powder
- 2 and ½ tablespoons olive oil
- Salt and black pepper to the taste
- 1 and ½ teaspoons garlic powder
- 1 tablespoon smoked paprika
- ½ cup chicken stock
- 1-pound chicken breasts, skinless, boneless and halved
- 2 teaspoons sherry vinegar
- 2 teaspoons hot sauce
- 2 teaspoons cumin, ground
- ½ cup black olives, pitted and sliced

Directions:
1. Warm up a pan with the oil over medium-high heat, add the chicken and brown for 3 minutes on each side.
2. Add the chili powder, salt, pepper, garlic powder and paprika, toss and cook for 4 minutes more.
3. Add the rest of the ingredients, toss, bring to a simmer and cook over medium heat for 15 minutes more.
Nutrition:
Calories:230,
Fat:18.4,
Fiber:9.4,
Carbs:15.3,
Protein:13.4

516. Chicken with Artichokes and Beans

Preparation Time: 10 Minutes
Cooking Time: 40 Minutes
Servings: 4
Ingredients:
- 2 tablespoons olive oil

- 2 chicken breasts, skinless, boneless and halved
- Zest of 1 lemon, grated
- 3 garlic cloves, crushed
- Juice of 1 lemon
- Salt and black pepper to the taste
- 1 tablespoon thyme, chopped
- 6 ounces canned artichokes hearts, drained
- 1 cup canned fava beans, drained and rinsed
- 1 cup chicken stock
- A pinch of cayenne pepper

Directions:
1. Warmth up a pan with the oil on medium-high heat, add chicken and brown for 5 minutes.
2. Add lemon juice, lemon zest, salt, pepper and the rest of the ingredients, bring to a simmer and cook over medium heat for 35 minutes.
3. Divide the mix between plates and serve right away.
Nutrition:
Calories:291,
Fat:14.9,
Fiber:10.5,
Carbs:23.8,
Protein:24.2

517. Quick Chicken Salad Wraps

Preparation time: 15 minutes
Cooking time: 0 minutes
Serving: 2
Ingredients:
Tzatziki Sauce:
- ½ cup plain Greek yogurt
- 1 tablespoon freshly squeezed lemon juice
- Pinch garlic powder
- 1 teaspoon dried dill
- Salt and freshly ground black pepper, to taste
Salad Wraps:
- 2 (8-inch) whole-grain pita bread
- 1 cup shredded chicken meat
- 2 cups mixed greens
- 2 roasted red bell peppers, thinly sliced
- ½ English cucumber, peeled if desired and thinly sliced
- ¼ cup pitted black olives
- 1 scallion, chopped

Direction:
1. Make the tzatziki sauce: In a bowl, whisk together the yogurt, lemon juice, garlic powder, dill, salt, and pepper until creamy and smooth.
2. Make the salad wraps: Place the pita bread on a clean work surface and spoon ¼ cup of the tzatziki sauce onto each piece of pita bread, spreading it all over. Top with the shredded chicken, mixed greens, red pepper slices, cucumber slices, black olives, finished by chopped scallion.
3. Roll the salad wraps and enjoy.
Nutrition Per Serving
calories: 428 | fat: 10.6g | protein: 31.1g | carbs: 50.9g | fiber: 6.0g | sodium: 675mg

518. Roasted Chicken Thighs With Basmati Rice

Preparation time: 15 minutes
Cooking time: 50 to 55 minutes
Serving: 2
Ingredients:
Chicken:

- ½ teaspoon cumin
- ½ teaspoon cinnamon
- ½ teaspoon paprika
- ¼ teaspoon ginger powder
- ¼ teaspoon garlic powder
- ¼ teaspoon coriander
- ¼ teaspoon salt
- 1/8 teaspoon cayenne pepper
- 10 ounces (284 g) boneless, skinless chicken thighs (about 4 pieces)

Rice:
- 1 tablespoon olive oil
- ½ small onion, minced
- ½ cup basmati rice
- 2 pinches saffron
- 1 cup low-sodium chicken stock
- ¼ teaspoon salt

Direction:

Make the Chicken

1. Preheat the oven to 350°F (180°C).
2. Combine the cumin, cinnamon, paprika, ginger powder, garlic powder, coriander, salt, and cayenne pepper in a small bowl.
3. Using your hands to rub the spice mixture all over the chicken thighs.
4. Transfer the chicken thighs to a baking dish. Roast in the preheated oven for 35 to 40 minutes, or until the internal temperature reaches 165°F (74°C) on a meat thermometer.

Make the Rice

5. Meanwhile, heat the olive oil in a skillet over medium-high heat.
6. Sauté the onion for 5 minutes until fragrant, stirring occasionally.
7. Stir in the basmati rice, saffron, chicken stock, and salt. Reduce the heat to low, cover, and bring to a simmer for 15 minutes, until light and fluffy.
8. Remove the chicken from the oven to a plate and serve with the rice.

Nutrition Per Serving

calories: 400 | fat: 9.6g | protein: 37.2g | carbs: 40.7g | fiber: 2.1g | sodium: 714mg

519. Panko Grilled Chicken Patties

Preparation time: 10 minutes
Cooking time: 8 to 10 minutes
Serving 4
Ingredients:
- 1-pound (454 g) ground chicken
- 3 tablespoons crumbled feta cheese
- 3 tablespoons finely chopped red pepper
- ¼ cup finely chopped red onion
- 3 tablespoons panko bread crumbs
- 1 garlic clove, minced
- 1 teaspoon chopped fresh oregano
- ¼ teaspoon salt
- 1/8 teaspoon freshly ground black pepper
- Cooking spray

Direction:

1. Mix together the ground chicken, feta cheese, red pepper, red onion, bread crumbs, garlic, oregano, salt, and black pepper in a large bowl, and stir to incorporate.
2. Divide the chicken mixture into 8 equal portions and form each portion into a patty with your hands.
3. Preheat a grill to medium-high heat and oil the grill grates with cooking spray.

4. Arrange the patties on the grill grates and grill each side for 4 to 5 minutes, or until the patties are cooked through.
5. Rest for 5 minutes before serving.

Nutrition Per Serving

calories: 241 | fat: 13.5g | protein: 23.2g | carbs:6.7g | fiber: 1.1g | sodium: 321mg

520. Moroccan Chicken

Preparation Time: 10 minutes
Cooking Time: 25 minutes
Servings: 6
Ingredients:
- 2 lbs chicken breasts, cut into chunks
- 1/2 tsp cinnamon
- 1 tsp turmeric
- 1/2 tsp ginger
- 1 tsp cumin
- 2 tbsp Dijon mustard
- 1 tbsp molasses
- 1 tbsp honey
- 2 tbsp tomato paste
- 5 garlic cloves, chopped
- 2 onions, cut into quarters
- 2 green bell peppers, cut into strips
- 2 red bell peppers, cut into strips
- 2 cups olives, pitted
- 1 lemon, peeled and sliced
- 2 tbsp olive oil
- Pepper
- Salt

Directions:

1. Add oil into the inner pot of instant pot and set the pot on sauté mode.
2. Add chicken and sauté for 5 minutes.
3. Add remaining ingredients and stir everything well.
4. Seal pot with a lid and select manual and set timer for 20 minutes.
5. Once done, release pressure using quick release. Remove lid.
6. Stir well and serve.

Nutrition: Calories 446 Fat 21.2 g Carbs 18.5 g Protein 45.8 g

521. Chicken and Olives Tapenade

Preparation Time: 10 Minutes
Cooking Time: 25 Minutes
Servings: 4
Nutrition:
Calories:291,
Fat:12.9,
Fiber:8.5,
Carbs:15.8,
Protein:34.2
Ingredients:
- 2 chicken breasts, boneless, skinless and halved
- 1 cup black olives, pitted
- ½ cup olive oil
- Salt and black pepper to the taste
- ½ cup mixed parsley, chopped
- ½ cup rosemary, chopped
- Salt and black pepper to the taste
- 4 garlic cloves, minced
- Juice of ½ lime

Directions:

1. In a blender, combine the olives with half of the oil and the rest of the ingredients except the chicken and pulse well.

2. Heat up a pan with the rest of the oil over medium-high heat, add the chicken and brown for 4 minutes on each side.

3. Add the olives mix, and cook for 20 minutes more tossing often.

522. Carrots and Tomatoes Chicken

Preparation Time: 10 Minutes
Cooking Time: 1 Hour 10 Minutes
Servings: 4
Nutrition:
Calories:309,
Fat:12.4,
Fiber:11.1,
Carbs:23.8,
Protein:15.3
Ingredients:
- 2 pounds chicken breasts, skinless, boneless and halved
- Salt and black pepper to the taste
- 3 garlic cloves, minced
- 3 tablespoons avocado oil
- 2 shallots, chopped
- 4 carrots, sliced
- 3 tomatoes, chopped
- ¼ cup chicken stock
- 1 tablespoon Italian seasoning
- 1 tablespoon parsley, chopped
Directions:

1. Warmth up a pan through the oil over medium-high heat, add the chicken, garlic, salt and pepper and brown for 3 minutes on each side.

2. Add the rest of the fixings excluding the parsley, bring to a simmer and cook over medium-low heat for 40 minutes.

523. Turkey Burgers with Mango Salsa

Preparation time: 15 minutes
Cooking time: 10 minutes
Servings: 6
INGREDIENTS:
- 1½ pounds ground turkey breast
- 1 teaspoon sea salt, divided
- ¼ teaspoon freshly ground black pepper
- 2 tablespoons extra-virgin olive oil
- 2 mangos, peeled, pitted, and cubed
- ½ red onion, finely chopped
- Juice of 1 lime
- 1 garlic clove, minced
- ½ jalapeño pepper, seeded and finely minced
- 2 tablespoons chopped fresh cilantro leaves
DIRECTIONS:

1. Form the turkey breast into 4 patties and season with ½ teaspoon of sea salt and pepper.

2. Heat the olive oil until it shimmers in a large nonstick skillet over medium-high heat.

3. Add the turkey patties and cook for about 5 minutes per side until browned.

4. While the patties cook, mix the mango, red onion, lime juice, garlic, jalapeño, cilantro, and remaining ½ teaspoon of sea salt in a small bowl. Spoon the salsa over the turkey patties and serve.

VARIATION TIP: Serve this salsa over grilled halibut. Heat the grill to medium-high heat and brush it with olive oil. Grill 4 (4- to 6-ounce) halibut fillets for about 6 minutes per side. Top with the salsa.

NUTRITION: Calories: 384g Protein: 34g Total Carbohydrates: 27g Sugars: 24g; Fiber: 3g Total Fat: 16g Saturated Fat: 3g Cholesterol: 84mg Sodium: 543mg

524. Herb-Roasted Turkey Breast

Preparation time: 15 minutes
Cooking time: 1½ hours (plus 20 minutes to rest)
Serving: 6
INGREDIENTS:
- 2 tablespoons extra-virgin olive oil
- 4 garlic cloves, minced
- Zest of 1 lemon
- 1 tablespoon chopped fresh thyme leaves
- 1 tablespoon chopped fresh rosemary leaves
- 2 tablespoons chopped fresh Italian parsley leaves
- 1 teaspoon ground mustard
- 1 teaspoon sea salt
- ¼ teaspoon freshly ground black pepper
- 1 (6-pound) bone-in, skin-on turkey breast
- 1 cup dry white wine
DIRECTIONS:

1. Preheat the oven to 325°F.

2. Place the olive oil, garlic, lemon zest, thyme, rosemary, parsley, mustard, sea salt, and pepper in a small cup.

3. Put the herb mixture evenly over the turkey breast's surface, loosen the skin, and rub underneath as well. Place the turkey breast in a roasting pan on a rack, skin-side up

4. Pour the wine into the pan. Roast for 1 to 1½ hours until the turkey reaches an internal temperature of 165°F. In a shallow cup, whisk together the olive oil, garlic, lemon zest, thyme, rosemary, parsley, mustard, sea salt, and pepper..

MAKE IT A MEAL: Serve alongside Sweet Potato Mash (here) and Easy Brussels Sprouts Hash (here) for a complete meal.

NUTRITION: Calories: 392 Protein: 84g Total Carbohydrates: 2g Sugars: <1g Fiber: <1g Total Fat: 6g Saturated Fat: <1g Cholesterol: 210m Sodium: 479mg

525. Chicken Sausage and Peppers

Preparation time: 10 minutes
Cooking time: 20 minutes
Serving: 6
INGREDIENTS:
- 2 tablespoons extra-virgin olive oil
- 6 Italian chicken sausage links
- 1 onion
- 1 red bell pepper
- 1 green bell pepper
- 3 garlic cloves, minced
- ½ cup dry white wine
- ½ teaspoon sea salt
- ¼ teaspoon freshly ground black pepper
DIRECTIONS:

1. Pinch red pepper flakes

2. Heat the olive oil until it shines in a large skillet over medium-high heat

3. Add the sausages and cook for 5 to 7 minutes, occasionally turning, until browned, and they reach an internal temperature of 165°F. With tongs, remove the link from the pan and set it aside on a platter, tented with aluminum foil to keep warm.

4. Return the skillet to heat and add the onion, red bell pepper, and green bell pepper. Cook, stirring regularly, for 5 to 7 minutes, until the vegetables begin to brown.

5. Add the garlic and simmer for 30 seconds, stirring continuously.

6. Stir in the wine, sea salt, pepper, and red pepper flakes. Using the spoon to scrape and fold in some browned fragments from the bottom of the plate. Simmer for about 4 minutes, stirring until the liquid decreases by half. Spoon the peppers over the sausages and serve.

SUBSTITUTION TIP: For a different flavor profile, add one fennel bulb, thinly shaved, in place of the green bell peppers—Cook as directed in the recipe.

NUTRITION: Calories: 173 Protein: 22g Total Carbohydrates: 6g Sugars: 2g Fiber: <1g Total Fat: 5g Saturated Fat: 1g Cholesterol: 85mg Sodium: 1,199mg

526. Chicken Piccata

Preparation time: 10 minutes
Cooking time: 15 minutes
Serving: 6
INGREDIENTS:
- ½ cup whole-wheat flour
- ½ teaspoon sea salt
- 1/8 teaspoon freshly ground black pepper
- 11/2 pounds of boneless, skinless chicken breasts, sliced into 6 pieces and pounded 1/2-inch-thick (see tip)
- 3 tablespoons extra-virgin olive oil
- 1 cup unsalted chicken broth
- ½ cup dry white wine
- Juice of 1 lemon
- Zest of 1 lemon
- ¼ cup capers drained and rinsed
- ¼ cup chopped fresh parsley leaves
DIRECTIONS:
1. In a shallow dish, whisk the flour, sea salt, and pepper. Dredge the chicken in the flour and tap off any excess.
2. Heat the olive oil until it shimmers in a large skillet over medium-high heat.
3. Add the chicken and cook for about 4 minutes per side until browned. To preserve temperature, remove the chicken from the pan and set aside, tented with aluminum foil.
4. Return the skillet to heat and add the broth, wine, lemon juice, lemon zest, and capers. Use the side of a spoon to scrape and fold in any browned bits from the pan's bottom. Simmer for 3 to 4 minutes, stirring, until the liquid thickens. Remove the skillet from the heat and return the chicken to the pan. Turn to coat. Stir in the parsley and serve.

COOKING TIP: To pound the chicken to an even thickness: Place the chicken between two pieces of plastic wrap or parchment paper and use a flat kitchen mallet or a smooth-bottomed heavy saucepan to pound until they reach the desired thickness. Use caution to avoid puncturing the plastic or paper.

NUTRITION: Calories: 153 Protein: 8g Total Carbohydrates: 9g Sugars: <1g Fiber: <1g Total Fat: 9g Saturated Fat: 1g Cholesterol: 19mg Sodium: 352mg

527. One-Pan Tuscan Chicken

Preparation time: 10 minutes
Cooking time: 25 minutes
Serving: 6
INGREDIENTS:
- ¼ cup extra-virgin olive oil, divided
- Skinless chicken breasts, 1 pound boneless, sliced into 3/4-inch pieces
- 1 onion, chopped
- 1 red bell pepper, chopped
- 3 garlic cloves, minced
- ½ cup dry white wine

- 1 (14-ounce) can crushed tomatoes, untrained
- 1 (14-ounce) can chopped tomatoes, drained
- 1 (14-ounce) can white beans, drained
- 1 tablespoon dried Italian seasoning
- ½ teaspoon sea salt
- 1/8 teaspoon freshly ground black pepper
- 1/8 teaspoon red pepper flakes
- ¼ cup chopped fresh basil leaves
DIRECTIONS:
1. Over medium-high pressure, heat 2 teaspoons of olive oil in a large skillet until it shimmers.
2. Add the chicken and cook for about 6 minutes, stirring, until browned. Remove the chicken from the skillet and set it aside on a platter, tented with aluminum foil to keep warm.
3. Return the skillet to heat and heat the remaining 2 tablespoons of olive oil until it shimmers.
4. Add the onion and red bell pepper. Cook for about 5 minutes, occasionally stirring, until the vegetables are soft.
5. Attach the garlic and fry, stirring continuously, for 30 seconds.
6. Stir in the wine, and use the spoon's side to scrape and fold in any browned bits from the bottom of the pan. Cook for 1 minute, stirring.
7. Add the crushed and chopped tomatoes, white beans, Italian seasoning, sea salt, pepper, and red pepper flakes. Bring it to a boil and bring the heat down to medium. Cook for 5 minutes, sometimes stirring.
8. Return to the skillet the chicken and any juices that have accumulated. Simmer for 1 to 2 minutes before the chicken heats up. Remove from the heat and before eating, mix in the basil.

VARIATION TIP: Add ½ cup chopped black or green olives and 1 cup thawed frozen spinach when you return the chicken to the pan. Note that the fat content will increase.

NUTRITION: Per Serving Calories: 271 Protein: 14g Total Carbohydrates: 29g Sugars: 8g Fiber: 8g Total Fat: 0g Saturated Fat: 1g Cholesterol: 14mg Sodium: 306mg

528. Chicken Kapama

Preparation time: 10 minutes
Cooking time: 2 hours
Serving: 4
INGREDIENTS:
- 1 (32-ounce) can chopped tomatoes, drained
- ¼ cup dry white wine
- 2 tablespoons tomato paste
- 3 tablespoons extra-virgin olive oil
- ¼ teaspoon red pepper flakes
- 1 teaspoon ground allspice
- ½ teaspoon dried oregano
- 2 whole cloves
- 1 cinnamon stick
- ½ teaspoon sea salt
- 1/8 teaspoon freshly ground black pepper
- 4 boneless, skinless chicken breast halves
DIRECTIONS:
1. Combine the tomatoes, wine, tomato paste, olive oil, red pepper flakes, allspice, oregano, garlic, cinnamon stick, sea salt and pepper in a big pot over medium-high heat. Bring to a boil, sometimes stirring.
2. Set the heat to medium-low and boil, stirring periodically for 30 minutes. Remove all the cloves and cinnamon sticks from the sauce and let the sauce cool.
3. Preheat the oven to 350°F.
4. Place the chicken in a 9-by-13-inch baking dish. Pour the sauce over the chicken and cover the pan with aluminum

foil—Bake for 40 to 45 minutes, or until the chicken reaches an internal temperature of 165°F.
MAKE IT A MEAL: Serve this dish spooned over ¾ cup (per serving) cooked whole-wheat pasta.
NUTRITION: 220; Protein: 8g Total Carbohydrates: 11g Sugars: 7g; Fiber: 3g Total Fat: 14g Saturated Fat: 3g Cholesterol: 19mg Sodium: 273mg

529. Spinach and Feta–Stuffed Chicken Breasts

Preparation time: 10 minutes
Cooking time: 45 minutes
Servings: 4
INGREDIENTS:
- 2 tablespoons extra-virgin olive oil
- 1-pound fresh baby spinach
- 3 garlic cloves, minced
- Zest of 1 lemon
- ½ teaspoon sea salt
- 1/8 teaspoon freshly ground black pepper
- ½ cup crumbled feta cheese
- 4 skinless, boneless chicken breast pieces, pounded to the thickness of 1/2 inch
DIRECTIONS:
1. Preheat the oven to 350°F.
2. Heat the olive oil until it shimmers in a large skillet over medium-high heat..
3. Add the spinach. Cook for 3 to 4 minutes, stirring until wilted.
4. Add the garlic, lemon zest, sea salt, and pepper. Cook for 30 seconds, stirring constantly. Cool slightly and mix in the cheese.
5. Spread spinach cheese mixture in an even layer over the chicken pieces and roll the breast around the filling. Hold closed with toothpicks or butcher's twine. Place breasts 9-by-13-inch baking dish and bakes for 30 to 40 minutes, or until the chicken reaches an internal temperature of 165°F.
6. Serve !
COOKING TIP: If you use toothpicks to hold the chicken rolls closed, soak them in water for about 5 minutes first to prevent burning.
NUTRITION: Calories: 263; Protein: 17g; Total Carbohydrates: 7g; Sugars: 3g; Fiber: 3g; Total Fat: 20g; Saturated Fat: 9g; Cholesterol: 63mg; Sodium: 901mg

530. Chicken Bruschetta

Preparation time: 10 minutes
Cooking time: 20 minutes
Servings: 2
Ingredients
- 5ml olive oil, divided
- 1 boneless, skinless chicken breast
- 80g cherry tomatoes
- 5ml balsamic vinegar
- 10g fresh basil leaves
- 1 small cloves garlic, minced
- 1 small onion, chopped
Direction:
1. In a pan, add half of the oil and cook the chicken over medium heat.
2. Meanwhile, slice the basil leaves into slivers and cook the vegetables.
3. Heat the remaining oil and bake for about 3 minutes with the garlic and onion.
4. For about 5 minutes, whisk in the basil and tomatoes.
5. Stir the vinegar in.

6. Cook until hot and serve the onion and tomato mixture topped with the chicken.
Nutrition Per Serving
calories: 95 | fat: 0.68g | protein: 4.16g | carbs:21.77g | fiber: 10.2g | sodium: 17mg

531. Coconut Chicken

Preparation time: 20 minutes
Cooking time: 10 minutes
Servings: 4
Ingredients
- 20g coconut, shredded
- 30g almond flour
- 1 tsp. sea salt
- 1 small egg
- 100g chicken breast, boneless, skinless
- 7.5 ml coconut oil
Direction:
1. Mix the shredded coconut, almond flour and sea salt in a dish.
2. Beat the egg in a separate bowl; dip the chicken in the egg and roll it until well coated in the flour mixture.
3. In a pan set over medium heat, add coconut oil and fry the chicken until the crust starts to brown.
4. Move the chicken to the oven and bake for approximately 10 minutes at 350 ° F.
Nutrition Per Serving
calories: 174 | fat: 7.74g | protein: 10.81g | carbs:16.2g | fiber: 5.2g | sodium: 1021mg

532. Turkey Burgers

Preparation time: 15 minutes
Cooking time: 10 minutes
Servings: 4
Ingredients
- 1 large egg white
- 1 cup red onion, chopped
- ¾ cup fresh mint, chopped
- ½ cup dried bread crumbs
- 1 tsp. dill, dried
- 1/3 cup feta cheese, crumbled
- ¾ kg turkey, ground
- Cooking spray
- 4 hamburger buns, split
- 1 red bell pepper, roasted and cut into strips
- 2 tbsp. fresh lime juice
Direction:
1. In a bowl, gently beat the egg white and add the onion, mint, breadcrumbs, dill, cheese, and turkey and lime juice, combine well, and then divide the turkey mixture into four equal burger patties.
2. On a medium-high setting, spray a large nonstick skillet with cooking spray and heat.
3. Place the patties carefully in the skillet and cook on each side for 8 minutes or according to preference.
4. Place the burgers on the sliced buns after cooking and top with pepper strips.
Nutrition Per Serving
calories: 846 | fat: 41.18g | protein: 79.26g | carbs:41.01g | fiber: 3g | sodium: 1486mg

533. Chicken with Greek Salad

Preparation time: 25 minutes
Cooking time: 0 minutes
Serving: 4
Ingredients
- 2 tbsp. extra virgin olive oil

- 1/3 cup red-wine vinegar
- 1 tsp. garlic powder
- 1 tbsp. chopped fresh dill
- ¼ tsp. sea salt
- ¼ tsp. freshly ground pepper
- 2 ½ cups chopped cooked chicken
- 6 cups chopped romaine lettuce
- 1 cucumber, peeled, seeded and chopped
- 2 medium tomatoes, chopped
- ½ cup crumbled feta cheese
- ½ cup sliced ripe black olives
- ½ cup finely chopped red onion

Direction:

1. Whisk the extra virgin olive oil, vinegar, garlic powder, dill, sea salt and pepper together in a large cup.
2. To combine well, add the chicken, lettuce, cucumber, tomatoes, feta, olives, and toss. Enjoy!

Nutrition Per Serving

calories: 460| fat: 37.94g | protein: 19.35g | carbs:10.49g | fiber: 3.8g | sodium: 559mg

534. Braised Chicken with Olives

Preparation time: 20 minutes
Cooking time: 1 hour 30 minutes
Servings: 4
Ingredients

- 1 tbsp. extra virgin olive oil
- 4 whole skinned chicken legs, cut into drumsticks and thighs
- 1 cup low-sodium canned chicken broth
- 1 cup dry white wine4 sprigs thyme
- 2 tbsp. chopped fresh ginger
- 2 garlic cloves, minced
- 3 carrots, diced
- 1 medium yellow onion, diced
- 3/4¾ cup chickpeas, drained, rinsed
- ½ cup green olives pitted and roughly chopped
- 1/3 cup raisins
- 1 cup water

Direction:

1. Preheat to 350°F in your oven.
2. Over medium heat, heat extra virgin olive oil in a Dutch oven or a large ovenproof skillet.
3. In the skillet, add the chicken pieces and sauté for around 5 minutes on each side or until browned on both sides and crisped.
4. To a tray, move the cooked chicken and set it aside.
5. Cook, stirring, for around 5 minutes or until the onion is translucent and soft. Lower heat to medium-low and add the garlic, onion, carrots and ginger to the same skillet.
6. Stir in sugar, broth of chicken and wine; bring to a gentle boil mixture.
7. Set the chicken back in the pot and stir in the thyme.
8. Return the mixture to the boil and cover.
9. For about 45 minutes, switch to the oven and braise.
10.   Take the pot out of the oven and add the chickpeas, olives, and grapes.
11.   Return to the oven and braise for 20 more minutes, uncovered.
12.   Take the skillet out of the oven, then discard the thyme.
13.   Instantly serve

Nutrition Per Serving

calories: 436| fat: 21.51g | protein: 36.69g | carbs:23.69g | fiber: 6.1g | sodium: 667mg

535. Braised Chicken with Mushrooms and Olives

Preparation time: 10 minutes
Cooking time: 35 minutes
Servings: 4
Ingredients

- 2 ½ pounds chicken, cut into pieces
- Sea salt
- Freshly ground pepper
- 1 tbsp. plus
- 1 tsp. extra virgin olive oil
- 16 cloves garlic, peeled
- 10 ounces cremini mushrooms, rinsed, trimmed, and halved
- ½ cup white wine
- 1/3 cup chicken stock
- ½ cup green olives pitted

Direction:

1. Over medium-high heat, prepare a large skillet.
2. Meanwhile, the chicken should be seasoned with sea salt and pepper.
3. To the heated skillet, add 1 tablespoon of extra virgin olive oil and add the chicken, skin side down; cook for around 6 minutes or until browned.
4. Move it to a dish and set it aside.
5. Add 1 teaspoon of the remaining extra virgin olive oil to the pan and sauté for around 6 minutes or until the garlic and mushrooms are browned.
6. Add the wine and bring to a boil, reduce the heat and cook for approximately 1 minute.
7. Send the chicken back to the pan and stir in the olives and chicken broth.
8. Return the mixture to a gentle boil, reduce heat and cook, covered, for about 20 minutes or until the chicken is thoroughly cooked.

Nutrition Per Serving

calories: 558| fat: 9.24g | protein: 65.93g | carbs:58.64g | fiber: 8.5g | sodium: 271mg

536. Chicken with Olives, Mustard Greens, and Lemon

Preparation time: 10 minutes
Cooking time: 30 minutes
Servings: 6
Ingredients

- 2 tbsp. extra virgin olive oil, divided
- 6 skinless chicken breast halves, cut in half crosswise
- ½ cup Kalamata olives pitted
- 1 tbsp. freshly squeezed lemon juice
- 1 1/2 pounds mustard greens, stalks removed and coarsely chopped
- 1 cup dry white wine
- 4 garlic cloves, smashed
- 1 medium red onion, halved and thinly sliced
- Sea salt
- Ground pepper
- Lemon wedges, for serving

Direction:

1. In a Dutch oven or large, heavy pot, heat 1 tablespoon of extra virgin olive oil over medium heat.
2. Rub the chicken with sea salt and pepper and add half of it to the mixing bowl; cook on all sides for about 8 minutes or until browned.
3. Switch to a plate with the cooked chicken and repeat with the remaining chicken and oil.

4. Add the garlic and onion to the pot and heat to medium; cook, stirring, until tender, or about 6 minutes.

5. Add the chicken and wine (with accumulated juices) and bring it to a boil.

6. Reduce the heat and cook for approximately 5 minutes, sealed.

7. On top of the chicken, add the greens and sprinkle it with sea salt and pepper.

8. Cook for 5 more minutes or until the greens are wilted, and the chicken is opaque.

9. Stir in the olives and lemon juice and remove the pot from the heat.

10. Serve drizzled and garnished with lemon wedges with the collected pan juices.

Nutrition Per Serving

calories: 122| fat: 7.66g | protein: 7.63g | carbs:8 .43g | fiber: 4.2g | sodium: 438mg

537. Delicious Mediterranean Chicken

Preparation time: 25 minutes
Cooking time: 30 minutes
Serving: 6
Ingredients
- 2 tsp. extra virgin olive oil
- ½ cup white wine, divided
- 6 chicken breasts, skinned and deboned
- 3 cloves garlic, pressed
- ½ cup onion, chopped
- 3 cups tomatoes, chopped
- ½ cup Kalamata olives
- ¼ cup fresh parsley, chopped
- 2 tsp. fresh thyme, chopped
- Sea salt to taste

Direction:

1. In a pan, heat the oil and 3 tablespoons of white wine over medium heat.

2. Add the chicken and cook until golden, on each side, for about 6 minutes.

3. Remove the chicken and place the chicken on a tray.

4. In the skillet, add the garlic and onions and sauté for approximately 3 minutes, then add the tomatoes.

5. Cook for five minutes, then the fire, add the remaining white wine and cook for 10 minutes.

6. Attach the thyme and cook for 5 minutes more.

7. Put the chicken back into the skillet and cook until the chicken is well cooked, on low heat.

8. Attach the parsley and olives, and cook for another 1 minute.

9. Stir in the salt and pepper, then serve.

Nutrition Per Serving

calories: 553| fat: 29.87g | protein: 62.67g | carbs:5 .43g | fiber: 1.6g | sodium: 304mg

538. Warm Chicken Avocado Salad

Preparation time: 15 minutes
Cooking time: 20 minutes
Servings: 4
Ingredients
- 2 tbsp. extra virgin olive oil, divided
- 500g chicken breast fillets
- 1 large avocado, peeled, diced
- 2 garlic cloves, sliced
- 1 tsp. ground turmeric
- 3 tsp. ground cumin
- 1 small head broccoli, chopped
- 1 large carrot, diced

- 1/3 cup currants
- 1 1/2 cups chicken stock
- 1 1/2 cups couscous
- Pinch of sea salt

Direction:

1. Heat 1 tablespoon of extra virgin olive oil in a large frying pan set over medium heat; add chicken and cook for about 6 minutes on each side or until cooked through; move to a plate and keep warm.

2. Meanwhile, in a heatproof dish, mix the currants and couscous; stir in the boiling stock and set aside, covered, for at least 5 minutes or until the liquid has been absorbed.

3. Separate the grains with a fork.

4. In a frying pan, add the remaining oil and add the carrots; cook for about 1 minute, stirring.

5. For about 1 minute, stir in the broccoli; add the garlic, turmeric, and cumin.

6. Cook for another 1 minute or so, then remove the pan from the oven.

7. Break the chicken into small slices and add to the mixture of broccoli; toss to combine; season with sea salt and serve with the sprinkled avocado on top.

Nutrition Per Serving

calories: 354| fat: 14.36g | protein: 28.34g | carbs: 29.77g | fiber: 5.7g | sodium: 1504mg

539. Chicken Stew

Preparation time: 20 minutes
Cooking time: 15 minutes
Servings: 4
Ingredients
- 1 tbsp. extra virgin olive oil
- 3 chicken breast halves (8 ounces each), boneless, skinless, cut into small pieces
- Sea salt
- Freshly ground pepper
- 1 medium onion, sliced
- 4 garlic cloves, sliced
- ½ tsp. dried oregano
- 1 ½ pounds escarole, ends trimmed, chopped
- 1 cup whole-wheat couscous, cooked
- 1 (28 ounces) can whole peeled tomatoes, pureed

Direction:

1. Heat the extra virgin olive oil in a big heavy pot or Dutch oven over medium-high heat.

2. Rub the sea salt and pepper with the chicken.

3. Cook the chicken in olive oil in batches, tossing periodically, for about 5 minutes or until browned; move to a dish and set aside.

4. Add the onion, garlic, oregano, tomatoes, sea salt and pepper to the mixing bowl and cook for 10 minutes or lightly browned.

5. Add the chicken and cook for about 4 minutes or until the mixture is opaque.

6. Fill the pot with escarole and cook until tender or around 4 minutes.

7. Serve over couscous with chicken stew.

Nutrition Per Serving

calories: 164| fat: 8.78g | protein: 4.67g | carbs: 18.35g | fiber: 8g | sodium: 1026mg

540. Chicken with Roasted Vegetables

Preparation time: 15 minutes
Cooking time: 40 minutes
Servings: 2
Ingredients
- 1 large zucchini, diagonally sliced

- 250g baby new potatoes, sliced
- 6 firm plum tomatoes, halved
- 1 red onion, cut into wedges
- 1 yellow pepper, seeded and cut into chunks
- 12 black olives, pitted
- 2 chicken breast fillets, skinless, boneless
- 1 rounded tbsp. green pesto
- 3 tbsp. extra virgin olive oil

Direction:

1. Preheat to 400 F in your oven.
2. In a roasting pan, spread the zucchini, potatoes, tomatoes, onion, and pepper and scatter with the olives.
3. Using sea salt and black pepper to season.
4. Cut four parts of each chicken breast and place them on top of the vegetables.
5. Combine the pesto and extra virgin olive oil in a small bowl and spread it over the
chicken. Cover with foil and cook for about 30 minutes in a preheated oven.
6. Uncover the pan and return to the oven; cook more or until the chicken is cooked through for about 10 minutes.
7. Enjoy!

Nutrition Per Serving

calories: 401| fat: 12.33g | protein: 6.86g | carbs: 71.61g | fiber: 8.2g | sodium: 407mg

541. Grilled Chicken with Olive Relish

Preparation time: 15 minutes
Cooking time: 6 minutes
Servings: 4
Ingredients

- 4 chicken breast halves, boneless, skinless
- ¾ cup extra virgin olive oil, divided
- Sea salt
- Freshly ground black pepper
- 2 tbsp. capers, rinsed, chopped
- 1 ½ cups green olives, rinsed, pitted, and chopped
- ¼ cup lightly toasted almonds, chopped
- 1 small clove garlic, mashed with sea salt
- 1 ½ tsp. chopped fresh thyme
- 2 ½ tsp. grated lemon zest
- 2 tbsp. chopped fresh parsley

Direction:

1. Heat the high-heat grill.
2. On one side of the plastic wrap, put 1 chicken breast and drizzle with about 1 teaspoon of extra virgin olive oil and fold the wrap over the chicken.
3. Pound the chicken to roughly 1/2-inch-thick with a large sauté pan or a meat mallet.
4. With the remaining chicken, repeat the procedure and remove the plastic wrap.
5. Sprinkle the chicken with sea salt and pepper and cover with around 2 tablespoons of extra virgin olive oil; set aside. Meanwhile, in a medium bowl, mix 1/2 cup of extra virgin olive oil, capers, olives, almonds, garlic, thyme, lemon zest, and parsley.
6. Grill the chicken on each side for about 3 minutes, then move it to a cutting board.
7. Let it cool down a little and cut into 1/2-inch-thick slices.
8. On four plates, arrange the chicken slices and spoon over the relish.
9. Instantly serve

Nutrition Per Serving

calories: 242| fat: 24.56g | protein: 4.09g | carbs: 2.65g | fiber: 1.3g | sodium: 508mg

542. Grilled Turkey with Salsa

Preparation time: 15 minutes
Cooking time: 35 minutes
Servings: 6
Ingredients
For the spice rub:

- 1 ½ tsp. garlic powder
- 1 ½ tsp. sweet paprika
- 2 tsp. crushed fennel seeds
- 2 tsp. dark brown sugar
- 1 tsp. sea salt
- 1 ½ tsp. freshly ground black pepper

For the salsa:

- 2 tbsp. drained capers
- ¼ cup pimento-stuffed green olives, chopped
- 2 scant cups cherry tomatoes, diced
- 1 ½ tbsp. extra virgin olive oil
- 1 large clove garlic, minced
- 2 tbsp. torn fresh basil leaves
- 2 tsp. Fresh lemon juice
- ½ tsp. finely grated lemon zest
- 6 turkey breast cutlets
- 1 cup diced red onion
- Sea salt
- Freshly ground black pepper

Direction:

1. In a small cup, combine the garlic powder, paprika, fennel seeds, brown sugar, salt and pepper.
2. Combine the capers, olives, tomatoes, onion, extra virgin olive oil, garlic, basil, lemon juice and zest, 1/4 teaspoon of sea salt and pepper in another bowl; set aside.
3. After dipping in the spice rub, grill the meat over medium-high heat for around 3 minutes per side or until browned on both sides.
4. Switch the grilled turkey to a serving plate and leave to rest for 5 minutes or so.
5. Serve with salsa.

Nutrition Per Serving

calories: 2113| fat: 24.56g | protein: 426.47g | carbs: 4.93g | fiber: 1.1g | sodium: 1900mg

543. Chicken Caper

Preparation time: 5 minutes
Cooking time: 25 minutes
Servings: 4
Ingredients:

- 2 pounds boneless chicken tenderloins, skinless, and excess fat removed
- 1 tbsp garlic gusto seasoning
- ½ cup chicken broth (low sodium)
- 2 tbsp fresh lemon juice
- 4 tbsp capers
- 2 tbsp butter (not margarine)
- ground pepper and natural sea salt - to taste

Directions:

1. In a single layer, place the chicken on the bottom of your pot. Add the broth, lemon juice, and garlic seasoning to a bowl and whisk.
2. Pour the mixture over the chicken and sprinkle over with the capers—cook on high for 10 minutes. Remove chicken and set it aside. Set to sauté and bring the liquid to a boil.
3. Add the butter and whisk together. Allow the sauce to cook until the liquid reduces to half. Spread the sauce over the chicken—season with pepper and salt. Serve.

Nutrition:

Calories: 262

Fat: 5.9g
Carbohydrates: 0.6g
Protein: 48.3g

544. Turkey Sausage Spaghetti

Preparation time: 10 minutes
Cooking time: 15 minutes
Servings: 4
Ingredients:
- 4 cups Zucchini, spiraled
- 1 ½ pound Lean turkey sausage
- 1 tbsp Tuscan seasoning
- 2 cups Tomato sauce (no added sugar)
- 8 tbsp fresh parmesan cheese (grated)

Directions:
1. Cut the turkey sausage into ½-inch chunks. Place the chunks in a pan and cook over medium-high heat for about 8 minutes, or until it turns brown. Stir occasionally.
2. Add the Tuscan seasoning and tomato sauce to the pan. Stir thoroughly to coat completely. Adjust heat to high and bring the batter to a boil, about 4 min.
3. Add the noodles and toss well—Cook for extra 2 minutes, or until the noodles become soft and the chicken fully cooked.
4. Transfer to your serving plates and sprinkle over with the parmesan cheese. Serve.

Nutrition:
Calories: 179
Fat: 8.5g
Carbohydrates: 8.5g
Protein: 19.3g

545. Spicy Turkey and Cauliflower

Preparation time: 10 minutes
Cooking time: 20 minutes
Servings: 4
Ingredients:
- 1 tbsp Roasted garlic oil (or another oil, with fresh garlic)
- 1 ½ pound Boneless turkey meat, skinless and cut into thin slices
- 1 tbsp Curry powder
- 4 cups Cauliflower florets
- 1 ½ cup Light coconut milk
- Ground pepper and natural sea salt - to taste

Directions:
1. Slice the turkey and set it aside. Chop the cauliflower into ½-inch florets. Add the garlic oil to your pan and heat on high.
2. Once the oil gets heated, add the turkey and sprinkle it over with curry. Stir thoroughly and cook for about 10 minutes.
3. Add the coconut milk and cauliflower. Cook until the turkey is fully cooked with cauliflower tender, about 10 minutes. Season with pepper and salt. Serve.

Nutrition:
Calories: 231
Fat: 5.4g
Carbohydrates: 6.3g
Protein: 38g

546. Spinach-Chicken Noodles

Preparation time: 15 minutes
Cooking time: 15 minutes
Servings: 3
Ingredients:
- 1 ½ lb. boneless chicken breasts, skinless
- 1 tbsp olive oil
- 1 cup plain Greek yogurt (low-fat)
- ½ cup chicken broth
- ½ tsp garlic powder
- ½ tsp Italian seasoning
- ¼ cup parmesan cheese
- 1 cup spinach, chopped
- 3-6 slices sun-dried tomatoes
- 1 tbsp garlic, chopped
- 1 ½ cup zucchini noodles

Directions:
1. For the chicken, heat-up oil over medium heat with your pan. Pat-dry the chicken breasts using a paper towel, and season with pepper and chicken.
2. Place in the pan and cook each side for about 5 minutes, or until it turns brown. Transfer the chicken from the pan to your plate.
3. Add the broth, yogurt, Italian seasoning, garlic powder, and parmesan cheese to the pan. Whisk and cook until it becomes slightly thick.
4. Add the tomatoes and spinach, and simmer until the spinach becomes wilted. Return the chicken and toss to coat well, then serve over the zoodles.
5. For the zoodles, preheat your oven to 350 degrees. Cut the zucchini into tiny spirals—place parchment paper on a baking sheet.
6. Spread the zucchini noodles on the sheet. Sprinkle sea salt and toss. Bake the zoodles for about 15 minutes or more, depending on how soft you want it. Serve.

Nutrition:
Calories: 414
Fat: 15g
Carbohydrates: 8g
Protein: 60g

547. Dijon Chicken Veggies

Preparation time: 5 minutes
Cooking time: 25 minutes
Servings: 4
Ingredients:
- 1 ½ pounds boneless chicken thighs (skinless)
- 1 tbsp Tuscan seasoning
- 4 tbsp balsamic
- 1 tbsp Dijon mustard
- 2 cups cherry/grape tomatoes (halved)
- 2 cups zucchini (sliced into 3/8-inch slices)
- 1/3 cup water

Directions:
1. Add the mustard, balsamic, and seasoning to a bowl and whisk together. Put the chicken in your bowl, then toss thoroughly.
2. Put it in your refrigerator to marinade, about 20 min to 8 hours. Preheat your oven to 425, then place your cast-iron skillet over medium-high heat.
3. Shake off any excess marinade and place the chicken in the skillet. Cook for about 5 min, or until seared. Do the same for the other side of the chicken.
4. Meanwhile, prepare the veggies. Add water to the marinade that remains in the bowl and whisk thoroughly to combine well.
5. Sprinkle the veggies around the skillet and season with a pinch of salt and pepper. Pour the marinade on the veggies and toss to combine everything.
6. Transfer to the oven and cook for extra 15 minutes. Remove from heat and serve.

Nutrition:
Calories: 280
Fat: 9.9g

Carbohydrates: 7.5g
Protein: 38.7g

548. Sesame Ginger Chicken

Preparation time: 10 minutes
Cooking time: 15 minutes
Servings: 4
Ingredients:
- 4 tsp Orange oil
- 1 ½ lb. Boneless chicken breast (skinless)
- 1 tbsp Toasted sesame ginger seasoning

Directions:
1. Put the chicken breast on a cutting board and flatten it to 3/8-inch-thick with your meat mallet. Sprinkle over with seasoning.
2. Add the orange oil to a nonstick pan and heat over medium-high heat. Add the chicken and cook each side for about 8 minutes, or until the chick is well cooked. Serve.

Nutrition:
Calories: 247
Fat: 9.9g
Carbohydrates: 0.5g
Protein: 36.5g

549. Creamy Garlic Sauce Turkey

Preparation time: 15 minutes
Cooking time: 28 minutes
Servings: 4
Ingredients:
- 1 ½ lb. Boneless turkey meat, skinless and cut into thin slices
- 2 tbsp Roasted garlic oil
- 1 medium onion, diced
- 1 tbsp Garlic and spring onion seasoning
- ½ cup Vegetable broth
- 1-2 tbsp Grass-fed butter

Directions:
1. Put the oil in your pan, then heat over medium-high heat. Add the onions to the pan and cook for 2 minutes. Add the turkey and cook for about 5 minutes. Stir occasionally.
2. Add the seasoning and cook for extra 20 minutes, or until the turkey is fully cooked. Add the broth and simmer for 1 more minute. Serve.

Nutrition:
Calories: 441
Carbs: 6g
Fat: 46g
Protein: 3g

550. Tomato Rotisserie

Preparation time: 15 minutes
Cooking time: 4 minutes
Servings: 5
Ingredients:
- 3 lb. Rotisserie chicken
- 15 Petite tomatoes, diced
- 9 Tortillas
- 1 cup shredded cheese
- ½ cup Plain Greek yogurt
- 1 Avocado
- 1 Lime

Directions:
1. Shred your chicken, then put it in a microwave-safe bowl. Add tomatoes and the seasoning to the bowl and mix.
2. Microwave for 4 minutes on high. Fill the tortillas with the chicken. Top with the remaining ingredients and spritz of lime.

Nutrition:
Calories: 170
Carbs: 1g
Fat: 11g
Protein: 15g

551. Balsamic Strawberry Chicken

Preparation time: 15 minutes
Cooking time: 20 minutes
Servings: 4
Ingredients:
- 1 ½ lb. boneless chicken breast, skinless
- 1 tbsp seasoning
- 1 cup fresh strawberries
- 1 tbsp balsamic mosto Cotto
- ½ tsp peppercorn
- 1 pinch sea salt
- 4 tbsp lemon oil

Directions:
1. Preheat your grill to medium-high heat. Season, the chicken with the seasoning. Place on the grill and cook each side for about 10 minutes. Remove from heat and set it aside.
2. For the dressing, add other ingredients to your food processor and puree until the mixture becomes smooth. Slice the chicken diagonally and drizzle the dressing over it. Serve.

Nutrition:
Calories: 367
Carbs: 17g
Fat: 11g
Protein: 45g

552. Cauliflower Tomato Shakshuka

Preparation time: 5 minutes
Cooking time: 20 minutes
Servings: 2
Ingredients:
- 1-pound Riced cauliflower
- 4 tsp extra virgin olive oil
- 4 tbsp Chopped onion
- 1 tbsp India seasoning
- 1 can diced tomatoes (with no added sugar)
- 1 can Pureed tomatoes (with no added sugar)
- 4 Fresh eggs

Directions:
1. Cook the cauliflower following the instructions on the package. Put the oil in your skillet and heat it over medium-high heat.
2. Stir in the onions and sauté for about 2 minutes, or until the onions become translucent. Sprinkle over the mixture with the spices and sauté for an extra 1 minute.
3. Now add the cooked cauliflower to the skillet and stir thoroughly. Add a pinch of natural salt. (optional)
4. Stir in the tomatoes and mix thoroughly. Boil the mixture in your skillet. Then simmer for an additional 5 minutes.
5. Open the pot and crack the eggs over the mixture—season with pepper and salt. Close the skillet and cook for 3 minutes to poach the egg. You can cook for about 6-7 for a hard-cooked egg. Turn off heat and serve.

Nutrition:
Calories: 228
Fat: 14.5g
Carbohydrates: 10.3g
Protein: 15.3g

553. Turkey Shrimp

Preparation time: 15 minutes
Cooking time: 30 minutes
Servings: 4
Ingredients:
- 2 tbsp roasted garlic oil
- 1 medium onion, diced
- 1 tbsp garlic gusto seasoning
- 1 lb. boneless turkey meat, skinless and cut into thin slices
- ½ lb. medium-size shrimp, precooked, peeled, with tails removed
- 3 scallions, chopped
- ¾ cup frank's red-hot seasoning
- lemon juice - splash

Directions:
1. Put the oil in your skillet and heat over medium-high heat. Add the onion and sauté until it becomes translucent, about 2 minutes.
2. Add the turkey and cook for about 10 minutes. Stir occasionally. Add the garlic seasoning and cook until the turkey is fully cooked about 12 minutes.
3. Add other ingredients and cook for about 5 minutes, or until the sauce begins to bubble. Serve.

Nutrition:
Calories: 361
Carbs: 0g
Fat: 8g
Protein: 22g

554. Broccoli Chicken Thighs

Preparation time: 5 minutes
Cooking time: 20 minutes
Servings: 4
Ingredients:
- 4 boneless chicken thighs, skinless
- 2 tsp seasoning, or use a mixture of garlic, salt, onion, pepper, and parsley
- 4 tbsp balsamic mosto cotto or use a balsamic reduction
- ¼ cup chicken broth, low sodium
- 4 cups steamed broccoli florets, crisp-tender

Directions:
1. Season the chicken thighs. Grease your pan with nonstick cooking spray. Place over high heat. Once it starts to shimmer, add the chicken.
2. Reduce the heat to medium and cook each side for about 7 min, or until it is well cooked. Remove the chicken and set it aside.
3. Add the broth and balsamic to the pan. Scrape all brown bits at the bottom of the pan. Once the sauce reduces by half, add the broccoli and chicken back to the pan. Toss to coat thoroughly. Serve immediately.

Nutrition:
Calories: 314
Fat: 10.8g
Carbohydrates: 8.8g
Protein: 43.6g

555. Bell Pepper Cashew Chicken

Preparation time: 10 minutes
Cooking time: 20 minutes
Servings: 4
Ingredients:
- 4 tsp lemon or roasted garlic oil or any other oil of choice
- 1 ½ lb. boneless chicken breast, skinless and sliced into thin strips
- 1 tbsp. Thai seasoning
- 2 cups of green bell pepper, thin strips
- 2 cups of red bell pepper, thin strips
- 3 scallions, sliced - put the greens and whites separate
- 24 cashews, chopped

Directions:
1. Over medium-high heat, heat the oil with your pan. Put the chicken strips to the pan and cook each side for about 5 min, or until it turns opaque.
2. Add the white scallions and peppers to the pan. Sprinkle seasoning over the mixture and stir thoroughly to combine.
3. Close the lid and cook for an extra 7 min over high heat until the chicken is well cooked. Stir occasionally.
4. Remove and sprinkle the scallion greens and nuts over. Serve hot. It can be served over rice cauliflower.

Nutrition:
Calories: 323
Fat: 13.1g
Carbohydrates: 12.3g
Protein: 38.7g

556. Tomato Puttanesca

Preparation time: 15 minutes
Cooking time: 0 minutes
Servings: 4
Ingredients:
- 4 tsp roasted garlic oil
- 1 ½ lb. boneless turkey meat, skinless and cut into thin slices
- 1 cup diced tomatoes
- 1 tsp Italian seasoning
- 1 tbsp garlic & spring onion seasoning
- 2 cups bell pepper, sliced
- 2 tbsp capers, drained

Directions:
1. Heat the oil in your pan until it starts to sizzle. Add the turkey and cook for about 5 minutes. Add other ingredients and reduce the heat to medium. Close the pan and sauté for 12 minutes or until the turkey is fully cooked. Serve.

Nutrition:
Calories: 70
Carbs: 8g
Fat: 3g
Protein: 2g

557. Herbed Lemon Chicken

Preparation time: 10 minutes
Cooking time: 30 minutes
Servings: 4
Ingredients:
- 1 ½ lb. Boneless chicken breasts, skinless
- 4 tsp Lemon oil or use oil with lemon juice and zest
- 1 tbsp Seasoning or use salt and pepper
- 2-3 tbsp Herbs (fresh chopped tarragon, parsley, rosemary, thyme, chives, etc., or combo)

Directions:
1. Preheat your grill to 350. Toss all the fixings in a bowl. Grill each side of the chicken within 9-11 minutes, or until the chicken is well cooked. Serve.

Nutrition:
Calories: 234
Fat: 8.8g
Carbohydrates: 0g
Protein: 36.1g

558. Phoenix Chicken Soup

Preparation time: 15 minutes
Cooking time: 20 minutes
Servings: 6
Ingredients:
- 4 tsp roasted garlic oil
- 1 ½ lb. boneless chicken breasts (skinless, sliced into thin strips)
- 4 minced scallions whites, and chopped greens
- 1 tbsp phoenix sunrise seasoning
- 1 tbsp garlic gusto seasoning
- 8 cups chicken broth
- ½ cup Roma or grape tomatoes, chopped
- 1/3 cup fresh chopped cilantro
- 1 lime, juiced
- 1 medium avocado, diced

Directions:
1. Put the oil in a pot and heat over medium-high heat. Add the scallions and chicken. Sauté for about 2 minutes. Add the broth, seasonings, and tomatoes. Stir and bring to a boil.
2. Lower the heat to medium. Simmer for about 15 minutes. Meanwhile, prepare the lime, cilantro, and avocado.
3. Add the lime juice and cilantro to the pot and stir. Add the avocado to the serving bowls. Scoop the soup onto the avocado and serve.

Nutrition:
Calories: 423
Carbs: 58g
Fat: 15g
Protein: 12g

559. Bell Pepper Turkey Sonoma

Preparation time: 15 minutes
Cooking time: 30 minutes
Servings: 4
Ingredients:
- 4 tsp roasted garlic oil or used any oil of your choice
- 1 cup scallions
- 1 cup red bell pepper, sliced thin
- 1 cup yellow bell pepper, sliced thin
- 20 oz boneless turkey meat, skinless and cut into thin slices
- 1 tbsp phoenix sunrise seasoning

Directions:
1. Heat the oil over medium-high heat with your pan. Add the scallions and cook for about 5 minutes. Add pepper and stir. Cook for 7 minutes.
2. Once done, transfer to your dish and keep it warm. Return the pan and add the sliced turkey. Sprinkle the seasoning over and cook for about 15-20 minutes. Stir often. Once the turkey is well cooked, add the pepper and stir well. Serve.

Nutrition:
Calories: 425
Carbs: 31g
Fat: 12g
Protein: 25g

560. Grilled Chicken

Preparation time: 15 minutes
Cooking time: 0 minutes
Servings: 3
Ingredients:
- 2 lb. boneless chicken breasts, skinless
- 1 ½ tbsp flavor quake seasoning
- 4 tsp roasted garlic oil

Directions:
1. Season the chicken in a bowl and allow it to sit for about 15 minutes or more in your refrigerator. Preheat your grill to 325 degrees.
2. Put the chicken on the preheated grill, cook each side for about 5 minutes, or until the chicken is fully cooked. Remove and let it cool, then serve.

Nutrition:
Calories: 110
Carbs: 0g
Fat: 3g
Protein: 22g

561. Creamy Chicken Asparagus

Preparation time: 10 minutes
Cooking time: 15 minutes
Servings: 4
Ingredients:
- 4 tsp Roasted garlic oil
- 1 ¾ lb. Boneless chicken breast, skinless, and chopped into 1-inch chunks
- ½ cup Chicken broth, low sodium
- 1 tbsp Garlic Gusto seasoning
- 8 tbsp Light cream cheese
- 4 cups fresh asparagus, chopped into 2-inch pieces
- Seasoning (salt, garlic, and pepper)

Directions:
1. Put the oil in your pan and heat it over medium-high heat. Stir in the chicken breast and cook for about 10 min, or until the chicken becomes slightly brown. Stir occasionally.
2. Put the chicken broth in the pan and scrape all the brown bits from the pan's bottom. Add the garlic seasoning, asparagus, and cream cheese.
3. Adjust to high and cook until the cream cheese completely melts. Stir frequently. Bring mixture to a boil.
4. Simmer until the sauce becomes thick. Equally, divide into 4 portions and sprinkle over with the seasoning. Serve hot.

Nutrition:
Calories: 302
Fat: 12.8g
Carbohydrates: 7.1g
Protein: 39g

562. Taco Tomato Seasoned Turkey

Preparation time: 5 minutes
Cooking time: 10 minutes
Servings: 4
Ingredients:
- 1 ½ pound Boneless turkey meat, skinless and cut into thin slices
- 1 tbsp Low salt tex-mex seasoning
- ½ cup Fresh tomatoes, chopped
- 1 tsp Seasoning (optional)
- Favorite taco condiments

Directions:
1. In a single layer, place the turkey in the bottom of your pot. Sprinkle the seasonings over the turkey. Spread the tomatoes over the turkey.
2. Cook on high for 10 minutes. Remove the chicken and shred it with your forks. Pour the sauce over and serve.

Nutrition:
Calories: 198
Fat: 4.3g
Carbohydrates: 0.9g
Protein: 36.3g

Chapter 8. Egg Recipes

563. Smoked Salmon and Poached Eggs on Toast

Preparation Time: 10 minutes
Cooking Time: 4 minutes
Serving: 2
Ingredients:

- 2 oz avocado smashed
- 2 slices of bread toasted
- Pinch of kosher salt and cracked black pepper
- 1/4 tsp freshly squeezed lemon juice
- 2 eggs see notes, poached
- 3.5 oz smoked salmon
- 1 TBSP. thinly sliced scallions
- Splash of Kikkoman soy sauce optional
- Microgreens are optional

Directions:

1. Take a small bowl and then smash the avocado into it. Then, add the lemon juice and also a pinch of salt into the mixture. Then, mix it well and set aside.
2. After that, poach the eggs and toast the bread for some time.
3. Once the bread is toasted, you will have to spread the avocado on both slices and after that, add the smoked salmon to each slice.
4. Thereafter, carefully transfer the poached eggs to the respective toasts.
5. Add a splash of Kikkoman soy sauce and some cracked pepper; then, just garnish with scallions and micro greens.

Nutrition: calories: 255| fat: 26.6g | protein: 19.28g | carbs: 14.83g | fiber: 2.8g | sodium: 465mg

564. Mediterranean Eggs White Breakfast Sandwich with Roasted Tomatoes

Preparation Time: 15 minutes
Cooking Time: 10 minutes
Servings: 2
Ingredients:

- Salt and pepper to taste
- ¼ cup egg whites
- 1 teaspoon chopped fresh herbs like rosemary, basil, parsley,
- 1 whole grain seeded ciabatta roll
- 1 teaspoon butter
- 1-2 slices Muenster cheese
- 1 tablespoon pesto
- About ½ cup roasted tomatoes
- 10 ounces grape tomatoes
- 1 tablespoon extra-virgin olive oil
- Black pepper and salt to taste

Directions:

1. First, you will have to melt the butter over medium heat in the small nonstick skillet.
2. Then, mix the egg whites with pepper and salt.
3. Then, sprinkle it with the fresh herbs
4. After that cook it for almost 3-4 minutes or until the eggs are done, then flip it carefully
5. Meanwhile, toast ciabatta bread in the toaster

6. After that, you will have to place the egg on the bottom half of the sandwich rolls, then top with cheese
7. Add roasted tomatoes and the top half of roll.
8. To make a roasted tomato, preheat the oven to 400 degrees.
9. Then, slice the tomatoes in half lengthwise.
10. Place on the baking sheet and drizzle with the olive oil.
11. Season it with pepper and salt and then roast in the oven for about 20 minutes. Skins will appear wrinkled when done.

Nutrition: calories: 328| fat: 15.51g | protein: 12.17g | carbs: 14.83g | fiber: 3.7g | sodium: 652mg

565. Mediterranean Feta and Quinoa Egg Muffins

Preparation Time: 15 minutes
Cooking Time: 15 minutes
Servings: 12
Ingredients:

- 2 cups baby spinach finely chopped
- 1 cup chopped or sliced cherry tomatoes
- 1/2 cup finely chopped onion
- 1 tablespoon chopped fresh oregano
- 1 cup crumbled feta cheese
- 1/2 cup chopped {pitted} kalamata olives
- 2 teaspoons high oleic sunflower oil
- 1 cup cooked quinoa
- 8 eggs
- 1/4 teaspoon salt

Directions:

1. Pre-heat oven to 350 degrees Fahrenheit, and then prepare 12 silicone muffin holders on the baking sheet, or just grease a 12-cup muffin tin with oil and set aside.
2. Finely chop the vegetables and then heat the skillet to medium.
3. After that, add the vegetable oil and onions and sauté for 2 minutes.
4. Then, add tomatoes and sauté for another minute, then add spinach and sauté until wilted, about 1 minute.
5. Place the beaten egg into a bowl and then add lots of vegetables like feta cheese, quinoa, veggie mixture as well as salt, and then stir well until everything is properly combined.
6. Pour the ready mixture into greased muffin tins or silicone cups, dividing the mixture equally. Then, bake it in an oven for 30 minutes or so, or until the eggs set nicely, and the muffins turn a light golden brown in color.

Nutrition : calories: 161| fat: 10.88g | protein: 9.48g | carbs: 6.47g | fiber: 1.5g | sodium: 293mg

566. Mediterranean Eggs

Preparation Time: 15 minutes
Cooking Time: 20 minutes
Servings: 2
Ingredients:

- 5 tbsp. of divided olive oil
- 2 diced medium sized Spanish onions

- 2 diced red bell peppers
- 2 minced cloves garlic
- 1 teaspoon cumin seeds
- 4 diced large ripe tomatoes
- 1 tablespoon of honey
- Salt
- Freshly ground black pepper
- 1/3 cup crumbled feta
- 4 eggs
- 1 teaspoon zaatar spice
- Grilled pita during serving

Directions:
1. To start with, you have to add 3 tablespoons of olive oil into a pan and heat it over medium heat. Along with the oil, sauté the cumin seeds, onions, garlic and red pepper for a few minutes.
2. After that, add the diced tomatoes and salt and pepper to taste and cook them for about 10 minutes till they come together and form a light sauce.
3. With that, half the preparation is already done. Now you just have to break the eggs directly into the sauce and poach them. However, you must keep in mind to cook the egg whites, but keep the yolks still runny. This takes about 8 to 10 minutes.
4. While plating adds some feta and olive oil with zaatar spice to further enhance the flavors. Once done, serve with grilled pita.

Nutrition: calories: 869| fat: 62.64g | protein: 38.37g | carbs: 42.43g | fiber: 7.2g | sodium: 486mg

567. Pastry-Less Spanakopita

Preparation Time: 5 minutes
Cooking Time: 20 minutes
Servings: 4
Ingredients:
- 1/8 teaspoons black pepper, add as per taste
- 1/3 cup of Extra virgin olive oil
- 4 lightly beaten eggs
- 7 cups of Lettuce, preferably a spring mix (mesclun)
- 1/2 cup of crumbled Feta cheese
- 1/8 teaspoon of Sea salt, add to taste
- 1 finely chopped medium Yellow onion

Directions:
1. For this delicious recipe, you need to first start by preheating the oven to 180C and grease the flan dish.
2. Once done, pour the extra virgin olive oil into a large saucepan and heat it over medium heat with the onions, until they are translucent. To that, add greens and keep stirring until all the ingredients are wilted.
3. After completing that, you should season it with salt and pepper and transfer the greens to the prepared dish and sprinkle on some feta cheese.
4. Pour the eggs and bake it for 20 minutes till it is cooked through and slightly brown.

Nutrition: calories: 272| fat: 21.53g | protein: 13.31g | carbs: 6.56g | fiber: 1.6g | sodium: 511mg

568. Greek Yogurt Pancakes

Preparation Time: 10 minutes
Cooking Time: 5 minutes
Servings: 2
Ingredients:
- 1 cup all-purpose flour

- 1 cup whole-wheat flour
- 1/4 teaspoon salt
- 4 teaspoons baking powder
- 1 Tablespoon sugar
- 1 1/2 cups unsweetened almond milk
- 2 teaspoons vanilla extract
- 2 large eggs
- 1/2 cup plain 2% Greek yogurt
- Fruit, for serving
- Maple syrup, for serving

Directions:
1. First, you will have to pour the curds into the bowl and mix them well until creamy.
2. After that, you will have to add egg whites and mix them well until combined.
3. Then take a separate bowl, pour the wet mixture into the dry mixture. Stir to combine. The batter will be extremely thick.
4. Then, simply spoon the batter onto the sprayed pan heated to medium-high.
5. The batter must make 4 large pancakes.
6. Then, you will have to flip the pancakes once when they start to bubble a bit on the surface. Cook until golden brown on both sides.

Nutrition: calories: 721| fat: 8.94g | protein: 18.24g | carbs: 145.4g | fiber: 9g | sodium: 444mg

569. Spinach and egg scramble with raspberries

Preparation Time: 10 minutes
Cooking Time: 10 minutes
Servings: 1
Ingredients:
- One teaspoon of canola oil
- One and a half cups of baby spinach (which is one and a half ounces)
- Two eggs, large and lightly beaten
- Kosher salt, a pinch.
- Ground pepper, a pinch
- One slice of whole-grain toasted bread
- Half cup of fresh and fine raspberries

Directions:
1. Heat the oil in a non-stick and small skillet at a temperature of medium-high.
2. Add spinach to the plate.
3. Cleanly wipe the pan and add eggs into the medium heated pan.
4. Stir and cook twice in order to ensure even-cooking for about two minutes.
5. Stir the spinach in and add salt and pepper into it.
6. Garnish it with raspberries and toast before eating.

Nutrition: calories: 532| fat: 16.33g | protein: 17.9g | carbs: 83.89g | fiber: 12.5g | sodium: 281mg

570. Egg Cauliflower Salad

Preparation Time: 10 minutes
Cooking Time: 14 minutes
Servings: 4
Ingredients:
- 4 eggs, hard-boiled, peeled and cubed
- 2 tbsp fresh parsley, chopped
- 1 tbsp vinegar
- 2 tbsp green onion, chopped

- 2 tbsp mayonnaise
- 1/2 cup heavy cream
- 1 1/2 cup vegetable stock
- 2 cups cauliflower florets
- 1/4 cup grape tomatoes, halved
- Pepper
- Salt

Directions:
1. Pour 1 1/2 cups of stock into the instant pot the place steamer basket in the pot.
2. Add cauliflower florets into the steamer basket.
3. Seal pot with lid and cook on high for 14 minutes.
4. Once done, allow to release pressure naturally for 10 minutes then release remaining using quick release. Remove lid.
5. Transfer cauliflower florets into the large mixing bowl. Add remaining ingredients into the bowl and mix well.
6. Serve and enjoy.

Nutrition: calories: 897| fat: 96.73g | protein: 8.42g | carbs: 6.79g | fiber: 1.5g | sodium: 178mg

571. Egg Salad

Preparation Time: 10 minutes
Cooking Time: 8 minutes
Servings: 4
Ingredients:
- 4 eggs
- 2 tablespoon mayonnaise
- ¼ cup fresh dill, chopped
- 1 avocado, chopped
- 1 teaspoon lime juice
- ¼ teaspoon ground black pepper
- 1 cup water, for cooking

Directions:
1. Pour water in the saucepan, add eggs and close the lid.
2. Boil the eggs for 8 minutes.
3. Meanwhile, in the salad bowl combine together avocado and chopped dill.
4. When the eggs are cooked, chill them in the ice water and peel.
5. Chop the eggs and add in the salad mixture.
6. Sprinkle the salad with lime juice, ground black pepper, and mayonnaise.
7. Mix up the salad carefully.

Nutrition: calories: 236| fat: 19.4g | protein: 10.5g | carbs: 5.94g | fiber: 3.5g | sodium: 165mg

572. Eggs In Zucchini Nests

Preparation Time: 10 minutes
Cooking Time: 7 minutes
Servings: 4
Ingredients:
- 4 teaspoons butter
- ½ teaspoon paprika
- ½ teaspoon black pepper
- ¼ teaspoon sea salt
- 4-ounces cheddar cheese, shredded
- 4 eggs
- 8-ounces zucchini, grated

Directions:
1. Grate the zucchini and place the butter in ramekins.
2. Add the grated zucchini in ramekins in the shape of nests. Sprinkle the zucchini nests with salt, pepper, and paprika. Beat the eggs and pour over zucchini nests.
3. Top egg mixture with shredded cheddar cheese. Preheat the air fryer basket and cook the dish for 7-minutes.
4. When the zucchini nests are cooked, chill them for 3-minutes and serve them in the ramekins.

Nutrition: calories: 227| fat: 16.27g | protein: 14.43g | carbs: 6.22g | fiber: 0.8g | sodium: 592mg

573. Herbed Breakfast Eggs

Preparation Time: 3 minutes
Cooking Time: 17 minutes
Servings: 2
Ingredients:
- 4 eggs
- 1 teaspoon oregano
- 1 teaspoon parsley, dried
- ½ teaspoon sea salt
- 1 tablespoon chives, chopped
- 1 tablespoon cream
- 1 teaspoon paprika

Directions:
1. Place the eggs in the air fryer basket and cook them for 17-minutes at 320°Fahrenheit. Meanwhile, combine the parsley, oregano, cream, and salt in shallow bowl.
2. Chop the chives and add them to cream mixture. When the eggs are cooked, place them in cold water and allow them to chill. After this, peel the eggs and cut them into halves.
3. Remove the egg yolks and add yolks to cream mixture and mash to blend well with a fork. Then fill the egg whites with the cream-egg yolk mixture. Serve immediately.

Nutrition: calories: 279| fat: 20.91g | protein: 18.41g | carbs: 3.38g | fiber: 0.7g | sodium: 790mg

574. Spinach Quiche

Preparation Time: 35 minutes
Cooking Time: 21 minutes
Servings: 6
Ingredients:
- 6-ounces cheddar cheese, shredded
- 1 teaspoon olive oil
- 3 eggs
- 1 teaspoon ground black pepper
- ½ yellow onion, diced
- ¼ cup cream cheese
- 1 cup spinach
- 1 teaspoon sea salt
- 4 tablespoons water, boiled
- ½ cup almond flour

Directions:
1. Combine the almond flour, water, and salt. Mix and knead the dough. Spray the inside of the fryer basket with olive oil. Set your air fryer to 375°Fahrenheit.
2. Roll the dough and place it in your air fryer basket tray in the shape of the crust.
3. Place air fryer basket tray inside of air fryer and cook for 5-minutes. Chop the spinach and

combine it with the cream cheese and ground black pepper.

4. Dice the yellow onion and add it to the spinach mixture and stir. Whisk eggs in a bowl. When the quiche crust is cooked—transfer the spinach filling.

5. Sprinkle the filling top with shredded cheese and pour the whisked eggs over the top. Set the air fryer to 350°Fahrenheit. Cook the quiche for 7-minutes.

6. Reduce the heat to 300°Fahrenheit and cook the quiche for an additional 9-minutes.

7. Allow the quiche to chill thoroughly and then cut it into pieces for serving.

Nutrition: calories: 156| fat: 11.03g | protein: 9.31g | carbs: 4.81g | fiber: 0.2g | sodium: 799mg

575. Seed Porridge

Preparation Time: 10 minutes
Cooking Time: 12 minutes
Servings: 3
Ingredients:
- 1 tablespoon butter
- ¼ teaspoon nutmeg
- 1/3 cup heavy cream
- 1 egg
- ¼ teaspoon salt
- 3 tablespoons sesame seeds
- 3 tablespoons chia seeds

Directions:
1. Place the butter in your air fryer basket tray. Add the chia seeds, sesame seeds, heavy cream, nutmeg, and salt. Stir gently.
2. Beat the egg in a cup and whisk it with a fork.
3. Add the whisked egg to air fryer basket tray.
4. Stir the mixture with a wooden spatula.
5. Preheat your air fryer to 375°F. Place the air fryer basket tray into air fryer and cook the porridge for 12-minutes.
6. Stir it about 3 times during the cooking process.
7. Remove the porridge from air fryer basket tray immediately and serve hot!

Nutrition: calories: 174| fat: 16.91g | protein: 4.95g | carbs: 1.71g | fiber: 1g | sodium: 267mg

576. Avocado Baked Eggs

Preparation Time: 10 minutes
Cooking Time: 25 minutes
Servings: 2
Ingredients:
- 2 eggs
- 1 medium sized avocado, halved and pit removed
- ¼ cup cheddar cheese, shredded
- Kosher salt and black pepper, to taste

Directions:
1. Preheat oven to 425 degrees and grease a muffin pan.
2. Crack open an egg into each half of the avocado and season with salt and black pepper.
3. Top with cheddar cheese and transfer the muffin pan in the oven.
4. Bake for about 15 minutes and dish out to serve.

Nutrition: calories: 299| fat: 24.42g | protein: 11.72g | carbs: 4.81g | fiber: 7.1g | sodium: 111mg

577. Cottage Cheese And Berries Omelet

Preparation Time: 2-3 minutes
Cooking Time: 4 minutes
Servings: 1
Ingredients:
- 1 egg, whisked
- 1 teaspoon cinnamon powder
- 1 tablespoon almond milk
- 3 ounces cottage cheese
- 4 ounces blueberries

Directions:
1. Scourge egg with the rest of the ingredients except the oil and toss.
2. Preheat pan with the oil over medium heat, add the eggs mix, spread, cook for 2 minutes on each side, transfer to a plate and serve.

Nutrition: calories: 327| fat: 13.89g | protein: 19.37g | carbs: 32.41g | fiber: 3.3g | sodium: 426mg

578. Almond Scramble

Preparation Time: 10 minutes
Cooking Time: 6 Hours
Servings: 4
Ingredients:
- 1 teaspoon almond butter
- 4 egg whites
- ¼ teaspoon salt
- ½ teaspoon paprika
- 2 tablespoons heavy cream

Directions:
1. Whisk the egg whites gently and add heavy cream.
2. Put the almond butter in the skillet and melt it.
3. Then add egg white mixture.
4. Sprinkle it with salt and cook for 2 minutes over the medium heat.
5. After this, scramble the egg whites with the help of the fork or spatula and sprinkle with paprika.
6. Cook the scrambled egg whites for 3 minutes more.
7. Transfer the meal into the serving plates.

Nutrition: calories: 52| fat: 3.59g | protein: 4.07g | carbs: 0.86g | fiber: 0.2g | sodium: 206mg

579. Poached Egg In Bell Pepper

Preparation Time: 10 minutes
Cooking Time: 15 minutes
Servings: 2
Ingredients:
- 2 eggs
- 2 bell peppers, ends sliced off
- 2 slices mozzarella cheese, shredded

Directions:
1. Pour 1 cup water inside the Instant Pot.
2. Add the steamer basket.
3. Carefully break an egg into each bell pepper cup.
4. Cover with foil.
5. Put on top of the basket.
6. Seal the pot.
7. Cook on low for 4 minutes.
8. Release the pressure naturally.
9. Top with the cheese and wait for it to melt.

Nutrition: calories: 148| fat: 9.73g | protein: 9.87g | carbs: 5.27g | fiber: 0.7g | sodium: 105mg

580. Eggs And Tomato Mix

Preparation Time: 5 minutes
Cooking Time: 5 minutes
Servings: 2
Ingredients:
- 1 tomato
- 2 eggs
- ¼ teaspoon chili flakes
- ¾ teaspoon salt
- ½ teaspoon butter

Directions:
1. Trim the tomato and slice it into 2 rings.
2. Remove the tomato flesh.
3. Toss butter in the skillet and melt it.
4. Then arrange the tomato rings.
5. Crack the eggs in the tomato rings. Sprinkle them with salt and chili flakes.
6. Cook the eggs for 4 minutes over the medium heat with the closed lid.
7. Transfer the cooked eggs into the serving plates with the help of the spatula.

Nutrition: calories: 150| fat: 10.79g | protein: 9.57g | carbs: 3.58g | fiber: 0.9g | sodium: 995mg

581. Baked Eggs With Cheddar And Beef

Preparation Time: 20 minutes
Cooking Time: 20 minutes
Servings: 2
Ingredients:
- 3 oz ground beef, cooked
- 2 organic eggs
- 2oz shredded cheddar cheese
- 1 tbsp olive oil

Directions:
1. Switch on the oven, then set its temperature to 390°F and let it preheat.
2. Meanwhile, take a baking dish, grease it with oil, add spread cooked beef in the bottom, then make two holes in it and crack an organic egg into each hole.
3. Sprinkle cheese on top of beef and eggs and bake for 20 minutes until beef has cooked and eggs have set.
4. When done, let baked eggs cool for 5 minutes and then serve straight away.
5. For meal prepping, wrap baked eggs in foil and refrigerate for up to two days.
6. When ready to eat, reheat baked eggs in the microwave and then serve.

Nutrition: calories: 380| fat: 31.67g | protein: 18.87g | carbs: 4.05g | fiber: 0g | sodium: 443mg

582. Eggs, Mint and Tomatoes

Preparation time: 10 minutes
Cooking time: 15 minutes
Servings: 2
Ingredients:
- 2 eggs, whisked
- 2 tomatoes, cubed
- 2 teaspoons olive oil
- 1 tablespoon mint, chopped
- 1 tablespoon chives, chopped
- Salt and black pepper to the taste
Directions:

1. Heat up a pan with the oil over medium heat, add the tomatoes and the rest of the ingredients except the eggs, stir and cook for 5 minutes.
2. Add the eggs, toss, cook for 10 minutes more, divide between plates and serve.
Nutrition: calories 300, fat 15.3, fiber 4.5, carbs 17.7, protein 11

583. Mediterranean Egg Muffins with Ham

Preparation time: 15 minutes
Cooking time: 15 minutes
Servings: 6
Ingredients:
- 9 Slices of thin cut deli ham
- 1/2 cup canned roasted red pepper, sliced + additional for garnish
- 1/3 cup fresh spinach, minced
- 1/4 cup feta cheese, crumbled
- 5 large eggs
- Pinch of salt
- Pinch of pepper
- 1 1/2 tbsp Pesto sauce
- Fresh basil for garnish
Directions:
1. Preheat oven to 400 degrees F. Spray a muffin tin with cooking spray, generously. Line each of the muffin tin with 1 ½ pieces of ham - making sure there aren't any holes for the egg mixture come out.
2. Place some of the roasted red pepper in the bottom of each muffin tin. Place 1 tbsp of minced spinach on top of each red pepper. Top the pepper and spinach off with a large 1/2 tbsp of crumbled feta cheese.
3. In a medium bowl, whisk together the eggs salt and pepper, divide the egg mixture evenly among the 6 muffin tins.
4. Bake for 15 to 17 minutes until the eggs are puffy and set. Remove each cup from the muffin tin. Allow to cool completely
5. Distribute the muffins among the containers, store in the fridge for 2 - 3days or in the freezer for 3 months.
Nutrition: Calories: 109 Carbs: 2g Fat: 6g Protein: 9g

584. Sun Dried Tomatoes, Dill and Feta Omelet Casserole

Preparation time: 15 minutes
Cooking time: 40 minutes
Servings: 6
Ingredients:
- 12 large eggs
- 2 cups whole milk
- 8 oz fresh spinach
- 2 cloves garlic, minced
- 12 oz artichoke salad with olives and peppers, drained and chopped
- 5 oz sun dried tomato feta cheese, crumbled
- 1 tbsp fresh chopped dill or 1 tsp dried dill
- 1 tsp dried oregano
- 1 tsp lemon pepper
- 1 tsp salt
- 4 tsp olive oil, divided
Directions:
1. Preheat oven to 375 degrees F. Chop the fresh herbs and artichoke salad. In a skillet over medium heat, add 1 tbsp olive oil.

2. Sauté the spinach and garlic until wilted, about 3 minutes. Oil a 9x13 inch baking dish, layer the spinach and artichoke salad evenly in the dish
3. In a medium bowl, whisk together the eggs, milk, herbs, salt and lemon pepper. Pour the egg mixture over vegetables, sprinkle with feta cheese.
4. Bake in the center of the oven for 35-40 minutes until firm in the center. Allow to cool, slice a and distribute among the storage containers. Store for 2-3 days or freeze for 3 months
Nutrition: Calories: 196 Carbohydrates: 5g Fat: 12g Protein: 10g

585. Egg White Scramble with Cherry Tomatoes & Spinach

Preparation Time: 5 minutes
Cooking Time: 8-10 minutes
Servings: 4
Ingredients:
- 1 tbsp. Olive oil
- 1 whole Egg
- 10 Egg whites
- ¼ tsp. Black pepper
- ½ tsp. Salt
- 1 garlic clove, minced
- 2 cups cherry tomatoes, halved
- 2 cups packed fresh baby spinach
- ½ cup Light cream or Half & Half
- ¼ cup finely grated parmesan cheese
Directions:
1. Whisk the eggs, pepper, salt, and milk. Prepare a skillet using the med-high temperature setting. Toss in the garlic when the pan is hot to sauté for approximately 30 seconds.
2. Pour in the tomatoes and spinach and continue to sauté it for one additional minute. The tomatoes should be softened, and the spinach wilted.
3. Add the egg mixture into the pan using the medium heat setting. Fold the egg gently as it cooks for about two to three minutes. Remove from the burner, and sprinkle with a sprinkle of cheese.
Nutrition: Calories 142 Protein: 15g Fat: 2g Carbs 4g

586. Bacon and Brie Omelet Wedges

Preparation time: 10 minutes
Cooking time: 10 minutes
Servings: 6
Ingredients:
- 2 tablespoons olive oil
- 7 ounces smoked bacon
- 6 beaten eggs
- Small bunch chives, snipped
- 3 ½ ounces brie, sliced
- 1 teaspoon red wine vinegar
- 1 teaspoon Dijon mustard
- 1 cucumber, halved, deseeded and sliced diagonally
- 7 ounces radish, quartered
Directions:
1. Turn your grill on and set it too high. Take a small-sized pan and add 1 teaspoon of oil, allow the oil to heat up. Add lardons and fry until crisp. Drain the lardon on kitchen paper.
2. Take another non-sticky cast iron frying pan and place it over grill, heat 2 teaspoons of oil. Add lardons, eggs, chives, ground pepper to the frying pan. Cook on low until they are semi-set.

3. Carefully lay brie on top and grill until the Brie sets and is a golden texture. Remove it from the pan and cut up into wedges.
4. Take a small bowl and create dressing by mixing olive oil, mustard, vinegar and seasoning. Add cucumber to the bowl and mix, serve alongside the omelet wedges.
Nutrition: Calories: 35 Fat: 31g Carbohydrates: 3g Protein: 25g

587. Mushroom Goat Cheese Frittata

Preparation time: 15 minutes
Cooking time: 35 minutes
Servings: 4
Ingredients:
- 1 tbsp olive oil
- 1 small onion, diced
- 10 oz cremini or your favorite mushrooms, sliced
- 1 garlic clove, minced
- 10 eggs
- 2/3 cup half and half
- 1/4 cup fresh chives, minced
- 2 tsp fresh thyme, minced
- 1/2 tsp kosher salt
- 1/2 tsp black pepper
- 4 oz goat cheese
Directions:
1. Preheat the oven to 375 degrees F. In an over safe skillet or cast-iron pan over medium heat, olive oil. Add in the onion and sauté for 3-5 mins until golden.
2. Add in the sliced mushrooms and garlic, continue to sauté until mushrooms are golden brown, about 10-12 minutes.
3. In a large bowl, whisk together the eggs, half and half, chives, thyme, salt and pepper. Place the goat cheese over the mushroom mixture and pour the egg mixture over the top.
4. Stir the MIXTURE in the pan and cook over medium heat until the edges are set but the center is still loose, about 8-10 minutes
5. Put the pan in the oven and finish cooking for an additional 8-10 minutes or until set. Allow to cool completely before slicing.
Nutrition: Calories: 243 Carbohydrates: 5g Fat: 17g Protein: 15g

588. Parmesan Omelet

Preparation Time: 5 minutes
Cooking Time: 10 minutes
Servings: 2
Ingredients:
- One tablespoon cream cheese
- Two eggs, beaten
- ¼ teaspoon paprika
- ½ teaspoon dried oregano
- ¼ teaspoon dried dill
- 1 oz Parmesan, grated
- One teaspoon coconut oil
Directions:
1. Mix up together cream cheese with eggs, dried oregano, and dill.
2. Put coconut oil in the frypan and heat it until it coats all the skillet.
3. Then pour the egg mixture into the skillet and flatten it.
4. Add grated Parmesan and close the lid.
5. Cook the omelet for 10 minutes over low heat.
6. Then transfer the cooked omelet to the serving plate and sprinkle with paprika.

Nutrition:
Calories: 148
Fat: 11.5 g
Fiber: 0.3 g
Carbs: 1.4 g
Protein: 10.6 g

589. Basil Scrambled Eggs

Preparation time: 5 minutes
Cooking time: 8 minutes
Serving: 2
Ingredients:

- 4 large eggs
- 2 tablespoons grated Gruyère cheese
- 2 tablespoons finely chopped fresh basil
- 1 tablespoon plain Greek yogurt
- 1 tablespoon olive oil
- 2 cloves garlic, minced
- Sea salt and freshly ground pepper, to taste

Direction:
1. In a large bowl, beat together the eggs, cheese, basil, and yogurt with a whisk until just combined.
2. Heat the oil in a large, heavy nonstick skillet over medium-low heat. Add the garlic and cook until golden, about 1 minute.
3. Pour the egg mixture into the skillet over the garlic. Work the eggs continuously and cook until fluffy and soft.
4. Season with sea salt and freshly ground pepper to taste. Divide between 2 plates and serve immediately.
Nutrition Per Serving
calories: 243 | fat: 19.7g | protein: 15.6g | carbs: 3.4g | fiber: 0.1g | sodium: 568mg

590. Potato Omelet

Preparation Time: 10 minutes
Cooking Time: 15 minutes
Serving: 4
Ingredients:

- ½ C. olive oil
- ½ lb. potatoes, sliced thinly
- Salt and freshly ground black pepper, to taste
- 1 large onion, sliced thinly
- 4 eggs
- 2 tomatoes, peeled, seeded and chopped roughly
- 2 scallions, chopped

Direction:
1. In a large skillet, heat the oil over medium-high heat and cook the potatoes with a little salt and black pepper for about 3-4 minutes or until golden brown and crisp.
2. Stir in the onion and cook for about 5 minutes, stirring occasionally.
3. Meanwhile, in a bowl, add the eggs, salt and black pepper and beat well.
4. Add the egg mixture into the skillet with potato mixture and gently stir to combine.
5. Reduce heat to low and cook until eggs begin to set on the bottom.
6. With a spatula, carefully flip the omelet and cook until eggs are set.
7. Serve warm with the garnishing of tomato and scallion.
Serving Suggestion: Serve with buttered toasts.
Variation Tip: Use a rubber spatula.
 Nutrition per Serving:
Calories per serving: 347; Carbohydrates: 15.7g; Fiber: 3.1g
Protein: 7.6g; Fat: 29.8g;

591. Veggie Omelet

Preparation Time: 15 minutes
Cooking Time: 15 minutes
Serving: 4
Ingredients:

- 1 tsp. olive oil
- 2 C. fresh fennel bulbs, sliced thinly
- ¼ C. canned artichoke hearts, rinsed, drained and chopped
- ¼ C. green olives, pitted and chopped
- 1 Roma tomato, chopped
- 6 eggs
- Salt and freshly ground black pepper, to taste
- ½ C. goat cheese, crumbled

Direction:
1. Preheat the oven to 325 °F.
2. In a large ovenproof skillet, heat the oil over medium-high heat and sauté the fennel bulb for about 5 minutes.
3. Stir in the artichoke, olives and tomato and cook for about 3 minutes.
4. Meanwhile, in a bowl, add the eggs, salt and black pepper and beat until well combined.
5. Place the egg mixture over veggie mixture and stir to combine.
6. Cook for about 2 minutes.
7. Sprinkle with the goat cheese evenly and immediately transfer the skillet into the oven.
8. Bake for about 5 minutes or until eggs are set completely.
9. Remove from the oven and carefully transfer the omelet onto a cutting board.
10.   Cut into desired sized wedges and serve.
Serving Suggestion: Serve alongside the caramelized onions.
Variation Tip: Feel free to use veggies of your choice.
Nutrition:
Calories per serving: 225; Carbohydrates: 6.6g; Fiber: 2.3g
Protein: 15.3g; Fat: 15.8g;

592. Slow-cooked Peppers Frittata

Servings: 6
Cooking Time: 3 Hours
Ingredients:

- ½ cup almond milk
- 8 eggs, whisked
- Salt and black pepper to the taste
- 1 teaspoon oregano, dried
- 1 and ½ cups roasted peppers, chopped
- ½ cup red onion, chopped
- 4 cups baby arugula
- 1 cup goat cheese, crumbled
- Cooking spray

Directions:
1. In a bowl, combine the eggs with salt, pepper and the oregano and whisk.
2. Grease your slow cooker with the cooking spray, arrange the peppers and the remaining ingredients inside and pour the eggs mixture over them.
3. Put the lid on and cook on Low for 3 hours.
4. Divide the frittata between plates and serve.
Nutrition: calories 259, fat 20.2, fiber 1, carbs 4.4, protein 16.3

593. Mediterranean Pancakes

Preparation time: 30 minutes
Cooking time: 20 minutes
Serving: 16 Pancakes
Ingredients
- 1 cup old-fashioned oats
- ½ cup all-purpose flour
- 2 tbsp. flax seeds
- 1 tsp. baking soda
- ¼ tsp. sea salt
- 2 tbsp. extra virgin olive oil
- 2 large eggs
- 2 cups nonfat plain Greek yogurt
- 2 tbsp. raw honey
- Fresh fruit, syrup, or other toppings

Direction:
1. Combine the oats, flour, flax seeds, baking soda, and sea salt in a blender; mix for 30 seconds or so.
2. Add extra virgin olive oil, eggs, honey and yogurt and continue to pulsate until very smooth.
3. For at least 20 minutes or until dense, let the mixture stand.
4. Over medium heat, position a large nonstick skillet and brush with extra virgin olive oil.
5. Scoop the batter into the skillet in batches of quarter-cup.
6. Cook the pancakes for about 2 minutes or until they are golden brown and bubbles appear.
7. Turn them over and cook for 2 more minutes or until the other sides are golden brown.
8. Put the cooked pancakes on a baking sheet and keep them warm in the oven.
9. Serve with the preferred toppings.

Nutrition: calories 57, fat 2.33, fiber 1.1, carbs 9.33, protein 2

594. Mediterranean Frittata

Preparation time: 10 minutes
Cooking time: 15 minutes
Servings: 4
Ingredients
- 3 tbsp. extra virgin olive oil, divided
- 1 cup chopped onion
- 2 cloves garlic, minced
- 8 eggs, beaten
- ¼ cup half-and-half, milk or light cream
- ½ cup sliced Kalamata olives
- ½ cup roasted red sweet peppers, chopped
- ½ cup crumbled feta cheese
- 1/8 tsp. black pepper
- ¼ cup fresh basil
- 2 tbsp. Parmesan cheese, finely shredded
- ½ cup coarsely crushed onion-and-garlic croutons
- Fresh basil leaves, to garnish

Direction:
1. Get your broiler preheated.
2. A broiler-proof skillet set over medium heat, heat 2 tablespoons extra virgin olive oil; sauté the onion and garlic for a few minutes or until tender.
3. Meanwhile, beat half-and-a-half eggs in a bowl until well mixed.
4. Stir in the olives, sweet roasted pepper, feta cheese, basil and black pepper.
5. Over the sautéed onion mixture, pour the egg mixture over and cook until almost set.
6. Raise the egg mixture with a spatula to allow the uncooked portion to flow underneath.

7. Continue to simmer for 2 more minutes or until set.
8. In a cup, blend the remaining extra virgin olive oil, parmesan cheese and crushed croutons; scatter the mixture over the frittata and broil for approximately 5 minutes or until the crumbs are golden and the top is set.
9. Break the frittata into wedges to serve and garnish it with fresh basil.

Nutrition: calories 412, fat 30.56, fiber 1.6, carbs 9.33, protein 22.66

595. Mediterranean Veggie Omelette

Preparation time: 15 minutes
Cooking time: 25 minutes
Servings: 4
Ingredients
- 1 tbsp. extra virgin olive oil
- 2 cups thinly sliced fresh fennel bulb
- ¼ cup chopped artichoke hearts, soaked in water, drained
- ¼ cup pitted green olives, brine-cured, chopped
- 1 diced Roma tomato6 eggs
- ¼ tsp. sea salt
- ½ tsp. freshly ground black pepper
- ½ cup goat cheese, crumbled
- 2 tbsp. freshly chopped fresh parsley, dill, or basil

Direction:
1. Preheat your oven to 325°F.
2. Over medium melt, heat extra virgin olive oil in an ovenproof skillet.
3. Sauté the fennel until tender, or for about 5 minutes.
4. Apply the heart, olives, and tomatoes to the artichoke and cook for 3 minutes or until softened.
5. Beat the eggs in a bowl; season with sea salt and pepper.
6. On top of the vegetables, add the egg mixture and stir for about 2 minutes.
7. Sprinkle over the Omelet with cheese and bake in the oven for about 5 minutes or until set and cooked through.
8. Place parsley, dill, or basil on top.
9. On a cutting board, move the Omelet, carefully cut into four wedges, and serve immediately.

Nutrition: calories 87, fat 4.29, fiber 4.1, carbs 9.49, protein 4.24

596. Breakfast Wrap

Preparation time: 5 minutes
Cooking time: 5 minutes
Servings: 2
Ingredients
- ½ cup fresh-picked spinach
- 4 egg whites
- 2 Bella sun-dried tomatoes
- 2 mixed-grain flax wraps
- ½ cup feta cheese crumbles

Directions
1. In a frying pan, cook the spinach, egg whites and tomatoes for approximately 4 minutes or lightly browned.
2. Flip it over and cook for 4 minutes or until nearly finished on the other side.
3. Microwave the wraps for approximately 15 seconds; remove from the microwave, fill the egg mixture with each wrap, sprinkle with crumbles of feta cheese and roll-up.
4. Each wrap is cut into two pieces and served.

Nutrition: calories 168, fat 10.44, fiber 1.66, carbs 9.49, protein 16.13

597. Garlicky Scrambled Eggs

Preparation time: 10 minutes
Cooking time: 15 minutes
Servings: 2
Ingredients
- ½ tsp. extra virgin olive oil
- ½ cup ground beef
- ½ tsp. garlic powder
- 3 eggs
- Salt Pepper

Direction:
1. Over medium heat, set the medium-sized pan.
2. Add extra virgin olive oil and keep warm, but do not smoke.
3. Stir in the ground beef and cook until almost cooked, or around 10 minutes.
4. Add the garlic and sauté for approximately 2 minutes.
5. Beat the eggs until almost frothy in a large bowl; season with salt and pepper.
6. With the cooked beef, add the egg mixture to the pan and scramble until ready.
7. Serve with toasted bread and olives to make your breakfast safe and satisfying.

Nutrition: calories 211, fat 0.5, fiber 1.66, carbs 4.33, protein 13.92

598. Egg and Sausage Breakfast Casserole

Preparation time: 20 minutes
Cooking time: 1 hour, 5 minutes
Servings: 12
Ingredients
The crust:
- 3 tbsp. olive oil, divided
- 2 lb. peeled and shredded russet potatoes
- ¾ tsp. ground pepper
- ¾ tsp. salt

The casserole:
- 12 oz. chopped turkey sausage
- 4 thinly sliced green onions
- ¼ cup diced bell pepper
- 1/3 cup skim milk
- 6 large eggs
- 4 egg whites
- ¾ cup shredded cheddar cheese
- 16 oz. low-fat cottage cheese

Direction:
The crust:
1. Preheat the oven to 425-degrees F. Grease a 9-13-inch baking dish lightly with 1tbsp. And set aside the olive oil.
2. With a kitchen towel or paper towel, suck the excess moisture out of the potato.
3. In a medium bowl, mix the potatoes, the remaining olive oil, salt and pepper together until they are well coated.
4. Move the mixture to the greased baking dish; press the mixture evenly on the sides and bottom of the dish and bake on the edges for approximately 20 minutes or until golden brown.

The casserole:
1. Decrease the heat of the oven to 375°F.
2. Cook the turkey sausage in a large skillet over medium-high heat for around 2 minutes or almost cooked through.
3. Attach the red bell pepper and green onions and continue cooking for 2 more minutes or until the bell pepper is tender.

4. Combine the skim milk, eggs, egg whites, and cheese.
5. Stir in the mixture of turkey sausage; pour over the potato's crust and bake for about 50 minutes. Cool slightly and slice into 12 bits. Enjoy

Nutrition: calories 305, fat 16.81, fiber 1.66, carbs 18.64, protein 19.93

599. Yogurt Pancakes

Preparation time: 10 minutes
Cooking time: 5 minutes
Servings: 5
Ingredients
- Whole-wheat pancake mix
- 1 cup yogurt
- 1 tbsp. baking powder
- 1 tbsp. baking soda
- 1 cup skimmed milk
- 3 whole eggs
- ½ tsp. extra virgin olive oil

Direction:
1. In a big bowl, combine the whole-wheat pancake recipe, yogurt, baking powder, baking soda, skimmed milk and eggs.
2. Stir until thoroughly blended.
3. Heat a pan that is lightly oiled with olive oil.
4. Pour 1/4 cup of batter onto the heated pan and cook for around 2 minutes or until some bubbles are on the pancake's surface.
5. Flip and continue cooking until it's browned on the underside.
6. With a cup of fat-free milk or two teaspoons of light maple syrup, serve the pancakes warmly.

Nutrition: calories 160, fat 9.75, fiber 0.3, carbs 9.22, protein 9.37

600. Breakfast Stir Fry

Preparation time: 5 minutes
Cooking time: 20 minutes
Servings: 4
Ingredients
- 1 tbsp. extra virgin olive oil
- 2 green peppers, sliced
- 2 small onions, finely chopped
- 4 tomatoes, chopped
- ½ tsp. sea salt
- 1 egg

Direction:
1. Heat the olive oil over medium-high heat in a medium-sized pan.
2. Stir in green pepper and sauté for 2 minutes or so.
3. Lower heat to medium and continue to cook for 3 more minutes, sealed.
4. Stir in the onion and cook until golden or around 2 minutes.
5. Stir in the tomatoes and the salt; cover and simmer to make the mixture moist and juicy.
6. Beat the egg in a bowl; drizzle the tomato mixture over it, and cook for about 1 minute. (Not to stir).
7. Serve with sliced cucumbers, black olives and feta cheese for a healthy meal.

Nutrition: calories 112, fat 5.75, fiber 2.4, carbs 10.44, protein 5.77

601. Greek Breakfast Pitas

Preparation time: 10 minutes
Cooking time: 10 minutes
Servings: 4
Ingredients
- ¼ cup chopped onion
- ¼ cup sweet red/black pepper, chopped
- 1 cup large egg
- 1/8 tsp. sea salt
- 1/8 tsp. black pepper
- 1 1/2 tsp. fresh basil, ground
- ½ cup baby spinach, freshly torn
- 1 red tomato, sliced
- 2 pita bread, whole
- 2 tbsp. feta cheese, crumbled

Direction:
1. Coat and place over medium heat with a sizeable nonstick skillet with cooking spray.
2. Attach the red peppers and onions and sauté for at least 3 minutes.
3. Combine the egg, pepper and salt in a small bowl and apply the mixture to the skillet.
4. Cook, constantly stirring, until ready.
5. Spoon the pitas with the basil, spinach, and tomatoes and cover with the egg mixture.
6. Sprinkle and serve with feta.
Nutrition: calories 439 fat 32.31, fiber 2.4, carbs 14.54, protein 21.92

602. Healthy Breakfast Scramble

Preparation time: 5 minutes
Cooking time: 15 minutes
Servings: 2
Ingredients
- 1 tsp. extra virgin olive
- 4 medium green onions, chopped
- 1 tsp. Dried basil leaves or 1 tbsp. fresh basil leaves, chopped
- 1 medium tomato, chopped
- 4 eggs
- Freshly ground pepper

Direction:
1. Heat olive oil over medium heat in a medium nonstick skillet; sauté the green onions, and occasionally, stirring for about 2 minutes.
2. Stir in the basil and tomatoes and cook, stirring periodically, for around 1 minute or until the tomatoes are fully cooked.
3. Beat the eggs thoroughly with a wire whisk or a fork in a small bowl and pour over the tomato mixture; cook for about 2 minutes.
4. Use the spatula to gently raise the cooked parts to allow the uncooked parts to flow to the bottom.
5. Continue to cook for about 3 minutes or until the eggs are completely cooked.
6. Season and serve with pepper.
Nutrition: calories 311 fat 20.23, fiber 2.4, carbs 12.83, protein 19.94

603. Pesto Scrambled Eggs

Preparation time: 10 minutes
Cooking Time: 10 Minutes
Servings: 2
Ingredients:
- 5 eggs
- 2 tablespoons butter
- 2 tablespoons pesto
- 4 tablespoons milk
- salt to taste
- pepper to taste

Directions:
1. Beat the eggs into a bowl and add salt and pepper as per your taste.
2. Then, heat a pan and add the butter, then the eggs, stirring continuously.
3. While stirring continuously, add the pesto.
4. Switch off the heat and quickly add the creamed milk and mix it well with eggs.
5. Serve hot.
Nutrition: Calories: 342, Total Fat: 29.8g, Saturated Fat: 12.3, Cholesterol: 44mg, Sodium: 345 mg, Total Carbohydrate: 3.4g, Dietary Fiber: 0.3 g, Total Sugars: 3.2 g, Protein: 16.8 g, Vitamin D: 47 mcg, Calcium: 148 mg, Iron: 2 mg, Potassium: 168 mg

604. Greek Frittata w/Zucchini, Tomatoes, Feta, and Herbs

Preparation Time: 10 minutes
Cooking Time: 18 minutes
Servings: 4
Ingredients:
- 6 Eggs
- 15 ounces of Diced Tomatoes 1 Diced Medium Zucchini
- 1 tbsp. of Olive Oil 2 Cloves of Minced Garlic
- 1/2 cup of Mozzarella Cheese 1 tbsp. of Cream
- 1/4 cup of Crumbled Feta Cheese 1/4 tsp. of Oregano
- 1/2 tsp. of Dried Basil
- 1 tsp. of Spike Seasoning Cracked Black Pepper

Directions:
1. Pour your tomatoes into your colander and allow them to drain out any liquid into your sink. Cut the ends off your zucchini and dice it into smaller pieces.
2. Preheat your broiler. Spray a frying pan with cooking spray—heat olive oil in your pan. Add the garlic, zucchini, spike seasoning, and dried herb. Sauté them for approximately 3 minutes. Add your tomatoes and cook an additional 3 to 5 minutes. All the liquid from your tomatoes should be evaporated.
3. While your vegetables are cooking, break your eggs in a bowl and beat them well. Pour your eggs into the pan with your vegetable mix and cook for an additional 2 to 3 minutes. Eggs should just be beginning to set.
4. Add half of your feta and mozzarella cheese. Stir them in gently—Cook for approximately 3 minutes. Sprinkle the rest of your feta and mozzarella cheese over the top and allow to cook for three more minutes with a lid covering your pan. Cheese should be mostly melted, and the eggs should be nearly set.
5. Place under your broiler until the top becomes browned slightly. It should only take a few minutes. Keep a close eye on it. Rotate the pan if necessary, to get an even browning.
6. Sprinkle any additional fresh herbs if you so desire. Cut into pie-shaped wedges.
7. Serve and Enjoy!
Nutrition
Calories: 333 kcal
Protein: 16.77 g
Fat: 26.28 g
Carbohydrates: 7.88 g

605. Mediterranean Scrambled Eggs w/Spinach, Tomato, and Feta

Preparation Time: 2 minutes
Cooking Time: 1 minute
Servings: 2
Ingredients:
- 3 Eggs
- 1/3 cup of Diced Tomatoes
- 1/8 cup of Cubed Feta Cheese
- 1 cup of Baby Spinach
- 1 tbsp. of Vegetable Oil Pepper
- Salt

Directions:
1. Put your oil in a pan on medium heat. Sauté your tomatoes and spinach until the spinach has wilted.
2. Add your eggs and mix to scramble. After approximately 30 seconds, add your feta cheese.
3. Cook until the eggs are done to your desired preference. Season with pepper and salt.
4. Serve and Enjoy!
Nutrition
Calories: 286 kcal
Protein: 15.48 g
Fat: 23.44 g
Carbohydrates: 3.42 g

606. Waffled Falafel

Preparation Time: 5 minutes
Cooking Time: 5 minutes
Servings: 4
Ingredients:
- Two cans of Garbanzo Beans
- 1 Chopped Medium Onion
2 Large Egg Whites
- 1/4 cup of Chopped Fresh Cilantro
- 1/4 cup of Chopped Fresh Parsley
- 1 1/2 tbsp. of All-Purpose Flour
- 3 Cloves of Roasted Garlic
- 2 tsp. of Ground Cumin
- 1 3/4 tsp. of Salt
- 1 tsp. of Ground Coriander
- 1/4 tsp. of Cayenne Pepper
- 1/4 tsp. of Ground Black Pepper
- Pinch of Ground Cardamom Cooking Spray

Directions:
1. Preheat your waffle iron. Spray inside of iron with your cooking spray.
2. Process your garbanzo beans in your food processor until they are coarsely chopped.
3. Add in your egg whites, onion, parsley, cilantro, flour, garlic, cumin, coriander, salt, cayenne pepper, black pepper, and ground cardamom to your garbanzo beans.
4. Pulse in your food processor until your batter resembles a coarse meal. Scrape down the sides while pulsing.
5. Put your batter into a bowl and stir it with your fork.
6. Spoon 1/4 cup of batter onto each piece of your waffle iron. Cook until they are evenly browned. It should take approximately 5 minutes. Repeat the process with batter until it has all been used.
7. Serve and Enjoy!
Nutrition
Calories: 243 kcal
Protein: 16.27 g
Fat: 5.99 g
Carbohydrates: 32.62 g

607. Omelet Provençale

Preparation Time: 5 minutes
Cooking Time: 10 minutes
Servings: 4
Ingredients:
- 2 tsp. for serving extra-virgin olive oil
- Two zucchinis, diced
- Two roasted drained red peppers from a jar, chopped finely
- One clove garlic, chopped finely
- ¼ cup chives, finely chopped
- Eight eggs
- ½ tsp. unrefined sea salt or salt
- ¼ tsp. freshly ground black pepper
- ½ cup goat cheese
- 2 tbsp. fresh basil, chopped finely
- 4 cups mixed field greens, such as baby spinach or arugula
- 1 tsp. lemon juice

Directions:
1. Put 2 tbsp. (30 ml) of oil in a prepared large skillet over medium heat. Add the zucchini, roasted red pepper, garlic, and chives, and then cook gently for about 10 minutes, until softened.
2. Break and put the eggs into a bowl, whisk lightly, and season with salt and pepper. Pour the eggs into the skillet, turn, and swivel to coat. Add knobs of the goat cheese over the top and sprinkle with basil.
3. Serve a slice of the omelet on the side.
Nutrition
Calories: 376 kcal
Protein: 19.37 g
Fat: 20.54 g
Carbohydrates: 30.22 g

608. Avocado Breakfast Sandwiches

Preparation Time: 5 minutes
Cooking Time: 5 minutes
Servings: 4
Ingredients:
- 4 Large Eggs
- 1 Sliced Avocado
- 1/4 cup of Light Mayonnaise 1 tsp. of Dijon Mustard
- 1/4 cup of Nonfat Plain Yogurt
- 1 tsp. of Lime Juice
- Four slices of Whole Grain Bread 1 Knorr Chipotle Mini Cube

Directions:
1. Heat your mayo, mustard, yogurt, lime juice, and Chipotle in a saucepan over low heat.
2. Cook your eggs to your desired preference.
3. Layer your eggs and avocado on toast. Drizzle with your sauce.
4. Serve and Enjoy!
Nutrition
Calories: 253 kcal
Protein: 9.77 g
Fat: 14.13 g
Carbohydrates: 23.68 g

609. Baked Mediterranean Frittata

Preparation Time: 5 minutes
Cooking Time: 30 minutes
Servings: 8
Ingredients:
- 4 Large Eggs

- 1 cup of Egg Whites
- 1 tbsp. of Olive Oil
- 1 Small Chopped Purple Onion
- 1 Large Chopped Red Bell Pepper
- 1 cup of Sliced Mushrooms
- 6 cups of Baby Spinach
- 1/2 tsp. of Baking Powder
- 1/3 cup of Whole Wheat Flour
- 1 tsp. of Dijon Mustard
- 1/2 tsp. of Red Pepper Flakes
- 1 cup of Crumbled Feta Cheese
- 1 cup of Cottage Cheese

Directions:

1. Preheat your oven to 350 degrees.
2. Heat your olive oil in a cast-iron pan. Sauté the garlic and onion. Add your sliced mushrooms, red pepper, and spinach. Cook them until soft. Turn off your heat.
3. In a mixing bowl, mix your egg whites and eggs with a whisk. Stir in your baking powder, flour, mustard, red pepper flakes, feta cheese, and cottage cheese.
4. Put your egg mixture into a cast iron pan. Bake an additional 25 minutes until they are golden brown and the center are set.
5. Remove from your oven and allow standing for 10 to 15 minutes. Cut into slices.
6. Serve and Enjoy!

Nutrition
Calories: 163 kcal
Protein: 11.85 g
Fat: 9.38 g
Carbohydrates: 8.38 g

610. Breakfast Toast

Preparation Time: 10 minutes
Cooking Time: 20 minutes
Servings: 6
Ingredients:
- Two eggs, beaten
- ½ cup of yogurt
- One banana, mashed
- ½ tsp. of ground cinnamon
- Six whole-grain bread slices
- 1 tbsp. of olive oil

Directions:

1. In the mixing bowl, mix up eggs, yogurt, ground cinnamon, add mashed banana.
2. Coat the bread in the egg mixture. Then heat olive oil.
3. Put the coated bread in the hot olive oil and roast for 3 minutes per side or light brown.

Nutrition:
Calories: 153
Protein: 6.2 g
Carbohydrates: 19.2 g
Fat: 5.6 g
Fiber: 2.6 g

611. Savory Egg Galettes

Preparation Time: 15 minutes
Cooking Time: 30 minutes
Servings: 4
Ingredients:
- ¼ cup of white onion, diced
- ¼ cup of bell pepper, chopped
- ½ tsp. of salt
- 1 tsp. of chili flakes
- 2 tbsp. of olive oil
- 1 tsp. of dried dill

- Six eggs, beaten
- 2 tbsp. of plain yogurt

Directions:

1. Mix up onion, bell pepper, salt, and chili flakes in the pan. Add olive oil and dried dill. Sauté the ingredients for 5 minutes.
2. Then pour the beaten eggs into the square baking mold. Add sautéed onion mixture and plain yogurt.
3. Flatten the mixture and bake in the preheated oven to 360 °F for 20 minutes. Cut the meal into galettes. Serve.

Nutrition:
Calories: 166
Protein: 9 g
Carbohydrates: 2.4 g
Fat: 13.5 g
Fiber: 0.3 g

612. Spinach Frittata

Preparation Time: 15 minutes
Cooking Time: 20 minutes
Servings: 6
Ingredients:
- ¼ cup of kalamata olives, pitted and chopped
- Eight eggs, beaten
- 2 cups of spinach, chopped
- 1 tbsp. of olive oil
- ½ tsp. of chili flakes
- 2 ounces feta cheese, crumbled
- ¼ cup of plain yogurt

Directions:

1. Brush the pan with olive oil. After this, mix up all the remaining ingredients in the mixing bowl, and pour them into the pan.
2. Bake the frittata for 20 minutes at 355 °F. Serve.

Nutrition:
Calories: 145
Protein: 9.6 g
Carbohydrates: 2.3 g
Fat: 10.9 g
Fiber: 0.4 g

613. Mushroom Casserole

Preparation Time: 15 minutes
Cooking Time: 60 minutes
Servings: 4
Ingredients:
- Two eggs, beaten
- 1 cup of mushrooms, sliced
- Two shallots, chopped
- 1 tsp. of marjoram, dried
- ½ cup of artichoke hearts, chopped
- 3 ounces cheddar cheese, shredded
- ½ cup of plain yogurt

Directions:

1. Mix up all ingredients in the casserole mold and cover it with aluminum foil.
2. Bake the casserole for 60 minutes at 355 °F.

Nutrition:
Calories: 156
Protein: 11.2 g
Carbohydrates: 6.2 g
Fat: 9.7 g
Fiber: 1.3 g

614. Baked Eggs with Parsley

Preparation Time: 15 minutes
Cooking Time: 20 minutes
Servings: 6
Ingredients:
- Two green bell peppers, chopped
- 3 tbsp. of olive oil
- One yellow onion, chopped
- 1 tsp. of sweet paprika
- Six tomatoes, chopped
- Six eggs
- ¼ cup of parsley, chopped

Directions:
1. Warm a pan with the oil over medium heat, add all ingredients except eggs and roast them for 5 minutes.
2. Stir the vegetables well and crack the eggs.
3. Transfer the pan with eggs in the preheated oven to 360 °F and bake them for 15 minutes.

Nutrition:
Calories: 167
Protein: 3 g
Carbohydrates: 10.2 g
Fat: 11.8 g
Fiber: 2.6 g

615. Artichoke Omelet

Preparation Time: 5 minutes
Cooking Time: 10 minutes
Servings: 4
Ingredients:
- Four eggs, beaten
- One tomato, chopped
- ½ cup of artichoke hearts, chopped
- 4 ounces goat cheese, crumbled
- 1 tbsp. of olive oil

Directions:
1. Mix up eggs, chopped artichokes, goat cheese, and tomato. Then brush the baking mold with olive oil and pour the mixture inside.
2. Bake the omelet for 10 minutes at 365 °F. Serve.

Nutrition:
Calories: 231
Protein: 14.9 g
Carbohydrates: 3.2 g
Fat: 18 g
Fiber: 1.1 g

616. Bell Pepper Frittata

Preparation Time: 10 minutes
Cooking Time: 15 minutes
Servings: 4
Ingredients:
- 1 cup of red bell pepper, chopped
- 1 tbsp. of olive oil, melted
- One tomato, sliced
- Four eggs, beaten
- ¼ tsp. of ground black pepper
- ¼ tsp. of salt

Directions:
1. Brush the baking pan with melted olive oil. Then add all remaining ingredients, mix gently and transfer in the preheated oven to 365 °F. Cook the frittata for 15 minutes.

Nutrition:
Calories: 105
Protein: 6 g
Carbohydrates: 3.3 g

Fat: 7.9 g
Fiber: 0.6 g

617. Fish Eggs

Preparation Time: 5 minutes
Cooking Time: 20 minutes
Servings: 4
Ingredients:
- 1 cup of sweet potato, chopped, cooked
- 1 tbsp. of avocado oil
- 10 ounces salmon fillet, chopped
- ¼ cup of cauliflower, chopped
- Four eggs, beaten

Directions:
1. Mash or crush the sweet potato, then mix it with chopped salmon and cauliflower. Then heat avocado oil in the pan.
2. Add mashed sweet potato mixture and cook it for 10 minutes. Stir to from time to time.
3. After this, add eggs, whisk the mixture gently. Close the lid and cook it for 10 minutes more.

Nutrition:
Calories: 208
Protein: 20.5 g
Carbohydrates: 11.2 g
Fat: 9.3 g
Fiber: 2 g

618. Arugula Frittata

Preparation Time: 15 minutes
Cooking Time: 25 minutes
Servings: 12
Ingredients:
- Three garlic cloves, minced
- 1 tbsp. of olive oil
- 1 cup of fresh arugula, chopped
- Eight eggs, beaten
- 1 tsp. of ground black pepper
- 1 cup of mozzarella cheese, shredded

Directions:
1. Warm the olive oil in the pan. Mix up eggs with ground black pepper, arugula, and garlic cloves.
2. Add arugula and pour the mixture into the hot pan. Top the egg mixture with mozzarella and transfer to the preheated 360 °F oven. Bake the frittata for 20 minutes. Serve.

Nutrition:
Calories: 61
Protein: 4.5 g
Carbohydrates: 0.7 g
Fat: 4.5 g
Fiber: 0.1 g

619. Mediterranean Diet Breakfast Tostadas

Preparation Time: 5 minutes
Cooking Time: 10 minutes
Servings: 4
Ingredients:
- Four corn tostadas
- ½ cup of roasted hummus, red pepper
- ½ cup of red pepper, diced
- ½ cup of green onions, chopped
- Eight large eggs, beaten
- ½ cup of milk, skim
- ½ tsp. of oregano
- ½ tsp. of garlic powder

- ¼ cup of feta cheese, crumbled
- ½ cup of cucumbers seeded, chopped
- ½ cup of ripe tomatoes, diced

Directions:

1. In a large-sized, non-stick skillet on medium heat, add red peppers. Cook for 2 to 3 minutes till they soften. Add milk, eggs, oregano, green onions, and garlic powder to the skillet while continually stirring until egg whites are no longer translucent anymore, e minutes or so.

2. Top tostadas with hummus, then egg mixture, tomatoes, feta cheese, and cucumbers. Serve promptly.

Nutrition:

Calories: 824

Fiber: 12 g

Fat: 48 g

Carbohydrates: 49 g

620. Mediterranean Egg Scramble

Preparation Time: 10 minutes

Cooking Time: 20 minutes

Servings: 2

Ingredients:

- 1 tbsp. of olive oil
- One yellow pepper, diced
- Two green onions, sliced
- Eight cherry tomatoes, quartered
- 2 tbsp. of black olives
- Four large eggs
- 1 tbsp. of capers
- ¼ tsp. of oregano, dried
- Ground pepper
- Fresh parsley, optional, for serving

Directions:

1. Heat oil in a frying pan. Add chopped onions and diced peppers. Cook for several minutes on medium heat till a bit soft. Add capers, tomatoes, and olives. Cook for 1 minute more.

2. Crack eggs into the pan. Scramble promptly with a spatula or spoon. Add ground pepper and oregano. Continue to stir till eggs have cooked fully. Top with parsley, as desired. Serve while warm.

Nutrition:

Calories: 247

Protein: 13.6 g

Fat: 16.5 g

Carbohydrates: 12.8 g

621. Greens & Eggs Mediterranean Breakfast

Preparation Time: 10 minutes

Cooking Time: 15 minutes

Servings: 2

Ingredients:

- 1 tbsp. of olive oil
- 2 cups of rainbow chard, stemmed, chopped
- 1 cup of spinach, fresh
- ½ cup of arugula
- Four large eggs, beaten
- Two garlic cloves, minced
- ½ cup of cheddar cheese, shredded
- Kosher salt, as desired
- Ground pepper, as desired

Directions:

1. Heat the oil in a saucepan placed on a medium-high heat. Sauté the arugula, chard, and spinach till tender, three

minutes or so. Add the garlic. Stir while cooking till fragrant, 2 to 3 minutes.

2. Mix cheese and eggs in a medium bowl. Add to spinach mixture.

3. Cover. Cook till mixture sets, 5 to 7 minutes. Season as desired and serve.

Nutrition:

Calories: 330

Protein: 22 g

Fat: 26.7 g

Carbohydrates: 4.4 g

622. Eggs with Zucchini Noodles

Preparation Time: 10 Minutes

Cooking Time: 11 Minutes

Servings: 2

Ingredients:

- Two tbsp. extra-virgin olive oil
- Three zucchinis, cut with a spiralizer
- Four eggs
- Salt and black pepper to the taste
- A pinch of red pepper flakes
- Cooking spray
- One tbsp. basil, chopped

Directions:

1. In a bowl, combine the zucchini noodles with salt, pepper, and olive oil and toss well.

2. Grease a baking sheet using cooking spray and divide the zucchini noodles into four nests on it.

3. Crash an egg on top of each nest, sprinkle salt, pepper, and pepper flakes on topmost, then bake at 350 degrees F for 11 minutes.

4. Divide the mix between plates, sprinkle the basil on top, and serve.

Nutrition:

Calories 296

Fat 23.6g

Fiber 3.3g

Carbs 10.6g

Protein 14.7 g

623. Veggie Bowls

Preparation Time: 10 Minutes

Cooking Time: 5 Minutes

Servings: 4

Ingredients:

- One tbsp. olive oil
- 1-pound asparagus, trimmed and roughly chopped
- 3 cups kale, shredded
- 3 cups Brussels sprouts, shredded
- ½ cup hummus
- One avocado, peeled, pitted, and sliced
- Four eggs, soft boiled, peeled and sliced

For the dressing:

- Two tbsp. lemon juice
- One garlic clove, minced
- Two tsp. Dijon mustard
- Two tbsp. olive oil
- Salt and black pepper to the taste

Directions:

1. Heat a pan put two tablespoon of oil over medium-high heat, then add the asparagus and sauté for 5 minutes, stirring often.

2. In a bowl, combine the other two tbsp. oil with the lemon juice, garlic, mustard, salt, and pepper and whisk well.

3. In a salad bowl, combine the asparagus with the kale, sprouts, hummus, avocado, and eggs and toss gently.

4. Add the dressing, toss, and serve for breakfast.
Nutrition:
Calories 323
Fat 21g
Fiber 10.9g
Carbs 24.8g

624. Breakfast Egg on Avocado

Preparation time: 10 minutes
Cooking Time: 15 minutes
Servings: 6
INGREDIENTS
- 1 tsp garlic powder
- 1/2 tsp sea salt
- 1/4 cup Parmesan cheese (grated or shredded)
- 1/4 tsp black pepper
- 3 medium avocados (cut in half, pitted, skin on)
- 6 medium eggs

DIRECTIONS
1. Prepare muffin tins and preheat the oven to 350oF.
2. To ensure that the egg would fit inside the cavity of the avocado, lightly scrape off 1/3 of the meat.
3. Place avocado on muffin tin to ensure that it faces with the top up.
4. Evenly season each avocado with pepper, salt, and garlic powder.
5. Add one egg on each avocado cavity and garnish tops with cheese.
6. Pop in the oven and bake until the egg white is set, about 15 minutes.
7. Serve and enjoy.

NUTRITION: Calories: 252; Protein: 14.0g; Carbs: 4.0g; Fat: 20.0g

625. Breakfast Egg-Artichoke Casserole

Preparation time: 30 minutes
Cooking Time: 35 minutes
Servings: 8
INGREDIENTS
- 16 large eggs
- 14 ounce can artichoke hearts, drained
- 10-ounce box frozen chopped spinach, thawed and drained well
  - cup shredded white cheddar
- 1 garlic clove, minced
- 1 teaspoon salt
- 1/2 cup parmesan cheese
- 1/2 cup ricotta cheese
- 1/2 teaspoon dried thyme
- 1/2 teaspoon crushed red pepper
- 1/4 cup milk
- 1/4 cup shaved onion

DIRECTIONS
1. Lightly grease a 9x13-inch baking dish with cooking spray and preheat the oven to 350oF.
2. In a large mixing bowl, add eggs and milk. Mix thoroughly.
3. With a paper towel, squeeze out the excess moisture from the spinach leaves and add to the bowl of eggs.
4. Into small pieces, break the artichoke hearts and separate the leaves. Add to the bowl of eggs.

5. Except for the ricotta cheese, add remaining ingredients in the bowl of eggs and mix thoroughly.
6. Pour egg mixture into the prepared dish.
7. Evenly add dollops of ricotta cheese on top of the eggs and then pop in the oven.
8. Bake until eggs are set and doesn't jiggle when shook, about 35 minutes.
9. Remove from the oven and evenly divide into suggested servings. Enjoy.

NUTRITION: Calories: 302; Protein: 22.6g; Carbs: 10.8g; Fat: 18.7g

626. Brekky Egg-Potato Hash

Preparation time: 15 minutes
Cooking Time: 25 minutes
Servings: 2,
INGREDIENTS
- 1 zucchini, diced
- 1/2 cup chicken broth
- ½ pound cooked chicken
- 1 tablespoon olive oil
- 4 ounces shrimp
- salt and ground black pepper to taste
- 1 large sweet potato, diced
- 2 eggs
- 1/4 teaspoon cayenne pepper
- 1 teaspoons garlic powder
- 1 cup fresh spinach (optional)

DIRECTIONS
1. In a skillet, add the olive oil.
2. Fry the shrimp, cooked chicken and sweet potato for 2 minutes.
3. Add the cayenne pepper, garlic powder and salt and toss for 4 minutes.
4. Add the zucchini and toss for another 3 minutes.
5. Whisk the eggs in a bowl and add to the skillet.
6. Season using salt and pepper. Cover with the lid.
7. Cook for 1 minute and add the chicken broth.
8. Cover and cook for another 8 minutes on high heat.
9. Add the spinach and toss for 2 more minutes.
10. Serve immediately.

NUTRITION: Calories: 190; Protein: 11.7g; Carbs: 2.9g; Fat: 12.3g

627. Cooked Beef Mushroom Egg

Preparation time: 10 minutes
Cooking Time: 15 minutes
Servings: 2
INGREDIENTS
- ¼ cup cooked beef, diced
- 6 eggs
- 4 mushrooms, diced
- Salt and pepper to taste
- 12 ounces spinach
- 2 onions, chopped
- A dash of onion powder
- ¼ green bell pepper, chopped
- A dash of garlic powder

DIRECTIONS
1. In a skillet, toss the beef for 3 minutes or until crispy.
2. Take off the heat and add to a plate.

3. Add the onion, bell pepper, and mushroom in the skillet.
4. Add the rest of the ingredients.
5. Toss for about 4 minutes.
6. Return the beef to the skillet and toss for another minute.
7. Serve hot.

NUTRITION: Calories: 213; Protein: 14.5g; Carbs: 3.4g; Fat: 15.7g

628. Curried Veggies and Poached Eggs

Preparation time: 10 minutes
Cooking Time: 45 minutes
Servings: 4
INGREDIENTS
- 4 large eggs
- ½ tsp white vinegar
- 1/8 tsp crushed red pepper – optional
- 1 cup water
- 1 14-oz can chickpeas, drained
- 2 medium zucchinis, diced
- ½ lb sliced button mushrooms
- 1 tbsp yellow curry powder
- 2 cloves garlic, minced
- 1 large onion, chopped
- 2 tsps. extra virgin olive oil

DIRECTIONS
1. On medium high fire, place a large saucepan and heat oil.
2. Sauté onions until tender around four to five minutes.
3. Add garlic and continue sautéing for another half minute.
4. Add curry powder, stir and cook until fragrant around one to two minutes.
5. Add mushrooms, mix, cover and cook for 5 to 8 minutes or until mushrooms are tender and have released their liquid.
6. Add red pepper if using, water, chickpeas and zucchini. Mix well to combine and bring to a boil.
7. Once boiling, reduce fire to a simmer, cover and cook until zucchini is tender around 15 to 20 minutes of simmering.
8. Meanwhile, in a small pot filled with 3-inches deep of water, bring to a boil on high fire.
9. Once boiling, reduce fire to a simmer and add vinegar.
10. Slowly add one egg, slipping it gently into the water. Allow to simmer until egg is cooked, around 3 to 5 minutes.
11. Remove egg with a slotted spoon and transfer to a plate, one plate one egg.
12. Repeat the process with remaining eggs.
13. Once the veggies are done cooking, divide evenly into 4 servings and place one serving per plate of egg.
14. Serve and enjoy.

NUTRITION: Calories: 215; Protein: 13.8g; Carbs: 20.6g; Fat: 9.4g

629. Dill and Tomato Frittata

Preparation time: 10 minutes
Cooking Time: 35 minutes
Servings: 6
INGREDIENTS
- pepper and salt to taste
- 1 tsp red pepper flakes
- 2 garlic cloves, minced
- ½ cup crumbled goat cheese – optional
- 2 tbsp fresh chives, chopped
- 2 tbsp fresh dill, chopped
- 4 tomatoes, diced
- 8 eggs, whisked
- 1 tsp coconut oil

DIRECTIONS
1. Grease a 9-inch round baking pan and preheat oven to 325F.
2. In a large bowl, mix well all ingredients and pour into prepped pan.
3. Pop into the oven and bake until middle is cooked through around 30-35 minutes.
4. Remove from oven and garnish with more chives and dill.

NUTRITION: Calories: 208 ; Protein: 13.43g ; Fat: 14.13g

630. Dill, Havarti & Asparagus Frittata

Preparation time: 20 minutes
Cooking Time: 20 minutes
Servings: 4,
INGREDIENTS
- 1 tsp dried dill weed or 2 tsp minced fresh dill
- 4-oz Havarti cheese cut into small cubes
- 6 eggs, beaten well
- Pepper and salt to taste
- 1 stalk green onions sliced for garnish
- 3 tsp. olive oil
- 2/3 cup diced cherry tomatoes
- 6-8 oz fresh asparagus, ends trimmed and cut into 1 ½-inch lengths

DIRECTIONS
1. On medium-high the fire, place a large cast-iron pan and add oil. Once oil is hot, stir-fry asparagus for 4 minutes.
2. Add dill weed and tomatoes. Cook for two minutes.
3. Meanwhile, season eggs with pepper and salt. Beat well.
4. Pour eggs over the tomatoes.
5. Evenly spread cheese on top.
6. Preheat broiler.
7. Lower the fire to low, cover pan, and let it cook for 10 minutes until the cheese on top has melted.
8. Turn off the fire and transfer pan in the oven and broil for 2 minutes or until tops are browned.
9. Remove from the oven, sprinkle sliced green onions, serve, and enjoy.

NUTRITION: Calories: 244; Protein: 16.0g; Carbs: 3.7g; Fat: 18.3g

631. Egg and Ham Breakfast Cup

Preparation time: 10 minutes
Cooking Time: 12 minutes
Servings: 12
INGREDIENTS
- 2 green onion bunch, chopped
- 12 eggs
- 6 thick pieces nitrate free ham

DIRECTIONS
1. Grease a 12-muffin tin and preheat oven to 4000F.
2. Add 2 hams per muffin compartment, press down to form a cup and add egg in middle. Repeat process to remaining muffin compartments.
3. Pop in the oven and bake until eggs are cooked to desired doneness, around 10 to 12 minutes.

4. To serve, garnish with chopped green onions.

NUTRITION: Calories: 92; Protein: 7.3g; Carbs: 0.8g; Fat: 6.4g

632. Egg Muffin Sandwich

Preparation time: 5 minutes
Cooking Time: 10 minutes
Servings: 2,
Muffin INGREDIENTS

- 1 large egg, free-range or organic
- 1/4 cup almond flour (25 g / 0.9 oz)
- 1/4 cup flax meal (38 g / 1.3 oz)
- 1/4 cup grated cheddar cheese (28 g / 1 oz)
- 1/4 tsp baking soda
- 2 tbsp heavy whipping cream or coconut milk
- 2 tbsp water
- pinch salt

Filing INGREDIENTS

- 1 tbsp butter or 2 tbsp cream cheese for spreading
- 1 tbsp ghee
- 1 tsp Dijon mustard
- 2 large eggs, free-range or organic
- 2 slices cheddar cheese or other hard type cheese (56 g / 2 oz)
- Optional: 1 cup greens (lettuce, kale, chard, spinach, watercress, etc.)
- salt and pepper to taste

DIRECTIONS
1. Make the Muffin: In a small mixing bowl, mix well almond flour, flax meal, baking soda, and salt. Stir in water, cream, and eggs. Mix thoroughly.
2. Fold in cheese and evenly divide in two single-serve ramekins.
3. Pop in the microwave and cook for 75 seconds.
4. Make the filing: on medium the fire, place a small nonstick pan, heat ghee and cook the eggs to the desired doneness. Season with pepper and salt.
5. To make the muffin sandwiches, slice the muffins in half. Spread cream cheese on one side and mustard on the other side.
6. Add egg and greens. Top with the other half of sliced muffin.
7. Serve and enjoy.

NUTRITION: Calories: 639; Protein: 26.5g; Carbs: 10.4g; Fat: 54.6g

633. Eggs Benedict and Artichoke Hearts

Preparation time: 15 minutes
Cooking Time: 30 minutes
Servings: 2,
INGREDIENTS

- Salt and pepper to taste
- ¾ cup balsamic vinegar
- 4 artichoke hearts
- ¼ cup bacon, cooked
- 1 egg white
- 8 eggs
- 1 tablespoon lemon juice
- ¾ cup melted ghee or butter

DIRECTIONS
1. Line a baking sheet with parchment paper or foil.
2. Preheat the oven to 3750F.
3. Deconstruct the artichokes and remove the hearts. Place the hearts in balsamic vinegar for 20 minutes. Set aside.

4. Prepare the hollandaise sauce by using four eggs and separate the yolk from the white. Reserve the egg white for the artichoke hearts. Add the yolks and lemon juice and cook in a double boiler while stirring constantly to create a silky texture of the sauce. Add the oil and season with salt and pepper. Set aside.
5. Remove the artichoke hearts from the balsamic vinegar marinade and place on the cookie sheet. Brush the artichokes with the egg white and cook in the oven for 20 minutes.
6. Poach the remaining four eggs. Turn up the heat and let the water boil. Crack the eggs one at a time and cook for a minute before removing the egg.
7. Assemble by layering the artichokes, bacon and poached eggs.
8. Pour over the hollandaise sauce.
9. Serve with toasted bread.

NUTRITION: Calories: 640; Protein: 28.3g; Carbs: 36.0g; Fat: 42.5g

634. Eggs over Kale Hash

Preparation time: 10 minutes
Cooking Time: 20 minutes
Servings: 4,
INGREDIENTS

- 4 large eggs
- 1 bunch chopped kale
- Dash of ground nutmeg
- 2 sweet potatoes, cubed
- 1 14.5-ounce can of chicken broth

DIRECTIONS
1. In a large non-stick skillet, bring the chicken broth to a simmer. Add the sweet potatoes and season slightly with salt and pepper. Add a dash of nutmeg to improve the flavor.
2. Cook until the sweet potatoes become soft, around 10 minutes. Add kale and season with salt and pepper. Continue cooking for four minutes or until kale has wilted. Set aside.
3. Using the same skillet, heat 1 tablespoon of olive oil over medium high heat.
4. Cook the eggs sunny side up until the whites become opaque and the yolks have set. Top the kale hash with the eggs. Serve immediately.

NUTRITION: Calories: 158; Protein: 9.8g; Carbs 18.5g; Fat: 5.6g

635. Eggs with Dill, Pepper, and Salmon

Preparation time: 15 minutes
Cooking Time: 15 minutes
Servings: 6,
INGREDIENTS

- pepper and salt to taste
- 1 tsp red pepper flakes
- 2 garlic cloves, minced
- ½ cup crumbled goat cheese
- 2 tbsp fresh chives, chopped
- 2 tbsp fresh dill, chopped
- 4 tomatoes, diced
- 8 eggs, whisked
- 1 tsp coconut oil

DIRECTIONS
1. In a big bowl whisk the eggs. Mix in pepper, salt, red pepper flakes, garlic, dill and salmon.

2. On low fire, place a nonstick fry pan and lightly grease with oil.
3. Pour egg mixture and whisk around until cooked through to make scrambled eggs.
4. Serve and enjoy topped with goat cheese.

NUTRITION: Calories: 141; Protein: 10.3g; Carbs: 6.7g; Fat: 8.5g

636. Fig and Walnut Skillet Frittata

Preparation time: 30 minutes
Cooking Time: 15 minutes
Servings: 4
INGREDIENTS
- 1 cup figs, halved
- 4 eggs, beaten
- 1 teaspoon cinnamon
- A pinch of salt
- 2 tablespoons almond flour
- 2 tablespoons coconut flour
- 1 cup walnut, chopped
- 2 tablespoons coconut oil
- 1 teaspoon cardamom
- 6 tablespoons raw honey

DIRECTIONS
1. In a mixing bowl, beat the eggs.
2. Add the coconut flour, almond flour, cardamom, honey, salt and cinnamon.
3. Mix well. Heat the coconut oil in a skillet over medium heat.
4. Add the egg mixture gently.
5. Add the walnuts and figs on top.
6. Cover and cook on medium low heat for about 10 minutes.
7. Serve hot with more honey on top.

NUTRITION: Calories: 221; Protein: 12.7g; Carbs: 5.9g; Fat: 16.3g

637. Frittata with Dill and Tomatoes

Preparation time: 20 minutes
Cooking Time: 35 minutes
Servings: 4,
INGREDIENTS
- pepper and salt to taste
- 1 tsp red pepper flakes
- 2 garlic cloves, minced
- ½ cup crumbled goat cheese – optional
- 2 tbsp fresh chives, chopped
- 2 tbsp fresh dill, chopped
- 4 tomatoes, diced
- 8 eggs, whisked
- 1 tsp coconut oil

DIRECTIONS
1. Grease a 9-inch round baking pan and preheat oven to 3250F.
2. In a large bowl, mix well all ingredients and pour into prepped pan.
3. Pop into the oven and bake until middle is cooked through around 30-35 minutes.
4. Remove from oven and garnish with more chives and dill.

NUTRITION: Calories: 309; Protein: 19.8g; Carbs: 8.0g; Fat: 22.0g

638. Italian Scrambled Eggs

Preparation time: 15 minutes

Cooking Time: 7 minutes
Servings: 1
INGREDIENTS
- 1 teaspoon balsamic vinegar
- 2 large eggs
- ¼ teaspoon rosemary, minced
- ½ cup cherry tomatoes
- 1 ½ cup kale, chopped
- ½ teaspoon olive oil

DIRECTIONS
1. Melt the olive oil in a skillet over medium high heat.
2. Sauté the kale and add rosemary and salt to taste. Add three tablespoons of water to prevent the kale from burning at the bottom of the pan. Cook for three to four minutes.
3. Add the tomatoes and stir.
4. Push the vegetables on one side of the skillet and add the eggs. Season with salt and pepper to taste.
5. Scramble the eggs then fold in the tomatoes and kales.

NUTRITION: Calories: 230; Protein: 16.4g; Carbs: 15.0g; Fat: 12.4g

639. Kale and Red Pepper Frittata

Preparation time: 15 minutes
Cooking Time: 23 minutes
Servings: 4
INGREDIENTS
- Salt and pepper to taste
- ½ cup almond milk
- 8 large eggs
- 2 cups kale, rinsed and chopped
- 3 slices of crispy bacon, chopped
- 1/3 cup onion, chopped
- ½ cup red pepper, chopped
- 1 tablespoon coconut oil

DIRECTIONS
1. Preheat the oven to 3500F.
2. In a medium bowl, combine the eggs and almond milk. Season with salt and pepper. Set aside.
3. In a skillet, heat the coconut oil over medium flame and sauté the onions and red pepper for three minutes or until the onion is translucent. Add in the kale and cook for 5 minutes more.
4. Add the eggs into the mixture along with the bacon and cook for four minutes or until the edges start to set.
5. Continue cooking the frittata in the oven for 15 minutes.

NUTRITION: Calories: 242; Protein: 16.5g; Carbs: 7.0g; Fat: 16.45g

640. Lettuce Stuffed with Eggs 'n Crab Meat

Preparation time: 20 minutes
Cooking Time: 10 minutes
Servings: 8
INGREDIENTS
- 24 butter lettuce leaves
- 1 tsp dry mustard
- ¼ cup finely chopped celery
- 1 cup lump crabmeat, around 5 ounces
- 3 tbsp plain Greek yogurt
- 2 tbsp extra virgin olive oil

- ¼ tsp ground pepper
- 8 large eggs
- ½ tsp salt, divided
- 1 tbsp fresh lemon juice, divided
- 2 cups thinly sliced radishes

DIRECTIONS

1. In a medium bowl, mix ¼ tsp salt, 2 tsps. juice and radishes. Cover and chill for half an hour.
2. On medium saucepan, place eggs and cover with water over an inch above the eggs. Bring the pan of water to a boil. Once boiling, reduce fire to a simmer and cook for ten minutes.
3. Turn off fire, discard hot water and place eggs in an ice water bath to cool completely.
4. Peel eggshells and slice eggs in half lengthwise and remove the yolks.
5. With a sieve on top of a bowl, place yolks and press through a sieve. Set aside a tablespoon of yolk.
6. On remaining bowl of yolks add pepper, ¼ tsp salt and 1 tsp juice. Mix well and as you are stirring, slowly add oil until well incorporated. Add yogurt, stir well to mix.
7. Add mustard, celery and crabmeat. Gently mix to combine. If needed, taste and adjust seasoning of the filling.
8. On a serving platter, arrange 3 lettuce in a fan for two egg slices. To make the egg whites sit flat, you can slice a bit of the bottom to make it flat. Evenly divide crab filling into egg white holes.
9. Then evenly divide into eight servings the radish salad and add on the side of the eggs, on top of the lettuce leaves. Serve and enjoy.

NUTRITION: Calories: 121; Protein: 10.0g; Carbs: 1.6g; Fat: 8.3g

641. Mixed Greens and Ricotta Frittata

Preparation time: 10 minutes
Cooking Time: 35 minutes
Servings: 8
INGREDIENTS

- 1 tbsp pine nuts
- 1 clove garlic, chopped
- ¼ cup fresh mint leaves
- ¾ cup fresh parsley leaves
- 1 cup fresh basil leaves
- 8-oz part-skim ricotta
- 1 tbsp red-wine vinegar
- ½ + 1/8 tsp freshly ground black pepper, divided
- ½ tsp salt, divided
- 10 large eggs
- 1 lb chopped mixed greens
- Pinch of red pepper flakes
- 1 medium red onion, finely diced
- 1/3 cup + 2 tbsp olive oil, divided

DIRECTIONS

1. Preheat oven to 350°F.
2. On medium high fire, place a nonstick skillet and heat 1 tbsp oil. Sauté onions until soft and translucent, around 4 minutes. Add half of greens and pepper flakes and sauté until tender and crisp, around 5 minutes. Remove cooked greens and place in colander. Add remaining uncooked greens in skillet and sauté until tender and crisp, when done add to colander. Allow cooked veggies to cool enough to handle, then squeeze dry and place in a bowl.

3. Whisk well ¼ tsp pepper, ¼ tsp salt, Parmesan and eggs in a large bowl.
4. In bowl of cooked vegetables, add 1/8 tsp pepper, ricotta and vinegar. Mix thoroughly. Then pour into bowl of eggs and mix well.
5. On medium fire, place same skillet used earlier and heat 1 tbsp oil. Pour egg mixture and cook for 8 minutes or until sides are set. Turn off fire, place skillet inside oven and bake for 15 minutes or until middle of frittata is set.
6. Meanwhile, make the pesto by processing pine nuts, garlic, mint, parsley and basil in a food processor until coarsely chopped. Add 1/3 cup oil and continue processing. Season with remaining pepper and salt. Process once again until thoroughly mixed.
7. To serve, slice the frittata in 8 equal wedges and serve with a dollop of pesto.

NUTRITION: Calories: 280; Protein: 14g; Carbs: 8g; Fat: 21.3g

642. Mushroom Tomato Frittata

Preparation time: 10 minutes
Cooking Time: 8 minutes
Servings: 8
INGREDIENTS

- ¼ cup mushroom, sliced
- 10 eggs
- 1 cup cherry tomatoes
- Salt
- Pepper
- 1 teaspoon olive oil

DIRECTIONS

1. Whisk the eggs in a bowl.
2. Add the eggs in a skillet.
3. Add the mushroom, cherry tomatoes and season using salt and pepper.
4. Cover with lid and cook for about 5 to 8 minutes on low heat.

NUTRITION: Calories: 190; Protein: 11.7g; Carbs: 2.9g; Fat: 12.3g

643. Leeks and Eggs Muffins

Preparation time: 10 minutes
Cooking time: 20 minutes
Servings: 2
Ingredients:

- 3 eggs, whisked
- ¼ cup baby spinach
- 2 tablespoons leeks, chopped
- 4 tablespoons parmesan, grated
- 2 tablespoons almond milk
- Cooking spray
- 1 small red bell pepper, chopped
- Salt and black pepper to the taste
- 1 tomato, cubed
- 2 tablespoons cheddar cheese, grated

Directions:

1. In a bowl, combine the eggs with the milk, salt, pepper and the rest of the ingredients except the cooking spray and whisk well.
2. Grease a muffin tin with the cooking spray and divide the eggs mixture in each muffin mould.
3. Bake at 380 degrees F for 20 minutes and serve them for breakfast.

Nutrition: calories 308, fat 19.4, fiber 1.7, carbs 8.7, protein 24.4

Chapter 9. Fish and Seafood Recipes

644. Speedy Tilapia with Red Onion and Avocado

Preparation Time: 10 minutes
Cooking Time: 5 minutes
Servings: 4
Ingredients:
- 1 tablespoon extra-virgin olive oil
- 1 tablespoon freshly squeezed orange juice
- ¼ teaspoon kosher or sea salt
- 4 (4-ounce) tilapia fillets, more oblong than square, skin-on or skinned
- ¼ cup chopped red onion
- 1 avocado

Directions:
1. In a 9-inch glass pie dish, combine together the oil, orange juice, and salt. Work on the fillet simultaneously, situate each in the pie dish and coat on all sides. Form the fillets in a wagon-wheel formation. Place each fillet with 1 tablespoon of onion, then fold the end of the fillet that's hanging over the edge in half over the onion. Once done, you should have 4 folded-over fillets with the fold against the outer edge of the dish and the ends all in the center.
2. Wrap the dish with plastic, leave small part open at the edge to vent the steam. Cook on high for about 3 minutes in microwave. When done it should separate into flakes (chunks) when pressed gently with a fork. Garnish the fillets with the avocado and serve.

Nutrition
200 Calories
3g Fat
4g Carbohydrates
22g Protein
811mg Sodium

645. Grilled Fish on Lemons

Preparation Time: 10 minutes
Cooking Time: 10 minutes
Servings: 4
Ingredients:
- 4 (4-ounce) fish fillets
- Nonstick cooking spray
- 3 to 4 medium lemons
- 1 tablespoon extra-virgin olive oil
- ¼ teaspoon freshly ground black pepper
- ¼ teaspoon kosher or sea salt

Directions:
1. Using paper towels, pat the fillets dry and let stand at room temperature for 10 minutes. Meanwhile, coat the cold cooking grate of the grill with nonstick cooking spray, and preheat the grill to 400°F, or medium-high heat.
2. Slice one lemon in half and set half aside. Slice the remaining half of that lemon and the remaining lemons into ¼-inch-thick slices. (You should have about 12 to 16 lemon slices.) Into a small bowl, squeeze 1 tablespoon of juice out of the reserved lemon half.
3. Add the oil to the bowl with the lemon juice, and mix well. Put both sides of the fish with the oil mixture, and sprinkle evenly with pepper and salt.
4. Carefully place the lemon slices on the grill (or the grill pan), arranging 3 to 4 slices together in the shape of a fish fillet, and repeat with the remaining slices. Place the fish fillets directly on top of the lemon slices, and grill with the

lid closed. (If you're grilling on the stove top, cover with a large pot lid or aluminum foil.) Flip the fish halfway through the cooking time only if the fillets are more than half an inch thick. It is cooked when it just starts to separate into flakes when pressed mildly with a fork.

Nutrition
147 Calories
5g Fat
1g Carbohydrates
22g Protein
917mg Sodium

646. Weeknight Sheet Pan Fish Dinner

Preparation Time: 10 minutes
Cooking Time: 10 minutes
Servings: 4
Ingredients:
- Nonstick cooking spray
- 2 tablespoons extra-virgin olive oil
- 1 tablespoon balsamic vinegar
- 4 (4-ounce) fish fillets (½ inch thick)
- 2½ cups green beans
- 1-pint cherry or grape tomatoes

Directions:
1. Preheat the oven to 400°F. Brush two large, rimmed baking sheets with nonstick cooking spray. In a small bowl, combine together the oil and vinegar. Set aside. Place two pieces of fish on each baking sheet.
2. In a large bowl, combine the beans and tomatoes. Pour in the oil and vinegar, and toss gently to coat. Pour half of the green bean mixture over the fish on one baking sheet, and the remaining half over the fish on the other. Turn the fish over, and rub it in the oil mixture to coat. Lay the vegetables evenly on the baking sheets so hot air can circulate around them.
3. Bake until the fish is just opaque. It is cooked when it just begins to separate into chunks when pricked gently with a fork.

Nutrition
193 Calories
8g Fat
3g Carbohydrates
23g Protein
811mg Sodium

647. Crispy Polenta Fish Sticks

Preparation Time: 15 minutes
Cooking Time: 10 minutes
Servings: 4
Ingredients:
- 2 large eggs, lightly beaten
- 1 tablespoon 2% milk
- 1-pound skinned fish fillets sliced into 20 (1-inch-wide) strips
- ½ cup yellow cornmeal
- ½ cup whole-wheat panko bread crumbs
- ¼ teaspoon smoked paprika
- ¼ teaspoon kosher or sea salt
- ¼ teaspoon freshly ground black pepper
- Nonstick cooking spray

Directions:
1. Situate a large, rimmed baking sheet in the oven. Preheat the oven to 400°F with the pan inside. In a large bowl,

combine the eggs and milk. Using a fork, add the fish strips to the egg mixture and stir gently to coat.

2. Put the cornmeal, bread crumbs, smoked paprika, salt, and pepper in a quart-size zip-top plastic bag. Using a fork or tongs, transfer the fish to the bag, letting the excess egg wash drip off into the bowl before transferring. Seal tight and shake gently to coat each fish stick completely.

3. With oven mitts, carefully remove the hot baking sheet from the oven and spray it with nonstick cooking spray. Using a fork or tongs, remove the fish sticks from the bag and arrange them on the hot baking sheet, with space between them so the hot air can circulate and crisp them up. Bake for 5 to 8 minutes, until gentle pressure with a fork causes the fish to flake, and serve.

Nutrition

256 Calories

6g Fat

2g Carbohydrates

29g Protein

667mg Sodium

648. Salmon Skillet Supper

Preparation Time: 15 minutes

Cooking Time: 15 minutes

Servings: 4

Ingredients:
- 1 tablespoon extra-virgin olive oil
- 2 garlic cloves minced
- 1 teaspoon smoked paprika
- 1-pint grape or cherry tomatoes, quartered
- 1 (12-ounce) jar roasted red peppers
- 1 tablespoon water
- ¼ teaspoon freshly ground black pepper
- ¼ teaspoon kosher or sea salt
- 1-pound salmon fillets, skin removed, cut into 8 pieces
- 1 tablespoon freshly squeezed lemon juice (from ½ medium lemon)

Directions:

1. Over medium heat, cook the oil in a skillet. Mix in the garlic and smoked paprika and cook for 1 minute, stirring often. Stir in the tomatoes, roasted peppers, water, black pepper, and salt. Adjust the heat to medium-high, simmer, and cook for 3 minutes and smash the tomatoes until the end of the cooking time.

2. Place the salmon to the skillet, and drizzle some of the sauce over the top. Cover and cook for 10 to 12 minutes (145°F using a meat thermometer) and just starts to flake.

3. Pull out the skillet from the heat, and sprinkle lemon juice over the top of the fish. Stir the sauce, then slice the salmon into chunks. Serve.

Nutrition

289 Calories

13g Fat

2g Carbohydrates

31g Protein

581mg Sodium

649. Tuscan Tuna and Zucchini Burgers

Preparation Time: 10 minutes

Cooking Time: 10 minutes

Servings: 4

Ingredients
- 3 slices whole-wheat sandwich bread, toasted
- 2 (5-ounce) cans tuna in olive oil
- 1 cup shredded zucchini
- 1 large egg, lightly beaten
- ¼ cup diced red bell pepper

- 1 tablespoon dried oregano
- 1 teaspoon lemon zest
- ¼ teaspoon freshly ground black pepper
- ¼ teaspoon kosher or sea salt
- 1 tablespoon extra-virgin olive oil
- Salad greens or 4 whole-wheat rolls, for serving (optional)

Directions

1. Crumble the toast into bread crumbs using your fingers (or use a knife to cut into ¼-inch cubes) until you have 1 cup of loosely packed crumbs. Pour the crumbs into a large bowl. Add the tuna, zucchini, egg, bell pepper, oregano, lemon zest, black pepper, and salt. Mix well with a fork. Divide the mixture into four (½-cup-size) patties. Place on a plate, and press each patty flat to about ¾-inch thick.

2. Over medium-high heat, cook the oil in a skillet. Add the patties to the hot oil, then turn the heat down to medium. Cook the patties for 5 minutes, flip with a spatula, and cook for an additional 5 minutes. Enjoy as is or serve on salad greens or whole-wheat rolls.

Nutrition

191 Calories

10g Fat

2g Carbohydrates

15g Protein

661mg Sodium

650. Mediterranean Cod Stew

Preparation Time: 10 minutes

Cooking Time: 20 minutes

Servings: 6

Ingredients:
- 2 tablespoons extra-virgin olive oil
- 2 cups chopped onion
- 2 garlic cloves, minced
- ¾ teaspoon smoked paprika
- 1 (14.5-ounce) can diced tomatoes, undrained
- 1 (12-ounce) jar roasted red peppers
- 1 cup sliced olives, green or black
- 1/3 cup dry red wine
- ¼ teaspoon freshly ground black pepper
- ¼ teaspoon kosher or sea salt
- 1½ pounds cod fillets, cut into 1-inch pieces
- 3 cups sliced mushrooms

Directions:

1. Cook the oil in a stockpot. Mix in the onion and cook for 4 minutes, stirring occasionally. Stir in the garlic and smoked paprika and cook for 1 minute, stirring often.

2. Mix in the tomatoes with their juices, roasted peppers, olives, wine, pepper, and salt, and turn the heat up to medium-high. Bring to a boil. Add the cod and mushrooms, and reduce the heat to medium.

3. Cook for about 10 minutes, stir occasionally, until the cod is cooked through and flakes easily, and serve.

Nutrition

220 Calories

8g Fat

3g Carbohydrates

28g Protein

583mg Sodium

651. Steamed Mussels in White Wine Sauce

Preparation Time: 5 minutes

Cooking Time: 10 minutes

Servings: 4

Ingredients:
- 2 pounds small mussels

- 1 tablespoon extra-virgin olive oil
- 1 cup thinly sliced red onion
- 3 garlic cloves, sliced
- 1 cup dry white wine
- 2 (¼-inch-thick) lemon slices
- ¼ teaspoon freshly ground black pepper
- ¼ teaspoon kosher or sea salt
- Fresh lemon wedges, for serving (optional)

Directions:

1. In a large colander in the sink, run cold water over the mussels (but don't let the mussels sit in standing water). All the shells should be closed tight; discard any shells that are a little bit open or any shells that are cracked. Leave the mussels in the colander until you're ready to use them.

2. In a large skillet, cook the oil. Mix in the onion and cook for 4 minutes, stirring occasionally. Place the garlic and cook for 1 minute, stirring constantly. Add the wine, lemon slices, pepper, and salt, and bring to a simmer. Cook for 2 minutes.

3. Add the mussels and cover. Cook until the mussels open their shells. Gently shake the pan two or three times while they are cooking.

4. All the shells should now be wide open. Using a slotted spoon, discard any mussels that are still closed. Spoon the opened mussels into a shallow serving bowl, and pour the broth over the top. Serve with additional fresh lemon slices, if desired.

Nutrition

222 Calories

7g Fat

1g Carbohydrates

18g Protein

708mg Sodium

652. Orange and Garlic Shrimp

Preparation Time: 20 minutes
Cooking Time: 10 minutes
Servings: 6
Ingredients:

- 1 large orange
- 3 tablespoons extra-virgin olive oil, divided
- 1 tablespoon chopped fresh rosemary
- 1 tablespoon chopped fresh thyme
- 3 garlic cloves, minced (about 1½ teaspoons)
- ¼ teaspoon freshly ground black pepper
- ¼ teaspoon kosher or sea salt
- 1½ pounds fresh raw shrimp, shells and tails removed

Directions:

1. Zest the entire orange using a citrus grater. Mix the orange zest and 2 tablespoons of oil with the rosemary, thyme, garlic, pepper, and salt. Stir in the shrimp, seal the bag, and gently massage the shrimp until all the ingredients are combined and the shrimp is completely covered with the seasonings. Set aside.

2. Heat a grill, grill pan, or a large skillet over medium heat. Brush on or swirl in the remaining 1 tablespoon of oil. Add half the shrimp, and cook for 4 to 6 minutes, or until the shrimp turn pink and white, flipping halfway through if on the grill or stirring every minute if in a pan. Handover the shrimp to a large serving bowl. Repeat, and place them to the bowl.

3. While the shrimp cook, peel the orange and cut the flesh into bite-size pieces. Place to the serving bowl, and toss with the cooked shrimp. Serve immediately or refrigerate and serve cold.

Nutrition

190 Calories

8g Fat

1g Carbohydrates

24g Protein

647mg Sodium

653. Roasted Shrimp-Gnocchi Bake

Preparation Time: 10 minutes
Cooking Time: 20 minutes
Servings: 4
Ingredients:

- 1 cup chopped fresh tomato
- 2 tablespoons extra-virgin olive oil
- 2 garlic cloves, minced
- ½ teaspoon freshly ground black pepper
- ¼ teaspoon crushed red pepper
- 1 (12-ounce) jar roasted red peppers
- 1-pound fresh raw shrimp, shells and tails removed
- 1-pound frozen gnocchi (not thawed)
- ½ cup cubed feta cheese
- 1/3 cup fresh torn basil leaves

Directions:

1. Preheat the oven to 425°F. In a baking dish, mix the tomatoes, oil, garlic, black pepper, and crushed red pepper. Roast in the oven for 10 minutes.

2. Stir in the roasted peppers and shrimp. Roast for 10 more minutes, until the shrimp turn pink and white.

3. While the shrimp cooks, cook the gnocchi on the stove top according to the package directions. Drain in a colander and keep warm. Remove the dish from the oven. Mix in the cooked gnocchi, feta, and basil, and serve.

Nutrition

277 Calories

7g Fat

1g Carbohydrates

20g Protein

711mg Sodium

654. Spicy Shrimp Puttanesca

Preparation Time: 5 minutes
Cooking Time: 15 minutes
Servings: 4
Ingredients:

- 2 tablespoons extra-virgin olive oil
- 3 anchovy fillets, drained and chopped
- 3 garlic cloves, minced
- ½ teaspoon crushed red pepper
- 1 (14.5-ounce) can low-sodium or no-salt-added diced tomatoes, undrained
- 1 (2.25-ounce) can black olives
- 2 tablespoons capers
- 1 tablespoon chopped fresh oregano
- 1-pound fresh raw shrimp, shells and tails removed

Directions:

1. Over medium heat, cook the oil. Mix in the anchovies, garlic, and crushed red pepper. Cook for 3 minutes, stirring frequently and mashing up the anchovies with a wooden spoon, until they have melted into the oil.

2. Stir in the tomatoes with their juices, olives, capers, and oregano. Turn up the heat to medium-high, and bring to a simmer.

3. When the sauce is lightly bubbling, stir in the shrimp. Select heat to medium, and cook the shrimp until they turn pink and white then serve.

Nutrition

214 Calories

10g Fat

2g Carbohydrates

26g Protein
591mg Sodium

655. Italian Tuna Sandwiches

Preparation Time: 10 minutes
Cooking Time: 0 minute
Servings: 4
Ingredients:
- 3 tablespoons freshly squeezed lemon juice
- 2 tablespoons extra-virgin olive oil
- 1 garlic clove, minced
- ½ teaspoon freshly ground black pepper
- 2 (5-ounce) cans tuna, drained
- 1 (2.25-ounce) can sliced olives
- ½ cup chopped fresh fennel, including fronds
- 8 slices whole-grain crusty bread

Directions:
1. Combine the lemon juice, oil, garlic, and pepper. Add the tuna, olives, and fennel. Using a fork, separate the tuna into chunks and stir to combine all the ingredients.
2. Divide the tuna salad equally among 4 slices of bread. Top each with the remaining bread slices. Let the sandwiches sit for at least 5 minutes so the zesty filling can soak into the bread before serving.

Nutrition
347 Calories
17g Fat
5g Carbohydrates
25g Protein
447mg Sodium

656. White Clam Pizza Pie

Preparation Time: 10 minutes
Cooking Time: 20 minutes
Servings: 4
Ingredients:
- 1 pound refrigerated fresh pizza dough
- Nonstick cooking spray
- 2 tablespoons extra-virgin olive oil, divided
- 2 garlic cloves, minced (about 1 teaspoon)
- ½ teaspoon crushed red pepper
- 1 (10-ounce) can whole baby clams, drained
- ¼ cup dry white wine
- All-purpose flour, for dusting
- 1 cup diced mozzarella cheese
- 1 tablespoon grated Pecorino Romano or Parmesan cheese
- 1 tablespoon chopped fresh flat-leaf (Italian) parsley

Directions:
1. Preheat the oven to 500°F. Brush large, rimmed baking sheet with nonstick cooking spray.
2. In a large skillet, cook 1½ tablespoons of the oil. Put the garlic and crushed red pepper and cook for 1 minute, stirring frequently to prevent the garlic from burning. Add the reserved clam juice and wine. Bring to a boil over high heat. Reduce to medium heat so the sauce is just simmering and cook for 10 minutes, stirring occasionally. The sauce will cook down and thicken.
3. Place the clams and cook for 3 minutes, stirring occasionally. While the sauce is cooking, on a lightly floured surface, form the pizza dough into a 12-inch circle or into a 10-by-12-inch rectangle with a rolling pin or by stretching with your hands. Situate the dough on the prepared baking sheet. Grease the dough with the remaining ½ tablespoon of oil. Set aside until the clam sauce is ready.

4. Spread the clam sauce over the prepared dough within ½ inch of the edge. Top with the mozzarella cheese, then sprinkle with the Pecorino Romano.
5. Bake for 10 minutes. Pull out the pizza from the oven and place onto a wooden cutting board. Top with the parsley, cut into eight pieces with a pizza cutter or a sharp knife, and serve.

Nutrition
541 Calories
21g Fat
1g Carbohydrates
32g Protein
688mg Sodium

657. Baked Bean Fish Meal

Preparation Time: 10 minutes
Cooking Time: 10 minutes
Servings: 4
Ingredients:
- 1 tablespoon balsamic vinegar
- 2 ½ cups green beans
- 1-pint cherry or grape tomatoes
- 4 (4-ounce each) fish fillets, such as cod or tilapia
- 2 tablespoons olive oil

Directions:
1. Preheat an oven to 400 degrees. Grease two baking sheets with some olive oil or olive oil spray. Arrange 2 fish fillets on each sheet. In a mixing bowl, pour olive oil and vinegar. Combine to mix well with each other.
2. Mix green beans and tomatoes. Combine to mix well with each other. Combine both mixtures well with each other. Add mixture equally over fish fillets. Bake for 6-8 minutes, until fish opaque and easy to flake. Serve warm.

Nutrition
229 Calories
13g Fat
8g Carbohydrates
2.5g Protein
559mg Sodium

658. Mushroom Cod Stew

Preparation Time: 10 minutes
Cooking Time: 20 minutes
Servings: 6
Ingredients:
- 2 tablespoons extra-virgin olive oil
- 2 garlic cloves, minced
- 1 can tomato
- 2 cups chopped onion
- ¾ teaspoon smoked paprika
- a (12-ounce) jar roasted red peppers
- 1/3 cup dry red wine
- ¼ teaspoon kosher or sea salt
- ¼ teaspoon black pepper
- 1 cup black olives
- 1 ½ pounds cod fillets, cut into 1-inch pieces
- 3 cups sliced mushrooms

Directions:
1. Get medium-large cooking pot, warm up oil over medium heat. Add onions and stir-cook for 4 minutes. Add garlic and smoked paprika; cook for 1 minute, stirring often. Add tomatoes with juice, roasted peppers, olives, wine, pepper, and salt; stir gently. Boil mixture. Add the cod and mushrooms; turn down heat to medium. Close and cook until the cod is easy to flake, stir in between. Serve warm.

Nutrition
238 Calories

7g Fat
15g Carbohydrates
3.5g Protein
772mg Sodium

659. Spiced Swordfish

Preparation Time: 10 minutes
Cooking Time: 15 minutes
Servings: 4
Ingredients:
- 4 (7 ounces each) swordfish steaks
- 1/2 teaspoon ground black pepper
- 12 cloves of garlic, peeled
- 3/4 teaspoon salt
- 1 1/2 teaspoon ground cumin
- 1 teaspoon paprika
- 1 teaspoon coriander
- 3 tablespoons lemon juice
- 1/3 cup olive oil

Directions:
1. Take a blender or food processor, open the lid and add all the ingredients except for swordfish. Close the lid and blend to make a smooth mixture. Pat dry fish steaks; coat evenly with the prepared spice mixture.
2. Add them over an aluminum foil, cover and refrigerator for 1 hour. Preheat a griddle pan over high heat, pour oil and heat it. Add fish steaks; stir-cook for 5-6 minutes per side until cooked through and evenly browned. Serve warm.
Nutrition
255 Calories
12g Fat
4g Carbohydrates
0.5g Protein
990mg Sodium

660. Anchovy Pasta Mania

Preparation Time: 10 minutes
Cooking Time: 20 minutes
Servings: 4
Ingredients:
- 4 anchovy fillets, packed in olive oil
- ½ pound broccoli, cut into 1-inch florets
- 2 cloves garlic, sliced
- 1-pound whole-wheat penne
- 2 tablespoons olive oil
- ¼ cup Parmesan cheese, grated
- Salt and black pepper, to taste
- Red pepper flakes, to taste

Directions:
1. Cook pasta as directed over pack; drain and set aside. Take a medium saucepan or skillet, add oil. Heat over medium heat. Add anchovies, broccoli, and garlic, and stir-cook until veggies turn tender for 4-5 minutes. Take off heat; mix in the pasta. Serve warm with Parmesan cheese, red pepper flakes, salt, and black pepper sprinkled on top.
Nutrition
328 Calories
8g Fat
35g Carbohydrates
7g Protein
834mg Sodium

661. Shrimp Garlic Pasta

Preparation Time: 10 minutes
Cooking Time: 15 minutes
Servings: 4
Ingredients:
- 1-pound shrimp, peeled and deveined

- 3 garlic cloves, minced
- 1 onion, finely chopped
- 1 package whole wheat or bean pasta of your choice
- 4 tablespoons olive oil
- Salt and black pepper, to taste
- ¼ cup basil, cut into strips
- ¾ cup chicken broth, low-sodium

Directions:
1. Cook pasta as directed over pack; rinse and set aside. Get medium saucepan, add oil then warm up over medium heat. Add onion, garlic and stir-cook until become translucent and fragrant for 3 minutes.
2. Add shrimp, black pepper (ground) and salt; stir-cook for 3 minutes until shrimps are opaque. Add broth and simmer for 2-3 more minutes. Add pasta in serving plates; add shrimp mixture over; serve warm with basil on top.
Nutrition
605 Calories
17g Fat
53g Carbohydrates
19g Protein
723mg Sodium

662. Berries and Grilled Calamari

Preparation Time: 10 minutes
Cooking Time: 5 minutes
Servings: 4
Ingredients:
- ¼ cup dried cranberries
- ¼ cup extra virgin olive oil
- ¼ cup olive oil
- ¼ cup sliced almonds
- ½ lemon, juiced
- ¾ cup blueberries
- 1 ½ lb. calamari tube, cleaned
- 1 granny smith apple, sliced thinly
- 1 tbsp. fresh lemon juice
- 2 tbsp. apple cider vinegar
- 6 cups fresh spinach
- Freshly grated pepper to taste
- Sea salt to taste

Directions:
1. In a small bowl, make the vinaigrette by mixing well the tbsp. of lemon juice, apple cider vinegar, and extra virgin olive oil. Season with pepper and salt to taste. Set aside.
2. Turn on the grill to medium fire and let the grates heat up for a minute or two.
3. In a large bowl, add olive oil and the calamari tube. Season calamari generously with pepper and salt.
4. Place seasoned and oiled calamari onto heated grate and grill until cooked or opaque. This is around two minutes per side.
5. As you wait for the calamari to cook, you can combine almonds, cranberries, blueberries, spinach, and the thinly sliced apple in a large salad bowl. Toss to mix.
6. Remove cooked calamari from grill and transfer on a chopping board. Cut into ¼-inch thick rings and throw into the salad bowl.
7. Drizzle with vinaigrette and toss well to coat salad.
8. Serve and enjoy!
Nutrition: Calories: 567; Fat: 24.5g; Protein: 54.8g; Carbs: 30.6g

663. Trout and Peppers Mix

Preparation Time: 10 minutes
Cooking Time: 20 minutes
Servings: 4
Ingredients:
- 4 trout fillets, boneless
- 2 tbsp. kalamata olives, pitted and chopped

- 1 tbsp. capers, drained
- 2 tbsp. olive oil
- A pinch of salt and black pepper
- 1 and ½ tsp. chili powder
- 1 yellow bell pepper, chopped
- 1 red bell pepper, chopped
- 1 green bell pepper, chopped

Directions:

1. Heat up a pan with the oil over medium-high heat, add the trout, salt and pepper and cook for 10 minutes.

2. Flip the fish, add the peppers and the rest of the ingredients, cook for 10 minutes more, divide the whole mix between plates and serve.

Nutrition: Calories 572, Fat 17.4g, Fiber 6g, Carbs 71g, Protein 33.7g

664. Vinegar Honeyed Salmon

Preparation Time: 10 minutes
Cooking Time: 5 minutes
Servings: 4
Ingredients:

- 4 (8-ounce) salmon fillets
- 1/2 cup balsamic vinegar
- 1 tablespoon honey
- Black pepper (ground) and sea salt, to taste
- 1 tablespoon olive oil

Directions:

1. In a mixing bowl, add honey and vinegar. Mix together well.

2. Season fish fillets with the black pepper (ground) and sea salt; brush with honey glaze. Take a medium saucepan or skillet, add oil. Heat over medium heat. Add salmon fillets and stir-cook until medium-rare in the center and lightly browned for 3-4 minutes per side. Serve warm.

Nutrition:
Calories: 481
Fat: 16g
Carbohydrates: 24g
Fiber: 1.5g

665. Orange Fish Meal

Preparation Time: 10 minutes
Cooking Time: 5 minutes
Servings: 4
Ingredients:

- ¼ teaspoon kosher or sea salt
- 1 tablespoon extra-virgin olive oil
- 1 tablespoon orange juice
- 4 (4-ounce) tilapia fillets, with or without skin
- ¼ cup chopped red onion
- 1 avocado, pitted, skinned, and sliced

Directions:

1. Take a baking dish of 9-inch; add olive oil, orange juice, and salt. Mix well. Add fish fillets and coat well. Add onions over fish fillets. Cover with plastic wrap.

2. Microwave for 3 minutes until fish is cooked well and easy to flake. Serve warm with sliced avocado on top.

Nutrition:
Calories: 231
Fat: 9g
Carbohydrates: 8g
Fiber: 2.5g

666. Shrimp Zoodles

Preparation Time: 10 minutes
Cooking Time: 5 minutes
Servings: 2
Ingredients:

- 2 tablespoons chopped parsley
- 2 teaspoons minced garlic
- 1 teaspoon salt
- ½ teaspoon black pepper
- 2 medium zucchinis, spiralized
- 3/4 pounds medium shrimp, peeled & deveined
- 1 tablespoon olive oil
- 1 lemon, juiced and zested

Directions:

1. Take a medium saucepan or skillet, add oil, lemon juice, and lemon zest. Heat over a medium heat. Add shrimps and stir-cook 1 minute per side. Add garlic and red pepper flakes; cook for 1 more minute.

2. Add zoodles and stir gently; cook for 3 minutes until cooked to satisfaction. Season with salt and black pepper and serve warm with parsley on top.

Nutrition:
Calories: 329
Fat: 12g
Carbohydrates: 11g
Fiber: 3g

667. Tuna Nutty Salad

Preparation Time: 10 minutes
Cooking Time: 0 minute
Servings: 4
Ingredients:

- 1 tablespoon chopped tarragon
- 1 stalk celery, trimmed and finely diced
- 1 medium shallot, diced
- 3 tablespoons chopped chives
- 1 (5-ounce) can tuna (covered in olive oil) drained and flaked
- 1 teaspoon Dijon mustard
- 2-3 tablespoons mayonnaise
- 1/4 teaspoon salt
- 1/8 teaspoon pepper
- 1/4 cup pine nuts, toasted

Directions:

1. In a large salad bowl, add tuna, shallot, chives, tarragon, and celery. Combine to mix well with each other. In a mixing bowl, add mayonnaise, mustard, salt, and black pepper. Combine to mix well with each other. Add mayonnaise mixture to a salad bowl; toss well to combine. Add pine nuts and toss again. Serve fresh.

Nutrition:
Calories: 236
Fat: 14g
Carbohydrates: 4g
Fiber: 1g

668. Asparagus Trout Meal

Preparation Time: 10 minutes
Cooking Time: 20 minutes
Servings: 4
Ingredients:

- 2 pounds trout fillets

- 1-pound asparagus
- Salt and ground white pepper, to taste
- 1 tablespoon olive oil
- 1 garlic clove, finely minced
- 1 scallion, thinly sliced (green and white part)
- 4 medium golden potatoes, thinly sliced
- 2 Roma tomatoes, chopped
- 8 pitted kalamata olives, chopped
- 1 large carrot, thinly sliced
- 2 tablespoons dried parsley
- ¼ cup ground cumin
- 2 tablespoons paprika
- 1 tablespoon vegetable bouillon seasoning
- ½ cup dry white wine

Directions:
1. In a mixing bowl, add fish fillets, white pepper, and salt. Combine to mix well with each other. Take a medium saucepan or skillet and add oil. Heat over a medium heat. Add asparagus, potatoes, garlic, and white part scallion, and stir-cook until the mixture becomes softened for 4-5 minutes. Add tomatoes, carrot, and olives; stir-cook for 6-7 minutes until tender. Add cumin, paprika, parsley, bouillon seasoning, and salt. Stir the mixture well.
2. Mix in white wine and fish fillets. Over a low heat, cover and simmer the mixture for about 6 minutes until fish is easy to flake, stirring in between. Serve warm with green scallions on top.

Nutrition:
Calories: 303
Fat: 17g
Carbohydrates: 37g
Fiber: 6g

669. Kale Olive Tuna

Preparation Time: 10 minutes
Cooking Time: 15 minutes
Servings: 6
Ingredients:
- 1 cup chopped onion
- 3 garlic cloves, minced
- 1 (2.25-ounce) can sliced olives, drained
- 1-pound kale, chopped
- 3 tablespoons extra-virgin olive oil
- ¼ cup capers
- ¼ teaspoon crushed red pepper
- 2 teaspoons sugar
- 1 (15-ounce) can cannellini beans or great northern beans, drained
- 2 (6-ounce) cans tuna in olive oil, un-drained
- ¼ teaspoon black pepper
- ¼ teaspoon kosher or sea salt

Directions:
1. Cook the kale in boiling water for 2 minutes; drain and set aside. Take a medium-large cooking pot or stockpot and heat the oil over z medium heat. Add onion and stir-cook until translucent and softened. Add garlic and stir-cook for 1 minute.
2. Add olives, capers, and red pepper, and stir-cook for 1 minute. Mix in cooked kale and sugar. Over a low heat, cover and simmer the mixture for about 8-10 minutes, stirring in between. Add tuna, beans, pepper, and salt. Stir well and serve warm.

Nutrition:
Calories: 242
Fat: 11g
Carbohydrates: 24g
Fiber: 7g

670. Tangy Rosemary Shrimps

Preparation Time: 10 minutes
Cooking Time: 10 minutes
Servings: 6
Ingredients:
- 1 large orange, zested and peeled
- 3 garlic cloves, minced
- 1 ½ pounds raw shrimp, shells, and tails removed
- 3 tablespoons olive oil
- 1 tablespoon chopped thyme
- 1 tablespoon chopped rosemary
- ¼ teaspoon black pepper
- ¼ teaspoon kosher or sea salt

Directions:
1. Take a zip-top plastic bag, add orange zest, shrimps, 2 tablespoons olive oil, garlic, thyme, rosemary, salt, and black pepper. Shake well and set aside to marinate for 5 minutes.
2. Take a medium saucepan or skillet, add 1 tablespoon olive oil. Heat over medium heat. Add shrimps and stir-cook for 2-3 minutes per side until totally pink and opaque. Slice the orange into bite-sized wedges and add in a serving plate. Add shrimp and combine well. Serve fresh.

Nutrition:
Calories: 187
Fat: 7g
Carbohydrates: 6g
Fiber: 0.5g

671. Asparagus Salmon

Preparation Time: 10 minutes
Cooking Time: 15 minutes
Servings: 2
Ingredients:
- 8.8-ounce bunch asparagus
- 2 small salmon fillets
- 1 ½ teaspoon salt
- 1 teaspoon black pepper
- 1 tablespoon olive oil
- 1 cup hollandaise sauce, low-carb

Directions:
1. Season salmon fillets with salt and black pepper. Take a medium saucepan or skillet, add oil. Heat over medium heat. Add salmon fillets and stir-cook until evenly seared and cooked well for 4-5 minutes per side. Add asparagus and stir cook for 4-5 more minutes. Serve warm with hollandaise sauce on top.

Nutrition:
Calories: 565
Fat: 7g
Carbohydrates: 8g
Fiber: 2.5g

672. Sicilian Kale and Tuna Bowl

Preparation Time: 15 minutes
Cooking Time: 15 minutes
Servings: 6
Ingredients:
- 1-pound kale

- 3 tablespoons extra-virgin olive oil
- 1 cup chopped onion
- 3 garlic cloves, minced
- 1 (2.25-ounce) can sliced olives, drained
- ¼ cup capers
- ¼ teaspoon crushed red pepper
- 2 teaspoons sugar
- 2 (6-ounce) cans tuna in olive oil, undrained
- 1 (15-ounce) can cannellini beans or great northern beans
- ¼ teaspoon freshly ground black pepper
- ¼ teaspoon kosher or sea salt

Directions:
1. Fill a large stockpot three-quarters full of water and bring to a boil. Add the kale and cook for 2 minutes. (This is to make the kale less bitter.) Drain the kale in a colander and set aside.
2. Set the empty pot back on the stove over medium heat and pour in the oil. Add the onion and cook for 4 minutes, stirring often. Add the garlic and cook for 1 minute, stirring often. Add the olives, capers, and crushed red pepper, and cook for 1 minute, stirring often. Add the partially cooked kale and sugar, stirring until the kale is completely coated with oil. Cover the pot and cook for 8 minutes.
3. Remove the kale from the heat, mix in the tuna, beans, pepper, and salt, and serve.

Nutrition:
Calories 265
Total Fat: 12g
Fiber: 7g
Protein: 16g

673. Greek Roasted Fish

Preparation Time: 5 minutes
Cooking Time: 30 minutes
Servings: 4
Ingredients:
- 4 salmon fillets
- 1 tablespoon chopped oregano
- 1 teaspoon dried basil
- 1 zucchini, sliced
- 1 red onion, sliced
- 1 carrot, sliced
- 1 lemon, sliced
- 2 tablespoons extra virgin olive oil
- Salt and pepper to taste

Directions:
1. add all the ingredients in a deep-dish baking pan.
2. Season with salt and pepper and cook in the preheated oven at 350F for 20 minutes.
3. Serve the fish and vegetables warm.

Nutrition:
Calories: 328
Fat: 13g
Protein: 38g
Carbohydrates: 8g

674. Tomato Fish Bake

Preparation Time: 5 minutes
Cooking Time: 30 minutes
Servings: 4
Ingredients:
- 4 cod fillets
- 4 tomatoes, sliced

- 4 garlic cloves, minced
- 1 shallot, sliced
- 1 celery stalk, sliced
- 1 teaspoon fennel seeds
- 1 cup vegetable stock
- Salt and pepper to taste

Directions:
1. Layer the cod fillets and tomatoes in a deep-dish baking pan.
2. Add the rest of the ingredients and add salt and pepper.
3. Cook in the preheated oven at 350F for 20 minutes.
4. Serve the dish warm or chilled.

Nutrition:
Calories: 299
Fat: 3g
Protein: 64g
Carbohydrates: 2g

675. Seafood Paella

Preparation Time: 5 minutes
Cooking Time: 45 minutes
Servings: 8
Ingredients:
- 2 tablespoons extra virgin olive oil
- 1 shallot, chopped
- 2 garlic cloves, chopped
- 1 red bell pepper, cored and diced
- 1 carrot, diced
- 2 tomatoes, peeled and diced
- 1 cup wild rice
- 1 cup tomato juice
- 2 cups chicken stock
- 1 chicken breast, cubed
- Salt and pepper to taste
- 2 monkfish fillets, cubed
- ½ pound fresh shrimps, peeled and deveined
- ½ pound prawns
- 1 thyme sprig
- 1 rosemary sprig

Directions:
1. Heat the oil in a skillet and stir in the shallot, garlic, bell pepper, carrot and tomatoes. Cook for a few minutes until softened.
2. Stir in the rice, tomato juice, stock, chicken, salt and pepper and cook on low heat for 20 minutes.
3. Add the rest of the ingredients and cook for 10 additional minutes.
4. Serve the paella warm and fresh.

Nutrition:
Calories: 245
Fat: 8g
Protein: 27g
Carbohydrates: 20.6g

676. Asparagus and Smoked Salmon Salad

Preparation Time: 15 minutes
Cooking Time: 10 minutes
Servings: 8
Ingredients:
- 1 lb. fresh asparagus, trimmed and cut into 1-inch pieces
- 1/2 cup pecans,
- 2 heads red leaf lettuce, rinsed and torn
- 1/2 cup frozen green peas, thawed
- 1/4 lb. smoked salmon, cut into 1-inch chunks
- 1/4 cup olive oil

- 2 tablespoons. lemon juice
- 1 teaspoon Dijon mustard
- 1/2 teaspoon salt
- 1/4 teaspoon pepper

Directions:

1. Boil a pot of water. Stir in asparagus and cook for 5 minutes until tender. Let it drain; set aside.

2. In a skillet, cook the pecans over medium heat for 5 minutes, stirring constantly until lightly toasted.

3. Combine the asparagus, toasted pecans, salmon, peas, and red leaf lettuce and toss in a large bowl.

4. In another bowl, combine lemon juice, pepper, Dijon mustard, salt, and olive oil. You can coat the salad with the dressing or serve it on its side.

Nutrition:

Calories: 159

Total Carbohydrate: 7 g

Cholesterol: 3 mg

Total Fat: 12.9 g

Protein: 6 g

Sodium: 304 mg

677. Shrimp Cobb Salad

Preparation Time: 25 minutes

Cooking Time: 10 minutes

Servings: 2

Ingredients:

- 4 slices center-cut bacon
- 1 lb. large shrimp, peeled and deveined
- 1/2 teaspoon ground paprika
- 1/4 teaspoon ground black pepper
- 1/4 teaspoon salt, divided
- 2 1/2 tablespoons. Fresh lemon juice
- 1 1/2 tablespoons. Extra-virgin olive oil
- 1/2 teaspoon whole grain Dijon mustard
- 1 (10 oz.) package romaine lettuce hearts, chopped
- 2 cups cherry tomatoes, quartered
- 1 ripe avocado, cut into wedges
- 1 cup shredded carrots

Directions:

1. In a large skillet over medium heat, cook the bacon for 4 minutes on each side till crispy.

2. Take away from the skillet and place on paper towels; let cool for 5 minutes. Break the bacon into bits. Pour out most of the bacon fat, leaving behind only 1 tablespoon. in the skillet. Bring the skillet back to medium-high heat. Add black pepper and paprika to the shrimp for seasoning. Cook the shrimp around 2 minutes each side until it is opaque. Sprinkle with 1/8 teaspoon of salt for seasoning.

3. Combine the remaining 1/8 teaspoon of salt, mustard, olive oil and lemon juice together in a small bowl. Stir in the romaine hearts.

4. On each serving plate, place on 1 and 1/2 cups of romaine lettuce. Add on top the same amounts of avocado, carrots, tomatoes, shrimp and bacon.

Nutrition:

Calories: 528

Total Carbohydrate: 22.7 g

Cholesterol: 365 mg

Total Fat: 28.7 g

Protein: 48.9 g

Sodium: 1166 mg

678. Coconut Salsa on Chipotle Fish Tacos

Preparation Time: 10 minutes

Cooking Time: 10 minutes

Servings: 4

Ingredients:

- ¼ cup chopped fresh cilantro
- ½ cup seeded and finely chopped plum tomato
- 1 cup peeled and finely chopped mango
- 1 lime cut into wedges
- 1 tbsp. chipotle Chile powder
- 1 tbsp. safflower oil
- 1/3 cup finely chopped red onion
- 10 tbsp. fresh lime juice, divided
- 4 6-oz boneless, skinless cod fillets
- 5 tbsp. dried unsweetened shredded coconut
- 8 pcs of 6-inch tortillas, heated

Directions:

1. Whisk well Chile powder, oil, and 4 tbsp. lime juice in a glass baking dish. Add cod and marinate for 12 − 15 minutes. Turning once halfway through the marinating time.

2. Make the salsa by mixing coconut, 6 tbsp. lime juice, cilantro, onions, tomatoes and mangoes in a medium bowl. Set aside.

3. On high, heat a grill pan. Place cod and grill for four minutes per side turning only once.

4. Once cooked, slice cod into large flakes and evenly divide onto tortilla.

5. Evenly divide salsa on top of cod and serve with a side of lime wedges.

Nutrition: Calories: 477; Protein: 35.0g; Fat: 12.4g; Carbs: 57.4g

679. Baked Cod Crusted with Herbs

Preparation Time: 5 minutes

Cooking Time: 10 minutes

Servings: 4

Ingredients:

- ¼ cup honey
- ¼ tsp. salt
- ½ cup panko
- ½ tsp. pepper
- 1 tbsp. extra virgin olive oil
- 1 tbsp. lemon juice
- 1 tsp. dried basil
- 1 tsp. dried parsley
- 1 tsp. rosemary
- 4 pieces of 4-oz cod fillets

Directions:

1. With olive oil, grease a 9 x 13-inch baking pan and preheat oven to 375°F.

2. In a zip top bag mix panko, rosemary, salt, pepper, parsley and basil.

3. Evenly spread cod fillets in prepped dish and drizzle with lemon juice.

4. Then brush the fillets with honey on all sides. Discard remaining honey if any.

5. Then evenly divide the panko mixture on top of cod fillets.

6. Pop in the oven and bake for ten minutes or until fish is cooked.

7. Serve and enjoy.

Nutrition: Calories: 137; Protein: 5g; Fat: 2g; Carbs: 21g

680. Cajun Garlic Shrimp Noodle Bowl

Preparation Time: 10 minutes
Cooking Time: 15 minutes
Servings: 2
Ingredients:
- ½ tsp. salt
- 1 onion, sliced
- 1 red pepper, sliced
- 1 tbsp. butter
- 1 tsp. garlic granules
- 1 tsp. onion powder
- 1 tsp. paprika
- 2 large zucchinis, cut into noodle strips
- 20 jumbo shrimps, shells removed and deveined
- 3 cloves garlic, minced
- 3 tbsp. ghee
- A dash of cayenne pepper
- A dash of red pepper flakes

Directions:
1. Prepare the Cajun seasoning by mixing the onion powder, garlic granules, pepper flakes, cayenne pepper, paprika and salt. Toss in the shrimp to coat in the seasoning.
2. In a skillet, heat the ghee and sauté the garlic. Add in the red pepper and onions and continue sautéing for 4 minutes.
3. Add the Cajun shrimp and cook until opaque. Set aside.
4. In another pan, heat the butter and sauté the zucchini noodles for three minutes.
5. Assemble by the placing the Cajun shrimps on top of the zucchini noodles.

Nutrition: Calories: 712; Fat: 30.0g; Protein: 97.8g; Carbs: 20.2g

681. Crazy Saganaki Shrimp

Preparation Time: 10 minutes
Cooking Time: 10 minutes
Servings: 4
Ingredients:
- ¼ tsp. salt
- ½ cup Chardonnay
- ½ cup crumbled Greek feta cheese
- 1 medium bulb. fennel, cored and finely chopped
- 1 small Chile pepper, seeded and minced
- 1 tbsp. extra virgin olive oil
- 12 jumbo shrimps, peeled and deveined with tails left on
- 2 tbsp. lemon juice, divided
- 5 scallions sliced thinly
- Pepper to Taste

Directions:
1. In medium bowl, mix salt, lemon juice and shrimp.
2. On medium fire, place a saganaki pan (or large nonstick saucepan) and heat oil.
3. Sauté Chile pepper, scallions, and fennel for 4 minutes or until starting to brown and is already soft.
4. Add wine and sauté for another minute.
5. Place shrimps on top of fennel, cover and cook for 4 minutes or until shrimps are pink.
6. Remove just the shrimp and transfer to a plate.
7. Add pepper, feta and 1 tbsp. lemon juice to pan and cook for a minute or until cheese begins to melt.
8. To serve, place cheese and fennel mixture on a serving plate and top with shrimps.

Nutrition: Calories: 310; Protein: 49.7g; Fat: 6.8g; Carbs: 8.4g

682. Creamy Bacon-Fish Chowder

Preparation Time: 10 minutes
Cooking Time: 30 minutes
Servings: 8
Ingredients:
- 1 1/2 lbs. cod
- 1 1/2 tsp. dried thyme
- 1 large onion, chopped
- 1 medium carrot, coarsely chopped
- 1 tbsp. butter, cut into small pieces
- 1 tsp. salt, divided
- 3 1/2 cups baking potato, peeled and cubed
- 3 slices uncooked bacon
- 3/4 tsp. freshly ground black pepper, divided
- 4 1/2 cups water
- 4 bay leaves
- 4 cups 2% reduced-fat milk

Directions:
1. In a large skillet, add the water and bay leaves and let it simmer. Add the fish. Cover and let it simmer some more until the flesh flakes easily with fork. Remove the fish from the skillet and cut into large pieces. Set aside the cooking liquid.
2. Place Dutch oven in medium heat and cook the bacon until crisp. Remove the bacon and reserve the bacon drippings. Crush the bacon and set aside.
3. Stir potato, onion and carrot in the pan with the bacon drippings, cook over medium heat for 10 minutes. Add the cooking liquid, bay leaves, 1/2 tsp. salt, 1/4 tsp. pepper and thyme, let it boil. Lower the heat and let simmer for 10 minutes. Add the milk and butter, simmer until the potatoes becomes tender, but do not boil. Add the fish, 1/2 tsp. salt, 1/2 tsp. pepper. Remove the bay leaves.
4. Serve sprinkled with the crushed bacon.

NUTRITION: Calories: 400; Carbs: 34.5g; Protein: 20.8g; Fat: 19.7g

683. Crisped Coco-Shrimp with Mango Dip

Preparation Time: 10 minutes
Cooking Time: 20 minutes
Servings: 4
Ingredients:
- 1 cup shredded coconut
- 1 lb. raw shrimp, peeled and deveined
- 2 egg whites
- 4 tbsp. tapioca starch
- Pepper and salt to taste
- Mango Dip INGREDIENTS:
- 1 cup mango, chopped
- 1 jalapeño, thinly minced
- 1 tsp. lime juice
- 1/3 cup coconut milk
- 3 tsp. raw honey

Directions:
1. Preheat oven to 400°F.
2. Ready a pan with wire rack on top.
3. In a medium bowl, add tapioca starch and season with pepper and salt.
4. In a second medium bowl, add egg whites and whisk.
5. In a third medium bowl, add coconut.
6. To ready shrimps, dip first in tapioca starch, then egg whites, and then coconut. Place dredged shrimp on wire rack. Repeat until all shrimps are covered.

7. Pop shrimps in the oven and roast for 10 minutes per side.
8. Meanwhile make the dip by adding all ingredients in a blender. Puree until smooth and creamy. Transfer to a dipping bowl.
9. Once shrimps are golden brown, serve with mango dip.
Nutrition: Calories: 294.2; Protein: 26.6g; Fat: 7g; Carbs: 31.2g

684. Seafood Souvlaki Bowl

Preparation Time: 20 minutes
Cooking Time: 20 minutes
Serving: 4
Ingredients
For salmon
- 1 pinch of salt
- 1 pinch of black pepper
- 1 tablespoon of fresh oregano
- 1 tablespoon of paprika
- 1 tablespoon of fresh dill
- 3 tablespoons of extra-virgin olive oil
- 2 tablespoons of balsamic vinegar
- 6 tablespoons of freshly squeezed lemon juice
- 2 cloves of garlic, minced
- 1 lb. of fresh salmon, cut into 4 fillets
Ingredients:
- 1 pinch of salt
- 1 pinch of black pepper
- 2 tablespoons of extra-virgin olive oil
- Juice of 1 lemon
- 2 red bell peppers, diced
- 1 large cucumber, diced
- 1 zucchini, sliced
- 1 cup of cherry tomatoes, halved
- ½ cup of kalamata olives, pitted and halved
- 1 cup of dry pearled couscous
- 8 g of feta, cubed
Directions:
1. Cook the couscous following the package instructions and set aside.
2. In a medium mixing bowl, add all the souvlaki ingredients apart from the fish. Combine well, then coat each fish fillet. Allow the fillets to rest in the bowl for 15 minutes.
3. In a separate mixing bowl, combine the sliced bell peppers and zucchini. Add two tablespoons of olive oil, salt, and pepper. Combine and set aside.
4. In a medium skillet over medium heat, cook the salmon until tender, then remove from the heat.
5. Add the sliced peppers and zucchini to the skillet and cook for three minutes until you see charring, then remove from the heat.
6. To serve, dish the couscous up into four serving bowls and top with the lemon juice. Add the cooked salmon, charred vegetables, cucumber, tomatoes, olives, and feta.
Nutrition:
159 calories
11g fat
2g protein
3g Carbohydrates

685. Baked Cod with Vegetables

Preparation Time: 15 minutes
Cooking Time: 25 minutes
Serving: 2
Ingredients:
- 1 pound (454 g) thick cod fillet, cut into 4 even portions
- ¼ teaspoon onion powder (optional)
- ¼ teaspoon paprika
- 3 tablespoons extra-virgin olive oil
- 4 medium scallions
- ½ cup fresh chopped basil, divided
- 3 tablespoons minced garlic (optional)
- 2 teaspoons salt
- 2 teaspoons freshly ground black pepper
- ¼ teaspoon dry marjoram (optional)
- 6 sun-dried tomato slices
- ½ cup dry white wine
- ½ cup crumbled feta cheese
- 1 (15-ounce / 425-g) can oil-packed artichoke hearts, drained
- 1 lemon, sliced
- 1 cup pitted kalamata olives
- 1 teaspoon capers (optional)
- 4 small red potatoes, quartered
Direction:
1. Set oven to 375°F (190°C).
2. Season the fish with paprika and onion powder (if desired).
3. Heat an ovenproof skillet over medium heat and sear the top side of the cod for about 1 minute until golden. Set aside.
4. Heat the olive oil in the same skillet over medium heat. Add the scallions, ¼ cup of basil, garlic (if desired), salt, pepper, marjoram (if desired), tomato slices, and white wine and stir to combine. Boil then removes from heat.
5. Evenly spread the sauce on the bottom of skillet. Place the cod on top of the tomato basil sauce and scatter with feta cheese. Place the artichokes in the skillet and top with the lemon slices.
6. Scatter with the olives, capers (if desired), and the remaining ¼ cup of basil. Pullout from the heat and transfer to the preheated oven. Bake for 15 to 20 minutes
7. Meanwhile, place the quartered potatoes on a baking sheet or wrapped in aluminum foil. Bake in the oven for 15 minutes.
8. Cool for 5 minutes before serving.
Nutrition:
1168 calories
60g fat
64g protein
5g Carbohydrates

686. Tuna Croquettes

Preparation Time: 40 minutes
Cooking Time: 25 minutes
Serving: 12
Ingredients:
- 6 tablespoons extra-virgin olive oil, plus 1 to 2 cups
- 5 tablespoons almond flour, plus 1 cup, divided
- 1¼ cups heavy cream
- 1 (4-ounce) can olive oil-packed yellowfin tuna
- 1 tablespoon chopped red onion
- 2 teaspoons minced capers
- ½ teaspoon dried dill
- ¼ teaspoon freshly ground black pepper
- 2 large eggs
- 1 cup panko breadcrumbs
Direction
1. In a huge skillet, heat 6 tablespoons olive oil over medium-low heat. Add 5 tablespoons almond flour and cook, stirring constantly, until a smooth paste forms and the flour browns slightly, 2 to 3 minutes.
2. Increase the heat to medium-high and gradually add the heavy cream, whisking constantly for 5 minutes.

3. Pull out from heat and stir in the tuna, red onion, capers, dill, and pepper.

4. Pour into 8-inch square baking dish that is well coated with olive oil and allow to cool to room temperature. Cover and chill for 4 hours.

5. To form the croquettes, set out three bowls. In one, beat together the eggs. In another, add the remaining almond flour. In the third, add the panko. Line a baking sheet with parchment paper.

6. Situate a tablespoon of cold prepared dough into the flour mixture and roll to coat. Shake off excess and, using your hands, roll into an oval.

7. Dip the croquette into the beaten egg, then lightly coat in panko. Set on lined baking sheet and repeat with the remaining dough.

8. In a small saucepan, cook 1 to 2 cups of olive oil over medium-high heat.

9. Once the oil is heated, fry the croquettes 3 or 4 at a time.

Nutrition:
245 Calories
22g Fat
6g Protein
8g Carbohydrates

687. Smoked Salmon Crudités

Preparation Time: 10 minutes
Cooking Time: 0 minute
Serving: 4
Ingredients:
- 6 ounces smoked wild salmon
- 2 tablespoons Roasted Garlic Aioli
- 1 tablespoon Dijon mustard
- 1 tablespoon chopped scallions
- 2 teaspoons chopped capers
- ½ teaspoon dried dill
- 4 endive spears or hearts of romaine
- ½ English cucumber

Direction:
1. Cut the smoked salmon. Add the aioli, Dijon, scallions, capers, and dill and mix well.

2. Top endive spears and cucumber rounds with a spoonful of smoked salmon mixture and enjoy chilled.

Nutrition:
92 Calories
5g Fat
9g Protein
7g Carbohydrates

688. Slow Cooker Salmon in Foil

Preparation Time: 5 minutes
Cooking Time: 2 hours
Serving: 2
Ingredients:
- 2 (6-ounce / 170-g) salmon fillets
- 1 tablespoon olive oil
- 2 cloves garlic, minced
- ½ tablespoon lime juice
- 1 teaspoon finely chopped fresh parsley
- ¼ teaspoon black pepper

Direction
1. Spread a length of foil onto a work surface and place the salmon fillets in the middle.

2. Blend olive oil, garlic, lime juice, parsley, and black pepper. Brush the mixture over the fillets. Fold the foil over and crimp the sides to make a packet.

3. Place the packet into the slow cooker, cover, and cook on High for 2 hours

4. Serve hot.
Nutrition:
446 calories
21g fat
65g protein
25g Carbohydrates

689. Dill Chutney Salmon

Preparation Time: 5 minutes
Cooking Time: 3 minutes
Serving: 2
Ingredients:
Chutney:
- ¼ cup fresh dill
- ¼ cup extra virgin olive oil
- Juice from ½ lemon
- Sea salt, to taste
Fish:
- 2 cups water
- 2 salmon fillets
- Juice from ½ lemon
- ¼ teaspoon paprika
- Salt and freshly ground pepper to taste

Direction:
1. Pulse all the chutney ingredients in a food processor until creamy. Set aside.

2. Add the water and steamer basket to the Instant Pot. Place salmon fillets, skin-side down, on the steamer basket. Drizzle the lemon juice over salmon and sprinkle with the paprika.

3. Secure the lid. Select the Manual mode and set the cooking time for 3 minutes at High Pressure.

4. Once cooking is complete, do a quick pressure release. Carefully open the lid.

5. Season the fillets with pepper and salt to taste. Serve topped with the dill chutney.

Nutrition
636 calories
41g fat
65g protein
45g Carbohydrates

690. Garlic-Butter Parmesan Salmon and Asparagus

Preparation Time: 10 minutes
Cooking Time: 15 minutes
Serving: 2
Ingredients:
- 2 (6-ounce / 170-g) salmon fillets, skin on and patted dry
- Pink Himalayan salt
- Freshly ground black pepper, to taste
- 1 pound (454 g) fresh asparagus, ends snapped off
- 3 tablespoons almond butter
- 2 garlic cloves, minced
- ¼ cup grated Parmesan cheese

Direction:
1. Prep oven to 400°F (205°C). Line a baking sheet with aluminum foil.

2. Season both sides of the salmon fillets.

3. Situate salmon in the middle of the baking sheet and arrange the asparagus around the salmon.

4. Heat the almond butter in a small saucepan over medium heat.

5. Cook minced garlic

6. Drizzle the garlic-butter sauce over the salmon and asparagus and scatter the Parmesan cheese on top.

7. Bake in the preheated oven for about 12 minutes. You can switch the oven to broil at the end of cooking time for about 3 minutes to get a nice char on the asparagus.
8. Let cool for 5 minutes before serving.
Nutrition:
435 calories
26g fat
42g protein
68g Carbohydrates

691. Lemon Rosemary Roasted Branzino

Preparation Time: 15 minutes
Cooking Time: 30 minutes
Serving: 2
Ingredients:
- 4 tablespoons extra-virgin olive oil, divided
- 2 (8-ounce) Branzino fillets
- 1 garlic clove, minced
- 1 bunch scallions
- 10 to 12 small cherry tomatoes, halved
- 1 large carrot, cut into ¼-inch rounds
- ½ cup dry white wine
- 2 tablespoons paprika
- 2 teaspoons kosher salt
- ½ tablespoon ground chili pepper
- 2 rosemary sprigs or 1 tablespoon dried rosemary
- 1 small lemon, thinly sliced
- ½ cup sliced pitted kalamata olives
Direction:
1. Heat a large ovenproof skillet over high heat until hot, about 2 minutes. Add 1 tablespoon of olive oil and heat
2. Add the Branzino fillets, skin-side up, and sear for 2 minutes. Flip the fillets and cook. Set aside.
3. Swirl 2 tablespoons of olive oil around the skillet to coat evenly.
4. Add the garlic, scallions, tomatoes, and carrot, and sauté for 5 minutes
5. Add the wine, stirring until all ingredients are well combined. Carefully place the fish over the sauce.
6. Preheat the oven to 450ºF (235ºC).
7. Brush the fillets with the remaining 1 tablespoon of olive oil and season with paprika, salt, and chili pepper. Top each fillet with a rosemary sprig and lemon slices. Scatter the olives over fish and around the skillet.
8. Roast for about 10 minutes until the lemon slices are browned. Serve hot.
Nutrition:
724 calories
43g fat
57g protein
24g Carbohydrates

692. Grilled Lemon Pesto Salmon

Preparation Time: 5 minutes
Cooking Time: 10 minutes
Serving: 2
Ingredients:
- 10 ounces (283 g) salmon fillet
- 2 tablespoons prepared pesto sauce
- 1 large fresh lemon, sliced
- Cooking spray
Direction:
1. Preheat the grill to medium-high heat. Spray the grill grates with cooking spray.
2. Season the salmon well. Spread the pesto sauce on top.
3. Make a bed of fresh lemon slices about the same size as the salmon fillet on the hot grill, and place the salmon on

top of the lemon slices. Put any additional lemon slices on top of the salmon.
4. Grill the salmon for 10 minutes.
5. Serve hot.
Nutrition:
316 calories
21g fat
29g protein
26g Carbohydrates

693. Steamed Trout with Lemon Herb Crust

Preparation Time: 10 minutes
Cooking Time: 15 minutes
Serving: 2
Ingredients:
- 3 tablespoons olive oil
- 3 garlic cloves, chopped
- 2 tablespoons fresh lemon juice
- 1 tablespoon chopped fresh mint
- 1 tablespoon chopped fresh parsley
- ¼ teaspoon dried ground thyme
- 1 teaspoon sea salt
- 1 pound (454 g) fresh trout (2 pieces)
- 2 cups fish stock
Direction:
1. Blend olive oil, garlic, lemon juice, mint, parsley, thyme, and salt. Brush the marinade onto the fish.
2. Insert a trivet in the Instant Pot. Fill in the fish stock and place the fish on the trivet.
3. Secure the lid. Select the Steam mode and set the cooking time for 15 minutes at High Pressure.
4. Once cooking is complete, do a quick pressure release. Carefully open the lid. Serve warm.
Nutrition:
477 calories
30g fat
52g protein
27g Carbohydrates

694. Roasted Trout Stuffed with Veggies

Preparation Time: 10 minutes
Cooking Time: 25 minutes
Serving: 2
Ingredient:
- 2 (8-ounce) whole trout fillets
- 1 tablespoon extra-virgin olive oil
- ¼ teaspoon salt
- 1/8 teaspoon black pepper
- 1 small onion, thinly sliced
- ½ red bell pepper
- 1 poblano pepper
- 2 or 3 shiitake mushrooms, sliced
- 1 lemon, sliced
Direction:
1. Set oven to 425ºF (220ºC). Coat baking sheet with nonstick cooking spray.
2. Rub both trout fillets, inside and out, with the olive oil. Season with salt and pepper.
3. Mix together the onion, bell pepper, poblano pepper, and mushrooms in a large bowl. Stuff half of this mix into the cavity of each fillet. Top the mixture with 2 or 3 lemon slices inside each fillet.
4. Place the fish on the prepared baking sheet side by side. Roast in the preheated oven for 25 minutes
5. Pullout from the oven and serve on a plate.

Nutrition:
453 calories
22g fat
49g protein
35g Carbohydrates

695. Lemony Trout with Caramelized Shallots

Preparation Time: 10 minutes
Cooking Time: 20 minutes
Serving: 2
Ingredients:
Shallots:
- 1 teaspoon almond butter
- 2 shallots, thinly sliced
- Dash salt
Trout:
- 1 tablespoon almond butter
- 2 (4-ounce / 113-g) trout fillets
- 3 tablespoons capers
- ¼ cup freshly squeezed lemon juice
- ¼ teaspoon salt
- Dash freshly ground black pepper
- 1 lemon, thinly sliced
Direction:
For Shallots
1. Situate skillet over medium heat, cook the butter, shallots, and salt for 20 minutes, stirring every 5 minutes.
For Trout
2. Meanwhile, in another large skillet over medium heat, heat 1 teaspoon of almond butter.
3. Add the trout fillets and cook each side for 3 minutes, or until flaky. Transfer to a plate and set aside.
4. In the skillet used for the trout, stir in the capers, lemon juice, salt, and pepper, then bring to a simmer. Whisk in the remaining 1 tablespoon of almond butter. Spoon the sauce over the fish.
5. Garnish the fish with the lemon slices and caramelized shallots before serving.
Nutrition:
344 calories
18g fat
21g protein
37g Carbohydrates

696. Easy Tomato Tuna Melts

Preparation Time: 5 minutes
Cooking Time: 4 minutes
Serving: 2
Ingredients:
- 1 (5-oz) can chunk light tuna packed in water
- 2 tablespoons plain Greek yogurt
- 2 tablespoons finely chopped celery
- 1 tablespoon finely chopped red onion
- 2 teaspoons freshly squeezed lemon juice
- 1 large tomato, cut into ¾-inch-thick rounds
- ½ cup shredded Cheddar cheese
Direction:
1. Preheat the broiler to High.
2. Stir together the tuna, yogurt, celery, red onion, lemon juice, and cayenne pepper in a medium bowl.
3. Place the tomato rounds on a baking sheet. Top each with some tuna salad and Cheddar cheese.
4. Broil for 3 to 4 minutes until the cheese is melted and bubbly. Cool for 5 minutes before serving.
Nutrition:

244 calories
10g fat
30g protein
26g Carbohydrates

697. Mackerel and Green Bean Salad

Preparation Time: 10 minutes
Cooking Time: 10 minutes
Serving: 2
Ingredients:
- 2 cups green beans
- 1 tablespoon avocado oil
- 2 mackerel fillets
- 4 cups mixed salad greens
- 2 hard-boiled eggs, sliced
- 1 avocado, sliced
- 2 tablespoons lemon juice
- 2 tablespoons olive oil
- 1 teaspoon Dijon mustard
- Salt and black pepper, to taste
Direction:
1. Cook the green beans in pot of boiling water for about 3 minutes. Drain and set aside.
2. Melt the avocado oil in a pan over medium heat. Add the mackerel fillets and cook each side for 4 minutes.
3. Divide the greens between two salad bowls. Top with the mackerel, sliced egg, and avocado slices.
4. Scourge lemon juice, olive oil, mustard, salt, and pepper, and drizzle over the salad. Add the cooked green beans and toss to combine, then serve.
Nutrition:
737 calories
57g fat
34g protein
45g Carbohydrates

698. Hazelnut Crusted Sea Bass

Preparation Time: 10 minutes
Cooking Time: 15 minutes
Serving: 2
Ingredients:
- 2 tablespoons almond butter
- 2 sea bass fillets
- 1/3 cup roasted hazelnuts
- A pinch of cayenne pepper
Direction
1. Ready oven to 425°F (220°C). Line a baking dish with waxed paper.
2. Brush the almond butter over the fillets.
3. Pulse the hazelnuts and cayenne in a food processor. Coat the sea bass with the hazelnut mixture, then transfer to the baking dish.
4. Bake in the preheated oven for about 15 minutes. Cool for 5 minutes before serving.
Nutrition:
468 calories
31g fat
40g protein
38g Carbohydrates

699. Shrimp and Pea Paella

Difficulty: Novice level
Preparation Time: 20 minutes
Cooking Time: 60 minutes
Serving: 2
Size/ Portion: 4 ounces
Ingredients:
- 2 tablespoons olive oil

- 1 garlic clove, minced
- ½ large onion, minced
- 1 cup diced tomato
- ½ cup short-grain rice
- ½ teaspoon sweet paprika
- ½ cup dry white wine
- 1¼ cups low-sodium chicken stock
- 8 ounces (227 g) large raw shrimp
- 1 cup frozen peas
- ¼ cup jarred roasted red peppers

Direction

1. Heat the olive oil in a large skillet over medium-high heat.
2. Add the garlic and onion and sauté for 3 minutes, or until the onion is softened.
3. Add the tomato, rice, and paprika and stir for 3 minutes to toast the rice.
4. Add the wine and chicken stock and stir to combine. Bring the mixture to a boil.
5. Cover and set heat to medium-low, and simmer for 45 minutes
6. Add the shrimp, peas, and roasted red peppers. Cover and cook for an additional 5 minutes. Season with salt to taste and serve.

Nutrition:

646 calories

27g fat

42g protein

41g Carbohydrates

700. Garlic Shrimp with Arugula Pesto

Preparation Time: 20 minutes

Cooking Time: 5 minutes

Serving: 2

Ingredients:

- 3 cups lightly packed arugula
- ½ cup lightly packed basil leaves
- ¼ cup walnuts
- 3 tablespoons olive oil
- 3 medium garlic cloves
- 2 tablespoons grated Parmesan cheese
- 1 tablespoon freshly squeezed lemon juice
- 1 (10-ounce) package zucchini noodles
- 8 ounces (227 g) cooked, shelled shrimp
- 2 Roma tomatoes, diced

Direction

1. Process the arugula, basil, walnuts, olive oil, garlic, Parmesan cheese, and lemon juice in a food processor until smooth, scraping down the sides as needed. Season
2. Heat a skillet over medium heat. Add the pesto, zucchini noodles, and cooked shrimp. Toss to combine the sauce over the noodles and shrimp, and cook until heated through.
3. Season well. Serve topped with the diced tomatoes.

Nutrition:

435 calories

30.2g fat

33g protein

38g Carbohydrates

701. Baked Oysters with Vegetables

Preparation Time: 30 minutes

Cooking Time: 17 minutes

Serving: 2

Ingredients:

- 2 cups coarse salt, for holding the oysters
- 1 dozen fresh oysters, scrubbed
- 1 tablespoon almond butter

- ¼ cup finely chopped scallions
- ½ cup finely chopped artichoke hearts
- ¼ cup finely chopped red bell pepper
- 1 garlic clove, minced
- 1 tablespoon finely chopped fresh parsley
- Zest and juice of ½ lemon

Direction:

1. Pour the salt into a baking dish and spread to fill the bottom of the dish evenly.
2. Using a shucking knife, insert the blade at the joint of the shell, where it hinges open and shut. Firmly apply pressure to pop the blade in, and work the knife around the shell to open. Discard the empty half of the shell. Using the knife, gently loosen the oyster, and remove any shell particles. Sprinkle salt in the oysters
3. Set oven to 425°F (220°C).
4. Heat the almond butter in a large skillet over medium heat. Add the scallions, artichoke hearts, and bell pepper, and cook for 5 to 7 minutes. Cook garlic
5. Takeout from the heat and stir in the parsley, lemon zest and juice, and season to taste with salt and pepper.
6. Divide the vegetable mixture evenly among the oysters. Bake in the preheated oven for 10 to 12 minutes.

Nutrition:

135 calories

7g fat

6g protein

7g Carbohydrates

702. Grilled Whole Sea Bass

Preparation Time: 5 minutes

Cooking Time: 15 minutes

Serving: 2

Ingredients:

- 1 (1-pound) whole lavraki
- ¼ cup extra-virgin olive oil
- 1 bunch fresh thyme
- ¼ cup chopped fresh parsley
- 2 teaspoons minced garlic
- 1 small lemon, cut into ¼-inch rounds

Direction:

1. Preheat a grill to high heat.
2. Rub the olive oil all over the fish's surface and in its middle cavity.
3. Season liberally with salt and pepper.
4. Stuff the inner cavity with the thyme, parsley, garlic, and lemon slices.
5. Set the lavraki on the grill (see Cooking tip). Cook for 6 minutes per side.
6. Remove the head, backbone, and tail. Carve 2 fillets from each side for serving.

Nutrition:

480 Calories

34g Fat

43g Protein

28g Carbohydrates

703. Pan-Cooked Fish with Tomatoes

Preparation Time: 20 minutes

Cooking Time: 45 minutes

Serving: 8

Ingredients:

- 1½ cups extra-virgin olive oil
- 1½ cups tomato juice
- 2 (12-ounce) cans organic tomato paste
- 2 teaspoons sea salt
- 2 teaspoons cane sugar

- 1 teaspoon black pepper
- 1 teaspoon dried Greek oregano
- 3 pounds fresh white fish fillets
- 2 large sweet onions
- 1 cup white wine
- 1½ cups bread crumbs
- 4 garlic cloves
- ½ cup fresh parsley
- 4 large, firm tomatoes

Direction
1. Preheat the oven to 325°F.
2. Blend olive oil, tomato juice, tomato paste, salt, sugar, pepper, and oregano. Rub small amount of the mixture onto the bottom of 9-by-13-inch roasting pan.
3. Lay the fresh fish fillets side by side on top of the tomato mixture.
4. Cover with the onion slices, overlapping them.
5. Sprinkle the wine evenly over each piece of fish.
6. Pour half of the tomato and olive oil mixture over the fish.
7. Blend bread crumbs, garlic, and parsley. Spread over the fish.
8. Lay the tomato slices, overlapping them, over the fish. Drizzle remaining tomato mixture over the top.
9. Bake for 40 to 45 minutes.
Nutrition:
908 Calories
55g Fat
51g Protein
68g Carbohydrates

704. Tuna Tacos

Preparation time: 15 minutes
Cooking time: 0 minutes
Servings: 4
Ingredients:
- 4 pitas
- 7 oz tuna, canned
- ½ teaspoon cayenne pepper
- ¼ cup corn kernels, cooked
- 3 tablespoons plain yogurt

Direction:
1. Shred the canned tuna and mix it with cayenne pepper, corn kernels, and plain yogurt.
2. Then fill the pittas with tuna mixture and roll into tacos.
Nutrition:
per serving: 274 calories, 19.6g protein, 36.2g carbohydrates, 5g fat, 1.6g fiber, 16mg cholesterol, 356mg sodium, 295mg potassium.

705. Thyme Seabass

Preparation time: 15 minutes
Cooking time: 12 minutes
Servings: 2
Ingredients:
- 1-pound seabass
- 1 tablespoon ground thyme
- 3 tablespoons olive oil
- 1 tablespoon lemon juice

Direction:
1. Peel and trim the seabass.
2. Then rub the fish with olive oil, lemon juice, and ground thyme.
3. Grill the seabass at 400F for 6 minutes per side.
Nutrition:

per serving: 301 calories, 0.2g protein, 4g carbohydrates, 24.2g fat, 0.5g fiber, 0mg cholesterol, 227mg sodium, 20mg potassium.

706. Salmon Skewers

Preparation time: 10 minutes
Cooking time: 6 minutes
Servings: 4
Ingredients:
- 12 oz salmon fillet, cubed
- 1 teaspoon plain yogurt
- 1 teaspoon ground coriander
- 1 teaspoon olive oil
- ½ teaspoon salt

Direction:
1. In the shallow bowl mix salt, olive oil, ground coriander, and plain yogurt.
2. Then mix plain yogurt mixture with salmon fillet cubes.
3. String the salmon cubes in the skewers and grill at 385F for 3 minutes per side.
Nutrition:
per serving: 123 calories, 16.6g protein, 0.1g carbohydrates, 6.4g fat, 0g fiber, 38mg cholesterol, 329mg sodium, 330mg potassium.

707. Lemon Squid Rings

Preparation time: 10 minutes
Cooking time: 7 minutes
Servings: 4
Ingredients:
- 1-pound squid, sliced
- 1 teaspoon garlic powder
- 1 tablespoon olive oil
- ½ teaspoon lemon zest, grated

Direction:
1. Melt olive oil in the skillet.
2. Add lemon zest and garlic powder.
3. Bring the liquid to boil.
4. Add sliced squid and cook it for 7 minutes.
Nutrition:
per serving: 138 calories,17.8g protein, 4.1g carbohydrates, 5.1g fat, 0.1g fiber, 265mg cholesterol, 51mg sodium, 289mg potassium.

708. Paprika Swordfish

Preparation time: 10 minutes
Cooking time: 10 minutes
Servings: 2
Ingredients:
- 2 swordfish fillets
- 1 teaspoon smoked paprika
- ½ teaspoon salt
- 1 tablespoon avocado oil

Direction:
1. Sprinkle the fish fillet with smoked paprika and salt from each side.
2. Preheat the avocado oil well and put the swordfish fillets in it.
3. Fry the fillets for 4 minutes per side or until they are light brown.
Nutrition: per serving: 177 calories, 27.2g protein, 1g carbohydrates, 6.5g fat, 0.7g fiber, 53mg cholesterol, 704mg sodium, 438mg potassium.

709. Coriander Shrimps

Preparation time: 10 minutes
Cooking time: 5 minute
Servings: 3
Ingredients:
- 1 teaspoon ground coriander
- 1-pound shrimps, peeled
- Cooking spray

Direction:
1. Mix shrimps with ground coriander and transfer in the skillet. Spray them with cooking spray.
2. Cook the shrimps for 2 minutes and them flip on another side.
3. Cook the shrimps for 1 minute more.
Nutrition:
per serving: 180 calories, 34.4g protein, 2.3g carbohydrates, 2.6g fat, 0g fiber, 318mg cholesterol, 369mg sodium, 257mg potassium.

710. Salmon Herbs de Province

Preparation time: 15 minutes
Cooking time: 40 minutes
Servings: 2
Ingredients:
- 15 oz salmon fillet
- 1 tablespoon herbs de province
- 2 tablespoons avocado oil
- ½ teaspoon salt

Direction:
1. Rub the salmon with salt and herbs de province. Leave the fish for 10 minutes to marinate.
2. Then brush it with avocado oil and wrap in the foil.
3. Bake the salmon for 40 minutes at 375F.
Nutrition:
per serving: 150 calories, 20.7g protein, 0.4g carbohydrates, 7.5g fat, 0.3g fiber, 47mg cholesterol, 338mg sodium, 430mg potassium.

711. Tilapia Under Cheese Blanket

Preparation time: 10 minutes
Cooking time: 18 minutes
Servings: 2
Ingredients:
- 10 oz tilapia fillet
- 2 tablespoons pesto sauce
- 2 oz Cheddar cheese, shredded

Direction:
1. Brush the fish with pesto sauce and put it in the tray.
2. Top it with Cheddar cheese and bake in the preheated to 375F oven for 18 minutes.
Nutrition:
per serving: 298 calories, 34.9g protein, 1.4g carbohydrates, 17.2g fat, 0.3g fiber, 103mg cholesterol, 321mg sodium, 28mg potassium.

712. Salmon in Orange Marinade

Preparation time: 20 minutes
Cooking time: 4 minutes
Servings: 4
Ingredients:
- 16 oz salmon fillet, cubed
- ½ cup of orange juice
- 1 teaspoon liquid honey
- 1 tablespoon olive oil
- ½ teaspoon dried rosemary

Direction:
1. Mix orange juice with honey, olive oil, and dried rosemary.
2. Then put the salmon cubes in the orange marinade and marinate for 15 minutes in the fridge.
3. Then grill the fish at 400F for 2 minutes per side.
Nutrition:
per serving: 200 calories, 22.2g protein, 4.8g carbohydrates, 10.6g fat, 0.1g fiber, 50mg cholesterol, 50mg sodium, 500mg potassium.

713. Yogurt Tilapia

Preparation time: 10 minutes
Cooking time: 10 minutes
Servings: 3
Ingredients:
- 3 tilapia fillets
- 3 tablespoons yogurt
- 1 teaspoon ground black pepper

Direction:
1. Preheat yogurt in the skillet until shimmering.
2. Then sprinkle the tilapia fillets with ground black pepper and put in the hot butter.
3. Cook the fish for 5 minutes from each side on low heat.
4. Serve the fish with hot remaining butter.
Nutrition:
per serving: 197 calories, 21.2g protein, 0.5g carbohydrates, 12.6g fat, 0.2g fiber, 86mg cholesterol, 122mg sodium, 12mg potassium.

714. Cod with Pomegranate Sauce

Preparation time: 10 minutes
Cooking time: 15 minutes
Servings: 4
Ingredients:
- 1-pound cod fillet
- ½ cup pomegranate juice
- ½ teaspoon dried mint
- 1 teaspoon whole-grain flour
- ½ teaspoon chili powder
- 1 teaspoon olive oil

Direction:
1. Chop the cod fillet roughly and roast with olive oil for 2 minutes per side.
2. Then mix pomegranate juice with dried mint, flour, and chili powder.
3. Pour the liquid over the fish and close the lid.
4. Simmer the fish for 10 minutes on low heat.
Nutrition:
per serving: 123 calories, 20.4g protein, 5.3g carbohydrates, 2.3g fat, 0.2g fiber, 56mg cholesterol, 76mg sodium, 85mg potassium.

715. Stuffed Branzino

Preparation time: 15 minutes
Cooking time: 30 minutes
Servings: 3
Ingredients:
- 10 oz branzino, trimmed
- 3 oz red kidney beans, canned
- 1 tablespoon olive oil
- ¼ teaspoon sesame seeds
- ½ teaspoon white pepper
- ½ teaspoon ground turmeric

Direction:
1. Mix ground turmeric, white pepper, and sesame seeds.

2. Rub the fish with spices and brush with olive oil.
3. Then fill the fish with red kidney beans and secure with toothpicks.
4. Wrap the branzino in the foil and bake at 400F for 30 minutes.
Nutrition:
per serving: 231 calories, 24g protein, 17.9g carbohydrates, 7.1g fat, 4.5g fiber, 38mg cholesterol, 66mg sodium, 400mg potassium.

716. Sheet-Pan Seabass

Preparation time: 10 minutes
Cooking time: 40 minutes
Servings: 3
Ingredients:
- 8 oz seabass, trimmed, chopped
- 1 bell pepper, roughly chopped
- 1 tomato, chopped
- 1 teaspoon allspices
- 2 tablespoons olive oil

Direction:
1. Line the baking tray with baking paper.
2. Put fish, bell pepper, and tomato in the tray.
3. Sprinkle the ingredients with allspices and olive oil. Gently stir them.
4. Bake the meal at 375F for 40 minutes.
Nutrition:
per serving: 282 calories, 0.6g protein, 9.1g carbohydrates, 14.3g fat, 0.9g fiber, 0mg cholesterol, 363mg sodium, 130mg potassium.

717. Fish Puttanesca

Preparation time: 10 minutes
Cooking time: 20 minutes
Servings: 2
Ingredients:
- ½ teaspoon mustard
- 1 tablespoon olive oil
- 2 oz onion, diced
- ¼ teaspoon garlic powder
- 1 teaspoon tomato paste
- 3 kalamata olives, sliced
- 1 teaspoon fresh cilantro, chopped
- 8 oz tilapia fillet
- ¼ cup of water

Direction:
1. Heat the oil in the skillet and add fish fillets. Roast them for 3 minutes per side.
2. Remove the fillets from the skillet.
3. Add all remaining ingredients in the skillet and roast them for 10 minutes.
4. Then stir well and add fish.
5. Close the lid and cook the meal for 7 minutes more.
Nutrition:
per serving: 180 calories, 21.9g protein, 4.1g carbohydrates, 9g fat, 1.1g fiber, 55mg cholesterol, 102mg sodium, 79mg potassium.

718. Fish with Pecan Gravy

Preparation time: 15 minutes
Cooking time: 15 minutes
Servings: 4
Ingredients:
- 15 oz salmon fillet, chopped
- 3 pecans, grinded
- ½ cup cream cheese

- 1 teaspoon dried thyme
- ½ teaspoon dried sage
- ¼ cup Cheddar cheese, shredded

Direction:
1. Bring the cream cheese to boil and add thyme and sage.
2. Add grinded pecans and salmon.
3. Simmer the meal for 10 minutes on medium heat.
4. Then add cheddar cheese, gently stir the ingredients and close the lid.
5. Cook it for 5 minutes or until cheese is dissolved.
6. Serve the fish with cheese gravy.
Nutrition:
per serving: 175 calories, 15.9g protein, 1.8g carbohydrates, 12.1g fat, 0.8g fiber, 40mg cholesterol, 67mg sodium, 315mg potassium.

719. Tomato Fish

Preparation time: 10 minutes
Cooking time: 25 minutes
Servings: 2
Ingredients:
- 7 oz halibut, chopped
- ½ cup tomatoes, chopped
- ½ white onion, diced
- 1 tablespoon olive oil
- 1 tablespoon avocado oil

Direction:
1. Heat avocado oil in the skillet.
2. Add chopped halibut and cook it for 2 minutes per side on high heat.
3. Then add white onion, olive oil, and tomatoes.
4. Sauté fish for 15 minutes on medium heat.
Nutrition:
per serving: 197 calories, 23.8g protein, 4.7g carbohydrates, 9.8g fat, 1.4g fiber, 35mg cholesterol, 64mg sodium, 169mg potassium.

720. Stuffed Mackerel

Preparation time: 15 minutes
Cooking time: 30 minutes
Servings: 4
Ingredients:
- 1 tablespoon capers, drained
- 1-pound mackerel fillet
- ½ teaspoon smoked paprika
- 1 tablespoon lemon juice
- 1 tablespoon olive oil
- ½ teaspoon chili powder

Direction:
1. Place the capers on the mackerel fillet.
2. Then roll it and secure it with toothpicks.
3. Gently rub the stuffed fish with smoked paprika, lemon juice, olive oil, and chili powder.
4. Put the stuffed mackerel in the tray and bake at 375F for 30 minutes.
5. Then remove the toothpicks and slice the fish into servings.
Nutrition:
per serving: 330 calories, 27.2g protein, 0.5g carbohydrates, 23.8g fat, 0.3g fiber, 85mg cholesterol, 162mg sodium, 473mg potassium.

721. Baked Tuna with Feta

Preparation time: 10 minutes
Cooking time: 40 minutes
Servings: 6

Ingredients:

- 12 oz tuna fillet, roughly chopped
- 1 teaspoon allspices
- 1 tablespoon olive oil
- ½ teaspoon dried rosemary
- 5 oz Feta, crumbled

Direction:

1. Sprinkle the tuna fillet cubes with allspices, dried rosemary, and olive oil.
2. Then line the baking tray with baking paper and put the fish inside. Flatten it in one layer.
3. Top the tuna with crumbled Feta and cook at 365F for 40 minutes.

Nutrition:

per serving: 289 calories, 15.3g protein, 1.3g carbohydrates, 25g fat, 0.1g fiber, 21mg cholesterol, 264mg sodium, 19mg potassium.

722. Salmon and Pineapple Skewers

Preparation time: 15 minutes
Cooking time: 6 minutes
Servings: 6
Ingredients:

- 1-pound salmon, cubed
- 1 tablespoon plain yogurt
- 1 teaspoon ground thyme
- ½ teaspoon chili powder
- 6 oz pineapple, peeled, cubed

Direction:

1. In the mixing bowl, mix plain yogurt, ground thyme, and chili powder.
2. Then rub evert salmon cube in plain yogurt mixture.
3. After this, string the salmon and pineapples into the skewers and grill at 400F for 3 minutes per side or until the fish and pineapple are light brown.

Nutrition:

per serving: 117 calories, 15g protein, 4.1g carbohydrates, 4.8g fat, 0.5g fiber, 33mg cholesterol, 38mg sodium, 333mg potassium.

723. Za'atar Tilapia

Preparation time: 10 minutes
Cooking time: 9 minutes
Servings: 2
Ingredients:

- 8 oz tilapia fillet
- 1 teaspoon za'atar
- 1 garlic clove, diced
- 1 tablespoon olive oil

Direction:

1. Melt the olive oil in the skillet and add za'atar. Roast it for 1 minute and add diced garlic.
2. Cook the mixture for 20 seconds.
3. Remove za'atar and garlic from skillet.
4. Put the tilapia fillets in the fragrant olive oil and cook for 3 minutes from both sides.

Nutrition:

per serving: 154 calories, 121.2g protein, 0.5g carbohydrates, 7.8g fat, 0g fiber, 55mg cholesterol, 40mg sodium, 6mg potassium.

Chapter 10. Sauce, Dip, And Dressing Recipes

724. Simple Italian Dressing

Preparation Time: 5 Minutes
Cooking Time: 0 Minutes
Servings: 12
Ingredients:
- ½ cup extra-virgin olive oil
- ¼ cup red wine vinegar
- 1 teaspoon dried Italian seasoning
- 1 teaspoon Dijon mustard
- ¼ teaspoon salt
- ¼ teaspoon freshly ground black pepper
- 1 garlic clove, minced

Directions:
1. Place all the fixings in a mason jar then cover. Shake vigorously for 1 minute until completely mixed.
2. Store in the refrigerator for up to 1 week.
Nutrition: Calories: 80 Fat: 8.6g Protein: 0g Carbs: 0g Fiber: 0g Sodium: 51m

725. Ranch-Style Cauliflower Dressing

Preparation Time: 10 Minutes
Cooking Time: 0 Minutes
Servings: 8
Ingredients:
- 2 cups frozen cauliflower, thawed
- ½ cup unsweetened plain almond milk
- 2 tablespoons apple cider vinegar
- 2 tablespoons extra-virgin olive oil
- 1 garlic clove, peeled
- 2 teaspoons finely chopped fresh parsley
- 2 teaspoons finely chopped scallions (both white and green parts)
- 1 teaspoon finely chopped fresh dill
- ½ teaspoon onion powder
- ½ teaspoon Dijon mustard
- ½ teaspoon salt
- ¼ teaspoon freshly ground black pepper

Directions:
1. Place all the fixings in a blender then pulse until creamy and smooth.
2. Serve instantly, or handover to an airtight container to refrigerate for up to 3 days.
Nutrition: Calories: 41 Fat: 3.6g Protein: 1.0g Carbs: 1.9g Fiber: 1.1g Sodium: 148mg

726. Asian-Inspired Vinaigrette

Preparation Time: 5 Minutes
Cooking Time: 0 Minutes
Servings: 2
Ingredients:
- ¼ cup extra-virgin olive oil
- 3 tablespoons apple cider vinegar
- 1 garlic clove, minced
- 1 tablespoon peeled and grated fresh ginger
- 1 tablespoon chopped fresh cilantro
- 1 tablespoon freshly squeezed lime juice
- ½ teaspoon sriracha

Directions:
1. Add all the fixings in a small bowl then stir to mix well.
2. Serve immediately, or store covered in the refrigerator and shake before using.
Nutrition: Calories: 251 Fat: 26.8g Protein: 0g Carbs: 1.8g Fiber: 0.7g Sodium: 3mg

727. Parsley Vinaigrette

Preparation Time: 5 Minutes
Cooking Time: 0 Minutes
Servings: 2
Ingredients:
- ½ cup lightly packed fresh parsley, finely chopped
- 1/3 cup extra-virgin olive oil
- 3 tablespoons red wine vinegar
- 1 garlic clove, minced
- ¼ teaspoon salt, plus additional as needed

Directions:
1. Place all the fixings in a mason jar then cover. Shake vigorously for 1 minute until completely mixed.
2. Taste and add additional salt as needed.
3. Serve immediately or serve chilled.
Nutrition: Calories: 92 Fat: 10.9g Protein: 0g Carbs: 0gFiber: 0g Sodium: 75mg

728. Homemade Blackened Seasoning

Preparation Time: 10 Minutes
Cooking Time: 0 Minutes
Servings: 2
Ingredients:
- 2 tablespoons smoked paprika
- 2 tablespoons garlic powder
- 2 tablespoons onion powder
- 1 tablespoon sweet paprika
- 1 teaspoon dried dill
- 1 teaspoon freshly ground black pepper
- ½ teaspoon ground mustard
- ¼ teaspoon celery seeds

Directions:
1. Add all the fixings to a small bowl then mix well.
2. Serve instantly, or handover to an airtight container and store in a cool, dry and dark place for up to 3 months.
Nutrition: Calories: 22 Fat: 0.9g Protein: 1.0g Carbs: 4.7g Fiber: 1.0g Sodium: 2mg

729. Not Old Bay Seasoning

Preparation Time: 10 Minutes
Cooking Time: 0 Minutes
Servings: 2
Ingredients:
- 3 tablespoons sweet paprika
- 1 tablespoon mustard seeds
- 2 tablespoons celery seeds
- 2 teaspoons freshly ground black pepper
- 1½ teaspoons cayenne pepper
- 1 teaspoon red pepper flakes
- ½ teaspoon ground ginger
- ½ teaspoon ground nutmeg
- ½ teaspoon ground cinnamon
- ¼ teaspoon ground cloves

Directions:
1. Mix together all the ingredients in an airtight container until well combined.
2. You can store it in a cool, dry, and dark place for up to 3 months.
Nutrition: Calories: 26 Fat: 1.9g Protein: 1.1g Carbs: 3.6g Fiber: 2.1g Sodium: 3mg

730. Tzatziki

Preparation Time: 15 Minutes
Cooking Time: 0 Minutes
Servings: 6
Ingredients:
- ½ English cucumber, finely chopped
- 1 teaspoon salt, divided
- 1 cup plain Greek yogurt
- 8 tablespoons olive oil, divided
- 1 garlic clove, finely minced
- 1 to 2 tablespoons chopped fresh dill
- 1 teaspoon red wine vinegar
- ½ teaspoon freshly ground black pepper

Directions:
1. In a food processor, beat the cucumber until puréed. Place the cucumber on several layers of paper towels lining the bottom of a colander and sprinkle with ½ teaspoon of salt. Allow to drain for 10 to 15 minutes. Using your hands, squeeze out any remaining liquid.
2. In a medium bowl, whisk together the cucumber, yogurt, 6 tablespoons of olive oil, garlic, dill, vinegar, remaining ½ teaspoon of salt, and pepper until very smooth.
3. Drizzle with the residual 2 tablespoons of olive oil. Serve instantly or chill until ready to serve.
Nutrition: Calories: 286 Fat: 29.0g Protein: 3.0g Carbs: 5.0g Fiber: 0g Sodium: 615mg

731. Pineapple Salsa

Preparation Time: 10 Minutes
Cooking Time: 0 Minutes
Servings: 6
Ingredients:
- 1 pound (454 g) fresh or thawed frozen pineapple, finely diced, juices reserved
- 1 white or red onion, finely diced
- 1 bunch cilantro or mint, leaves only, chopped
- 1 jalapeño, minced (optional)
- Salt, to taste

Directions:
1. Stir together the pineapple with its juice, onion, cilantro, and jalapeño (if desired) in a medium bowl. Season with salt to taste and serve.
2. The salsa can be refrigerated in an airtight container for up to 2 days.
Nutrition: Calories: 55 Fat: 0.1g Protein: 0.9g Carbs: 12.7g Fiber: 1.8g Sodium: 20mg

732. Creamy Grapefruit and Tarragon Dressing

Preparation Time: 5 Minutes
Cooking Time: 0 Minutes
Servings: 6
Ingredients:
- ½ cup avocado oil mayonnaise
- 2 tablespoons Dijon mustard
- ½ teaspoon salt
- 1 teaspoon dried tarragon
- Zest and juice of ½ grapefruit
- ¼ teaspoon freshly ground black pepper
- 1 to 2 tablespoons water (optional)

Directions:
1. In a mason jar with lid, combine the mayonnaise, Dijon, tarragon, grapefruit zest and juice, salt, and pepper and whisk well with a fork until smooth and creamy. If a thinner dressing is preferred, thin out with water.

2. Serve instantly or chill until ready to serve.
Nutrition: Calories: 86 Fat: 7.0g Protein: 1.0g Carbs: 6.0g Fiber: 0g Sodium: 390mg

733. Ginger Teriyaki Sauce

Preparation Time: 5 Minutes
Cooking Time: 0 Minutes
Servings: 2
Ingredients:
- ¼ cup pineapple juice
- ¼ cup low-sodium soy sauce
- 2 tablespoons packed coconut sugar
- 1 tablespoon grated fresh ginger
- 1 tablespoon arrowroot powder or cornstarch
- 1 teaspoon garlic powder

Directions:
1. Whisk the pineapple juice, soy sauce, coconut sugar, ginger, arrowroot powder, and garlic powder together in a small bowl.
2. Stock in a wrapped vessel in the fridge for up to 5 days.
Nutrition: Calories: 37 Fat: 0.1g Protein: 1.1g Carbs: 12.0g Fiber: 0g Sodium: 881mg

734. Hot Pepper Sauce

Preparation Time: 10 Minutes
Cooking Time: 20 Minutes
Servings: 8
Ingredients:
- 2 red hot fresh chiles, deseeded
- 2 dried chiles
- 2 garlic cloves, peeled
- ½ small yellow onion, roughly chopped
- 2 cups water
- 2 cups white vinegar

Directions:
1. Place all the fixings excluding the vinegar in a medium saucepan over medium heat. Allow to simmer for 20 minutes until softened.
2. Transfer the mixture to a food processor or blender. Stir in the vinegar and pulse until very smooth.
3. Serve immediately or transfer to a sealed container and refrigerate for up to 3 months.
Nutrition: Calories: 20 Fat: 1.2g Protein: 0.6g Carbs: 4.4g Fiber: 0.6g Sodium: 12mg

735. Lemon-Tahini Sauce

Preparation Time: 10 Minutes
Cooking Time: 0 Minutes
Servings: 4
Ingredients:
- 1/2 cup tahini
- 1 garlic clove, minced
- Juice and zest of 1 lemon
- ½ teaspoon salt, plus more as needed
- ½ cup warm water, plus more as needed

Directions:
1. Combine the tahini and garlic in a small bowl.
2. Add the lemon juice and zest and salt to the bowl and stir to mix well.
3. Fold in the warm water and whisk until well combined and creamy. Feel free to add more warm water if you like a thinner consistency.
4. Taste and add additional salt as needed.
5. Stock the sauce in a sealed container in the fridge for up to 5 days.
Nutrition: Calories: 179 Fat: 15.5g Protein: 5.1g Carbs: 6.8g Fiber: 3.0g Sodium: 324mg

736. Peri-Peri Sauce

Preparation Time: 10 Minutes
Cooking Time: 5 Minutes
Servings: 4
Ingredients:
- 1 tomato, chopped
- 1 red onion, chopped
- 1 red bell pepper, deseeded and chopped
- 1 red chile, deseeded and chopped
- 4 garlic cloves, minced
- 2 tablespoons extra-virgin olive oil
- Juice of 1 lemon
- 1 tablespoon dried oregano
- 1 tablespoon smoked paprika
- 1 Teaspoon Sea Salt

Directions:
1. Process all the fixings in a food processor or a blender until smooth.
2. Transfer the mixture to a small saucepan over medium-high heat and bring to a boil, stirring often.
3. Reduce the heat to medium and allow to simmer for 5 minutes until heated through.
4. You can store the sauce in an airtight container in the refrigerator for up to 5 days.
Nutrition: Calories: 98 Fat: 6.5g Protein: 1.0g Carbs: 7.8g Fiber: 3.0g Sodium: 295mg

737. Peanut Sauce with Honey

Preparation Time: 5 Minutes
Cooking Time: 0 Minutes
Servings: 4
Ingredients:
- ¼ cup peanut butter
- 1 tablespoon peeled and grated fresh ginger
- 1 tablespoon honey
- 1 tablespoon low-sodium soy sauce
- 1 garlic clove, minced
- Juice of 1 lime
- Pinch red pepper flakes

Directions:
1. Whisk all the fixings in a small bowl until well incorporated.
2. Transfer to an airtight container and refrigerate for up to 5 days.
Nutrition: Calories: 117 Fat: 7.6g Protein: 4.1g Carbs: 8.8g Fiber: 1.0g Sodium: 136mg

738. Cilantro-Tomato Salsa

Preparation Time: 10 Minutes
Cooking Time: 0 Minutes
Servings: 6
Ingredients:
- 2 or 3 medium, ripe tomatoes, diced
- 1 serrano pepper, seeded and minced
- ½ red onion, minced
- ¼ cup minced fresh cilantro
- Juice of 1 lime
- ¼ teaspoon salt, plus more as needed

Direction:
1. Place the tomatoes, serrano pepper, onion, cilantro, lime juice, and salt in a small bowl and mix well.
2. Taste and add additional salt, if needed.
3. Store in a sealed vessel in the refrigerator for up to 3 days.
Nutrition: Calories: 17 Fat: 0g Protein: 1.0g Carbs: 3.9g Fiber: 1.0g Sodium: 83mg

739. Cheesy Pea Pesto

Preparation Time: 5 Minutes
Cooking Time: 0 Minutes
Servings: 4
Ingredients:
- ½ cup fresh green peas
- ½ cup grated Parmesan cheese
- ¼ cup extra-virgin olive oil
- ¼ cup pine nuts
- ¼ cup fresh basil leaves
- 2 garlic cloves, minced
- ¼ teaspoon sea salt

Directions:
1. Add all the fixings to a food processor or blender then pulse until the nuts are chopped finely.
2. Transfer to an airtight container and refrigerate for up to 2 days. You can also store it in ice cube trays in the freezer for up to 6 months.
Nutrition: Calories: 247 Fat: 22.8g Protein: 7.1g Carbs: 4.8g Fiber: 1.0g Sodium: 337mg

740. Guacamole

Preparation Time: 10 Minutes
Cooking Time: 0 Minutes
Servings: 6
Ingredients:
- 2 large avocados
- ¼ white onion, finely diced
- 1 small, firm tomato, finely diced
- ¼ cup finely chopped fresh cilantro
- 2 tablespoons freshly squeezed lime juice
- ¼ teaspoon salt
- Freshly ground black pepper, to taste

Directions:
1. Slice the avocados in half and take away the pits. Using a large spoon to scoop out the flesh and add to a medium bowl.
2. Mash the avocado flesh with the back of a fork, or until a uniform consistency is achieved. Add the onion, tomato, cilantro, lime juice, salt, and pepper to the bowl and stir to combine.
3. Serve instantly, or transfer to a sealed vessel and refrigerate until chilled.
Nutrition: Calories: 81 Fat: 6.8g Protein: 1.1g Carbs: 5.7g Fiber: 3.0g Sodium: 83mg

741. Lentil-Tahini Dip

Preparation Time: 10 Minutes
Cooking Time: 15 Minutes
Servings: 8
Ingredients:
- 1 cup dried green or brown lentils, rinsed
- 2½ cups water, divided
- 1/3 cup tahini
- 1 garlic clove
- ½ teaspoon salt, plus more as needed

Directions:
1. Add the lentils in addition 2 cups of water to a medium saucepan and bring to a boil over high heat.
2. Once it twitches to boil, lessen the heat to low, and then cook for 14 minutes, stirring occasionally, or the lentils become tender but still hold their shape. You can drain any excess liquid.
3. Transfer the lentils to a food processor, along with the remaining water, tahini, garlic, and salt and process until smooth and creamy.

4. Taste and adjust the seasoning if needed. Serve immediately.
Nutrition: Calories: 100 Fat: 3.9g Protein: 5.1g Carbs: 10.7g Fiber: 6.0g Sodium: 106mg

742. Lemon-Dill Cashew Dip

Preparation Time: 10 Minutes
Cooking Time: 0 Minutes
Servings: 4
Ingredients:
- ¾ cup cashews, saturated in water for at minimum 4 hours and drained well
- ¼ cup water
- Juice and zest of 1 lemon
- 2 tablespoons chopped fresh dill
- ¼ teaspoon salt, plus more as needed
Directions:
1. Put the cashews, water, lemon juice and zest in a blender and blend until smooth.
2. Add the dill and salt to the blender and blend again.
3. Taste and adjust the seasoning, if needed.
4. Transfer to an airtight container and refrigerate for at least 1 hour to blend the flavors.
5. Serve chilled.
Nutrition: Calories: 37 Fat: 2.9g Protein: 1.1g Carbs: 1.9g Fiber: 0g Sodium: 36mg

743. Creamy Cucumber Dip

Preparation Time: 10 Minutes
Cooking Time: 0 Minutes
Servings: 6
Ingredients:
- 1 medium cucumber, peeled and grated
- ¼ teaspoon salt
- 1 cup plain Greek yogurt
- 2 garlic cloves, minced
- 1 tablespoon extra-virgin olive oil
- 1 tablespoon freshly squeezed lemon juice
- ¼ teaspoon freshly ground black pepper
Directions:
1. Put the grated cucumber in a colander set over a bowl and season with salt. Allow the cucumber to stand for 10 minutes. Using your hands, squeeze out as much liquid from the cucumber as possible. Transfer the grated cucumber to a medium bowl.
2. Add the yogurt, garlic, olive oil, lemon juice, and pepper to the bowl and stir until well blended.
3. Conceal the bowl with plastic wrap and refrigerate for at least 2 hours to blend the flavors.
4. Serve chilled.
Nutrition: Calories: 47 Fat: 2.8g Protein: 4.2g Carbs: 2.7g Fiber: 0g Sodium: 103mg

744. Basic Tahini Sauce

Preparation time: 5 minutes
Cooking time: 0 minutes
Serving: 1¼ cups
Ingredients:
- ½ cup tahini
- ½ cup water
- ¼ cup lemon juice
- 2 garlic cloves, minced
- Salt and pepper, to taste
Direction:
1. Whisk tahini, water, lemon juice, and garlic together in bowl until combined. Season with salt and pepper to taste.

Let sit until flavors meld, about 30 minutes. (Sauce can be refrigerated for up to 4 days.)
Nutrition: Calories: 755 Fat: 64.83g Protein: 21.67g Carbs: 36.08g Fiber: 12.3g Sodium: 316mg

745. Tahini-Greek Yogurt Sauce

Preparation time: 5 minutes
Cooking time: 0 minutes
Serving: 1 cup
Ingredients:
- 1/3 cup tahini
- 1/3 cup plain Greek yogurt
- ¼ cup water
- 3 tablespoons lemon juice
- 1 garlic clove, minced
- Salt and pepper, to taste
Direction:
1. Whisk tahini, yogurt, water, lemon juice, garlic, and ¾ teaspoon salt together in bowl until combined. Season with salt and pepper to taste. Let sit until flavors meld, about 30 minutes. (Sauce can be refrigerated for up to 4 days.)
Nutrition: Calories: 1462 Fat: 129.29g Protein: 41.82g Carbs: 59.47g Fiber: 23.4g Sodium: 452mg

746. Cilantro Yogurt Sauce

Preparation time: 5 minutes
Cooking time: 0 minutes
Serving: 1 cup
Ingredients:
- 1 cup plain yogurt
- 2 tablespoons minced fresh cilantro
- 2 tablespoons minced fresh mint
- 1 garlic clove, minced
- Salt and pepper, to taste
Direction:
1. Whisk yogurt, cilantro, mint, and garlic together in bowl until combined. Season with salt and pepper to taste. Let sit until flavors meld, about 30 minutes. (Sauce can be refrigerated for up to 2 days.)
Nutrition: Calories: 173 Fat: 8.13g Protein: 9.41g Carbs: 16.94g Fiber: 1g Sodium: 288mg

747. Minty Lemon-Yogurt Sauce

Preparation time: 5 minutes
Cooking time: 0 minutes
Serving: 1 cup
Ingredients:
- 1 cup plain yogurt
- 1 tablespoon minced fresh mint
- 1 teaspoon grated lemon zest plus 2 tablespoons juice
- 1 garlic clove, minced
- Salt and pepper, to taste
Direction:
1. Whisk yogurt, mint, lemon zest and juice, and garlic together in bowl until combined. Season with salt and pepper to taste. Let sit until flavors meld, about 30 minutes. (Sauce can be refrigerated for up to 2 days.)
Nutrition: Calories: 174 Fat: 8.14g Protein: 9.38g Carbs: 17.22g Fiber: 1g Sodium: 287mg

748. Cucumber-Dill Yogurt Sauce

Preparation time: 10 minutes
Cooking time: 0 minutes
Serving: 2½ cups
Ingredients:
- 1 cup plain Greek yogurt
- 2 tablespoons extra-virgin olive oil

- 2 tablespoons minced fresh dill
- 1 garlic clove, minced
- 1 cucumber, peeled, halved lengthwise, seeded, and shredded
- Salt and pepper, to taste

Direction:

1. Whisk yogurt, oil, dill, and garlic together in medium bowl until combined. Stir in cucumber and season with salt and pepper to taste. (Sauce can be refrigerated for up to 1 day.)

Nutrition: Calories: 98 Fat: 7.2g Protein: 2.13g Carbs: 8.54g Fiber: 2.6g Sodium: 210mg

749. Napoli Sauce

Preparation time: 10 minutes
Cooking time: 30 minutes
Serving: 4
Ingredients:

- 1-pound (454 g) mushrooms
- 2 cups canned tomatoes, diced
- 1 carrot, chopped
- 1 onion, chopped
- 1 celery stick, chopped
- 1 tablespoon olive oil
- 1 teaspoon salt
- ½ teaspoon paprika
- 1 teaspoon fish sauce
- 1 cup water

Direction:

1. Heat olive oil on Sauté. Stir-fry carrot, onion, celery, and paprika, for 5 minutes. Add all remaining ingredients, except for the tomatoes, and cook for 5-6 more minutes, until the meat is slightly browned. Seal the lid.

2. Cook on High Pressure for 20 minutes. When done, release the steam naturally, for about 10 minutes. Hit Sauté, and cook for 7-8 minutes, to thicken the sauce.

Nutrition: Calories: 402 Fat: 4.79g Protein: 12.26g Carbs: 93.36g Fiber: 15.3g Sodium: 751mg

750. Classic Tzatziki Sauce

Preparation time: 10 minutes
Cooking time: 0 minutes
Serving: 2
Ingredients:

- 1 medium cucumber, peeled, seeded and diced
- ½ teaspoon salt, divided, plus more
- ½ cup plain, unsweetened, full-fat Greek yogurt
- ½ lemon, juiced
- 1 tablespoon chopped fresh parsley
- ½ teaspoon dried minced garlic
- ½ teaspoon dried dill
- Freshly ground black pepper, to taste

Direction:

1. Put the cucumber in a colander. Sprinkle with ¼ teaspoon of salt and toss. Let the cucumber rest at room temperature in the colander for 30 minutes.

2. Rinse the cucumber in cool water and place in a single layer on several layers of paper towels to remove the excess liquid.

3. In a food processor, pulse the cucumber to chop finely and drain off any extra fluid.

4. Pour the cucumber into a mixing bowl and add the yogurt, lemon juice, parsley, garlic, dill, and the remaining ¼ teaspoon of salt. Season with salt and pepper to taste and

whisk the ingredients together. Refrigerate in an airtight container.

Nutrition: calories: 77 | fat: 2.9g | protein: 6.1g | carbs: 6.2g | fiber: 1.2g | sodium: 607mg

751. Aïoli

Preparation time: 10 minutes
Cooking time: 0 minutes
Serving: 1¼ cups
Ingredients:

- 2 large egg yolks
- 2 teaspoons Dijon mustard
- 2 teaspoons lemon juice
- 1 garlic clove, minced
- ¾ cup vegetable oil
- 1 tablespoon water
- Salt and pepper, to taste
- ¼ cup extra-virgin olive oil

Direction:

1. Process egg yolks, mustard, lemon juice, and garlic in food processor until combined, about 10 seconds. With processor running, slowly drizzle in vegetable oil, about 1 minute.

Transfer mixture to medium bowl and whisk in water, ½ teaspoon salt, and ¼ teaspoon pepper. Whisking constantly, slowly drizzle in olive oil until emulsified. (Aïoli can be refrigerated for up to 4 days.)

Nutrition: calories: 1760| fat: 196.24g | protein: 6.88g | carbs: 7.96g | fiber: 1.4g | sodium: 765mg

752. Green Jalapeño Sauce

Preparation time: 10 minutes
Cooking time: 2 minutes
Serving: 4
Ingredients:

- 4 ounces (113 g) green jalapeno peppers, chopped
- 1 green bell pepper, chopped
- 2 garlic cloves, crushed
- ½ cup white vinegar
- 1 tablespoon apple cider vinegar
- 1 teaspoon sea salt
- 4 tablespoons water

Direction:

1. Add all ingredients to the instant pot. Seal the lid and cook on High Pressure for 2 minutes. When done, release the steam naturally, for about 5 minutes.

2. Transfer to a blender, pulse until combined and store in jars.

Nutrition: calories: 26 | fat: 0.09g | protein: 0.89g | carbs: 4.96g | fiber: 0.6g | sodium: 586mg

753. Zhoug Sauce

Preparation time: 10 minutes
Cooking time: 1 minute
Serving: ½ cup
Ingredients:

- 6 tablespoons extra-virgin olive oil
- ½ teaspoon ground coriander
- ¼ teaspoon ground cumin
- ¼ teaspoon ground cardamom
- ¼ teaspoon salt
- Pinch ground cloves
- ¾ cup fresh cilantro leaves
- ½ cup fresh parsley leaves
- 2 green Thai chiles, stemmed and chopped

- 2 garlic cloves, minced

Direction:

1. Microwave oil, coriander, cumin, cardamom, salt, and cloves in covered bowl until fragrant, about 30 seconds; let cool to room temperature.

2. Pulse oil-spice mixture, cilantro, parsley, chiles, and garlic in food processor until coarse paste forms, about 15 pulses, scraping down sides of bowl as needed. (Green Zhoug can be refrigerated for up to 4 days.)

Nutrition: calories: 1007 | fat: 71.2g | protein: 82.42g | carbs: 4.89g | fiber: 1.7g | sodium: 1498mg

754. Harissa Paste

Preparation time: 10 minutes
Cooking time: 0 minutes
Serving: ½ cup
Ingredients:

- 6 tablespoons extra-virgin olive oil
- 6 garlic cloves, minced
- 2 tablespoons paprika
- 1 tablespoon ground coriander
- 1 tablespoon ground dried Aleppo pepper
- 1 teaspoon ground cumin
- ¾ teaspoon caraway seeds
- ½ teaspoon salt

Direction:

1. Combine all ingredients in bowl and microwave until bubbling and very fragrant, about 1 minute, stirring halfway through microwaving; let cool to room temperature. (Harissa can be refrigerated for up to 4 days.)

Nutrition: calories: 522 | fat: 38.64g | protein: 5.01g | carbs: 19.31g | fiber: 6.7g | sodium: 1902mg

755. Rasel Hanout Spice Mix

Preparation time: 10 minutes
Cooking time: 2 minutes
Serving: ½ cup
Ingredients:

- 16 cardamom pods
- 4 teaspoons coriander seeds
- 4 teaspoons cumin seeds
- 2 teaspoons anise seeds
- ½ teaspoon allspice berries
- ¼ teaspoon black peppercorns
- 4 teaspoons ground ginger
- 2 teaspoons ground nutmeg
- 2 teaspoons ground dried Aleppo pepper
- 2 teaspoons ground cinnamon

Direction:

1. Toast cardamom, coriander, cumin, anise, allspice, and peppercorns in small skillet over medium heat until fragrant, shaking skillet occasionally to prevent scorching, about 2 minutes. Let cool to room temperature.

2. Transfer toasted spices, ginger, nutmeg, Aleppo, and cinnamon to spice grinder and process to fine powder. (Ras el hanout can be stored at room temperature in airtight container for up to 1 year.)

Nutrition: calories: 166 | fat: 6.05g | protein: 6.11g | carbs: 30.62g | fiber: 10.8g | sodium: 28mg

756. Za'atar Spice

Preparation time: 5 minutes
Cooking time: 0 minutes
Serving: ½ cup
Ingredients:

- ½ cup dried thyme, ground

- 2 tablespoons sesame seeds, toasted
- 1½ tablespoons ground sumac

Direction:

1. Combine all ingredients in bowl. (Za'atar can be stored at room temperature in airtight container for up to 1 year.)

Nutrition: calories: 120 | fat: 10.12g | protein: 4.34g | carbs: 6.57g | fiber: 4.5g | sodium: 9mg

757. Dukkah Spice

Preparation time: 10 minutes
Cooking time: 40 minutes
Serving: 2 cups
Ingredients:

- 1 (15-ounce / 425-g) can chickpeas, rinsed
- 1 teaspoon extra-virgin olive oil
- ½ cup shelled pistachios, toasted
- 1/3 cup black sesame seeds, toasted
- 2 1/2 tablespoons coriander seeds, toasted
- 1 tablespoon cumin seeds, toasted
- 2 teaspoons fennel seeds, toasted
- 1½ teaspoons pepper
- 1¼ teaspoons salt

Direction:

1. Adjust oven rack to middle position and heat oven to 400°F (205°C). Pat chickpeas dry with paper towels and toss with oil. Spread chickpeas into single layer in rimmed baking sheet and roast until browned and crisp, 40 to 45 minutes, stirring every 5 to 10 minutes; let cool completely.

2. Process chickpeas in food processor until coarsely ground, about 10 seconds; transfer to medium bowl. Pulse pistachios and sesame seeds in now-empty food processor until coarsely ground, about 15 pulses; transfer to bowl with chickpeas. Process coriander, cumin, and fennel seeds in again-empty food processor until finely ground, 2 to 3 minutes; transfer to bowl with chickpeas. Add pepper and salt and whisk until mixture is well combined. (Dukkah can be refrigerated for up to 1 month.)

Nutrition: calories: 770 | fat: 51.29g | protein: 28.31g | carbs: 62.63g | fiber: 26.3g | sodium: 1820mg

758. Herbes de Provence Blend

Preparation time: 5 minutes
Cooking time: 0 minutes
Serving: ½ cup
Ingredients:

- 2 tablespoons dried thyme
- 2 tablespoons dried marjoram
- 2 tablespoons dried rosemary
- 2 teaspoons fennel seeds, toasted

Direction:

1. Combine all ingredients in bowl. (Herbes de Provence can be stored at room temperature in airtight container for up to 1 year.)

Nutrition: calories: 32 | fat: 1.11g | protein: 1.44g | carbs: 6.03g | fiber: 4.1g | sodium: 7mg

759. Marinara Sauce

Preparation time: 10 minutes
Cooking time: 36 minutes
Serving: 8 cups
Ingredients:

- 1 small onion, diced
- 1 small red bell pepper, stemmed, seeded and chopped

- 2 tablespoons plus ¼ cup extra-virgin olive oil, divided
- 2 tablespoons butter
- 4 to 6 garlic cloves, minced
- 2 teaspoon salt, divided
- ½ teaspoon freshly ground black pepper
- 2 (32-ounce / 907.2-g) cans crushed tomatoes (with basil, if possible), with their juices
- ½ cup thinly sliced basil leaves, divided
- 2 tablespoons chopped fresh rosemary
- 1 to 2 teaspoons crushed red pepper flakes (optional)

Direction:

1. In a food processor, combine the onion and bell pepper and blend until very finely minced.
2. In a large skillet, heat 2 tablespoons olive oil and the butter over medium heat. Add the minced onion, and red pepper and sauté until just starting to get tender, about 5 minutes.
3. Add the garlic, salt, and pepper and sauté until fragrant, another 1 to 2 minutes.
4. Reduce the heat to low and add the tomatoes and their juices, remaining ¼ cup olive oil, ¼ cup basil, rosemary, and red pepper flakes (if using). Stir to combine, then bring to a simmer and cover. Cook over low heat for 30 to 60 minutes to allow the flavors to blend.
5. Add remaining ¼ cup chopped fresh basil after removing from heat, stirring to combine.

Nutrition Per Serving (1 cup)

calories: 265 | fat: 19.9g | protein: 4.1g | carbs: 18.7g | fiber: 5.1g | sodium: 803mg

760. Basic Vinaigrette

Preparation time: 5 minutes
Cooking time: 0 minutes
Serving: ¼ cup
Ingredients:

- 1 tablespoon wine vinegar
- 1½ teaspoons minced shallot
- ½ teaspoon low fat yogurt
- ½ teaspoon Dijon mustard
- 1/8 teaspoon salt
- Pinch pepper
- 3 tablespoons extra-virgin olive oil

Direction:

1. Whisk vinegar, shallot, low fat yogurt, mustard, salt, and pepper together in bowl until smooth. Whisking constantly, slowly drizzle in oil until emulsified. (Vinaigrette can be refrigerated for up to 2 weeks.)

Nutrition: calories: 188 | fat: 18.22g | protein: 1.36g | carbs: 5.03g | fiber: 0.9g | sodium: 704mg

761. Lemony Vinaigrette

Preparation time: 10 minutes
Cooking time: 0 minutes
Serving: ¼ cup
Ingredients:

- ¼ teaspoon grated lemon zest plus
- 1 tablespoon juice
- ½ teaspoon low fat yogurt
- ½ teaspoon Dijon mustard
- 1/8 teaspoon salt
- Pinch pepper
- Pinch sugar
- 3 tablespoons extra-virgin olive oil

Direction:

1. Whisk lemon zest and juice, low fat yogurt, mustard, salt, pepper, and sugar together in bowl until smooth. Whisking constantly, slowly drizzle in oil until emulsified. (Vinaigrette can be refrigerated for up to 2 weeks.)

Nutrition: calories: 192 | fat: 18.24g | protein: 1.33g | carbs: 6.62g | fiber: 0.8g | sodium: 704mg

762. Dijon Balsamic Vinaigrette

Preparation time: 10 minutes
Cooking time: 0 minutes
Serving: ¼ cup
Ingredients:

- 1 tablespoon balsamic vinegar
- 2 teaspoons Dijon mustard
- 1½ teaspoons minced shallot
- ½ teaspoon low fat yogurt
- ½ teaspoon minced fresh thyme
- 1/8 teaspoon salt
- Pinch pepper
- 3 tablespoons extra-virgin olive oil

Direction:

1. Whisk vinegar, mustard, shallot, low fat yogurt, thyme, salt, and pepper together in bowl until smooth. Whisking constantly, slowly drizzle in oil until emulsified. (Vinaigrette can be refrigerated for up to 2 weeks.)

Nutrition: calories: 204 | fat: 18.47g | protein: 1.74g | carbs: 8.25g | fiber: 1.2g | sodium: 789mg

763. Walnut Oil Vinaigrette

Preparation time: 10 minutes
Cooking time: 0 minutes
Serving: ¼ cup
Ingredients:

- 1 tablespoon wine vinegar
- 1½ teaspoons minced shallot
- ½ teaspoon low fat yogurt
- ½ teaspoon Dijon mustard
- 1/8 teaspoon salt
- Pinch pepper
- 1½ tablespoons roasted walnut oil
- 1½ tablespoons extra-virgin olive oil

Direction:

1. Whisk vinegar, shallot, low fat yogurt, mustard, salt, and pepper together in bowl until smooth. Whisking constantly, slowly drizzle in oils until emulsified. (Vinaigrette can be refrigerated for up to 2 weeks.)

Nutrition: calories: 287 | fat: 29.62g | protein: 1.28g | carbs: 5.03g | fiber: 0.9g | sodium: 524mg

764. Tomato Basil Sauce Recipe

Preparation time: 10 minutes
Cooking time: 5 minutes
Servings: 8
Ingredients:

- Tomatoes; diced (8 lb.)
- bay leaves (2)
- chopped basil (1 cup)
- Two onions; diced
- 1 tbsp. of pepper
- Italian seasoning (3 tbsp.)
- olive oil
- garlic cloves (1/2); minced
- salt
- Ground peppers (1/2 tsp)
- vinegar

- Garlic powder (1 tbsp.)

Directions:

1. Put the oil within your instant pot & choose the *Sauté* mode.
2. Later, combine the onions, oil & garlic; stir-fry for almost 5 minutes.
3. Add all the leftover components besides the basil into your instant pot.
4. Close your instant pot with the lid & utilize the pressure discharge holder through the sealed region.
5. Choose the *Manual* mode; fix into high pressure & set the timer for almost 10 minutes.
6. While listening to the beeps, then the pressure discharge naturally & uncover your instant pot cap.
7. Mix them well; discard the bay leaves & put the basil into the sauce.
8. Use instantly or store into a container for later.

Nutrition:
Calories: 101
Sodium: 3mg
Carbohydrates: 23.9g
Fat: 0.1g
Sugar: 18.8g
Protein: 0.2g

765. Barbeque Sauce Recipe

Preparation time: 10 minutes
Cooking time: 13 minutes
Servings: 5
Ingredients:
- Sesame seed oil (2 tbsp.)
- Onions (2); coarsely chopped.
- white vinegar (1/2 cup)
- honey
- Granulated garlic (1 tsp.)
- hot sauce
- Liquid smoke (2 tsp.)
- 1/4 tsp. of clove ground
- water
- Cumin powder (1/4 tsp.)
- Salt
- tomato puree
- seedless plums (1½ cups), dried

Direction:

1. Put the onion, garlic & oil into your instant pot & *Sauté* for almost 3 minutes.
2. Add all the leftover Components, mix well.
3. Close your instant pot with the lid & utilize the pressure discharge holder through the sealed region.
4. Choose the *Manual* mode; fix into high pressure & set the timer for around 10 minutes.
5. While listening to the beeps let the pressure discharge quickly & uncover your instant pot cap.
6. Shift the sauce into your blender & mix thoroughly to develop a creamy mixture.
7. Use instantly or store into a container for further use.

Nutrition:
Calories: 105
Sodium: 3mg
Carbohydrates: 23.9g
Fat: 0.1g
Sugar: 16g
Protein: 0.2g

766. Orange Cranberry Sauce

Preparation time: 5 minutes
Cooking time: 5 minutes
Servings: 30
Ingredients:
- orange juice (1 cup)
- sugar
- cranberries (12 oz)
- orange zest (½ tsp)

Direction:

1. Add all components within your instant pot; stir thoroughly.
2. Close your instant pot with the lid.
3. Cook for almost 5 minutes.
4. Discharge the pressure utilizing the quick release system, and then uncover your pot.
5. Let the sauce cool entirely & store.

Nutrition:
Protein: 0.1g
Sugar: 7.8g
Calories: 35
Sodium: 0mg
Carbohydrates: 8.6g
Fat: 0g

767. Super Quick Garlic Sauce Recipe

Preparation time: 5 minutes
Cooking time: 3 minutes
Servings: 2
Ingredients:
- garlic powder
- Chopped garlic (4 tbsp.)
- Salt
- Parsley (2 tbsp.)
- water
- Cornstarch (4 tbsp.)
- pepper
- heavy cream (4 cups)

Direction:

1. Put the garlic, pepper, garlic powder, water, cream & salt within your instant pot.
2. Close your instant pot with the lid & utilize the pressure discharge holder through the sealed region.
3. Choose the *Manual* mode; fix into high pressure & set the timer for almost 3 minutes.
4. While listening to the beeps, then the pressure discharges quickly & uncovers your instant pot cap.
5. Combine the cornstarch & the leftover water.
6. Later, combine the slurry into the garlic sauce, put it into the parsley.
7. Use instantly or store into a container for later.

Nutrition:
Calories: 91
Sodium: 1mg
Carbohydrates: 27g
Fat: 0.1g
Sugar: 0g
Protein: 0.2g

768. Marinara Sauce Recipe

Preparation time: 10 minutes
Cooking time: 16 minutes
Servings: 6
Ingredients:
- garlic; minced (2 cloves)
- butter

- onions (2); chopped
- Parsley
- Two carrots; diced
- black pepper, crushed
- tomatoes (4 cans); diced
- salt
- Basil dried (3 tsp.)
- olive oil
- Oregano, dried (3 tsp.)

Direction:
1. Put the oil within your instant pot & choose the *Sauté* mode.
2. Later, combine the vegetables; stir-fry for almost 5 minutes.
3. Add all the leftover components besides the basil into your instant pot.
4. Close your instant pot with the lid & utilize the pressure discharge holder through the sealed region.
5. Choose the *Manual* mode; fix into high pressure & set the timer for almost 10 minutes.
6. While listening to the beeps, then the pressure discharge naturally & uncover your instant pot cap.
7. Utilize an immersion blender to blend them toward a creamy paste.
8. Combine the black pepper & butter; cook for almost 1 minute at *Sauté* mode.
9. Stir thoroughly & serve with the pasta.
10. Or, use instantly or store into a container for later.

Nutrition:
Calories: 98
Sodium: 2mg
Carbohydrates: 23.9g
Fat: 0.3g
Sugar: 0g
Protein: 0.2g

769. Apple Cranberry Sauce

Preparation time: 5 minutes
Cooking time: 5 minutes
Servings: 8
Ingredients:
- One apple, stripped & chopped
- orange juice (1)
- maple syrup (½ cup)
- cranberries (12 oz)
- apple cider (½ cup)
- orange zest (1)

Direction:
1. Add all components into your instant pot & mix thoroughly.
2. Seal your Instant Pot with the lid; cook for almost 5 minutes on high
3. Let the pressure discharge naturally for nearly 5 minutes.
4. Later, utilizing a quick discharge system for pressure loosens.
5. Leave to chill entirely & store.

Nutrition:
Calories: 101
Sodium: 3mg
Carbohydrates: 23.9g
Fat: 0.1g
Sugar: 18.8g
Protein: 0.2g

770. Bolognese Sauce

Preparation time: 10 minutes
Cooking time: 8 minutes
Servings: 4
Ingredients:
- ground beef (1 lb)
- parsley, minced (3 tbsp)
- marinara sauce (14 oz)
- garlic, minced (1 ½ tsp)

Direction:
1. Add all components within your instant pot, mix thoroughly.
2. Seal your pot with the lid & then cook for almost 8 minutes at high.
3. Let the pressure discharge utilizing the quick-release system, then uncover the lid.
4. Stir thoroughly & serve.

Nutrition:
Carbohydrates: 14.2g
Sugar: 8.8g
Calories: 300
Protein: 36.3g
Sodium: 483mg
Fat: 9.8g

771. Cheese Onion Sauce

Preparation time: 10 minutes
Cooking time: 25 minutes
Servings: 5
Ingredients:
- onion (1), chopped
- olive oil
- parsley (2 tsp)
- vegetable stock (1 cup)
- cream cheese (2 cups)
- onion powder (1 tsp)

Direction:
1. Put the oil into your instant pot & select sauté mode.
2. Put the onion & sauté for nearly 10 minutes.
3. Add leftover components & mix thoroughly.
4. Close your Instant pot with the lid, cook for almost 10 minutes on Manual settings.
5. Let the pressure discharge utilizing the quick release system, then uncover the lid.
6. Permit to calm entirely & then store.

Nutrition:
Protein: 7.3g
Sugar: 1.7g
Calories: 385
Sodium: 420mg
Fat: 3804g
Carbohydrates: 5.3g

772. Spicy Indian Sauce

Preparation time: 10 minutes
Cooking time: 25 minutes
Serving: 3
Ingredients:
- olive oil
- onions (1½), diced
- 1½ garlic cloves, finely chopped
- ground turmeric
- ½ length knob ginger, stripped & grated
- ground cumin (½ tablespoon)
- water

- cayenne pepper (½ teaspoon)
- ground coriander
- sweet paprika (½ tablespoon)
- Salt
- Whole tomatoes (28 oz.)

Direction:
1. Put the oil within your instant pot & choose the *Sauté* mode.
2. Later, combine the onions, oil & garlic; stir-fry for almost 5 minutes.
3. Then, combine all the vegetables inside your pot and stir-fry for extra 5 minutes.
4. Add all the leftover components besides the basil into your instant pot.
5. Close your instant pot with the lid & utilize the pressure discharge holder through the sealed region.
6. Choose the *Manual* mode; fix into high pressure & set the timer for almost 15 minutes.
7. While listening to the beeps, then the pressure discharges quickly & uncovers your instant pot cap.
8. Mix them well; discard the bay leaves & put the basil into the sauce.
9. Use instantly or store into a container for later.

Nutrition:
Carbohydrate: 9.8g
Sugar: 2.5g
Calories: 83
Protein: 1.6g
Sodium: 181mg
Fat: 3.9g

773. Roasted Tomato Sauce

Preparation time: 10 minutes
Cooking time: 10 minutes
Serving: 4
Ingredients:
- red onion (1), chopped
- salt
- bell pepper (1), diced
- water
- garlic cloves-Eight
- Four chipotle chilies into adobo sauce
- jalapeño pepper (1), sliced
- powdered cumin (2tsp)
- Mexican red chili powder (4tsp)
- Fire-roasted, tomatoes diced (28 oz.)

Direction:
1. Add all components into your instant pot & mix thoroughly.
2. Close your instant pot with the lid & utilize the pressure discharge holder through the sealed region.
3. Choose the *Manual* mode; fix into high pressure & set the timer for almost 10 minutes.
4. While listening to the beeps, then the pressure discharge naturally & uncover your instant pot cap.
5. Use instantly or store into a container for later.

Nutrition:
Protein: 3.9g
Sugar: 7.9g
Carbohydrate: 18.4g
Calories: 96
Sodium: 2109mg
Fat: 1.4g

774. Strawberry Sauce

Preparation time: 02 minutes
Cooking time: 08 minutes
Serving: 5
Ingredients:
- pressed orange juice (½ cup)
- Strawberries (8 oz.)
- raw honey
- cinnamon (½ teaspoon)
- stevia

Direction:
1. Set all components into the instant pot.
2. Close your instant pot with the lid & utilize the pressure discharge holder through the sealed region.
3. Choose the *Manual* mode; fix into high pressure & set the timer for almost 8 minutes.
4. While listening to the beeps, then the pressure loosens quickly & uncovers your instant pot cap.
5. Utilize your blender to puree them.
6. Use instantly or store into a container for later.

Nutrition:
Carbohydrate: 15.6g
Sodium: 4mg
Protein: 0.5g
Fat: 0.1g
Calories: 63
Sugar: 13.9g

775. Enchilada Sauce

Preparation time: 10 minutes
Cooking time: 10 minutes
Servings: 8
Ingredients:
- chipotle chilies within adobo sauce
- roasted tomatoes (14 oz)
- garlic (3 cloves)
- chili powder (1 tsp)
- jalapeno pepper (½), sliced
- water
- bell pepper (½), minced
- salt
- onion (½), diced

Direction:
1. Put all components within your instant pot.
2. Put the tomatoes toward the top.
3. Close your instant pot with the lid.
4. Cook for almost 10 minutes on High.
5. Let the pressure discharge utilizing the quick release system, then uncover the lid.
6. Utilize your blender to mix the sauce & reserve.

Nutrition:
Calories: 20
Fat: 0.1g
Sugar: 1.9g
Carbohydrates: 4.2g
Sodium: 408mg
Protein: 0.7g

776. Creamy Artichoke Dip

Preparation Time: 10 minutes
Cooking Time: 5 minutes
Servings: 8
Ingredients
- 28 oz. can artichoke hearts, drain and quartered
- 1 1/2 cups parmesan cheese, shredded

- 1 cup sour cream
- 1 cup mayonnaise
- oz. can green chilies
- 1 cup of water
- Pepper
- Salt

Directions

1. Add artichokes, water, and green chilies into the instant pot.
2. Seal pot with the lid and select manual and set timer for 1 minute.
3. Once done, release pressure using quick release. Remove lid. Drain excess water.
4. Set instant pot on sauté mode. Add remaining ingredients and stir well and cook until cheese is melted.
5. Serve and enjoy.

Nutrition:
Calories 262 Fat 7.6 g Carbohydrates 14.4 g Sugar 2.8 g Protein 8.4 g Cholesterol 32 mg

777. Garlic Pinto Bean Dip

Preparation Time: 10 minutes
Cooking Time: 43 minutes
Servings: 6
Ingredients
- 1 cup dry pinto beans, rinsed
- 1/2 tsp. cumin
- 1/2 cup salsa
- 2 garlic cloves
- 2 chipotle peppers in adobo sauce
- 5 cups vegetable stock
- Pepper
- Salt

Directions

1. Add beans, stock, garlic, and chipotle peppers into the instant pot.
2. Seal pot with lid and cook on high for 43 minutes.
3. Once done, release pressure using quick release. Remove lid.
4. Drain beans well and reserve 1/2 cup of stock.
5. Transfer beans, reserve stock, and remaining ingredients into the food processor and process until smooth.
6. Serve and enjoy.

Nutrition:
Calories 129 Fat 0.9 g Carbohydrates 23 g Sugar 1.9 g Protein 8 g Cholesterol 2 mg

778. Creamy Eggplant Dip

Preparation Time: 10 minutes
Cooking Time: 20 minutes
Servings: 4
Ingredients
- 1 eggplant
- 1/2 tsp. paprika
- 1 tbsp. olive oil
- 1 tbsp. fresh lime juice
- 2 tbsp. tahini
- 1 garlic clove
- 1 cup of water
- Pepper
- Salt

Directions

1. Add water and eggplant into the instant pot.
2. Seal pot with the lid and select manual and set timer for 20 minutes.
3. Once done, release pressure using quick release. Remove lid.

4. Drain eggplant and let it cool.
5. Once the eggplant is cool then remove eggplant skin and transfer eggplant flesh into the food processor.
6. Add remaining ingredients into the food processor and process until smooth.
7. Serve and enjoy.

Nutrition:
Calories 108 Fat 7.8 g Carbohydrates 9.7 g Sugar 3.7 g Protein 2.5 g Cholesterol 0 mg

Chapter 11. Snack Recipes

779. Citrus-Marinated Olives

Preparation time: 10 minutes + 4 hours
Cooking time: 0 minutes
Servings: 4
Ingredients:
- 2 cups mixed green olives with pits
- ¼ cup red wine vinegar
- ¼ cup extra-virgin olive oil
- 4 garlic cloves, finely minced
- Zest and juice orange
- 1 teaspoon red pepper flakes
- 2 bay leaves
- ½ teaspoon ground cumin
- ½ teaspoon ground allspice

Directions:
1. In a jar, mix olives, vinegar, oil, garlic, orange zest and juice, red pepper flakes, bay leaves, cumin, and allspice.
2. Cover and chill for 4 hours, tossing again before serving.

Nutrition:
Calories: 133
Fat: 14 g
Protein: 1 g

780. Olive Tapenade with Anchovies

Preparation time: 70 minutes
Cooking time: 0 minutes
Servings: 4
Ingredients:
- 2 cups pitted Kalamata olives
- 2 anchovy fillets
- 2 teaspoons capers
- 1 garlic clove
- 1 cooked egg yolk
- 1 teaspoon Dijon mustard
- ¼ cup extra-virgin olive oil

Directions:
1. Wash olives in cold water and drain well.
2. In a food processor, mix drained olives, anchovies, capers, garlic, egg yolk, and Dijon.
3. With the food processor running, slowly stream in the olive oil.
4. Wrap and refrigerate for at least 1 hour. Serve with Seedy Crackers.

Nutrition:
Calories: 179
Fat: 19 g
Protein: 2 g

781. Greek Deviled Eggs

Preparation time: 45 minutes
Cooking time: 15 minutes
Servings: 4
Ingredients:
- 4 large hardboiled eggs
- 2 tablespoons Roasted Garlic Aioli
- ½ cup feta cheese
- 8 pitted Kalamata olives
- 2 tablespoons chopped sun-dried tomatoes
- 1 tablespoon minced red onion
- ½ teaspoon dried dill
- ¼ teaspoon black pepper

Directions:
1. Slice the hardboiled eggs in half lengthwise, remove the yolks, and place them in a medium bowl. Reserve the egg white halves and set them aside.
2. Smash the yolks well with a fork. Add the aioli, feta, olives, sun-dried tomatoes, onion, dill, and pepper and stir to combine until smooth and creamy.
3. Spoon the filling into each egg white half and chill for 30 minutes, or up to 24 hours, covered.

Nutrition:
Calories: 147
Fat: 11 g
Protein: 9 g

782. Manchego Crackers

Preparation time: 55 minutes
Cooking time: 15 minutes
Servings: 4
Ingredients:
- 4 tablespoons butter, at room temperature
- 1 cup Manchego cheese
- 1 cup almond flour
- 1 teaspoon salt, divided
- ¼ teaspoon black pepper
- 1 large egg

Directions:
1. Using an electric mixer, scourge butter, and shredded cheese.
2. Mix almond flour with ½ teaspoon salt and pepper. Mix almond flour mixture to the cheese, mixing constantly to form a ball.
3. Situate onto plastic wrap and roll into a cylinder log about 1½ inches thick. Wrap tightly and refrigerate for at least 1 hour.
4. Preheat the oven to 350°F. Prep two baking sheets with parchment papers.
5. For egg wash, blend egg and remaining ½ teaspoon salt.
6. Slice the refrigerated dough into small rounds, about ¼ inch thick, and place on the lined baking sheets.
7. Egg wash the tops of the crackers and bake for 15 minutes. Pull out from the oven and situate in a wire rack.
8. Serve.

Nutrition:
Calories: 243
Fat: 23 g
Protein: 8 g

783. Burrata Caprese Stack

Preparation time: 5 minutes
Cooking time: 0 minutes
Servings: 4
Ingredients:
- 1 large organic tomato
- ½ teaspoon salt
- ¼ teaspoon black pepper
- 1 (4-ounce) ball burrata cheese
- 8 fresh basil leaves
- 2 tablespoons extra-virgin olive oil
- 1 tablespoon red wine

Directions:
1. Slice the tomato into 4 thick slices, removing any tough center core, and sprinkle with salt and pepper. Place the tomatoes, seasoned side up, on a plate.

2. On a separate rimmed plate, slice the burrata into 4 thick slices and place one slice on each tomato slice. Top each with one-quarter of the basil and pour any reserved burrata cream from the rimmed plate over the top.

3. Serve with a fork and knife, drizzled with olive oil and vinegar.

Nutrition:

Calories: 153

Fat: 13 g

Protein: 7 g

784. Zucchini-Ricotta Fritters with Lemon-Garlic Aioli

Preparation time: 30 minutes

Cooking time: 25 minutes

Servings: 4

Ingredients:

- 1 large zucchini
- 1 teaspoon salt, divided
- ½ cup whole-milk ricotta cheese
- 2 scallions
- 1 large egg
- 2 garlic cloves
- 2 tablespoons fresh mint (optional)
- 2 teaspoons grated lemon zest
- ¼ teaspoon freshly ground black pepper
- ½ cup almond flour
- 1 teaspoon baking powder
- 8 tablespoons extra-virgin olive oil
- 8 tablespoons Roasted Garlic Aioli

Directions:

1. Toss the shredded zucchini in a colander or a stack of paper towels. Sprinkle with ½ teaspoon salt and let sit for 10 minutes. Using another layer of paper towel, press down on the zucchini to release any excess moisture and pat dry.

2. In a large bowl, combine the drained zucchini, ricotta, scallions, egg, garlic, mint (if using), lemon zest, remaining ½ teaspoon salt, and pepper and stir well.

3. Blend the almond flour and baking powder. Mix in flour mixture into the zucchini mixture and let rest for 10 minutes.

4. In a large skillet, working in four batches, fry the patties. For each batch of four, heat two tablespoons olive oil over medium-high heat. Add 1 heaping tablespoon of zucchini batter per fritter, pressing down with the back of a spoon to form 2- to 3-inch fritters. Cover and let fry 2 minutes before flipping. Fry another 2 to 3 minutes, covered.

5. Repeat for the remaining three batches, using 2 tablespoons of olive oil for each batch.

6. Serve with aioli.

Nutrition:

Calories: 448

Fat: 42 g

Protein: 8 g

785. Salmon-Stuffed Cucumbers

Preparation time: 10 minutes

Cooking time: 0 minutes

Servings: 4

Ingredients:

- 2 large cucumbers, peeled
- 1 (4-ounce) can red salmon
- 1 medium very ripe avocado
- 1 tablespoon extra-virgin olive oil
- Zest and juice of 1 lime
- 3 tablespoons chopped fresh cilantro

- ½ teaspoon salt
- ¼ teaspoon black pepper

Directions:

1. Slice the cucumber into 1-inch-thick segments and, using a spoon, scrape seeds out of the center of each piece and stand up on a plate.

2. In a medium bowl, mix salmon, avocado, olive oil, lime zest and juice, cilantro, salt, and pepper.

3. Spoon the salmon mixture into the center of each cucumber segment and serve chilled.

Nutrition:

Calories: 159

Fat: 11 g

Protein: 9 g

786. Instant Pot Salsa

Preparation time: 9 minutes

Cooking time: 22 minutes

Servings: 12

Ingredients:

- 12 cups seeded diced tomatoes
- 6 ounces tomato paste
- 2 medium yellow onions
- 6 small jalapeño peppers
- 4 cloves garlic
- ¼ cup white vinegar
- ¼ cup lime juice
- 2 tablespoons granulated sugar
- 2 teaspoons salt
- ¼ cup chopped fresh cilantro

Directions:

1. Place tomatoes, tomato paste, onions, jalapeños, garlic, vinegar, lime juice, sugar, and salt in the Instant Pot and stir well. Close it, situate steam release to Sealing. Click the Manual button and time to 20 minutes.

2. Once the timer beeps, quick-release the pressure. Open, stir in cilantro, and press the Cancel button.

3. Let salsa cool to room temperature, about 40 minutes, then transfer to a storage container and refrigerate overnight.

Nutrition:

Calories: 68

Fat: 0.1 g

Protein: 2 g

787. Sfougato

Preparation time: 9 minutes

Cooking time: 13 minutes

Servings: 4

Ingredients:

- ½ cup crumbled feta cheese
- ¼ cup breadcrumbs
- 1 medium onion
- 4 tablespoons all-purpose flour
- 2 tablespoons fresh mint
- ½ teaspoon salt
- ½ teaspoon ground black pepper
- 1 tablespoon dried thyme
- 6 large eggs, beaten
- 1 cup water

Directions:

1. In a medium bowl, mix cheese, breadcrumbs, onion, flour, mint, salt, pepper, and thyme. Stir in eggs.

2. Spray an 8" round baking dish with nonstick cooking spray. Pour egg mixture into the container.

3. Place rack in the Instant Pot® and add water. Fold a long piece of foil in half lengthwise. Lay foil over a rack to form a

sling and top with a dish. Cover loosely with foil. Seal lid, put the steam release in Sealing, select Manual, and time to 8 minutes.

4. When the timer alarms, release the pressure. Uncover. Let stand 5 minutes, then remove the dish from the pot.

Nutrition:
Calories: 274
Fat: 14 g
Protein: 17 g

788. Goat Cheese–Mackerel Pâté

Preparation time: 10 minutes
Cooking time: 0 minutes
Servings: 4
Ingredients:
- 4 ounces olive oil-packed wild-caught mackerel
- 2 ounces goat cheese
- Zest and juice of 1 lemon
- 2 tablespoons chopped fresh parsley
- 2 tablespoons chopped fresh arugula
- 1 tablespoon extra-virgin olive oil
- 2 teaspoons chopped capers
- 2 teaspoons fresh horseradish (optional)

Directions:
1. In a food processor, blender, or large bowl with an immersion blender, combine the mackerel, goat cheese, lemon zest and juice, parsley, arugula, olive oil, capers, and horseradish (if using). Process or blend until smooth and creamy.
2. Serve with crackers, cucumber rounds, endive spears, or celery.

Nutrition:
Calories: 118
Fat: 8 g
Protein: 9 g

789. Hummus

Preparation time: 10 minutes
Cooking time: 0 minutes
Servings: 16
Ingredients:
- 1 (14-ounce) can chickpeas, drained
- 3 garlic cloves, minced
- 2 tablespoons tahini
- 2 tablespoons extra-virgin olive oil
- Juice of 1 lemon
- Zest of 1 lemon
- ½ teaspoon sea salt
- Pinch cayenne pepper
- 2 tablespoons chopped fresh Italian parsley leaves

Directions:
1. Mix the chickpeas, garlic, tahini, olive oil, lemon juice and zest, sea salt, and cayenne pepper in a blender. Blend for about 60 seconds until smooth.
2. Garnish with parsley and serve.

Nutrition:
Calories: 118
Protein: 5 g
Total Fat: 5 g

790. Baba Ganoush

Preparation time: 10 minutes
Cooking time: 15 minutes
Servings: 6
Ingredients:
- 1 eggplant, peeled and sliced
- ¼ cup tahini

- ½ teaspoon sea salt
- Juice of 1 lemon
- ¼ teaspoon ground cumin
- 1/8 teaspoon freshly ground black pepper
- 2 tablespoons extra-virgin olive oil
- 2 tablespoons sunflower seeds (optional)
- 2 tablespoons fresh Italian parsley leaves (optional)

Directions:
1. Preheat the oven to 350°F.
2. On a baking sheet, spread the eggplant slices in an even layer. Bake for about 15 minutes until soft. Cool slightly and roughly chop the eggplant.
3. In a blender, blend the eggplant with tahini, sea salt, lemon juice, cumin, and pepper for about 30 seconds. Transfer to a serving dish.
4. Before eating, drizzle with olive oil and top with sunflower seeds and parsley.

Nutrition:
Calories: 121
Protein: 3 g
Total Fat: 10 g

791. Spiced Almonds

Preparation time: 10 minutes
Cooking time: 7 minutes
Servings: 8
Ingredients:
- 2 cups raw unsalted almonds
- 1 tablespoon extra-virgin olive oil
- 1 teaspoon ground cumin
- ½ teaspoon garlic powder
- ½ teaspoon sea salt
- 1/8 teaspoon cayenne pepper

Directions:
1. Preheat a large nonstick skillet over high heat, cook the almonds for about 3 minutes, shaking the pan constantly until the almonds become fragrant. Transfer to a bowl and set aside.
2. In the same skillet over medium-high heat, heat the olive oil until it shimmers.
3. Add the cumin, garlic powder, sea salt, and cayenne. Heat for 30 to 60 seconds, or until the spices have produced their fragrance.
4. Add the almonds to the skillet. Cook for about 3 minutes more, stirring until the spices coat the almonds.
5. Let cool before serving.

Nutrition:
Calories: 154
Protein: 14 g
Total Fat: 14 g

792. Sweet-and-Savory Popcorn

Preparation time: 5 minutes
Cooking time: 15 minutes
Servings: 8
Ingredients:
- 8 cups air-popped popcorn
- 2 tablespoons extra-virgin olive oil
- 2 tablespoons packed brown sugar
- 2 tablespoons Chinese five-spice powder
- ¼ teaspoon sea salt

Directions:
1. Preheat the oven to 350°F.
2. Put the popcorn in a large bowl. Set aside.
3. Whisk together the olive oil, brown sugar, five-spice powder, and sea salt in a small cup.

4. Pour the mixture over the popcorn, tossing to coat. Transfer to a 9-by-13-inch baking dish.

5. Bake the popcorn for 15 minutes, stirring every 5 minutes or so. Serve hot or cool and store in resealable bags in single-serve (1-cup) batches.

Nutrition:

Calories: 131

Protein: 3 g

Total Fat: 5 g

793. Baked Apples with Walnuts and Spices

Preparation time: 10 minutes

Cooking time: 45 minutes

Servings: 4

Ingredients:

- 4 apples
- ¼ cup chopped walnuts
- 2 tablespoons honey
- 1 teaspoon ground cinnamon
- ¼ teaspoon ground nutmeg
- ¼ teaspoon ground ginger
- Pinch sea salt

Directions:

1. Preheat the oven to 375°F.

2. Cut the tops off the apples and scrape the cores with a metal spoon or paring knife, leaving the bottoms of the apples intact. Place the apple cut-side up in a 9-by-9-inch baking pan.

3. In a small bowl, stir together the walnuts, honey, cinnamon, nutmeg, ginger, and sea salt. Fill the apples' centers with the mixture. Bake the apples for about 45 minutes until browned, soft, and fragrant. Serve warm.

Nutrition:

Calories: 199

Protein: 5 g

Total Fat: 5 g

794. Marinated Olives

Preparation time: 10 minutes

Cooking time: 0 minutes

Servings: 8

Ingredients:

- ¼ cup extra-virgin olive oil
- ¼ cup red wine vinegar
- 3 garlic cloves, minced
- 2 tablespoons chopped fresh rosemary leaves
- 1 tablespoon chopped fresh thyme leaves
- Zest of 1 lemon
- ½ teaspoon sea salt
- 2 cups black or green olives, drained and rinsed

Directions:

1. Whisk together the olive oil, vinegar, garlic, rosemary, thyme, lemon zest, and sea salt in a small cup.

2. Add the olives to your container and pour the marinade over the top. Seal and refrigerate for at least 2 hours. The olives will keep refrigerated for up to 2 weeks.

3. MAKE IT A MEAL: Include the olives as part of a festive smorgasbord with sliced veggies, or use them as treats for dipping in Hummus (here) or Baba Ganoush (here).

Nutrition:

Calories: 103

Protein: 10 g

Fat: 10 g

795. Tzatziki Sauce

Preparation time: 10 minutes

Cooking time: 0 minutes

Servings: 8

Ingredients:

- 1 cup unsweetened nonfat plain Greek yogurt
- 1 cucumber, peeled and grated
- 1 tablespoon chopped fresh dill
- 1 garlic clove, minced
- ¼ teaspoon sea salt
- 1/8 teaspoon freshly ground black pepper

Directions:

1. In a small bowl, whisk the yogurt, cucumber, dill, garlic, sea salt, and pepper. Cover and refrigerate for 1 hour or more before serving.

SUBSTITUTION TIP: To make this dairy-free, substitute a nondairy plain yogurt, such as coconut or almond milk yogurt.

INGREDIENT TIP: For some reason, the garlic essence in tzatziki sauce lingers. You may want to have breathed mints on hand, even the next day! A nontraditional addition that can help mitigate this is chopped fresh parsley.

Nutrition:

Calories: 29

Protein: 2 g

Total Fat: 1 g

796. Easy Trail Mix

Preparation time: 10 minutes

Cooking time: 0 minutes

Servings: 8

Ingredients:

- ½ cup unsalted roasted cashews
- ¼ cup dried cranberries
- ¼ cup dried apricots
- ½ cup walnut halves
- ½ cup toasted hazelnuts

Directions:

1. In a bowl, combine all ingredients. Store in ¼ cup servings in resealable bags for up to six weeks.

VARIATION TIP: Replace the apricots and cranberries with ½ cup of dried apples.

Nutrition:

Calories: 144

Protein: 4 g

Total Fat: 11 g

797. Cucumber Sandwich Bites

Preparation Time: 5 minutes

Cooking Time: 0 minutes

Servings: 12

Ingredients:

- 1 cucumber, sliced
- 8 slices whole wheat bread
- 2 tablespoons cream cheese, soft
- 1 tablespoon chives, chopped
- ¼ cup avocado, peeled, pitted and mashed
- 1 teaspoon mustard
- Salt and black pepper to the taste

Directions:

1. Spread the mashed avocado on each bread slice, also spread the rest of the ingredients except the cucumber slices.

2. Divide the cucumber slices on the bread slices, cut each slice in thirds, arrange on a platter and serve as an appetizer.

Nutrition:
Calories 187;
Fat 12.4 g;
Fiber 2.1 g;
Carbs 4.5 g;
Protein 8.2 g

798. Chili Mango and Watermelon Salsa

Preparation Time: 5 minutes
Cooking Time: 0 minutes
Servings: 12
Ingredients:
- 1 red tomato, chopped
- Salt and black pepper to the taste
- 1 cup watermelon, seedless, peeled and cubed
- 1 red onion, chopped
- 2 mangos, peeled and chopped
- 2 chili peppers, chopped
- ¼ cup cilantro, chopped
- 3 tablespoons lime juice
- Pita chips for serving

Directions:
1. In a bowl, mix the tomato with the watermelon, the onion and the rest of the ingredients except the pita chips and toss well.
2. Divide the mix into small cups and serve with pita chips on the side.
Nutrition:
Calories 62;
Fat 4g;
Fiber 1.3 g;
Carbs 3.9 g;
Protein 2.3 g

799. Creamy Spinach and Shallots Dip

Preparation Time: 10 minutes
Cooking Time: 0 minutes
Servings: 4
Ingredients:
- 1-pound spinach, roughly chopped
- 2 shallots, chopped
- 2 tablespoons mint, chopped
- ¾ cup cream cheese, soft
- Salt and black pepper to the taste

Directions:
1. In a blender, combine the spinach with the shallots and the rest of the ingredients, and pulse well.
2. Divide into small bowls and serve as a party dip.
Nutrition:
Calories 204;
Fat 11.5 g;
Fiber 3.1 g;
Carbs 4.2 g;
Protein 5.9 g

800. Feta Artichoke Dip

Preparation Time: 10 minutes
Cooking Time: 30 minutes
Servings: 8
Ingredients:
- 8 ounces artichoke hearts, drained and quartered
- ¾ cup basil, chopped
- ¾ cup green olives, pitted and chopped
- 1 cup parmesan cheese, grated
- 5 ounces feta cheese, crumbled

Directions:
1. In your food processor, mix the artichokes with the basil and the rest of the ingredients, pulse well, and transfer to a baking dish.

2. Introduce in the oven, bake at 375° F for 30 minutes and serve as a party dip.
Nutrition:
Calories 186;
Fat 12.4 g;
Fiber 0.9 g;
Carbs 2.6 g;
Protein 1.5 g

801. Avocado Dip

Preparation Time: 5 minutes
Cooking Time: 0 minutes
Servings: 8
Ingredients:
- ½ cup heavy cream
- 1 green chili pepper, chopped
- Salt and pepper to the taste
- 4 avocados, pitted, peeled and chopped
- 1 cup cilantro, chopped
- ¼ cup lime juice

Directions:
1. In a blender, combine the cream with the avocados and the rest of the ingredients and pulse well.
2. Divide the mix into bowls and serve cold as a party dip.
Nutrition:
Calories 200;
Fat 14.5 g;
Fiber 3.8 g;
Carbs 8.1 g;
Protein 7.6 g

802. Goat Cheese and Chives Spread

Preparation Time: 10 minutes
Cooking Time: 0 minute
Servings: 4
Ingredients:
- 2 ounces goat cheese, crumbled
- ¾ cup sour cream
- 2 tablespoons chives, chopped
- 1 tablespoon lemon juice
- Salt and black pepper to the taste
- 2 tablespoons extra virgin olive oil

Directions:
1. In a bowl, mix the goat cheese with the cream and the rest of the ingredients and whisk really well.
2. Keep in the fridge for 10 minutes and serve as a party spread.
Nutrition:
Calories 220;
Fat 11.5 g;
Fiber 4.8 g;
Carbs 8.9 g;
Protein 5.6 g

803. Fluffy Bites

Preparation Time: 20 minutes
Cooking Time: 60 minutes
Servings: 12
Ingredients:
- 2 teaspoons cinnamon
- 2/3 cup sour cream
- 2 cups heavy cream
- 1 teaspoon scraped vanilla bean
- ¼ teaspoon cardamom
- 4 egg yolks
- Stevia to taste

Directions:

1. Start by whisking your egg yolks until creamy and smooth.
2. Get out a double boiler, and add your eggs with the rest of your ingredients. Mix well.
3. Remove from heat, allowing it to cool until it reaches room temperature.
4. Refrigerate for an hour before whisking well.
5. Pour into molds, and freeze for at least an hour before serving.

Nutrition:
Calories: 363
Protein: 2 g
Fat: 40 g
Carbohydrates: 1 g

804. Coconut Fudge

Preparation Time: 20 minutes
Cooking Time: 60 minutes
Servings: 12
Ingredients:
• 2 cups coconut oil
• ½ cup dark cocoa powder
• ½ cup coconut cream
• ¼ cup almonds, chopped
• ¼ cup coconut, shredded
• 1 teaspoon almond extract
• Pinch of salt
• Stevia to taste

Directions:

1. Pour your coconut oil and coconut cream in a bowl, whisking with an electric beater until smooth. Once the mixture becomes smooth and glossy, do not continue.
2. Begin to add in your cocoa powder while mixing slowly, making sure that there aren't any lumps.
3. Add in the rest of your ingredients, and mix well.
4. Line a pan with parchment paper, and freeze until it sets.
5. Slice into squares before serving.

Nutrition:
Calories: 172
Fat: 20 g
Carbohydrates: 3 g

805. Nutmeg Nougat

Preparation Time: 30 minutes
Cooking Time: 60 minutes
Servings: 12
Ingredients:
• 1 cup heavy cream
• 1 cup cashew butter
• 1 cup coconut, shredded
• ½ teaspoon nutmeg
• 1 teaspoon vanilla extract, pure
• Stevia to taste

Directions:

1. Melt your cashew butter using a double boiler, and then stir in your vanilla extract, dairy cream, nutmeg, and stevia. Make sure it's mixed well.
2. Remove from heat, allowing it to cool down before refrigerating it for half an hour.
3. Shape into balls, and coat with shredded coconut. Chill for at least two hours before serving.

Nutrition:
Calories: 341
Fat: 34 g
Carbohydrates: 5 g

806. Premium Roasted Baby Potatoes

Preparation Time: 10 Minutes
Cooking Time: 35 Minutes
Servings: 4
Ingredients:
• 2 pounds new yellow potatoes, scrubbed and cut into wedges
• 2 tablespoons extra virgin olive oil
• 2 teaspoons fresh rosemary, chopped
• 1 teaspoon garlic powder
• 1 teaspoon sweet paprika
• ½ teaspoon sea salt
• ½ teaspoon freshly ground black pepper

Directions:
1. Pre-heat your oven to 400 degrees Fahrenheit.
2. Take a large bowl and add potatoes, olive oil, garlic, rosemary, paprika, sea salt and pepper.
3. Spread potatoes in single layer on baking sheet and bake for 35 minutes.
4. Serve and enjoy!
Nutrition: Calories: 225 Fat: 7g Carbohydrates: 37g Protein: 5g

807. Fig with Yogurt and Honey

Preparation time: 5 minutes
Cooking time: 0 minutes
Servings: 2
Ingredients:
• 6 dried figs, sliced
• 4 teaspoons honey
• 1 1/3 cups low- fat plain Greek style yogurt

Directions:
1. Divide the figs into 2 bowls. Add honey and yogurt into a bowl and stir. Pour over the figs and serve.
Nutrition: Calories 208 Fat 3 g Carbohydrate 39 g Protein 9 g

808. Greek Fava

Preparation time: 10 minutes
Cooking time: 30 minutes
Servings: 4
INGREDIENTS:
• 2 cups Santorini fava (yellow split peas), rinsed
• 2 medium onions, chopped
• 2 ½ cups water
• 2 cups +2 tablespoons vegetable broth
• 1 teaspoon salt or Himalayan pink salt
• To garnish:
• Lemon juice as required
• Chopped parsley

Directions:
1. Place fava in a large pot. Add onions, broth, water and salt and stir. Place over medium heat. When it begins to boil, reduce the heat and cook until fava is tender.
2. Remove from heat and cool. Blend until creamy. Ladle into small plates. Add lemon juice and stir. Garnish with parsley and serve.
Nutrition: Calories 405 Fat 1 g Carbohydrate 75 g Protein 25 g

809. Hummus, Feta & Bell Pepper Crackers

Preparation time: 10 minutes
Cooking time: 0 minutes
Servings: 2
Ingredients:
- 4 tablespoons hummus
- 2 large whole grain crisp bread
- 4 tablespoons crumbled feta
- 1 small bell pepper, diced

Directions:
1. Top the pieces of crisp bread with hummus. Sprinkle feta cheese and bell peppers and serve.
Nutrition: Calories 136 Fat 7 g Carbohydrate 13 g Protein 6 g

810. Tomato & Basil Bruschetta

Preparation time: 10 minutes
Cooking time: 10 minutes
Servings: 3
Ingredients:
- 3 tomatoes, finely chopped
- 1 clove garlic, minced
- ¼ teaspoon garlic powder (optional)
- A handful basil leaves, coarsely chopped
- Salt to taste
- Pepper to taste
- ½ teaspoon olive oil
- ½ tablespoon balsamic vinegar
- ½ tablespoon butter
- ½ baguette French bread or Italian bread, cut into ½ inch thick slices

Directions:
1. Add tomatoes, garlic and basil in a bowl and toss well. Add salt and pepper. Drizzle oil and vinegar and toss well. Set aside for an hour.
2. Melt the butter and brush it over the baguette slices. Place in an oven and toast the slices. Sprinkle the tomato mixture on top and serve right away.
Nutrition: Calories 162 Fat 4 g Carbohydrate 29 g Protein 4 g

811. Lemon-Pepper Cucumbers

Preparation time: 5 minutes
Cooking time: 0 minutes
Servings: 2
Ingredients:
- 1 large cucumber, sliced
- Lemon juice, to taste
- Freshly ground pepper to taste

Directions:
1. Place cucumber slices on a serving platter. Trickle lemon juice over it. Garnish with pepper and serve.
Nutrition: Calories 24 Fat 0 g Carbohydrate 6 g Protein 1 g

812. Falafel

Preparation time: 30 minutes
Cooking time: 15 minutes
Servings: 2
Ingredients:
- 1 cup dried chickpeas (do not use cooked or canned)
- ½ cup fresh parsley leaves, discard stems
- ¼ cup fresh dill leaves, discard stems
- ½ cup fresh cilantro leaves
- 4 cloves garlic, peeled
- ½ tablespoon ground black pepper
- ½ tablespoon ground coriander
- ½ tablespoon ground cumin
- ½ teaspoon cayenne pepper (optional)
- ½ teaspoon baking powder
- ¼ teaspoon baking soda
- Salt to taste
- 1 tablespoon toasted sesame seeds
- Oil, as required

Directions:
1. Rinse chickpeas and soak in water overnight. Cover with at least 3 inches of water. Drain and dry by patting with a kitchen towel.
2. Add all the fresh herbs into a food processor. Process until finely chopped. Add chickpeas, spices and garlic and pulse for not more than 40 seconds each time until smooth.
3. Transfer into a container. Cover and chill for at least 1 hour or until use. Divide the mixture into 12 equal portions and shape into patties.
4. Place a deep pan over medium heat. Pour enough oil to cover at least 3 inches from the bottom of the pan.
5. When the oil is well heated, but not smoking, drop falafel, a few at a time and fry until medium brown.
6. Remove with a spoon and place on a plate lined with paper towels. Serve with a dip of your choice.
Nutrition: Calories 93 Fat 3.8 g Carbohydrate 1.3 g Protein 3.9 g

813. Walnut-Feta Yogurt Dip

Preparation time: 15 minutes + chilling
Cooking time: 0 minutes
Servings: 8 (2 tablespoons dip without vegetable sticks)
Ingredients:
- 2 cups plain low-fat yogurt
- ¼ cup crumbled feta cheese
- 3 tablespoons chopped walnuts or pine nuts
- 1 teaspoon chopped fresh oregano or marjoram or ½ teaspoon dried oregano or marjoram, crushed
- Freshly ground pepper to taste
- Salt to taste
- 1 tablespoon snipped dried tomatoes (not oil packed)
- Salt to taste
- Walnut halves to garnish
- Assorted vegetable sticks to serve

Directions:
1. For yogurt dip, place 3 layers of cotton cheesecloth over a strainer. Place strainer over a bowl. Add yogurt into the strainer. Cover the strainer with cling wrap. Refrigerate for 24-48 hours.
2. Discard the strained liquid and add yogurt into a bowl. Add feta cheese, walnuts, seasoning, and herbs and mix well. Cover and chill for an hour.
3. Garnish with walnut halves. Serve with vegetable sticks.
Nutrition: Calories 68 Fat 4 g Carbohydrate 5 g Protein 4 g

814. Date Wraps

Preparation time: 10 minutes
Cooking time: 0 minutes
Servings: 8
Ingredients:
- 8 whole dates, pitted
- 8 thin slices prosciutto
- Freshly ground pepper to taste

Directions:
1. Take one date and one slice prosciutto. Wrap the prosciutto around the dates and place on a serving platter. Garnish with pepper and serve.
Nutrition: Calories 35 Fat 1 g Carbohydrate 6 g Protein 2 g

815. Clementine & Pistachio Ricotta

Preparation time: 5 minutes
Cooking time: 0 minutes
Servings: 2
Ingredients:
- 2/3 cup part-skim ricotta
- 2 clementine's, peeled, separated into segments, deseeded
- 4 teaspoons chopped pistachio nuts
Directions:
1. Place 1/3 cup ricotta in each of 2 bowls. Divide the clementine segments equally and place over the ricotta. Sprinkle pistachio nuts on top and serve.
Nutrition: Calories 178 Fat 9 g Carbohydrate 15 g Protein 11 g

816. Serrano-Wrapped Plums

Preparation time: 10 minutes
Cooking time: 0 minutes
Servings: 4
Ingredients:
- 2 firm ripe plums or peaches or nectarines, quartered
- 1 ounce thinly sliced Serrano ham or prosciutto or jamón Ibérico, cut into 8 pieces
Directions:
1. Take one piece of ham and one piece of fruit. Wrap the ham around the fruit and place on a serving platter. Serve.
Nutrition: Calories 30 Fat 1 g Carbohydrate 4 g Protein 2 g

817. Easy Salmon Burger

Preparation Time: 15 minutes
Cooking Time: 15 minutes
Servings: 6
Ingredients:
- 16 ounces pink salmon, minced
- 1 cup prepared mashed potatoes
- 1 medium onion, chopped
- 1 stalk celery, finely chopped
- 1 large egg, lightly beaten
- 2 tablespoons fresh cilantro, chopped
- 1 cup breadcrumbs
- Vegetable oil, for deep frying
- Salt and freshly ground black pepper
Directions:
1. Combine the salmon, mashed potatoes, onion, celery, egg, and cilantro in a mixing bowl. Season to taste and mix thoroughly.
2. Spoon about 2 tablespoon mixture, roll in breadcrumbs, and then form into small patties.
3. Heat oil in a non-stick frying pan. Cook your salmon patties for 5 minutes on each side or until golden brown and crispy. Serve in burger buns and with coleslaw on the side if desired.
Nutrition:
Calories 230
Fat 7.9 g
Carbs 20.9 g
Protein 18.9 g

818. Salmon Sandwich with Avocado and Egg

Preparation Time: 15 minutes
Cooking Time: 10 minutes
Servings: 4
Ingredients:
- 8 ounces smoked salmon, thinly sliced
- 1 medium ripe avocado, thinly sliced
- 4 large poached eggs
- 4 slices whole-wheat bread
- 2 cups arugula or baby rocket
- Salt and freshly ground black pepper
Directions:
1. Place 1 bread slice on a plate top with arugula, avocado, salmon, and poached egg. Season with salt and pepper. Repeat the procedure for the remaining ingredients. Serve and enjoy.
Nutrition:
Calories: 310
Fat: 18.2 g
Carbohydrates: 16.4 g
Protein: 21.3 g

819. Salmon Spinach and Cottage Cheese Sandwich

Preparation Time: 15 minutes
Cooking Time: 10 minutes
Servings: 4
Ingredients:
- 4 ounces of cottage cheese
- 1/4 cup chives, chopped
- 1 teaspoon capers
- 1/2 teaspoon grated lemon rind
- 4 smoked salmon
- 2 cups loose baby spinach
- 1 medium red onion, sliced thinly
- 8 slices rye bread
- Kosher salt and freshly ground black pepper
Directions:
1. Preheat your griddle or Panini press. Mix cottage cheese, chives, capers, and lemon rind in a small bowl.
2. Spread and divide the cheese mixture on 4 bread slices. Top with spinach, onion slices, and smoked salmon.
3. Cover with remaining bread slices. Grill the sandwiches until golden and grill marks form on both sides. Transfer to a serving dish. Serve and enjoy.
Nutrition:
Calories: 261
Fat 9.9 g
Carbohydrates 22.9 g
Protein 19.9 g

820. Salmon Feta and Pesto Wrap

Preparation Time: 15 minutes
Cooking Time: 10 minutes
Servings: 4
Ingredients:
- 8 ounces smoked salmon fillet, thinly sliced
- 1 cup feta cheese
- 8 Romaine lettuce leaves
- 4 pita bread
- 1/4 cup basil pesto sauce
Directions:
1. Place 1 pita bread on a plate. Top with lettuce, salmon, feta cheese, and pesto sauce. Fold or roll to enclose filling. Repeat the procedure for the remaining ingredients. Serve and enjoy.
Nutrition:
Calories: 379
Fat 17.7 g
Carbohydrates: 36.6 g
Protein: 18.4 g

821. Salmon Cream Cheese and Onion on Bagel

Preparation Time: 15 minutes
Cooking Time: 10 minutes
Servings: 4
Ingredients:
- 8 ounces smoked salmon fillet, thinly sliced
- 1/2 cup cream cheese
- 1 medium onion, thinly sliced
- 4 bagels (about 80g each), split
- 2 tablespoons fresh parsley, chopped
- Freshly ground black pepper, to taste

Directions:
1. Spread the cream cheese on each bottom's half of bagels. Top with salmon and onion, season with pepper, sprinkle with parsley, and then cover with bagel tops. Serve and enjoy.

Nutrition:
Calories: 309
Fat 14.1 g
Carbohydrates 32.0 g
Protein 14.7 g

822. Greek Baklava

Preparation Time: 20 minutes
Cooking Time: 20 minutes
Servings: 18
Ingredients:
- 1 package phyllo dough
- 1 lb. chopped nuts
- 1 cup butter
- 1 teaspoon ground cinnamon
- 1 cup of water
- 1 cup white sugar
- 1 teaspoon. vanilla extract
- 1/2 cup honey

Directions:
1. Warm oven to 175°C or 350°Fahrenheit. Spread butter on the sides and bottom of a 9-in by the 13-in pan.
2. Chop the nuts, then mix with cinnamon; set it aside. Unfurl the phyllo dough, then halve the whole stack to fit the pan. Use a damp cloth to cover the phyllo to prevent drying as you proceed.
3. Put two phyllo sheets in the pan, then butter well. Repeat to make eight layered phyllo sheets. Scatter 2-3 tablespoons of the nut mixture over the sheets
4. Place two more phyllo sheets on top; butter, then sprinkle with nuts. Layer as you go. The final layer should be six to eight phyllo sheets deep.
5. Make square or diamond shapes with a sharp knife up to the bottom of the pan. You can slice into four long rows for diagonal shapes. Bake until crisp and golden for 50 minutes.
6. Meanwhile, boil water and sugar until the sugar melts to make the sauce; mix in honey and vanilla. Let it simmer for 20 minutes.
7. Take the baklava out of the oven, then drizzle with sauce right away; cool. Serve the baklava in cupcake papers. You can also freeze them without cover. The baklava will turn soggy when wrapped.

Nutrition:
Calories: 393
Carbohydrate: 37.5 g
Fat: 25.9 g
Protein: 6.1 g

823. Glazed Bananas in Phyllo Nut Cups

Preparation Time: 30 minutes
Cooking Time: 45 minutes
Servings: 6.
Ingredients:
- 3/4 cup shelled pistachios
- 1/2 cup sugar
- 1 teaspoon. ground cinnamon
- 4 sheets phyllo dough (14 inches x 9 inches)
- 1/4 cup butter, melted
Sauce:
- 3/4 cup butter, cubed
- 3/4 cup packed brown sugar
- 3 medium firm bananas, sliced
- 1/4 teaspoon. ground cinnamon
- 3 to 4 cups of vanilla ice cream

Directions:
1. Finely chop sugar and pistachios in a food processor; move to a bowl, then mix in cinnamon. Slice each phyllo sheet into 6 four-inch squares, get rid of the trimmings. Pile the squares, then use plastic wrap to cover.
2. Slather melted butter on each square one at a time, then scatter a heaping tablespoonful of pistachio mixture. Pile 3 squares, flip each at an angle to misalign the corners.
3. Force each stack on the sides and bottom of an oiled eight-oz. Custard cup. Bake for 15-20 minutes in a 350 degrees F oven until golden; cool for 5 minutes. Move to a wire rack to cool completely.
4. Melt and boil brown sugar and butter in a saucepan to make the sauce; lower heat. Mix in cinnamon and bananas gently; heat thoroughly.
5. Put ice cream in the phyllo cups until full, then put banana sauce on top. Serve right away.

Nutrition:
Calories: 735
Carbohydrate: 82 g
Fat: 45 g
Protein: 7 g

824. Salmon Apple Salad Sandwich

Preparation Time: 15 minutes
Cooking Time: 10 minutes
Servings: 4
Ingredients:
- 4 ounces canned pink salmon, drained and flaked
- 1 medium red apple, cored and diced
- 1 celery stalk, chopped
- 1 shallot, finely chopped
- 1/3 cup light mayonnaise
- 8 slices whole-grain bread, toasted
- 8 Romaine lettuce leaves
- Salt and freshly ground black pepper

Directions:
1. Combine the salmon, apple, celery, shallot, and mayonnaise in a mixing bowl. Season with salt and pepper.
2. Put 1 slice of bread on your plate, top with lettuce and salmon salad, and then covers with another piece of bread—repeat the procedure for the remaining ingredients. Serve and enjoy.

Nutrition:
Calories: 315
Fat 11.3 g
Carbohydrates 40.4 g
Protein 15.1 g

825. Smoked Salmon and Cheese on Rye Bread

Preparation Time: 15 minutes
Cooking Time: 10 minutes
Servings: 4
Ingredients:
- 8 ounces smoked salmon, thinly sliced
- 1/3 cup mayonnaise
- 2 tablespoons lemon juice
- 1 tablespoon Dijon mustard
- 1 teaspoon garlic, minced
- 4 slices cheddar cheese
- 8 slices rye bread
- 8 Romaine lettuce leaves
- Salt and freshly ground black pepper

Directions:
1. Mix the mayonnaise, lemon juice, mustard, and garlic in a small bowl. Flavor with salt plus pepper and set aside.
2. Spread dressing on 4 bread slices. Top with lettuce, salmon, and cheese. Cover with remaining rye bread slices. Serve and enjoy.

Nutrition:
Calories: 365
Fat: 16.6 g
Carbohydrates: 31.6 g
Protein: 18.8 g

826. Bulgur Lamb Meatballs

Preparation Time: 10 minutes
Cooking Time: 15 minutes
 Servings: 6
Ingredients:
- 1 and ½ cups Greek yogurt
- ½ teaspoon cumin, ground
- 1 cup cucumber, shredded
- ½ teaspoon garlic, minced
- A pinch of salt and black pepper
- 1 cup bulgur
- 2 cups of water
- 1-pound lamb, ground
- ¼ cup parsley, chopped
- ¼ cup shallots, chopped
- ½ teaspoon allspice, ground
- ½ teaspoon cinnamon powder
- 1 tablespoon olive oil

Directions:
1. In a bowl, mix the bulgur with the water, cover the bowl, leave aside for 10 minutes, drain and transfer to a bowl.
2. Add the meat, the yogurt, and the rest of the ingredients except the oil, stir well and shape medium meatballs out of this mix.
3. Heat-up a pan with the oil over medium-high heat, add the meatballs, cook them for 7 minutes on each side, arrange them all on a platter and serve as an appetizer.

Nutrition:
Calories 300
Fat 9.6 g
Carbs 22.6 g
Protein 6.6 g

827. Cucumber Bites

Preparation Time: 10 minutes
Cooking Time: 0 minutes
Servings: 12
Ingredients:
- 1 English cucumber, sliced into 32 rounds

- 10 ounces hummus
- 16 cherry tomatoes, halved
- 1 tablespoon parsley, chopped
- 1-ounce feta cheese, crumbled

Directions:
1. Spread the hummus on each cucumber round, divide the tomato halves on each. Sprinkle the cheese and parsley on to, and serve.

Nutrition:
Calories 162
Fat 3.4 g
Fiber 2 g
Carbs 6.4 g
Protein 2.4 g

828. Stuffed Avocado

Preparation Time: 10 minutes
Cooking Time: 0 minute
Servings: 2
Ingredients:
- 1 avocado, halved and pitted
- 10 ounces of canned tuna, drained
- 2 tablespoons sun-dried tomatoes, chopped
- 1 and ½ tablespoon basil pesto
- 2 tablespoons black olives, pitted and chopped
- Salt and black pepper to the taste
- 2 teaspoons pine nuts, toasted and chopped
- 1 tablespoon basil, chopped

Directions:
1. In a bowl, mix the tuna plus sun-dried tomatoes and the rest of the ingredients except the avocado and stir. Stuff the avocado halves with the tuna mix and serve as an appetizer.

Nutrition:
Calories 233
Fat 9 g
Carbs 11.4 g
Protein 5.6 g

829. Hummus with Ground Lamb

Preparation Time: 10 minutes
Cooking Time: 15 minutes
Servings: 8
Ingredients:
- 10 ounces hummus
- 12 ounces lamb meat, ground
- ½ cup pomegranate seeds
- ¼ cup parsley, chopped
- 1 tablespoon olive oil
- Pita chips for serving

Directions:
1. Heat-up pan with the oil over medium-high heat, add the meat, and brown for 15 minutes, stirring often.
2. Spread the hummus on a platter, spread the ground lamb all over, also spread the pomegranate seeds and the parsley, and serve with pita chips as a snack.

Nutrition:
Calories 133
Fat 9.7 g
Carbs 6.4 g
Protein 5 g

830. Wrapped Plums

Preparation Time: 5 minutes
Cooking Time: 0 minutes
Servings: 8
Ingredients:
- 2 ounces prosciutto, cut into 16 pieces

- 4 plums, quartered
- 1 tablespoon chives, chopped
- A pinch of red pepper flakes, crushed

Directions:

1. Wrap each plum quarter in a prosciutto slice, arrange them all on a platter, sprinkle the chives and pepper flakes all over, and serve.

Nutrition:

Calories 30

Fat 1 g

Carbs 4 g

Protein 2 g

831. Veggie Fritters

Preparation Time: 10 minutes

Cooking Time: 10 minutes

Servings: 4

Ingredients:

- 2 garlic cloves, minced
- 2 yellow onions, chopped
- 4 scallions, chopped
- 2 carrots, grated
- 2 teaspoons cumin, ground
- ½ teaspoon turmeric powder
- Salt and black pepper to the taste
- ¼ teaspoon coriander, ground
- 2 tablespoons parsley, chopped
- ¼ teaspoon lemon juice
- ½ cup almond flour
- 2 beets, peeled and grated
- 2 eggs, whisked
- ¼ cup tapioca flour
- 3 tablespoons olive oil

Directions:

1. In a bowl, combine the garlic, onions, scallions, and the rest of the ingredients except the oil, stir well and shape medium fritters out of this mix.

2. Heat oil in a pan over medium-high heat, add the fritters, cook for 5 minutes on each side, arrange on a platter and serve.

Nutrition:

Calories 209

Fat 11.2 g

Carbs 4.4 g

Protein 4.8 g

832. White Bean Dip

Preparation Time: 10 minutes

Cooking Time: 0 minute

Servings: 4

Ingredients:

- 15 oz white beans, drained & rinsed
- 6 ounces canned artichoke hearts, drained and quartered
- 4 garlic cloves, minced
- 1 tablespoon basil, chopped
- 2 tablespoons olive oil
- Juice of ½ lemon
- Zest of ½ lemon, grated
- Salt and black pepper to the taste

Directions:

1. In your food processor, combine the beans, artichokes, and the rest of the ingredients except the oil and pulse well. Add the oil gradually, pulse the mix again, divide into cups, and serve as a party dip.

Nutrition:

Calories 274

Fat 11.7 g

Carbs 18.5 g

Protein 16.5 g

833. Eggplant Dip

Preparation Time: 10 minutes

Cooking Time: 40 minutes

Servings: 4

Ingredients:

- 1 eggplant, poked with a fork
- 2 tablespoons tahini paste
- 2 tablespoons lemon juice
- 2 garlic cloves, minced
- 1 tablespoon olive oil
- Salt and black pepper to the taste
- 1 tablespoon parsley, chopped

Directions:

1. Put the eggplant in a roasting pan, bake at 400° F for 40 minutes, cool down, peel and transfer to your food processor.

2. Add the remaining ingredients except for the parsley, pulse well, divide into small bowls and serve as an appetizer with the parsley sprinkled on top.

Nutrition:

Calories 121

Fat 4.3 g

Carbs 1.4 g

Protein 4.3 g

834. Cucumber Rolls

Preparation Time: 5 minutes

Cooking Time: 0 minutes

Servings: 6

Ingredients:

- 1 big cucumber, sliced lengthwise
- 1 tablespoon parsley, chopped
- 8 ounces canned tuna, drained and mashed
- Salt and black pepper to the taste
- 1 teaspoon lime juice

Directions:

1. Arrange cucumber slices on a working surface, divide the rest of the ingredients, and roll. Arrange all the rolls on a surface and serve.

Nutrition:

Calories 200

Fat 6 g

Carbs 7.6 g

Protein 3.5 g

835. Olives and Cheese Stuffed Tomatoes

Preparation Time: 10 minutes

Cooking Time: 0 minutes

Servings: 24

Ingredients:

- 24 cherry tomatoes, top cut off, and insides scooped out
- 2 tablespoons olive oil
- ¼ teaspoon red pepper flakes
- ½ cup feta cheese, crumbled
- 2 tablespoons black olive paste
- ¼ cup mint, torn

Directions:

1. In a bowl, mix the olives paste with the rest of the ingredients except the cherry tomatoes and whisk. Stuff the cherry tomatoes with this mix, arrange them all on a platter, and serve.

Nutrition:

Calories 136

Fat 8.6 g

Carbs 5.6 g

Protein 5.1 g

836. Tomato Salsa

Preparation Time: 5 minutes
Cooking Time: 0 minutes
Servings: 6
Ingredients:
- 1 garlic clove, minced
- 4 tablespoons olive oil
- 5 tomatoes, cubed
- 1 tablespoon balsamic vinegar
- ¼ cup basil, chopped
- 1 tablespoon parsley, chopped
- 1 tablespoon chives, chopped
- Salt and black pepper to the taste
- Pita chips for serving

Directions:
1. Mix the tomatoes plus garlic in a bowl, and the rest of the ingredients except the pita chips, stir, divide into small cups and serve with the pita chips on the side.

Nutrition:
Calories 160
Fat 13.7 g
Carbs 10.1 g
Protein 2.2

837. Mini Burgers and Sauce

Preparation time: 5 minutes
Cooking time: 6 minutes
Servings: 16
Ingredients:
For the sauce:
- ¾ cup Greek yogurt
- 1 teaspoon lemon zest, grated
- 1 garlic clove minced
- ¼ teaspoon dill, chopped
- A pinch of salt and black pepper
For the burgers:
- 1-pound beef, ground
- ¼ cup bread crumbs
- 2 teaspoons lemon juice
- 1 tablespoon balsamic vinegar
- 1 teaspoon oregano, dried
- 1 teaspoon thyme, chopped
- 3 garlic cloves, minced
- 16 mini pita bread, sliced in halves horizontally
- Cooking spray
- 1 cucumber, sliced

Directions:
1. In a bowl, mix the yogurt with the lemon zest and the other ingredients for the sauce, whisk and leave aside for now.
2. In a separate bowl mix the meat with the bread crumbs and the other ingredients except the pita bread, cucumber and cooking spray stir well and shape 16 small burgers out of this mix.
3. Place the mini burgers on your preheated grill, grease them with cooking spray and cook for 3 minutes on each side.
4. Divide the burgers on 16 of the pita bread halves, spread the sauce all over, divide the cucumber slices over the burgers and tip with the other pita halves, arrange on a platter and serve as an appetizer.

Nutrition: calories 210, fat 11, fiber 5, carbs 12, protein 7

838. Tuna Rolls

Preparation time: 10 minutes
Cooking time: 0 minutes
Servings: 6
Ingredients:
- 1 big cucumber, sliced lengthwise
- 1 tablespoon cilantro, chopped
- 1 tablespoon cranberries, dried
- 4 ounces canned sardines, drained and flaked
- 3 ounces canned tuna pate
- Salt and black pepper to taste
- 1 teaspoon lemon juice

Directions:
1. In a bowl, mix sardines with tuna paste, salt and pepper to taste and lemon juice and mash everything well.
2. Spoon this mix on each cucumber slice, add the rest of the ingredients on top, roll, arrange on a platter and serve.

Nutrition: calories 80, fat 1, fiber 2, carbs 2, protein 1

839. Cheese Stuffed Tomatoes

Preparation time: 10 minutes
Cooking time: 2minutes
Servings: 24
Ingredients:
- 24 cherry tomatoes, top cut off and insides scooped out
- 2 tablespoons olive oil
- A pinch of salt
- ¼ teaspoon red pepper flakes
- ½ cup feta cheese, cut into 24 pieces
- 1 tablespoon black olive paste
- 1 tablespoon water
- ¼ cup mint, torn

Directions:
1. Season each tomato with pepper flakes and drizzle half of the oil.
2. Insert a feta cheese cube in each tomato, place them under preheated broiler over medium heat and broil them for 2 minutes.
3. In a bowl, mix the rest of the ingredients except the mint, whisk, spread on a platter, arrange the tomatoes on top and serve. with the mint sprinkled on top.

Nutrition: calories 110, fat 1, fiber 2, carbs 2, protein 2

840. Tomato Toasts

Preparation time: 10 minutes
Cooking time: 5 minutes
Servings: 6
Ingredients:
- 1 garlic clove, minced
- 4 tablespoons olive oil
- 5 tomatoes, chopped
- 1 tablespoon balsamic vinegar
- ¼ cup basil, chopped
- A pinch of red pepper flakes
- 14 slices whole wheat baguette
- Salt and black pepper to taste

Directions:
1. In a bowl, mix tomatoes with 3 tablespoons oil and the other ingredients except the baguette and stir.
2. Arrange bread slices on a lined baking sheet, place them in the oven at 350 degrees F, toast for 5 minutes, arrange on a platter, divide tomato mix on them, drizzle the remaining oil all over and serve as an appetizer.

Nutrition: calories 84, fat 1, fiber 1, carbs 1, protein 1

841. Tomato and Watermelon Salsa

Preparation time: 2 hours and 5 minutes
Cooking time: 0 minutes
Servings: 16
Ingredients:
- 3 yellow tomatoes, seedless and chopped
- 1 red tomato, seedless and chopped
- Salt and black pepper to taste
- 1 cup watermelon, seedless and chopped
- 1/3 cup red onion, chopped
- 1 mango, peeled, seedless and chopped
- 2 jalapeno peppers, chopped
- ¼ cup cilantro, chopped
- 3 tablespoons lime juice
- 2 teaspoons honey

Directions:
1. In a bowl, combine the tomatoes with the watermelon and the other ingredients, toss, keep in the fridge for 2 hours and then serve.
Nutrition: calories 83, fat 2, fiber 1, carbs 2, protein 1

842. Green Dip

Preparation time: 15 minutes
Cooking time: 0 minutes
Servings: 4
Ingredients:
- 1 bunch spinach, roughly chopped
- 1 scallion, sliced
- 2 tablespoons mint, chopped
- ¾ cup sour cream
- Salt and black pepper to taste

Directions:
1. Put some water in a saucepan, bring to a boil over medium heat, add spinach, cook for 20 seconds, rinse and drain well, chop and put in a bowl.
2. Add the rest of the ingredients, blend with an immersion blender, stir well, leave aside for 15 minutes and then serve.
Nutrition: calories 110, fat 1, fiber 1, carbs 1, protein 5

843. Basil Artichoke Spread

Preparation time: 10 minutes
Cooking time: 30 minutes
Servings: 10
Ingredients:
- 8 ounces artichoke hearts
- ¾ cup basil, chopped
- ¾ cup green olive paste
- 1 cup parmesan cheese, grated
- 5 ounces garlic and herb cheese

Directions:
1. In a food processor, mix artichokes with basil and the other ingredients, pulse well and spread into a baking dish,
2. Place in the oven at 375 degrees F and bake for 30 minutes. Serve warm.
Nutrition: calories 152, fat 2, fiber 3, carbs 3, protein 1

844. Lemon Cilantro and Avocado Dip

Preparation time: 10 minutes
Cooking time: 0 minutes
Servings: 8
Ingredients:
- ½ cup sour cream
- 1 chili pepper, chopped
- Salt and pepper to taste
- 4 avocados, pitted, peeled and chopped
- 1 cup cilantro, chopped
- ¼ cup lemon juice
- Carrot sticks for serving

Directions:
1. Put avocados in a blender and pulse a few times.
2. Add the rest of the ingredients, pulse well, transfer to a bowl and serve as a snack.
Nutrition: calories 112, fat 1, fiber 2, carbs 2, protein 4

845. Potato Chips and Dip

Preparation time: 10 minutes
Cooking time: 10 minutes
Servings: 4
Ingredients:
- 2 ounces goats cheese, soft
- ¾ cup sour cream
- 1 shallot, minced
- 1 tablespoon chives, chopped
- 1 tablespoon lemon juice
- Salt and black pepper to taste
- ½ pound potatoes, sliced
- ½ pound purple potatoes, sliced
- 2 tablespoons extra virgin olive oil

Directions:
1. In a bowl, mix the chives with the cream and the other ingredients except the potatoes and the oil and whisk.
2. In another bowl, mix potato slices with salt and olive oil and toss to coat.
3. Heat up a grill pan over medium high heat, add potato slices, grill for 5 minutes on each side, transfer them to a bowl and serve with the dip on the side.
Nutrition: calories 110, fat 2, fiber 2, carbs 2, protein 5

846. Chickpeas and Arugula Salsa

Preparation time: 10 minutes
Cooking time: 0 minutes
Servings: 6
Ingredients:
- 4 scallions, sliced
- 1 cup arugula, chopped
- 15 ounces canned chickpeas, chopped
- Salt and black pepper to taste
- 2 jarred red peppers, roasted and chopped
- 2 tablespoons olive oil
- 2 tablespoons lemon juice

Directions:
1. In a bowl, mix the chickpeas with the arugula and the other ingredients, toss and serve.
Nutrition: calories 74, fat 2, fiber 2, carbs 6, protein 2

847. Dill Dip

Preparation time: 10 minutes
Cooking time: 0 minutes
Servings: 8
Ingredients:
- 1 garlic clove, minced
- 2 cups Greek yogurt
- ¼ cup dill, chopped
- ¼ cup walnuts, chopped
- Salt and black pepper to taste

Directions:
1. In a bowl, mix the yogurt with the dill and the other ingredients, whisk well, stir again and serve.
Nutrition: calories 73, fat 2, fiber 1, carbs 2, protein 3

848. Goats Cheese Dip

Preparation time: 10 minutes
Cooking time: 0 minutes
Servings: 4
Ingredients:
- ¼ cup mixed parsley and chives, chopped
- 8 ounces goat cheese, soft
- Black pepper to taste
Directions:
1. In a food processor mix the parsley with the cheese and black pepper, pulse well, divide into bowls and serve as a snack.
Nutrition: calories 152, fat 2, fiber 2, carbs 2, protein 1

849. Cannelini Beans Dip

Preparation time: 10 minutes
Cooking time: 0 minutes
Servings: 8
Ingredients:
- 19 ounces canned cannellini beans, drained
- 3 scallions, chopped
- 1 garlic clove, minced
- 3 tablespoons olive oil
- Salt and black pepper to taste
- 1 tablespoon lemon juice
- 2 ounces prosciutto, chopped
Directions:
1. In a bowl, combine the beans with the scallions and the other ingredients, whisk well, divide into bowls and serve.
Nutrition: calories 62, fat 4, fiber 1, carbs 1, protein 3

850. Cream Cheese Dip

Preparation time: 10 minutes
Cooking time: 0 minutes
Servings: 6
Ingredients:
- 12 ounces Greek cream cheese
- 1 big tomato, cut in quarters
- ¼ cup mayonnaise
- 2 garlic clove, minced
- 2 tablespoons yellow onion, chopped
- 1 celery stalk, chopped
- 1 teaspoon sugar
- 2 tablespoons lemon juice
- Salt and black pepper to taste
- 4 drops hot sauce
Directions:
1. In a blender, mix the cream cheese with the tomato and the other ingredients and pulse well.
2. Transfer to a bowl and serve.
Nutrition: calories 74, fat 3, fiber 1, carbs 3, protein 4

851. Pesto Dip

Preparation time: 10 minutes
Cooking time: 0 minutes
Servings: 6
Ingredients:
- 1 cup mayonnaise
- 7 ounces Greek basil pesto sauce
- Salt and black pepper to taste
- 1 cup sour cream
Directions:
1. In a bowl, combine the mayo with the pesto and the other ingredients, whisk and keep in the fridge until ready to serve.
Nutrition: calories 87, fat 2, fiber 0, carbs 1, protein 2

852. Chips and Vinaigrette

Preparation time: 1 hour and 10 minutes
Cooking time: 30 minutes
Servings: 4
Ingredients:
- 2 beets, sliced
- A pinch of sea salt
For the vinaigrette:
- 1/3 cup champagne vinegar
- A pinch of black pepper
- 1 cup olive oil
- 1 teaspoon green tea powder
Directions:
1. Put the vinegar in a small saucepan and heat over medium heat.
2. Add salt, pepper and green tea powder, whisk and keep in the fridge for 1 hour.
3. Add beets slices and a pinch of salt, arrange them on a lined baking sheet and bake at 350 degrees F for 30 minutes.
4. Leave them to cool down completely before serving with the vinaigrette on the side for your next party as a snack.
Nutrition: calories 100, fat 2, fiber 2, carbs 3, protein 2

853. Cucumber Cups

Preparation time: 10 minutes
Cooking time: 0 minutes
Servings: 20
Ingredients:
- 2 big cucumbers, cut into ½ inch thick slices and seeds scooped out
- 2 cups canned chickpeas, drained
- 7 ounces canned red peppers, roasted, drained and chopped
- ¼ cup lemon juice
- 1/3 cup tahini paste
- 1 garlic clove, minced
- Salt and black pepper to taste
- ¼ teaspoon cumin, ground
- 3 tablespoons olive oil
- 1 tablespoon hot water
Directions:
1. In a food processor, mix red peppers with chickpeas with the oil and the other ingredients except the cucumber cups and pulse well.
2. Arrange cucumber cups on a platter, fill each with chickpeas mix and serve right away as an appetizer.
Nutrition: calories 182, fat 1, fiber 3, carbs 4, protein 2

854. Salmon Platter

Preparation time: 7 minutes
Cooking time: 0 minutes
Servings: 44
Ingredients:
- 1 big long cucumber, sliced into 44 pieces
- 2 teaspoons lemon juice
- 4 ounces sour cream
- 1 teaspoon lemon zest, finely grated
- Salt and black pepper to taste
- 2 teaspoons dill, chopped
- 4 ounces smoked salmon, cut into 44 strips
Directions:
1. In a bowl, mix lemon juice with lemon zest and the other ingredients except the cucumber and salmon strips and stir.
2. Arrange cucumber and salmon stirps on a platter, add ½ teaspoon cream mix on each and serve.

855. Eggplant Meatballs

Preparation time: 15 minutes
Cooking time: 1 hour
Servings: 6
Ingredients:
- 4 cups eggplants, cubed
- 3 tablespoons olive oil
- 3 garlic cloves, minced
- 1 tablespoon water
- 2 eggs, whisked
- Salt and black pepper to taste
- 1 cup parsley, chopped
- ½ cup parmesan cheese, finely grated
- ¾ cups breadcrumbs

Directions:
1. Heat a pan with the oil over medium high heat, add garlic and eggplant, stir and brown it for a few minutes.
2. Add water, stir, reduce heat to low, cover pan, cook for 20 minutes and transfer them to a bowl.
3. Add the rest of the ingredients except the parmesan, stir well, shape medium balls and arrange them on a lined baking sheet.
4. Place them in oven at 350 degrees F and bake for 30 minutes.
5. Sprinkle parmesan, arrange on a platter and serve as an appetizer.

Nutrition: calories 142, fat 1, fiber 3, carbs 2, protein 3

856. Eggplant Platter

Preparation time: 10 minutes
Cooking time: 15 minutes
Servings: 8
Ingredients:
- 2 eggplants, cut into 20 slices
- A drizzle of olive oil

For the tapenade:
- 2 tablespoons olive oil
- ½ cup bottled roasted peppers, chopped
- ½ cup kalamata and black olives, pitted and chopped
- 1 tablespoon lemon juice
- 1 teaspoon red pepper flakes, crushed
- Salt and black pepper to the taste
- 2 tablespoons mixed mint, parsley, oregano and basil, chopped

For serving:
- 2 tablespoons pine nuts, toasted
- 4 tablespoons feta cheese, crumbled
- A drizzle of olive oil

Directions:
1. In a bowl, mix roasted peppers with 2 tablespoons oil and the other ingredients for the tapenade, stir well and keep in the fridge.
2. Brush eggplant slices with a drizzle of olive oil on both sides, place them on preheated grill pan over medium high heat, cook for 7 minutes on each side and transfer them to a platter.
3. Top each eggplant slice with the tapenade mix, also sprinkle the rest of the ingredients and serve.

Nutrition: calories 132, fat 2, fiber 3, carbs 4, protein 4

Chapter 12. Dessert Recipes

857. Banana, Cranberry, and Oat Bars

Preparation time: 15 minutes
Cooking time: 40 minutes
Servings: 16 bars
INGREDIENTS:
- 2 tablespoon extra-virgin olive oil
- 2 medium ripe bananas, mashed
- ½ cup almond butter
- ½ cup maple syrup
- 1/3 cup dried cranberries
- 1½ cups old-fashioned rolled oats
- ¼ cup oat flour
- ¼ cup ground flaxseed
- ¼ teaspoon ground cloves
- ½ cup shredded coconut
- ½ teaspoon ground cinnamon
- 1 teaspoon vanilla extract

DIRECTIONS:
1. Preheat the oven to 400°F (205°C). Line an 8-inch square pan with parchment paper, then grease with olive oil.
2. Combine the mashed bananas, almond butter, and maple syrup in a bowl. Stir to mix well. Mix in the remaining ingredients and stir to mix well until thick and sticky.
3. Spread the mixture evenly on the square pan with a spatula, then bake in the preheated oven for 40 minutes or until a toothpick inserted in the center comes out clean.
4. Remove them from the oven and slice into 16 bars to serve.

NUTRITION: Calories: 145 Fat: 7.2g Protein: 3.1g Carbs: 18.9g

858. Berry and Rhubarb Cobbler

Preparation time: 15 minutes
Cooking time: 35 minutes
Servings: 8
INGREDIENTS:
Cobbler:
- 1 cup fresh raspberries
- 2 cups fresh blueberries
- 1 cup sliced (½-inch) rhubarb pieces
- 1 tablespoon arrowroot powder
- ¼ cup unsweetened apple juice
- 2 tablespoons melted coconut oil
- ¼ cup raw honey
Topping:
- 1 cup almond flour
- 1 tablespoon arrowroot powder
- ½ cup shredded coconut
- ¼ cup raw honey
- ½ cup coconut oil

DIRECTIONS:
1. Preheat the oven to 350°F (180°C). Grease a baking dish with melted coconut oil. Combine the ingredients for the cobbler in a large bowl. Stir to mix well. Spread the mixture in the single layer on the baking dish. Set aside.
2. Combine the almond flour, arrowroot powder, and coconut in a bowl. Stir to mix well. Fold in the honey and coconut oil. Stir with a fork until the mixture crumbled.
3. Spread the topping over the cobbler, then bake in the preheated oven for 35 minutes or until frothy and golden brown. Serve immediately.

NUTRITION: Calories: 305 Fat: 22.1g Protein: 3.2g Carbs: 29.8g

859. Citrus Cranberry and Quinoa Energy Bites

Preparation time: 15 minutes
Cooking time: 0 minutes
Servings: 12 bites
INGREDIENTS:
- 2 tablespoons almond butter
- 2 tablespoons maple syrup
- ¾ cup cooked quinoa
- 1 tablespoon dried cranberries
- 1 tablespoon chia seeds
- ¼ cup ground almonds
- ¼ cup sesame seeds, toasted
- Zest of 1 orange
- ½ teaspoon vanilla extract

DIRECTIONS:
1. Line a baking sheet with parchment paper. Combine the butter and maple syrup in a bowl. Stir to mix well.
2. Fold in the remaining ingredients and stir until the mixture holds together and smooth. Divide the mixture into 12 equal parts, then shape each part into a ball.
3. Arrange the balls on the baking sheet, then refrigerate for at least 15 minutes. Serve chilled.

NUTRITION: Calories: 110 Fat: 10.8g Protein: 3.1g Carbs: 4.9g

860. Easy Blueberry and Oat Crisp

Preparation time: 15 minutes
Cooking time: 20 minutes
Servings: 4
INGREDIENTS:
- 2 tablespoons coconut oil, melted, plus additional for greasing
- 4 cups fresh blueberries
- Juice of ½ lemon
- 2 teaspoons lemon zest
- ¼ cup maple syrup
- 1 cup gluten-free rolled oats
- ½ cup chopped pecans
- ½ teaspoon ground cinnamon
- Sea salt, to taste

DIRECTIONS:
1. Preheat the oven to 350°F (180°C). Grease a baking sheet with coconut oil. Combine the blueberries, lemon juice and zest, and maple syrup in a bowl. Stir to mix well, then spread the mixture on the baking sheet.
2. Combine the remaining ingredients in a small bowl. Stir to mix well. Pour the mixture over the blueberry's mixture.
3. Bake in the preheated oven for 20 minutes or until the oats are golden brown. Serve immediately with spoons.

NUTRITION: Calories: 496 Fat: 32.9g Protein: 5.1g Carbs: 50.8g

861. Lemony Blackberry Granita

Preparation time: 15 minutes
Cooking time: 0 minutes
Servings: 4
INGREDIENTS:
- 1 pound (454 g) fresh blackberries
- 1 teaspoon chopped fresh thyme
- ¼ cup freshly squeezed lemon juice
- ½ cup raw honey
- ½ cup water

DIRECTIONS:

1. Put all the ingredients in a food processor, then pulse to purée. Pour the mixture through a sieve into a baking dish. Discard the seeds remain in the sieve.

2. Put the baking dish in the freezer for 2 hours. Remove the dish from the refrigerator and stir to break any frozen parts.

3. Return the dish back to the freezer for an hour, then stir to break any frozen parts again. Return the dish to the freezer for 4 hours until the granita is completely frozen.

4. Remove it from the freezer and mash to serve.

NUTRITION: Calories: 183 Fat: 1.1g Protein: 2.2g Carbs: 45.9g

862. Yogurt Dip

Preparation Time: 10 minutes
Cooking Time: 0 minutes
Servings: 6
INGREDIENTS:
- 2 cups Greek yogurt
- 2 tablespoons pistachios, toasted and chopped
- A pinch of salt and white pepper
- 2 tablespoons mint, chopped
- 1 tablespoon kalamata olives, pitted and chopped
- ¼ cup zaatar spice
- ¼ cup pomegranate seeds
- 1/3 cup olive oil

DIRECTIONS:

1. Mix the yogurt with the pistachios and the rest of the ingredients, whisk well,

2. Divide into small cups and serve with pita chips on the side.

NUTRITION: Calories 294 Fat 18g Carbohydrates 2g Protein 10g

863. Mint Banana Chocolate Sorbet

Preparation time: 4 hours & 5 minutes
Cooking time: 0 minutes
Servings: 1
INGREDIENTS:
- 1 frozen banana
- 1 tablespoon almond butter
- 2 tablespoons minced fresh mint
- 2 to 3 tablespoons dark chocolate chips (60% cocoa or higher)
- 2 to 3 tablespoons goji (optional)

DIRECTIONS:

1. Put the banana, butter, and mint in a food processor. Pulse to purée until creamy and smooth. Add the chocolate and goji, then pulse for several more times to combine well.

2. Pour the mixture in a bowl or a ramekin, then freeze for at least 4 hours before serving chilled.

NUTRITION: Calories: 213 Fat: 9.8g Protein: 3.1g Carbs: 2.9g

864. Pecan and Carrot Cake

Preparation time: 15 minutes
Cooking time: 45 minutes
Servings: 12
INGREDIENTS:
- ½ cup coconut oil, at room temperature, plus more for greasing the baking dish
- 2 teaspoons pure vanilla extract
- ¼ cup pure maple syrup
- 6 eggs
- ½ cup coconut flour
- 1 teaspoon baking powder
- 1 teaspoon baking soda
- ½ teaspoon ground nutmeg
- 1 teaspoon ground cinnamon
- 1/8 teaspoon sea salt
- ½ cup chopped pecans
- 3 cups finely grated carrots

DIRECTIONS:

1. Preheat the oven to 350°F (180°C). Grease a 13-by-9-inch baking dish with coconut oil. Combine the vanilla extract, maple syrup, and ½ cup of coconut oil in a large bowl. Stir to mix well.

2. Break the eggs in the bowl and whisk to combine well. Set aside. Combine the coconut flour, baking powder, baking soda, nutmeg, cinnamon, and salt in a separate bowl. Stir to mix well.

3. Make a well in the center of the flour mixture, then pour the egg mixture into the well. Stir to combine well.

4. Add the pecans and carrots to the bowl and toss to mix well. Pour the mixture in the single layer on the baking dish.

5. Bake in the preheated oven for 45 minutes or until puffed and the cake spring back when lightly press with your fingers.

6. Remove the cake from the oven. Allow to cool for at least 15 minutes, then serve.

NUTRITION: Calories: 255 Fat: 21.2g Protein: 5.1g Carbs: 12.8g

865. Raspberry Yogurt Basted Cantaloupe

Preparation time: 15 minutes
Cooking time: 0 minutes
Servings: 6
INGREDIENTS:
- 2 cups fresh raspberries, mashed
- 1 cup plain coconut yogurt
- ½ teaspoon vanilla extract
- 1 cantaloupe, peeled and sliced
- ½ cup toasted coconut flakes

DIRECTIONS:

1. Combine the mashed raspberries with yogurt and vanilla extract in a small bowl. Stir to mix well.

2. Place the cantaloupe slices on a platter, then top with raspberry mixture and spread with toasted coconut. Serve immediately.

NUTRITION: Calories: 75 Fat: 4.1g Protein: 1.2g Carbs: 10.9g

866. Simple Apple Compote

Preparation time: 15 minutes
Cooking time: 10 minutes
Servings: 4
INGREDIENTS:
- 6 apples, peeled, cored, and chopped
- ¼ cup raw honey
- 1 teaspoon ground cinnamon
- ¼ cup apple juice
- Sea salt, to taste

DIRECTIONS:

1. Put all the ingredients in a stockpot. Stir to mix well, then cook over medium-high heat for 10 minutes or until the apples are glazed by honey and lightly saucy.

2. Stir constantly. Serve immediately.

NUTRITION: Calories: 246 Fat: 0.9g Protein: 1.2g Carbs: 66.3g

867. Peanut Butter and Chocolate Balls

Preparation time: 45 minutes
Cooking time: 0 minutes
Servings: 15 balls
INGREDIENTS:
- ¾ cup creamy peanut butter
- ¼ cup unsweetened cocoa powder
- 2 tablespoons softened almond butter
- ½ teaspoon vanilla extract
- 1¾ cups maple sugar

DIRECTIONS:
1. Line a baking sheet with parchment paper. Combine all the ingredients in a bowl. Stir to mix well.
2. Divide the mixture into 15 parts and shape each part into a 1-inch ball. Arrange the balls on the baking sheet and refrigerate for at least 30 minutes, then serve chilled.
NUTRITION: Calories: 146 Fat: 8.1g Protein: 4.2g Carbs: 16.9g

868. Spiced Sweet Pecans

Preparation time: 15 minutes
Cooking time: 17 minutes
Servings: 4
INGREDIENTS:
- 1 cup pecan halves
- 3 tablespoons almond butter
- 1 teaspoon ground cinnamon
- ½ teaspoon ground nutmeg
- ¼ cup raw honey
- ¼ teaspoon sea salt

DIRECTIONS:
1. Preheat the oven to 350°F (180°C). Line a baking sheet with parchment paper. Combine all the ingredients in a bowl. Stir to mix well, then spread the mixture in the single layer on the baking sheet with a spatula.
2. Bake in the preheated oven for 16 minutes or until the pecan halves are well browned. Serve immediately.
NUTRITION: Calories: 324 Fat: 29.8g Protein: 3.2g Carbs: 13.9g

869. Lemon Crockpot Cake

Preparation Time: 15 minutes
Cooking Time: 3 hours
Servings: 8
INGREDIENTS:
- ½ cup coconut flour
- 1 ½ cup almond flour
- 3 tbsps. stevia sweetener
- 2 tsps. baking powder
- ½ tsp. xanthan gum
- ½ cup whipping cream
- ½ cup butter, melted
- 1 tbsp. juice, freshly squeezed
- Zest from one large lemon
- 2 eggs

DIRECTIONS:
1. Grease the inside of the Crockpot with a butter or cooking spray. Mix together coconut flour, almond flour, stevia, baking powder, and xanthan gum in a bowl.
2. In another bowl, combine the whipping cream, butter, lemon juice, lemon zest, and eggs. Mix until well combined.
3. Pour the wet ingredients to the dry ingredients gradually and fold to create a smooth batter. Spread the batter in the Crockpot and cook on low for 3 hours
NUTRITION: Calories: 350 Carbohydrates: 11.1g Protein: 17.6g Fat: 32.6g

870. Lemon and Watermelon Granita

Preparation Time: 10 minutes + 3 hours to freeze
Cooking Time: 0 minutes
Servings: 4
INGREDIENTS:
- 4 cups watermelon cubes
- ¼ cup honey
- ¼ cup freshly squeezed lemon juice

DIRECTIONS:
1. In a blender, combine the watermelon, honey, and lemon juice. Purée all the ingredients, then pour into a 9-by-9-by-2-inch baking pan and place in the freezer.
2. Every 30 to 60 minutes, run a fork across the frozen surface to fluff and create ice flakes. Freeze for about 3 hours total and serve.
NUTRITION: Calories: 153 Carbohydrates: 39g Protein: 2g Fat: 1g

871. Mascarpone and Fig Crostini

Preparation Time: 10 minutes
Cooking Time: 10 minutes
Servings: 6-8
INGREDIENTS:
- 1 long French baguette
- 4 tablespoons (½ stick) salted butter, melted
- 1 (8-ounce) tub mascarpone cheese
- 1 (12-ounce) jar fig jam or preserves

DIRECTIONS:
1. Preheat the oven to 350°F. Slice the bread into ¼-inch-thick slices. Lay out the sliced bread on a single baking sheet and brush each slice with the melted butter.
2. Put the single baking sheet in the oven and toast the bread for 5 to 7 minutes, just until golden brown.
3. Let the bread cool slightly. Spread it about a tea spoon or so of the mascarpone cheese on each piece of bread. Top with a teaspoon or so of the jam. Serve immediately.
NUTRITION: Calories 445 Fat 24g Carbs 48g Protein 3g

872. Mini Nuts and Fruits Crumble

Preparation time: 15 minutes
Cooking time: 15 minutes
Servings: 6
Ingredients:
- Topping:
- ¼ cup coarsely chopped hazelnuts
- 1 cup coarsely chopped walnuts
- 1 teaspoon ground cinnamon
- Sea salt, to taste
- 1 tablespoon melted coconut oil
- Filling:
- 6 fresh figs, quartered
- 2 nectarines, pitted and sliced
- 1 cup fresh blueberries
- 2 teaspoons lemon zest
- ½ cup raw honey
- 1 teaspoon vanilla extract

Directions:
1. Combine the ingredients for the topping in a bowl. Stir to mix well. Set aside until ready to use.
2. Preheat the oven to 375°F (190°C). Combine the ingredients for the fillings in a bowl. Stir to mix well. Divide the filling in six ramekins, then divide and top with nut topping.
3. Bake in the preheated oven for 15 minutes or until the topping is lightly browned and the filling is frothy. Serve immediately.
Nutrition: Calories: 336 Fat: 18.8g Protein: 6.3g Carbs: 41.9g

873. Traditional Mediterranean Lokum

Preparation Time: 25 minutes
Cooking Time: 0 minutes
Servings: 20
Ingredients
- 1-ounce confectioners' sugar
- 3 ½ ounces cornstarch
- 20 ounces caster sugar
- 4 ounces pomegranate juice
- 16 ounces cold water
- 3 tablespoons gelatin, powdered

Directions
1. Line a baking sheet with a parchment paper.
2. Mix the confectioners' sugar and 2 ounces of cornstarch until well combined.
3. In a saucepan, heat the caster sugar, pomegranate juice and water over low heat.
4. In a mixing bowl, combine 4 ounces of cold water with the remaining cornstarch. Stir the mixture into the sugar syrup.
5. Slowly and gradually, add in the powdered gelatin and whisk until smooth and uniform.
6. Bring the mixture to a boil, turn the heat to medium and continue to cook for another 18 minutes, whisking constantly, until the mixture has thickened.
7. Scrape the mixture into the baking sheet and allow it to set in your refrigerator.
8. Cut your lokum into cubes and coat with the confectioners' sugar mixture. Bon appétit!
Nutrition: Calories: 208; Fat: 0.5g; Carbs: 54.4g; Protein: 0.2g

874. Mixed Berry and Fig Compote

Preparation Time: 20 minutes
Cooking Time: 0 minutes
Servings: 5
Ingredients
- 2 cups mixed berries
- 1 cup figs, chopped
- 4 tablespoons pomegranate juice
- 1/2 teaspoon ground cinnamon
- 1/2 teaspoon crystalized ginger
- 1/2 teaspoon vanilla extract
- 2 tablespoons honey

Directions
1. Place the fruit, pomegranate juice, ground cinnamon, crystalized ginger, vanilla extract in a saucepan; bring to medium heat.
2. Turn the heat to a simmer and continue to cook for about 11 minutes, stirring occasionally to combine well. Add in the honey and stir to combine.
3. Remove from the heat and keep in your refrigerator. Bon appétit!
Nutrition: Calories: 150; Fat: 0.5g; Carbs: 36.4g; Protein: 1.4g

875. Creamed Fruit Salad

Preparation Time: 10 minutes
Cooking Time: 0 minutes
Servings: 2
Ingredients
- 1 orange, peeled and sliced
- 2 apples, pitted and diced
- 2 peaches, pitted and diced
- 1 cup seedless grapes
- 3/4 cup Greek-style yogurt, well-chilled
- 3 tablespoons honey

Directions
1. Divide the fruits between dessert bowls.
2. Top with the yogurt. Add a few drizzles of honey to each serving and serve well-chilled.
3. Bon appétit!
Nutrition: Calories: 250; Fat: 0.7g; Carbs: 60g; Protein: 6.4g

876. Almond Cookies

Preparation Time: 5 minutes
Cooking Time: 10 minutes
Servings: 4-6
Ingredients:
- ½ cup sugar
- 8 tablespoons (1 stick) room temperature salted butter
- 1 large egg
- 1½ cups all-purpose flour
- 1 cup ground almonds or almond flour

Directions:
1. Preheat the oven to 375°F. Using a mixer, cream together the sugar and butter. Add the egg and mix until combined.
2. Alternately add the flour and ground almonds, ½ cup at a time, while the mixer is on slow.
3. Once everything is combined, line a baking sheet with parchment paper. Drop a tablespoon of dough on the baking sheet, keeping the cookies at least 2 inches apart.
4. Put the single baking sheet in the oven and bake just until the cookies start to turn brown around the edges for about 5 to 7 minutes.
Nutrition: Calories 604 Fat 36g Carbs 63g Protein 11g

877. Chocolate Ganache

Preparation Time: 10 minutes
Cooking Time: 3 minutes
Servings: 16
Ingredients
- 9 ounces bittersweet chocolate, chopped
- 1 cup heavy cream
- 1 tablespoon dark rum (optional)

Direction
1. Put the chocolate in a medium bowl. Heat the cream in a small saucepan over medium heat.
2. Bring to a boil. When the cream has reached a boiling point, pour the chopped chocolate over it and beat until smooth. Stir the rum if desired.
3. Allow the ganache to cool slightly before you pour it on a cake. Begin in the middle of the cake and work outside. For a fluffy icing or chocolate filling, let it cool until thick and beat with a whisk until light and fluffy.
Nutrition
142 calories
10.8g fat
1.4g protein

878. Chocolate Covered Strawberries

Preparation Time: 15 minutes
Cooking Time: 4 minutes
Servings: 24
Ingredients
- 16 ounces milk chocolate chips
- 2 tablespoons shortening
- 1-pound fresh strawberries with leaves

Direction
1. In a bain-marie, melt chocolate and shortening, occasionally stirring until smooth. Pierce the tops of the strawberries with toothpicks and immerse them in the chocolate mixture.

2. Turn the strawberries and put the toothpick in Styrofoam so that the chocolate cools.
Nutrition
115 calories
7.3g fat
12.7g carbohydrates

879. Strawberry Angel Food Dessert

Preparation Time: 15 minutes
Cooking Time: 0 minute
Servings: 18
Ingredients
- angel cake (10 inches)
- packages of softened cream cheese
- 1 container (8 oz.) of frozen fluff, thawed
- 1 liter of fresh strawberries, sliced
- 1 jar of strawberry icing
Direction
1. Crumble the cake in a 9 x 13-inch dish.
2. Beat the cream cheese and 1 cup sugar in a medium bowl until the mixture is light and fluffy. Stir in the whipped topping. Crush the cake with your hands, and spread the cream cheese mixture over the cake.
3. Combine the strawberries and the frosting in a bowl until the strawberries are well covered. Spread over the layer of cream cheese. Cool until ready to serve.
Nutrition
261 calories
11g fat
3.2g protein

880. Key Lime Pie

Preparation Time: 8 minutes
Cooking Time: 9 minutes
Servings: 8
Ingredients
- (9-inch) prepared graham cracker crust
- 2 cups of sweetened condensed milk
- 1/2 cup sour cream
- 3/4 cup lime juice
- 1 tablespoon grated lime zest
Direction
1. Preheat the oven to 175 ° C (350 ° F).
2. Combine the condensed milk, sour cream, lime juice, and lime zest in a medium bowl. Mix well and pour into the graham cracker crust.
3. Bake in the preheated oven for 5 to 8 minutes until small hole bubbles burst on the surface of the cake.
4. Cool the cake well before serving. Decorate with lime slices and whipped cream if desired.
Nutrition:
553 calories
20.5g fat
10.9g protein

881. Ice Cream Sandwich Dessert

Preparation Time: 20 minutes
Cooking Time: 0 minute
Servings: 12
Ingredients
- 22 ice cream sandwiches
- Frozen whipped topping in 16 oz. container, thawed
- 1 jar (12 oz.) Caramel ice cream
- 1 1/2 cups of salted peanuts
Direction
1. Cut a sandwich with ice in two. Place a whole sandwich and a half sandwich on a short side of a 9 x 13-inch baking dish. Repeat this until the bottom is covered; alternate the full sandwich, and the half sandwich.

2. Spread half of the whipped topping. Pour the caramel over it. Sprinkle with half the peanuts. Repeat the layers with the rest of the ice cream sandwiches, whipped cream, and peanuts.
3. Cover and freeze for up to 2 months. Remove from the freezer 20 minutes before serving. Cut into squares.
Nutrition:
559 calories
28.8g fat
10g protein

882. Bananas Foster

Preparation Time: 5 minutes
Cooking Time: 5 minutes
Servings: 4
Ingredients
- 2/3 cup dark brown sugar
- 1/2 teaspoons vanilla extract
- 1/2 teaspoon of ground cinnamon
- bananas, peeled and cut lengthwise and broad
- 1/4 cup chopped nuts, butter
Direction
1. Melt the butter in a deep-frying pan over medium heat. Stir in sugar, 3 ½ tbsp. of rum, vanilla, and cinnamon.
2. When the mixture starts to bubble, place the bananas and nuts in the pan. Bake until the bananas are hot, 1 to 2 minutes. Serve immediately with vanilla ice cream.
Nutrition:
534 calories
23.8g fat
4.6g protein

883. Rhubarb Strawberry Crunch

Preparation Time: 15 minutes
Cooking Time: 45 minutes
Servings: 18
Ingredients
- 3 tablespoons all-purpose flour
- 3 cups of fresh strawberries, sliced
- 3 cups of rhubarb, cut into cubes
- 1/2 cup flour
- 1 cup butter
Direction
1. Preheat the oven to 190 ° C.
2. Combine 1 cup of white sugar, 3 tablespoons flour, strawberries and rhubarb in a large bowl. Place the mixture in a 9 x 13-inch baking dish.
3. Mix 1 1/2 cups of flour, 1 cup of brown sugar, butter, and oats until a crumbly texture is obtained. You may want to use a blender for this. Crumble the mixture of rhubarb and strawberry.
4. Bake in the preheated oven for 45 minutes or until crispy and light brown.
Nutrition:
253 calories
10.8g fat
2.3g protein

884. Frosty Strawberry Dessert

Preparation Time: 5 minutes
Cooking Time: 21 minutes
Servings: 16
Ingredients
- cup flour, white sugar, whipped cream
- 1/2 cup chopped walnuts, butter
- cups of sliced strawberries
- tablespoons lemon juice

- 1/4 cup brown sugar

Direction

1. Preheat the oven to 175 ° C (350 ° F).
2. Mix the flour, brown sugar, nuts, and melted butter in a bowl. Spread on a baking sheet and bake for 20 minutes in the preheated oven until crispy. Remove from the oven and let cool completely.
3. Beat the egg whites to snow. Keep beating until you get firm spikes while slowly adding sugar. Mix the strawberries in the lemon juice and stir in the egg whites until the mixture turns slightly pink. Stir in the whipped cream until it is absorbed.
4. Crumble the walnut mixture and spread 2/3 evenly over the bottom of a 9-inch by 13-inch dish. Place the strawberry mixture on the crumbs and sprinkle the rest of the crumbs. Place in the freezer for two hours. Take them out of the freezer a few minutes before serving to facilitate cutting.

Nutrition:

184 calories

9.2g fat

2.2g protein

885. Dessert Pie

Preparation Time: 16 minutes

Cooking Time: 18 minutes

Servings: 12

Ingredients

- cup all-purpose flour
- 1 package of cream cheese
- 8 oz. whipped cream topping
- 1 (4-oz) package of instant chocolate pudding
- 1/2 cup butter, white sugar

Direction

1. Preheat the oven to 175 ° C (350 ° F).
2. In a large bowl, mix butter, flour and 1/4 cup sugar until the mixture looks like coarse breadcrumbs. Push the mixture into the bottom of a 9 x 13-inch baking dish. Bake in the preheated oven for 15 to 18 minutes or until lightly browned to allow cooling to room temperature.
3. In a large bowl, beat cream cheese and 1/2 cup sugar until smooth. Stir in half of the whipped topping. Spread the mixture over the cooled crust.
4. Mix the pudding in the same bowl according to the instructions on the package. Spread over the cream cheese mixture.
5. Garnish with the remaining whipped cream. Cool in the fridge.

Nutrition:

376 calories

23g fat

3.6g protein

886. Sugar-Coated Pecans

Preparation Time: 15 minutes

Cooking Time: 1 hour

Servings: 12

Ingredients

- egg white
- 1 tablespoon water
- 1-pound pecan halves
- 1 cup white sugar
- 1/2 teaspoon ground cinnamon

Directions

1. Preheat the oven to 120 ° C (250 ° F). Grease a baking tray.
2. In a bowl, whisk the egg whites and water until frothy. Combine the sugar, ¾ tsp. salt, and cinnamon in another bowl.

3. Add the pecans to the egg whites and stir to cover the nuts. Remove the nuts and mix them with the sugar until well covered. Spread the nuts on the prepared baking sheet.
4. Bake for 1 hour at 250 ° F (120 ° C). Stir every 15 minutes.

Nutrition:

328 calories

27.2g fat

3.8g protein

887. Jalapeño Popper Spread

Preparation Time: 10 minutes

Cooking Time: 3 minutes

Servings: 32

Ingredients

- 2 packets of cream cheese, softened
- cup mayonnaise
- 1 (4-gram) can chopped green peppers, drained
- grams diced jalapeño peppers, canned, drained
- 1 cup grated Parmesan cheese

Direction

1. In a large bowl, mix cream cheese and mayonnaise until smooth. Stir the bell peppers and jalapeño peppers.
2. Pour the mixture into a microwave oven and sprinkle with Parmesan cheese.
3. Microwave on maximum power, about 3 minutes.

Nutrition:

110 calories

11.1g fat

2.1g protein

888. Brown Sugar Smokies

Preparation Time: 10 minutes

Cooking Time: 4 minutes

Servings: 12

Ingredients

- 1-pound bacon
- (16 ounces) package little smoky sausages
- 1 cup brown sugar, or to taste

Direction

1. Preheat the oven to 175 ° C (350 ° F).
2. Cut the bacon in three and wrap each strip around a little sausage. Place sausages wrapped on wooden skewers, several to one place the kebabs on a baking sheet and sprinkle generously with brown sugar.
3. Bake until the bacon is crispy, and the brown sugar has melted.

Nutrition:

356 calories

27.2g fat

9g protein

889. Fruit Dip

Preparation Time: 5 minutes

Cooking Time: 0 minute

Servings: 12

Ingredients

- (8-oz) package cream cheese, softened
- 1 (7-oz) jar marshmallow crème

Direction

1. Use an electric mixer to combine the cream cheese and marshmallow
2. Beat until everything is well mixed.

Nutrition:

118 calories

6.6g fat

13.4g carbohydrates

890. Banana & Tortilla Snacks

Preparation Time: 5 minutes
Cooking Time: 0 minute
Servings: 1
Ingredients
• flour tortilla (6 inches)
• tablespoons peanut butter
• 1 tablespoon honey
• 1 banana
• tablespoons raisins
Directions
1. Lay the tortilla flat. Spread peanut butter and honey on the tortilla. Place the banana in the middle and sprinkle the raisins. Wrap and serve.
Nutrition:
520 calories
19.3g fat
12.8g protein

891. Caramel Popcorn

Preparation Time: 30 minutes
Cooking Time: 1 hour
Servings: 20
Ingredients
• 2 cups brown sugar
• 1/2 cup of corn syrup
• 1/2 teaspoon baking powder
• teaspoon vanilla extract
• 5 cups of popcorn
Direction
1. Preheat the oven to 95° C (250° F). Put the popcorn in a large bowl.
2. Melt 1 cup of butter in a medium-sized pan over medium heat. Stir in brown sugar, 1 tsp. of salt, and corn syrup. Bring to a boil, constantly stirring — Cook without stirring for 4 minutes. Then remove from heat and stir in the soda and vanilla. Pour in a thin layer on the popcorn and stir well.
3. Place in two large shallow baking tins and bake in the preheated oven, stirring every 15 minutes for an hour. Remove from the oven and let cool completely before breaking into pieces.
Nutrition:
14g fat
253 calories
32.8g carbohydrates

892. Apple and Berries Ambrosia

Preparation Time: 15 minutes
Cooking Time: 0 minutes
Serving: 4
Ingredients:
• 2 cups unsweetened coconut milk, chilled
• 2 tablespoons raw honey
• 1 apple, peeled, cored, and chopped
• 2 cups fresh raspberries
• 2 cups fresh blueberries
Direction
1. Spoon the chilled milk in a large bowl, and then mix in the honey. Stir to mix well.
2. Then mix in the remaining ingredients. Stir to coat the fruits well and serve immediately.
Nutrition
386 calories
21.1g fat
4.2g protein

893. Chocolate, Almond, and Cherry Clusters

Preparation Time: 15 minutes
Cooking Time: 3 minutes
Serving: 5
Ingredients:
• 1 cup dark chocolate (60% cocoa or higher), chopped
• 1 tablespoon coconut oil
• ½ cup dried cherries
• 1 cup roasted salted almonds
Direction
1. Line a baking sheet with parchment paper.
2. Melt the chocolate and coconut oil in a saucepan for 3 minutes. Stir constantly.
3. Turn off the heat and mix in the cherries and almonds.
4. Drop the mixture on the baking sheet with a spoon. Place the sheet in the refrigerator and chill for at least 1 hour or until firm.
5. Serve chilled.
Nutrition
197 calories
13.2g fat
4.1g protein

894. Chocolate and Avocado Mousse

Preparation Time: 40 minutes
Cooking Time: 5 minutes
Serving: 5
Ingredients:
• 8 ounces (227 g) dark chocolate (60% cocoa or higher), chopped
• ¼ cup unsweetened coconut milk
• 2 tablespoons coconut oil
• 2 ripe avocados, deseeded
• ¼ cup raw honey
Direction:
1. Put the chocolate in a saucepan. Pour in the coconut milk and add the coconut oil.
2. Cook for 3 minutes or until the chocolate and coconut oil melt. Stir constantly.
3. Put the avocado in a food processor, and then drizzle with honey and melted chocolate. Pulse to combine until smooth.
4. Pour the mixture in a serving bowl, then sprinkle with salt. Refrigerate to chill for 30 minutes and serve.
Nutrition
654 calories
46.8g fat
7.2g protein

895. Coconut Blueberries with Brown Rice

Preparation Time: 55 minutes
Cooking Time: 10 minutes
Serving: 4
Ingredients:
• 1 cup fresh blueberries
• 2 cups unsweetened coconut milk
• 1 teaspoon ground ginger
• ¼ cup maple syrup
• 2 cups cooked brown rice
Direction
1. Put all the ingredients, except for the brown rice, in a pot. Stir to combine well.

2. Cook over medium-high heat for 7 minutes or until the blueberries are tender.
3. Pour in the brown rice and cook for 3 more minute or until the rice is soft. Stir constantly.
4. Serve immediately.
Nutrition:
470 calories
24.8g fat
6.2g protein

896. Glazed Pears with Hazelnuts

Preparation Time: 10 minutes
Cooking Time: 20 minutes
Serving: 4
Ingredients:
• 4 pears, peeled, cored, and quartered lengthwise
• 1 cup apple juice
• 1 tablespoon grated fresh ginger
• ½ cup pure maple syrup
• ¼ cup chopped hazelnuts
Direction
1. Put the pears in a pot, then pour in the apple juice. Bring to a boil over medium-high heat, and then reduce the heat to medium-low. Stir constantly.
2. Cover and simmer for an additional 15 minutes or until the pears are tender.
3. Meanwhile, combine the ginger and maple syrup in a saucepan. Bring to a boil over medium-high heat. Stir frequently. Turn off the heat and transfer the syrup to a small bowl and let sit until ready to use.
4. Transfer the pears in a large serving bowl with a slotted spoon, then top the pears with syrup.
5. Spread the hazelnuts over the pears and serve immediately.
Nutrition:
287 calories
3.1g fat
2.2g protein

897. Italian Apple Olive Oil Cake

Preparation Time: 20 minutes
Cooking Time: 45 minutes
Serving 12
Ingredients
• Gala apples, as thinly peeled and chopped as possible, 2 large
• Orange juice, to soak apples
• All-purpose flour, 3 cups
• The ground cinnamon, 1/2 tsp
• Ground nutmeg, 1/2 tsp
• 1 tsp baking powder
• 1 tsp of baking soda
• 1 cup of sugar
• 1 cup of extra virgin olive oil
• Large eggs 2
• 2/3 cup gold raisins, immersed for 15 minutes in warm water and then drained.
• For dusting, Confectioner' sugar
Direction:
1. Preheat the oven to 400 degrees F.
2. To stop browning, put the sliced apples in a large bowl, add orange juice; just enough juice to toss and cover the apples.
3. Sift together the cinnamon, baking powder, flour, nutmeg, and baking soda in a big mixing bowl. For now, put aside it.

4. Add the sugar and extra virgin olive oil to the bowl of a stand mixer fitted with a whisk.
For 2 minutes, mix on low until well-combined
5. Add the eggs one by one while the mixer is on, and proceed to blend for extra 2 minutes till the volume of the mixture rises (it should be denser but still soft)
6. Build a well in the middle of the flour mixture in a large bowl with the dried ingredients. Through the well, add the wet mixture (the sugar and olive oil mixture). Stir until just mixed, using a wooden spoon; it will be a dense batter (do not add anything to loosen it).
7. Fully drain the raisins (which were soaked in water) and extract the excess juice apples. Add all raisins and apples to the batter and blend until well-combined with a spoon. Once again, the batter would be very dense.
8. Using parchment paper to cover a 9-inch cake sheet. Spoon the pan with a dense batter, and level the top with the wooden spoon's back.
9. Bake for 45 minutes at 350 degrees F or until an inserted wooden skewer or toothpick comes out clean.
10.   Cool completely in the pan. Simply lift the parchment to move the cake into a serving plate when ready.   Sprinkle with confectioner's sugar. Otherwise, to serve on top, heat some dark honey (those with a sugary tooth like this option.)
Nutrition: Per serving: Kcal 295, Fat: 11g, Net Carbs: 47.9g, Protein: 5.3g

898. Gluten-free fig almond olive oil cake

Preparation Time: 15 minutes
Cooking Time: 35 minutes
Serving 8
Ingredients
• Fresh lemon juice 2 tablespoons/30ml
• Zest of 1 small lemon
• 1/4 cup/84g of honey
• 1/4 cup/60ml of extra virgin olive oil
• 2 large eggs
• Salt, 1 pinch
• 1 1/2 cups/168g of fine almond flour
• 1 1/2 tsp baking powder
• 8-10 fresh, sliced figs
Direction:
1. Preheat the oven to 350 degrees F. Grease an 8-inch cake pan and use parchment paper to line the bottom.
2. Mix the lemon juice, eggs, lemon zest, honey, olive oil, and salt in a large bowl. Add the baking powder and almond flour; whisk again until mixed.
3. Into the prepared pan, pour the batter and top with fig slices. Bake for 35 minutes or so until the top is golden and the middle is set. Place the cake on a rack and let it cool.
4. Run a knife around the edge of a tray, put the cake on a cooling rack and allow it to cool fully.
Nutrition: Per serving: Kcal 275, Fat: 19g, Net Carbs: 23g, Protein: 6g

899. Olive Oil Chocolate Chip Cookies

Preparation Time: 18 minutes
Cooking Time: 12 minutes
serving 24
Ingredients
• 1 cup of extra virgin olive oil
• 1 tablespoon of pure vanilla extract
• Granulated sugar 3/4 cup
• 3/4 cup of golden-brown sugar
• 1 tsp, with additional kosher salt for garnish
• Large egg 1

- All-purpose flour 2 cups
- 1/2 teaspoon Baking soda
- 2 cups of semisweet chocolate chips

Direction:

1. Preheat the oven to 400 ° F, then use parchment paper to cover two baking sheets. Only set aside.
2. In a medium mixing bowl, add the sugar, olive oil, vanilla, and 1 teaspoon of salt. Mix so there's a smooth consistency for you.
3. Mix the egg in. Blend until it's smooth again, completely.
4. Add the baking soda and flour to the bowl and mix until it is thoroughly mixed and no dry spots of flour are seen.
5. Fold in the chocolate chips.
6. Use your hands, about 2 tablespoons each, to form the batter into balls. (Your hands may be greasy from the grease, but I think hands are better for this recipe.) Add the rounded dough balls to the baking sheets lined with parchment as you go. Between them, they should have at least 2 inches, around a dozen per sheet.
7. Using the palm of your hand, just about halfway, to softly flatten the batter's balls.
8. Then sprinkle each one gently with kosher salt.
9. In the preheated 400 ° F oven, put the baking sheets until the cookies around the edges are golden brown, 10 to 12 minutes. Let them cool for approximately 5 minutes on the baking sheet, then put them on a cooling rack to reach room temperature.

Nutrition: Per serving: Kcal 187, Fat: 9g, Net Carbs: 18g, Protein: 8g

900. Maple Vanilla Baked Pears

Preparation Time: 5 minutes
Cooking Time: 25 minutes
Serving: 4
Ingredients
- 4 D'Anjou pears
- Pure Maple Syrup 1/2 cup (120ml)
- Ground cinnamon 1/4 teaspoon
- 1 teaspoon of pure vanilla extract
- Optional toppings: Greek yogurt, maple pecan granola

Direction:

1. Preheat the oven to 190°C (375°F).
2. Cut the pears, and cut a small sliver from the underside so that when set upright on the baking sheet, the pears sit flat. Core out the seeds using a big or medium cookie scoop and melon scoop (or even a teaspoon). Arrange the pears on the baking dish, face up. Sprinkle with cinnamon uniformly- if you like, feel free to add more cinnamon.
3. In a small bowl, mix the maple syrup and vanilla extract. Drizzle much of it all over the
pears, reserving only 2 tablespoons for baking after the pears are completed.
4. Bake the pears for about 25 minutes, until the sides are soft and lightly browned. Remove from the oven and drizzle instantly with any leftover mixture of maple syrup. With the granola and yogurt, serve warm. Store the leftovers for up to 5 days in the refrigerator.

Nutrition Per serving: Kcal 153, Fat: 6g, Net Carbs: 16g, Protein: 6g

901. Mediterranean Pistachio No-Bake Snack Bars

Preparation Time: 5 minutes
Cooking Time: 5 minutes
serving 8
Ingredients
- Pitted Dates 20

- 1 1/4 cups of Roasted & Salted Pistachios no-shell
- 1 cup rolled gluten-free old-fashioned oats, if necessary,
- 2 tbsp. of pistachio butter
- 1/4 cup of unsweetened applesauce
- Vanilla extract 1 teaspoon

Direction:

1. Add the dates to a food processor equipped with a metal blade and process for 30 to 45 seconds before purifying. Add Pistachios and oats pulse 2 to 3 times in 15-second intervals before crumbly, coarse consistency is reached.
2. The processor put the applesauce, pistachio butter, vanilla extract and pulse for 20 to 30 seconds until the dough is slightly sticky.
3. Cover a sheet of 8 x 8 inches of parchment paper.
4. Take the dough from the processor with a spatula and pour it into the pan. Push down tightly with another sheet of parchment paper to spread the dough evenly in the pan.
5. Lift the paper and place it on the top of the dough thinly over the remaining 1/4 cup of no-shell Pistachios.
6. Place parchment paper on top of the pan in the freezer and set free for at least one hour before cutting.
7. Cut into 8 bars and place for up to one week in an airtight jar in the refrigerator.

Nutrition: Per serving: Kcal 220, Fat: 12g, Net Carbs: 26g, Protein: 6g

902. Lemon Olive Oil Cake Recipe

Preparation Time: 5 minutes
Cooking Time: 50 minutes
Serving: 8
Ingredients
For cake:
- 1 cup of unsweetened almond milk
- 1 tablespoon of lemon zest
- 1 tablespoon of lemon juice
- 3/4 cup turbinado sugar
- 1/3 cup of olive oil
- 2 cups of whole wheat pastry flour
- 1 teaspoon of baking soda
- 1/2 teaspoon of salt
For glaze:
- 1 cup of powdered sugar
- Lemon juice 1-2 tablespoons
- 1/2 teaspoon of vanilla extract

Direction:

For the cake:

1. Preheat the oven to 350°F. Line a 9-inch parchment paper loaf pan and cover with nonstick cooking spray.
2. In a small cup, whisk together the almond milk, lemon zest, and 1 tablespoon of lemon juice to make vegan buttermilk. Place it aside for 5 minutes to mix.
3. Meanwhile, in a big cup, whisk the sugar and olive oil together until creamy. Whisk in a paste of buttermilk.
4. Mix the baking soda, flour, and salt in a medium bowl. Fold in the mixture of buttermilk and whisk until it is only mixed.
5. Pour the batter and smooth the top into the prepared pan. Bake until the inserted toothpick comes out clean, about 45 minutes, with a few crumbs attached.
6. Take from the oven and refrigerate in a pan for at least 10 minutes. Remove and cool absolutely on a cooling rack set over a baking sheet.
For the glaze:
1. Whisk the remaining lemon juice, powdered sugar, and vanilla together until tender. Pour over the cooled cake, allowing the excess to spill onto the baking sheet beneath the cake.

Nutrition: Per serving: Kcal 347, Fat: 9.7g, Net Carbs: 62.1g, Protein: 3.1g

903. Whole Grain Citrus And Olive Oil Muffins

Preparation Time: 13 minutes
Cooking Time: 19 minutes
Serving: 12
Ingredients
• Flour 1 1/2 cups
• 1/4 cup of rolled oats
• 2 1/2 teaspoons of baking powder
• 1/2 teaspoon of sea salt
• Cinnamon 1/2 teaspoon
• 1 egg
• 1/3 cup of extra virgin olive oil
• 1/3 cup of orange juice, freshly squeezed (about 1 to 2 medium oranges)
• 1/3 cup of unsweetened almond milk
• 1/3 cup of maple syrup
• 1/2 teaspoon of vanilla extract (or powder)
• 1/2 of a tablespoon of orange zest (from about 1 medium orange)
• 1 grated carrot
• 1/4 cup chopped almonds (optional)
Direction:
1. Preheat the oven to 375 degrees F. Line up and set aside a muffin tin with liners.
2. In a medium cup, whisk together the flour, salt, rolled oats, baking powder, and cinnamon.
3. Whisk together the egg, olive oil, vanilla, orange juice, almond milk, maple syrup, and orange zest in another medium bowl. For the dry ingredients, add to the bowl and mix until just combined. Fold in the carrot gently.
4. Scoop the batter into the muffin tins prepared, filling each around 3/4 full. If needed, dust the tops of the muffins with chopped almonds.
5. Bake until a toothpick inserted into the middle comes out clean, around 16 to 19 minutes. Let the muffins cool for five minutes, then remove them from the wire rack to cool completely.
Nutrition: Per serving: Kcal 347, Fat: 9.7g, Net Carbs: 62.1g, Protein: 3.1g

904. Easy Roasted Fruit Recipe

Preparation Time: 10 minutes
Cooking Time: 20 minutes
serving 4
Ingredients
• Peaches 4, peeled & sliced
• Fresh blueberries 1 1/2 cups
• Ground cinnamon 1/8 teaspoon
• 3 tablespoons of brown sugar
Direction:
1. Preheat the oven to 350°F.
2. In a baking dish, spread the sliced peaches & blueberries. Sprinkled with brown sugar and cinnamon.
3. Bake for about 20 minutes at 350 degrees F, then change the oven settings to a low grill and broil for about five min, or until sparkling.
4. Serve warm, cover and refrigerate, or let cool.
Nutrition: Per serving: Kcal 256, Fat: 9g, Net Carbs: 25g, Protein: 4g

905. Apricot Balls with Dates, Cashews, & Coconut

Preparation Time: 5 minutes
Cooking Time: 5 minutes
serving 20
Ingredients
• 2 cups of raw, unsalted cashew nuts
• 1 cup of dried apricots
• 1/3 cup of unsweetened shredded coconut
• 1/4 cup of dates chopped
• Zest of 1 orange, 1 teaspoon
• Zest of 1 lemon, 1 teaspoon
• 1/2 teaspoon of cinnamon
• 1/2 teaspoon of ground ginger
• Salt 1/8 teaspoon
Direction:
1. Add in a food processor, a bowl of coconut, cashew nuts, apricots, and dates. Pulse the ingredients until the mix is crumbly.
2. Add a mixture of spices, citrus zest, and salt. Combine the pulse ingredients well and process them at high speed until the mixture begins to stick together.
3. Line a parchment paper tray. Shape the mixture with clean hands into 20 1-inch balls.
4. Stored in a sealed jar in the refrigerator for up to 3 days. Or, keep it in the freezer for up to three weeks.
Nutrition: Per serving: Kcal 102, Fat: 6g, Net Carbs: 9g, Protein: 2g

906. Balsamic Berries with Honey Yogurt

Preparation Time: 5 minutes
Cooking Time: 10 minutes
serving 4
Ingredients
• 8 ounces of hulled strawberries, and halved or, if very large, quartered (approximately 1 1/2 cups)
• 1 cup of blueberries
• 1 cup of raspberries
• Balsamic vinegar 1 tablespoon
• 2/3 cup plain Greek yogurt
• 2 teaspoons of honey
Direction:
1. In a large bowl, toss the blueberries, strawberries, and raspberries along with the balsamic vinegar. Let them sit for 10 minutes. In a small bowl, stir the yogurt and honey together. Divide the berries among bowls or glasses to serve and top each one with a dollop of yogurt or honey.
Nutrition: Per serving: Kcal 111, Fat: 3g, Net Carbs: 18.6g, Protein: 4.6g

907. Chocolate Almond Butter Fruit Dip

Preparation Time: 15 minutes
Cooking Time: 0 minutes
serving 14
Ingredients
• 1 cup Greek plain yogurt
• 1/2 cup of almond butter
• 1/3 cup of chocolate-hazelnut spread
• 1 tablespoon of honey
• 1 teaspoon of vanilla
• Fresh fruit such as apples, pears, apricots, and bananas in slices
Direction:
1. Whisk the first five ingredients together in a medium dish (through vanilla). (Place in a blender or food processor for

a lighter, cleaner dip; cover & pulse until smooth). With fruit, serve it.

Nutrition: Per serving: Kcal 115, Fat: 8g, Net Carbs: 8g, Protein: 4g

908. Lemon-Cream Pavlova with Berries

Preparation Time: 10 minutes
Cooking Time: 1 hour 30 minutes
Serving 12
Ingredients
- Egg whites 6
- Cream of tartar ¼ teaspoon
- Sugar 1 1/2 cups
- 3 teaspoons of vanilla
- 1 tablespoon of cornstarch
- 1 cup of heavy cream
- 1 tablespoon of sugar
- 1 lemon curd recipe or Lemon Curd Jar one 10-oz.
- Fresh raspberries
- Finely sliced pistachio (optional)

Direction:
2. Enable the egg whites to remain at room temperature for 30 minutes in an extra-large bowl. Meanwhile, with parchment paper, cover a baking sheet. Draw on paper a 9-inch circle; invert paper on a baking sheet.
3. Place the baking rack in the oven's middle. Preheat the oven to 250 degrees F. Add the tartar cream to the egg whites for the meringue. Beat on medium with a mixer until soft peaks develop (tips curl). Stir in 1 1/2 cups of sugar, 1 Tbsp. Beating on high till stiff peaks form at a time (tips stand straight). Beat 2 tsp. In Vanilla, sear cornstarch into beaten egg whites; softly fold in.
4. Using a large spoon, place meringue on paper around a circle, slightly shaping edges to create a shell. Bake for 1 1/2 hours, then (do not open door). Turn the oven off; let the meringue stand for 1 hour in the oven with the door closed.
5. Meanwhile, for topping, beat 1 Tbsp. Of cream in a large chilled bowl. Sugar, plus an extra 1 tsp. Vanilla with medium-sized chilled clean beaters before rigid peaks form (tips stand straight). Fold in Lemon Curd.
6. Lift the shell of meringue off the paper and pass it to a plate. Spread with raspberries and, if needed, pistachios with topping and sprinkle.

Nutrition: Per serving: Kcal 273, Fat: 12g, Net Carbs: 38g, Protein: 3g

909. Strawberry Greek Frozen Yogurt

Preparation Time: 4 hours
Cooking Time: 0 minutes
serving 16
Ingredients
- Plain yogurt, Greek low-fat (2%) 3 cups
- 1 cup of sugar
- 1/4 cup of lemon juice, freshly squeezed
- 2 teaspoons of vanilla
- 1/8 teaspoon of salt
- 1 cup of Strawberries Sliced

Direction:
1. Combine the vanilla, yogurt, milk, lemon juice, and salt in a medium bowl. Until smooth, whisk it.
2. According to the manufacturer's instructions, in a 1 1/2- to 2-quart ice cream maker, freeze the yogurt mixture, adding the last minute of sliced strawberries. Transfer to an airtight jar and freeze before serving for 2 to 4 hours. Until eating, let it settle at room temperature for 15 minutes.

Nutrition: Per serving: Kcal 86, Fat: 1g, Net Carbs: 16g, Protein: 4g

910. Triple Chocolate Tiramisu

Preparation Time: 6 hours
Cooking Time: 0 minutes
serving 12
Ingredients
- 2 3-ounce ladyfingers package, split
- 1/4 cup of espresso brewed or strong coffee
- 1 8 ounces mascarpone carton cheese
- 1 cup of whipped cream
- 1/4 cup of sugar powdered
- 1 teaspoon of vanilla
- 1/3 cup of chocolate liqueur
- White baking bars of 1 ounce, grated
- 1 ounce bittersweet, grated chocolate
- Unsweetened cocoa powdered
- Chopped coffee beans covered in chocolate (optional)

Direction:
1. With some of the ladyfingers, line the bottom of an 8x8x2-inch baking pan, cutting to fit as required. Drizzle over the ladyfingers with half of the espresso; set aside.
2. Beat together the mascarpone cheese, powdered sugar, whipped cream, and vanilla with an electric mixer in a medium mixing cup, only before stiff peaks develop. Up until now combined, beat in the chocolate liqueur. Spoon half of the mascarpone combination, pouring evenly around the ladyfingers. Sprinkle over the mascarpone mixture of white chocolate and bittersweet chocolate. Top with a different layer of ladyfinger (reserve any leftover ladyfingers for another use). A layer with the remaining mixture of espresso and mascarpone cheese.
3. For 6 to 24 hours, cover and chill. Sift the cocoa powder over the dessert top. Garnish with cocoa beans, if desired. Make twelve squares.

Nutrition: Per serving: Kcal 256, Fat: 19g, Net Carbs: 17g, Protein: 6g

911. Sweet Ricotta and Strawberry Parfaits

Preparation Time: 4 hours
Cooking Time: 30 minutes
serving 6
Ingredients
- 1 pound of fresh, trimmed strawberries, halved or quartered
- Sugar 1 teaspoon
- 1 tablespoon of freshly snipped mint
- 1 15 ounces part-skim ricotta cheese carton
- Light agave nectar 3 tablespoons
- Vanilla 1/2 teaspoon
- 1/4 teaspoon of lemon peel, finely shredded
- Fresh mint

Direction:
1. Combine the strawberries, honey, and 1 tablespoon of snipped mint in a medium bowl; blend gently to mix. Let the berries stand for around 10 minutes or before they soften and begin to release their juices.
2. Mix the vanilla, ricotta, agave nectar, and lemon peel in a medium dish. Beat at medium speed for 2 minutes using an electric mixer.
3. Scoop 1 tbsp. Of the ricotta mix. Into each of six parfait glasses for assembly. Top each glass of the ricotta mixture with a big spoonful of a strawberry mixture. For the remaining ricotta mixture or strawberry mixture, repeat the layers. Garnish with fresh mint also. Serve or cover immediately and chill for up to 4 hours.

Nutrition: Per serving: Kcal 157, Fat: 6g, Net Carbs: 18g, Protein: 9g

912. Melomakarona (Greek Honey-Dipped Cookies)

Preparation Time: 1 hour
Cooking Time: 15 minutes
serving 60
Ingredients
- 1 3/4 cups of olive oil with a mild flavor
- 11/4 cups of sugar
- 1 tablespoon of finely shredded orange peel
- 1/2 cup of orange juice
- 2 teaspoons of cognac or orange juice
- 2 teaspoons of ground cinnamon
- 1 1/2 teaspoons of baking soda
- Freshly grated nutmeg 3/4 teaspoon
- 1/4 teaspoon of salt
- ¼ teaspoon of ground cloves
- 7 cups all-purpose flour
- 1/2 cup of sugar
- Ground cinnamon 1/2 teaspoon
- 1 white egg, gently beaten
- Sliced almonds 1/4 cup
- 1 Spiced Honey Glaze

Direction:
1. Preheat the oven to 375° F. Mix the oil, 1-1/4 cups of sugar, orange peel, orange juice, cognac, salt, 2 teaspoons of cinnamon, baking soda, nutmeg, and cloves in a very big bowl until well mixed. Using a wooden spoon, stir in the flour. The dough would be stiff.
2. On a lightly floured surface, turn out the dough and knead for 5 minutes. When you knead it, the dough can get crumbly? Form the dough into a ball.
3. Then add 1/2 cup of sugar and 1/2 teaspoon of cinnamon in a small bowl. Form the dough into 2-1/2x1-1/2-inch oval shapes, 1/4- 1/2-inch thick, using a lightly rounded tbsp. Of dough for each cookie. Dip the dough ovals in the mixture of cinnamon-sugar, rotating both sides to coat. Place the ovals on an ungreased baking sheet 1-inch apart. Brush the oval tops rather gently with the white beaten egg. Place 2 to 3 slices of almond on top of each cookie and gently press on the cookies.
4. When gently touched and the tops are lightly browned, bake for 9 to 11 minutes or until the edges are only firm. Cool the cookies for 1 minute on the cookie sheet. To cool completely, transfer cookies to wire racks.
5. Atop waxed paper or sheets of parchment, set up cooling racks. Dip cooled cookies, turning to coat both ends, into Spiced Honey Glaze. Remove with two forks from the syrup, allowing the excess syrup to drip off. Place cookies on cooling racks that have been packed. Before eating, let it stand for 30 minutes.
Nutrition: Per serving: Kcal 123, Fat: 7g, Net Carbs: 19g, Protein: 11g

913. Rosé-Poached Peaches

Preparation Time: 12 minutes
Cooking Time: 6 minutes
serving 6
Ingredients
- Rose' wine 1/2 cup
- 1 tablespoon of sugar
- 1 whole pink, black, or green peppercorn teaspoon, crushed
- 1 pound of fresh, pitted and sliced peaches

Direction:
1. Stir the sugar, rose, and crushed peppercorns together in a medium saucepan. Bring it to a boil; reduce the heat. Simmer, 5 minutes, uncovered. Add the peaches; softly stir. Return to the boil. Cook, uncovered, for another 1 minute. Transfer the mixture into a medium dish. Chill, covered, for up to three days.
Nutrition: Per serving: Kcal 54, Fat: 0g, Net Carbs: 10g, Protein: 1g

914. Almond Biscotti

Preparation Time: 55 minutes
Cooking Time: 55 minutes
serving 36
Ingredients
- 1 cup raw whole almonds
- 2 1/4 cups of flour
- 1 1/2 tsp baking powder
- 1/2 tsp of salt
- 1/2 cup of sugar granulated
- 3/4 cup of brown sugar
- Large eggs 3 (room temperature)
- 1/2 cup of olive oil
- 1 tablespoon of pure almond extract
- Pure vanilla extract 1/2 teaspoon
- Lemon zest 1 teaspoon

Direction:
1. Preheat the oven to 325 degrees F. Position the rack in the center.
2. Spread the almonds on a baking sheet and toast for 12-15 minutes in the oven.
3. Meanwhile, whisk the dry ingredients together in a medium bowl (flour, baking powder, salt and sugars).
4. Whisk the eggs together in a large bowl. Add olive oil, zest, and extracts. Whisk together lightly.
5. Remove from the oven till the almonds are toasted, then chop coarsely.
6. Line the parchment paper baking sheet.
7. Add the flour mixture to the egg mixture; stir until just mixed, using a wooden spoon.
8. Fold in almonds chopped (make sure they have cooled off before incorporating them in the batter).
9. To scoop the dough out, use a medium serving spoon and place it on the parchment-lined cookie sheet. On the cookie sheet, add a scoop next to the batter and keep going till 2 logs are formed. Shape it into a log shape with wet fingers.
10. Bake for about 30 minutes or until golden brown and solid in color. Allow about 10 minutes to cool slightly.
11. Remove and transfer from the baking sheet to the cutting board.
12. Slice cookies at an angle of between 1/2 - 3/4 inches deep using a serrated knife.
13. Place the slices back on the baking sheets and placed them back in the oven for another 20 minutes (the longer they stay in the oven, the crispier they get). At the halfway mark, turn them over.
14. Place it to cool on a wire rack.
Nutrition: Per serving: Kcal 112, Fat: 5g, Net Carbs: 14g, Protein: 2g

915. Easy Strawberry Crepes Recipe

Preparation Time: 7 minutes
Cooking Time: 5 minutes
serving 12
Ingredients
- 2 cups of sliced frozen strawberries, thawed
- 2 tablespoons of sugar

- Orange zest 1/2 teaspoon, optional
- 3 cups of fresh strawberries, diced
- Large eggs 2
- 2 tablespoons butter, slightly melted and cooled
- 2 cups of milk
- 1 teaspoon of vanilla
- 1 tablespoon of sugar
- 1/2 tsp of salt
- 1 1/2 cups flour

Direction:

For Strawberry filling

1. Gently puree the strawberries to thaw. Stir in honey, orange zest if using, and fresh sliced strawberries. Serve at room temperature with a strawberry filling.

For Crêpes

1. In the order listed, add the ingredients to the blender jar, cover and blend until smooth.

2. Until cooking, refrigerate overnight or for 1 hour. (Or you can strain any lumps and use them immediately if you'd prefer.)

3. Over medium heat, heat the crepe pan or an 8-inch skillet and brush loosely with butter or cooking spray. Pour 1/4 cup of batter into the middle of the skillet with each crepe and then roll the pan, so the batter covers the skillet's bottom with a thin layer. Cook for about 1 minute, before light brown and the top, starts to dry out. Flip and boil for an extra 30 seconds.

4. Repeat for the batter that remains. Pile the completed crepes on a tray. (Place wax paper between the crepes if the crepes hold together.) In a 200 degrees C oven, you should put crepes to stay warm before ready to serve.

5. With a strawberry filling, fill each crepe and roll-up. With whipped cream, serve it.

Nutrition: Per serving: Kcal 120, Fat: 7g, Net Carbs: 18g, Protein: 6g

916. Greek Yogurt Parfait

Preparation Time: 5 minutes
Cooking Time: 10 sec.
serving 1
Ingredients
- 1 cup of Plain Greek Yogurt
- Almond Butter 1 cup
- Fresh Fruit 1 tbsp.

Direction:

1. Combine a tbsp. of almond butter with Greek yogurt.
2. In a cup or bowl, place it.
3. Cover with yogurt and add fresh fruit.
4. Heat an extra tbsp. of almond butter for 10 seconds in the microwave.
5. Drizzle over the yogurt with soft almond butter.

Nutrition Per serving: Kcal 165, Fat: 8g, Net Carbs: 21g, Protein: 8g

917. Fruit Nut Bowl

Preparation Time: 10 minutes
Cooking Time: 10 minutes
Servings: 2
Ingredients:
- 1/4 cup pecans, chopped
- 1/4 cup shredded coconut
- 1 cup of water
- 3 tbsp coconut oil
- 1/2 tsp cinnamon
- 1 pear, chopped
- 1 plum, chopped

- 2 tbsp Swerve
- 1 apple, chopped

Directions:
1. In a heat-safe dish add coconut, coconut oil, pear, apple, plum, and swerve and mix well.
2. Pour water into the instant pot then place the trivet in the pot.
3. Place dish on top of the trivet.
4. Seal pot with lid and cook on high for 10 minutes.
5. Once done, release pressure using quick release. Remove lid.
6. Remove dish from pot carefully. Top with pecans and serve.

Nutrition:
Calories: 338
Carbs: 47.2 g
Protein: 1.4 g
Fat: 25.4 g

918. Applesauce

Preparation Time: 10 minutes
Cooking Time: 1 minute
Servings: 12
Ingredients:
- 3 lbs. apples, peeled, cored, and diced
- 1/3 cup apple juice
- 1/2 tsp ground cinnamon

Directions:
1. Add all ingredients into the instant pot and stir well.
2. Seal pot with lid and cook on high for 1 minute.
3. Once done, allow to release pressure naturally. Remove lid.
4. Blend apple mixture using an immersion blender until smooth.
5. Serve and enjoy.

Nutrition:
Calories: 32
Carbs: 8.6 g
Protein: 0.2 g
Fat: 0.1 g

919. Sweet Coconut Raspberries

Preparation Time: 10 minutes
Cooking Time: 2 minutes
Servings: 12
Ingredients:
- 1/2 cup dried raspberries
- 3 tbsp swerve
- 1/2 cup shredded coconut
- 1/2 cup coconut oil
- 1/2 cup coconut butter

Directions:
1. Set instant pot on sauté mode.
2. Add coconut butter into the pot and let it melt.
3. Add raspberries, coconut, oil, and swerve and stir well.
4. Seal pot with lid and cook on high for 2 minutes.
5. Once done, release pressure using quick release. Remove lid.
6. Spread berry mixture on a parchment-lined baking tray and place in the refrigerator for 3-4 hours.
7. Slice and serve.

Nutrition:
Calories: 101
Carbs: 6.2 g
Protein: 0.3 g
Fat: 10.6 g

920. Creamy Fruit Bowls

Preparation Time: 10 minutes
Cooking Time: 1 minute
Servings: 4
Ingredients:
- 1 cup heavy cream
- 1 cup grapes, halved
- 1 avocado, peeled and cubed
- 3 cups pineapple, peeled and cubed
- 1 cup mango, peeled and cubed
- 1/2 tsp vanilla

Directions:
1. Add mango, pineapple, avocado, and grapes into the instant pot and stir well.
2. Seal pot with lid and cook on high for 1 minute.
3. Once done, release pressure using quick release. Remove lid.
4. Stir in vanilla and heavy cream.
5. Serve and enjoy.

Nutrition:
Calories: 309
Carbs: 31.6 g
Protein: 2.7 g
Fat: 21.3 g

921. Delicious Berry Crunch

Preparation Time: 10 minutes
Cooking Time: 4 minutes
Servings: 2
Ingredients:
- 2 tbsp almond flour
- 1 tsp cinnamon
- 1/2 cup pecans, chopped
- 2 tbsp coconut oil
- 1/4 tsp Xanthan gum
- 1/4 cup Erythritol
- 1 tsp vanilla
- 20 blackberries

Directions:
1. Add blackberries, vanilla, erythritol, and xanthan gum into the heat-safe dish. Stir well.
2. Mix together almond flour, cinnamon, pecans, and coconut oil and sprinkle over blackberry mixture. Cover dish with foil.
3. Pour 1 cup of water into the instant pot then place the trivet in the pot.
4. Place dish on top of the trivet.
5. Seal pot with lid and cook on high for 4 minutes.
6. Once done, release pressure using quick release. Remove lid.
7. Serve and enjoy.

Nutrition:
Calories: 224
Carbs: 40.3 g
Protein: 2.9 g
Fat: 19.8 g

922. Cinnamon Apple

Preparation Time: 10 minutes
Cooking Time: 20 minutes
Servings: 4
Ingredients:
- 4 apples, cored and cut into chunks
- 1/2 cup apple juice
- 1 tsp liquid stevia
- 2 tsp cinnamon

Directions:
1. Add all ingredients into the instant pot and stir well.
2. Seal pot with lid and cook on low pressure for 20 minutes.
3. Once done, release pressure using quick release. Remove lid.
4. Serve and enjoy.

Nutrition:
Calories: 133
Carbs: 35.2 g
Protein: 0.7 g
Fat: 0.5 g

923. Sweet Vanilla Pears

Preparation Time: 10 minutes
Cooking Time: 15 minutes
Servings: 4
Ingredients:
- 4 pears, cored & cut into wedges
- 1 tsp vanilla
- 2 tbsp maple syrup
- 1/4 cup raisins
- 1 cup apple juice

Directions:
1. Add all ingredients into the instant pot and stir well.
2. Seal pot with lid and cook on high for 15 minutes.
3. Once done, release pressure using quick release. Remove lid.
4. Serve and enjoy.

Nutrition:
Calories: 205
Carbs: 52.8 g
Protein: 1.1 g
Fat: 0.4 g

924. Tapioca Pudding

Preparation Time: 10 minutes
Cooking Time: 10 minutes
Servings: 4
Ingredients:
- 2 1/2 cups almond milk
- 1 tsp cinnamon
- 1 tsp liquid stevia
- 1/2 cup quinoa
- 1/3 cup tapioca pearls, rinsed
- Pinch of salt

Directions:
1. Spray instant pot from inside with cooking spray.
2. Add all ingredients into the inner pot of instant pot and stir well.
3. Seal pot with lid and cook on high for 10 minutes.
4. Once done, allow to release pressure naturally for 10 minutes then release remaining using quick release. Remove lid.
5. Stir well and serve.

Nutrition:
Calories: 470
Carbs: 33.7 g
Protein: 6.5 g
Fat: 37.1 g

925. Apple Orange Stew

Preparation Time: 10 minutes
Cooking Time: 10 minutes
Servings: 4
Ingredients:
- 4 apples, cored and cut into wedges
- 1 tsp liquid stevia
- 1/2 cup orange juice
- 1 cup apple juice
- 1 tsp vanilla

Directions:
1. Add all ingredients into the inner pot of instant pot and stir well.
2. Seal pot with lid and cook on high for 10 minutes.
3. Once done, allow to release pressure naturally for 10 minutes then release remaining using quick release. Remove lid.
4. Stir well and serve.

Nutrition:
Calories: 161
Carbs: 41.2 g
Protein: 0.9 g
Fat: 0.5 g

926. Lime Pears

Preparation Time: 10 minutes
Cooking Time: 10 minutes
Servings: 4
Ingredients:
- 4 pears, cored & cut into wedges
- 1/2 tsp vanilla
- 1 cup apple juice
- 1 tsp lime zest, grated
- 1 lime juice

Directions:
1. Add all ingredients into the inner pot of instant pot and stir well.
2. Seal pot with lid and cook on high for 10 minutes.
3. Once done, allow to release pressure naturally for 10 minutes then release remaining using quick release. Remove lid.
4. Stir and serve.

Nutrition:
Calories: 151
Carbs: 39.9 g
Protein: 0.9 g
Fat: 0.4 g

927. Italian Apple - Olive Oil Cake

Preparation Time: 15 minutes
Cooking Time: 1 hour
Servings: 12
Ingredients:
- Gala apples (2 large)
- Orange juice - for soaking apples
- All-purpose flour (3 cups)
- Ground cinnamon (.5 tsp.)
- Nutmeg (.5 tsp.)
- Baking powder (1 tsp.)
- Baking soda (1 tsp.)
- Sugar (1 cup)
- Olive oil (1 cup)
- Large eggs (2)
- Gold raisins (.66 cup)
- Confectioner's sugar - for dusting
- Also Needed: 9-inch baking pan

Directions:
1. Peel and finely chop the apples. Drizzle the apples with just enough orange juice to prevent browning.
2. Soak the raisins in warm water for 15 minutes and drain well.
3. Sift the baking soda, flour, baking powder, cinnamon, and nutmeg. Set it to the side for now.
4. Pour the olive oil and sugar into the bowl of a stand mixer. Mix on the low setting for 2 minutes or until well combined.
5. Blend it while running, break in the eggs one at a time and continue mixing for 2 minutes. The mixture should increase in volume; it should be thick - not runny.
6. Combine all of the ingredients well. Begin by making a hole in the center of the flour mixture and add in the olive and sugar mixture.
7. Remove the apples of any excess of juice and drain the raisins that have been soaking. Add them together with the batter, mixing well.
8. Prepare the baking pan with parchment paper. Scoop the batter into the pan and level it with the back of a wooden spoon.
9. Bake it for 45 minutes at a 350° Fahrenheit.
10. When ready, remove the cake from the parchment paper and place it into a serving dish. Dust with the confectioner's sugar. Heat dark honey to garnish the top.

Nutrition:
Calories: 294
Protein: 5.3 g
Fat: 11 g

928. Strawberry Ricotta Parfaits

Preparation Time: 30 minutes + 4 hours to chill
Cooking Time: 0 minutes
Servings: 4
Ingredients:
- Fresh strawberries (1 lb.)
- Sugar (1 tsp.)
- Fresh mint (1 tbsp.)
- Part-skim ricotta cheese (15 oz.)
- Light agave nectar (3 tbsp.)
- Vanilla (.5 tsp.)
- Shredded lemon peel (.25 tsp.)

Directions:
1. Combine the berries, mint, and sugar. Gently stir and marinate about 10 minutes until the berries soften.
2. Combine the ricotta, lemon peel, agave, and vanilla with an electric mixer for two minutes using the medium speed.
3. Assemble into chilled parfait glasses. Layer the ricotta mixture and top it off with the berries, alternating as desired.
4. Chill and cover for four hours.

Nutrition:
Calories: 157
Protein: 9 g
Fat: 6 g

929. Vanilla Greek Yogurt Affogato

Preparation Time: 10 minutes
Cooking Time: None
Servings: 4
Ingredients:
- Vanilla Greek yogurt (24 oz.)
- Sugar (2 tsp.)
- Hot espresso (4 Shots) or (0.75 of a cup) strong brewed coffee
- Chopped - unsalted pistachios (4 tbsp.)
- Dark chocolate chips or shavings (4 tbsp.)

Directions:
1. Spoon the yogurt into four tall chilled glasses.
2. Mix .5 teaspoon of sugar into each of the espresso shots.
3. Pour one shot of hot espresso or 1.5 ounces of coffee into each of the yogurt glasses.
4. Garnish each one off with the chocolate chips and pistachios before serving.

Nutrition:
Calories: 270
Protein: 11 g
Fat: 10 g

930. Watermelon Cups

Preparation Time: 10 minutes
Cooking Time: 15 minutes
Servings: 16
Ingredients:
- Seedless watermelon cubes (16 - 1-inch)
- Finely chopped cucumber (.33 cup)
- Finely chopped red onion (5 tsp.)
- Minced fresh mint (2 tsp.)
- Lime juice (.5 to 1 tsp.)
- Freshly minced cilantro (2 tsp.)

Directions:
1. Use a measuring spoon or a small melon baller to remove the center of each of the watermelon cubes. Leave a ¼-inch shell. Use the pulp another time.
2. In a small dish, mix the remaining fixings. Spoon into the watermelon cubes and serve.

Nutrition:
Calories: 7
Protein: 0 g
Fat: 0 g

931. Chocolate Nut Spread

Preparation Time: 10 minutes
Cooking Time: 10 minutes
Servings: 4
Ingredients:
- 1/4 cup unsweetened cocoa powder
- 1/4 tsp nutmeg
- 1 tsp vanilla
- 1/4 cup coconut oil
- 1 tsp liquid stevia
- 1/4 cup coconut cream
- 3 tbsp walnuts
- 1 cup almonds

Directions:
1. Add walnut and almonds into the food processor and process until smooth.

2. Add oil and process for 1 minute. Transfer to the bowl and stir in vanilla, nutmeg, and liquid stevia.
3. Add coconut cream into the instant pot and set the pot on sauté mode.
4. Add almond mixture and cocoa powder and stir well and cook for 5 minutes.
5. Pour into the container and store it in the refrigerator for 30 minutes.

Nutrition:
Calories: 342
Carbs: 9.6 g
Protein: 7.8 g
Fat: 33.3 g

932. Greek Coconut Cake With Syrup

Preparation Time: 10 minutes
Cooking Time: 30 minutes
Servings: 8-10
Ingredients:
- Eggs (4 separated)
- Salt (1 pinch)
- Margarine/butter - softened (0.33 lb. or 0.66 cup)
- Sugar (1 cup)
- Whole milk (.5 cup)
- Self-rising flour (1.5 cups)
- Baking powder (1 tbsp.)
- Shredded coconut (1.5 cups)

For the Syrup:
- Water (2.5 cups)
- Sugar (1.5 cups)
- Lemon juice (1 tbsp.)
- Whole cloves (3)
- Lemon zest (.5 tbsp.)
- Stick of cinnamon (1)
- Butter/Margarine - for baking pan (1 tbsp.)
- Flour - needed for the baking pan (2 tbsp.)

Directions:
1. Combine each of the syrup fixings in a saucepan to boil for seven to eight minutes. Transfer the pan from the burner and set it aside to cool.
2. Warm the oven at 340° Fahrenheit.
3. Whisk the egg whites with salt to form the stiff peak stage.
4. In a separate mixing container, whisk the egg yolks, sugar, and margarine, until it's smooth and mix in milk.
5. Whisk the baking powder and flour and beat into the mixture. Stir in the coconut.
6. Lastly, fold in the whisked egg whites.
7. Lightly grease a 15x10-inch baking pan with butter. Lightly coat it with flour, shaking the pan, discarding the excess flour.
8. Transfer the cake batter to the pan. Bake at 340° Fahrenheit until it's golden, and the cake starts to pull away from the sides of the pan (40-45 min.).
9. Remove the pan from the oven, cut it into pieces, and while it's hot - pour the cooled syrup evenly over the cake. Begin around the edges and move it to the center.
10. Sprinkle the top with 4 to 5 tablespoons of shredded coconut.
11. Wait for two to three hours before serving so the cake can absorb the deliciousness.

Nutrition:
Calories: 479
Protein: 6 g
Fat: 23 g

933. Greek Semolina Cake with Orange Syrup - Revani

Preparation Time: 15 minutes
Cooking Time: 50 minutes
Servings: 15
Ingredients:
- Flour (1 cup)
- Baking powder (1 tbsp.)
- Fine semolina (1 cup)
- Unsalted butter (0.5 cup/1 stick)
- Sugar (1 cup)
- Eggs (3 separated)
- Milk (1 cup)
- Vanilla extract (1 tsp.)
- Zest of 1 lemon
- Sugar (1.5 cups)
- Salt (1 pinch)
- Water (1.5 cups)
- Two 3-inch strips of orange zest
- Fresh lemon juice (1 tsp.)

Optional:
- Ground cinnamon
- Powdered sugar
- Almonds - blanched - lightly toasted and chopped (.5 cup)
- Also Needed: 9 x 13 pan

Directions:
1. Set the oven to 350° Fahrenheit. Lightly grease the baking pan and then set it aside.
2. Mix the semolina, flour, and baking powder in a mixing container.
3. Cream the butter with some sugar until it becomes light and fluffy using an electric mixer. With the mixer running, break in the egg yolks one by one. Continue mixing it until the batter becomes light yellow color, and toss in the lemon zest and vanilla extract.
4. With the mixer on low speed, add the flour mixture in three batches alternating the sequence using the milk.
5. Beat the egg whites in a separate bowl with a pinch of salt until soft peaks form. Fold the egg whites into the batter until just blended. (Don't mix too much or you will "flatten" your egg whites.)
6. Pour the batter into the pan to bake for 45 minutes or until the cake is a golden color.
7. Prepare the syrup by adding the orange zest, sugar, and water to a saucepan. Wait for it to boil and set a timer for it to simmer for five minutes. Add the lemon juice and cool.
8. Cover the cake with the syrup while the cake is still warm. After the cake cools, sprinkle it as desired using the cinnamon, powdered sugar, or almonds.

Nutrition:
Calories: 318
Protein: 5 g
Fat: 12 g

934. Greek Strawberry Frozen Yogurt

Preparation Time: 15 minutes
Cooking Time: 2-4 hours
Servings: 16/1 quart
Ingredients:
- Fresh lemon juice (.25 cup)
- Salt (.125 tsp.)
- Sugar (1 cup)
- Vanilla (2 tsp.)
- 2% plain Greek yogurt (3 cups)
- Sliced strawberries (1 cup)
- Also Needed: 1.5 to 2-quart ice cream maker

Directions:
1. Whisk the vanilla, salt, lemon juice, yogurt, and sugar until it's creamy.
2. Put the mixture in the ice cream maker. Prepare the yogurt according to the manufacturer's instructions.
3. Toss in the sliced berries for the last minute of the cycle. Empty into a container and freeze for two to four hours before serving.
4. Let the ice cream sit out at room temperature for about 5 to 15 minutes before serving.

Nutrition:
Calories: 86
Protein: 4 g
Fat: 1 g

935. Grilled Angel Food Cake Kebabs

Preparation Time: 5 minutes
Cooking Time: 15 minutes
Servings: 4
Ingredients:
- Whole strawberries (1 cup)
- Peach slices (1 cup)
- Angel food cake (1 cup of 1-inch cubes)
- Sugar (1 tbsp.)
- Ground cinnamon (.25 tsp.)
- Light white chocolate strawberry yogurt - ex. Yoplait (1 container - 6 oz.)

Directions:
1. Heat a charcoal or gas grill.
2. Place the cake cubes, berries, and peaches alternately on the skewers.
3. Combine the cinnamon and sugar. Sprinkle over the kebabs.
4. Grill using the medium heat temperature setting.
5. Close the lid and cook about two minutes, turning once.
6. Serve with the yogurt when ready.

Nutrition:
Calories: 100
Protein: 2 g
Fat: 0 g

936. Grilled Stone Fruit With Whipped Ricotta

Preparation Time: 5 minutes
Cooking Time: 15 minutes
Servings: 4
Ingredients:
- Apricots/plums - 8 or Peaches/nectarines (4 - halved & pitted)
- Olive oil (2 tsp.)
- Whole-milk ricotta cheese (.75 cup)
- Honey (1 tbsp.)
- Freshly grated nutmeg (.25 tsp.)
- Optional Garnish: Mint sprigs (4)

Directions:
1. Spray a grill pan or cold grill with a spritz of nonstick cooking spray. Heat up the grill using the medium heat temperature setting.

2. Place a large bowl in the fridge to chill.
3. Use oil to brush over the fruit and place onto the grill or pan with the cut side down. Cook it for three to five minutes or until the grill marks appear on the skin.
4. Use tongs and turn the fruit over.
5. Cover with a lid for four to six minutes or until the skin is easily cut away. Set aside to cool.
6. Take the bowl out of the fridge and add the ricotta. Beat the ricotta using the high speed of an electric beater for about two minutes.
7. Pour in the honey and nutmeg. Continue cooking for another minute.
8. Divide the room temperature/warm fruit into serving dishes.
9. Garnish with the ricotta concoction and a sprig of mint. Serve.

Nutrition:
Calories: 176
Protein: 7 g
Fat: 9 g

Chapter 13. Drinks and Smoothies

937. Hemp Milk Smoothie

Preparation time: 10 minutes
Cooking time: 10 minutes
Servings: 2
Ingredients
- 1 cup shelled hemp seeds
- 3-4 cups water

Directions:
1. Hemp milk does not need to be strained through a nut milk bag.
2. Simply blend well, and store in a tightly closed jar in the refrigerator.

Nutrition: calories 120, fat 2, fiber 4, carbs 26.0, protein 7

938. Raspberry Spinach Smoothie

Preparation time: 10 minutes
Cooking time: 5 minutes
Servings: 2
Ingredients:
- 3 cups raspberries
- 1 cup of coconut water
- 1 cup unsweetened coconut milk
- 2 cups spinach
- 1 tsp vanilla extract
- 1 tbsp chia seeds

Directions:
1. Soak chia seeds in milk for overnight.
2. Add all ingredients into the blender and blend until smooth and creamy.
3. Serve and enjoy.

Nutrition: calories 320, fat 2, fiber 4, carbs 27., protein 12

939. Blueberry Red Cabbage Smoothie

Preparation time: 10 minutes
Cooking time: 5 minutes
Servings: 2
Ingredients:
- 1/2 small red cabbage, sliced
- 1 1/2 cups water
- 1 banana
- 1 cup blueberries

Directions:
1. Add all ingredients into the blender and blend until smooth and creamy.
2. Serve and enjoy.

Nutrition: calories 120, fat 2, fiber 4, carbs 27.protein 2

940. Blackberry Lime Kale Smoothie

Preparation time: 10 minutes
Cooking time: 10 minutes
Servings: 2
Ingredients:
- 1 1/2 cups blackberries
- 1 cup kale
- 1 cup of coconut water
- 1 fresh lime juice
- 1 banana

Directions:
1. Add all ingredients into the blender and blend until smooth and creamy.
2. Serve and enjoy.

Nutrition: calories 160, fat 4, fiber 4, carbs 37.protein 3

941. Blackberry Smoothie

Preparation time: 10 minutes
Cooking time: 5minutes
Servings: 2
Ingredients:
- 1 cup blackberries
- 1 cup spinach
- 1 fresh lime juice
- 1 banana
- 1/2 tsp lime zest

Directions:
1. Add all ingredients into the blender and blend until smooth and creamy.
2. Serve and enjoy.

Nutrition: calories 420, fat 32, fiber 4, carbs 37.protein 8

942. Power Booster Smoothie

Preparation time: 10 minutes
Cooking time: 10 minutes
Servings: 2
Ingredients:
- Kale-2/3 cups
- Light coconut milk-1 cup
- Water-1 cup
- Frozen mango-1 cup
- Persimmons-2 piece
- Banana-1 piece
- Shredded coconut-3tbsp

Directions:
1. Place all the ingredients in you blender and turn it on.
2. Blend it for around 3 minutes.

Nutrition: calories 220, fat 1, fiber 4, carbs 27.protein 2

943. Cherry with Kale Smoothie

Preparation time: 10 minutes
Cooking time: 5 minutes
Servings: 2
Ingredients:
- Kale-2 cup
- Almond milk-2 cup
- Pineapple-2 cup
- Mango mix-2 cup
- Cherry-1 cup

Directions:
1. You don't need both pineapple and mango for this smoothie. You can use any one of them.
2. You have to use unsweetened almond milk.
3. Put everything in blender and turn it on.
4. Blend everything for two-three minutes.
5. Take it out and use ice to make it cold. Enjoy.

Nutrition: calories 190, fat 2, fiber 4, carbs 47.protein 2

944. Almond Nut Milk Smoothie

Preparation time: 10 minutes
Cooking time: 5 minutes
Servings: 2
Ingredients:
- 2 cups almonds (soaked overnight and rinsed well)
- 1 whole vanilla bean (cut into small pieces)
- 5 dates (pitted)

- 3 cups filtered water – more or less depending on how creamy you like it

Directions:
1. Place everything in the blender and blend until liquefied.
2. Use a nut milk bag to strain and store in a sealed jar/bottle in your refrigerator.
3. This is really good on granola or "raw porridge". Will keep 3-5 days in the fridge.

Nutrition: calories 60, fat 2, fiber 4, carbs 17.protein 4

945. Cashew Nut Milk Smoothie

Preparation time: 10 minutes
Cooking time: 7 minutes
Servings: 2
Ingredients:
- 2 cups soaked cashews (soaked 8 hours and rinsed well)
- 5 dates (pitted)
- 1 whole vanilla bean (cut into small pieces)
- 3 cups of water – more or less depending on how creamy you like it

Directions:
1. Blend all ingredients until well liquefied.
2. Using a nut milk bag, strain. Store in a sealed jar/bottle. Will keep 3-4 days in the fridge.
3. This is awesome in raw shakes and Irish moss drinks too!
4. You don't have to limit yourself to one-nut milks. You can mix and match to create unique flavors.

Nutrition: calories 150, fat 2, fiber 4, carbs 32.protein 3

946. Hazelnut Milk Smoothie

Preparation time: 10 minutes
Cooking time: 5 minutes
Servings: 2
Ingredients:
- 2 cups Hazelnuts (soaked 8 hours and rinsed well)
- 2 cups filtered water
- 1 vanilla pod (cut into small pieces)
- 4 dates (pitted)

Directions:
1. Add all ingredients to the blender and blend until liquefied.
2. Using a nut milk bag strain. Store in a sealed jar/bottle.
3. Will keep up to 5 days in the fridge.

Nutrition: calories 380, fat 7, fiber 4, carbs 27.protein 11

947. Pecan Nut Milk Smoothie

Preparation time: 10 minutes
Cooking time: 5 minutes
Servings: 2
Ingredients:
- 1 cup Pecans
- 2 cups filtered water
- 1 vanilla pod (cut into small pieces)
- 4 dates

Directions:
1. Blend all ingredients until liquefied. Store in a sealed jar/bottle.
2. Will keep up to 5 days in the fridge.

Nutrition: calories 320, fat 2, fiber 4, carbs 47.protein 5

948. Sunflower Seed Milk Smoothie

Preparation time: 10 minutes
Cooking time: 5 minutes
Servings: 2
Ingredients:
- 2 cups seeds (soaked 8-10 hours and rinsed well)
- 3 cup filtered water
- 1 vanilla pod (cut into small pieces)
- 4 dates

Directions:
1. Blend all ingredients until liquefied. Store in a sealed jar/bottle.
2. Will keep up to 4 days in the fridge.

Nutrition: calories 120, fat 2, fiber 4, carbs 27.protein 2

949. Refreshing Green Mint Smoothie

Preparation time: 10 minutes
Cooking time: 0 minutes
Servings: 2
- Ingredients:
- 1/4 cup fresh mint leaves
- 1/2 cup parsley
- 1 avocado
- 1 cucumber, chopped
- 1 lemon juice
- 1 cup of water
- 4 cups baby spinach
- 1/2 cup ice cubes
- 1 tbsp ginger

Directions:
1. Add all ingredients into the blender and blend until smooth and creamy.
2. Serve and enjoy.

Nutrition: calories 120, fat 2, fiber 4, carbs 27.protein 2

950. Kale Coconut Basil Smoothie

Preparation time: 10 minutes
Cooking time: 0 minutes
Servings: 2
Ingredients:
- 1 cup kale
- 1 1/2 cups unsweetened coconut milk
- 3 strawberries
- 1/2 banana
- 1 tbsp flax seeds
- 1/4 cup basil

Directions:
1. Add all ingredients into the blender and blend until smooth and creamy.
2. Serve and enjoy.

Nutrition: calories 120, fat 2, fiber 4, carbs 27.protein 2

951. Spinach Grapefruit Smoothie

Preparation time: 10 minutes
Cooking time: 0 minutes
Servings: 2
Ingredients:
- 2 grapefruits, peeled and deseeded
- 10 drops of liquid stevia
- 2 cups baby spinach
- 1 avocado
- 4 oz water

Directions:
1. Add all ingredients into the blender and blend until smooth and creamy.
2. Serve and enjoy

Nutrition: calories 120, fat 2, fiber 4, carbs 27.protein 2

952. Smoothie with Cinnamon

Preparation time: 5 minutes
Cooking time: 10 minutes
Servings: 2
Ingredients:
- 3 dessertspoons porridge oats
- 1 large ripe fig
- 6 ¾ oz. orange juice
- 3 rounded dessertspoons Greek yogurt
- ½ teaspoon ground cinnamon
- 3 ice cubes

Directions:
1. Wash and dry the fig and chop roughly. Reserve some for topping.
2. Add all ingredients to a blender, except for the ice cubes.
3. Add a little water to thin the smoothie and add an ice cube at the end.
4. Top with some cinnamon, a teaspoon of yogurt, and reserved fig. Finally, serve.

Nutrition: calories 120, fat 2, fiber 4, carbs 27.protein 2

953. Avocado Smoothie

Preparation time: 10 minutes
Cooking time: 0 minutes
Servings: 2
Ingredients
- 1 large avocado
- 1½ cups unsweetened coconut milk
- 2 tablespoons honey

Directions
Place all ingredients in a blender and blend until smooth and creamy.
Serve immediately

Nutrition: calories 120, fat 2, fiber 4, carbs 27.protein 2

954. Spinach Tomato Smoothie

Preparation time: 10 minutes
Cooking time: 0 minutes
Servings: 2
Ingredients:
- 1 carrot, chopped
- ½ celery rib, chopped
- ½ cup of chopped spinach
- 3 tomatoes, make halves
- ½ cup of mint leaves

Directions:
1. Take your blender or processor; one by one add the smoothie ingredients.
2. Blend or process the ingredients for 20-30 seconds to combine well and make a smooth mixture. (If using processor, process over high speed setting.)
3. Pour this fresh smoothie mixture in a serving glass.
4. Enjoy your fresh smoothie!

Nutrition: calories 120, fat 2, fiber 4, carbs 27.protein 2

955. Groovy Green Smoothie

Preparation time: 10 minutes
Cooking time: 0 minutes
Servings: 2
Ingredients
- 1 banana, cut in chunks
- 1 cup grapes
- 1 (6 ounces) tub vanilla yogurt
- 1/2 apple, cored and chopped
- 1 1/2 cups fresh spinach leaves

Direction:
1. Put the banana, grapes, yogurt, apple, and spinach in a blender. Cover and mix until smooth.
2. Pour into glasses and serve.

Nutrition:
Per serving: 205 calories; 1.9 g fat; 45 g carbohydrates; 6.1 g of protein; 4 mg cholesterol; 76 mg of sodium.

956. Sun Juice

Preparation time: 10 minutes
Cooking time: 0 minutes
Servings: 1
Ingredients
- 2 oranges, peeled and sliced
- 1/2 cup fresh raspberries
- 1 medium-sized banana, peeled
- 3 fresh mint leaves

Direction:
1. Juice everything in the juice machine. Pour on the ice to serve.

Nutrition:
Per serving: 293 calories; 1.1 g of fat; 73.6 g carbohydrates; 5 g of protein; 0 mg of cholesterol; 1 mg of sodium

957. Sweet Kale Smoothie

Preparation Time: 10 minutes
Cooking time: 15 minutes
Servings: 2
Ingredients:
- 1 cup low-fat plain Greek yogurt
- ½ cup apple juice
- 1 apple, cored and quartered
- 4 Medjool dates
- 3cups packed coarsely chopped kale
- Juice of ½ lemon
- 4 ice cubes

Directions:
1. In a blender, combine the yogurt, apple juice, apple, and dates and pulse until smooth.
2. Add the kale and lemon juice and pulse until blended. Add the ice cubes and blend until smooth and thick. Pour into glasses and serve.

Nutrition:
Calories: 355 | Total fat: 2g | Saturated fat: 1g; | Carbohydrates: 77g; | Sugar: 58g | Fiber: 8g; | Protein: 11g

958. Gingerbread & Pumpkin Smoothie

Preparation Time: 15 minutes
Cooking time: 50 minutes
Servings: 1
Ingredients:
- 1 cup almond milk, unsweetened
- 2 teaspoons chia seeds
- 1 banana

- ½ cup pumpkin puree, canned
- ¼ teaspoon ginger, ground
- ¼ teaspoon cinnamon, ground
- 1/8 teaspoon nutmeg, ground

Directions:

1. Start by getting out a bowl and mix your chia seeds and almond milk. Allow them to soak for at least an hour, but you can soak them overnight. Transfer them to a blender.
2. Add in your remaining ingredients, and then blend until smooth. Serve chilled.

Nutrition:

250 Calories | 13g Fats | 26g protein

959. Walnut & Date Smoothie

Preparation Time: 10 minutes
Cooking time: 0 minute
Servings: 2
Ingredients:

- 4 dates, pitted
- ½ cup milk
- 2 cups Greek yogurt, plain
- 1/2 cup walnuts
- ½ teaspoon cinnamon, ground
- ½ teaspoon vanilla extract, pure
- 2-3 ice cubes

Directions:

1. Blend everything until smooth, and then serve chilled.

Nutrition:

109 Calories | 11g Fats | 29g protein

960. Avocado-Blueberry Smoothie

Preparation Time: 5 minutes
Cooking time: 0 minutes
Servings: 2
Ingredients:

- ½ cup unsweetened vanilla almond milk
- ½ cup low-fat plain Greek yogurt
- 1 ripe avocado, peeled, pitted, and coarsely chopped
- 1 cup blueberries
- ¼ cup gluten-free rolled oats
- ½ teaspoon vanilla extract
- 4 ice cubes

Directions:

1. In a blender, combine the almond milk, yogurt, avocado, blueberries, oats, and vanilla and pulse until well blended.
2. Add the ice cubes and blend until thick and smooth. Serve.

Nutrition:

Calories: 273 | Total fat: 15g | Saturated fat: 2g; | Carbohydrates: 28g; | Sugar: 10g; | Fiber: 9g; | Protein: 10g

961. Cranberry-Pumpkin Smoothie

Preparation Time: 5 minutes
Cooking time: 0 minutes
Servings: 2
Ingredients:

- 2 cups unsweetened almond milk
- 1 cup pure pumpkin purée
- ¼ cup gluten-free rolled oats
- ¼ cup pure cranberry juice (no sugar added)
- 1 tablespoon honey

- ¼ teaspoon ground cinnamon
- Pinch ground nutmeg

Directions:

1. In a blender, combine the almond milk, pumpkin, oats, cranberry juice, honey, cinnamon, and nutmeg and blend until smooth.
2. Pour into glasses and serve immediately.

Nutrition:

Calories: 190 | Total fat: 7g | Saturated fat: 0g; | Carbohydrates: 26g; | Sugar: 12g | Fiber: 5g; | Protein: 4g

962. Green Juice

Preparation Time: 5 minutes
Cooking time: 0 minute
Servings: 1
Ingredients:

- 3 cups dark leafy greens
- 1 cucumber
- ¼ cup fresh Italian parsley leaves
- ¼ pineapple, cut into wedges
- ½ green apple
- ½ orange
- ½ lemon
- Pinch grated fresh ginger

Directions:

1. Using a juicer, run the greens, cucumber, parsley, pineapple, apple, orange, lemon, and ginger through it, pour into a large cup, and serve.

Nutrition:

200 Calories | 14g Fats | 27g protein

963. Sweet Cranberry Nectar

Preparation Time: 8 minutes
Cooking time: 5 minutes
Servings: 4
Ingredients:

- 4 cups fresh cranberries
- 1 fresh lemon juice
- ½ cup agave nectar
- 1 piece of cinnamon stick
- 1-gallon water, filtered

Directions:

1. Add cranberries, ½ gallon water, and cinnamon into your pot
2. Close the lid
3. Cook on HIGH pressure for 8 minutes
4. Release the pressure naturally
5. Firstly, strain the liquid, then add the remaining water
6. Cool, add agave nectar and lemon
7. Served chill and enjoy!

Nutrition: (Per Serving)

Calories: 184 | Fat: 0g | Carbohydrates: 49g | Protein: 1g

964. Hearty Pear and Mango Smoothie

Preparation Time: 10 minutes
Cooking time: 0 minute
Servings: 1
Ingredients:

- 1 ripe mango, cored and chopped
- ½ mango, peeled, pitted, and chopped
- 1 cup kale, chopped
- ½ cup plain Greek yogurt
- 2 ice cubes

Directions:

1. Add pear, mango, yogurt, kale, and mango to a blender and puree.
2. Add ice and blend until you have a smooth texture.
3. Serve and enjoy!

Nutrition: (Per Serving)

Calories: 293 | Fat: 8g | Carbohydrates: 53g | Protein: 8g

965. Breakfast Almond Milk Shake

Preparation Time: 4 minutes

Cooking time: 0 minute

Servings: 2

Ingredients:

- 3 cups almond milk
- 4 tbsp heavy cream
- ½ tsp vanilla extract
- 4 tbsp flax meal
- 2 tbsp protein powder
- 4 drops of liquid stevia
- Ice cubes to serve

Directions:

1. In the bowl of your food processor, add almond milk, heavy cream, flax meal, vanilla extract, collagen peptides, and stevia.
2. Blitz until uniform and smooth, for about 30 seconds.
3. Add a bit more almond milk if it's very thick.
4. Pour in a smoothie glass, add the ice cubes and sprinkle with cinnamon.

Nutrition:

Calories 326, | Fat: 27g; | Net Carbs: 6g; | Protein: 19g

966. Chocolate Banana Smoothie

Preparation Time: 5 minutes

Cooking time: 0 minutes

Servings: 2

Ingredients:

- 2 bananas, peeled
- 1 cup unsweetened almond milk, or skim milk
- 1 cup crushed ice
- 3 tablespoons unsweetened cocoa powder
- 3 tablespoons honey

Directions:

1. In a blender, combine the bananas, almond milk, ice, cocoa powder, and honey. Blend until smooth.

Nutrition:

Calories: 219; | Protein: 2g | Total Carbohydrates: 57g | Sugars: 40g | Fiber: 6g | Total Fat: 2g | Saturated Fat: <1g | Cholesterol: 0mg | Sodium: 4mg

967. Fruit Smoothie

Preparation Time: 5 minutes

Cooking time: 0 minutes

Servings: 2

Ingredients:

- 2 cups blueberries (or any fresh or frozen fruit, cut into pieces if the fruit is large)
- 2 cups unsweetened almond milk
- 1 cup crushed ice
- ½ teaspoon ground ginger (or other dried ground spice such as turmeric, cinnamon, or nutmeg)

Directions:

1. In a blender, combine the blueberries, almond milk, ice, and ginger. Blend until smooth.

Nutrition:

Calories: 125; | Protein: 2g | Total Carbohydrates: 23g | Sugars: 14g | Fiber: 5g | Total Fat: 4g; | Fat: <1g | Cholesterol: 0mg | Sodium: 181mg

968. Chia-Pomegranate Smoothie

Preparation Time: 5 minutes

Cooking time: 0 minutes

Servings: 2

Ingredients:

- 1 cup pure pomegranate juice (no sugar added)
- 1 cup frozen berries
- 1 cup coarsely chopped kale
- 2 tablespoons chia seeds
- 3 Medjool dates, pitted and coarsely chopped
- Pinch ground cinnamon

Directions:

1. In a blender, combine the pomegranate juice, berries, kale, chia seeds, dates, and cinnamon and pulse until smooth. Pour into glasses and serve.

Nutrition:

Calories: 275 | Total fat: 5g | Saturated fat: 1g; | Carbohydrates: 59g; | Sugar: 10g | Fiber: 42g; | Protein: 5g

969. Honey and Wild Blueberry Smoothie

Preparation Time: 5 minutes

Cooking time: 10 minutes

Servings: 2

Ingredients:

- 1 whole banana
- 1 cup of mango chunks
- ½ cup wild blueberries
- ½ plain, nonfat Greek yogurt
- ½ cup milk (for blending)
- 1 tablespoon raw honey
- ½ cup of kale

Directions:

1. Add all the above ingredients into an instant pot Ace blender. Add extra ice cubes if needed.
2. Process until smooth.

Nutrition:

Calories: 223 | Protein: 9.4 grams | Total Fat: 1.4 grams | Carbohydrates: 46.8 grams

970. Pina Colada Smoothie

Preparation Time: 10 minutes

Cooking time: 0 minutes

Servings: 4

Ingredients:

- 4 bananas
- 2 cups pineapple, peeled and sliced
- 2 cups mangoes, cored and diced
- 1 cup ice
- 4 tablespoons flaxseed
- 1¼ cups coconut milk

Directions:

1. Put all the ingredients in a blender and blend until smooth.
2. Pour into 4 glasses and immediately serve.

Nutrition: calories 120, fat 2, fiber 4, carbs 27.protein 2

971. Kiwi Smoothie

Preparation Time: 10 minutes
Cooking time: 0 minutes
Servings: 2
Ingredients:
- 1 cup basil leaves
- 2 bananas
- 1 cup fresh pineapple
- 10 kiwis

Directions:
1. Put all the ingredients in a blender and blend until smooth.
2. Pour into 2 glasses and immediately serve

Nutrition: calories 120, fat 2, fiber 4, carbs 27.protein 2

972. Grape Green Smoothie

Preparation time: 10 minutes
Cooking time: 0 minutes
Servings: 2
Ingredients:
- Cantaloupe-½ of amount
- Grapes-1 cup
- Coconut oil-2 tbs
- Water-½ cup
- Almond milk-1 cup
- Spinach-2 cup

Directions:
1. Pour water in the blender and place spinach and almond milk in it.
2. Make sure the almond milk is unsweetened.
3. Now add the other items in the blender and blend again for 3 minutes.
4. Use a frozen ingredient to make it cool.

Nutrition: calories 120, fat 2, fiber 4, carbs 27.protein 2

973. Tropical Smoothie

Preparation time: 10 minutes
Cooking time: 0 minutes
Servings: 2
Ingredients:
- Mango-1 big piece
- Pineapple-1 cup
- Kale-2 handful
- Orange-half cup

Directions:
1. Remove the seeds from the orange and peel it properly.
2. Place all the ingredients in your blender and turn it on.

Nutrition: calories 120, fat 2, fiber 4, carbs 27.protein 2

974. Peach Juice with Mint

Preparation time: 5 minutes
Cooking time: 0 minutes
Servings: 1
Ingredients
- 3 large peaches or nectarines, diced
- 1 large apple, in quarters
- 1 lime
- 2 sprigs of fresh mint

Direction:
1. Squeeze the peaches, apples, and lime into a juice. Pour the juice into a blender with the mint leaves. Mix.

Nutrition:
Per serving: 0.5 g fat; 60.8 g carbohydrates; 232 calories; 1.3 g of protein; 0 mg cholesterol; 19 mg of sodium.

975. Matcha Coconut Smoothie

Preparation time: 10 minutes
Cooking time: 0 minutes
Servings: 1
Ingredients
- 1 banana, 1 cup frozen mango chunks
- 2 leaves kale, torn into several pieces
- 3 tablespoons white beans, drained
- 2 tablespoons unsweetened shredded coconut
- 1 cup water, 1/2 teaspoon matcha green tea powder

Direction:
1. Combine banana, mango, kale, white beans, coconut, and matcha powder in a blender; add water. Blend the mixture until smooth.

Nutrition:
Per serving: 367 calories; 8.8 g fat; 72.4 g carbohydrates; 8 g protein; 0 mg cholesterol; 36 mg sodium.

976. Thick Pomegranate Cherry Smoothie

Preparation time: 10 minutes
Cooking Time: 5 Minutes
Servings: 4
Ingredients:
- 16 ounces frozen dark cherries
- ¾ cup pomegranate juice
- 1 teaspoon vanilla extract
- 6 ice cubes
- ½ cup pomegranate seeds
- 1 1/2 cups Greek yogurt, plain
- 1/3 cup milk
- ¾ teaspoon ground cinnamon
- ½ cup pistachios, chopped

Directions:
1. Add the ice cubes, cherries, pomegranate juice, yogurt, vanilla, milk, and cinnamon into a blender. Mix until the ingredients are smooth. It is thicker than your average smoothie.
2. Instead of a cup, divide the smoothie into four bowls.
3. Sprinkle chopped pistachios and pomegranate seeds on top of the smoothie.
4. Serve and enjoy!

Nutrition Info: calories: 212, fats: 7 grams, carbohydrates: 3grams, protein: 4 grams.

977. Raspberry Vanilla Smoothie

Preparation time: 5 minutes
Cooking time: 0 minutes
Serving: over 2 cups
Ingredients:
- 1 cup frozen raspberries
- 6-ounce container of vanilla Greek yogurt
- ½ cup of unsweetened vanilla almond milk

Direction:
1. Take all of your ingredients and place them in an instant pot Ace blender.
2. Process until smooth and liquified.

Nutrition:
Calories: 155
Protein: 7 grams
Total Fat: 2 grams
Carbohydrates: 30 grams

978. Blueberry Banana Protein Smoothie

Preparation time: 5 minutes
Cooking time: 0 minutes
Servings: 1
Ingredients:
- ½ cup frozen and unsweetened blueberries
- ½ banana slices up
- ¾ cup plain nonfat Greek yogurt
- ¾ cup unsweetened vanilla almond milk
- 2 cups of ice cubes

Direction:
1. Add all of the ingredients into an instant pot ace blender.
2. Blend until smooth.

Nutrition:
Calories: 230
Protein: 19.1 grams
Total Fat: 2.6 grams
Carbohydrates: 32.9 grams

979. Oats Berry Smoothie

Preparation time: 10 minutes
Cooking Time: 0 Minutes
Servings: 2
Ingredients:
- 1 cup of frozen berries
- 1 cup Greek yogurt
- ¼ cup of milk
- ¼ cup of oats
- 1 teaspoon honey

Direction:
1. Place all ingredients in an instant pot Ace blender and blend until smooth.

Nutrition:
Calories: 295
Protein: 18 grams
Total Fat: 5 grams
Carbohydrates: 44 grams

980. Kale-Pineapple Smoothie

Preparation Time: 5 Minutes
Cooking time: 0 minutes
Servings: 2
Ingredients:
- 1 Persian cucumber
- fresh mint
- 1 cup of coconut milk
- 1 tablespoon honey
- 1 ½ cups of pineapple pieces
- ¼ pound baby kale

Direction:
1. Cut the ends off of the cucumbers and then cut the whole cucumber into small cubes. Strip the mint leaves from the stems.
2. Add all of the ingredients to your instant pot Ace blender and blend until smooth.

Nutrition:
Calories: 140
Protein: 4 grams
Total Fat: 2.5 grams
Carbohydrates: 30 grams

981. Moroccan Avocado Smoothie

Preparation Time: 5 Minutes
Cooking time: 0 minutes
Servings: 4
Ingredients:
- 1 ripe avocado, peeled and pitted
- 1 overripe banana
- 1 cup almond milk, unsweetened
- 1 cup of ice

Direction:
1. Place the avocado, banana, milk, and ice into your instant pot Ace blender.
2. Blend until smooth with no pieces of avocado remaining.

Nutrition:
Calories: 100
Protein: 1 gram
Total Fat: 6 grams
Carbohydrates: 11 grams

982. Mediterranean Smoothie

Preparation Time: 5 Minutes
Cooking time: 0 minutes
Servings: 2
Ingredients:
- 2 cups of baby spinach
- 1 teaspoon fresh ginger root
- 1 frozen banana, pre-sliced
- 1 small mango
- ½ cup beet juice
- ½ cup of skim milk
- 4-6 ice cubes

Direction:
1. Take all ingredients and place them in your instant pot Ace blender.

Nutrition:
Calories: 168
Protein: 4 grams
Total Fat: 1 gram
Carbohydrates: 39 grams

983. Mango Strawberry Smoothie With Greek Yogurt

Preparation time: 10 minutes
Cooking Time: 0 Minutes
Servings:2
Ingredients:
- 1 banana
- ½ cup frozen strawberries
- ½ cup frozen mango
- ½ cup Greek yogurt
- ¼ cup almond milk
- ¼ teaspoon turmeric
- ¼ teaspoon ginger
- 1 tablespoon honey

Direction:
1. Place all of these ingredients into your instant pot ace blender and blend until smooth.
2. Pour in a glass and serve.

Nutrition:
Calories: 184.9
Protein: 18.9 grams
Total Fat: 1 grams
Carbohydrates: 27.5 grams

984. Anti-Inflammatory Blueberry Smoothie

Preparation Time: 5 Minutes
Cooking time: 0 minutes
Servings: 1
Ingredients:
- 1 cup of almond milk
- 1 frozen banana
- 1 cup frozen blueberries
- 2 handfuls of spinach
- 1 tablespoon almond butter
- ¼ teaspoon cinnamon
- ¼ teaspoon cayenne
- 1 teaspoon maca powder

Direction:
1. Combine all of these ingredients into your instant pot Ace blender and blend until smooth.

Nutrition:
Calories: 340
Protein: 9 grams
Total Fat: 13 grams
Carbohydrates: 55 grams

985. Healthy Breakfast Smoothie

Preparation Time: 3 Minutes
Cooking time: 0 minutes
Servings: 1
Ingredients:
- 1 medium banana
- ½ cup sliced strawberries
- ¼ cup 2% Greek yogurt
- 1 tablespoon of almond butter
- ½ cup baby spinach
- ½ cup of unsweetened almond milk

Direction:
1. Place all of the ingredients into your instant pot ace blender and blend until smooth.

Nutrition:
Calories: 300
Protein: 12.5 grams
Total Fat: 11 grams
Carbohydrates: 40 grams

986. Super Nutrient Smoothie

Preparation Time: 5 Minutes
Cooking time: 0 minute
Servings: 1
Ingredients:
- ½ cup of frozen blueberries
- ½ cup of frozen pineapple
- ¼ cup of spinach
- 1 tablespoon of honey
- ½ cup of water

Direction:
1. Combine all of the ingredients into your instant pot Ace blender and blend until smooth.

Nutrition:
Calories: 214
Protein: 6 grams
Total Fat: 4 grams
Carbohydrates: 41 grams

987. Raspberries and Yogurt Smoothie

Preparation Time: 5 minutes
Cooking Time: 0 minutes
Servings: 2
Ingredients:
- 2 cups raspberries
- ½ cup Greek yogurt
- ½ cup almond milk
- ½ tsp vanilla extract

Directions:
1. In your blender, combine the raspberries with the milk, vanilla, and the yogurt, pulse well, divide into 2 glasses and serve for breakfast.

Nutrition: Calories 245 Fat: 9.5g Carbs: 5.6g Protein: 1.6g

988. Avocado and Apple Smoothie

Preparation time: 5 minutes
Cooking time: 0 minutes
Servings: 2
Ingredients:
- 3 cups spinach
- 1 green apple, cored and chopped
- 1 avocado, peeled, pitted and chopped
- 3 tablespoons chia seeds
- 1 teaspoon honey
- 1 banana, frozen and peeled
- 2 cups coconut water

Directions:
1. In your blender, combine the spinach with the apple and the rest of the ingredients, pulse, divide into glasses and serve.

Nutrition: calories 168, fat 10.1, fiber 6, carbs 21, protein 2.1

989. Pear and Mango Smoothie

Preparation time: 5 minutes
Cooking time: 0 minutes
Servings: 1
Ingredients:
- 1 ripe mango, cored and chopped
- ½ mango, peeled, pitted and chopped
- 1 cup kale, chopped
- ½ cup plain Greek yogurt
- 2 ice cubes

Directions:
1. Add pear, mango, yogurt, kale, and mango to a blender and puree. Add ice and blend until you have a smooth texture. Serve and enjoy!

Nutrition: Calories: 293 Fat: 8g Carbohydrates: 53g Protein: 8g

990. Mango Pear Smoothie

Preparation Time: 5 minutes
Cooking Time: 0 minute
Servings: 1
Ingredients:
- 2 ice cubes
- ½ cup Greek yogurt, plain
- ½ mango, peeled, pitted & chopped
- 1 cup kale, chopped
- 1 pear, ripe, cored & chopped

Directions:
1. Take all ingredients and place them in your blender. Blend together until thick and smooth. Serve.

Nutrition: Calories 350 Protein 40g Fats 12g Carbohydrates: 11 g

991. Strawberry-Rhubarb Smoothie

Preparation Time: 5 minutes
Cooking Time: 3 minutes
Servings: 1
Ingredients:
- 1 rhubarb stalk, chopped
- 1 cup sliced fresh strawberries
- ½ cup plain Greek yogurt
- 2 tablespoons honey
- Pinch ground cinnamon
- 3 ice cubes

Directions:
1. Place a small saucepan filled with water over high heat and bring to a boil. Add the rhubarb and boil for 3 minutes. Drain and transfer the rhubarb to a blender.
2. Add the strawberries, yogurt, honey, and cinnamon and pulse the mixture until it is smooth. Add the ice and blend until thick, with no ice lumps remaining. Pour the smoothie into a glass and enjoy cold.

Nutrition: Calories: 295 Fat: 8g Carbohydrates: 56g Protein: 6g

992. Smoothie of Kiwi Berry

Preparation time: 10 minutes
Cooking time: 0 minutes
Servings: 2
Ingredients:
- Blueberry-1 cup
- Mixed berry-1 cup
- Banana-1 piece
- Kiwi-1 piece
- Avocado-½ amount
- Spinach-2 cups

Directions:
1. Firstly blend the spinach and water till it get smoothed.
2. The next task is to add the other ingredients in the blender.
3. Now blend it again for 2-3 minutes. It will be done.

Nutrition: calories 120, fat 2, fiber 4, carbs 27.protein 2

993. Peachy Strawberry Green Smoothie

Preparation time: 10 minutes
Cooking time: 0 minutes
Servings: 2
Ingredients:
- Strawberry-1 cup
- Peach-2 cup
- Almond milk-2 cups
- Bok choy-2 cups

Directions:
1. Make sure the almond milk is unsweetened. Turn the blender on and put bok choy and almond milk in it.
2. Now blend it for two minutes.
3. Now you can put other ingredients in blender. Blend everything for 2 minutes.

Nutrition: calories 120, fat 2, fiber 4, carbs 27.protein 2

994. Cherry with Berry Green

Preparation time: 10 minutes
Cooking time: 0 minutes
Servings: 2
Ingredients:
- Mixed berry-1 cup
- Cherry-1 cup
- Banana-1 cup
- Water-2 cup
- Spinach-2 cup

Directions:
1. Firstly, take the spinach and water and blend them together.
2. Now add the other things into the blender and blend it again. Use a frozen fruit to make the smoothie cool.
3. Remember that you need to take out cherry pits before you make the smoothie.

Nutrition: calories 120, fat 2, fiber 4, carbs 27.protein 2

995. Broccoli Cucumber Smoothie

Preparation time: 10 minutes
Cooking time: 0 minutes
Servings: 2
Ingredients:
- ½ medium cucumber, make slices
- 1 celery stalk, diced
- ½ cup of broccoli florets
- Coconut water as needed

Directions:
1. Take your blender or processor; add the cucumber, celery, broccoli, and coconut water one by one.
2. Blend or process all the ingredients for 15-20 seconds to combine well and make a smooth mixture. (If using processor, process over high speed setting.)
3. Pour this fresh smoothie mixture in a serving glass.
4. Enjoy your fresh smoothie!

Nutrition: calories 120, fat 2, fiber 4, carbs 27.protein 2

996. Cucumber Smoothie

Preparation time: 10 minutes
Cooking time: 0 minutes
Servings: 2
Ingredients:
- ½ medium cucumber, diced
- 1 handful kale, torn
- 2 tbs. of lemon juice
- 1 tsp. of maple syrup

Directions:
1. Take your blender or processor; add the kale, cucumber, lemon juice, maple syrup, and water one by one.
2. Blend or process all the ingredients for 15-20 seconds to combine well and make a smooth mixture. (If using processor, process over high speed setting.)
3. Pour this fresh smoothie mixture in a serving glass.
4. Top with a slice of cucumber or lemon.
5. Enjoy your fresh smoothie!

Nutrition: calories 120, fat 2, fiber 4, carbs 27.protein 2

997. Fig Smoothie with Cinnamon

Preparation time: 10 minutes
Cooking Time: 0 minutes
Servings: 1
Ingredients:
- One large fig (ripe)
- Three dessertspoons porridge oats

- 200ml orange juice
- Three rounded dessertspoons thick, plain yogurt
- Three ice cubes
- Half tsp. ground cinnamon

Directions:
1. Rinse and dry the figs, then coarsely chop them. Reserving a small amount for sprinkling on top of the smoothie.
2. In an electric blender, combine all ingredients. Blend thoroughly, progressing to the milkshake settings on your blender, if it has them. If not, omit the ice cubes and substitute a little water for the ice cubes, and serve with an ice cube whole at the end, particularly if having this in the summer months.
3. To serve, spoon a tsp. of the yogurt on top, along with some additional chopped fig and ground cinnamon.

Nutrition: Calories: 54 Fat: 0.22g Carbohydrates: 14.37g Protein: 0.58g

998. Simple Green Juice

Preparation Time: 15 minutes
Cooking time: 0 minutes
Servings: 2
Ingredients:
- One bunch kale
- One large apple
- One piece peeled fresh ginger (one inch)
- Five celery stalks
- Handful fresh parsley
- Half large English cucumber

Directions:
1. Prepare the vegetables by washing and preparing them.
2. Juice in the ingredients.
3. If using a juicer, add the green juice directly into glasses and serve immediately. The juice will be thicker if you use a blender. You should strain it through a fine-mesh sieve and press the fiber into the sieve with the back of a spoon to remove as much liquid as possible. Strain the juice into glasses and serve!

Nutrition: Calories: 18 Fat: 0.24g Carbohydrates: 3.28g Protein: 0.88g

999. Oregano Tea

Preparation time: 20 minutes
Cooking Time: 0 minutes
Servings: 1
Ingredients:
- 1 cup boiling water
- 2 tbsps. fresh oregano

Directions:
1. In a mug, cup, or teapot, place the herbs. Cover with a lid and add the boiling water over the herbs. Allow fifteen minutes for steeping. Before drinking, strain.

Nutrition: Calories: 0 Fat: 0.g Carbohydrates: 0g Protein: 0g

1000. Bone Broth

Preparation Time: 10 minutes
Cooking time: 72 hours
Servings: 4
Ingredients:
- Two pounds bones (lamb)

- One-gallon water
- One-fourth cup apple cider vinegar
- One bay leaf
- Six sprigs fresh parsley
- Two springs fresh rosemary
- Six sprigs fresh thyme
- Two sprigs fresh sage

Directions:
1. In a slow cooker, combine the vinegar and bones with plenty of water to cover by about an inch. Cook on high heat until the liquid starts to boil, then reduce to low and cook for a minimum of 48 hours and a maximum of 72 hours. The water rate will decrease as the broth cooks; include hot water as required to maintain the water level above the bones. Do not be concerned if the bones rise to the surface of the broth; this is not the same as there is insufficient water to cover them.
2. Add the parsley, rosemary, sage, thyme, and bay leaf to the broth when it is about 2 to 3 hours from completion.
3. When it is finished cooking, remove it from the heat and set it aside to cool slightly. Place a colander over a stockpot and strain the broth. The broth will be transferred to the pot below, while the herbs and bones will stay in the colander.
4. Allow the broth to cool fully before moving to storage containers.

Nutrition: Calories: 171 Fat: 5.34g Carbohydrates: 7.02g Protein: 24g

1001. Turmeric Fire Cider

Preparation Time: 15 minutes
Cooking time: 0 minutes
Servings: 2
Ingredients:
- Half cup onion (chopped)
- One-fourth cup fresh ginger (grated)
- Half cup garlic (chopped)
- Two to four tbsps. raw honey
- One-fourth cup horseradish root (grated)
- One-fourth tsp. ground dried cayenne
- One and a half tbsp. ground dried turmeric
- Raw apple cider vinegar

Directions:
1. In a glass container, combine the garlic, onion, turmeric, horseradish, ginger, and cayenne pepper to taste. Sufficient vinegar should be added to cover all of the ingredients fully.
2. Seal the pot. Since vinegar corrodes metal, use a plastic or glass lid or place a layer of waxed paper in between the lid and the liquid when making infused vinegar.
3. Put the mixture in a dark, cold place for four weeks to steep.
4. Using a fine-mesh strainer, fine cheesecloth, or cotton muslin, strain out the herbs.
5. Add honey to taste, mixing vigorously to dissolve.

Nutrition: Calories: 228 Fat: 1.66g Carbohydrates: 51.51g Protein: 7.47g

1002. Mediterranean Pink Lady

Preparation Time: 5 minutes
Cooking time: 0 minutes
Servings: 1
Ingredients:
- One and a half oz. gin

- One-fourth oz. limoncello
- Half oz. Cointreau
- Ice
- One-fourth oz. Campari
- 1 large egg white
- Half oz. fresh lemon juice
- Four thin strips of lemon zest

Directions:
1. Shake all the ingredients in a cocktail shaker with ice until they are thoroughly mixed, then strain into a chilled glass.
2. An additional piece of ice should be added, and the mixture should be shaken.
3. Using a strainer, strain lemon juice into a chilled glass and garnish with lemon zest

Nutrition: Calories: 32 Fat: 2.55g Carbohydrates: 57.01g Protein: 11.36g

1003. Grapefruit Cocktail

Preparation Time: 5 minutes
Cooking time: 0 minutes
Servings: 1
Ingredients:
- Three oz. Grapefruit juice
- Ice
- One oz. Vodka
- Salt for decorating rim of glass

Directions:
1. Rub a slice of grapefruit around the rim of a bottle.
2. Dip the rim of the glass in a deep bowl of salt.
3. Fill the glass halfway with ice
4. Combine vodka and grapefruit juice.
5. Gently stir and enjoy!

Nutrition: Calories: 32 Fat: 1.91g Carbohydrates: 3.59g Protein: 0.48g

1004. Avocado and Banana Smoothie

Preparation Time: 5 minutes
Cooking time: 0 minutes
Servings: 4
Ingredients:
- One peeled banana
- One lemon juice

- One cored and peeled avocado
- A pinch of pure Himalayan crystal salt
- One large peeled and cored green apple (quartered)
- Two cups coconut water
- A peeled piece of ginger
- One tablespoon organic thyme honey
- Half cup of ice

Directions:
1. Combine the ginger, half cup coconut water, lemon juice, apple, and ice in a blender. Blend until entirely smooth.
2. Combine the remaining ingredients, including the coconut water and ice, in a blender. Blend once more until smooth.
3. Serve right away.

Nutrition: Calories: 162 Fat: 7.62g Carbohydrates: 25.31g Protein: 1.65g

1005. Healthy Whipped Coffee

Preparation Time: 6 minutes
Cooking time: 0 minutes
Servings: 1
Ingredients:
- Two tsps. sugar
- Two tsps. cool water
- Two tsps. instant coffee
- One-fourth tsps. vanilla
- Half cup milk (reduced-fat)
- Half tsps. cocoa powder
- Several ice cubes

Directions:
1. Combine the coffee, sugar, and water in a big cup. Whisk vigorously into a dense foam using a milk frother, wire whisk, or electric beater. Using a whisk would take approximately 3 minutes.
2. Fill a glass halfway with milk and ice. Spoon the whipped coffee carefully over the milk.

Nutrition: Calories: 231 Fat: 14.04g Carbohydrates: 11.66g Protein: 14.09g

Chapter 14. 14-Day Meal Plan

Day	Breakfast	Lunch	Dinner	Dessert
1	Mediterranean Bowl	Italian Broccoli And Potato Soup	Tasty Beef And Broccoli	Banana, Cranberry, And Oat Bars
2	Berry Oats	Broccoli Soup With Gorgonzola	Beef Corn Chili	Berry And Rhubarb Cobbler
3	Stuffed Tomatoes	Comfort Food Soup	Balsamic Beef Dish	Citrus Cranberry And Quinoa Energy Bites
4	Watermelon "Pizza"	Comfy Meal Stew	Soy Sauce Beef Roast	Easy Blueberry And Oat Crisp
5	Avocado Chickpea Pizza	Exciting Chickpeas Soup	Rosemary Beef Chuck Roast	Lemony Blackberry Granita
6	Stuffed Sweet Potato	Classic Napoli Sauce	Pork Chops And Tomato Sauce	Yogurt Dip
7	Tuna Salad	Winter Dinner Stew	Slow Cooker Mediterranean Beef Hoagies	Mint Banana Chocolate Sorbet
8	Veggie Quiche	Meatless-Monday Chickpeas Stew	Roasted Sirloin Steak	Pecan And Carrot Cake
9	Veggie Stuffed Hash Browns	Fragrant Fish Stew	Lemon Pepper Pork Tenderloin	Raspberry Yogurt Basted Cantaloupe
10	Feta And Pepper Frittata	Bright Green Soup	Jalapeno Lamb Patties	Simple Apple Compote
11	Tomato, Herb, And Goat Cheese Frittata	Parsley Garden Vegetable Soup	Lemon Chicken With Asparagus	Peanut Butter And Chocolate Balls
12	Prosciutto Breakfast Bruschetta	Lamb And Spinach Soup	Tender Chicken Quesadilla	Spiced Sweet Pecans
13	Prosciutto, Avocado, And Veggie Sandwiches	Effortless Chicken Rice Soup	Chicken And Chorizo Casserole	Lemon Crockpot Cake
14	Apple Muffins	Spanish Fall Soup	Chorizo White Bean Stew	Lemon And Watermelon Granita

Conclusion

The Mediterranean diet is a diet that includes lots of fruits, vegetables, whole grains, and plant-based oils, while it eliminates foods that are rich in sugar and saturated fats. The diet also includes lean sources of protein such as fish, poultry, or red meat.

The Mediterranean diet is ideal for those people who are trying to lose weight or maintain a healthy weight because it emphasizes eating fewer animal fats and less sugar while emphasizing healthier foods.

Here are different components of the Mediterranean diet:

Fruits: fruits that grow above ground like blueberries, blackberries, grapes, and bananas are good to eat in moderation. Fruits to avoid include watermelon, pineapples, mangoes, and more exotic fruits such as avocados. Fruits with seeds such as mangoes and papayas should be eaten in moderation. A fruit that is the exception to this rule should be apples. It is okay to eat a whole apple, but it should not be peeled or the skin eaten. Apples are rich in fiber and antioxidants that help prevent heart disease and cancer.

Fats: Olive oil, canola oil, peanut oil, and flaxseed oil are good oils for cooking and salad dressings. They also are great for drizzling over vegetables or pasta dishes in place of mayonnaise or butter, although they can never replace mayonnaise completely when making a sandwich or salad. These oils are good for cooking because they have a high smoke point. They are also better for baking low-fat cakes and cookies because they do not solidify easily.

Fish: Fish used in the Mediterranean diet include salmon, tuna, herring, and mackerel. The best fish to eat is definitely tuna, which can be baked or grilled lightly.

Refined Sugar: Sugar does not belong in a Mediterranean diet. But honey can be eaten sparingly because it contains important antioxidants that help boost the immune system and fight infections.

Grains: Whole grains such as barley, rye, or oatmeal, and whole-grain pasta should be eaten instead of white flour pasta. Whole-grain bread such as pumpernickel is better than white bread because they contain more fiber than white bread. White rice, like brown rice, has little nutritional value compared to other foods, but white rice is acceptable in a Mediterranean diet because it has no saturated fat content as long as it is not cooked in vegetable oil or used to make crispy fried foods like French fries.

Nuts: Nuts such as almonds, peanuts, macadamia nuts, or pine nuts are allowed in the Mediterranean diet but should be eaten sparingly because they are high in fat.

Vegetables: Vegetables that grow under the ground like potatoes, sweet potatoes, and carrots have been excluded from the Mediterranean diet because they contain a large amount of starch and sugar. But celery, green beans, and bell peppers are good vegetables to eat if you are doing a Mediterranean diet.

Dairy Products: Dairy products like milk cheeses and yogurt are acceptable to eat in moderation.

Meat & Poultry: Some meats, such as lamb, are allowed in the Mediterranean diet but should be eaten sparingly. Sausage and kabobs are good examples of foods that can be eaten frequently. Other meats such as chicken and beef should be eaten less often or not at all because these meats are high in saturated fat and cholesterol.

Candy: Candy can be included in a Mediterranean diet if it is sugar-free. Jelly beans or hard candies with nuts in them are better than regular candies like gumdrops for dessert because they contain more nutritional value than regular candies.

Sweets: Sweets such as chocolate or ice cream are not part of the Mediterranean diet. The only sweets that are allowed on a Mediterranean diet are sugar-free candies and jelly beans.

Alcohol: Wine is a good source of antioxidants and has fewer calories than any carbohydrate-based alcohol like beer or vodka. Drinking a glass of wine in moderation, one to two times per week, is acceptable. Red wine is the best choice over white wine because red wine contains more antioxidants and polyphenols, which help fight cancer when consumed in moderation.

Printed in Great Britain
by Amazon